300 Ways to Ask The Four Questions:
From Zulu to Abkhaz*
The Second Edition

An Extraordinary Survey of the World's Languages Through the Prism of the Haggadah

By
Murray Spiegel
and Rickey Stein

*Or rather,
374 Ways to Ask The Four Questions,
but Who's Counting?!

Abkhaz
Adhola
Adyghe
Afrikaans
Akan/Fanti/Twi
Akha
Akkadian, Ancient
Albanian
Alemannisch/Swiss German
American Sign Language
Amharic
Apache, Western
Arabic
Arabic, Judeo-Iraqi
Arabic, Judeo-Yemeni/Yemenite
Aramaic, Ancient
Aramaic, Lishanid Noshan
Aramaic, Zakho/Kurdish
Armenian
Arrernte, Eastern
Assamese
Assyrian, Old
Assyrian/Neo-Aramaic
Asturian
Avar
Awutu/Efutu
Azerbaijani
Bali
Basque/Eskara
Bassa
Batak Toba
Belarussian/Belarusan
Bemba
Bengali
Bete-Bendi/Mbete
Bezhta
Bhojpuri
Bicolano, Albay/Bikol Albay
Bicolano, Central/Bikol Naga
Binary
Blues
Braille
Braille, Hebrew
Braille, Sanskrit
Breton
Bukharic/Judeo-Tajik
Bulgarian
Buriat/Buryat
Burmese
Cajun French
Catalan
Cebuano
Chaouia/Tachawit
Chechen
Cherokee
Cheyenne
Chibcha/Muisca
Chickasaw
Chinese, Hakka

Chinese, Mandarin
Chinese, Min Bei/Foochow
Chinese, Min Nan/Taiwanese
Chinese, Nuosu/Sichuan
Chinese, Wu/Wuu
Chinese, Xiang/Hunan
Chinese, Yue/Cantonese
Chinook Wawa
Choctaw
Cofán
Coptic
Coptic
Cornish
Corsican
Crioulo, Upper Guinea
Croatian
Country Western
Crow
Czech
Dagaare, Southern
Dagbani
Danish
Degema
Dene/Chipewyan
Diriku/Rugciriku/Mbogedu
Dogri
Do (Dough) Re Mi
Dutch
Ebira
Egyptian, Late
Egyptian, Middle
Elmer Fudd
English
English, Middle
English, Old
Esperanto
Estonian
Ewondo/Beti
Éwé/Ewe
Faroese
Farsi, Eastern/Dari
Farsi, Western/Persian
Fijian
Finnish
Finnish, Tornedalen
Flemish/Vlaams
Fon/Fongbe
Frafra/Gurenne/Talensi
French
French Sign Language
Frisian, Western
Ga/Accra
Gaddang
Galician
Ganda/Luganda
Garifuna
Georgian
German
Gĩkũyũ/Kikuyu
Gilbert & Sullivan Operettas

Gogo/Kigogo
Gothic
Greek
Greek, Ancient
Gronings
Gua
Gujarati
Gulla
Gurage, Sebat Bet
Gusii/Kisii/Ekegusii
Gwere/Lugwere
Haitian Creole French
Hawaiian
Haya/Kihaya
Hebrew
Hebrew Semaphore
Hehe/Kihehe
Herero/Ochiherero
Hiligaynon
Hindi/Hindustani
Huichol
Ibanag
Icelandic
Igbo
Ilocano
Indonesian
Interlingua
Inuktitut, Eastern/Eskimo
Irish Gaelic/Erse/Connemara
Irish, Old
Israeli Sign Language
Italian
Jamaican Creole English
Jamaican Reggae
Japanese
Java Language
Java Script
Javanese
Jibberish
Judeo-Greek/Romaniote
Juwri/Judeo-Tat
Kabardian
Kabyle/Tamazight
Kamba
Kanjobal, Eastern/Q'anjob'al
Kanjobal, Western/Akateko
Kannada
Kashmiri
Kazakh
Kei
Khmer
Khoekhoegowab/Hottentot
Kilivila/Kiriwina
Kinaray-A
Kisar/Meher
Klingon

Kodava/Kodagu
Koongo
Korean
Krio
Kwangali/Sikwangali
Kwanyama
Ladin
Ladino
Lak
Lakota
Lao
Latvian
Lawyer Speak
Leti
Lingala
Lithuanian
Lozi/Silozi
Luiseño
Luo/Dholuo
Luxembourgish
Maasai
Macedonian
Maithili
Makonde/Kimakonde
Malagasy, Plateau
Malay
Malayalam
Malinke/Maninkakan/N'ko
Maltese
Manx
Maori
Mapudungun
Marathi
Maritime Signal Flags
Marshallese
Marwari/Marvari
Masaaba/Lugisu
Masalit/Massaleit
Maya, Mopán/Mayan
Mbukushu/Thimbukushu
Mingrelian
Miscellaneous Mideast les
Mohawk/Iroquois
Mongolian
Mongolian, Ancient
Morse Code
Morse Code, Hebrew
Mungaka/Bali
Munsee/Lenape/Unami
Nahuatl, Eastern Huasteca
Navajo
Na'vi
Ndebele/Sindebele
Ndonga/Oshindonga
Nenets
Nepali
Newari/Nepal Bhasha

Norwegian
Norwegian, Nynorsk
Nyakyusa-Ngonde
Nyamwezi/Kinyamwezi
Nyanja
Nzema
Okinawa
Oneida
Oriya
Oromo, West Central/
Oromo
Pali
Panjabi, Eastern
Papiamentu
Pashto, Northern
PCS
Phoenician/Canaanite
Piemontese
Pig Latin
Pipil/Nahuat/Nawat
Pitcairn
Poetry, E. B. Browning
Pohnpeian
Pontic
Portuguese
Provençal
Pulaar/Fulfulde/Fuuta Jalon
Q'oqchi'/Kekchi
Quechua, Ayacucho
Quechua, Cuzco
Quechua, Huanca
Quechua, Napo Lowland
Quechua, South Bolivian
Quenya
Qumran, Hebrew
Rap
Romani, Vlax
Romanian
Romansch
Russian
Saami, North/Lapp
Saamia/Luyia/Lusamia
Samaritan
Sambal, Tina
Samoan
Sandorian
Sanskrit
Sardinian
Scots
Secoya
Serbian
Sheng
Shona

Slovenian/Slovene
SMS Messaging/Twitter
Sociology Professor
Somali
Sorbian, Upper/Wendish
Sotho, Southern
Spanish
Stenography, Heb Translit
Structured Query Language
Sukuma/Kisukuma
Sullen Teenager Language
Sumerian
Susu/Sousou
Swabian
Swahili
Swedish
Sylheti
Symbolic Logic
Tabassaran
Tachelhit
Tagalog
Tamasheq
Tamil
Tarifit
Telugu
Teso/Ateso
Tetum/Tetun/Dili
Thai
Thai, Northern
Tibetan
Tigrinya/Tigrigna
Tlingit
Tswana/Setswana
Tulu
Turkish
Tuvin
Ugaritic
Ukrainian
Uncle Eli/Dr Seuss style
Upper East Side
Urdu
Urkers
Ute/Southern Paiute
Uzbek, Northern
Valley Girl
Veluws
Vietnamese
Waray-Waray
Welsh
Xhosa
Yiddish, Eastern
Yoruba
Yucatan Maya/Yucatán/Yucateco
Yupik, Central
Zarma
Zulu

Cover Artist: Alysa Lerman
Page Design: Randi E Spiegel
Design Adviser: Joe Buchwald Gelles
Design Assistants: Larry Edlavitch, Barbara Shopiro
Editors: Randi E Spiegel, Toby Lee Spiegel

ISBN 978-0-615-15063-5

Printed in China.

We dedicate this book to our wives, Randi Spiegel and Dana Stein,
and to all the guests at our annual Seders, past, present and future.

We love them more than 300 Ways.

Clockwise from top: Following the Seder, by Jackson Salter, 5th grade, W Caldwell, NJ;
Moses parting the Red Sea, by Samantha Gilbert, 4th grade, N Caldwell, NJ;
Having a hand in the Seder, by Paulina Berse, 4th grade, N Caldwell, NJ

300 Ways to Ask The Four Questions: From Zulu to Abkhaz

Contents

Index of Languages

Abkhaz
Adhola
Adyghe
Afrikaans
Akan/Fanti/Twi
Akha
Akkadian, Ancient
Albanian
Alemannisch/Alsatian/Swiss German
American Sign Language/ASL
Amharic
Apache, Western
Arabic
Arabic, Judeo-Iraqi
Arabic, Judeo-Yemeni/Yemenite
Aramaic, Ancient
Aramaic, Lishanid Noshan/Koi Sanjaq
Aramaic, Zakho/Kurdish
Armenian
Arrernte, Eastern
Assamese
Assyrian, Old
Assyrian/Assyrian Neo-Aramaic
Asturian
Avar
Awutu/Efutu
Azerbaijani
Bali
Basque/Eskara
Bassa
Batak Toba
Belarussian/Belarusan
Bemba
Bengali
Bete-Bendi/Mbete
Bezhta
Bhojpuri
Bicolano, Albay/Bikol Albay
Bicolano, Central/Bikol Naga
Breton
Bukharic/Judeo-Tajik
Bulgarian
Buriat/Buryat
Burmese
Cajun French
Catalan/Catalan-Valencian-Balear
Cebuano

Chaouia/Tachawit
Chechen
Cherokee
Cheyenne
Chibcha/Muisca
Chickasaw
Chinese, Hakka
Chinese, Mandarin
Chinese, Min Bei/Foochow
Chinese, Min Nan/Taiwanese/Fukienese
Chinese, Nuosu/Sichuan
Chinese, Wu/Wuu
Chinese, Xiang/Hunan/Xiang
Chinese, Yue/Cantonese/Yue
Chinook Wawa
Choctaw
Cofán
Coptic, Bohairic
Coptic, Sahidic
Cornish
Corsican
Crioulo, Upper Guinea
Croatian
Crow
Czech
Dagaare, Southern
Dagbani
Danish
Degema
Dene/Chipewyan
Diriku/Rugciriku/Mbogedu
Dogri
Dutch
Ebira
Egyptian, Late
Egyptian, Middle
English
English, Middle
English, Old
Estonian
Ewondo/Beti
Éwé/E<u>we</u>
Faroese
Farsi, Eastern/Dari
Farsi, Western/Persian
Fijian
Finnish

Finnish, Tornedalen
Flemish/Vlaams
Fon/Fongbe
Frafra/Gurenne/Talensi
French
French Sign Language
Frisian, Western
Ga/Ga-Adangme-Krobo/Accra
Gaddang
Galician
Ganda/Luganda
Garífuna
Georgian
German
Gĩkũyũ/Kikuyu
Gogo/Kigogo
Gothic
Greek
Greek, Ancient
Gronings
Gua
Gujarati
Gulla
Gurage, Sebat Bet
Gusii/Kisii/Ekegusii
Gwere/Lugwere
Haitian Creole French/Haitian Creole
Hausa
Hawaiian
Haya/Kihaya
Hebrew
Hehe/Kihehe
Herero/Ochiherero
Hiligaynon
Hindi/Hindustani
Hopi
Huichol
Hungarian
Ibanag
Icelandic
Igbo
Ilocano
Indonesian
Inuktitut, Eastern Canadian/Eskimo
Irish Gaelic/Erse/Connemara
Irish, Old
Israeli Sign Language/Hebrew Sign Language

Italian
Jamaican Creole English
Japanese
Javanese
Judeo-Greek/Romaniote
Juwri/Judeo-Tat
Kabardian
Kabyle/Tamazight
Kamba
Kanjobal, Eastern/Q'anjob'al
Kanjobal, Western/Akateko
Kannada
Kashmiri
Kazakh
Kei
Khmer
Khoekhoegowab/Hottentot/Bushman
Kilivila/Kiriwina
Kinaray-A
Kisar/Meher
Kodava/Kodagu
Koongo
Korean
Krio
Kwangali/Sikwangali/Rukwangali
Kwanyama
Ladin
Ladino
Lak
Lakota
Lao
Latin
Latvian
Leti
Lingala
Lithuanian
Lozi/Silozi
Luiseño
Luo/Dholuo
Luxembourgish/Luxembourgeois
Maasai/Maa
Macedonian
Makhuwa/Makhuwa-Metto
Makonde/Kimakonde
Malagasy, Plateau
Malay
Malayalam
Malinke/Maninkakan/N'ko
Maltese

Manx
Maori
Mapudungun
Marathi
Marshallese
Marwari/Marvari
Masaaba/Lugisu
Masalit/Massaleit
Maya, Mopán/Mayan
Mbukushu/Thimbukushu
Mende/Boumpe
Mingrelian
Mirandese/Mirandes
Moabite
Mohawk/Iroquois
Mongolian
Mongolian, Ancient
Mungaka/Bali
Munsee/Lenape/Unami
Nahuatl, Eastern Huasteca
Navajo
Ndebele/Sindebele
Ndonga/Oshindonga
Nenets
Nepali
Newari/Nepal Bhasha
Norwegian, Bokmål/Norwegian
Norwegian, Nynorsk
Nyakyusa-Ngonde/Kinyakyusa
Nyamwezi/Kinyamwezi
Nyanja
Nzema
Okinawan, Central
Oneida
Oriya
Oromo, West Central/Oromoo
Pampangan
Panjabi, Eastern
Papiamentu
Pashto, Northern
Phoenician/Canaanite
Piemontese
Pipil/Nahuat/Nawat
Pitcairn
Polish
Pontic
Portuguese
Provençal
Pulaar/Fulfulde/Fuuta Jalon

Q'eqchi'/Kekchi
Quechua, Ayacucho
Quechua, Cuzco
Quechua, Huanca
Quechua, Napo Lowland/Quichua
Quechua, South Bolivian
Qumran, Hebrew
Romani, Vlax
Romanian
Romansch
Russian
Saami, North/Lapp
Saamia/Luyia/Lusamia
Samaritan
Sambal, Tina
Samoan
Sanskrit
Sardinian
Scots
Secoya
Serbian
Sherpa
Shona
Sicilian
Signed English
Sindhi
Sinhala
Slovak
Slovenian/Slovene
Somali
Sorbian, Upper/Wendish
Sotho, Southern
Spanish
Sranan
Sukuma/Kisukuma
Sumerian
Susu/Sousou
Swabian
Swahili
Swedish
Sylheti/Sylhetti
Tabassaran
Tachelhit
Tagaloq
Tamasheq
Tamil
Tarifit
Telugu
Teso/Ateso

Tetum/Tetun/Dili
Thai
Thai, Northern
Tibetan
Tigrinya/Tigrigna
Tlingit
Tswana/Setswana
Tulu
Turkish

Tuvin
Ugaritic
Ukrainian
Urdu
Urkers
Ute/Southern Paiute
Uzbek, Northern
Veluws
Vietnamese

Waray-Waray
Welsh
Xhosa
Yiddish, Eastern
Yoruba
Yucatan Maya/Yucatán/Yucateco
Yupik, Central
Zarma
Zulu

Index of Languages by Country *

Afghanistan
Farsi, Eastern/Dari
Albania
Albanian
Algeria
Chaouia/Tachawit; Kabyle/Tamazight
Angola
Kwanyama
Armenia
Armenian
Australia
Arrernte, Eastern; Pitcairn
Azerbaijan
Azerbaijani; Juwri/Judeo-Tat
Bangladesh
Bengali; Sylheti/Sylhetti
Belarus
Belarussian/Belarusan
Belgium
Flemish/Vlaams
Belize
Garífuna; Maya, Mopán/Mayan; Q'eqchi'/Kekchi;
Yucatan Maya/Yucatán/Yucateco
Benin
Fon/Fongbe
Bolivia
Quechua, South Bolivian
Botswana
Tswana/Setswana
Brazil
Portuguese

Bulgaria
Bulgarian
Cambodia
Khmer
Cameroon
Ewondo/Beti; Mungaka/Bali
Canada
Chinook Wawa; Dene/Chipewyan;
Inuktitut, Eastern Canadian/Eskimo; Lakota;
Mohawk/Iroquois; Munsee/Lenape/Unami;
Oneida
Chile
Mapudungun
China
Chinese: Hakka, Mandarin, Min Bei/Foochow,
Min Nan/Taiwanese/Fukienese, Nuosu/Sichuan,
Wu/Wuu, Xiang/Hunan/Xiang, Yue/Cantonese/
Yue; Tibetan
Croatia
Croatian
Czech Republic
Czech
Dagestan
Juwri/Judeo-Tat
Democratic Republic of the Congo
Koongo; Lingala
Denmark
Danish; Faroese
Ecuador
Cofán; Secoya
Egypt
Arabic

El Salvador
Pipil/Nahuat/Nawat
Estonia
Estonian
Ethiopia
Amharic; Gurage, Sebat Bet;
Oromo, West Central/Oromoo; Tigrinya/Tigrigna
Faroe Islands
Faroese
Fiji
Fijian
Finland
Finnish
France
Breton; Corsican; Provençal; French;
French Sign Language
Georgia
Abkhaz; Georgian; Mingrelian
Germany
German; Sorbian, Upper/Wendish; Swabian;
Yiddish, Eastern
Ghana
Akan/Fanti/Twi; Awutu/Efutu;
Dagaare, Southern; Dagbani; Éwé/Ewe;
Frafra/Gurenne/Talensi; Ga/Accra; Gua; Nzema
Greece
Greek; Judeo-Greek/Romaniote; Pontic
Guatemala
GarífunaKanjobal, Eastern/Q'anjob'al;
Kanjobal, Western/Akateko; Q'eqchi'/Kekchi
Guinea
Susu/Sousou

*Country where language originated
and where most speakers live.

Guinea-Bissau
Crioulo, Upper Guinea
Haiti
Haitian Creole French/Haitian Creole
Honduras
Garífuna
Hungary
Hungarian
Iceland
Icelandic
India
Assamese; Bhojpuri; Dogri; Gujarati;
Hindi/Hindustani; Kannada; Kashmiri;
Kodava/Kodagu; Malayalam; Marathi;
Marwari/Marvari; Oriya; Panjabi, Eastern;
Sanskrit; Tamil; Telugu; Tulu; Urdu
Indonesia
Bali; Batak Toba; Indonesian; Javanese; Kei;
Kisar/Meher; Leti; Tetum/Tetun/Dili;
Iraq
Arabic, Judeo-Iraqi; Aramaic, Zakho/Kurdish;
Assyrian/Assyrian Neo-Aramaic;
Farsi, Western/Persian
Ireland
Irish Gaelic/Erse/Connemara
Israel
Arabic, Judeo-Iraqi;
Arabic, Judeo-Yemeni/Yemenite;
Aramaic, Lishanid Noshan/Koi Sanjaq;
Aramaic, Zakho/Kurdish; Bukharic/Judeo-Tajik;
Hebrew; Israeli Sign Language;
Judeo-Greek/Romaniote; Juwri/Judeo-Tat;
Ladino; Yiddish, Eastern
Italy
Italian; Ladin; Piemontese; Sardinian; Sicilian
Ivory Coast
Bete-Bendi/Mbete; Lingala
Jamaica
Jamaican Creole English
Japan
Japanese; Okinawan, Central
Kazakhstan
Kazakh

Kenya
Gĩkũyũ/Kikuyu; Gusii/Kisii/Ekegusii; Kamba;
Luo/Dholuo; Maasai/Maa
Korea
Korean
Laos
Lao
Latvia
Latvian
Lesotho
Sotho, Southern
Liberia
Bassa
Lithuania
Lithuanian
Luxembourg
Luxembourgish/Luxembourgeois
Macedonia
Macedonian
Madagascar
Malagasy, Plateau
Malawi
Nyanja
Malaysia
Malay
Mali
Tamasheq
Malta
Maltese
Marshall Islands
Marshallese
Mexico
Huichol; Nahuatl, Eastern Huasteca; Spanish;
Yucatan Maya/Yucatán/Yucateco
Mongolia
Buriat/Buryat; Mongolian
Montenegro
Serbian
Morocco
Tachelhit; Tarifit
Mozambique
Makhuwa/Makhuwa-Metto
Myanmar
Akha; Burmese

Namibia
Diriku/Rugciriku/Mbogedu; Herero/Ochiherero;
Khoekhoegowab/Hottentot/Bushman;
Kwangali/Sikwangali/Rukwangali; Kwanyama;
Mbukushu/Thimbukushu; Ndonga/Oshindonga
Nepal
Nepali; Newari/Nepal Bhasha; Sherpa
Netherlands
Dutch; Frisian, Western; Gronings; Urkers;
Veluws
Netherlands Antilles
Papiamentu
New Zealand
Maori
Niger
Zarma
Nigeria
Bete-Bendi/Mbete; Degema; Ebira; Hausa; Igbo;
Yoruba
Norfolk and Pitcairn Islands
Pitcairn
Norway
Norwegian, Bokmål/Norwegian;
Norwegian, Nynorsk; Saami, North/Lapp
Pakistan
Pashto, Northern; Sindhi; Urdu
Papua New Guinea
Kilivila/Kiriwina
Peru
Quechua, Ayacucho; Quechua, Cuzco;
Quechua, Huanca;
Quechua, Napo Lowland/Quichua
Philippines
Bicolano, Albay/Bikol Albay;
Bicolano, Central/Bikol Naga; Cebuano;
Gaddang; Hiligaynon; Ibanag; Ilocano;
Kinaray-A; Pampangan; Sambal, Tina; Tagalog;
Waray-Waray
Poland
Polish
Portugal
Mirandese/Mirandes; Portuguese
Romania
Romani, Vlax; Romanian

Z
Y
X
W
V
U
T
S
R
Q
P
O
N
M
L
K
J
I
H
G
F
E
D
C
B
A

Russia
Adyghe; Avar; Bezhta; Chechen; Kabardian;
Lak; Nenets; Russian; Tabassaran; Tuvin
Samoa
Samoan
Saudi Arabia
Arabic
Scotland
Scots
Senegal
Malinke/Maninkakan/N'ko;
Pulaar/Fulfulde/Fuuta Jalon
Serbia
Serbian
Sierra Leone
Krio; Mende/Boumpe
Singapore
Chinese: Min Bei/Foochow
Slovakia
Slovak
Slovenia
Slovenian/Slovene
Somalia
Somali
South Africa
Afrikaans; Xhosa; Zulu
Spain
Asturian; Basque/Eskara; Catalan; Galician;
Spanish

Sri Lanka
Sinhala
Sudan
Masalit/Massaleit
Suriname
Sranan
Sweden
Finnish, Tornedalen; Swedish
Switzerland
Alemannisch/Alsatian/Swiss German; Romansch
Tanzania
Gogo/Kigogo; Haya/Kihaya; Hehe/Kihehe;
Makonde/Kimakonde; Nyakyusa-Ngonde/
Kinyakyusa; Nyamwezi/Kinyamwezi; Sukuma/
Kisukuma; Swahili
Thailand
Thai; Thai, Northern
Tibet
Tibetan
Turkey
Turkish
Tuva
Tuvin

USA
American Sign Language/ASL;
Apache, Western; Cajun French; Cherokee;
Cheyenne; Chickasaw; Choctaw; Crow; English;
Gulla; Hawaiian; Hopi; Judeo-Greek/Romaniote;
Lakota; Luiseño; Navajo; Signed English; Tlingit;
Ute/Southern Paiute; Yiddish, Eastern;
Yupik, Central
Uganda
Adhola; Ganda/Luganda; Gwere/Lugwere;
Masaaba/Lugisu; Saamia/Luyia/Lusamia;
Teso/Ateso
Ukraine
Ukrainian
United Kingdom
Cornish; English; Scots; Welsh
Uzbekistan
Bukharic/Judeo-Tajik; Uzbek, Northern
Vietnam
Vietnamese
Wales
Welsh
Yemen
Arabic, Judeo-Yemeni/Yemenite
Zambia
Bemba; Lozi/Silozi; Nyanja
Zimbabwe
Ndebele/Sindebele; Shona

Ancient Languages

Akkadian; **Akkad**
Ancient Aramaic; **Middle East**
Ancient Greek; **Greece**
Ancient Mongolian; **Mongolia**
Chibcha; **Columbia**
Coptic, Bohairic; **Egypt**
Coptic, Sahidic; **Egypt**

Gothic; **Germany**
Late Egyptian Hieroglyphics; **Egypt**
Latin; **Italy**
Manx; **Isle Of Man**
Middle Egyptian Hieroglyphics; **Egypt**
Middle English; **Merrie Olde England**
Moabite; **Jordan**

Old Assyrian; **Mesopotamia/Nineveh**
Old English; **Merrie Olde England**
Old Irish; **Ireland**
Phoenician; **Syria/Lebanan/Israel**
Samaritan; **Israel**
Sumerian; **Sumer**
Ugaritic; **Ugarit**

Sign Languages

American Sign Language / ASL
Israeli Sign Language / Hebrew Sign Language

French Sign Language
Signed English

Constructed Languages and Fun Parodies

Binary
Braille
Braille, Hebrew
Braille, Sanskrit
Country-Western
Do (Dough) Re Mi
Elmer Fudd
Esperanto
Gilbert and Sullivan Operettas
Haiku
Interlingua (Scientific and Technical use)
Ithig
Jamaican Reggae
Java Programming Language

Java Script
Jibberish/Ubbi Dubbi
Klingon (from *Star Trek*)
Lawyerese / Legalese
Leet Speak
Maritime Signal Flags
Morse Code, English
Morse Code, Hebrew
Na'vi (from *Avatar*)
Picture Communication Symbols
Pig Latin
Poetry, E. B. Browning
Quenya (Tolkien Elvish)
Rap

Sandorian
Semaphore, Hebrew
Sfat Habet (Abanibi)
Shakespearean
SMS/Twitter
Sociology Professor
Stenography, Transliterated Hebrew
Structured Query Language (SQL)
Sullen Teenager
Symbolic Logic
Uncle Eli (Dr Seuss style)
Upper East Side
Valley Girl

Music, Games, Culture - CD & DVD Content

Chants
  Aramaic Chant
  Bukharic Chant
  Judeo-Greek / Romaniote Chant
  Judeo-Iraqi Chants (multiple)
  Judeo-Indian (Cochin)
  Ladino (Judeo-Spanish)
  Libyan Chant
  Turkish Chant
  Yemenite Chant
  Yiddish Cheder Chant

Kiddush and Other Prayers
  Bukharan, Judeo-Greek, Libyan, Yemenite ...
Cultural Stories
  Suriname History
  Ugandan Jews History

Games
  Hebrew Semaphore Game
  Four Questions Language Quizzes
Music and Singing
  Continuous Breathing, Flute
  Mongolian Throat Singing
  Madagascar Music
  Soviet Georgia Music
Click Languages
  Xhosa Tongue Twisters
  Click Language Examples

Drawing: Alara Rothstein, 5th grade, W Caldwell, NJ

The symbols of Passover

Clockwise from top: Having a hand in the Seder, by Paulina Berse, 4th grade, N Caldwell, NJ
The themes of Passover, by Alexandra Mayer, 3rd grade, W Caldwell, NJ;
Symbols of Passover, by Jacob 'Jake' Carino, 5th grade, W Orange, NJ

Foreword

At the outset I will ask the Fifth Question: On all other nights we recite the Questions in one language only (when in Israel) or in two languages at most (when in the Diaspora) but on this night we use hundreds? Would one or two not have permitted us to say Dayenu - it is enough?

Well, obviously not.

While the 4 Questions are part of the recitation at the Passover table, they are decidedly not liturgical. Quite the contrary, they represent an innocent child's inquiry about the meaning of some rites and customs at Passover. This is neither a prayer, nor a supplication or a thanksgiving; it is the prelude to a discussion about the meaning of freedom from slavery, the freedom for which Passover is the paradigm. Along with prayer around the table there is banter in which people of any age are encouraged to participate.

There are works that have seen translations into more languages than what follows in these pages. The most translated work on record is the Bible. The entire Bible, comprising the Old and New Testaments, is available in 459 languages; the New Testament standing alone has been rendered into 1,213 languages at last count. The difference between those translations and this work is that those translations have a missionary agenda and this work does not. With the exception of historic records in ancient Aramaic, Chaldaic, Greek and Latin, the translations of the Bible are directed at living native speakers. The clear purpose of all these is study, prayer and worship for Christians or tools of conversion directed at non-Christians.

That is a far cry from the light-hearted purpose of *300 Ways to Ask the Four Questions*. Not that it lacks scholarship; it is clearly the product of painstaking research. But just as the child asking the questions takes delight in the recital, so does this publication find joy in the fun of rendering innocent passages into obscure idioms, including archaic and extinct languages, and even into literary Shakespearean pastiche. And let us not forget the spoken renditions, a priceless bonus.

The linguist in me takes great delight in this book. In the past the science of Linguistics used to be called philology. This more aptly described what is happening here and what it is that so delights me. The term philology is derived from the Greek and means not just study of language but love of the word.

How is this night different? On all other nights we may fill our mind with the word or hunger for the word. On this night we feast on it.

Theodore Bikel
May 2, 2006

Theodore Bikel is star of screen (African Queen, My Fair Lady, Moulin Rouge, The Enemy Below, The Defiant Ones), stage (Broadway's Sound of Music, Zorba the Greek, Fiddler on the Roof – portraying Tevye over 2000 times) and music (dozens of albums, founder of Newport Folk Festival) He is one of the most versatile, well-loved actors of our generation, appearing in over 50 movies and starring in a great number of dramatic shows on TV.

Data on Bible translations were updated for this new edition.

Preface

The authors are indebted to a wondrous variety of individuals from the mundane to the exotic: a computer techie for a bank in Brussels; scholars of ancient Greek, ancient Egyptian and Old English; a Tuvin throat singer; a news broadcaster in Northern Siberia; linguists from all over the planet; a Circassian princess from the Caucasian community; famous Jewish singers in Bukharan and Djuwri cultural performing groups; African Jews who had no contact with the rest of the Judaic world until the 1920s; an Orthodox Jewish Tamil speaker; a barber; the President of the Foundation for Endangered Languages; the Chief Editor of the Oxford English Dictionary; a Professor at the Russian Academy of Sciences; the first native Mayan novelist; the Native American musician who played in the opening ceremony at the Salt Lake City Olympics; a junior Maasai warrior; people whose long-lost cousins lived in remote areas; signal processing experts at Bell Laboratories; students, teachers, dancers, journalists, custodians and many many others. Viewed any way, nearly every one of the over 700 people who helped us is special.

We recommend that you welcome some of these remarkable people as guests to your next Seder!

We have begun this book with what is normally put in an Acknowledgments section. Although it was our idea to collect hundreds of translations of an ancient ceremonial text, it would have remained a dream without our contributors. It is the motions of their hands you see. It is their voices you hear. The debt we owe to them is incalculable ... this book is their book.

Actually, setting out to collect hundreds of translations wasn't an idea either of us had originally planned. We each started this as a private and personal activity, gathering a few languages from friends, for friends. The two of us became acquainted after we joined the same choir. Amazingly, several years passed before we discovered our shared secret passion. If two people in a small choir were interested in this, how many more people around the world might be interested? The answer might still be "Only two!" But from the interest in our project we found during its preparation, we suspect not. After we joined forces, the project took on a life of its own. In receiving contributions from hundreds of people, we should say it has taken on hundreds of lives.

While we were fascinated by the idea of recording Jews from around the world saying the *Ma Nishtana*, we also asked ourselves the question, what would the Four Questions sound like in languages that don't typically have Jewish communities? This question led to the book you now hold.

When you look at the translations in this book, what might first strike you is the amazing variation in typography used by the world's languages. In most cases, we've entered the translations into a computer font, but we've published some handwritten (and calligraphied!) versions. More than the languages themselves, the written text is more permanent and enduring – you may never have dreamed there were so many different writing styles. Typography is a fascinating field of study in itself. Some writing styles grew out of pressing shaped stones into clay; others developed from the constraints of scratching their letters on palm leaves, which tear if too many straight lines are used.

When you play the CD and DVD, your first impression might be the variety of voices: young kids, elderly folk, gravelly voices, melodic voices. But there's a deeper insight – these are the voices of seamstresses, priests, royalty, engineers, accountants, museum guides, students, teachers, editors, linguists, professional translators, poets, actors, artists, musicians and choreographers. Isn't it always the case that digging beneath first impressions often reveals remarkable facts about people we've met? We include some information about each speaker to help you connect with them.

You may also notice the amazing variety of sounds in the languages: weird consonant clusters, strange sounding vowels, melodies and clicks. Even though everyone uses the same physical apparatus – mouth, jaw, tongue, larynx and chest – it's quite astounding how different people around the world sound; our languages seem so strange. Yet the important elements underlying communication – each language's syntax (nouns, verbs), grammar (ordering of words) and vocabulary – convey meaning in much the same manner. We're all different, but also similar.

This book is a modern-day Rosetta stone – all the languages and tongues living together in the same document, all trying to convey more or less the same thing. Having the same text conveyed in a variety of languages is a good way to see the similarities and differences between languages.

Of course, this isn't the first time the Four Questions have been translated into (say) Hungarian or Swedish: there are Hungarian and Swedish Haggadahs. The Jewish Theological Seminary in New York contains the largest collection of Haggadahs anywhere in the world – its library contains Haggadahs for at least 27 foreign languages: Arabic, possibly several varieties of Judeo-Arabic, Czech, Kurdish, Marathi, Persian and Slovenian among them. But you hold in your hands the largest number of languages for anything connected to Passover; quite possibly for any ceremonial text.

Introduction

Why Translate the Four Questions?

Since beginning this project more than 30 years ago, the authors have found many families who have taken it on their own to translate the Four Questions into foreign languages. Some try to add another language each year; others try to make the Seder into a multi-language fest. One person said: "It's not that I go looking for people to invite [to our Seder] based on what languages they speak ... and yet ..."

Of all portions of the Seder, why is this text so often chosen? One reason is the Four Questions are a highlight of the Seder. Everyone's attention focuses on the youngest child able to recite them. The child has practiced saying the Four Questions for weeks and we adults remember the anxiety (and pride) we experienced when it was our turn, many years ago. Also, reciting the Four Questions occurs early in the Seder (though this was not always the case). We are all still fresh with the excitement of gathering together, anticipating the tradition, dialogue (and good food!) that is before us. Another reason is the Seder is educational, the telling of a story so that as a people We May Never Forget. To keep the education process interesting we seek ways to make it fresh, different, novel. One way to achieve this is finding someone who speaks another language – something not too hard to do – and have them render the questions in that language.

But whatever the reason, Seder participants always enjoy the Four Questions. And asking not only the traditional questions, but also asking how they would be said in another country, another culture, another time and place.

Originally, questions occurred throughout the Seder whenever something unusual happened, from the pouring of the second cup of wine onward. This makes more sense: how strange is it to expect a child to ask 'Why are we doing these strange things tonight?' before any of them have happened! "On all other nights, we do not dip even once, but I predict we will be dipping our food two times by the end of the evening."

The *Ma Nishtana* (and any question) was to be asked by the son – and in those days, only the sons participated in this. And if the son could not ask, his father teaches him to ask questions. But at the end of the Seder, many children were tired or already asleep. (Murray writes: One of my earliest Seder memories was sleeping in my grandmother's bed after drinking too much wine.) It's likely the Rabbis, who wrote the "example" *Ma Nishtana* questions we now use, moved them to the top of the Seder, so that children would still be awake and alert for the *Ma Nishtana*.

And so, this is how we've ended up with our very traditional and very confusing ritual. The youngest child (now, no longer just male) asks questions about activities that have not yet been performed. And out of respect to tradition, we haven't changed the text to future tense. This is but one story of how rituals evolve over the centuries. The *Ma Nishtana*, like a lot of the Seder's texts, is like a house constructed of ancient timbers and stones, continually reconstructed, refashioned and recycled.

History of the Project

Rickey's story:
You may well ask what was the גרעין ('nucleus') upon which my adventure was built and how did it start to grow and flower. My interests involve two major areas – one of Judaism and the second of language. I first recognized my fascination with languages as a young child sitting with my grandfather. Reading a comic book I came across a page that had translations for Happy New Year in more than a dozen languages. I showed it to my grandfather and he immediately identified and read the Russian. Then, to my surprise, he proceeded to do the same with most of the other languages on the page. I already knew that my grandfather spoke Russian. How many times had he told me he was a 'White Russian' and came to the United States from Odessa in Besarabia. What I did not know at that time was that he spoke quite a number of languages. As a young man he was the representative for the Singer Sewing Machine Company in Eastern Europe before his emigration from Odessa to America.

Traveling over a wide area of Europe and Asia, and having to deal with speakers of many languages and dialects, he learned to read and write an awesome number of languages. Shortly after this I received a short-wave radio and was again fascinated by the many voices and sounds I could hear on that radio. Here was a panoply of different tongues and my most fervent wish was to twist the dial, and then, no matter where it stopped, to be able to understand fully what was being said. The truth is, that somewhere deep down in my psyche, I still harbor this desire. Perhaps working with these 300 languages has assuaged and fulfilled a bit of that desire.

The love for Judaism and interest in Passover was always there. As a young married couple, Dana and I moved back to the New Brunswick area. We joined Anshe Emeth Memorial Temple in New Brunswick where she had grown up. We quickly became part of the temple family. During earlier college years there were many invitations to Seders from family and friends. Most of these Seders seemed to lack any originality. Most were dull and spiritless. Very few spurred any kind of excitement in the attendees.

In 1972 we and our three young children were invited to a Seder by the Levines, friends and members of the temple family. After the youngest child sang the Four Questions in Hebrew, Alan turned to me and asked me to do them in Spanish. He knew I spoke Spanish but I had never thought about doing the Four Questions in any other language but the Hebrew/Aramaic or English that I had learned as a child. I did it and we all laughed and went on with the Seder. We were invited back the following year and I was again asked to recite the Four Questions in Spanish. I did it again and then someone tried it in French, another in Yiddish and a third person with a bit of knowledge of Italian also tried. What a great idea I thought. Everyone enjoyed doing or hearing the questions done this way. None of us knew it at the time but both a tradition and a 35-year adventure had begun.

It sparked interest in both kids and adults and lead to a discussion of where Jews had lived in past ages and what languages they might have brought to the Seder table. The following year we had our own Seder and added yet another language. This was to be a pattern we followed for the next 25 years – adding at least one new language to our repertoire. We didn't do all of them each year but did select a few. The entire family was enlisted in the search for new languages. When my daughters went to Israel as high school exchange students, each brought with them a copy of the Four Questions. And when they met other students from Denmark or Sweden or wherever, they would sit the other student down and get a translation. People we worked with were all fair game and after 25 years we had collected more than 25 translations. It was at that time that I met Murray.

Murray's story:
From my earliest childhood memories, I know I've always loved Passover. It was a joyous time when the entire extended family came together, from guests whose names I never remembered from far-away towns, to my favorite cousins. My tiny grandmother brought out endless platters and trays and plates piled high with food; it seem like magic – how was it possible for her tiny kitchen to contain so much bounty? One year my grandfather dyed his white hair to pink – he's going though his second childhood, my parents explained. The Afikomen hunts were especially fun.

I drifted away a bit from Judaism during college; other things were more important to me. I didn't fully return until after graduate school. It was my immersion into Israeli folkdance that did it: I loved the music, I loved the movements, I loved learning the words and singing along, I loved the people I met. But even when furthest away from Judaism, I had my attachment to Passover Seders.

Starting in graduate school, lonely for my family Seders, I began to lead my own Seders. I invited loads of friends, as my wife Randi and I still do, and tried each year to do something novel.

I started adding recordings of people doing odd versions of the Four Questions to my Seders in the late 1980s. A friend recited them as would be chanted by a Hebrew-speaking Donald Duck, a regular at our Seder sang them in Ladino, another friend recorded Spanish, and so on. Like Rickey, my inspiration was to make the Seder more interesting.

A critical event for our project occurred when I discovered that the world's "most accomplished speaker of Klingon", an Orthodox Jew, worked in my company. He developed a translation for Klingon in 1994. Although Rickey and I sang in the same Jewish choir, remarkably we didn't know about each other's passion. He overheard me talking about the Klingon translation and asked me what I was doing, not believing anyone else would do such a thing. He'd been collecting the text and I, only audio, so we joined forces and began obtaining translations with renewed passion. Within one year we had over 50 translations, within 10 years we had 250.

Why are there Five Questions?
(or) The History of the Questions

Why do we have five questions, when all Haggadahs show just four? Even our book title refers to The Four Questions.

Our explanation begins by noting the actual content of the *Ma Nishtana* has changed over the years. The original fourth question, found in the Mishnah, was: "On all other nights, we eat meat roasted, stewed or boiled; on this night, only roasted." This roasted meat served at the Seder was a reminder of the sacrifice of a lamb at the Holy Temple. However, as no Jewish Temple currently exists and no sacrifices take place, many years ago (around the 4th century) Rabbinic authorities replaced that question with another, referring to the reclining posture representing free people.

Some modern movements have changed this last, less ancient, question to be more representative of the entire holiday (this isn't a normal meal, but a ceremonial one). We see this in English as well as Russian and French Haggadahs. As the Hebrew hasn't been changed in modern times, only its translation, it might be considered to be less grounded. But some communities use this, so we consider it authentic and educational to include it. Rather than decide which final question to use and slight the tradition whose question was left out, we include both.

Moses Maimonides, in his 12th Century Code (Laws of Chametz and Matzah 10:2), has both Roast and Reclining (in that order), so his version has five questions altogether – though he points out that the 'Roast' question was deleted after the destruction of the Temple.

In fact, originally the questions didn't number four. Only three questions were customarily used when the Mishnah (*Pesachim 10:4*) first listed them: dipping, Matzah and roasted meat. (The question about Maror, bitter herbs, was added in later printed texts of the Mishnah.) Some Haggadahs have even fewer. For instance, the oldest surviving Haggadah is a small folio found in the Cairo Geniza. This 15-page book dating from the 10th or 11th century contains only questions about dipping and roasted meat. Researchers suspect this was a copyist's error, but several ancient Haggadahs show only two questions.

Foreign language Haggadahs. From top left:
Danish, Spanish (Cuba), Farsi (Iran),
Russian, Swedish, Amharic (Ethiopia),
Turkish, Marathi (India), Japanese,
Georgian, Ladino, Italian, Greek, German

About the Translations

How Translations Were Obtained

We obtained translations through every means possible. In spite of the world becoming more interconnected each day, with billions of instant messages whizzing wirelessly around, often the personal connection was key: experts recommended by linguists, friends of friends, chance encounters, donations of professional translation services, contacts made during vacations, message board postings, websites and concert notices. Recordings came via CD, email, tape cassettes and dictation micro-cassettes. We even shipped tape recorders to Romania and Myanmar because language sources there had no means for recording. (The tape recorder continued to be used in Myanmar for linguistics research.)

This project started prior to the Internet, using personal connections. Friends, colleagues, the United Nations and national consulates were very helpful. But it was a great boon to finally find language resources via the web. Researching connections between Germany and Namibia, we found the online site for Namibia's national newspaper. We contacted its editor regarding Herero and other Namibian languages. The editor said he'd put a notice in the paper. We soon started receiving letters from people all over Namibia. One of the most fruitful resources there was Gamsberg Macmillan, a publisher of African textbooks, who provided nine languages spoken throughout Africa.

The translators reflect a wide range of expertise. Some were world experts, a few had only marginal fluency (nonetheless, the best we could obtain). However, most translators had reasonably comfortable competence skills for their language. The translations, too, span a wide range in depth of erudition. A small number of texts had little forethought – for instance, one was done verbatim while the speaker was driving a van through forest trails. Many others contain unparalleled scholarship. Some translators wrote 6 pages (or more) to explain word choices, grammar, phrasing and parallelism to native ceremonies. Some experts returned to their translation several times over the course of many weeks, refining and correcting the text. We provided a Biblical concordance for unusual terms, and many researched how these phrases are translated in their own Norwegian, Lithuanian or Inuit Bibles. For all these efforts we are eternally grateful, and you all are the beneficiaries.

The Task of Translation

Most people are familiar with the game of Telephone, where each person attempts to convey the gist of a story to the next person in the line. The original story is often distorted by the time the story reaches the last person. (The proverb "Out of sight, out of mind," might become, the old joke goes, "Blind idiot.")

Most translators worked very hard to keep faithful to the original. But, like the Telephone game, translating a text from one language to another nearly always involves some distortion or loss or addition of information.

Some languages have no words for some of the concepts. One writer told us that his was a rice-based culture and in his Dravidian language there was no word for bread other than borrowed words from Hindi. Even most Indian languages have no generic all-encompassing word for bread, so there's no way to express 'bread with yeast' (leavened bread) without mentioning the name of a specific bread (Roti, Naan, Paratha, Puri, Phulka, Bhatura, Bati, Choorma, etc.). They have borrowed both the French [pain] and the Hindi [roti]. This is somewhat surprising since Alford and Duguid, in their book *Flatbreads and Flavors*, write that "Flatbreads can be made from every grain imaginable: wheat, rye, corn, oats, millet, sorghum, teff, rice and buckwheat. They can also be made from tubers, such as potatoes, and from legumes such as chickpeas and lentils." Some peoples have no general word for herbs or spices. Yet others do not dip foods. Still others felt mentioning dipping foods was strange because they dip food at almost every meal. The concept of reclining, itself an archaic reference to how the Romans ate while lying on pillows, led to convoluted expressions in some translations.

Several translators complained about the text. "It's too vague ... our language can't say 'we dip twice' without giving the verb and object, explaining what is dipped." "It will sound like you are dipping yourself." "We've used the word for 'night', but we would *never* eat then." We developed a translator's guide to provide paths around some of the difficulties. The guide mentioned the usual difficulties (night vs. evening, leaning, what is different or what is changed, unleavened bread, descriptions of herbs, dipping and what is dipped) as well as the symbolism underpinning the phrases.

The single word 'reclining' led to several interpretations. The word in the text is מסבין (m'subin). The root סבב (sovev, 'to go around') is puzzling – what did going around have to do with leaning? The original inspiration was a Roman custom of the wealthy and free of eating while lying on a comfortable couch, the *lectus triclinaris*. Three *lecti* were arranged in the shape of a horseshoe around a *mensa* – a round table – to allow the slaves to serve. Slaves had to stand. By custom all heads were oriented towards the central table, with left elbows propped on a cushion. Thus, current custom, based on Rabbinic interpretation, is to lean to the left while drinking the cups of wine. Yet, in translating 'reclining', translators either could get overly specific (drink while leaning to the left), or use their language's term for leaning. The gist for these words sometimes means 'leaning over', 'leaning sideways', 'lying down' or 'slouching'. Don't be offended that the translations imply that we slouch while we eat or we eat off the floor. Remember there are reclining chairs (though these lean back rather than to the left).

Yes, the text *is* vague; it *does* have strange constructions; it *is* a bit contradictory – that's part of what makes our table discussions so interesting.

For most languages, a decision needed to be made: Are we seeking a culturally acceptable translation (not mentioning bread if it is not customary to eat bread for dinner) or a linguistic one (convey the words without respect to how odd the actions may seem)? Some of the translators wrote pages to explain why particular words and phrases were chosen. Most often a linguistic translation was given, for the Four Questions refer to a symbolism-rich ceremony. Activities that may seem odd often *do* occur in ceremonies!

Even in English translations, we have considerable variation. As an example, in some Haggadahs the English states we dip twice, without mentioning what is dipped. Some use the general word 'vegetables', while others specify horseradish and parsley. Thus, our translations, where (for instance) no suitable word for herbs could be found in the language, and the word vegetables was used instead, are quite adequately correct.

The typical English translation may even perpetuate an error in translating the original Hebrew. The opening phrase, "*Ma nishtana halaylah hazeh*", is most faithfully translated as "How different [is] tonight from all nights", and is not a question at all! The subsequent phrases are then understood as a listing of four of the ways tonight is different.

We don't know when the English translation was first rendered as "Why is this night different from all other nights?" Yet, this (mis)translation is very commonly used. So we decided to adopt it rather than introduce the confusion that would be caused by bucking the conventional concepts of the Four Questions. (See Sidebar: Rabbinic interpretations of Why, What, How.)

Rabbinic interpretations of Why, What, How

Dr. Lawrence A. Hoffman, of the Hebrew Union College in New York, writes:

The complete sentence from the original source is, "And here the son asks his father, and if the son lacks knowledge (of how to do so?) his father teaches him *Ma Nishtana* (e.g., how is this night is different from all the other nights)." The 16th-century commentator, Bertinoro, says that by his day, the son was actually saying *Ma Nishtana* (as is our custom) but he knew that in ancient days, the adult male who said kiddush [the blessing over the wine, e.g. the leader of the Seder] said that prayer.

The so-called 'questions' in other words were not necessarily questions at all in antiquity. They were comments on "How this night is different (*Ma nishtana halaylah hazeh*) from other nights!"

Rabbi Neil Gillman, of the Jewish Theological Seminary in New York, adds this elaboration:

"Why translate it 'What is different ...' [eg: as a question]? Probably because the Mishnah says 'Then the son asks the father ...' In other words, the Mishnah misleads us to understand what the child says is a question – when it really is an exclamation."

This 'What vs. How' confusion is reflected in modern Haggadahs. A Dutch Haggadah of ours has an exclamation point (implying How) after the Hebrew, yet it uses a question mark (implying Why) after its Dutch translation. Many linguists say the proper translation of the first line is not "Why is this night different from ..." but "What distinguishes this night from all other nights?" or even "What has changed this night from all other nights?" While more technically correct, such subtleties might make the English more difficult to understand for our foreign translators. And this change from the standard English translation may still not have been conveyed in other languages. Thus, we used the de-facto standard translation, and accompanied it with our translator's guide.

Most translations are more than one language removed from the original Hebrew. In some cases, these translations are three "language removes" away. For example, because our Piemontese speaker did not know English, he worked from the Italian translation of the English translation of the Hebrew. Similarly, the Tarafit speaker worked from the Arabic; the Oriya is based on the Hindi; Mapudungun on the Spanish; and so on. The source languages used were Arabic, Bengali, Burmese, Dutch, English, French, Hebrew, Hindi, Indonesian, Italian, Portuguese, Russian and Spanish.

In the final analysis, what you hold can only be considered just one suggestion of the many ways to convey the questions in the various languages.

Kindness and Interest of People

Most people were delighted to help this project. We can't count the number of times the translators thanked *us* for including them in our project. Those representing lesser-used languages were happy for even a momentary focus on their 'little' language. A small number said they were very busy, but participated anyway; very few people outright declined to help. Many people went to extraordinary measures to assist the project – time taken from vacations, expensive and extensive long distance phone calls, research to find community centers or community leaders, even overcoming the loss of treasured recordings and personal artifacts when luggage was stolen. The sheer number of languages represented in this collection, and the even larger number of people who helped us, shows that people like to help others. It is a reflection of the hope we all feel for cooperation towards peaceful co-existence. May it soon blossom.

While the overwhelming majority of people did translations gratis, some received reimbursement for telephone expenses, an honorarium, or gifts of rugs, artwork, mugs.

Many people enjoyed the project, respected the connections to tradition and ceremony, and appreciated the attention to their language and culture. Listen to them ...

Nenets: "Anastasia and I went through your text, which she found very beautiful and touching."

Cheyenne: "[Louise] will enjoy translating the Seder service since she (and a number of us in Busby, Montana) participate in a Seder service each Passover season. How interesting to have a Native American translating an ancient Jewish spiritual ceremony! Cheyennes have deep respect for spiritual ceremonies."

Apache: The linguist working with the speaker said "most Apaches I have talked to feel a kinship with the Jewish experience, since both peoples have been kicked around a lot in deserts (and other places)."

Malinke: "Fodé was interested in translating this text because his first visit to the USA involved flying 14 hours from Guinea to Newark Airport and driving directly to a Passover Seder in Princeton."

Mongolian: "I [am] prompted to help people who are trying to assess my heritage and my culture. I am proud that I was born to this rich culture and it is a privilege to share my knowledge with anyone who is interested about it. It has been truly a pleasure to work for your project."

Luiseño: "Thank you for creating such a wonderful project. We were very happy to participate."

Makhuwa: "I like very much to know about other countries, cultures, languages and peoples. Always [after] I had a conversation with you, I felt special moments and thought that really the earth is round."

Cornish: "I feel a connection to Judaism, and I was very happy to be asked to participate in this project. Thanks again for letting me take part!"

Several people gave us more than we asked for. The DVD contains samples of songs, chants, music and history for several of the cultures. One story of generosity was Manahem's, the Bukharan we asked to record the Four Questions as it was chanted in his community. "Only the *Ma Nishtana*?!" Manahem asked incredulously, in Hebrew, our only jointly understood language (severely hampered by our own limited vocabulary). "*Keyn, keyn*" (Yes, yes). When he received our 20-minute cassette tape, he complained it was too small. Sure enough, when we received his recording, we understood. He'd started with the Kiddish, the beginning of the Seder, continued with the blessings that followed and the *Ha Lachma*. Recording on both sides, Manahem ran out of tape before getting to the Four Questions! We called again to say "*Rak Ma Nishtana*" (Only the *Ma Nishtana*) – he was clearly disappointed to do so little. He had wanted to record the entire Bukharan Seder for us!

A collection of this size would have not been possible had our world not become so connected in recent years. But that is a trite comment, because the world has always been connected. The friend-of-an-associate-of-a-friend-of-a-cousin always could extend our reach far away from our home town.

In traditional cultures, the connectedness <u>within</u> villages is very high, and the connectedness <u>between</u> villages is low. Yet people who share traditions, concerns, pursuits and even commercial (trading) interests are likely to know each other. A Russian friend explains that the sheep herders on top of each mountain know each other, the farmers in each valley know each other, but the herders on the mountains don't know the farmers in the valleys as well. (See Sidebar: Six Degrees of Separation.) A linguist consultant said this project might become easier over time. Although seeking rarer and rarer languages, we might more easily find informants for those rare languages as the Internet connects more of the world's people.

If truth be told, without the computer and the Internet this enterprise would have ended up between impossible and not completed. It took the addition of the computer to our daily lives to allow us the ability to contact a large number of people around the globe and the facility to manipulate the very letters we type into this machine. By the time we realized our common interest, the Internet had begun to blossom. We went out onto the old Usenet and posted a request to a number of social groups. We asked, with a little additional background, "Have you ever done the Four Questions in [*insert language*] or would you be willing to try it"? We received many responses (and one asking "What is the Four Questions??") but most were quite positive and helpful, including several from an Esperanto group.

By far the strangest but ultimately one of the most interesting replies came back with the heading 'Fir Kashes' ["Four Questions" in Yiddish]. Fir Kashes wasn't mentioned in our requests (See Sidebar: Fir Kashes vs. Qushiyot) but it was a legitimate response. It was the sender's *name* that was the surprise – P.V. Viswanath. We later learned that P.V., who goes by the name Meylekh, was a devout Jew and a speaker of Tamil. His 7-year old daughter Meena, <u>trilingually</u> fluent in Tamil, Yiddish and English, was the youngest speaker in our collection.

Dialects and Languages

When two people speak differently, are they speaking different languages, or different dialects of the same language? The greater the difference, the more likely linguists are to say that two different languages are involved, but the boundary between "different dialects" and "different languages" is a fuzzy one. Some people place the boundary at "mutual intelligibility" – if two people can converse with each other, like a New Yorker and an Alabamian, they are speaking the same language, though they may be speaking different dialects of that language. This is not a clean definition, however, since intelligibility depends heavily on how slowly and clearly a person speaks.

Another confounding factor is political considerations. An old joke among linguists is that a language is a dialect with an Army and a Navy. So we commonly refer to Swedish and Norwegian as different languages, even though they are largely mutually intelligible, while some southern Italian "dialects" are unintelligible to northern Italians unfamiliar with those dialects.

What We Did Not Collect

Our project tried not to gather different dialects for several reasons. First and foremost was the labor involved for verification. It was hard enough to get all the languages we have properly entered, proofed, recorded and edited. In some cases, the languages with harder-to-reach experts took several years to be proofed.

Second is the pragmatic issue of "how much difference" in speech, syntax, vocabulary, etc. is required to consider one village's speech a different dialect from a neighboring one's. This question, at the language level, is one that linguists continually debate. There are so many dialects, and ways of making a dialect, that some linguists do not attempt a definition. We mean no offense to any one group of peoples – we respect and treasure all dialects and languages. But, we needed to draw the line somewhere. Otherwise, this project would have never seen the light of day.

Our collection is, however, inconsistent with respect to these goals. Sometimes in pursuing a given language, several people were asked on our behalf to teach us the translation. This sometimes resulted in two translations for the same language, differing in dialect. We included both in the recordings, rather than choose one dialect as the one true representative for a language. This was especially important when the language was rare and generally interesting to the world at large.

Themes of Passover
Drawings by (clockwise from top): Joseph Salter, 3rd grade, W Caldwell, NJ;
Eital Schattner-Elmaleh, 5th grade, Montclair, NJ; Tatiana Mickley, 4th grade, W Caldwell, NJ

The Seder

Oppression as a Theme in the Seder

The Seder tells a story of oppression. A cold-hearted and evil Pharaoh enslaves a people, punishes its women, and refuses to let go of his slaves when confronted by the signs and wonders of the Almighty.

When relating this ancient story of oppression to more modern times, we unfortunately find many echos throughout history. Translations in other languages is enough for some to remember unfortunate events in the lives of other peoples: "I think of the stories (of oppression) ... Creole (slave uprisings, unthinkable poverty); Farsi (revolutions and religious fundamentalism), Irish (potato famine and British imperialism), Yiddish (don't ask!)."

Oppression of peoples is also evidenced in the life stories of our translators. The Kabyle linguist spoke of French Colonial authorities refusing to accept his family's name, instead assigning a name based on their village. Some speakers were told not to use their language at school; Canada's earlier policy tried to eradicate the Mohawk language – our speaker saw many people abused when they were caught speaking it. Our speaker of Eastern Kanjobal is a well-known poet and author, who has written about the oppression of being Mayan in Guatemala. When the translator for Eastern Farsi and Dari attended medical school in Kabul, he ran into political problems with the Soviet's installed government and was forced to leave Kabul and then Afghanistan. The Gĩkũyũ speaker was raised in a detention camp where his parents were incarcerated during Kenya's struggle for independence.

Mystique of the Number Four

It has been written that no other Jewish holiday is so involved with and so dependent upon numbers as is Passover. Numbers are used both to count and to express ideas. We create portraits and images with numbers and also teach with them. In all religions and civilizations there have been numbers which were considered mystical. In both the East and the West the numbers three and seven hold special powers. We see this for example in 'Three Coins in the Fountain', the three wishes the Genie gives to Aladdin, the triton of the Roman god Neptune, or Cerberus, the three-headed dog, which, in Greek tradition, guards the entrance to Hades. There are Seven Hills of Rome and seven days of the week and even Snow White's seven dwarfs.

These numbers are also seen in many parts of our Jewish tradition. We have three Patriarchs, all the world rests on three things [*Al Shlosha D'varim*] and the Priestly [*Aharonic*] Blessing has three statements. Numbers are used throughout the Passover Seder but by far the number four is seen most often in the Haggadah. As the dominant recurring number, four is obviously an important mnemonic and acts as a kind of link connecting the commentaries, subjects and ideas of the holiday.

Looking at the basic structure of the Passover Seder, these are the recurring symbols and themes: four questions, four cups of wine, four sons, four matriarchs, four core symbols on the Seder table, four promises of redemption and four Hebrew names for the holiday of Passover.

So what is this mystique with the number four?

All rituals have an organizing principal and Passover is no exception. The rituals of the Seder have been well defined and structured by the Rabbis who codified the service. Often we must look at the beliefs at the time that a process is put together to better understand its component parts. In the first and second centuries CE, four was a critical number, and so it was for the Rabbis too. It was well known by the mathematicians of the second century CE that using just *four* fours, one could find simple mathematical expressions for every integer from 0 to at least 112, something that cannot be done with any other number. This became the puzzle of the Four Fours and today there are a number of websites which discuss the subject including *The Definite Four Fours Answer Key*. The solutions for integers from 0 to 40,000 are shown at www.dwheeler.com/fourfours.

In the second century CE, the thinking went like this: the number one was considered only as a single point. Two was two points connected by a line and virtually no space was created. Three was three points, which created an irregular shape – the triangle. Four was four points, the first number that created a whole space when connected by lines. Within the whole space the participant is guided along the way as he or she moves in the cycle from slavery to freedom, from exile to redemption, from oppression to independence. The participant can experience and remember each move, step by step. Perhaps the Rabbis of the time were fascinated by the Four Fours puzzle, giving the number a special place in the Seder.

The Questions

Community Variations in the Text

The text that is used for the questions differs from community to community. In various Judeo-Spanish (Ladino) and Judeo-Iraqi versions, מַטְבִּילִין (matbilin) is מְטַבְּלִין (metablin), אוֹכְלִין (okhlin) is אוֹכְלִין וְשׁוֹתִין (okhlin veshotin, 'eat and drink'), and חָמֵץ וּמַצָּה (chameits u'matsah) is חָמֵץ אוֹ מַצָּה (chameits o matsah). These variations can be clearly heard in the recordings; for instance, some of the highlights recordings on the CD.

Some Haggadahs add the word כֻּלוֹ (kulo, 'only') prior to Maror, in addition to before Matzah.

Even something as simple as the vowels used for אֶחָת (echat, 'once') reflect regional differences. In classical Hebrew, at the end of a phrase the vowels for אַחַת (achat) shift to אֶחָת (echat). Some communities follow the Mishnah's Classical Hebrew form (פַּעַם אֶחָת, pa'am echat, 'one time'), while others (פַּעַם אַחַת, pa'am achat) follow modern Hebrew conventions.

> ### Classical אֶחָת (echat) vs. modern אַחַת (achat)
> From a sample of more than 3 dozen Haggadahs, 10 used *achat*: Cuban, Ethiopian, Farsi, Greek, Italian, Judeo-Iraqi, Ladino, Marathi, one published in 1814 in Hungary and even one published in 1739 in Denmark followed so-called "modern" conventions. This difference does not follow strict Sephardi/Ashkenazi divisions, as some Sephardi editions used *echat*.

The Order of Questions

As well as having different versions of the text, different communities have a different order for the questions. In most Sephardi Haggadahs, the question referring to dipping is moved to the beginning. That is, the Sephardi order (relative to the Ashkenazi) is #3, #1, #2 then #4. The Amharic community uses the order of leaning, matzah, maror, dipping (e.g., #4, #1, #2, #3).

Bread on Passover?

Early Printer Errors

Does your Haggadah tell you to eat bread for Passover? Probably not, but there have been Haggadahs in the past which have told their readers to do this very thing. How can that be?

It has to do with something called עירוב תבשילין (Eruv tavshilin, 'a mixture of dishes'). An *Eruv tavshilin* is a halachic device which allows one to cook food on a Festival for use on the Shabbat that immediately follows the festival. Permission to prepare food on holy (Festival) days is restricted only to food required for those days and the food must be consumed on that day itself. But if a *Yom Tov* (Holy Day) falls on Friday the problem arises of how to prepare food for the Shabbat which follows. The answer and solution to the problem is in an exception to the exception and that is in the enactment of *Eruv tavshilin*. On the day before the Festival, one sets aside some bread [in the case of Passover, some Matzah] and a cooked dish. This symbolically serves as the preparation of the food for Shabbat.

In the Diaspora, if the first two days of Passover fall on a Thursday and Friday, one must prepare an *Eruv tavshilin* on the afternoon before Passover so that one can cook on the Festival for Shabbat. Note that in Israel, one need never prepare an *Eruv tavshilin* on the day before Passover because the first day of Passover never falls on a Friday. It is possible, however, for the last day of Passover to fall on a Friday. Thus, in Israel as well, there are times when one would have to prepare an *Eruv tavshilin* on the last of the intermediate days. So how did this error make its way in those Haggadahs? The *Eruv tavshilin* is not a part of the Haggadah recital and at times was not mentioned at all. In order to make the Haggadah more practical for use, the benediction for the *Eruv tavshilin* was added to the Haggadah. The benediction, with an explanation, was meant for the whole year and not for Passover. Some publishers of early Haggadahs added translations of the Hebrew: "Take some prepared food and a piece of bread…" and this caused the error.

On Language

Fluency

Murray's comment:

Each time I listen to one of these recordings, where the speaker haltingly speaks the words, I'm reminded of my own difficulties with speaking Hebrew, the language of my 'tribe'. I had several years of relatively intensive Hebrew instruction as a child, and well into middle age I regularly recite prayers in our temple. Yet, I still stumble over similar-looking words, transpose vowels, and mumble over longer words when I am hurried along.

How much more difficult it was for our translators! For some had even less familiarity with their languages; in all cases, they were speaking words and phrases they had never used before. We have nothing but admiration and the highest praise for them and their willingness to share their knowledge, to teach us a little bit of their language.

Language Extinction

Just as some of the wildlife on this planet is endangered and may not be around for future generations, some of the languages in this collection are endangered too. Our 'most endangered list' in this collection includes Lenape, with only 6 speakers left. Linguists estimate 400-500 of the world's languages are within a generation of dying, and without sustained conservation efforts, possibly half of the world's 5,000-7,000 languages will be gone in a hundred years. Fluent speakers of many languages are all old; younger speakers have limited opportunities for discourse – they are increasingly attracted to the larger world outside their community. Linguists and ethnographers decry the loss of culture, stories, art, music, poetry, historical documents and ordinary conversations associated with each language. However, language preservation – formal and informal – is ongoing for many of these languages.

Prior to Hebrew's revival in the late 1880s it had been a dead language also, used only for religious purposes, literature and learning. Until Eliezer Ben-Yehuda promoted Hebrew for daily use in 1881, Hebrew had not been a living, spoken language for as many as 1,800 years. The successful revival of Hebrew can be an inspiration for all peoples who see the steady extinction of their language as native-speaking elders die away.

What can I do?

■ Pick a language (or two!) that intrigues you, find a web resource or college where the language is taught, and inquire how you can help.

■ Make a personal connection with a speaker of another language. Don't hold prejudices against people who speak English with an accent. Change your perspective: a person with a foreign accent is probably someone who speaks multiple languages.

■ Find someone who speaks a different language from you. Ask the custodian from Ghana, the librarian from Hungary, the salesgirl from Indonesia, the waitress from Pakistan: What languages do you speak? When and how did you learn them? When was the last time you went home? Who in your family is still there? What do you miss about your home culture?

■ Perhaps you can make a contribution to a preservation office far away from you, or perhaps you can volunteer time at a college office closer to you. Here are some suggested resources:

Endangered Language Fund, Inc.
300 George St., Suite 900
New Haven, CT 06511

Foundation for Endangered Languages
Batheaston Villa, 172 Bailbrook Lane,
Bath BA1 7AA England

Summer Institute of Linguistics
International Academic Bookstore
7500 W. Camp Wisdom Road
Dallas, TX 75236

Also, search the web for Tribal and Native American colleges.

Drawing by Zak Klein, 5th grade, Pine Brook, NJ

Crossing the Red Sea

Suggestions for Use

Personalize your Seder! There are limitless ways of using the material contained in this book, its CD and DVD. Add educational and cultural elements to the Four Questions. What follows are suggestions based on how the authors and their friends incorporated these translations into their Seders, teaching materials and school projects. We hope these suggestions inspire you to develop additional innovative uses. We'd love to hear your ideas; contact us on our website.

■ Ask someone who knows a foreign language to read it at your Seder. Read (or play) one new translation each year.

■ Illustrate your family's genealogy. Did Grandma come from Hungary? Did Great-Grandpa come from Ukraine or Poland? Show the languages that your family's ancestors spoke.

■ Illustrate all participants' genealogies. Prior to the Seder, ask each participant where their grandparents/great-grandparents came from. Prepare a copy of the language from that country for them to read.

■ Entertain by playing some of the CD's Highlights tracks: this is a famous Mayan poet; here is a Circassian princess; this fellow is the Chief Editor of the Oxford English Dictionary (he'd never said "Matzah" before); and now a young girl who is an Orthodox tri-lingual Tamil speaker ...

■ Play or learn the Bukharan Kiddish. Explore and explain the history and special culture of the Jews living in Uzbekistan. Next year, do the same for the Libyan Kiddish (or Four Questions) – how long did Jews live in Libya? Or play the songs and chants – explore what life was like for Jews in Yemen, Iraq, Uganda, Turkey, Romania, Bulgaria ...

■ Play or learn the Japanese Four Questions and the Japanese transliteration of the Hebrew. Show page from Japanese Haggadah. Explore how Jews traveled there, beginning with early settlements in the 1860s through Jews escaping Nazi Europe. Next year, explore other areas of the Judaic world.

■ Guess the mystery language. Give a language to someone ahead of time – ask them to learn the pronunciation from the recording. Have them read it during the Seder, while others guess where it's from: Native American, European, African, etc.

■ Provide a different language for each participant, spanning the world.

■ The Hebrew Semaphore was actually used by the Israeli Navy. Imagine you're on a ship in the Mediterranean Sea. You can't do the whole Seder in Semaphore, but you can "act out" the Four Questions! Get small Israeli flags, available from flag stores or your local Jewish community center. Give each guest a diagram for a different letter, and spell *Ma Nishtana* around the room! Or have one person wave the whole sequence of letters.

■ Decorate your Israeli Naval ship: put Maritime Signal flags on your walls.

■ Show or play the Egyptian to give a sense of the location and time of Exodus.

■ Guess which translation is Old English (the CD quiz): since the sound is part-Dutch, part-German, with very few English-sounding words, it's fun to hear the similarities between languages.

■ Compare ancient languages with modern counterparts, providing a sense of how languages evolve: ancient Greek/modern Greek; Gothic/German; Latin/Italian; Old English/English or German. Or use modern dialects of ancient languages: Bohairic, Coptic and Sahidic Aramaic (Kurdish).

■ Show or play some of the minority languages: relate the theme of the Seder to modern struggles for independence or survival. Discuss what causes languages to become endangered and disappear – compare the fate of Ladino to Yiddish: why might one die out sooner?

■ Choose languages and countries to illuminate and relate to current events. Counter bad news from halfway around the world with the generosity of someone there who provided a translation for this book. Expand on current news with cultural explanations of the people living there.

■ Read some of the African languages, and relate the story of Nelson Mandela's struggle to win freedom and rights through the African National Congress.

■ Use a translation to welcome a guest from another country, or someone who has married into your family.

■ Use the translations to make school reports more interesting and personal.

■ Play "Guess the Language" games contained in the book, CD and DVD.

■ Make a poster of the first lines of common languages – order them in an interesting way. Can you identify them from their words and scripts?

Lighthearted Fare

While collecting these translations, communicating with people all around the world, we had many humorous exchanges, misunderstandings and accidental insights. We share with you some of these for your interest and enjoyment. May you also have the privilege of speaking with people from 120 countries.

Uzbek: Howie asked his Uzbek-speaking co-worker Boris if he could do the translation into Uzbek. After a long time, Howie asked Boris if he was done. No, I'm not ready yet. Again, Howie waited a reasonable time, then asked Boris about it. No, Boris said, "I took it to a Rabbi." Why, Howie asked, was there something about the text he didn't understand? No, Boris had taken the Four Questions text to his Rabbi to get the answers!

Marathi: Sanjay stopped by one day and saw the Marathi translation (which uses Hindi chararacters) and tried reading it. As he only understood a little of the language, he asks "What is this, a diet?" (Sanjay later helped refine the Hindi translation.)

Cofan: Our guide in the Ecuadorian jungle helped obtain the Cofan translation from a schoolteacher we'd met. When the guide faxed the translation, he ended his letter with this accidental philosophical mantra:
THE ANSWERS ARE THE QUESTIONS.
I HOPE YOU UNDERSTAND WHAT SHE DID.

Yup'ik: A linguistics student at Alaska University in Fairbanks agreed to do the translation. Studying both Yup'ik and English, her second language, Monica said she planned to have another person help her who was less influenced by English as she was. We never received responses to emails and letters, and we gave up after two years. Three years from our initial contact, we received a voicemail: "Hi, This is Monica. I finally got someone to record the translation. Sorry it took so long. Do you still want this?? I guess I'll send it to you." (When it came, the translation had intersperced our explanation of the text, along with the actual text.)

Ugandan languages: A friend in Boston mentioned a community of Jews in Uganda he'd heard about, saying a web search for Abayudaya would locate them. Murray wrote to Matthew, a person who'd posted a lot about them. Matthew responded that the community gets lots of 'research' requests all the time, but as he'd spent much time there, we should mention we were Matthew's friends. Doing so, two months later we received four translations in the local Ugandan languages, with cassette tape recordings. Rabbi Gershom Sizomu ended the tape with a thank you and *Chag Sameach* in his inimitable Ugandan accent. Laughing, we wrote to our friend in Boston, who found it remarkable that sitting at a computer terminal in NJ, we were able to receive translations from Uganda in such a short time.

Four years later, in January 2003 Gershom and his brother JJ toured the USA and came to Murray's community. Meeting him at a reception that evening, he showed the translations to Gershom and asked "Do you remember this?" Gershom enthusiastically hugged him and said how glad he was to meet him. Murray responded "You're glad to meet *me*?! I'm so thrilled to meet you!!"

Murray and his wife Randi were taken by Gershom's infectious and sincere passion for Judaism and decided to do something for the community. Murray got copying permission from two Haggadah publishers and received a donation of 400 Haggadahs from their local ShopRite supermarket. He modified the Four Questions page in each one to include translations into the four Ugandan languages used by their community. Supplementing the hundreds of tiresome hours spent formatting, cutting, reassembling and stapling the newly customized-for-Uganda Haggadahs, they got funding from various people in their community for copying and shipping. In October 2003, the Ugandans received over 500 Haggadahs, more than enough for every adult there.

Oriya: One of our longest-sought Indian languages was Oriya (because it was fairly common, we figured it would be easy to obtain). An Indian fellow knew someone who knew someone who knew someone who did the translation and collected it.

But then he lost it – looked all over his house for it. He couldn't contact the translator who'd moved back to India. A month later, he showed up at Murray's office with the Oriya translation. Where had it been? In a pocket of his baby's diaper bag!

Makhuwa: At one point the email link for the translator, Loubato, was down for several days. Dan, who knows Spanish and a little Portuguese, called Loubato in Portugal to answer his questions about 'unleavened bread'. During the call, Loubato tried to get a sense of what this 'Matzah' was like. He asked if it was good or bad. Dan, who isn't Jewish, said bad (having in mind that one wouldn't want to eat it if it weren't a religious observance). Loubato asked if it was horrible, and Dan said 'yes, horrible' – obviously there are many attitudes to Matzah.

Latvian: The translator wrote: "My mother and I had fun translating the text a couple of weekends ago when I visited there. We were scanning through the Old Testament for pointers on how certain things were translated there, such as the bitter herbs. My mother knew that there was a reference to it in the Old Testament, but at first couldn't remember where, so she phoned the Dean of our Latvian church, who was unfortunately out, then tried one of the Reverends who lives in London, also without success, and was just about to ring a lay preacher she knows when we found it! We learnt a lot, including the fact that we didn't know we had so many Bibles at home, in Latvian and English! We had never known the Latvian word for Passover, for example. It took my mum back, as she remembered stuff she had been taught in religious education at refugee camps after the war!"

Gronings: When perfecting the translation, John-Luc found the following rule of thumb: "Groningers make short sentences; eight words per sentence is almost too much." On his translation, John-Luc indicated how much shorter each Gronings line was relative to the Dutch.

Old English: Marcia teaches a class on translation issues at NYC's New School. "[Seeing the Old English,] I get a real kick out of thinking of folks sitting around the mead hall reciting these – then they open the door for Elijah, and Grendel comes in!"

Buriat: When meeting Sayan a year after he translated the text, his first question (in Russian) was: What number language was Buriat in our collection! He remembered it immediately as the text with *Matzu* in it.

Irish Gaelic: Pat wrote: "I have a question about the text side of things. Faxing is not an option – I'm afraid I cannot justify a fax to the United States to my employer." So, he put the Gaelic script on a web page for us to download! At the time, the web was new and the concept of a web page for a single individual to view was very strange.

Marathi: Kirthika was asked to type the hand-written Marathi translation. We asked what the translation meant, to see how accurate it was. The introduction was good: "Why is this night so special compared to other nights?" But the first question was awful: "In the other nights, we do have a sumptuous meal not even once; but this night we have a sumptuous meal twice."

But the rest was faithfully translated, so we asked about 'sumptuous meal'. Does it really say that? "It's a colloquial expression, but yes." "Well, it's supposed to say, 'On all other nights, we do not dip even ...'" She interrupted with "Yes, yes, that's what it says." "But why did you say sumptuous meal?"

Kirthika answers: "Because in Marathi, and only in Marathi, when you talk about dipping foods, that's a colloquial expression that implies a sumptuous feast!"

Yemenite: In seeking the Yemenite chant, we first approached Moshiko, a famous Israeli folkdance choreographer, Yemenite and 8th generation Sabra. "Please, Moshiko, sing the *Ma Nishtana* as you sang it as a child." Moshiko started singing, and it was the traditional Askenazi melody! "No, no, the way Yemenites do it." "This is the only one I know." "*NOooo!*" (disbelief that he didn't know it). His rendition is in the recordings.

It was nine (!) years later that we finally located a Yemenite singer, from the group Moshav Amka, who sent us the Yemenite chant.

Cornish: Briony Williams, a linguist studying Welsh and related languages, originally had helped with the Welsh translation. Meeting her again at a speech conference, she continually tried to find a language that we didn't have. [Spoken in a very proper, detached British accent] "Have you Gaelic Scots?" (Yes) "Do you have Manx?" (Yes) "Well, how about Cornish?" (No). "I put in a research proposal for Cornish that was rejected, but I still have a few contacts there." She sent a request to the Secretary of the Cornish Language Board, who forwarded it to their "official" translator. He quickly worked on the translation and sent it to his colleague Benjamin at Harvard, who finished it up. Briony's kind generosity to keep helping our project was greatly appreciated.

Breads: Recently a co-worker was asked if there was a generic word for bread in any of the several languages she spoke or was familiar with. A wonderful cook, born and raised in the State of Gujarat in India, she responded that there was no one word for bread in any of the 18 official languages of India but rather there were a number of words. These words [*roti, naan, poori, paratha, phielka*] actually described either the grain or legume used or the method of cooking. The closest word that might be considered as a generic term is *chiapatti,* but this is a word that does not come from any Indian language. It was one of several words made up for the British during the British rule (the *Raj*). She also had a problem with 'leavening', since yeast was not something she used in cooking. She said the word for yeast in a number of Indian languages is yeast – again, no native word for this product. She used baking soda in her *poori* because these breads needed to balloon during cooking. When no baking soda was available, her mother would use a commercial antacid, *Sal Heptica* or *Eno* [both once available in the United States]. Laughing, she told us the disadvantage here was, in addition to the sodium bicarbonate, there were other ingredients in these products that turned the bread a purple color.

Don't Give Up in the Face of Rejection!

Moses and Aaron didn't give up when Pharaoh said he would not Let Our People Go. If something fuels your passion, pursue it. You may not succeed the first time you try, but persist in your quest. History proved Moses, a shy stutterer from the Land of Goshen, could overcome his inabilities with the help of God.

So may you, with the help of God, achieve your goals and dreams!

THE WHITE HOUSE
WASHINGTON

Dear Dr. Spiegel:

Thank you for your kind invitation to President Clinton. The President has asked us to convey his appreciation for your offer.

At this time, we are unable to make a commitment to your request. However, please be assured that we will keep your invitation on file for further consideration.

On behalf of the President, thank you again for your thoughtful invitation and best wishes.

Sincerely,

Stephanie S. Streett
Director of Scheduling

Anne Walley
Director of Scheduling

OFFICE OF RONALD REAGAN

Thank you for your interest which led you to write to President Reagan.

Unfortunately, this must be a disappointing response to your request. President Reagan receives a large volume of similar appeals. Surely, you will understand that, in all fairness, we must take care not to single out any individual request for special attention.

However, the President would like to convey his appreciation for thinking of him and wishes you every success in your endeavors.

Boston University

University Professors
745 Commonwealth Avenue
Boston, Massachusetts 02215

Elie Wiesel, *Andrew W. Mellon Professor in the Humanities*

Dear Dr. Spiegel:

Thanks for your recent letter regarding your Passover translation project. I wish I could participate, but I am already so overcommitted and overextended that it is simply impossible. I hope you understand.

With best, best wishes –

Elie Wiesel

THE CARTER CENTER

Dear Dr. Spiegel:

Thank you for your recent letter inviting President Carter to make a recording of his voice to be used as an official example of the English language.

As much as President Carter appreciates your offering him this opportunity, I regret that he will be unable to participate in your project due to his many other commitments and responsibilities. However, he has asked that I extend his best wishes.

Sincerely,

Deanna Congileo
Acting Director
Public Information
404/420-5108

MINISTRY OF FOREIGN AFFAIRS
FOREIGN MINISTER'S BUREAU

משרד החוץ
לשכת השר

Dear Dr. Spiegel:

Prime Minister Shimon Peres has asked me to respond to your very interesting proposal regarding the "Mah Nishtanah". Unfortunately, recent tragic events and the pressing responsibilities of the coming weeks and months make it unlikely that Mr. Peres will be able to participate in this worthy project.

The Prime Minister wishes you every success in this endeavor.

Sincerely,

Martin Peled-Flax
Assistant to the Minister of Foreign Affairs

ITZHAK PERLMAN

Dear Dr. Spiegel,

Thank you for your letter requesting my participation in your project to translate the Ma Nishtana into as many languages as possible. As much as I would like to help you, I cannot. My schedule is of such a magnitude that I just do not have the time required to take on any new projects. I do hope that you understand my situation.

Good luck.

Sincerely yours,

Itzhak Perlman

Office of George Bush

Dear Dr. Spiegel: July 29, 1996

President Bush is travelling and asked me to acknowledge your letter of July 11. He appreciated your offering him the opportunity to be a part of Bellcore's international cross-cultural linguistics project.

Unfortunately, President Bush must respectfully decline your invitation. He and Mrs. Bush have a firm policy of not participating in such projects, except for a few charitable causes. Certainly, Mr. Bush wishes you well with this effort and thanks you for remembering him so thoughtfully.

Tamil

இன்றிரவுக்கும் மற்றிரவுகளுக்கும் என்ன வித்தியாசம்? *
■ inDRiravukkum maRRiravugaLukkum enna viththiyAsam?
■ What is the difference between this night and other nights?

வழக்கமாக இரவில் நாம் மாத்ஸாவும் ஹாமேத்ஸூம் சாப்பிடுவோம்;
இன்றிரவு மாத்ஸா மட்டும் சாப்பிடுகிறோம். இது ஏன்?
■ vazhakkamAga iravil nAm mAthsAvum hAmEthsum chappiDuvOm;
inRiravu mAthsA mattum chAppiDugiROm. idhu En?
■ Customarily, at night, we eat matza and khometz (leaven) ... ;
this night we eat matza only. Why is this so?

வழக்கமாக இரவில் நாம் பலவிதமான காய்கறிகள் சாப்பிடுவோம்;
இன்றிரவு மாரோர் மட்டும் சாப்பிடுகிறோம். இது ஏன்?
■ vazhakkamAga iravil nAm palavidhamAna kAygaRigaL chappiduvOm;
inRi...
■ Cus...
this...

வழக்கமாக ... சாப்பிடு மட்டே ...
இன்றிரவு ... சாப்பிடுகிறோம். இது ஏன்?
■ vazhakkamAga iravil nAm chAppATTup poruTkaLai kuzhambugaLil mukkich chAppiDa mATTOm -
inRiravu iraNDu thaDavai mukki chAppiDugiROm -
oru thaDavai upputh thaNNIrilum, oru thaDavai hArOysassilum. idhu En?
■ Customarily, ... up the eatables in sauces while eating th...
... khorosess. Why is this so?

வழக்கமாக இ... ... ர்ந்தும்
சாப்பிடுவோ...
இன்றிரவு சாய்ந்து உட்கார்நது மட்டுமே சாப்பிடுகிறோம். இது ஏன்?
■ vazhakkamAga iravil nAm chila shamayam nErAga uTkArndhum, chila shamayam shAyndhu
uTkArndhum shAppiDugiROm; inRiravu shAyndhu uTkArndhu maTTumE chAppiDugiROm. idhu En?
... night, we sometimes eat sitting straight up and sometimes reclining;
... at reclining one. Why is this so?

அப்பா இந்த கேள்விகளுக்கு பதில் கூறுவீர்களா?
■ appA, indha kELvigaLukku badhil kURuvIrgaLA?
... would you answer these questions?

Not contained in audio recording

Capital vowels indicate long vowels; lower case letters are short vowels. Capital consonants generally indicate retroflexes, with the following exception: R = somewhat trilled, retroflex version of English 'r' • zh = close to an American 'r' • th = dental (unvoiced) version of English 't' • dh = dental voiced version of English 'd' • 'r' is more like a Spanish 'r' than an American 'r', but dental rather than retroflex.

ABOUT THE LANGUAGE:

Tamil
Number of speakers: 65,675,200
Rank: 18

Tamil is one of the national languages of India. It is also spoken in Australia, Bahrain, Canada, Fiji, Germany, Malaysia, Mauritius, the Netherlands, Qatar, Réunion, Singapore, South Africa, Sri Lanka, Thailand, United Arab Emirates, United Kingdom and the USA.

... at C CE.

P V (Meylekh) Viswanath
Age: 40   Translated: 1995
Towns: Palghat, India / Teaneck, NJ

P.V. was born in Palghat, India (near the Kerala-... at age 20. He is Professor of Finance at Pace ... ... Director of ... both graduate and undergraduate students. ... the author of numerous educational publications, research articles and papers.

Translation © 1995 P.V. Viswanath. Used with his kind permission.

ABOUT THE SPEAKER:
Meena Viswanath
Age: 7 Recorded: 1995
Town: Teaneck, NJ

Meena Viswanath is the daughter of PV Viswanath. She is trilingual (Tamil, English and Yiddish). Meena is the youngest speaker in this collection of languages.

Top line is the translation. Lines underneath may show an English transliteration as a guide for pronunciation, and a gloss, which gives the sense of the translation. Shown last is the source language on which the translation was based. English was used most often, but you'll see translations based on Arabic, Dutch, French, Italian, Portuguese, Spanish, Russian and even Burmese, Greek, Hindi and Indonesian.

Information about the language and writing system. Shows number of speakers (often derived from census figures), rank ordering (Mandarin, the language spoken by the most people, is ranked #1), and other interesting facts. Information based on SIL (Summer Inst. of Linguistics) and omniglot.com. Used by permission.

Shaded scroll bar tracks where you are in the alphabet. A/E represents Ancient and Extinct languages. C represents Constructed (Man-made) languages.

Information about the translator and speaker in the recordings. Age shown and biographical information is at the time of translation and recording.

A/E

Z
Y
X
W
V
U
T
S
R
Q
P
O
N
M
L
K
J
I
H
G
F
E
D
C
B
A

C

Having a hand in the Seder, asking the Four Questions
Drawings by (clockwise from upper left): Jared Lake, age 9, Towaco, NJ; Kloe Rosenbloom, age 8, Towaco, NJ;
Zoe Elfenbein, age 10, N Caldwell, NJ; and Rachel E. Scheckman, age 8, W Orange, NJ

Introduction to Ancient / Extinct Languages

Our first section shows translations in Ancient and Extinct Languages. The translations were often obtained from accomplished experts in the field. Our earliest languages, Akkadian, Middle Egyptian Hieroglyphics and Sumerian, are over 4000 years old. The "youngest" extinct languages, Chibcha and Manx, became extinct in the 18th and 20th centuries. (The last native Manx speaker died in 1974, but several hundred people have learned it in school.)

This book has recordings for many of the ancient languages. How do we know what an ancient language sounds like?

The short answer is, no one knows for sure. But a language leaves hints of its speech from words that rhymed in its poetry; there are also contemporary descriptions of how ancient languages were spoken. Linguists can reconstruct a language based on its remnants within languages that followed it in time and also via comparative scholarship of similar languages. But there's no way anyone can be sure of the standard pronunciation of an extinct language. (This is why linguists now record native speakers of endangered languages, before all records of a language disappear.) Our readings of the text in long-extinct languages are "best guesses," but they are usually guesses by some of the best experts for each language.

So, look at the symbols used by civilizations now known only in museums, listen to the sounds of languages lost many centuries ago to this earth. Imagine the lives of their peoples, saving thoughts for all time via chiseled stone or clay pressings. Think about the long history that spans languages such as Sumerian Cuneiform – the first written language; Egyptian Hieroglyphics – on monuments to the ancient Pharaohs; Ancient Hebrew – the language of the Old Testament; Aramaic – the people's language at the time of Christ; Ancient Greek and Latin – spoken throughout vast stretches of the ancient world; Old Church Slavonic – which developed into our modern Russian, Polish and other Slavic languages; Anglo-Saxon – which developed into modern Dutch, English and other Germanic languages.

The translation pages often include a gloss to help us understand compromises created by the translation. The gloss gives the gist of the translation. It shows what, for example, the Chibcha translation would have looked like to native speakers of Chibcha.

Look and listen, as each of the hundreds of languages ask the same questions spoken by children around the world every year at the Seder table ...

"The 𓀀 is silent."

Ugaritic

𒀀𒀭𒋾 [Ugaritic cuneiform]

■ lm ll hnd bl km kl llm?
lemā lêlu hānādū bal kimā kulli lêlīma?
■ Why is this night not like every night?

[Ugaritic cuneiform]

■ bkl llm nlḥm blḥm áy. bll hnd nlḥm blḥm d l ynpʻ.
bikulli lêlīma nilḥamu bilaḥmi ʻayyi.
bilêli hānādū nilḥamu bilaḥmi dī lā yinnapiʻu.
■ On all nights we eat all kinds of bread;
on this night we eat bread that does not rise.

[Ugaritic cuneiform]

■ bkl llm nlḥm bybl árṣ áy. bll hnd nlḥm bybl mr.
bikulli lêlīma nilḥamu biyabūli ʻarṣi ʻayyi. bilêli hānādū nilḥamu biyabūli marri.
■ On all nights we eat all kinds of the produce of the field;
on this night we eat bitter produce.

[Ugaritic cuneiform]

■ bkl llm l nṭbl áp pámm. bll hnd pámt tn.
bikulli lêlīma lā naṭblu ʻap paʻamêma. bilêli hānādū paʻmāti tn.
■ On all nights we do not wet food even once; on this night twice.

[Ugaritic cuneiform]

■ bkl llm nlḥm ytbn wškbn. bll hnd škbn.
bikulli lêlīma nilḥamu yātibūna ušākibūna. bilêli hānādū šākibūna.
■ On all nights we eat sitting or reclining; on this night, reclining.

[Ugaritic cuneiform]

■ bkl llm nlḥm bálkt ʻyt. bll hnd ky l nlḥm.
bikulli lêlīma nilḥamu biʻalakti ʻayyati. bilêli hānādū kī lā nilḥamu.
■ On all other nights we eat in any manner;
on this night, we do not eat in this way.

Translation notes: There is no attested word for 'manner' in Ugaritic.
The term used 𒁉𒀠𒆠 (biʻalakti) was taken from the Akkadian
translation. Ugaritic character 𒁹 is typically used as a word separator.

Provided under Creative Commons
Attribution ShareAlike 2.0 France License

List of Ugarit gods

Sumerian

■ limmu èn...tar
■ Four Questions

■ ə.nə.əm ğál ən.ú.sə... ne.en
kəm.ta ri ən.ú.sə... ən.ú.sə...ene
■ Why is night this
different from other night night [all nights]?

■ ri ən.ú.sə... gu₇ nində.ğiš šu...bəl
■ Other night eat bread or

■ ri ən.ú.sə... ...sù ___ dis.nə;
ne.en ən.ú.sə... ...sù min.nə
■ Other night dip [not] once;
this night dip twice

■ ri ən.ú.sə... dúr...ğar ri...ši
■ Other night sit lean

The translation is incomplete because not all the terms have been attested – no authority can say for certain which, if any, symbols genuinely represent the missing words. Subscripts are used to distinguish multiple symbols pronounced the same: e.g. gu₇ represents the 7th symbol sounded as 'gu'. Unknown pronunciations are indicated as ... and ___ denotes an unknown symbol. ğ is nasalized g; š is 'sh'; ə is schwa (as in first syllable of about).

The house of the Mukhtar of Jerwan, Iraq, is built of blocks from the aqueduct of Sennacherib (7th C BCE). One block (lower right) has Cuneiform inscriptions (1933 photo)

ABOUT THE LANGUAGE:

Sumerian

Status: Extinct   Time Period: 2500 BCE – 1600 BCE

Sumerian is usually described as the first writing system to develop in the world. Sumerian was spoken in Sumer (Southern Mesopotamia, Aram Naharayim, the land between the rivers Tigris and Euphrates), which is present-day Iraq. From the time period of 3200 BCE onwards, Sumerian used pictographs. Around 2500 BCE, the pictographs were completely replaced by Cuneiform, wedge-shaped strokes in soft clay that were baked into solid tablets. Texts in Sumerian have been found in modern Turkey, Egypt, Syria, Iraq and Iran. Sumerian is not a Semitic language – as compared to a neighboring Semitic language, Akkadian, which was spoken north of Sumer.

Modern knowledge of Cuneiform dates from 1835 when Henry Rawlinson, an English army officer, found inscriptions on a Persian cliff. The inscriptions date from the reign of Persia's King Darius (522-486 BCE) and consisted of identical texts in Old Persian, Babylonian and Elamite. Within 16 years, Rawlinson had deciphered 200 signs.

In ancient terms, the amount of Sumerian is huge; at least 100,000 excavated documents are in museums throughout the world. There are an estimated hundreds of thousands of texts still awaitng discovery, mostly in Iraqi and Syrian ruins.

ABOUT THE TRANSLATOR:

Dr. David Blumsohn

Age: 72   Translated: 2004
Town: Johannesburg, South Africa

David was born in Johannesburg where he still works as a specialist physician at Baragwanath Hospital and the University of the Witwatersrand. He studied Semitic and non-Semitic languages at the University of South Africa (UNISA), obtaining a D. Litt. et Phil. His thesis was on the Egyptian language at the time of the Nineteenth Dynasty. The signs shown here are one of many variants used over the Sumerian time period.

Courtesy of the Oriental Institute

Sumerian statues excavated from Tell Asmar, Iraq (1934 photo)

Samaritan, Hebrew

ABOUT THE LANGUAGE AND PEOPLE:

Samaritan

Time Period: Possibly Kingdom of Judea to present day
Script used by: 656 people

Samaritans are a group of monotheists worshipping on Israel's Mount Gerizim. They are related to, but not identical with, the inhabitants of ancient Samaria. Samaritanism resembles Judaism, but there are several differences.

Samaritans think that the Holy Temple should not be on Mount Zion in Jerusalem, but on Mount Gerizim near modern Nablus (ancient Sh'chem); they believe that their line of priests is the legitimate one, as opposed to the line of priests in Jerusalem; and they accept only the Law of Moses (*Genesis, Exodus, Leviticus, Numbers, Deuteronomy*) as authoritative, and have a slightly different text of these books. The writings of Prophets and other books are not recognized as divinely inspired.

It is claimed in the 4th and 5th centuries there were over 1 million Samaritans living from southern Syria to northern Egypt. Over the centuries, persecution and conversions reduced their numbers, until in 1917 there were only 147 left. Samaritans began increasing in the 1930s; there were 656 Samaritans in 2003 living in Holon and near Mount Gerizim.

Their Passover Sacrifice of a lamb is separate from their Feast of *Matzot*. Neither ceremony uses the traditional Four Questions. This page shows how the Four Questions would be written in the ancient Hebrew script.

ABOUT THE SPEAKER:

Benyamim Sedaka

Age: 61   Recorded: 2006
Town: Nablus / Holon, Israel

Benny is the conductor of the Samaritan Choir. He was born in Nablus (Sh'chem in Samaria) and at age 17 moved to Holon, near Tel Aviv. He was educated at the Hebrew University of Jerusalem, with a specialty in the History of *Tehilla Israel* (Community of Israel). Like all Samaritan children, Benny learned Ancient Hebrew from Samaritan teachers from age 6 till age 13 and uses it in his daily prayers.

In the recordings: Benyamim sings the Samaritan chant for the first 2 verses of the Song of the Sea (Exodus, Chapter 15). They claim this is the actual melody used when Miriam, the Prophetess, praised God after the people of Israel crossed the Red Sea. The recording also contains the chant for the first two verses of the Aramaic alphabet acrostic "God the Merciful", written by Samaritan Amram Dareh in the 3rd C CE. This poem is sung during the Samaritan's Passover Sacrifice ceremony.

Photo courtesy of Benyamim Sedaka

The entrance to the Samaritan Synagogue in Holon, Israel. The seven candle Menorah is the national symbol of the Samaritans. On the right side of the gate is engraved "You are blessed while coming" [Deut. xxviii.6] and on the left "You are blessed while leaving" [Deut. xxviii.6]. On the Rainbow is engraved in the ancient Hebrew still used only by Samaritans, "You will erect a Temple and I will settle among you" [Samaritan version of the Torah, Ex. xxv.8]

Qumran, Hebrew

מהנשתנהחלילהחחזחהמעלהחלילותשבעלהחלילותאנואועליהמקומעחלילהחחזחעלימעלימעליהדמקומעחלילהחחזחעלימעליה
אנואועליהשארירקותהחלילהחחזחמרורשבעלהחלילותאינואנומטבילימאפילופעמאתהחלילהחחזחשתיפע
מימשבעלהחלילותאנואועליהחלילותשבעלהחלילותמסבינומסביהחלילהחחזחעלימסביוביושביוישבייושבימעליהאנואועליהבצורה
רגילהחלילהחחזחהברוכטקסיית

ABOUT THE PEOPLE:

Qumran

Status: Extinct
Time Period: Approximately 130 BCE – 70 CE

Qumran is a ruin from the days of the Second Temple. The caves at Qumran became world famous in 1947 when a number of ancient manuscripts were found by two Bedouin shepherds. The manuscripts, now called the Dead Sea Scrolls, are housed in the Shrine of the Book at the Israel Museum.

Many scrolls and thousands of fragments were found in 11 caves, constituting all the books of the Bible except for the Book of Esther. Although Passover is mentioned, e.g. in Leviticus, no texts unique to the Haggadah are found. The text shown here represent the Four Questions as they would have been written using a script typical of the Qumran scrolls, specifically that in '1QISa', the Great Isaiah Scroll. Words and sentences are not separated by spaces in the Dead Sea scrolls. Changes in color here indicate the individual phrases of the Four Questions.

Photo © Philip Greenspun

The caves at Qumran

Phoenician

ABOUT THE LANGUAGE:

Phoenician / Canaanite

Status: Extinct
Time Period: 11th C BCE - 1st C CE

The Semitic language of ancient Phoenician was spoken in the coastal region called Canaan (*Pūt* in Ancient Egyptian). Its closest living relative is Hebrew. Of all the ancient languages in this book, Phoenician and Moabite are the most likely witnesses as to how biblical Hebrews would have asked the Four Questions.

The Phoenician civilization was an enterprising maritime trading culture that spread across the Mediterranean. Phoenicians were some of the greatest traders of their time, and obtained considerable prosperity.

Phoenician's phonetic alphabet – the first widely-used alphabetic script – is considered the ancestor of almost all modern alphabets.

Phoenicians mostly carved their script into stone, so the final strokes are non-connecting; Hebrews wrote with ink on leather and pottery shards, changing the script into a cursive, with final strokes connecting to the following letter.

ABOUT THE TRANSLATOR AND SPEAKER:

Rabbi Allen Darnov

Age: 53   Recorded: 2010
Towns: Los Angeles / Marlboro, NJ

A graduate of UCLA, Rabbi Allen Darnov was ordained by the Hebrew Union College-Jewish Institute of Religion in New York, and currently serves as Rabbi at the Reform Temple of Putnam Valley. Due to great admiration for the ancient world and biblical civilization in particular, Rabbi Darnov earned a doctorate in the field of Hebrew Bible and Ancient Semitics at the Jewish Theological Seminary of America. He taught biblical topics at several leading rabbinical schools in New York City.

The translation's consonants were checked by **Professor David Marcus**, Professor of Bible studies at New York's Jewish Theological Seminary.

ha·lêlōt 'aharay ba·kōl ze ha·lêl šōniy ma

■ How is this night different from all other nights?

wa·maṣṣōt laḥm 'ōklīm 'anaḥnū lêl middê lêl kī

laḥōdáyya maṣṣōt ze ha·lêl

■ For every night we eat leavened and unleavened bread; this night we eat only unleavened bread.

pērōt ba·kol 'ōklīm 'anaḥnū lêl middê lêl kī

marōt pērōt ze wa·ha·lêl

■ For every night we eat fruit of all kinds; but this night we eat bitter fruit.

'aḥat pa`m 'ap pērōt ṭōblīm bal 'anaḥnū lêl middê lêl kī

šatêm pa`mōt ze wa·ha·lêl

■ For every night we do not dip fruit even one time; but on this night two times.

wa·šōkbīm yōšbīm 'ōklīm 'anaḥnū lêl middê lêl kī

šōkbīm 'anaḥnū ze ha·lêl

■ For every night we eat sitting or reclining; this night we recline.

A Phoenician coin showing an image of a ship

Pronunciation notes: š=sh; ṣ=ts; ḥ=ch in *Bach*; ī=in *ski*; i=in *bid*; ê=in *they*; ē longer than ê; á=primary stress; final y=consonant "y" with a slight release. Doubled letters (e.g., ṣ) are longer.

Translation notes: Rabbi Darnov's extensive references for the words are contained on the DVD.

Mongolian, Ancient

ABOUT THE TRANSLATORS:

Tonglaga Bao, Solongo Chuluunbaatar, Tsendsuren Tumnee and Mikael A Thompson
Age: All in their 20s   Translated: 1997-2004
Towns: China / Ulaanbaatar, Mongolia / Laie, HI / Provo, UT /
          Bloomington, IN

Translation and proofreading took the most effort of all languages in this book. Tonglaga Bao, from China, and Solongo Chuluunbaatar, born in Ulaanbaatar, Mongolia's capital, first worked on it. Tsendsuren Tumnee, born in Sukhbaatar, Mongolia, helped proofread the computer text. All three were students at Brigham Young University in Hawaii; Mikael A Thompson, a doctoral linguistics student at the University of Indiana Bloomington specializing in north Asian languages, completed the proofreading.

See main Mongolian entry for speaker information.

ABOUT THE LANGUAGE:

Ancient Mongolian

Script: Ancient Mongolian
The ancient Mongolian alphabet was adapted from the *Uighur* alphabet in the 12th C. *Uighur*, itself derived from the *Sogdian* alphabet, ultimately came from Aramaic. From 13th-15th C, Mongolian was written using Chinese, Arabic and also Tibetan characters. The Mongolian government abolished the traditional alphabet in 1941, but since 1994 has tried to re-establish use of the ancient script. It is read vertically, from left to right.

Moabite

ABOUT THE LANGUAGE:

Moabite

Status: Extinct
Time Period: 12th C BCE – 1st C CE

Moabite is a dialect of ancient Canaanite, closely related to Hebrew. It was used in the area of Moab, east of the Dead Sea (south-central area of present-day Jordan).

The main evidence for the Moabite language is the 34-line inscription that appears on the Mesha Stele (bottom right). Its author, King Mesha of Moab, mentioned in the Bible in 2 Kings 3, reigned in the middle of the 9th C BCE. The stele's inscription details the wars between Moab and Israel, with specific mentions of King Omri of Israel, YHWH (the deity of Israel) and the "House of David" (with reference to the kingdom of Judah).

The Moabite alphabet is essentially the same one used by the Hebrews and the Phoenicians.

ABOUT THE SPEAKER:

Gary A Rendsburg

Age: 56   Recorded: 2010
Town: Highland Park, NJ

Dr. Rendsburg is Professor of Jewish Studies at Rutgers University, with a specialty in the Bible, the history of the Hebrew language and ancient Semitic languages. He received his BA in English from the University of North Carolina, and his MA and PhD from New York University in Hebrew. Professor Rendsburg is the author of six books and more than 100 scholarly articles, plus he has produced two courses for The Teaching Company's "Great Courses" program: "The Book of Genesis" and "The Dead Sea Scrolls." The translation was checked by **Professor Aaron Rubin**.

Translation notes: Professor Rendsburg's references are contained on the DVD.

Pronunciation notes:
š=sh; ṣ=ts; ḥ=ch in *Bach*; ē=as in *they*; e=in *bed*;
ī=in *ski*; i=in *bid*. Doubled letters (e.g., ṣ) are longer.

hal-lēlōt mik-kul ze hal-lēla mištanē ma

■ How is this night different from all other nights?

wa-maṣṣat laḥm 'ōkilīn naḥnū hal-lēlōt bi-kul kī

maṣṣat raq ze hal-lēla

■ For on every night we eat leavened bread and unleavened bread; this night only unleavened bread.

yiraqōt kul 'ōkilīn naḥnū hal-lēlōt bi-kul kī

marōr raq ze hal-lēla

■ For on every night we eat all vegetables; this night only bitter herbs.

'aḥat pa`m 'ap tōbilīn 'ēninū hal-lēlōt bi-kul kī

pa`mēn ze hal-lēla

■ For on every night we do not dip, not even one time; this night twice.

šōkibīn gam yōšibīn gam 'ōkilīn naḥnū hal-lēlōt bi-kul kī

šōkibīn raq ze hal-lēla

■ For on every night we eat, even sitting, even reclining; this night only reclining.

Moabite kingdom map

The Mesha Stele, now in the Louvre, was found at Dibon (modern-day Dhiban, Jordan) in 1868. It stands over a meter high

Manx

Cre'n fa ta'n oie shoh ancasley rish dagh ooilley oieghyn elley?

■ *Why is this night different from all other nights?*

Er dagh ooilley oieghyn elley, ta shin g'ee arran soorit ny arran gyn soorid;
er yn oie shoh, cha nel agh arran gyn soorid.

■ *On all other nights we eat either leavened bread or matzah;*
on this night only matzah.

Er dagh ooilley oieghyn elley, ta shin g'ee dagh sorch dy lossreeyn;
er yn oie shoh, cha nel agh lossreeyn sharroo.

■ *On all other nights we eat all kinds of herbs;*
on this night only bitter herbs.

Er dagh ooilley oieghyn elley, cha nel shin thummey eer un cheayrt;
er yn oie shoh, ta shin thummey daa cheayrt.

■ *On all other nights we do not dip even once;*
on this night we dip twice.

Er dagh ooilley oieghyn elley, ta shin g'ee nyn soie ny nyn lieh-lhie;
er yn oie shoh, ta shin nyn lieh-lhie.

■ *On all other nights we eat either sitting up or reclining;*
on this night we recline.

Er dagh ooilley oieghyn elley, ta shin g'ee ayns aght erbee cadjin;
er yn oie shoh, ta shin g'ee lesh formoilid er-lheh.

■ *On all other nights we eat in an ordinary manner;*
on this night we dine with special ceremony.

ABOUT THE LANGUAGE:

Manx

Status: Nearly extinct

Manx was spoken on the Isle of Man. The last native speaker died in 1974, at which point the language was declared extinct. However, through recent efforts to revive it, several hundred of the current 77,000 residents have learned it as a second language. It is now used for some public functions.

Manx emerged as a distinct language in the 13th-14th C after the collapse of the Norse kingdom of Mann and the Isles, prior to a long settled period of English control. Manx was first written using an orthography based on Welsh around 1610, when John Phillips, the Welsh Bishop of Sodor and Mann, translated the Book of Common Prayer into Manx.

Courtesy of flagspot.net

The national flag of the Isle of Man. The three-legged man is one of mankind's oldest symbols, first found in prehistoric cave drawings in Italy, perhaps as a symbol of pagan Sun worship. The Legs appear on all the Island's currency notes and on some coins and postage stamps

ABOUT THE TRANSLATOR AND SPEAKER:

Phil Kelly

Age: 48   Recorded: 1997
Location: Isle of Man

Phil Kelly grew up and still resides on the Isle of Man. Manx is his second language, with English as his first.

Latin

CUR HAEC NOX AB OMNIBUS ALIIS NOCTIBUS DIFFERT

■ *Why is this night different from all other nights?*

OMNIBUS ALIIS NOCTIBUS PANEM MATZAMVE EDIMUS

HAC NOCTE MATZAM SOLUM

■ *On all other nights we eat either leavened bread or matzah;*
on this night only matzah.

OMNIBUS ALIIS NOCTIBUS OMNIA GENERA HERBARUM EDIMUS

HAC NOCTE PRAECIPUE AMARAS

■ *On all other nights we eat all kinds of herbs;*
on this night only bitter herbs.

OMNIBUS ALIIS NOCTIBUS HERBAS NON SEMEL ETIAM MERGIMUS

HAC NOCTE BIS

■ *On all other nights we do not dip even once;*
on this night we dip twice.

OMNIBUS ALIIS NOCTIBUS SEDENTES AUT RECUMBENTES EDIMUS

HAC NOCTE RECUMBIMUS

■ *On all other nights we eat either sitting up or reclining;*
on this night we recline.

OMNIBUS ALIIS NOCTIBUS EX CONSUETUDINE EDIMUS

HAC NOCTE EXIMIO RITU

■ *On all other nights we eat in an ordinary manner;*
on this night we dine with special ceremony.

ABOUT THE LANGUAGE:

Latin

Status: Extinct   Time Period: 6th C BCE – 15th C CE

Latin is the language of ancient Italy, still used in Roman Catholic liturgy. The earliest known Latin inscriptions date from the 6th C BCE and were written in various versions of the Greek alphabet, which was brought to Italy by Greek colonists. Over the centuries the spoken varieties of Latin continued to move away from the literary standard and eventually evolved into the modern Italic/Romance languages (Italian, French, Spanish, Portuguese, Romanian, etc).

Even after the collapse of the western Roman Empire in 476 CE, Latin continued to be used as a literary language throughout western and central Europe until it began losing its dominance during the 15th C.

ABOUT THE TRANSLATOR:

Katherine Olstein

Age: Unavailable   Translated: 1995
Town: New Brunswick, NJ

Dr. Olstein obtained her PhD in Greek and Latin Studies from Columbia University in 1973. She was a Professor at Tufts University and also taught Greek studies at Rutgers University. Katherine presently teaches Latin at the high school level in NJ. The translation was also worked on by **Astrid Werner**, a grade-school student who studied Latin at the Princeton Latin Academy since age 8; **Ed Kahn** of the Illinois Institute of Technology; and **Martin Wallraff** in the United Kingdom.

ABOUT THE CHANTER:

Gill Diamond

Age: 30s   Recorded: 1996
Town: Millburn, NJ

Dr. Diamond is a world-renowned genetics biochemist working at the University of Medicine and Dentistry of NJ, where he is an Associate Professor. Using his training in classical singing, Gill set the Latin translation to an ancient Recessional melody.

Ur haec nox ab omnibus a-liis noctibus dif-fert?

Irish, Old

THE FOUR QUESTIONS

Ceirṫ, cid deiligedar in n-aidchi-re fri cach n-aidchi n-aili?
- Ceist cid deiligedar in n-aidchi-se fri cach n-aidchi n-aili?
- *Why is this night different from all other nights?*

Ní anrae rodbo arán nemderctháe nó arán for derctháib n-ethmae cacha aidche aile; acht ir arán nemderctháe nammá n-ethmae ind adaig-re.
- Ní ansae rodbo arán nemdescthae nó arán for descthaib n-ethmae cacha aidche aile; acht is arán nemdescthae nammá n-ethmae ind adaig-se.
- *On all other nights, we eat either leavened bread or matzah; on this night, only matzah.*

Cacha aidche aile ethmai cach cenél lubae; acht it luba rerba nammá n-ethmae ind adaig-re.
- Cacha aidche aile ethmai cach cenél lubae; acht it luba serba nammá n-ethmae ind adaig-se.
- *On all other nights, we eat all kinds of herbs; on this night, only bitter herbs.*

Cacha aidche aile ní tummam cid óenḟecht; acht ir fo dí tummai ind adaig-re.
- Cacha aidche aile ní tummam cid óenfecht; acht is fo dí tummai ind adaig-se.
- *On all other nights, we do not dip even once; on this night, we dip twice.*

Cacha aidche aile rodbo innar ruidiu díriuch nó innar ligiu ethmai; acht ir innar ligiu ethmai ind adaig-re.
- Cacha aidche aile rodbo innar suidiu díriuch nó innar ligiu ethmai; acht is innar ligiu ethmai ind adaig-se.
- *On all other nights, we eat either sitting up or reclining; on this night, we recline.*

Cacha aidche aile ethmai fo gnáthbéraib; acht ir raintomalt do-melam in fleid ind adaig-re.
- Cacha aidche aile ethmai fo gnáthbésaib; acht is saintomalt do-melam in fleid ind adaig-se.
- *On all other nights, we eat in an ordinary manner; on this night, we dine with special ceremony.*

Stones outside of Beaufort, County Kelly, Ireland with 4th-7th C Ogham writing

Greek, Ancient

διὰ τί ἥδε ἡ νὺξ διαφέρει τῶν ἄλλων νυκτῶν;

- dia ti háde ha nyx diaférei ton állon nyktón?
- *Why is this night different from all other nights?*

πασῶν τῶν μὲν ἄλλων νυκτῶν ἢ ἄρτον ζυμίτη ἢ ἄζυμα ἐσθίομεν·
τῇδε τῇ νυκτὶ μόνον ἄζυμα.

- pasón ton men állon nyktón e árton zymíte e ázyma esthíomen;
  téde te nyktí de mónon ázyma.

- *On all other nights we eat either leavened bread or matzah;*
  on this night only matzah.

πασῶν τῶν μὲν ἄλλων νυκτῶν πάντες τοὺς χόρτους ἐσθίομεν·
τῇδε τῇ νυκτὶ ἐξαιρέτως πικρούς.

- pasón ton men állon nyktón pántes tus hórtus esthíomen;
  téde te nyktí exairétos pikrús.

- *On all other nights we eat all kinds of herbs;*
  on this night only bitter herbs.

πασῶν τῶν μὲν ἄλλων νυκτῶν οὐκ ἐμβαπτίζομεν τοὺς χόρτους·
τῇδε τῇ νυκτὶ δὲ δίς ἐμβαπτίζομεν.

- pasón ton men állon nyktón uk embaptízomen tus hórtus;
  téde te nyktí dis embaptízomen.

- *On all other nights we do not dip even once;*
  on this night we dip twice.

πασῶν τῶν μὲν ἄλλων νυκτῶν καθίζοντες ὀρθῶς ἢ κατακλίνοντες ἐσθίομεν·
τῇδε τῇ νυκτὶ κατακλίνομεν.

- pasón ton men állon nyktón kathídzontes orthós e kataklinontis esthíomen;
  téde te nyktí kataklínomen.

- *On all other nights we eat either sitting up or reclining;*
  on this night we recline.

πασῶν τῶν μὲν ἄλλων νυκτῶν τρόπῳ συνήθει ἐσθίομεν·
τῇδε τῇ νυκτὶ πανηγυρικῶς δειπνοῦμεν.

- pasón ton men állon nyktón trópo synéthei esthíomen;
  téde te nyktí panegyrikós deipnúmen.

- *On all other nights we eat in an ordinary manner;*
  on this night we dine with special ceremony.

> The punctuation is correct: Ancient and Modern Greek use a semicolon to represent a question mark and a raised dot for commas. **In the recordings**: The Professor's reading is slightly different because the text was corrected later by Dr. Deborah Beck.

About the Language:

Ancient Greek

Status: Extinct   Time Period: 5th C BCE

This form of ancient Greek is from the time period around the 5th C BCE. The Greek alphabet has been in continuous use since about 750 BCE. For more information, see main entry under modern Greek.

About the Translator and Speaker:

Minas Kostis

Age: Unavailablle   Recorded: 1999
Town: Rhodes, Greece

Professor Minas Kostis is a scholar of Ancient Greek from Rhodes. The translation was also worked on by **Martin Wallraff** of Cambridge, Britain and **Dr. Deborah Beck** who received her PhD in Classical Philology from Harvard and is Assistant Professor in the Department of Classics, Swarthmore College.

The Parthenon in Athens, built 448–432 BCE

Gothic

𐍈𐌰 𐍆𐌹𐌳𐍅𐍉𐍂 𐍆𐍂𐌰𐌹𐌷𐌰𐌽𐍉𐌽𐌰

Þo fidwor fraihanona — *The Four Questions*

𐌳𐌿𐍈𐌴 𐍃𐍉 𐌽𐌰𐌷𐍄𐍃 𐌽𐌹𐍃𐍄 𐌲𐌰𐌻𐌴𐌹𐌺𐌰 𐌰𐌻𐌻𐌰𐌹𐌼 𐌰𐌽𐌸𐌰𐍂𐌰𐌹𐌼 𐌽𐌰𐌷𐍄𐌰𐌼

■ Duhwe so nahts nist galeika allaim anþaraim nahtam?

■ *Why is this night different from all other nights?*

𐌰𐌻𐌻𐌰𐌹𐌼 𐌰𐌽𐌸𐌰𐍂𐌰𐌹𐌼 𐌽𐌰𐌷𐍄𐌰𐌼 𐌼𐌰𐍄𐌲𐌰𐌼 𐌰𐌽𐌳𐌹𐌶𐌿𐌷
𐌷𐌻𐌰𐌹𐍆 𐌲𐌰𐌱𐌴𐌹𐍃𐍄𐌹𐌳𐌰𐌽𐌰 𐌰𐌹𐍈𐍈𐌰𐌿 𐌿𐌽𐌱𐌴𐌹𐍃𐍄𐌲𐍉𐌳𐌰𐌽𐌰
𐍈𐌹𐌶𐌰𐌹 𐌽𐌰𐌷𐍄 𐍈𐌰𐍄𐌰𐌹𐌽𐌴𐌹 𐌷𐌻𐌰𐌹𐍆 𐌿𐌽𐌱𐌴𐌹𐍃𐍄𐌲𐍉𐌳𐌰𐌽𐌰

■ Allaim anþaraim nahtam, matjam andizuh hlaif gabeistidana aiþþau unbeistjodana;
þizai naht, þatainei hlaif unbeistjodana.

■ *On all other nights we eat either leavened bread or matzah; on this night only matzah.*

𐌰𐌻𐌻𐌰𐌹𐌼 𐌰𐌽𐌸𐌰𐍂𐌰𐌹𐌼 𐌽𐌰𐌷𐍄𐌰𐌼 𐌼𐌰𐍄𐌲𐌰𐌼 𐌼𐌹𐍃𐍃𐌰𐌻𐌴𐌹𐌺𐌰 𐌲𐍂𐌰𐍃𐌰
𐍈𐌹𐌶𐌰𐌹 𐌽𐌰𐌷𐍄 𐍈𐌰𐍄𐌰𐌹𐌽𐌴𐌹 𐌱𐌰𐌹𐍄𐍂𐌰 𐌲𐍂𐌰𐍃𐌰

■ Allaim anþaraim nahtam, matjam missaleika grasa;
þizai naht, þatainei baitra grasa.

■ *On all other nights we eat all kinds of herbs; on this night only bitter herbs.*

𐌰𐌻𐌻𐌰𐌹𐌼 𐌰𐌽𐌸𐌰𐍂𐌰𐌹𐌼 𐌽𐌰𐌷𐍄𐌰𐌼 𐌽𐌹 𐌳𐌰𐌿𐍀𐌾𐌰𐌼 𐌰𐌹𐌽𐌰𐌼𐌼𐌰 𐍃𐌹𐌽𐍈𐌰
𐍈𐌹𐌶𐌰𐌹 𐌽𐌰𐌷𐍄 𐌳𐌰𐌿𐍀𐌾𐌰𐌼 𐍄𐍅𐌰𐌹𐌼 𐍃𐌹𐌽𐍈𐌰𐌼

■ Allaim anþaraim nahtam, ni daupjam ainamma sinþa;
þizai naht, daupjam twaim sinþam.

■ *On all other nights we do not dip even once; on this night we dip twice.*

𐌰𐌻𐌻𐌰𐌹𐌼 𐌰𐌽𐌸𐌰𐍂𐌰𐌹𐌼 𐌽𐌰𐌷𐍄𐌰𐌼 𐌼𐌰𐍄𐌲𐌰𐌼 𐌰𐌽𐌳𐌹𐌶𐌿𐌷 𐍃𐌹𐍄𐌰𐌽𐌳𐌰𐌽𐍃
𐌰𐌹𐍈𐍈𐌰𐌿 𐌰𐌽𐌰𐌺𐌿𐌼𐌱𐌲𐌰𐌽𐌳𐌰𐌽𐍃
𐍈𐌹𐌶𐌰𐌹 𐌽𐌰𐌷𐍄 𐌰𐌽𐌰𐌺𐌿𐌼𐌱𐌲𐌰𐌼

■ Allaim anþaraim nahtam, matjam andizuh sitandans aiþþau anakumbjandans;
þizai naht, anakumbjam.

■ *On all other nights we eat either sitting up or reclining; on this night we recline.*

𐌰𐌻𐌻𐌰𐌹𐌼 𐌰𐌽𐌸𐌰𐍂𐌰𐌹𐌼 𐌽𐌰𐌷𐍄𐌰𐌼 𐌼𐌰𐍄𐌲𐌰𐌼 𐍃𐍅𐌴 𐌱𐌹𐌿𐌷𐍄𐍃 𐌹𐍃𐍄
𐍈𐌹𐌶𐌰𐌹 𐌽𐌰𐌷𐍄 𐌼𐌰𐍄𐌲𐌰𐌼 𐌼𐌹𐍈 𐍅𐌿𐌻𐌸𐌰𐌿

■ Allaim anþaraim nahtam, matjam swe biuhts ist;
þizai naht, matjam miþ wulþau.

■ *On all other nights we eat in an ordinary manner;
on this night we dine with special ceremony.*

In the recordings: Tom begins his recording
with The Four Asked [Things] spoken in Gothic.

ABOUT THE LANGUAGE:

Gothic

Status: Extinct   Time Period: 4th – 10th C CE

The Gothic language is the earliest recorded Germanic language that has come down to us. Knowledge is derived primarily from the remains of a Bible translation made in the 4th C by the Visigothic bishop *Wulfila* or *Ulfilas*, although the surviving manuscripts are not originals but much later copies thought to have been written in northern Italy during the period of *Ostrogothic* rule (first half of the 6th C).

Gothic is an ancient language, spoken in the areas of modern day Ukraine, Bulgaria and the Crimea. This translation shows the ancient Gothic script followed by a more modern transcription. The Old English translation was used as a reference.

ABOUT THE TRANSLATOR AND SPEAKER:

Tom De Herdt

Age: Unavailable   Recorded: 1997
Town: Destelbergen, Belgium

Tom studied Germanic languages (German and Swedish) at the University of Ghent, Belgium (1991-1996). He became interested in comparative linguistics, with a preference for Old Germanic languages, and wrote his final paper on word constructions in the Gothic Bible.

Tom later became interested in Computer Science, working at the computer department of a bank in Brussels.

Tom's background for the Gothic language and research into its pronunciation, too extensive to show here, can be found on the DVD.

Explanation of some word choices from Tom: "**herbs**": The Gothic word *gras* usually translates Greek *khórtos*, grass, but is also used for Greek *lákhanon*, greens, vegetables or herbs. "**all kinds of**": The Old English translation *we etaþ mislice wyrta* provides a good solution for Gothic too: *missaleiks* translates Greek *poikilos*, various. "**dip**": I chose the verb *daupjan*, which is the etymological counterpart of *to dip*. Unfortunately, the verb already has a specific, religious meaning in Wulfilian Gothic: to baptize. However, a better translation couldn't be found; the only alternative [*uf-*]*saggqjan* is not an accurate translation either. "**once, twice**": *Ainamma sinþa, twaim sinþam* is a common construction in Gothic, literally one time, two times. "**recline**": Gothic verb *anakumbjan* seems a perfect translation. The word is derived from Latin *accumbere*, and thus refers to the "Roman" way of dining, i.e. easily sitting around on a pillow. "**special ceremony**": I couldn't directly translate *special* nor *ceremony*; searching the Bible doesn't yield any results for Gothic. The Old English translation *on aenlicre wisan* ("in a special way") avoids the word ceremony and is a good starting point – *way* or *manner* could be translated using an adverb. Unfortunately, the word "special" was still problematic. I considered a free translation: *miþ wulþau*, literally *with glory, greatness, splendour*. The word *wulþus* (Greek *dóxa*) might be a bit too glorious for special ceremonies, but this was the best solution.

English, Old

ÞA FEOꝰER FRIᵹNUNᵹE   THA FEOWER FRIGNUNGE
The Four Questions

Foꞃ hƿı ıꞃ þeoꞃ nıht unᵹelıc eallum oꝺꝥum nıhtum?
- For hwi is theos niht ungelic eallum othrum nihtum?
- **Why is this night different from all other nights?**

On eallum oþþum nıhtum ƿe etaꝺ hlaꝼ ꞃƿa ᵹehaꝼene ꞃƿa þeoꞃꝼne;
on þıꞃꞃe nıhte, þeoꞃꝼne anan.
- On eallum othrum nihtum we etath hlaf swa gehafene swa theorfne;
  on thisse nihte, theorfne anan.
- **On all other nights we eat either leavened bread or matzah;**
  on this night only matzah.

On eallum oþþum nıhtum ƿe etaꝺh mıꞃlıce ƿyꞃta;
on þıꞃꞃe nıhte, bıtꞃe ƿyꞃta anan.
- On eallum othrum nihtum we etath mislice wyrta; on thisse nihte, bitre wyrta anan.
- **On all other nights we eat all kinds of herbs; on this night only bitter herbs.**

On eallum oþþum nıhtum ne ꝺyppaꝺ ƿe ꞃƿa oꝼt ꞃƿa aneꞃ;
on þıꞃꞃe nıhte, ƿe ꝺyppaꝺ tuƿa.
- On eallum othrum nihtum ne dyppath we swa oft swa anes;
  on thisse nihte, we dyppath tuwa.
- **On all other nights we do not dip even once; on this night we dip twice.**

On eallum oþþum nıhtum ƿe etaꝺ ꞃƿa ꞃıttende ꞃƿa hleomende;
on þıꞃꞃe nıhte, ealle ƿe hleomıaꝺ.
- On eallum othrum nihtum we etath swa sittende swa hleoniende;
  on thisse nihte, ealle we hleoniath.
- **On all other nights we eat either sitting up or reclining; on this night we recline.**

On eallum oþþum nıhtum ƿe etaꝺ on ᵹeƿunelıcꞃe ƿıꞃan;
on þıꞃꞃe nıhte, ƿe etaꝺ on ænlıcꞃe ƿıꞃan.
- On eallum othrum nihtum we etath on gewunelicre wisan;
  on thisse nihte, we etath on aenlicre wisan.
- **On all other nights we eat in an ordinary manner;**
  on this night we dine with special ceremony.

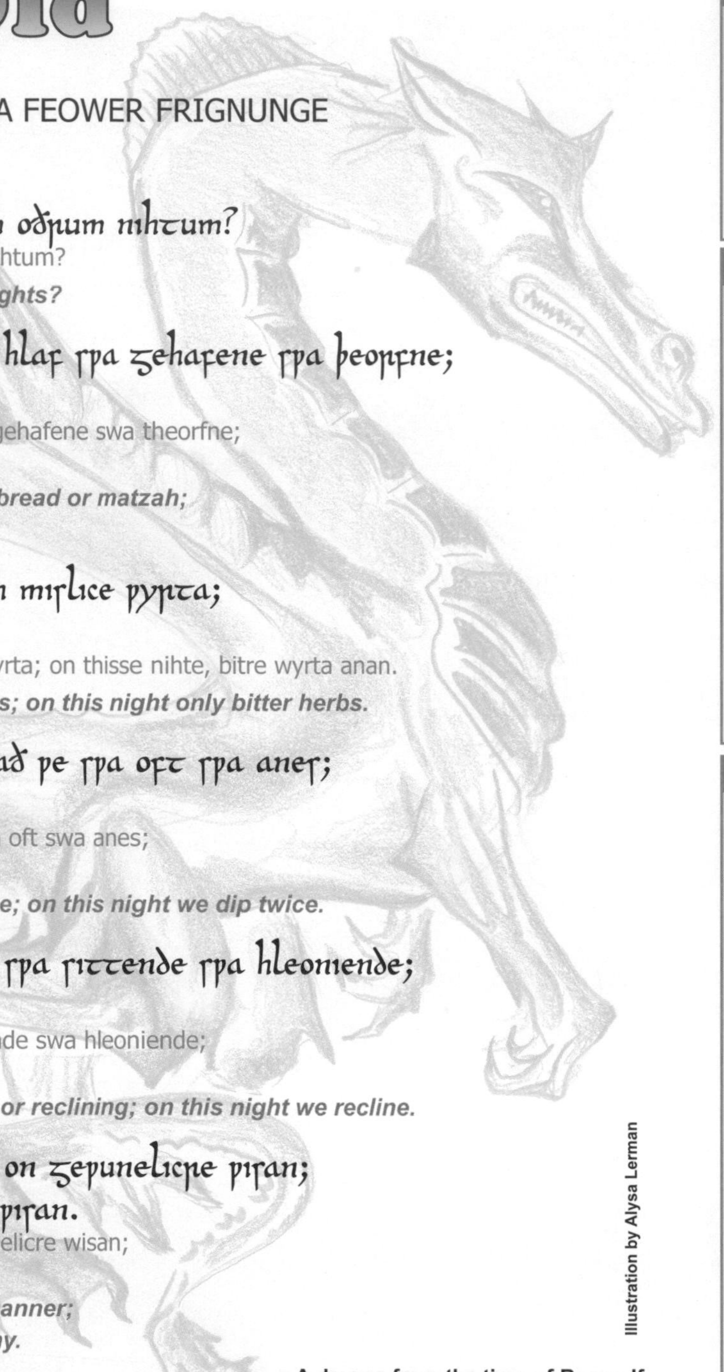

Illustration by Alysa Lerman

A dragon from the time of Beowulf

ABOUT THE LANGUAGE:

Old English

Status: Extinct   Time Period: Through 10th C

Old English (OE), the language of Beowulf, is the ancient English spoken around the 10th C. (Chaucer [1340-1400] spoke Middle English.) OE's Insular Uncial script shown here is followed by its modern counterpart.

ABOUT THE SPEAKER:

Duncan MacRae Gibson

Age: Unavailable   Recorded: 1997
Location: England

Dr. Gibson holds the title of Honorary Reader in English, University of Aberdeen, Scotland. Duncan has a long professional career in the study and teaching of OE. He is an author or part-author of three instructional courses in OE and part-author of Critical Discography of Readings in Old English, which required listening critically to all recorded readings in OE then accessible. Duncan is *Heahwita* (chief counsellor) and *Cwidewissa* (linguistic adviser) of *Tha Engliscan Gesithas,* for whom he has made many OE recordings.

ABOUT THE TRANSLATORS:

The Old English translation was developed by a group of English professors, students and linguists, contributing to the recently established ENGLISC-listserv newsgroup. They had been wondering what to do with their Old English listserv when our request appeared and they worked on it with gusto.

Dr. Cathy Ball, Associate Professor of Linguistics, Georgetown University, Washington, DC; **Melissa Bernstein**, English PhD Student, University of Rochester, Rochester, NY; **Dr. Patrick Conner**, Associate Professor of English, West Virginia University, Morgantown, WV; **Dr. Edwin Duncan**, Associate Professor of English, Towson State University, Baltimore, MD; **Dr. Sarah Higley**, Associate Professor of English, University of Rochester, Rochester, NY; **Dr. Joyce Lionarons**, Associate Professor of English, Ursinus College, Collegeville, PA; **Dr. Miriam Youngerman Miller**, Prof of English, University of New Orleans, New Orleans, LA.

English, Middle

The Foure Questiouns
- The Foure Questiouns

Why is this nyght unlyk alle othere nyghtes?
- Why is this nyght unlyk alle othere nyghtes?

Alle othere nyghtes we eten breed eyther bermed or withouten; berm;this nyght but breed unbermed.
- Alle othere nyghtes we eten breed eyther bermed or withouten berm; this nyght but breed unbermed.

Alle othere nyghtes we ete alle manere herbes; this nyght oonly bitter herbes.
- Alle othere nyghtes we ete alle manere herbes; this nyght oonly bitter herbes.

Alle othere nyghtes ne dyppen we nat ones; this nyght we dyppen twyes.
- Alle othere nyghtes ne dyppen we nat ones; this nyght we dyppen twyes.

Alle othere nyghtes eten we sittynge or liggynge adoun; this nyght we lye adoun.
- Alle othere nyghtes eten we sittynge or liggynge adoun; this nyght we lye adoun.

Alle othere nyghtes we ete in commune wyse; this nyght we dine with rytes especial.
- Alle othere nyghtes we ete in commune wyse; this nyght we dine with rytes especial.

ABOUT THE LANGUAGE:

Middle English

Status: Extinct
Time Period: 1066 to mid-to-late 15th C

Middle English is the ancient English that began under the influence of the Norman Conquest and roughly ended a century before Shakespeare. There were few silent letters in Middle English: knight was pronounced with a <k> and a <gh> as the ch in Bach.

Chancery Standard, the official written form, was developed by the government to counter the varying English dialects spoken and written around the country.

ABOUT THE TRANSLATOR AND SPEAKER:

Professor George Petty

Age: 80   Recorded: 2008
Town: Denville, NJ

George Petty is Professor Emeritus of English from Montclair State University, having taught English for 35 years there and at SUNY Stony Brook. His specialty is Old and Middle English studies. He also has been an aviation mechanic, Flight Engineer, union president, newspaper reporter, tennis coach, poet, and associate naturalist for the New Jersey Audubon Society.

The largest collection of Middle English writings come from the pen of Geoffrey Chaucer (1343 –1400). His most famous work is *The Canterbury Tales*, stories told by fictional pilgrims near Canterbury

Egyptian, Middle

In the recordings: Geoffrey ends his recordings with the names of the languages (in Middle and Late Egyptian).

mak <u>g</u>araa<u>h</u>pihn <u>ch</u>an'u ihrkyu<u>g</u>araa<u>h</u>u <u>h</u>ar<u>maa</u>

■ Why is this night different from all other nights?

wan<u>aa</u>mun tal up<u>h</u>ar <u>kih</u>fnu ihmkyu<u>g</u>araa<u>h</u>u <u>nih</u>bu as'ch wan<u>aa</u>mun <u>kih</u>fnu wa'<u>ay</u>tu ihm<u>g</u>araa<u>h</u>pihn

■ On all other nights we eat bread or matzah; but on this night we eat only matzah.

wan<u>aa</u>mun ih<u>lk</u>awa na<u>k</u>atnihb ihmkyu<u>g</u>araa<u>h</u>u <u>nih</u>bu as'ch wan<u>aa</u>mun smut<u>har</u> wa'<u>ay</u>tu ihm<u>g</u>araa<u>h</u>pihn

■ On all other nights we eat vegetables of all kinds; but on this night we eat only bitter herbs.

<u>naa</u>sap <u>h</u>arapnan smu ihmkyu<u>g</u>araa<u>h</u>u <u>nih</u>bu as'ch <u>h</u>arpun sen sap<u>snee</u>yu ihm<u>g</u>araa<u>h</u>pihn

■ On all other nights we do not dip herbs even once; but on this night we dip them twice.

wan<u>aa</u>mun <u>ma</u>kun <u>h</u>amsu<u>ween</u> up<u>h</u>ar sach<u>ra</u>wee ihmkyu<u>g</u>araa<u>h</u>u <u>nih</u>bu as'ch <u>sa</u>chrun ihm<u>g</u>araa<u>h</u>pihn

■ On all other nights we eat while seated or reclining; but on this night we recline.

wan<u>aa</u>mun Hyasih<u>Har</u> niHyara<u>har</u>wu ihmkyu<u>g</u>araa<u>h</u>u <u>nih</u>bu as'ch wan<u>aa</u>mun Hyasih<u>Har</u> n<u>ih</u>aab <u>chaa</u>sar im<u>g</u>araa<u>h</u>pihn

■ On all other nights we eat in the fashion of every day; but on this night we eat with holy ceremony.

Hieroglyphics are found on many pillars and walls in the temples at Luxor, Valley of the Kings, Egypt

Photo by Stephanie Goldhuber

ABOUT THE TRANSLATOR AND SPEAKER:

Geoffrey Graham

Age: Unknown   Recorded: 1998
Towns: Berkeley, CA / Austin, TX / Cairo, Egypt / New Haven, CT

Geoffrey has a Master of Philosophy in Egyptology from Yale University. He pursued Middle East Studies with a focus on Islamic Art as an undergraduate, obtained a BA in Egyptology from University of California, Berkeley, and later focused on Arabic and Islamic Art at the American University in Cairo. He is particularly interested in Egyptian religious iconography, the historical linguistics of Egyptian, and the creation of teaching tools in the field of Egyptology. Geoffrey helped create the new Mummies Gallery at Boston's Museum of Fine Arts.

Geoffrey's partner, the son of a Rabbi in Cincinnati's Hebrew Union College, is a student of Middle Eastern Culture, learned Kurdish and follows Iranian customs in his own Seders.

Egyptian, Late

taywuHee sehtehnyut eh'enkyu enweHeeyu ħiaH

■ Why is this night different from all other nights?

eh'aren waanem 'ayku emerpeh kihfnu emenkyu enweHeeyu ehteeru Hihsuwa eh'aren waanem kihfnu wa'aytu emtaywuHee waa'aytes

■ On all other nights we eat bread or matzah; but on this night we eat only matzah.

eh'aren waanem eeka emkeenihb emenkeeyu enweHeeyu ehteeru Hihsuwa eh'aren waanem nehsmeh t'ha wa'aytu emtaywuHee waa'aytes

■ On all other nights we eat vegetables of all kinds; but on this night we eat only bitter herbs.

eh'aren temhaarep emensmeh sap waa'aytih emenkeeyu enweHeeyu ehteeru Hihsuwa eh'aren harpu sapsnihyu emtaywuHee waa'aytes

■ On all other nights we do not dip herbs even once; but on this night we dip them twice.

eh'aren waanem tenħmoset emerpeh tens'cheeyut emenkeeyu enweHeeyu ehteeru Hihsuwa eh'aren s'cha emtaywuHee waa'aytes

■ On all other nights we eat while seated or reclining; but on this night we recline.

eh'aren waanem HyasHa entihnhawu emenkeeyu enweHeeyu ehteeru Hihsuwa eh'aren waanem HyaHa' chaasa emtaywuHee waa'aytes

■ On all other nights we eat in the fashion of every day; but on this night we eat with holy ceremony.

ABOUT THE LANGUAGES:

Late and Middle Egyptian

Status: Extinct   Time Period: 3400 BCE – 300s CE

Moses and the Israelites probably saw and heard Late Egyptian (1700 – 800 BCE, which includes the Ramesside Period – e.g., the Exodus). Egyptian was an Afro-Asiatic language spoken in Egypt possibly as early as 3400 BCE until the 4th C CE. Its continued use by Egyptian Christians, as a liturgical language, modified into Coptic forms still used today. Middle Egyptian is dated from 2160 – 1780 BCE, but its hieroglyphics continued to be used in Greco-Roman temples until 450 CE.

The earliest known examples of Egyptian hieroglyphics date from 3400 BCE, possibly pre-dating Sumerian Cuneiform writing. The hieroglyphics were used mainly for formal inscriptions on the walls of temples and tombs. Some inscriptions have glyphs that are very detailed and in full color; in others they are simple outlines.

In 1799, Napoleon's soldiers discovered the Rosetta Stone, which had the same text written in three languages (an Egyptian script called Demotic script, Coptic Greek and Hieroglyphics). Knowledge of hieroglyphics was lost until the French Egyptologist Jean-Francois Champollion worked on the Rosetta Stone. Thus, Champollion became the first human in 1400 years to read hieroglyphics when he decoded them in the 1820s.

Coptic, Sahidic

ⲈⲦⲂⲈ ⲞⲨ ⲦⲀⲒ-ⲨⲰⲎ ⲰⲂⲂⲒⲀⲈⲒⲦ Ⲉ-Ⲛ̄-ⲔⲈ-ⲨⲰⲎ ⲦⲎⲢⲞⲨ

- etb̲e ū taywše š̲ebyayt eꜣenkewše tēru

- Why is this night different from all other nights?

Ⲉ-ⲰⲀⲚ-ⲞⲨⲰⲘ Ⲛ̄-ⲌⲚ̄-ⲞⲈⲒⲔ Ⲏ ⲌⲚ̄-ⳋⲰⲰⲖⲈ Ⲛ̄-ⲌⲚ̄-Ⲛ̄-ⲔⲈ-ⲨⲰⲎ ⲦⲎⲢⲞⲨ
Ⲉ-ⲰⲀⲚ-ⲞⲨⲰⲘ ⲆⲈ Ⲛ̄-ⲌⲚ̄-ⳋⲰⲰⲖⲈ ⲌⲰⲰⲞⲨ ⲌⲚ̄-ⲦⲀⲒ-ⲨⲰⲎ

- ešanwōm ᵉnhᵉnoyk ē ᵉnhᵉnkʸōꜣle hᵉnᵉnkewše tēru
  ešanwōm de ᵉnhᵉnkʸōꜣle hōꜣu hᵉntaywše

- On other nights we eat bread or matzah;
  but on this night we eat only matzah.

Ⲉ-ⲰⲀⲚ̄-ⲞⲨⲰⲘ Ⲛ̄-Ⲛ̄-ⲎⳓⲈ Ⲛ̄-ⳓⲒ ⲚⲒⲘ ⲌⲚ̄-Ⲛ̄-ⲔⲈ-ⲨⲰⲎ ⲦⲎⲢⲞⲨ
Ⲉ-ⲰⲀⲚ-ⲞⲨⲰⲘ ⲆⲈ Ⲛ̄-ⲚⲈ-ⲤⲘⲈ ⲈⲦⲦⲌⲞ ⲌⲰⲰⲞⲨ ⲌⲚ̄-ⲦⲀⲒ-ⲨⲰⲎ

- ešanwōm ᵉnᵉnēkʸe ᵉnkꜟ nim hᵉnᵉnkewše tēru
  ešanwōm de ᵉnnesme ettho hōꜣu hᵉntaywše

- On other nights we eat vegetables of all kinds;
  but on this night we eat only bitter herbs.

Ⲉ-ⲰⲀⲚ̄-ⲤⲰⲠ Ⲛ̄-ⲚⲈ-ⲤⲘⲈ Ⲛ̄-ⲤⲞⲠ ⲘⲀⲨⲀⲦ̄ϥ̄ ⲌⲚ̄-Ⲛ̄-ⲔⲈ-ⲨⲰⲎ ⲦⲎⲢⲞⲨ
Ⲉ-ⲰⲀⲚ-ⲤⲞⲠⲞⲨ ⲆⲈ Ⲛ̄-ⲤⲞⲠ ⲤⲚⲀⲨ Ⲛ̄-ⲦⲀⲒ-ⲨⲰⲎ

- emensōp ᵉnnesme ᵉnsop mawatᵉf hᵉnᵉnkewše tēru
  ešansopu de ᵉnsop snaw ᵉntaywše

- On other nights we do not dip herbs even once;
  but on this night we dip them twice.

Ⲉ-ⲰⲀⲚ̄-ⲞⲨⲰⲘ ⲈⲦⲚ̄-ⲌⲘⲞⲤⲦ Ⲏ ⲈⲦⲚ̄-ⲰⲬⲎⲨⲦ ⲌⲚ̄-Ⲛ̄-ⲔⲈ-ⲨⲰⲎ ⲦⲎⲢⲞⲨ
Ⲉ-ⲰⲀⲚ-ⲰⲬⲞ ⲆⲈ ⲌⲚ̄-ⲦⲀⲒ-ⲨⲰⲎ

- ešanwōm etᵉnhmosᵉt ē etᵉnščēwt hᵉnᵉnkewše tēru
  ešanščo de hᵉntaywše

- On other nights we eat while seated or reclining;
  but on this night we recline.

Ⲉ-ⲰⲀⲚ̄-ⲞⲨⲰⲘ Ⲙ̄-Ⲡ-ⲢⲎⲦⲈ Ⲛ̄-ⲌⲞⲞⲨ ⲚⲒⲘ ⲌⲚ̄-Ⲛ̄-ⲔⲈ-ⲨⲰⲎ ⲦⲎⲢⲞⲨ
Ⲉ-ⲰⲀⲚ-ⲞⲨⲰⲘ ⲆⲈ ⲌⲚ̄-ⲞⲨ-ⲰⲀ ⲈⲦ-ⲞⲨⲀⲀⲂ ⲌⲚ̄-ⲦⲀⲒ-ⲨⲰⲎ

- ešanwōm ᵉmpᵉrēte ᵉnhow nim hᵉnᵉnkewše tēru
  ešanwōm de hᵉnuša etwaꜣb hᵉntaywše

- On other nights we eat in the fashion of every day;
  but on this night we eat with holy ceremony.

The Coptic Saint Shenouda (born in 348 CE), ruled over 4000 monks and nuns as Abbot of the White Monastery of Atripe in the desert of Thebes

ABOUT THE LANGUAGE:

Sahidic Coptic

Status: Extinct   Time Period: 3rd CE – 8th C CE

Sahidic Coptic was spoken in Ancient Egypt in the period from 3rd CE to 8th CE. The language was the classical koine (the *lingua franca*) of Egypt during the time period. Sahidic was replaced by other dialects until the 13th C, when Arabic came into use. *Coptic* derives from the Greek word for Egyptian, *Aigyptioi;* it became *Qibt* in Arabic and was Latinized to *Copt*.

ABOUT THE TRANSLATOR AND SPEAKER:

Geoffrey Graham

Age: Unavailable   Recorded: 1998
Towns: Berkeley, CA / Austin, TX / Cairo, Egypt / New Haven, CT

Geoffrey obtained a Masters of Philosophy (specializing in Egyptology) from Yale University. He was raised in Berkeley, California. His undergraduate and graduate studies (and travels to Europe and the Middle East) allowed him to pursue interests in Islamic and Arabic Art, Delta Archaeology, Epigraphy, Egyptian religious iconography, historical linguistics of Egyptian, and developing teaching tools in the field of Egyptology. Geoffrey assisted in the creation of a new Mummies Gallery at Boston's Museum of Fine Arts.

Geoffrey writes "On the whole, it is always good for one's mastery of the language to practice translating ideas from one's native language into the one we study."

Geoffrey's partner, the son of a Rabbi in Cincinnati's Hebrew Union College, is a student of Middle Eastern Culture, learned Kurdish and follows Iranian customs in his own Seders.

Coptic, Bohairic

ⲈⲦⲂⲈ ⲞⲨ ⲠⲀⲒⲈⲭⲰⲢⲢ ⳘⲪⲢⲎ⳿Ⲧ ⲀⲚ ⲚⲚⲒⲔⲈⲈⲭⲰⲢⲢ ⲦⲎⲢⲞⲨ?

■ Why is this night not like all the other nights?

ϦⲈⲚ ⲚⲒⲔⲈⲈⲭⲰⲢⲢ ⲦⲎⲢⲞⲨ ⲦⲈⲚⲞⲨⲰⳘ ⲚⳤⲀⲚⲰⲒⲔ ⲚϢⲈⳘⲎⲢ ⲒⲈ ⳤⲀⲚⲰⲒⲔ ⲚⲀⲦϢⲈⳘⲎⲢ;
ϦⲈⲚ ⲠⲀⲒⲈⲭⲰⲢⲢ (ⲦⲈⲚⲞⲨⲰⳘ) ⲚⳤⲀⲚⲰⲒⲔ ⲚⲀⲦϢⲈⳘⲎⲢ ⳘⳘⲀⲨⲀⲦϤ;

■ In all other nights we eat leavened bread or unleavened bread;
  in this night (we eat) unleavened bread only.

ϦⲈⲚ ⲚⲒⲔⲈⲈⲭⲰⲢⲢ ⲦⲎⲢⲞⲨ ⲦⲈⲚⲞⲨⲰⳘ ⲈⲂⲞⲖ ⳤⲒ ⲚⲒⲤⳘⲈⳤ ⲦⲎⲢⲞⲨ;
ϦⲈⲚ ⲠⲀⲒⲈⲭⲰⲢⲢ (ⲦⲈⲚⲞⲨⳘ ⲈⲂⲞⲖ ⳤⲒ) ⳤⲀⲚⲤⳘⲈⳤ ⲚⲈⲚϢⲀϢⲒ ⳘⳘⲀⲨⲀⲦϤ.

■ In all other nights we eat from all the herbs;
  in this night (we eat from) bitter herbs only).

ϦⲈⲚ ⲚⲒⲔⲈⲈⲭⲰⲢⲢ ⲦⲎⲢⲞⲨ ⲚⲦⲈⲚⲤⲰⲠ ⲔⲀⲚ ⲞⲨⲀⲒ ⲀⲚ;
ϦⲈⲚ ⲠⲀⲒⲈⲭⲰⲢⲢ ⲦⲈⲚⲤⲰⲠ ⲚⲤⲞⲠ ⲤⲚⲀⲨ.

■ In all other nights we do not dip even once;
  in this night we dip two times.

ϦⲈⲚ ⲚⲒⲔⲈⲈⲭⲰⲢⲢ ⲦⲎⲢⲞⲨ ⲦⲈⲚⲞⲨⲰⳘ ⲈⲚⳤⲈⳘⲤⲒ ⲒⲈ ⲈⲚⲢⲰⲦⲈⲂ;
ϦⲈⲚ ⲠⲀⲒⲈⲭⲰⲢⲢ ⲦⲈⲚⲢⲰⲦⲈⲂ.

■ In all other nights we eat while sitting or reclining;
  in this night we recline.

ϦⲈⲚ ⲚⲒⲔⲈⲈⲭⲰⲢⲢ ⲦⲎⲢⲞⲨ ⲦⲈⲚⲞⲨⲰⳘ ϦⲈⲚ ⲞⲨⲢⲎ⳿Ⲧ ⲚⲔⲞⲒⲚⲞⲤ;
ϦⲈⲚ ⲠⲀⲒⲈⲭⲰⲢⲢ ⲦⲈⲚⲞⲨⲰⳘ ϦⲈⲚ ⲞⲨⲀⲢⲒⲤⲦⲞⲚ ⳘⳘⲞⲚⲞⲚ.

■ In all other nights we eat in an ordinary manner;
  in this night we eat in a special banquet.

ABOUT THE LANGUAGE:

Bohairic Coptic

Time period: 5th C CE to present day

Coptic was spoken in Ancient Egypt and is the liturgical language of the Coptic Church. There are approximately 6,500,000 Coptic Christians worldwide. Although classified as an extinct language, the Bohairic dialect survives to the present day.

ABOUT THE TRANSLATOR AND SPEAKER:

Hany N Takla

Age: 43   Recorded: 1998
Towns: Cairo, Egypt / Los Angeles, CA

Hany was born in Cairo, Egypt and left for the USA in 1970. Hany serves as President of the St. Shenouda the Archimandrite Coptic Society.

Photo by Stephanie Goldhuber

Cairo man, accompanied by his grandchild, smokes from a hookah

Chibcha

Ia hac aguens fazinaz ataguê uchas zinaz puynuca micagê?

■ How is it and on this night [early evening] is one, all other nights is another?

Uchas zinaca puynucan funbi chibgysqua bizcochobixin chibcasqua; fazinacan bizcochocu chibcasqua.

■ On all other nights we eat bread or bizcocho;
on this night bizcocho.

Uchas zinaca puynucan muyne ipquac aguenynga xin chibsosqua; fazinacan muyne aquyhyquynancu chibsosqua.

■ On all other nights we eat herbs whatever they may be;
on this night herbs only if they are bitter.

Uchas zinaca puynucan iotuque chibgasquan etaquyn magueza; fazinacan iotuque chibgasqua boza gue.

■ On all other nights we do not dip even once;
on this night we dip twice.

Uchas zinaca puynucan hischanbi quychebixin chibiza chiquychyquysuca; fazinacan quyche chibiza chiquychyquysuca.

■ On all other nights we eat either sitting up or reclining;
on this night we recline.

Uchas zinaca puynucan yscuc aguecua cuhuc chiquychyquysuca; fazinacan atuc aguecua cuhuc chiquychyquysuca.

■ On all other nights we eat in a way that always is;
on this night we eat in a way that is one/other.

Spelling and pronunciation notes: The spelling is based on 17th C Spanish. "qu" is [k] except before "a", when it is pronounced [kw]. "y" appears to have been a high schwa sound. "z" may have been affricated and unvoiced [ts]. "h" would have been pronounced [h]. Final "e" is probably schwa.

Language and translation Notes:
"How is it and on this night is one, all other nights is another?" This phraseology is drawn from one of the Confessionals, where it is used to translate "...el Dios de los Españoles es diferente del Dios de los Yndios ..." (The god of the Spaniards is different from the god of the Indians.)

Bizcocho was the unleavened bread known to the Spaniards in America. Note that there is a different word in Chibcha for eating bread (and root vegetables) as against hard things like bizcocho. It is different again from the verb for eating herbs (in the next question) and yet again for eating intransitive, irrespective of object (seen further down.)

Atuc aguecua used for "that is one" and "that is other". No Chibcha word for "ceremony" was found.

The main problem in writing Chibcha is arbitrary gaps in the known vocabulary and in examples of the syntax of words when the words are known. All information comes from (Dominican) missionary grammars of the 17th C.
All connected Chibcha text probably amounts to no more than 20,000 words.

Dr. Ostler writes: From a purist's viewpoint, it is very egoistic to put one's own cultural expression into other languages, but I'm happy to help with Chibcha. This is an extinct language. It won't be much of a change for this poor language, since 98% of its extant literature is translations of another culture's liturgy.

ABOUT THE LANGUAGE:

Chibcha

Status: Extinct   Time Period: Through 18th C

Chibcha, also called Muisca, was spoken by the Chibcha Indians of Colombia. Chibcha people are still located near towns of Tocancipa, Cota, Gachancipa and Tenjo. There were once 1 million speakers prior to its extinction, sometime during the 18th C.

ABOUT THE TRANSLATOR AND SPEAKER:

Nicholas Ostler

Age: Unavailable   Recorded: 1999
Towns: Tonbridge / Bath, England

Dr. Ostler, as President of the Foundation for Endangered Languages, is a linguist working to preserve languages that are in danger of extinction and is an expert on several rarely used languages. Nick had visited Colombia seven times in the 1990s and knows Chibcha exclusively through manuscripts and published sources of texts obtained in Colombia. Dr. Ostler was recently working on a reference grammar of the language, including historical comparisons. He is also studying Chibcha's closest modern relative, Tunebo, spoken in the foothills of the Andes on the Colombia-Venezuela border.

Colorful houses on Calle Vicaria Santa Teresa in Cartagena's El Centro

Photo by Bernard Cloutier (berclo.net)

Assyrian, Old

ܐܱܪܒܥܰܐ ܫܸܛܐܠܶܐ `arbʕa šṭ'ale   *Four Questions*

مِهَل مَنَا فَرِیشَا هَو لِلَیَا هَانَا مِن کَتَلَوَاثَا ئَسَرَی؟
- "muṭṭul māna priša-w lilya hāna min laylawatha xrāne?
- *Why is this night different from all other nights?*

- bxulhun laylawatha xrāne laʕsinan laxma xmiṣa ʿaw paṭṭira; bram bhan lilya laxma paṭṭira balxṭdh.
- *On all other nights we eat either leavened bread or matzah; on this night only matzah.*

- bxulhun laylawatha xrāne ʿaxlinan kulhun ʿadše d yarqe; bram bhan lilya yarqe marire balxṭdh.
- *On all other nights we eat all kinds of herbs; on this night only bitter herbs.*

- bxulhun laylawatha xrāne la n ṭammiš xnān ʿapla xdha zwatta; bram bhan lilya tartēn zawnatha.
- *On all other nights we do not dip even once; on this night we dip twice.*

- bxulhun laylawatha xrāne laʕsinan waxnān tiwin ʿaw smixin; bram bhan lilya smixin hwen xnān.
- *On all other nights we eat either sitting up or reclining; on this night we recline.*

- bxulhun laylawatha xrāne laʕsinan bazna ʕyadhāya; bram bhan lilya ʿaxlinan bzawxa priša."
- *On all other nights we eat in an ordinary manner; on this night we dine with special ceremony.*

About the Language:

Old Assyrian

Status: Extinct, liturgical
Time Period: Through 16th C

Old Assyrian (Syriac) was spoken in Mesopotamia (modern-day Iraq) until the 16th C and is still used in religious ceremonies.

About the Translator and Speaker:

Daniel Benjamin

Age: 73   Recorded: 2000
Towns: Mosul / Kirkuk, Iraq / Kuwait / Des Plaines, IL

Daniel is a native speaker of modern Assyrian. He was born in Mosul, in northern Iraq. He completed his studies of the Assyrian language at the Assyrian Seminary, run by the famous Assyrian Scholar, Reverend Joseph De Kelaita. He moved to Kirkuk, Iraq and later lived in Kuwait. Daniel moved to the USA in 1988.

Courtesy of the Oriental Institute

(Left) Human-headed Winged Bull from Khorsabad, Mesopotamia; reign of Sargon II (721-705 BCE)

(Right) Clay prism of Assyrian King Sennacherib (ca. 689 BCE) describes eight military campaigns, including a siege of Jerusalem and imposition of heavy tribute on Hezekiah, King of Judah; the Biblical account (II Kings 18-19) has a different ending

In the recordings: Daniel ends his recording with his name and that of the language, both spoken in Old Assyrian.

Pronunciation guide:
ā = vowels with macron indicates lengthening
š = "sh"
th = "th" as in thing
dh = "th" as in this
` = glottal stop
x = "ch" as in German word "nacht" or Arabic خ
ʕ = voiced pharyngeal fricative shown by Arabic ع
ṭ = an emphatic "t" found in Semitic languages shown by Arabic ط
q = hard guttural sound found in Semitic languages shown by Arabic ق

Aramaic, Ancient

Translated from Hebrew

אֲפַאי אִשְׁתְּנִי הָא לֵילְיָא מִכֻּלְהוּ לֵילְוָתָא؟

■ מַה נִּשְׁתַּנָּה הַלַּיְלָה הַזֶּה מִכָּל הַלֵּילוֹת؟

About the Translators:

Rabbi Alex Heppenheimer and Rabbi Judy Weiss

Age: 31 (Alex) / 49 (Judy)   Translated: 2003
Towns: Brooklyn, NY (Alex) / Millburn, NJ (Judy)

Rabbi Heppenheimer is a former Yeshiva student who spent 14 years studying the Talmud full-time. He received his Rabbinical ordination at Central Yeshiva Tomchei T'mimim, in Brooklyn, NY. Alex can read Talmudic Aramaic fairly fluently.

Rabbi Weiss was born and raised in Cleveland. She received a BA in History and French, a Master's in Accounting, and received her Rabbinic ordination from the Academy for Jewish Religion in New York. Judy is currently pursuing a Doctorate in Bible and Ancient Semitic Languages from NY's Jewish Theological Seminary.

The ancient Aramaic is our only translation that shows the original final question about Roasted Meat, which is found in the Talmud in the laws regarding Passover (Mishna *Pesachim* 10:4). Roasted meat at the Seder was symbolic of the Passover sacrifice. When the Second Temple was destroyed in 70 CE, Temple sacrifices were no longer possible. Because reclining symbolizes freedom, the motif of the Passover Seder, Rabbinic authorities substituted the question about roasted meat with the final question that is currently used.

דִּבְכֻלְּהוּ לֵילְוָתָא אֲכְלֵינַן חֲמִירָא וּפַטִּירָא؛
בְּהָא לֵילְיָא - כֻּלֵּה פַּטִּירָא.

■ שֶׁבְּכָל הַלֵּילוֹת אָנוּ אוֹכְלִין חָמֵץ וּמַצָּה؛
הַלַּיְלָה הַזֶּה כֻּלּוֹ מַצָּה؛

דִּבְכֻלְּהוּ לֵילְוָתָא אֲכְלֵינַן שְׁאָר יַרְקַיָּא؛
בְּהָא לֵילְיָא - כֻּלֵּה מְרִרְיָתָא.

■ שֶׁבְּכָל הַלֵּילוֹת אָנוּ אוֹכְלִין שְׁאָר יְרָקוֹת؛
הַלַּיְלָה הַזֶּה מָרוֹר؛

דִּבְכֻלְּהוּ לֵילְוָתָא לָא מַטְבְּלֵינַן אֲפִילּוּ חֲדָא זִימְנָא؛
בְּהָא לֵילְיָא - תְּרֵי זִימְנֵי.

■ שֶׁבְּכָל הַלֵּילוֹת אֵין אָנוּ מַטְבִּילִין אֲפִילוּ פַּעַם אֶחָת؛
הַלַּיְלָה הַזֶּה שְׁתֵּי פְעָמִים؛

דִּבְכֻלְּהוּ לֵילְוָתָא אֲכְלֵינַן אִי יָתְבֵי אִי מְסַחֲרֵי؛
בְּהָא לֵילְיָא - כֻּלָּנָא מְסַחֲרִינַן.

■ שֶׁבְּכָל הַלֵּילוֹת אָנוּ אוֹכְלִין בֵּין יוֹשְׁבִין וּבֵין מְסֻבִּין؛
הַלַּיְלָה הַזֶּה כֻּלָּנוּ מְסֻבִּין؛

About the Language:

Ancient Aramaic *

Status: Extinct
Time Period: 3rd C BCE – 5th C CE

Aramaic was spoken in (Ancient) Middle East (3rd C BCE – 5th C CE, with a span that is possibly as great as 10th BCE – 7th C).

Illustration by Alysa Lerman

דִּבְכֻלְּהוּ לֵילְוָתָא אֲכְלֵינַן בִּשְׂרָא טַוְיָא שְׁלִיקָא וּמְבַשְׁלָא؛
בְּהָא לֵילְיָא - כֻּלֵּה טַוְיָא؛

■ שֶׁבְּכָל הַלֵּילוֹת אָנוּ אוֹכְלִין בָּשָׂר צָלִי שָׁלוּק וּמְבוּשָׁל؛
הַלַּיְלָה הַזֶּה כֻּלּוֹ צָלִי؛

■ On all other nights we eat meat roasted, stewed or boiled;
on this night only roasted.

דִּבְכֻלְּהוּ לֵילְוָתָא אֲכְלֵינַן בִּשְׁאָר דִּרְכַיָּא؛
בְּהָא לֵילְיָא - חֲדָא דִּרְכָּא؛

■ *On all other nights we eat in any ordinary manner;
on this night we dine with special ceremony.*

*** For additional information, see
"*Focus on ... pages.pdf*" on the DVD.**

54 Spiegel & Stein, *300 Ways to Ask the Four Questions*

Akkadian

am- me- ni mu- šu an- nu ina ka- al mu- ši šá- ni

■ **ammēni mūšu annû ina kal mūšī šani?**

■ Why is this night different from all other nights?

ina mu- ši al- lu- ti NINDA ù ku- si- pa nik- kal

ina mu- ši an- ni ku- si- pa ed- iš

■ **ina mūšī allûti akāla u kusīpa nikkal; ina mūši annî kusīpa ēdiš.**

■ On all other nights we eat either bread or flat bread; on this night only flat bread.

ina mu- ši al- lu- ti ka- al ar- qi nik- kal

ina mu- ši an- ni ar- qa mar- ra ed- iš

■ **ina mūšī allûti kal arqi nikkal; ina mūši annî arqa marra ēdiš.**

■ On all other nights we eat all kinds of vegetables; on this night only bitter herbs.

ina mu- ši al- lu- ti iš- ti- iš- šu la ni- ra- am- muk

ina mu- ši an- ni ši- na ni- ra- am- muk

■ **ina mūšī allûti ištiššu lā nirammuk; ina mūši annî šina nirammuk.**

■ On all other nights we do not dip even once; on this night twice.

ina mu- ši al- lu- ti ina KÚ- i nu- uš- šá- ab ù ni- im- mi- id

ina mu- ši an- ni ka- lu- ni ni- im- mi- id

■ **ina mūšī allûti ina akāli nuššab u nimmid; ina mūši annî kalūni nimmid.**

■ On all other nights we eat either sitting up or reclining;
on this night we all recline.

ina mu- ši al- lu- ti ina ka- al al- ak- ti nik- kal

ina mu- ši an- ni ina al- ak- ti ma- ag- ir- ti

■ **ina mūšī allûti ina kal alakti nikkal; ina mūši annî ina alakti magirti.**

■ On all other nights we eat in any manner;
on this night we eat in a special ceremony.

ABOUT THE TRANSLATOR:

Rabbi Judy Weiss

Age: 49   Translated: 2003
Towns: Cleveland, OH / New York, NY / Millburn, NJ

Rabbi Weiss was born and raised in Cleveland. She received a BA in History and French, a Master's in Accounting, and received her Rabbinic ordination from the Academy for Jewish Religion in New York. Judy is currently pursuing a Doctorate in Bible and Ancient Semitic Languages from NY's Jewish Theological Seminary, where she studied Akkadian for one year. Her Akkadian translation was modified by **Professor David Marcus**, a world expert in Akkadian and related ancient languages at the JTS.

The translation is typical of Standard Babylonian, which is a style dating to the end of the second millennium and the first millennium.

ABOUT THE LANGUAGE:

Akkadian

Status: Extinct   Time Period: 2600 BCE – 50 CE

Akkadian was spoken in Akkad (Northern Mesopotamia), which was located in the area of modern day Iraq. It is the oldest of the group of Semitic languages; it is classified as an East Semitic language. Largely because of its extraordinarily long history – over 2500 years – Akkadian had many dialects and different forms of the Cuneiform script.

An Akkadian greeting was the first of 55 languages etched into gold-plated copper records that were sent into space in 1977 by NASA on the Voyager 1 and 2 spacecraft.

Pronunciation note: The first line shows a symbol-by-symbol transliteration, the second shows normalization, as the text would be spoken. Capital words indicate logograms, Sumerian words written as one sign, rather than via syllables. Hyphens show syllables that form a word (e.g. am- me- ni forms the single word ammeni).

Courtesy of the Oriental Institute

Cylinder seal, Sun God's boat journey, Tell Asmar; (Akkadian Period 2300–2155 BCE); rolled out inscription shown on left

Introduction to Living Languages

This section presents the translations for living languages – those with native-born speakers somewhere in the world. The world's most commonly spoken language is Mandarin Chinese, with about 1 billion speakers. At the other extreme, many Native American languages are close to extinction. One of the rarest, Lenape, is in our collection. At publication time, there were only six native speakers left. Lenape's youngest native speaker participated in our project – she was 61 at the time. Without dedicated education efforts, lesser-used languages frequently become extinct languages.

Data shown for each language:

Number of speakers: In most cases, the number is an estimate for native (first language) speakers of a language, as indicated by the Summer Institute of Linguistics (SIL). This number is assembled from surveys, governments and linguists. But the statistics are not that reliable and perfect. The numbers clearly show too much precision: most certainly there aren't exactly 66,305,890 speakers of Korean, for instance. Even if one discounts the variations in population surveys, a topic of considerable statistical research, one can't assume all people within a linguistically homogeneous area have proficiency in a language. Some people may be blind, deaf and mute; others may lack the intellectual power to grasp a language. It may be more appropriate to cite "about 66 million" Korean speakers. This book didn't modify SIL's numbers, because we don't know how much precision was warranted: Does one report about 66,*306*,000 for Korean; about 66,*300*,000; or maybe "around 65,000,000"?

Rounding off obscures ranking differences between the languages. Although both Jamaican Creole and Albanian each have approximately 3 million speakers, Jamaican Creole (rank 176) probably does have more speakers than Albanian (rank 187) because Jamaica's population is considerably bigger. So this book uses SIL's "overly precise" numbers.

There is yet another important consideration regarding numbers of speakers for a language. Often numbers are underestimated or inflated for political purposes. In many areas of the world, there is a tradition to belittle minority populations. One example is provided by our Assyrian translator, Daniel Benjamin: Iraq often denied the strong historical connection that Assyrians and Arameans have with the ancient population of Mesopotamia. On the other hand, speaker numbers can be inflated. Some populations resist division by linguists into separate languages, as they lose political influence when viewed as smaller populations. Laura Martin provides this example of Mayans in Guatemala: the proliferation of names for separate languages had weakened the power of the Mayan groups to act jointly, and so began the current movement to reverse earlier separations.

Rank: The rank of the language indicates how common the language is, relative to all other languages. Mandarin, the language spoken by the most people on Earth, is rank 1, ahead of others at rank 2, 3 and so on. While serving as a general guide, rank numbers are less reliable as one approaches the bottom. In addition, two languages in this collection – Nynorsk (Norway) and Veluws (Netherlands) – have no rank numbers, because there are no reliable estimates for the number of speakers.

Most pages show a transliteration or transcription, teaching us non-natives how to say the foreign sounds (just as '*Ma Nishtana*' shows how to say the Hebrew). The transliterations are approximations: most languages have sounds not easily conveyed in (English) spelling. Each translator used their own scheme: a few used the International Phonetic Alphabet, while most used common-sense spellings. Many pages show a gloss, which gives the gist of the translation back into English.

Zulu

Kugani lobubusuku behlukile kobunye na?

■ *Why is this night different from all other nights?*

**Ngabo bonke obunye unusuku sidla isinkwa esivutshelwe noma isinkwa esingavutshelwe;
ngalobubusuku sidla imatsa kuphela.**

■ *On all other nights we eat either leavened bread or matzah;
on this night only matzah.*

**Ngabo bonke obunye unusuku sidla zonke izinhlobo semifino;
ngalobubusuku sidla imifino emuncu kuphela.**

■ *On all other nights we eat all kinds of herbs;
on this night only bitter herbs.*

**Ngabo bonke obunye unusuku asiyigcobhozi nakanye imifino;
ngalobubusuku siyigcibhoza kabili.**

■ *On all other nights we do not dip even once;
on this night we dip twice.*

**Ngabo bonke obunye unusuku sidla sihleli siqondile noma siqhiyeme;
ngalobubusuku siyaqhiyama.**

■ *On all other nights we eat either sitting up or reclining;
on this night we recline.*

**Ngabo bonke obunye unusuku sidla nganoma iyiphi indlela;
ngalobubusuku sidla emkhosini obalulekile.**

■ *On all other nights we eat in an ordinary manner;
on this night we dine with special ceremony.*

ABOUT THE LANGUAGE:

Zulu

Number of speakers: 10,349,100
Rank: 77

Zulu, called Isizulu or Zunda by its speakers, is spoken in South Africa, primarily in Zululand and northern Natal. There are a significant number of speakers also in Swaziland, Malawi and Mozambique.

During the early 19th C, Christian missionaries devised the first writing system for Zulu. The first Zulu booklet *Incwadi Yokuqala Yabafundayo* was written between 1837-1838 and explained the spelling of Zulu words and the history of the Old Testament.

ABOUT THE TRANSLATOR AND SPEAKER:

Derek Mbatha

Age: Unavailable   Recorded: 1997
Towns: Durban, South Africa / New York, NY

Derek grew up in Durban and came to the USA as an adult. He works at the United Nations.

Photo by Stephanie Goldhuber

Elephants on the African Savanna

Zarma

Ifo se cin wo sin himar nda ciine fay kulu?

■ *Why is this night different from all other nights?*

Bon ciine hinka kulu, iri nwa walla buuru wala matzah; ciine wo kala matzah.

■ *On all other nights we eat either leavened bread or matzah; on this night only matzah.*

Bon ciine hinka kulu, iri nwa kulu subu dumi-dumi; ciine wo kala subu mooro nda fottu.

■ *On all other nights we eat all kinds of herbs; on this night only bitter herbs.*

Bon ciine hinka kulu, iri nwa kulu subu dumi-dumi; ciine wo kala subu mooro nda fottu.

■ *On all other nights we do not dip even once; on this night we dip twice.*

Bon ciine hinka kulu, iri nwa walla gorey wala kani; ciine wo iri kani.

■ *On all other nights we eat either sitting up or reclining; on this night we recline.*

Bon ciine hinka kulu, iri nwa "in an ordinary manner"; ciine wo iri nwa nda "special ceremony".

■ *On all other nights we eat in an ordinary manner; on this night we dine with special ceremony.*

Translation note: Dr. Alidou was unable to find Zarma words to faithfully translate some words in the last question.

ABOUT THE LANGUAGE:

Zarma

Number of speakers: 2,438,400
Rank: 207

Zarma (also called Adzerma and Djerma) is spoken in southwest Niger, surrounding Niger's capital of Niamey. It is also spoken in the neighboring countries Burkina Faso, Mali and in Nigeria. Dialects from the languages of Dendi and Songai blend into Zarma. It is taught in primary school. Zarma is written in Latin script (shown here) as well as the Ajami style of Arabic script.

ABOUT THE TRANSLATOR:

Dr. Ousseina Alidou

Age: Unavailable   Translated: 2010

Towns: Niamey, Niger / Bloomington, IN / New Brunswick, NJ

Dr. Alidou is director of African Languages and Literature in the Department of African Studies at Rutgers University. She has two Masters degrees in Linguistics and Applied Linguistics, and a PhD in Theoretical Linguistics. Her main area of research concerns women's writing practices in African societies.

Dr. Alidou at a conference in Pumwani, Kenya

Photo by Roland Huziker.
Provided under Creative Commons
Attribution 2.0 Generic License

The Grand Mosque in Niger's capital, Niamey. The top of its minaret is reached by climbing 171 steps

Yup'ik, Central

The Passover Seder Ceremony

Why is this night different from all other nights?
Although the ceremony and eating takes place during the evening,
the word 'night' is used.

On all other nights we eat either leavened bread or matzah;
'bread with yeast' could replace 'leavened bread'.
On this night only matzah.
Bread without yeast or incorporate 'matzah' into Yup'ik.

On all other nights we eat all kinds of herbs;
'greens' may be substituted.
on this night only bitter herbs.
very unappetizing, distasteful food.

On all other nights we do not dip even once;
original doesn't mention what is dipped.
Dip refers to dipping parsley greens into salt water.
on this night we dip twice.

On all other nights we eat either sitting up or reclining;
on this night we recline.
Refers to eating while leaning sideways in a relaxed manner.

On all other nights we eat in an ordinary manner;
on this night we dine with special ceremony.

In the recordings: The extracts from the Translator's Guide, shown above, accompanied the tape. It is likely the 4-minute recording is a translation of these explanations, interspersed with the Yup'ik translation. One can hear the words "Passover Seder ceremony" at the beginning.

ABOUT THE LANGUAGE:

Central Yup'ik

Number of speakers: 16,900
Rank: 2,574

Central Yup'ik (also written Yupik) is spoken in Alaska, on Nunivak Island, the coast from Bristol Bay to Unalakleet on Norton Sound and inland along the Nushagak, Kuskokwim and Yukon rivers.

ABOUT THE TRANSLATOR AND SPEAKER:

Denis David Shelden

Age: 55   Recorded: 2001
Town: Alakanuk, AK

Denis lives in Alakanuk, Alaska. His first language is Yupik and he learned English at a mission school when he was 6 years old. Denis serves as the Catholic Deacon in the village of Alakanuk and is manager of Alakanuk Native Corporation.

Alakanuk is in western Alaska at the entrance of Alakanuk Pass, the major south-west channel of the Yukon River, 15 miles from the Bering Sea. Alakanuk was originally settled in 1899. The settlement had only 7 cabins in 1936; today there are 140 occupied "housing units".

Yukon River near Carcross [Caribou Crossing], Alaska, near its easternmost extent (the other end of the Yukon River from Alakanuk Pass)

Z Y X W V U T S R Q P O N M L K J I H G F E D C B A

Yucatacán Maya

Bas tun eh akkam ulela umpaz que tu lac aka?

■ *Why is this night different from all other nights?*

U lac a akā, kik hantic wah.

■ *On all other nights we eat either leavened bread or matzah; on this night only matzah.*

U lac a akā, kik hantic lea che.

■ *On all other nights we eat all kinds of herbs; on this night only bitter herbs.*

U lac a akā, machik zulic bele tic zulac ca pak.

■ *On all other nights we do not dip even once; on this night we dip twice.*

U lac a akā, kik hanā culanō wa nacā bele tic nacahba.

■ *On all other nights we eat either sitting up or reclining; on this night we recline.*

U lac a akā, kik hanā bīsakile bele tic hana ma basha malobi.

■ *On all other nights we eat in an ordinary manner; on this night we dine with special ceremony.*

Photo by Robyn Stein

The Mayan feathered serpent head of Quetzalcoatl in Teotihuacan, Mexico. From 300 CE.

ABOUT THE LANGUAGE:

Yucatán Maya

Number of speakers: 706,000
Rank: 449

Yucatán Maya (also called Yucateco) is spoken primarily in Mexico; Belize has a small population of Yucatán Maya speakers.

The early Mayan civilization lasted from 500 BCE to 1200 CE, with a classical period from 300 to 900 CE. The earliest known writing in the Mayan script dates from about 250 BCE, but the script is thought to have developed at an earlier date. The Yucatec Maya continued to use the Mayan logographic/syllabary script until at least the 16th C. Recently, their descendants have started to learn the script once again from the scholars who have deciphered it. The spelling system shown here is more commonly used.

ABOUT THE TRANSLATOR AND SPEAKER:

Aurora Garcia Saqui

Age: 31   Recorded: 1998
Town: Cayo District, Belize

Aurora was raised in Cayo District and lives in Maya Center, Belize. She is one of the Garcia sisters who are famous in the Cayo District. Their father developed (and his daughters continued) a new art form: slate carving. (The slate is taken from the rivers, carved by locals with Mayan symbols and motifs, then rubbed with black shoe polish; this art is currently sold all over Belize and is a hot tourist item.) She married Ernesto Saqui [translator for Mopan Maya] in 1992 and moved to Maya Center. Their two sons, ages 3 and 5, speak 5 languages: English, Belizean Creole, Spanish, Mopan Maya and Yucateco Maya.

Aurora has developed thriving businesses in a guest house, restaurant and herbal medicine. In 5 years she earned the respect of her husband's community and was elected to the Maya Center Village Council.

Translation notes: The first phrases have the appearance of being incomplete. First phrases may only be a translation of "On all other nights we ..." Last phrases have *bele tic*, perhaps meaning "on this night."

Several inconsistencies were corrected: Although only last 2 phrases had accents, they were added to analogous words in prior lines. The translator used *akābo* on each line and crossed off *bo* on all lines except the last – by analogy *bo* was removed everywhere. The third question had *bele ik* whereas last two had *bele tic* – the authors assumed the third should be also be *bele tic*.

Yorùbá

Èé ṣe tí òru òní fi yàtò̩ sí gbogbo òru t' ó kù?

■ Why be that night today happen different from all nights that they remain?

Ní gbogbo óru t'ó kù, a ñ jẹ ìwukàrà tàbí mátísà;
Ṣùgbó̩n ní òru òní, mátísà nìkan ni.

■ On/at all nights that they remain, we are eating swollen-cake or matzah; but at/on night today, matzah be-alone be.

Ní gbogbo óru t'ó kù, a ñ jẹ gbogbo oríṣiríṣi ewéko;
Ṣùgbó̩n ní òru òní, ewéko kíkorò nìkan ni.

■ On/at all nights that they remain, we are eating all kinds (of) herbs; but at/on night today, herbs bitter be-alone be.

Ní gbogbo óru t'ó kù, a ñ jẹ run ọbè̩ lé̩è̩kan rárá;
Ṣùgbó̩n ní òru òní, a n run lé̩è̩mejì.

■ On/at all nights that they remain, we not be dipping-into stew at-one-time at-all but at/on night today, we be dipping-into at-two-times.

Ní gbogbo óru t'ó kù, a ñ jẹ jẹun ní ìjókòó tàbí ní ìdùbúlè̩;
Ṣùgbó̩n ní òru òní, a n dùbúlè̩ ni.

■ On/at all nights that they remain, we are eating-food at sitting or at reclining; but at/on night today, we are reclining be.

Ní gbogbo óru t'ó kù, a n jẹun ní ọ̀nà t'ó wù wá;
Ṣùgbó̩n ní òru òní, a n jẹun pè̩lú àriyá àkànṣe.

■ On/at all nights that they remain, we are eating in way/manner that it please us; but at/on night today, we are eating-food with ceremony special.

ABOUT THE LANGUAGE:

Yorùbá

Number of speakers: 19,380,800
Rank: 51

Yorùbá, also called Yooba and Yariba, is one of the four official languages of Nigeria. It is primarily spoken in Nigeria's Oyo, Ogun, Ondo Osun, Kwara, Lagos and Kogi states. It is also spoken in Benin, Togo, United Kingdom and the USA. It is a language with three tones (upward accent, downward accent and unmarked letters).

Yorùbá first appeared in writing during the 19th C. The first Yorùbá publications were a number of teaching booklets produced by John Raban between 1830-1832.

ABOUT THE TRANSLATOR AND SPEAKER:

Yiwola Awoyale

Age: 50s   Recorded: 1997
Towns: Igbesi/Ilorin, Nigeria

Dr. Awoyale is Professor and Head of the Department of Linguistics and Nigerian Languages at the University of Ilorin, Nigeria. Yiwola lived in Nigeria all his life except for the four years (in his 30s) he spent at the University of Illinois earning his PhD in Linguistics. His birthplace, Igbesi, is in Kwara state, 50 km from Ilorin.

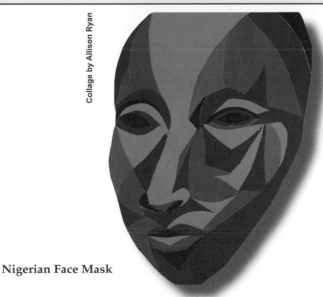

Collage by Allison Ryan

Nigerian Face Mask

Translator's notes: Yorùbá does not express present tense, only future vs. non-future tense. *tí* covers both "that" and all elements of Wh-questions in English (Why, What, Where, etc). "This" can be translated as *èyí/yìí* but *òní* refers to this given night. *òru* is the word for night; evening is *alé*. *Ìwukàrà* ("swollen cake") is derived from *Ì wu àkàrà*. *Àkàrà* is made of ground bean powder which swells up after steaming or frying. As wheat flower is not indigenous to Nigeria, the Yorùbá bible translates leavened bread as *Ìwukàrà*. *ewéko* is derived from *ewé-oko* ("leaves/plants of the bush") for herbs, as opposed to *ewébe* ("leaves for stew") for vegetables. Stew is the only food we dip into; not water, tea, etc.

Yiddish

ABOUT THE LANGUAGE:

Yiddish

Number of speakers: 1,762,320
Rank: 258

Yiddish, a language of Eastern Europe, is spoken in Israel and in Argentina, Australia, Belarus, Belgium, Canada, Estonia, Hungary, Latvia, Lithuania, Moldova, Panama, Poland, Puerto Rico, Romania, Russia, South Africa, Ukraine, Uruguay and the USA.

Yiddish is commonly thought to be a mixture of Hebrew and German; however, most dialects borrowed from any language of the local community. The name comes from the German word for Jewish, *jüdisch*.

ABOUT THE TRANSLATOR:

Rebecca Levine

Age: 71   Translated: 2003
Towns: Brooklyn, NY / White Meadow Lake, NJ

Rebecca is a well-known Yiddish instructor in the northern NJ area, with 40 years experience. She was raised in Brooklyn, NY by Polish parents (currently Belarus). Yiddish is her first language and was also studied in elementary and high school. Most of the translation text is traditional.

ABOUT THE SPEAKER:

Theodore Bikel

Age: 79   Recorded: 2003
Towns: Vienna / Palestine / London / Los Angeles, CA

Theodore Bikel is a famous movie, TV, Broadway and recording star. Born in Vienna, he moved to Israel (then Palestine) at age 14 and then to London at age 21. He moved to the USA when he was 30. He is fluent in 6 languages.

Theodore has been in over 50 movies and 75 notable TV appearances. Notable roles: Broadway: Sound of Music (Captain Von Trapp in original Broadway show), national tours of Zorba and Fiddler on the Roof. He's played Tevye more than 2000 times (top right). Movies: The African Queen, Moulin Rouge, My Fair Lady, The Enemy Below and The Defiant Ones. Recordings: Dozens of albums, including folk songs in nearly 20 languages. Folk Music: 50-60 concerts annually, founder of Newport Folk Festival.

טאַטע, איך וועל דיך פֿרעגן די פֿיר קשיאות.

- Tateh, ikh vel dikh fregn dee fir kashes.
- *Father, I will ask the Four Questions.*

פֿאַרװאָס איז די נאַכט פֿון פּסח פֿון אַנדערש פֿון אַלע אַנדערע נעכט?

- Farvos iz dee nakht fun peysakh andersh fun aleh andereh nekht?
- *Why is this night different from all other nights?*

אַלע נעכט פֿון אַ גאַנץ יאָר עסן מיר חמץ און מצה,
אָבער די נאַכט פֿון פּסח עסן מיר נאָר מצה.

- Aleh nekht fun a gants yor ess-n mir khomets un matseh;
  ober dee nakht fun peysakh ess-n mir nor matseh.
- *On all other nights we eat either leavened bread or matzah; on this night only matzah.*

אַלע נעכט פֿון אַ גאַנץ יאָר עסן מיר אלערליי גרינמן,
אָבער די נאַכט פֿון פּסח עסן מיר נאָר מרור.

- Aleh nekht fun a gants yor ess-n mir aler-ley grin-sn;
  ober dee nakht fun peysakh ess-n mir nor morer.
- *On all other nights we eat all kinds of herbs; on this night only bitter herbs.*

אַלע נעכט פֿון אַ גאַנץ יאָר טונקען מיר ניט אַיין אַפֿילו איין מאָל,
אָבער די נאַכט פֿון פּסח טונקען מיר אַיין צוויי מאָל.

- Aleh nekht fun a gants yor tunken mir nit ayn afileh eyn mol;
  ober dee nakht fun peysakh tunken mir ayn tsvey mol.
- *On all other nights we do not dip even once; on this night we dip twice.*

אַלע נעכט פֿון אַ גאַנץ יאָר עסן מיר סיי זיצענדיק און סיי אָנגעלענט,
אָבער די נאַכט פֿון פּסח עסן מיר נאָר אָנגעלענט.

- Aleh nekht fun a gants yor ess-n mir say zitsendik un say on-ge-lent;
  ober dee nakht fun peysakh ess-n mir nor on-ge-lent.
- *On all other nights we eat either sitting up or reclining; on this night we recline.*

אַלע נעכט פֿון אַ גאַנץ יאָר עסן מיר אין אַ געוויינטלעכן אופֿן,
אָבער די נאַכט פֿון פּסח עסן מיר מיט באַזונדערע מינהגים.

- Aleh nekht fun a gants yor ess-n mir in a geveyntlekhn oyfn;
  ober dee nakht fun peysakh ess-n mirmit bazyndere minhogm.
- *On all other nights we eat in an ordinary manner; on this night we dine with special ceremony.*

Photos used by permission of Theodore Bikel

Xhosa

Obu busuku bohluke njani na kubo bonke obunye ubusuku?

■ *Why is this night different from all other nights?*

Ngabo bonke obunye ubusuku, sitya isonk' esingenagwele okanye imathsa; ngobu ubusuku, (sitya) imathsa kuphela.

■ *On all other nights we eat either leavened bread or matzah; on this night only matzah.*

Ngabo bonke obunye ubusuku, sitya zonk' intlobo zemifuno; ngobu ubusuku, kuphela imifuno ekrakrayo.

■ *On all other nights we eat all kinds of herbs; on this night only bitter herbs.*

Ngabo bonke obunye ubusuku, asincindi nkqu nakanye; ngobu ubusuku, sincinda kabini.

■ *On all other nights we do not dip even once; on this night we dip twice.*

Ngabo bonke obunye ubusuku, sitya sihleli okanye singqiyamile; ngobu ubusuku, siyangqiyama.

■ *On all other nights we eat either sitting up or reclining; on this night we recline.*

Ngabo bonke obunye ubusuku, sitya nje ngesiqhelo; ngobu ubusuku, sifumana isidlo kumnyadala owodwa (otyhulu).

■ *On all other nights we eat in an ordinary manner; on this night we dine with special ceremony.*

ABOUT THE LANGUAGE:

Xhosa

Number of speakers: 7,817,300
Rank: 97

Xhosa, also written !Hosa and called Isixhosa by its speakers, is one of the official languages of South Africa. It is primarily spoken in southwest Cape Province and Transkei, and also spoken in Botswana and Lesotho.

Xhosa is possibly the most famous of South Africa's click languages. The X or ! symbol stands for a click, which functions as a consonant.

ABOUT THE TRANSLATOR AND SPEAKER:

Sindiwe Magona

Age: 54   Recorded: 1997
Towns. Umtata, South Africa / NY / South Africa

A South African writer, Sindiwe grew up in Cape Town's black townships and came to the USA at age 38, receiving a Masters in Organizational Social Work and worked many years at the United Nations. She has taught Xhosa to children and adults. She is the author of two autobiographical books, two books of short stories, a novel and a language book on Xhosa.

Photo by Stephanie Goldhuber

Elephants at Lake Kariba

Bonus in the recordings: Sindiwe recites a tongue twister in Xhosa, one of the longest and most complicated in the world.

Welsh

Pam mae'r noson hon yn wahanol i bob noson arall?

■ *Why is this night different from all other nights?*

Rydyn ni'n bwyta naill ai bara wedi'u lefeinio neu bara heb lefain ar bob noson arall; dim ond bara heb lefain y noson hon.

■ *On all other nights we eat either leavened bread or matzah; on this night only matzah.*

Rydyn ni'n bwyta pob fath o lysieuyn blas ar bob noson arall; dim ond llysiau chwerw y noson hon.

■ *On all other nights we eat all kinds of herbs; on this night only bitter herbs.*

Dydyn ni ddim yn trochi'r llysiau o gwbl ar bob noson arall; rydyn ni'n eu trochi dwywaith y noson hon.

■ *On all other nights we do not dip even once; on this night we dip twice.*

Rydyn ni'n bwyta naill ai yn sefyll neu'n gogwyddo ar bob noson arall; rydyn ni'n gogwyddo y noson hon.

■ *On all other nights we eat either sitting up or reclining; on this night we recline.*

Photo courtesy of Mary Parry

Interior of Swansea's Synagogue in Wales

ABOUT THE LANGUAGE:

Welsh

Number of speakers: 537,870
Rank: 524

The Celtic language Welsh is spoken in northern, western and southern Wales. There are also speakers in Scotland, Argentina, Canada, USA, Australia and New Zealand. Welsh is fairly closely related to Cornish and Breton, and more distantly related to the Irish, Manx and Scottish Gaelics.

At the beginning of the 20th C about half of the population of Wales spoke Welsh as an everyday language. Towards the end of the century, the proportion of Welsh speakers had fallen to about 20%.

The earliest known examples of Welsh literature are poems of Taliesin mentioning a 6th C King (Urien of Rheged) and Aneirin's *Y Gododdin*, a description of a battle between Celts and Northumbrians which occurred around 600 CE.

ABOUT THE TRANSLATOR AND SPEAKER:

Rhys James Jones

Age: 33   Recorded: 2006
Towns: Carmarthen / Oxford / Swansea, Wales

Rhys was born in Carmarthen, Wales. He moved to Drefach at age three, later moved to Oxford and then finally to Swansea as an adult. Rhys obtained a PhD from the University of Wales on the speech recognition of Welsh.

In the recordings: Rhys ends his recording with his name and the name of the language, spoken in Welsh.

Waray-Waray

Kay ano nga iba ini nga gab-i han ngatanan nga mga naglabay nga gab-i?

■ *Why is this night different from all other nights?*

**Ha ngatanan nga mga gab-i kumakaon kita hin pinaalsa nga tinapay,
kon usahay naman dire pinaalsa;
yana nga gab-i dire la pinaalsa.**

■ *On all other nights we eat either leavened bread or matzah;
on this night only matzah.*

**Kada gab-i kumakaon kita hin sarsalado nga mga utanon;
yana nga gab-i mapait la nga utanon an aton kinaon.**

■ *On all other nights we eat all kinds of herbs;
on this night only bitter herbs.*

**Ha ngatanan nga gab-i waray kita pagtulnob bisan makausa;
yana nga gab-i tinulnob kita makaduha.**

■ *On all other nights we do not dip even once;
on this night we dip twice.*

**Ha ngatanan nga gab-i pwede kita kumaon hin maupay nga kalingkod,
hin usahay naman nakasandig;
yana nga gab-i nakasandig kita kumaon.**

■ *On all other nights we eat either sitting up or reclining;
on this night we recline.*

**Ha ngatanan nga gab-i ordinaryo la an aton pangaon;
yana nga gab-i may seremonyas an aton pangaon.**

■ *On all other nights we eat in an ordinary manner;
on this night we dine with special ceremony.*

ABOUT THE LANGUAGE:

Waray-Waray

Number of speakers: 2,570,000
Rank: 204

Waray-Waray is spoken in the Philippines, in northern and eastern Samar-Leyte. It is also called Samareño and Samaran.

ABOUT THE TRANSLATOR AND SPEAKER:

Kobla Grace May A Leaño

Age: 38   Recorded: 1999
Town: Borongan, Eastern Samar / Manila, Philippines

Grace, a native speaker of Waray-Waray, was raised in Borongan and is now a guidance counselor in Manila.

Photo by Rody Torres

Traditional Philippines New Year's Eve fireworks display, Tondo, Manila. The firework is often placed at the end of a bamboo pole and paraded around

Vietnamese

Bốn Câu Hỏi – The Four Questions

Sao đêm nay lại khác mọi đêm qua?
- Why is this night different than all the other nights?

**Vì như mọi đêm ta có thể ăn mọi loại bánh;
nhưng đêm nay chỉ duy nhất bánh mì cứng.**
- On all other nights we can eat all kinds of bread;
  but tonight only hard bread.

**Như mọi đêm ta ăn mọi thứ rau thơm;
nhưng đêm nay chỉ rau nào đắng ta mới ăn.**
- On all other nights we can eat all kinds of herbs;
  but tonight we eat only bitter herbs.

**Như mọi đêm ta chẳng hề nhúng rau thơm vào nước muối;
còn đêm nay ta sẽ làm như thế đúng hai lần.**
- On all other nights we would not dip the herbs in salt water;
  but tonight we dip twice.

**Vì mọi đêm ta có thể vừa ăn ngã nghiêng hay ngồi thẳng;
còn đêm nay ta sẽ nghiêng mình.**
- On all other nights we can eat sitting upright or reclining;
  but tonight only reclining.

**Như mọi đêm ta ăn một buả ăn bình thường;
nhưng đêm nay nghi lễ trang trọng.**
- On all other nights we eat an ordinary supper;
  but tonight with special ceremony.

Floating villages in Ha Long Bay

Translation notes: All breads known in Vietnam are leavened bread. Luan used words that represent 'hard bread' instead of 'Matzah'. The translation uses words for specific types of herbs known in Vietnam: *rau thơm* represents fresh, green herbs; while *gia vị* means bottled/dried/ground (e.g., not fresh) herbs.

The recording uses both *ngã nghiêng* (relaxed leaning) and *ngiêng mình* (formal leaning – bowing); *ngã nghiêng* is used both times in the text. The fifth question was not recorded. Instead, the fourth question was introduced with the phrase: *Và không như mọi đêm, cỗ đêm nay sẽ trong nghi lễ đặc biệt*, which means "Unlike all other nights tonight's supper follows a special tradition".

Photo by Stephanie Goldhuber

ABOUT THE LANGUAGE:

Vietnamese

Number of speakers: 68,634,000
Rank: 14

Vietnamese, also called Kinh, Gin, Jing and Ching, is the national language of Vietnam. It is also spoken in 19 other countries – a significant number of speakers are in China.

Vietnamese was originally written with a Chinese-like script known as *Chữ'-nôm* or *Nôm*. During the 17th C, Roman Catholic missionaries introduced Latin-based spelling for Vietnamese, *Quốc Ngữ'*. During the early 20th C, the *Quốc Ngữ'* completely replaced *Nôm*.

ABOUT THE TRANSLATOR AND SPEAKER:

Cong Luan Ngo Tran

Age: Unavailable   Recorded: 1995
Locations: Vietnam / United Kingdom

Cong Luan Ngo Tran, who goes by the name Luan, was studying for a doctorate in Civil Engineering at Oxford University at the time of the recording, but now is back working in Vietnam. The text was entered with assistance by **Luan Lam Doniger**, who also provided the translation of the fifth question.

Veluws

Translated from Dutch

Waarüm is disse avend so anders as andere avenden?

■ *Waarom is het vanavond anders dan andere avonden?*

Up alle andere avenden atten wy of eresen brood of matzah; vanavend allin matzah.

■ *Op alle andere avonden aten we of gerezen brood of matzoh; vanavond alleen matzoh.*

Up alle andere avenden atten wy verschillende soorten kruyden; vanavend allin bittere kruyden.

■ *Op alle andere avonden aten we verschillende soorten specerijen; vanavond alleen bittere specerijen.*

Up alle andere avenden dippen wy de kruyden höylmaal ny; vanavend dippen wy et twee keer.

■ *Op alle andere avonden dippen we de specerijen helemaal niet; vanavond dippen we ze twee keer.*

Up alle andere avenden sitten wy rechtup of loenen wy achterover; up disse avend loenen wy achterover.

■ *Op alle andere avonden zitten we rechtop of leunen we achterover; op deze avond leunen we achterover.*

Up alle andere avenden atten wy soas altyd; vanavend dineern wy up ceremoniële wyse.

■ *Op alle andere avonden aten we zoals altijd; vanavond dineren we op ceremoniële wijze.*

ABOUT THE TRANSLATOR AND SPEAKER:

Stefan Lauvie

Age: 20s   Recorded: 2005
Towns: Zeewolde, Netherlands / St. Frances Bay, South Africa

Stefan is a language student who knows Dutch, Afrikaans, English, Low Saxon and Veluws. Though he was born in Zeewolde, Stefan learned Veluws from his grandfather and so his speech resembles dialects spoken in Nunspeet and Putten.

The Veluws translation was based on the Dutch, referencing the Afrikaans and English translations.

ABOUT THE LANGUAGE:

Northern Veluws

Number of speakers: Unknown
Rank: N/A

Veluws is spoken in the Netherlands. It belongs to the class of languages classified as Low Saxon. The writing system used here is called *Algemene Schryvwyse* ("common writing system"). The language's rank is artificially high because the number of speakers is unknown.

In the recordings: Stefan ends his recording with his name and the name of the language, spoken in Veluws.

Haggadah from the collection of Rabbi Arnold Zoref

Cover of Haggadah published in the Netherlands

Uzbek

Translated from Russian

Нима Фарқи бор бу кеча бошқа кечалардан?
■ Чем отличается эта ночь от всех других ночей?

Хар бошқалардан кеча бизлар емиз нон;
ва маца бу кеча Факат маца.
■ Во все другие ночи мы едим либо квашеный хлеб либо мацу;
а в эту ночь-только мацу.

Хар бошқалардан кеча бизлар емиз кук нарса Фаркм ёк;
бу кеча Факат очиқ, кук нарса.
■ Во все другие ночи мы едим любую зелень;
а в эту-только горькую.

Хар бошқалардан кеча бизлар ботермастан емиз кук нарса;
бу кеча ботерамнз ики- марта.
■ Во все другие ночи мы вообще не обмакиваем зелени;
а в эту ночь-обмакиваем ее дважды.

Хар бошқалардан кеча бизлар утириб емиз ва ёнбошлаб;
бу кеча ёнбошлаб емиз.
■ Во все другие ночи мы едим сидя или возлегая;
а в эту ночь-возлегая.

Хар бошқалардан кеча бизлар емиз;
бу кеча байрамча ухшаб емиз.
■ Во все другие ночи мы едим как обыденно;
а сегодня у нас ритуадьная трапеза.

ABOUT THE LANGUAGE:

Northern Uzbek

Number of speakers: 18,817,600
Rank: 52

Northern Uzbek (also called Özbek) is the national language of Uzbekistan. (The Southern version is primarily spoken in Aghanistan.) Uzbek is spoken throughout the Asian republics of the former USSR, east of the Amu Darya and around the southern Aral Sea, as well as in Australia, China, Israel, Kazakhstan, Kyrgyzstan, Russia, Tajikistan, Turkey, Turkmenistan, Ukraine and the USA.

An early Arabic script form of Uzbek (named *Chagatai* after a son of Genghis Khan) was developed in the 14th C. A version using the Latin alphabet replaced the script in 1927, which was in turn replaced by the Cyrillic alphabet in 1940.

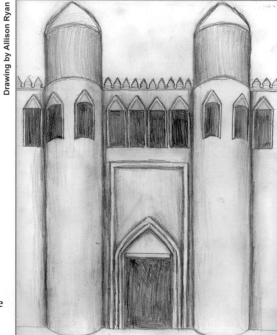

Drawing by Allison Ryan

The Ark Citadel in Bukhara, Uzbekistan dates from before the 1st C CE. Destroyed many times and restored to its present state in the 16th C, the museum inside holds 92,000 articles of historical interest

ABOUT THE TRANSLATOR AND SPEAKER:

Boris Bababekov

Age: Unavailable   Recorded: 2001
Towns: Uzbekistan / New York, NY

Boris was born and raised in Uzbekistan. He was 45 years old when he emigrated to the USA.

Ute

Hadeyach ich duwachget gumachayuvay ich duwachget?

■ *Why is this night different from all other nights?*

Note: The recordings contain the full translation.

**Aldean Ketchum and family
in the Kelly Lodge**

Photos by Janice Allen

ABOUT THE TRANSLATOR AND SPEAKER:

Aldean (Lightning Hawk) Ketchum

Age: Unavailable   Recorded: 2004
Town: White Mesa, UT

Aldean is a master flute maker and player. He was given the honor of playing the first flute note in the opening ceremonies of 2002 Salt Lake City International Winter Olympics. With others in their family, Aldean and his wife perform widely throughout the region as the Ketchum Family. They perform traditional songs and dances for Anglos and their own communities. At the time of this recording, the family had performed over 9 years and recorded 2 CDs. Although they have no children of their own, Aldean and his wife raised 7 nieces and nephews.

The story about Aldean playing at the 2002 Winter Olympics opening ceremonies was written in the Cortez Journal: www.cortezjournal.com/archives/1news2073.htm.

Aldean's traditional name (Lightning Hawk) was given to him by his grandfather, when he was an adult. Traditionally, names were only known by the family. If an enemy knew your name, they'd be able to call you while sneaking up on you.

ABOUT THE LANGUAGE:

Ute

Number of speakers: 1,980
Rank: 4,608

Ute is spoken in southern Colorado, Utah, northern Arizona, southern Nevada and lower Colorado River, California.

The name of the state Utah is taken from the Ute tribe.

Ute is primarily a spoken language. There are few written texts and very few Utes can write the language.

Urkers

Woromme is disse aved angers as alle angere aveden?

■ *Why is this evening different from all other evenings?*

Woromme eten we allieneg matzes in gien brood?

■ *Why do we eat just matzot and no bread?*

Woromme eten we allienig bittere kruien in gien angere gruunte?

■ *Why do we eat only bitter herbs and no other vegetables?*

Woromme stippen we et eeten twie keer?

■ *Why do we dip the food twice?*

Woromme leggen of zitten we elleke aved an tafel, maar vanaved leggen we allemoal?

■ *Why do we sit or recline at the table every evening, but tonight we all recline?*

Woromme is et vles normoal eroosterd, mariniert of ekookt, maar vanaved is et allemoal eroosterd?

■ *Why is the food normally roasted, marinated or cooked, but this evening it is all roasted?*

ABOUT THE TRANSLATOR AND SPEAKER:

Bert de Jong

Age: 32   Recorded: 2010

Towns: Amsterdam / Urk, The Netherlands

Bert's mother tongue is both Urkers and standard Dutch, having lived in Urk from age 5 until 25. Bert's interest in languages extends to English, Spanish, Russian, French, German, Hebrew and even Swahili. Bert's translation explicitly asks a question for each phrase, and translates the original final question about roasted meat (see Ancient Aramaic). Bert was once a computer programmer, but now gives tours of Amsterdam's Jewish neighborhoods.

ABOUT THE DIALECT:

Urkers

Number of speakers: 17,000 (estimate)

Equivalent Rank: 2573

Urkers is spoken in Urk, a village that used to be an island in The Netherlands. Urkers is one of the oldest and most distinctive dialects of Dutch, having been isolated from the rest of the country – no other dialect of Dutch has as many vowels sounds.

In historical times, young girls frequently left the island to become domestic servants around Amsterdam. They often served with Jewish families. After a few years, they would return home to Urk. As a result, the Urkers absorbed the Amsterdam dialect of Dutch as well as some loan-words from Yiddish (eg: Kalletje = Challah). In addition, Jewish traditions have pervaded the Christian population: without knowing why, the housewives of Urk turn their houses upside down around Easter (and, thus, Passover) and clean everything so meticulously.

A sizeable community of Jews live in Urk. The residents have a strong connection to Israel – everyone follows the tradition to try to visit Israel at least once in their lifetime.

Provided under Creative Commons Attribution-Share Alike 2.5 Generic License

The harbor of the former island of Urk

Urdu

ABOUT THE LANGUAGE:

Urdu *

Number of speakers: 60,586,800
Rank: 21

Urdu is spoken in Pakistan, India, Mauritius, South Africa and 16 other countries.

Urdu has been written in Perso-Arabic script since the 12th C and is normally written in *Nastaliq* style. The word Urdu is Turkish for 'foreign' or 'horde'.

The Urdu, Hindi and Hindustani are sometimes considered co-dialects (they are mutually intelligible), but as they have important sociolinguistic differences, they are usually considered separate languages. In addition, a lot of Urdu vocabulary comes from Persian and Arabic, which is not the case for Hindi.

ABOUT THE TRANSLATOR AND SPEAKER:

Khurram Haneef

Age: 26   Recorded: 1999
Towns: Karachi, Pakistan / Morris Plains, NJ

Khurram was born in Karach and came to the USA in 1995. He is a native speaker of Urdu.

The translation was also worked on by **Rashid Ansari**, originally from Purna, India, now living in Chicago, IL. Rashid is a Professor of Electrical Engineering at the University of Illinois, with degrees from the Indian Institute of Technology (Kanpur, India) and a PhD from Princeton University.

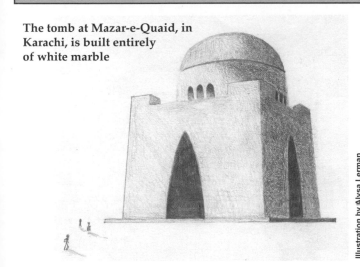

The tomb at Mazar-e-Quaid, in Karachi, is built entirely of white marble

Illustration by Alysa Lerman

یہ رات اور سب راتوں سے مختلف کیوں ہے؟

■ Yeh ra'at aur sab raaton se mukhtalif kyun hai?

■ *Why is this night different from all other nights?*

اور سب راتوں کو ہم یا تو اُبھری ہوئی یا بغیر اُبھری ہوئی روٹی کھاتے ہیں؛
اس رات کو صرف بغیر اُبھری ہوئی روٹی

■ Aur sab raaton ko hum ya to ubhri hui ya baghair ubhri huwi roti khate hain;
Is ra'at ko sirf baghair ubrhi huwi roti.

■ *On all other nights we eat either leavened bread or matzah;*
on this night only matzah.

اور سب راتوں کو ہم ہر قسم کے مصالحے کھاتے ہیں؛
اس رات کو صرف کڑوے مصالحے

■ Aur sab raaton ko hum har kisam ke masalay khate hain;
Is ra'at ko sirf karway masalay.

■ *On all other nights we eat all kinds of herbs;*
on this night only bitter herbs.

اور سب راتوں کو ہم ایک بار بھی نہیں ڈبوتے؛
اس رات کو دو بار ڈبوتے ہیں

■ Aur sab raaton ko hum aik bar bhi nahein dabote;
Is ra'at ko do baar dabote hain.

■ *On all other nights we do not dip even once;*
on this night we dip twice.

اور سب راتوں کو ہم یا سیدھے بیٹھ کر یا جھک کر کھاتے ہیں؛
اس رات کو جھک کر

■ Aur sab raaton ko hum ya seedhe baithkar ya jhuk kar khate hain;
Is raat ko jhuk kar.

■ *On all other nights we eat either sitting up or reclining;*
on this night we recline.

اور سب راتوں کو ہم کسی بھی عام طریقے سے کھاتے ہیں؛
اس رات کو خاص رسم سے کھاتے ہیں

■ Aur sab raaton ko hum kisi bhi aam tareqe se khate hain;
Is raat ko khas rasm se khate hain.

■ *On all other nights we eat in any ordinary manner;*
on this night we dine with special ceremony.

> * For additional information, see "*Focus on ... pages.pdf*" on the DVD.

Ukrainian

Чим відрізняється ця ніч від інших ночей?
- Chim vidriznyayetza tzya nich vid inshih nochey?
- *Why is this night different from all other nights?*

Кожної ночі ми їмо хліб чи мацу;
цієї ночі-тільки мацу.
- Kozhnoyi nochee mi yimo hleeb chi matzu;
  tziyeyi nochee tilkee matzu.
- *On all other nights we eat either leavened bread or matzah;*
  on this night only matzah.

Кожної ночі ми їмо всяку зелень;
цієї ночі-гірке.
- Kozhnoyi nochee mi yimo vsyaku zelen';
  tziyeyi nochee-ghirkeh.
- *On all other nights we eat all kinds of herbs;*
  on this night only bitter herbs.

Кожної ночі ми не макаємо жодного разу;
цієї ночі-двічі.
- Kozhnoyi nochee mi ne makayemo zhodnogho razu;
  tziyeyi nochee-dvichee.
- *On all other nights we do not dip even once;*
  on this night we dip twice.

Кожної ночі ми сидимо рівно чи напів-лежачи;
цієї ночі-напів лежачи.
- Kozhnoyi nochee mi sidimo reevno chi napiv-lezhachi;
  tziyeyi nochee-mapiv lezhachi.
- *On all other nights we eat either sitting up or reclining;*
  on this night we recline.

Кожної ночі ми просто їмо;
а сьогодні у нас ритуальна вечеря.
- Kozhnoyi nochee mi prosto yimo;
  a syogodnee u nas ritualna vecherya.
- *On all other nights we eat in an ordinary manner;*
  on this night we dine with special ceremony.

Photo © Barry Hantman

Kiev's 11th C Pecherskaya Lavra monastery

ABOUT THE LANGUAGE:

Ukrainian

Number of speakers: 37,029,730
Rank: 30

Ukrainian is spoken in western Ukraine and adjacent republics. It is spoken in about 25 other countries, primarily Poland and Slovakia. Ukrainian is closely related to Russian and Belarussian.

The recorded history of Ukrainian began in 988, when the principality of Kiev was converted to Christianity. Ukrainian religious material, including translations of the Bible, was written in Old Slavonic, the language used by missionaries to spread Christianity to the Slavic peoples.

A decree in 1876 banned the printing or importing of Ukrainian books. In spite of this, there was a revival of Ukrainian poetry and historiography during the 19th C.

ABOUT THE TRANSLATOR AND SPEAKER:

Alex Gelman

Age: 50s   Recorded: 1996
Towns: Chernovtsy, Ukraine / Brooklyn, NY

Dr. Gelman was born in Chernovtsy, western Ukraine, Northern Bukovina. He is a world-renowned communications engineer. Alex is Vice President of the Communication Society of IEEE.

Tuvin

Бо дун өске дуннерден чуте билгалын турарыл?
■ *Why is this night different from all other nights?*

**Өске дуннерде бис дрожхи - биле кылган хлеб азы матза чиир бис;
бо дуне чугле матза.**
■ *On all other nights we eat either leavened bread or matzah;
on this night only matzah.*

**Өске дуннерде бис кандыг-даа оът-сиген чиир бис;
бо дуне чугле ажыг оът-сиген.**
■ *On all other nights we eat all kinds of herbs;
on this night only bitter herbs.*

**Өске дуннерде бис чандгыс каттап безин сукпас бис;
бо дуне ийи каттап сугар бис.**
■ *On all other nights we do not dip even once;
on this night we dip twice.*

**Өске дуннерде бис дорт олурупкали азы дорт эвес олурупкали чемненир бис;
бо дуне бис дорт эвес елур бис.**
■ *On all other nights we eat either sitting up or reclining;
on this night we recline.*

**Өске дуннерде бис анаа чемненир бис;
бо дуне бис байырлап чемненир бис.**
■ *On all other nights we eat in an ordinary manner;
on this night we dine with special ceremony.*

ABOUT THE LANGUAGE:

Tuvin

Number of speakers: 264,400
Rank: 757

Tuvin (also spelled Tuvan) is spoken in the Russian republic of Tuva and in Mongolia; there are a few speakers in China. Until 1944, Tuva (spelled **Tyva** in Cyrillic) was an independent state.

ABOUT THE TRANSLATOR AND SPEAKER:

Chodura N Khandy

Age: Unavailable   Recorded: 1993
Towns: Kyzl, Tuva / Arlington, VA

Chodura was born in Kyzl, the capital of Tuva. She was recently studying business administration at North Virginia Community College.

Postcard showing Lenin Street in Kyzl, the capital of Tuva

Bonus in the recordings: Tuva is famous for an unusual form of singing usually called throat singing, where one singer produces multiple tones, up to tour at a time. Many of the world's best throat singers come from Tuva. The recordings contain examples of the throat singing of singers from the neighboring republic of Buriat.

Turkish

Bu gece neden bütün öbür gecelerden farklıdır?

■ *Why is this night different from all other nights?*

Bütün öbür gecelerde mayalı veya mayasız ekmek yiyoruz; fakat bu gece sadece mayasız ekmek yiyoruz.

■ *On all other nights we eat either leavened bread or matzah; on this night only matzah.*

Bütün öbür gecelerde her türlü baharatları yiyoruz; fakat bu gece sadece acılı baharatları yiyoruz.

■ *On all other nights we eat all kinds of herbs; on this night only bitter herbs.*

Bütün öbür gecelerde otları hiç batırmıyoruz; fakat bu gece iki defa batırıyoruz.

■ *On all other nights we do not dip even once; on this night we dip twice.*

Bütün öbür gecelerde düz oturarak veya dayanarak yiyoruz; fakat bu gece sadece dayanıyoruz.

■ *On all other nights we eat either sitting up or reclining; on this night we recline.*

Bütün öbür gecelerde düz her zamanki gibi alelade yiyoruz; fakat bu gece özel bir kutlama ile yiyoruz.

■ *On all other nights we eat in an ordinary manner; on this night we dine with special ceremony.*

Girls from Yasaçal village in traditional costume

ABOUT THE LANGUAGE:

Turkish

Number of speakers: 50,750,120
Rank: 23

Turkish, called Türkçe by its speakers, is the national language of Turkey. It is spoken in 35 other countries, primarily in Bulgaria, Macedonia/Yugoslavia, Uzbekistan, Cyprus, Romania and Greece.

Until 1928, Turkish was written with a version of the Perso-Arabic script known as the Ottoman Turkish script. In 1928, as part of his efforts to modernize Turkey, President Mustafa Kemal Atatürk issued a decree replacing the Arabic script with a version of the Latin alphabet, which has been used ever since.

ABOUT THE TRANSLATOR AND SPEAKER:

Işıl Sebüktekin

Age: 40s   Recorded: 1998
Towns: Ankara, Turkey / Parsippany, NJ

Dr. Sebüktekin grew up in Ankara, Turkey. She has a PhD in Electrical Engineering from Lehigh University. Işıl is a Senior Research Scientist working in the field of Internet and Wireless Networks. The translation was also worked on by **Laura Bloomenthal**, a student of the Turkish language.

Istanbul's *Ayasofya*, now a mosque, was the world's largest church for 1000 years

Tulu

ಇನಿತ್ತ ಇರ್ಲ್ ಬೇತೆ ಇರ್ಲ್ತಲೆಕ್ಕೊ ಇಜ್ಜಿ ದಾಯೆ ?

■ maata raatriDduh ii raatri beete daayaguh?

■ *Why is this night different from all other nights?*

ಬಾಕಿ ಇರ್ಲ್ ಲಿಟ್ ಉರ್ಬೂನ ರೊಟ್ಟಿ ತಿನ್ಪೊ.
ಇನಿತ್ತ ಇರ್ಲ್ ಉರ್ಬಂತ್ನ ರೊಟ್ಟಿ ತಿನ್ಪೊ.

■ beete raatri enkulu rooTi tinpa;
aaND ii raatri enkulu 'matzah' rooTi maatra tinoDu.

■ *On all other nights we eat either leavened bread or matzah;
on this night only matzah.*

ಬೇತೆ ಇರ್ಲ್ಡ್ ಬೇತೆ ಬೇತೆ ತರೊತ್ತ ಸಪ್ಪುಲೆನ್ ತಿನ್ಪೊ.
ಇನಿತ್ತ ಇರ್ಲ್ ಕೈಪೆ ಸಪ್ಪುಲೆನ್ ತಿನ್ಪೊ.

■ beete raatri enkulu maata kaayikajipu tinpa;
ii raatri kaipeda kaayikajipu tinoDu.

■ *On all other nights we eat all kinds of herbs; on this night only bitter herbs.*

ಬೇತೆ ಇರ್ಲ್ಡ್ ಸಪ್ಪುನ್ ಮುರ್ಕಾವಂತೆ ತಿನ್ಪ.
ಇನಿತ್ತ ಇರ್ಲ್ ರಡ್ಡ್ ಸರ್ತಿ ಮುರ್ಕಾವೊಂತ್ ತಿನ್ಪ.

■ beete raatri kaayikajipuDu rooTi paaDinijji;
aaNDa ii raatri tinpinaga rooTi kaayikajipuDu raDDuh sartuh paaDoDu.

■ *On all other nights we do not dip even once; on this night we dip twice.*

ಬೇತೆ ಮಾಂತ ಇರ್ಲ್ಡ್ ನೇರ್ಪ ಕುಲ್ಲ್ತ್ ಇಜ್ಸಾಂಡ ಪುಸೊರ್ತ್ ಡ್ ವಗೊ̂ರೊಂತ್ ತಿನ್ಪ.
ಇನಿತ್ತ ಇರ್ಲ್ ಪುಸೊರ್ತ್ತಾಂಡ್

■ ii raatri enkulu visheeshada riti naDakondu tinpa.

■ *On all other nights we eat either sitting up or reclining; on this night we recline.*

ಬೇತೆ ಇರ್ಲ್ಡ್ ಮಾಮೂಲ್ ವಳಾಸ್ ಮಾಲ್ಪ.
ಇನಿತ್ತ ಇರ್ಲ್ಡ್ ಗಡ್ಡ್ ವಳಾಸ್ ಮಾಲ್ಪ.

■ beete raatri sartuh kuludu tinoli baguhduh kuludu tinoli;
ii raatri baguhduh kuludu tinoDu.

■ *On all other nights we eat in an ordinary manner;
on this night we dine with special ceremony.*

ABOUT THE LANGUAGE:

Tulu

Number of speakers: 1,950,000
Rank: 241

Tulu, also called Tal and Thalu, is an Indian language spoken primarily in the southern state of Karnataka, as well as in Andhra Pradesh, Kerala, Tamil Nadu, Maharashtra and Meghalaya.

Tulu is written using the *Kannada* alphabet, which developed from the *Kadamba* and *Cālukya* scripts, descendents of *Brahmi* that were used between the 5th and 7th centuries CE. These scripts developed into the *Old Kannada* script, which by about 1500 had morphed into the *Kannada* and *Telugu* scripts. Under the influence of Christian missionary organizations, *Kannada* and *Telugu* scripts were standardized at the beginning of the 19th C.

ABOUT THE TRANSLATOR AND SPEAKER:

K Krishna Naik

Age: Unavailable   Recorded: 1995
Towns: Ishwaramangala, Puttur Taluk / Bangalore / Bengaluru, India

Krishna is a native speaker of Tulu. He was born in Ishwaramangala and now lives in Bangalore, India. The text was typed by **Maya Yajnik**.

In the recordings: Krishna ends his recording with his name, birthplace and current location, spoken in Tulu.

Translation and transliteration notes: Double vowels are long vowels. Upper case consonants are retroflex (tip of tongue curled back). "uh" is pronounced as vowel of "hut".

The word *rooTi* includes breads (wheat, unless otherwise specified) both leavened or not. Hence, *matzah rooTi* must serve for the specialty bread.

Tulu (and other Indian languages) have two first-person-plural forms. One includes the listener (*nama*) and one excludes the listener (*enkulu* above). In explaining an American custom to a non-American we'd use the <u>exclusive</u> (meaning 'we-Americans'), but when speaking of a similar custom with another American we'd use the <u>inclusive</u>, since we (both speaker and listener) are American. The word *nama* may be substituted for all occurrences of *enkulu*, if more appropriate. The words for "herbs" presumed 'vegetables' or at least 'vegetal food stuff' (as opposed to meats).

The translator added that "some of these sentences are ones not likely to occur in Tulu in any natural context. For instance, Tuluvas eat almost exclusively rice [and] they mix their curries using their fingers; they don't often use breads to dip into the other foods."

Z Y X W V U T S R Q P O N M L K J I H G F E D C B A

Tswana

Ke ka ntlha ya eng bosigo jo bo farologana le masigo a mangwe otlhe?

■ *Why is this night different from all other nights?*

Masigo a mangwe otlhe, re ja senkgwe se se tlhabegilweng gongwe senkgwe se se sa tlhabegiwang;
Mme mo bosigong jo, gone re ja senkgwe se se sa tlhabegiwang fela.

■ *On all other nights we eat either leavened bread or matzah;*
on this night only matzah.

Masigo a mangwe otlhe, re ja mefuta yotlhe ya merogo;
Mme mo bosigong jo, re ja merogo e e galakang fela.

■ *On all other nights we eat all kinds of herbs;*
on this night only bitter herbs.

Masigo a mangwe otlhe, re ja inele le e seng gangwe;
Mme mo bosigong jo, re inela gabedi.

■ *On all other nights we do not dip even once;*
on this night we dip twice.

Masigo a mangwe otlhe, re ja re ntse ka marago kgotsa re sekame;
Mme mo bosigong jo, re a rapama.

■ *On all other nights we eat either sitting up or reclining;*
on this night we recline.

Masigo a mangwe otlhe, re ja ka mokgwa wa tlwaelo;
Mme mo bosigong jo, re ja semodiro o o kgethegileng.

■ *On all other nights we eat in an ordinary manner;*
on this night we dine with special ceremony.

ABOUT THE LANGUAGE:

Tswana

Number of speakers: 4,521,700
Rank: 142

Tswana, called Setswana by its speakers, is spoken throughout Botswana. It is also spoken in Namibia, South Africa and by the Bakaka in Zimbabwe. Tswana is largely intelligible with Sotho (Northern and Southern), but have generally been considered separate languages.

ABOUT THE TRANSLATOR AND SPEAKER:

Moshê M Baitsewe

Age: Unavailable   Recorded: 1998
Towns: Kimberly, South Africa / Bachbrecht, Namibia

Moshê was born and raised in Kimberly, South Africa. He now works at a radio station in Namibia using Setswana.

Photo by Stephanie Goldhuber

Giraffes on the African Savanna in Botswana

Tlingit

Wáasá yá xáanaa tlél tatgé xáana yáx utí.

■ What is different this evening that was not like last evening?

Ldakát xáanaa sakwnéin tooxáa nooch;
yáa xáanaa ku.aa máatsa gaxtooxáa.

■ In every evening we eat bread;
   but this evening we will eat Maatsa.

Ldakát xáanaa yáa kayaaní tooxáa nooch;
yáa xáanaa ku.aa si.áax'u kayaaní gaxtooxáa.

■ Every evening we eat leaves (spices);
   this evening however we eat sour leaves.

Ldakát xáanaa yáa s'íx' tóodein tooteech nuch haa atxaayí, tléix' dahéen;
Yáa xáanaa ku.aa déix dahéen s'íx' tóodei gaxtoo.

■ Each night we dip our food into the bowl not one time;
   tonight however we will dip it in twice.

Ldakát xáanaa k'idéin yéi tookéech nuch atooxaayí;
yáa xáanaa ku.aa ch'a koogéi yéi gaxtookée.

■ Each evening we sit up straight to eat our food;
   this night however we will sit any old way.

Ldakát xáanaa ch'a tlákw k'idéin at tooxáa nooch;
yáa xáanaa ku.aa k'idéin aax sateeyích kúnáx k'idéin at gaxtooxáa.

■ Each evening we eat good;
   but this evening we will eat special food.

ABOUT THE LANGUAGE:

Tlingit

Number of speakers: 1,430
Rank: 4,796

Tlingit is spoken southeast Alaska (surrounding Sitka), and Yakutat south to the Canadian border at Portland Canal. There are a couple hundred speakers in British Columbia: Yukon and Carcross. The name of the language sounds like *Klinkit*, *Thlinkit* or beginning with the "ch" sound of Bach.

ABOUT THE TRANSLATOR AND SPEAKER:

Ethel Daasdiyaa Joseph

Age: 79   Recorded: 2008
Town: Sitka, AK

Ethel, a native speaker of Tlingit, is an Elder in Sitka's Tlingit tribe.

The translation was written by **Roby Koolyeik Littlefield**, a student of Ethel's. Roby has taught Tlingit in the local school district for 12 years, and has worked with Ethel on language projects for over 20 years.

Photo by Roby Littlefield

Sheet'ka Kwáan Naa Kahídi
Performing Arts Theater

In the recordings: Ethel ends her recording with "Daasdiyáa yóo xat duwasáakw. L'uknax.ádi áyá xat, Lingít xat sitee, Sheet'káa dáu."
(My name is *Daasdiyáa*. I am a Tlingit Coho lady from Sitka.)
"L'uknax.ádi Naatláa áyá xat sitee." (I am a *L'uknax.ádi* clan mother.)
"Át xoowaatch atwuskoowú." (You grow into being an elder.)

Tlingit dancers of the Raven and Eagle moiety (kinship group) performing in Sitka's Clan House

Tigrinya

Translated from Hebrew

እንታየ ኸይና እዚ ምሸት ታብኩሉ ምሸት።

זְמֶשֶת תַבחולוּ מֶשֶת אִיזִי הוֹינוּ אַנטַ'ה ∎

∎ מַה נִשְתַנָּה הַלַּיְלָה הַזֶּה מִכָּל הַלֵּילוֹת?

ታብኩሉ ምሸት ንኽና ንበላ ሓሙጽ ቅጣ፤
ታብዚ ምሸት ኹሉ ቀጣ።

תִּטַה הוֹלוּ מֶשֶת טבזִי קטה חַמוּצ נִבֶלָה נְחֵנַה מֶשֶת תַבחוּלוּ.

∎ שֶׁבְּכָל הַלֵּילוֹת אָנוּ אוֹכְלִין חָמֵץ וּמַצָּה.
הַלַּיְלָה הַזֶּה כֻּלּוֹ מַצָּה:

ታብኩሉ ምሸት ንኽና ንበላ ኻልኢ ፍረፍሪ፤
ታብዚ ምሸት መሪር።

מַרִיר מֶשֶת טבזִי פְּרְפְּרֶה חֶלְאִי נִבֶלָה נְחֵנַה מֶשֶת תַבחוּלוּ.

∎ שֶׁבְּכָל הַלֵּילוֹת אָנוּ אוֹכְלִין שְׁאָר יְרָקוֹת.
הַלַּיְלָה הַזֶּה מָרוֹר:

ታብኩሉ ምሸት ንኽና አይ ዳሓሱ አ ን ሽኺና ሓንቲኻ፤
ታብዚ ምሸት ቅልጠኻ።

רְלַתְשֶׁה מֶשֶת טבזִי הַנָנְשָׁה סֶרְחִינוּ אֶנִי דַח'סוּ אַיַה נְחֵנַה מֶשֶת תַבחוּלוּ.

∎ שֶׁבְּכָל הַלֵּילוֹת אֵין אָנוּ מַטְבִּילִין אֲפִילוּ פַּעַם אֶחָת.
הַלַּיְלָה הַזֶּה שְׁתֵּי פְּעָמִים:

ታብኩሉ ምሸት ንኽና ንበላ ምስ ኻፈልና ምስ መጋደም፤
ታብዚ ምሸት ልና መጋደም።

מֶגְדֶם חוּלְנַה מֶשֶת טבזִי מֶגְדֶם מְסַה חְפַלְנַה מסַה נִבֶלָה נְחֵנַה מֶשֶת תַבחוּלוּ.

∎ שֶׁבְּכָל הַלֵּילוֹת אָנוּ אוֹכְלִין בֵּין יוֹשְׁבִין וּבֵין מְסֻבִּין.
הַלַּיְלָה הַזֶּה כֻּלָּנוּ מְסֻבִּין:

ታብኩሉ ምሸት ንኽና ንበላ ቆቆም ተፈለጠ፤
ታብዚ ምሸት ኻፈልና ሓለ።

הַלִי חְפַלְנַה מֶשֶת טבזִי טפֶלֶטֶה קוֹמַה נִבֶלָה נְחֵנַה מֶשֶת תַבחוּלוּ.

∎ שֶׁבְּכָל הַלֵּילוֹת אָנוּ אוֹכְלִין בְּצוּרָה רְגִילָה.
הַלַּיְלָה הַזֶּה בְּרוֹב טֶקְסִיוֹת:

∎ On all other nights we eat in a regular way;
on this night we eat in an unusual way.

Native hut near Finchawa, Ethiopia, midway between Sashemane and Moyale

ABOUT THE LANGUAGE:

Tigrinya

Number of speakers: 5,791,710
Rank: 120

Tigrinya (also called Tigrigna and Tigray) is one of the national languages of Ethiopia. It is spoken in Tigray province. There are also speakers in Eritrea and Israel. The liturgy of those in Beta Israel who speak Tigrinya is written in Geez, which is an ancient language of the Aksumites. It is also the official liturgical language of the Ethiopian Orthodox Church.

ABOUT THE TRANSLATOR:

Yehonathan Menegistu

Age: Unavailable   Translated: 2005
Towns: Ethiopia / Petah Tikvah, Israel

Yehonathan, a native speaker of Tigrinya, lives in Petah Tikvah. The text also shows a Hebrew transliteration, e.g. a pronunciation guide to the Tigrinya for Hebrew speakers. The transliteration is to be read left to right, as is Tigrinya, opposite of Hebrew's normal reading direction.

Before the final question was translated into Trigrinya, it was translated from English to a nonstandard Hebrew for this project; the rest was translated directly from the Hebrew. The text was entered with the assistance of Dr. Yemani Mesfun.

ABOUT THE SPEAKER:

Dr. Yemani Mesfun

Age: 49   Recorded: 2006
Towns: Eritrea / Addis Ababa, Ethiopia / NJ

Dr. Mesfun, a native speaker of Tigrinya, was born and raised in Eritrea, but moved to Ethiopia's capital, Addis Ababa when he was a teenager. At age 29, he moved to the USA. Dr. Mesfun is a veterinarian working in West Caldwell, NJ.

Yemani explained that his dialect is most certainly different from that of the translator, Yehonathan.

Photo by Bernard Cloutier (berclo.net)

Tibetan

༄༅། །ཅིའི་ཕྱིར་མཚན་མོ་འདི་ནི་མཚན་མོ་གཞན་པ་ཀུན་དང་མཚུངས་མ་ཡིན།

■ chee-chir tshan-mo dee-ni tshan-mo shan-pa kun-dang tshung ma-yin?

■ ***Why is this night different from all other nights?***

།མཚན་མོ་གཞན་པ་ཀུན་ཏུ་ང་ཚོས་བག་ལེབ་སྐྱུར་སོབ་ཡིན་མིན་གཉིས་ཀ་ཟ།

།མཚན་མོ་འདི་ལ་ང་ཚོས་བག་ལེབ་སྐྱུར་སོབ་མ་ཡིན་ཁོ་ན་ཟ།

■ tshan-mo shan-pa kun-tu nga-tshoe pag-leb kyur-sob yin-min nyi-ka sa;
tshan-mo dee-la nga-tshoe pag-leb kyur-sob ma-yin kho-na sa.

■ ***On all other nights we eat either leavened bread or matzah; on this night only matzah.***

།མཚན་མོ་གཞན་པ་ཀུན་ཏུ་ང་ཚོས་ཟས་སྤྱོད་སྣ་ཚོགས་ཟ།

།མཚན་མོ་འདི་ལ་ང་ཚོས་ཟས་སྤྱོད་ཁ་བོ་ཁོ་ན་ཟ།

■ tshan-mo shan-pa kun-tu nga-tshoe se-pod na-tshog sa;
tshan-mo dee-la nga-tshoe sed-pod kha-wo kho-na sa.

■ ***On all other nights we eat all kinds of herbs; on this night only bitter herbs.***

།མཚན་མོ་གཞན་པ་ཀུན་ཏུ་ང་ཚོས་ཐེངས་གཅིག་ཙམ་ཡང་སྦྲེ་བ་ར་མི་བྱེད་དེ།

།མཚན་མོ་འདི་ལ་ང་ཚོས་ལན་གཉིས་སྦྲེབར་བྱེད།

■ tshan-mo shan-pa kun-tu nga-tshoe theng-chig tsam-yang dre-war mee-ched de;
tshan-mo dee-la nga-tshoe lan-nyi dre-war ched.

■ ***On all other nights we do not dip even once; on this night we dip twice.***

།མཚན་མོ་གཞན་པ་ཀུན་ཏུ་ང་ཚོའི་ལུས་པོ་དྲང་པོར་སྡོད་དམ་བསྙེས་ནས་བཟའ་བཏུང་བསྟེན་ཆོག་སྟེ།

།མཚན་མོ་འདི་ལ་ང་ཚོའི་ལུས་པོ་བསྙེས་ནས་སྡོད།

■ tshan-mo shan-pa kun-tu nga-tshoe lue-po drang-por dod-tam nye-nay za-tung ten chog te;
tshan-mo dee-la nga-tshoe lue-po nye-ne dod.

■ ***On all other nights we eat either sitting up or reclining; on this night we recline.***

།མཚན་མོ་གཞན་པ་ཀུན་ཏུ་ང་ཚོས་ཟས་སྤྱོད་ཅི་དགར་བསྟེན་ཆོག་སྟེ།

།མཚན་མོ་འདི་ལ་ང་ཚོའི་ནུབ་ཚར་རྟེན་འབྲེལ་ཅོ་ག་སྔོན་ལ་གཏོང་།།

■ tshan-mo shan-pa kun-tu nga-tshoe se-chod chi-gar ten chog te;
tshan-mo dee-la nga-tshoe nub-tshar ten-drel cho-ga ngon-la tong.

■ ***On all other nights we eat in an ordinary manner; on this night we dine with special ceremony.***

About the Language:

Tibetan

Number of speakers: 1,277,620
Rank: 308

Tibetan is spoken in Tibet and China (Sichuan and Qinghai). It has significant numbers of speakers in Nepal, India and Bhutan; it is also spoken in Norway, Switzerland, Taiwan and the USA.

Tibet is the highest continent in the world and is commonly described as the most isolated.

About the Translator and Speaker:

Pema Bhum

Age: Unavailable Recorded: 2000
Towns: Rebgong, Tibet / Bloomington, IN

Pema is a Lecturer in Tibetan Studies at Indiana University's Department of Central Eurasian Studies. He was born and raised in Rebgong, which is in the region of Amdo, Tibet.

Additional Information:

Tibet's Dalai Lama, while exiled from his country by China, has developed an interest in other religions. His interest in Judaism is based on its ability to retain its identity and faith while in exile for thousands of years. Since the Seder is a key ingredient to how Jews have maintained their traditions, the Dalai Lama attended a Passover Seder when he was in Washington, DC in 1997. We sent this translation to the Dalai Lama so that it would increase his appreciation of his visit and connection to what he experienced.

Priest Tenzin Sangpo of the Nitsan Tibetan Temple in Howell, NJ

Thai, Northern

เยี้ยฮือคืนนี้บ่เหมือนคืนอื่นๆ

■ Yiá huu3 khuu3n nií bɔ̀ɔ muán khuùn 'uùn 'uùn?

■ *Why is this night different from all other nights?*

ในคืนอื่นๆเฮากิ๊นคะหนมปังฟูกาคะหนมปังบ่ฟู
คืนนี้มีก้าคะหนมปังบ่ฟู

■ Nǎy khuūn 'uùn'uùn hāw kǐn khā'nŏmpāyfuū kaā khā'nŏm pāy bɔ̀ɔ fuū; khuūn nií mií kaâ khā'nŏm pāy bɔ̀ɔ fuū.

■ *On all other nights we eat either leavened bread or matzah; on this night only matzah.*

ในคืนอื่นๆเฮากิ๊นพักชีกั๊บพืธสมุนไพรอื่นตุ๊กชนิต
ในคืนนี้มีก้าสมุนไพรขม

■ Nǎy khuūn 'uùn'uùn hǎw kǐn phákchǐi káp phuût sà'mǔnphāy túk chā'nìt; nǎy khuūn nií mǐi kaâ sàmǔnphāy khŏm.

■ *On all other nights we eat all kinds of herbs; on this night only bitter herbs.*

ในคืนอื่นๆเฮาบ่ต้องจิ้มอาหารกิ๊น
ในคืนนี้เฮาต้องจิ้มอาหารกิ๊นสองครั้ง

■ Nǎy khuūn 'uùn'uùn hāw bɔ̀ɔ tɔ̀ɔn cîm 'aāhaǎn kǐn; nǎy khuūn nií hāw tɔ̀n cîm 'aāhaǎn kǐn sɔ̀ɔŋ khâŋ.

■ *On all other nights we do not dip even once; on this night we dip twice.*

ในคืนอื่นๆเฮาจะนั่งกิ๊นกานอนต๋ามสบายกิ๊นก่อได้
ในคืนนี้เฮานอนต๋ามสบายกิ๊น

■ Nǎy khuūn 'uùn'uùn hāw cǎ nây kǐn kaā nɔɔn taǎm sā baāy kǐn kɔ̀ dây; nǎy khuūn nií hāw nɔɔn taǎm sà baāy kǐn.

■ *On all other nights we eat either sitting up or reclining; on this night we recline.*

ในคืนอื่นๆเฮากิ๊นแบบธรรมดา
ในคืนนี้เฮากิ๊นอย่างมีพิธีรีตอง

■ Nǎy khuūn 'uùn'uùn hāw kǐn bɛɛìp thāmmādaā; nǎy khuūn nií kaâ kǐn yaàn miī phí'thiī riī'tɔɔŋ.

■ *On all other nights we eat in an ordinary manner; on this night we dine with special ceremony.*

ABOUT THE LANGUAGE:

Northern Thai

Number of speakers: 6,009,400
Rank: 118

Northern Thai, called Phasaa Nua by its speakers, is spoken in several regions of Thailand and in Laos.

Northern Thai had used the *Yuan* script for a long time, but it is not used much now and few can read it. Standard Thai script has been used for literature in Northern Thai, although it lacks some necessary contrasts.

ABOUT THE TRANSLATOR AND SPEAKER:

Khun Namrin Dampan

Age: Unavailable   Recorded: 1999
Towns: Chiang Mai, Thailand / Bangkok

Khun ("Mrs") Namrin Dampan grew up in Chiang Mai, but at time of the recording, lived in Bangkok. Both Northern Thai and Thai are first languages for her – Namrin's mother spoke Northern Thai while her father spoke (Central) Thai. Northern Thai was exclusively spoken in many of the neighboring homes of her childhood.

The transliteration's accents show tone markings for each syllable.

Photo by Stephanie Goldhuber

Bangkok's Grand Palace – detail

Thai

ทำไมคืนนี้ไม่เหมือนคืนอื่นๆ

■ Tammai kuen nee mai muan kuen eun eun?

■ *Why is this night different from all other nights?*

ไนคืนอื่นๆเรากินขนมปังฟูหรือขนมปังไม่ฟู
คืนนนี้มีเพียงขนมปังไม่ฟู

■ Nai kuen eun eun rao kin kanompang foo rue kanompang mai foo;
kuen nee me pieng ksnompsng mai foo.

■ *On all other nights we eat either leavened bread or matzah; on this night only matzah.*

ในคืนอื่นเราฑานสมุนไพรทุกชนิต
แต่ในคืนนี้เราฑานสมุนไพรรศขมเฑานั้น

■ Nai kuen eun eun rao kin pakchee lae puet samunprai eun took chanit;
kuen nee me pieng samunprai kome.

■ *On all other nights we eat all kinds of herbs; on this night only bitter herbs.*

ในคืนอื่นเราไม่จุ่มสมุนไพรในน้ำเกลือ
แต่ในคืนนี้เราจุ่มสองครั้ง

■ Nai kuen eun eun rao mai tong jim aharn kin; kuen nee rao tong jim Hrn kin song krang.

■ *On all other nights we do not dip even once; on this night we dip twice.*

ในคืนอื่นเรานั่งฑานหรือนอฑาน
แต่ในคืนนี้เรานอนฑาน

■ Nai kuen eun eun rao ja nang kin rue nawn ekkanek ikin koh dai; nai kuen nee rao nawn ekkanek kin.

■ *On all other nights we eat either sitting up or reclining; on this night we recline.*

ในคืนอื่นเราฑานแบบปกติธรรมดา
แต่ในคืนนี้เราฑานด้วยพิธีรีตองเป็นพิเศษ

■ Nai kuen eun eun rao kin bab tamada; nai kuen nee rao rappratan yang mee piti ree trong.

■ *On all other nights we eat in an ordinary manner; on this night we dine with special ceremony.*

A slightly different version was recorded: Thammai khun-ni jung tang jak khun-un?
Nai khun-un rai than khanom-pang sai chua-fu ru khanom-pang rai-chua; tae khun-ni rao kin khanom-pang rai-chua thao-nan.
Nai khun-un rao than samunphrai thuk thuk chanit; tae khun-ni rao samunphrai rot khom thao-nan.
Nai khun-un rao mai jum samunphrai nai nam-klua; tae nai khun-ni rao chum song khrang
Nai khun-un rao nang than ru non than; tae nai khun-ni rao non than.
Nai khun-un rao than baeb pokati thammada; tae khun-ni rao duay phithi-ri-tong pen phiset.

Translation note: The question about dipping food seems strange, since Thais dip their food at almost every meal!

ABOUT THE LANGUAGE:

Thai

Number of speakers: 20,362,390
Rank: 50

Thai is spoken in the central regions of Thailand, centered in Bangkok. It is also spoken in Midway Islands, Singapore, United Arab Emirates and the USA. Its speakers are sometimes called the Siamese.

It is claimed King Ramkhamhaeng (1275-1317) created an alphabet for Siamese language in 1292, which later developed into the modern Thai alphabet.

ABOUT THE TRANSLATOR AND SPEAKER:

Benjawan Kanyaphan

Age: Unavailable   Recorded: 1999
Town: Unavailable

Benjawan Kanyaphan (pronounced Kanyapan), who works for the Asian translation service in Midvale, UT kindly provided this translation. The translation was also worked on by **Ronald Jay Cristal**, born in Brooklyn and living 30 years in Thailand since age 27, by his company law attorney, **Sompol Piromyothee**, native born in Bangkok and by **Somchart Chantasiriwan**. The transliteration is by **Karla Allan** and Karla's teacher, **Khun Bang-On** in Bangkok, Thailand.

Photo by Stephanie Goldhuber

Bangkok's Grand Palace

Z Y X W V U T S R Q P O N M L K J I H G F E D C B A

Tetum

Translated from Indonesian

Tansá kalan ida-ne'e oin-seluk ho kalan molok sira?
- Mengapa malam ini berbeda dari malam-malam sebelumnya?
- Why does this night have a different face from the previous night?

Kalan molok sira, ita han paun hodi fermentu ka paun laho fermentu; kalan ida-ne'e mak paun laho fermentu de'it.
- Malam-malam sebelumnya, kita makan roti atau matsa; malam ini, hanya matsa.
- The previous nights we eat bread with yeast or bread without yeast; this night (it is) bread without yeast.

Kalan molok sira, ita han du'ut-morin oioin; kalan ida-ne'e ita han mak ai-dila tahan de'it.
- Malam-malam sebelumnya, kita makan berbagai jamu; malam ini, hanya jamu pahit.
- Previous nights we eat all kinds of herbs (= fragrant grass); this night we eat just pawpaw leaves.

Kalan molok sira, ita hamout ladún dala ida; kalan ida-ne'e mak ita hamout dala rua.
- Malam-malam sebelumnya, sekalipun kita tidak mencelupkan; malam ini, kita mencelupkan dua kali.
- Previous nights, we inundate not even once; this night it is that we inundate twice.

Kalan molok sira, ita han tuur loloos ka saderek; kalan ida-ne'e mak ita tuur saderek.
- Malam-malam sebelumnya, kita makan sambil duduk atau bersandar santai; malam ini, kita bersandar santai.
- Previous nights we eat sitting straight or reclining; this night it is that we sit reclining.

Kalan molok sira, ita han hanesan baibain; kalan ida-ne'e mak ita han hodi serimonia espesiál.
- Malam-malam sebelumnya, kita makan secara biasa; malam ini, kita santap dengan upacara khusus.
- Previous nights we eat as usual; this night it is we eat using a special ceremony.

ABOUT THE LANGUAGE:

Tetum

Number of speakers: 450,000
Rank: 583

Tetum is spoken in Indonesia's Timor and Timor Lorosae. Tetum speakers live in the central Timor corridor from coast to coast, east of Atoni, west of Bunak, around Batibo and in the south coast around Viqueque and Soibada.

ABOUT THE TRANSLATOR:

Aone Thomas van Engelenhoven

Age: 43   Translated: 2005
Towns: Halsteren / Leiden, Netherlands

Dr. van Engelenhoven is an Astronesian linguistics professor in Leiden University's Department of Languages & Culture Southeast Asia & Oceania. Aone is of mixed Indonesian (Letinese) and Dutch descent, and is bilingual in Dutch and Malay (Indonesian).

He reports the text was vaguely familiar because of very remote Jewish relatives of whom this ritual has been reported to him. A Tetum translation was also developed by one of his students, a native Tetum speaker from East Timor.

Photo by Aone van Engelenhoven

A traditional house in Lospalos, East Timor, where Tetum and Portuguese are the two co-official languages

Teso

Kanukinyobo ejai nat kware egelara kaecekwarekere?

■ *Why is this night different from all other nights?*

Ecekwarekere inyamit iso emugaati kede ainyales naarai ematsa; nat kware matsacut.

■ *On all other nights we eat either leavened bread or matzah; on this night only matzah.*

Ecekwarekere inyamit iso idiasyokere; nat kware idasyo edwar.

■ *On all other nights we eat all kinds of herbs; on this night only bitter herbs.*

Ecekwarekere mam aicunyakin iso irwana idiopet; nat kware aicunyakin iso irwana iaarei.

■ *On all other nights we do not dip even once; on this night we dip twice.*

Ecekwarekere iboikin iso ainyam; nat kware ainiaar iso.

■ *On all other nights we eat either sitting up or reclining; on this night we recline.*

Ecekwarekere inyamit iso loduc; nat kware inyamit iso kede asuban.

■ *On all other nights we eat in an ordinary manner; on this night we dine with special ceremony.*

ABOUT THE LANGUAGE:

Teso

Number of speakers: 1,849,000
Rank: 252

Teso is spoken in east Uganda, in the Katakwi, Soroti, Kaberamaido, Kumi, Pallisa and Tororo districts. There are also over 250,000 speakers in Kenya. It is called Ateso, Bakedi, Elgumi and several other names by its speakers.

ABOUT THE TRANSLATOR:

Rishi Desai

Age: Unavailable   Translated: 2010
Locations: WV / Chicago, IL

Rishi worked as a Peace Corps trainer in the Kumi district of Uganda. Rishi is not a native speaker, but learned Teso while working in Uganda.

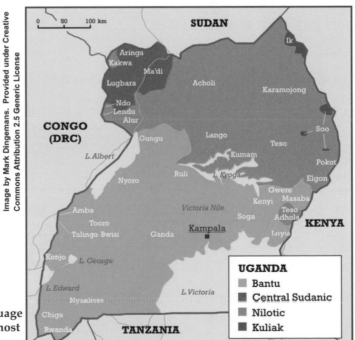

Image by Mark Dingemans. Provided under Creative Commons Attribution 2.5 Generic License

Map of Uganda, showing language families (color) and names of most of Uganda's languages

UGANDA
- Bantu
- Central Sudanic
- Nilotic
- Kuliak

Telugu

ఎందుకో యీ రాత్రి ఇతర రాత్రులకంటె వేరుగాపుంది?
- Enduko e raatri itara raatrulakante vaerugaavundi?
- *Why is this night different from all other nights?*

ప్రతి రాత్రి తింతాము మేము పులిని వొంగిన రొట్టెనో పులవని రొట్టెనో;
ఈ రాత్రి మాత్రం పులవని రొట్టెనే.
- Prati raatri tintaamu maemu pulisi pongina rotteno pulavani rotteno;
  e raatri maatram pulavani rottene.
- *On all other nights we eat either leavened bread or matzah;
  on this night only matzah.*

ప్రతి రాత్రి తింతాము మేము అన్నిరకముల మూలికలను;
ఈ రాత్రి మాత్రం చేదు మూలికలనే.
- Prati raatri tintaamu maemu annirakamula moolikalanu;
  e raatri maatram chedu moolikalane.
- *On all other nights we eat all kinds of herbs; on this night only bitter herbs.*

ప్రతి రాత్రి ముంచము మేమెకనారి కూద;
ఈ రాత్రి మాత్రం ముంచుతాము రెండునార్లు.
- Prati raatri munchamu maemokasaari kooda;
  e raatri maatram munchutaamu rendusaarlu.
- *On all other nights we do not dip even once; on this night we dip twice.*

ప్రతి రాత్రి మేము భోజనం చేస్తాము కూర్చుని గాని నడుము వాల్చిగాని;
ఈ రాత్రి నడుము వాలుస్తాము.
- Prati raatri maemu bhojanam chaestaamu koorchuni gaani nadumu vaallchigaani;
  e raatri nadumu vaalustamu.
- *On all other nights we eat either sitting up or reclining; on this night we recline.*

ప్రతి రాత్రి మేము భోజనం చేస్తాము నిరాడంబరంగా;
ఈ రాత్రి మాత్రం ఎందారగిస్తాము ప్రత్యేక వేడుకగా.
- Prati raatri maemu bhojanam chaestaamu niraadambaranga;
  e raatri maatram vindaaragistaamu pratyeka vaedukaga.
- *On all other nights we eat in an ordinary manner;
  on this night we dine with special ceremony.*

ABOUT THE LANGUAGE:

Telugu

Number of speakers: 69,758,890
Rank: 13

Telugu is chiefly spoken in the southern state of Andhra Pradesh and neighboring states. It is also spoken in Bahrain, Fiji, Malaysia, Mauritius, Singapore and the United Arab Emirates. Telugu is the mother tongue of the ethnic groups Yanadi and Bagata.

The Telugu alphabet is a descendant of the *Brahmi* script of ancient India. It is closely related to the *Kannada* alphabet. The earliest known inscriptions in the Telugu language date from the 6th C CE and Telugu poetry started to appear during the 11th C.

Prior to the 20th C, Telugu was written in an archaic style very different from the commonly spoken language. During the second half of the century, a new written standard arose that was based on the spoken language.

ABOUT THE TRANSLATOR AND SPEAKER:

Prakasa Rao

Age: Unavailable   Recorded: 1994
Town: Bangalore, India

Prakasa was raised in Bangalore and is a native speaker of Telugu.

Photo by Tony DeJoie

Tigers in Bannerghatta National Sanctuary outside Bangalore

Tarifit

Translated from Arabic

mayemmi thamedditha war thedji amashnaw thimeddithin nneDhni?

■ لماذا تختلف هذه الليلة عن كل الليالى الاخرى؟

**Dhi thmeddithin nneDhni nttett aghrum iggwin s untun (slexmira)
nigh wenni yeggwin bra antun;
Dhi thmeddithа nttet aghrum yeggwin bra yantun waha.**

■ فى كل الليالة أخرى نأكلالخبز المخمر أو الخبز الفطير
فى هذه الليلة فقط نأكل خبز الفطير .

**Dhi thmeddithin nneDhni nttet re'shub izegzawen mamesh ma ggin;
Dhi thmedditha nttet re'shub yarZgen waha.**

■ فى كل الليالى الاخرى نأكلجميع أدواع التوابل الخضراء
فى هذه الليلة نأكل فقط التوابل المره .

**Dhi thmeddithin nneDhni war nessisin re'shub ura d ij umur;
Dhi thmedditha nssisin re'shub marthayen.**

■ فى كل الليالى اخرى لا نغمس التوابل حتى لمرة واحدة
فى هذه الليلة نغمس التوابل مرتين .

**Dhi thmeddithin nneDhni nttet s ughimi nigh nsennedh;
Dhi thmedditha nttet nsennedh waha.**

■ فى كل الليالى الاخرى نأكلجالسين منتصبين أو متكئين .
فى هذه الليلة نأكل متكئين .

**Dhi thmeddithin nneDhni nttet bra fishta;
Dhi thmedditha ntteet s fishta.**

■ *On all other nights we eat in an ordinary manner;
on this night we dine with special ceremony.*

In the recordings: Abderrahman ends his recording with "The translation in Tarifit. Berber of the Rif," meaning a Berber language of the Rif area of northern Morocco.

Transliteration notes:
Capital letters indicate that a sound is pharyngealized (articulated with back of the tongue against the pharynx) – not found in English or any European language
'th' is the same as the English fricative 'th' in fifth
'dh' is same as English 'th' in there
'gh' is a velar like the famous French R of Edith Piaf
Quote (') indicates an 'ayn', pharyngeal voiced fricative
No word for ceremony in Berber languages was found. Although the Arabic word *h'efla* is sometimes used, Abderrahman selected the Spanish loan word *fishta*, denoting feast

ABOUT THE LANGUAGE:

Tarifit

Number of speakers: 1,700,000
Rank: 263

Tarifit (*Rifia* in Arabic) is a Berber language spoken in the Rif area of northern Morocco, as well as Algeria, France and the Netherlands.

Tarifit has no written version. A partial phonetic version of the words is shown here.

ABOUT THE TRANSLATOR AND SPEAKER:

Abderrahman El Aissati

Age: Unavailable   Recorded: 1997
Towns: Rif area, Morocco / Tilburg, Netherlands

Dr. El Aissati is an Assistant Professor of linguistics, specializing in Berber and Arabic languages at Tilburg University in The Netherlands. Tarifit is Abderrahman's first language. The final question was translated from English.

Photo by Stephanie Goldhuber

Traditional
Moroccan
hospitality

Tamil

இன்றிரவுக்கும் மற்றிரவுகளுக்கும் என்ன வித்தியாசம்? *
- ■ inDRiravukkum maRRiravugaLukkum enna viththiyAsam?
- ■ What is the difference between this night and other nights?

வழக்கமாக இரவில் நாம் மாத்ஸாவும் ஹாமேத்ஸும் சாப்பிடுவோம்;
இன்றிரவு மாத்ஸா மட்டும் சாப்பிடுகிறோம். இது ஏன்?
- ■ vazhakkamAga iravil nAm mAthsAvum hAmEthsum chappiDuvOm;
  inRiravu mAthsA mattum chAppiDugiROm. idhu En?
- ■ Customarily, at night, we eat matza and khamets (leavened bread);
  this night we eat matza only. Why is this so?

வழக்கமாக இரவில் நாம் பலவிதமான காய்கறிகள் சாப்பிடுவோம்;
இன்றிரவு மாரோர் மட்டும் சாப்பிடுகிறோம். இது ஏன்?
- ■ vazhakkamAga iravil nAm palavidhamAna kAygaRigaL chappiduvOm;
  inRiravu mArOr maTTum chappiDugiROm. idhu En?
- ■ Customarily, at night, we eat many kinds of vegetables;
  this night we eat maror only. Why is this so?

வழக்கமாக இரவில் நாம் சாப்பாட்டுப் பொருட்களை குழம்புகளில் முக்கிச் சாப்பிட மாட்டோம்;
இன்றிரவு இரண்டு தடவை முக்கிச் சாப்பிடுகிறோம் –
ஒரு தடவை உப்புத் தண்ணீரிலும், ஒரு தடவை ஹாரோய்ஸஸ்ஸிலும். இது ஏன்?
- ■ vazhakkamAga iravil nAm chAppATTup poruTkaLai kuzhambugaLil mukkich chAppiDa mATTOm;
  inRiravu iraNDu thaDavai mukki chAppiDugiROm -
  oru thaDavai upputh thaNNIrilum, oru thaDavai hArOysassilum. idhu En?
- ■ Customarily, at night, we do not dip the eatables in sauces while eating them;
  this night we dip them twice while eating – once in salt water and once in kharoses. Why is this so?

வழக்கமாக இரவில் நாம் சில சமயம் நேராக உட்கார்ந்தும், சில சமயம் சாய்ந்து உட்கார்ந்தும் சாப்பிடுவோம்;
இன்றிரவு சாய்ந்து உட்கார்ந்து மட்டுமே சாப்பிடுகிறோம். இது ஏன்?
- ■ vazhakkamAga iravil nAm chila shamayam nErAga uTkArndhum, chila shamayam shAyndhu
  uTkArndhum shAppiDugiROm; inRiravu shAyndhu uTkArndhu maTTumE chappiDugiROm. idhu En?
- ■ Customarily, at night, we sometimes eat sitting straight up and sometimes reclining;
  this night we eat reclining one. Why is this so?

அப்பா இந்த கேள்விகளுக்கு பதில் கூறுவீர்களா?
- ■ appA, indha kELvigaLukku badhil kURuvIrgaLA?
- ■ Father, would you answer these questions?

*** Not contained in audio recording**

Capital vowels indicate long vowels; lower case letters are short vowels. Capital consonants generally indicate retroflexes, with the following exception: R = somewhat trilled, retroflex version of English 'r' • zh = close to an American 'r' • th = dental (unvoiced) version of English 't' • dh = dental voiced version of English 'd' • 'r' is more like a Spanish 'r' than an American 'r', but dental rather than retroflex.

ABOUT THE LANGUAGE:

Tamil *

Number of speakers: 65,675,200
Rank: 18

Tamil is one of the national languages of India. It is also spoken in Australia, Bahrain, Canada, Fiji, Germany, Malaysia, Mauritius, the Netherlands, Qatar, Réunion, Singapore, South Africa, Sri Lanka, Thailand, United Arab Emirates, United Kingdom and the USA.

The Tamil alphabet is descended from the *Brahmi* script. Tamil has been used since at least the 3rd C BCE; its literature is from 1st C CE.

ABOUT THE TRANSLATOR:

P V (Meylekh) Viswanath

Age: 40   Translated: 1995
Towns: Palghat, India / Teaneck, NJ

P.V. was born in Palghat, India (near the Kerala-Madras border) in 1954 and moved to the USA at age 20. He is Professor of Finance at Pace University's School of Business and is Director of its Global Portfolio Analysis Center. PV teaches both graduate and undergraduate students. He is the author of numerous educational publications, research articles and papers.

Translation © 1995 P.V. Viswanath. Used with his kind permission.

ABOUT THE SPEAKER:

Meena Viswanath

Age: 7 Recorded: 1995
Town: Teaneck, NJ

Meena Viswanath is the daughter of PV Viswanath. She is trilingual (Tamil, English and Yiddish). Meena is the youngest speaker in this collection of languages.

* For additional information, see *"Focus on ... pages.pdf"* on the DVD.

Tamasheq

Mamous awayaboudin ihadi adhadan wihadni?

■ *Why is this night different from all other nights?*

Ehadi buru adsan ehadwahadn nikshe asbanan; ehadwa burwahineksh bwartihawele.

■ *On all other nights we eat either leavened bread or matzah; on this night only matzah.*

Ehadn ikul saba antat woreyhawele; ehadi tey she sumath aheynaksh.

■ *On all other nights we eat all kinds of herbs; on this night only bitter herbs.*

Ehadn ikul saba antat woreyhawele; ehadi tey she sumath aheynaksh.

■ *On all other nights we eat either sitting up or reclining; on this night we recline.*

Ehad kul anoosee eyin antat; ehadi amonsee bohizoo antat.

■ *On all other nights we eat in an ordinary manner; on this night we dine with special ceremony.*

The translation received did not contain the dipping question.

ABOUT THE LANGUAGE:

Tamasheq

Number of speakers: 281,200
Rank: 742

Tamasheq is a national language of Mali, primarily spoken around the capital city of Lukasa. It has speakers throughout North and West Africa. Tamasheq and related Berber languages are spoken by Tuaregs, an ancient nomadic community that once lived throughout the Sahara.

ABOUT THE TRANSLATOR:

Agadi Mohamed Iknen Issm Ali

Age: Unavailable   Translated: 2010
Town: Niamey, Zambia

Agadi works as a night watchman for the African meteorological company ACMAD in Niamey, the capital of Zambia. He is a Tuareg.

The market in Ayorou features goods brought by several different tribes, each with their own distinctive dress and behavior

Photos by Bernard Cloutier (berclo.net)

Camels share space with humans crossing the Niger river in the capital city of Niamey

Tagalog

Bakit ang gabing ito ay kaiba sa mga gabing nagdaan?

■ *Why is this night different from all other nights?*

**May gabing kumakain tayo ng tinapay o matzah;
pero ngayong gabi ay matzah lang.**

■ *On all other nights we eat either leavened bread or matzah;
on this night only matzah.*

**May gabing ang kinakain natin ay halos lahat ng uri ng damo;
at sa gabing tulad nito ay karaniwang nating kinakain ay ang
mapait na damo.**

■ *On all other nights we eat all kinds of herbs;
on this night only bitter herbs.*

**May gabing ang kinakain natin sinasawsaw ang damo;
pero ngayon dalawang beses nating ginawa ito.**

■ *On all other nights we do not dip even once;
on this night we dip twice.*

**Karaniwang gabi tayo ay kumakain nang nakaupo ng
directo o nakasandal;
pero ngayong gabing ito tayo 'y nakasandal.**

■ *On all other nights we eat either sitting up or reclining;
on this night we recline.*

**Karaniwang gabi tayo ay kumakain na ordinaryo lang;
pero ngayon ay kakaiba atspesyal.**

■ *On all other nights we eat in an ordinary manner;
on this night we dine with special ceremony.*

ABOUT THE LANGUAGE:

Tagalog

Number of speakers: 23,853,200
Rank: 44

Tagalog, also called Filipino, is spoken in the Philippines (Manila, most of
Luzon and Mindoro). It is also spoken in Canada, Guam, Midway Islands,
Saudi Arabia, United Arab Emirates, United Kingdom and the USA.

ABOUT THE TRANSLATOR AND SPEAKER:

Beth Chia-Rubin

Age: Unavailable   Recorded: 2001
Towns: Jolo, Philippines / Saddle Brook, NJ

Beth Chia-Rubin grew up in Jolo, Philippines. She works at the United
Nations. An earlier version of the translation was worked on by **Mahalia
(Mai) Caliolio**.

Photo by Rody Torres

**Stores and street vendors on
Carriedo Street, one of Manila's
busiest commercial districts**

Tachelhit

Translated from Arabic

magh alig imzalag yttendagh g f weyat atnin?

■ لماذا تختلف هذه الليلة عن كل الليالى الاخرى؟

ko ittan atnin da ntseta aghrum ikermen, n'ghad aghroum nlefTour;
get idag day qa ntich aghroum n lefTour.

■ فى كل الليالة أخرى نأكل الخبز المخمر أو الخبز الفطير
فى هذه الليلة فقط نأكل خبز الفطير .

ko ittan atnin da ntseta kulshi lanwa' n issafarn izegzawen;
get idag day ntseta issafarn iHerran.

■ فى كل الليالى الاخرى نأكل جميع أنواع التوابل الخضراء
فى هذه الليلة نأكل فقط التوابل المره .

ko ittan atnin our da nssouy issafarn aoudit tikelt;
get idag da nssouy issafarn snat tikal.

■ فى كل الليالى اخرى لا نغمس التوابل حتى لمرة واحدة .
فى هذه الليلة نغمس التوابل مرتين .

ittan atnin da ntseta s iqimi negh nsenned;
get idag da ntseta nsenned.

■ فى كل الليالى الاخرى نأكل جالسين منتصبيين أو متكئين .
فى هذه الليلة نأكل متكئين .

ABOUT THE LANGUAGE:

Tachelhit

Number of speakers: 3,000,000
Rank: 193

Tachelhit, one of the major Berber languages, is spoken in southwestern Morocco, from the coast south to Ifni and north to near Agadir, northeast to outskirts of Marrakech, and east to Draa, including the valley of the Sous and south near the border. It is also spoken in Algeria and France. While many men speak both Arabic and Tachelhit, many of the women only learn Tachelhit.

Tachelhit has no written version. A partial phonetic version of the words is shown here.

ABOUT THE TRANSLATOR AND SPEAKER:

Hassan Ournahim

Age: 40   Recorded: 1997
Towns: Ouarzazate, Morocco / Tilburg, Netherlands

Hassan is a linguistics student of Dr. Abderrahman El Aissati of Tilburg University (a Berber languages specialist), through whom we obtained this translation.

Photo by Stephanie Goldhuber

Fez's Kairouyine Mosque (built in 810) has been the center of Islamic learning in Morocco for over 1000 years

Transliteration notes: Capital letters indicate that a sound is pharyngealized (articulated with root of the tongue against the pharynx). 'gh' is a velar, like the famous French 'R' of Edith Piaf. Quote (') indicates 'ayn', a pharyngeal voiced fricative.

Z Y X W V U T S R Q P O N M L K J I H G F E D C B A

Tabassaran

Вари імбу иишвари учу ужагъ уъл вая лечІшу уъл (кал) ипІурача;
гьаму иишwан - анжагъ лечІшу кал.

■ *Why is this night different from all other nights?*

Вари імбу иишвари учу вари жюрийрін укІар иптІурача;
гьаму иишwан - анжагъ кьуткьліб.

■ *On all other nights we eat either leavened bread or matzah;*
on this night only matzah.

Вари імбу иишвари учу сабакьан (ипІруб кыілак) кубсрадарча (кубсрі
шулдарча);
гьаму иишwан учу кьюбан кубсрача.

■ *On all other nights we eat all kinds of herbs;*
on this night only bitter herbs.

Вари імбу иишвари учу я деъну, я(-сана) гьюн иібку дахъну ипІурча
(ипІурі шулча);
гьаму иишwан учу ілжігъурча (ілжігъну дахъруча).

■ *On all other nights we do not dip even once;*
on this night we dip twice.

Вари імбу иишвари учу аьдатнан саягъніінді (гьаргансі) ипІурача;
гьаму иишwан учу махсус шадлугъ серенжемдіз (мажлісдіз)
таьлукь вуді ипІурача.

■ *On all other nights we eat either sitting up or reclining;*
on this night we recline.

Translation note: The initial question was not translated.

ABOUT THE LANGUAGE:

Tabassaran

Number of speakers: 128,900
Rank: 1,093

Tabassaran is spoken in southern Dagestan, as well as in Azerbaijan, Kazakhstan, Turkmenistan and Uzbekistan.

ABOUT THE TRANSLATOR:

Mikhail Alekseev

Age: Unavailable   Translated: 1996
Town: Moscow, Russia

Dr. Alekseev, also known as Michael Alekseyev, is a Daghestanian language specialist at the Institute of Linguistics Russian Academy of Sciences, in Moscow.

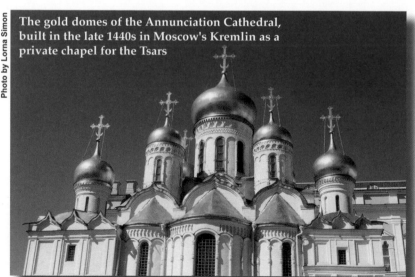

Photo by Lorna Simon

The gold domes of the Annunciation Cathedral, built in the late 1440s in Moscow's Kremlin as a private chapel for the Tsars

Sylheti

আজ রাত অন্নো কোন রাতের থেকে আলাদা কেন?

■ Why is tonight different than all other nights?

অন্য কোন রাতে আমরা রুটি মাট্সা খাই।
কিন্তু আজ রাতে আমরা শুধু মাট্সা খাই।

■ On other night we eat bread [made from wheat or rice flower] or matzah; but tonight we eat only matzah.

অন্য কোন রাতে আমরা নানান রকমের শাক সজ্জী খাই।
কিন্তু আজ রাতে আমরা বিশেষ রকমের ভেঁতো শাক খাই।

■ On other night we eat variety of leaves/herbs and vegetables; but tonight we eat a special variety of bitter leaves/herbs.

অন্য কোন রাতে আমরা হাগ ডুবিয়ে খাই।
কিন্তু আজ রাতে আমরা হাগ ডুবিয়ে খাই।

■ On other night we do not eat dipping leaves/herbs at all; but tonight we eat leaves/herbs by dipping it.

অন্য রাতে আমরা বসে বা শুয়ে খাই।
কিন্তু আজ রাতে আমরা শুয়ে শুয়ে খাই।

■ On other night we eat either sitting up or reclining; but tonight we eat reclining only.

অন্য রাতে আমরা সাধারণভাবে খাই।
কিন্তু আজ রাতে আমরা ফূর্তি ও উৎসবের সঙ্গে খাই।

■ On other night we eat in an ordinary manner; but tonight we eat with joy and happiness [ceremony].

ABOUT THE LANGUAGE:

Sylheti

Number of speakers: 10,300,000
Rank: 79

Sylheti is spoken in the districts of Sylhet, Sunamgani, Habigani, Moulvibazar in Bangladesh. It is also spoken in Australia, Canada, India (where 3 million speakers live), Italy, Malaysia, Myanmar, Singapore, United Kingdom and the USA.

ABOUT THE TRANSLATOR AND SPEAKER:

Friend of **Tafiqual Islam**

Age: Unavailable   Recorded: 2001
Towns: Bangladesh / Queens, NY

Information about the translator and speaker of Sylheti is very incomplete. She is the wife of Tafiqual Islam's co-worker. She lives in Elmhurst (Queens), NY. The text was typed by **Subir Das**.

Photo c/o U.N. World Food Programme

Bangladesh receiving food aid after the 1998 floods, which submerged 75% of the country and affected 30 million people

Swedish

Varför är denna natt annorlunda än alla andra nätter?

■ Vaufor air denna not annorlunda anne alla andra netter?

■ *Why is this night different from all other nights?*

På alla andra nätter äter vi antingen jäst bröd eller matzah; på denna natt endast matzah.

■ Paw alla andra netter airtter vi antinyen yes brerd eller matzah; paw denna not endast matzah.

■ *On all other nights we eat either leavened bread or matzah; on this night only matzah.*

På alla andra nätter äter vi alla sorts kryddor; på denna natt äter vi bittra kryddor.

■ Paw alla andra netter etter vi alla sorchs kreedor; paw denna not etter vi bettra kreedor.

■ *On all other nights we eat all kinds of herbs; on this night only bitter herbs.*

På alla andra nätter doppar vi inte vår mat i kryddor; på denna natt doppar vi maten två gånger.

■ Paw alla andra netter doppar vi inta aws ee kreedor; paw denna not doppar vi dem tavauw gonyer.

■ *On all other nights we do not dip even once; on this night we dip twice.*

På alla andra nätter sitter vi upprätt eller lutar oss; på denna natt lutar vi oss alla.

■ On all other nights we either sit up or recline; on this night we recline.

■ Paw alla andra netter sitter vi uppratt eller lutar oss; paw denna natt lutar vi oss alla.

På alla andra nätter äter vi på ett vanligt sätt; på denna natt äter vi med en speciell cermoni.

■ Paw alla andra netter airtter vi paw et vonlit sett; paw denna not airtter vi med en speciel cermoni.

■ *On all other nights we eat in an ordinary manner; on this night we dine with special ceremony.*

ABOUT THE LANGUAGE:

Swedish

Number of speakers: 8,311,739
Rank: 94

Swedish, called Svenska by its speakers, is the national language of Sweden. It is also spoken in Canada, Finland, Norway, United Arab Emirates and the USA. There are many different dialects (Gutniska, Överkalixmål, Pitemål, Nörpes and Skåne) within and outside of Sweden.

Like several other languages that share borders, the Norwegian and Swedish languages are mutually intelligible (Swedish and Norwegian speakers can understand each other) because they share much the same vocabulary; however, the languages have different syntax and grammar.

ABOUT THE TRANSLATOR AND SPEAKER:

Ted Folke

Age: Unavailable   Recorded: 2000
Towns: Stockholm, Sweden / Westport, CT

Ted was raised in Stockholm, the capital of Sweden. As an adult, he moved to the USA and works at the United Nations. The translation differs in only minor ways from a Swedish Haggadah. In the recording, the final question was read by Mr. Folke at a later time. The final question was modified by American-born **Debbie Gerber**, who lived in Sweden 27 years.

Swedish Haggadah from the collection of Rabbi Arnold Zoref

Stockholm's Old City

הַגָּדָה שֶׁל פֶּסַח

Hagada shel Pesach

Swahili

Kwanini usiku huu ni tofauti na usiku mwingine wowote?

■ *Why is this night different from all other nights?*

**Siku zote usiku huwa tunakula mkate wenye hamira au usiyo hamira;
Usiku huu, tunakula matzah tu.**

■ *On all other nights we eat either leavened bread or matzah;
on this night only matzah.*

**Siku zote usiku huwa tunakula aina zote za mboga;
usiku huu huwa, tunakula mboga chungu tu.**

■ *On all other nights we eat all kinds of herbs;
on this night only bitter herbs.*

**Siku zote usiku huwa hatuchovyi mboga kabisa hata mara moja;
usiku huu, tunachovya mara mbili tu.**

■ *On all other nights we do not dip even once;
on this night we dip twice.*

**Siku zote usiku huwa tunaketi wima au tunapumzika wakati tunakula;
usiku huu, tunapumzika tu.**

■ *On all other nights we eat either sitting up or reclining;
on this night we recline.*

**Siku zote usiku huwa tunakula kama kawaida;
usiku huu, tunakula chakula maalum.**

■ *On all other nights we eat in an ordinary manner;
on this night we dine with special ceremony.*

ABOUT THE LANGUAGE:

Swahili

Number of speakers: 787,630
Rank: 428

Swahili, called Kiswahili by its speakers, is spoken throughout Tanzania, in the coastal areas and Zanzibar. It is also has many speakers in Kenya and Somalia (where speakers are called the Baraawe); it is a required subject in Uganda's schools; there are also a few speakers in Mayotte, Mozambique and South Africa.

ABOUT THE TRANSLATOR AND SPEAKER:

Godfrey Ndagala

Age: Unavailable   Recorded: 2001
Town: Dar es Salaam, Tanzania

Godfrey was raised in Dar es Salaam. His father is a government minister and ex-professor. The translation was also worked on by language enthusiast **David Lowe**.

Images of the Serengeti. From left: Oldupai Gorge, location of earliest Hominid footprints; Zebras in the Ngorongoro Conservation Area; and a sunset at Ndutu Conservation Area

Photos by Joan Hantman

Swabian

Wa'sch heit nacht andrsch wiε én ällé andré nächt?

■ *Why is this night different from all other nights?*

**Én ällé andré nächt èss'mr gseirts brot odr ao matzε;
én dèrε nacht bloss matzε.**

■ *On all other nights we eat either leavened bread or matzah;
on this night only matzah.*

**En ällé andré nächt ké'mr ällé kreitr èssε;
én dèrε nacht bloss bittrré.**

■ *On all other nights we eat all kinds of herbs;
on this night only bitter herbs.*

**En ällé andré nächt tonk'mr nix ε oisigs mål ai;
én dèrε nacht tonk'mr d pflanzε zwoimål ai.**

■ *On all other nights we do not dip even once;
on this night we dip twice.*

**En ällé andré nächt hock'mr ons zom èssε nå, odr abr mr liigεt;
én dèrε nacht lég mr ons nå drzuε.**

■ *On all other nights we eat either sitting up or reclining;
on this night we recline.*

**En ällé andré nächt èss'mr ganz normal;
én dèrε nacht èss'mr zom feirε uf ε ganz bsondré weis.**

■ *On all other nights we eat in an ordinary manner;
on this night we dine with special ceremony.*

**Kiddush, from the 15th C
illustrated Darmstadt Haggadah**

ABOUT THE LANGUAGE:

Swabian

Number of speakers: 819,000
Rank: 412

Swabian is spoken in southwest Germany, the eastern part of Baden-Wuerttemberg, Wuerttemberg, Schwaben and western Bavaria. It is a variety of Highest Alemannisch.

ABOUT THE TRANSLATOR AND SPEAKER:

Markus Hiller

Age: Unavailable   Recorded: 1997
Town: near Tübingen, Germany

Markus is a native speaker of Swabian, living near Tübingen, Germany. The dialect represented here is spoken in southwest Germany and Switzerland.

Markus states there isn't a standard writing system for Swabian. He used standard German spelling to capture the sound of Swabian. (Not obvious from Markus' spellings is that Swabian, even before vowels, pronounces "t" and "d" as [t] and "p" and "b" as [p]). Because he was uncomfortable representing five different vowel sounds with the same symbol, Markus used diacritics (àááèé). These don't indicate stress or tones or length; for the most part, vowel length is the same as the corresponding words in Standard German. Marcus wrote the central vowel (schwa) as ε. He expects native speakers could read this fairly fluently.

Susu

Munse yi koe noun bore koe taguirassakhi?

■ *Why is this night different from all other nights?*

Bore koe ye birin, mukhu lebini tami nan doma, khana mara lebini tami mu nakhan ma;
to koe, lebini mouna tami nakhanma moukhou nanan doma.

■ *On all other nights we eat either leavened bread or matzah;*
   on this night only matzah.

Bore koe ye birin, mukhu sekhe mole birin nan doma;
to koe, mukhu seke khonoe nan toun doma.

■ *On all other nights we eat all kinds of herbs;*
   on this night only bitter herbs.

Bore koe ye birin, mukhu n'yan moe a bounda ma hali samaya kere;
to koe, moukhou a boundamane sammaya firin.

■ *On all other nights we do not dip even once;*
   on this night we dip twice.

Bore koe ye birin, mukhu degemane mukhu dokhi, khanamara mukhu yi talakhi;
to koe, mukhu mukhuye talamane.

■ *On all other nights we eat either sitting up or reclining;*
   on this night we recline.

Bore koe ye birin, mukhu moukhoun mou deguemane alo moukhou darikhi a khounma ki nakhe;
to koe, moukhou mou deguema binye ki nun a keyna nanma.

■ *On all other nights we eat in an ordinary manner;*
   on this night we dine with special ceremony.

ABOUT THE LANGUAGE:

Susu

Number of speakers: 1,060,280
Rank: 342

Susu, also called Soso and similar variants, is spoken in western and southwest Guinea. It is also spoken in Guinea-Bissau, Sierra Leone. Many people write Susu in both Latin (shown here) and Arabic scripts.

Susu does not yet have standardized spelling; note that *moukhou* and *mukhu* are variant phonetic spellings for the same word.

ABOUT THE TRANSLATOR AND SPEAKER:

Souleymane Camara

Age: Unavailable   Recorded: 2000
Town: Conakry, Guinea

Souleymane, a native speaker of Susu, was raised in Conakry, Guinea.

Photo by Boris Kester

View of Faranah in central Guinea, founded in the 1890s as a French outpost on the Niger river

Sukuma

Kolowake obuchiko bolelo botikolile na bushiko bungi?

■ *Why is this night different from all other nights?*

Kila lochiko tokolyaga ngate gotolile hamira au ngate gotatolile hamira; obushiko obo tolelya ngate botena amira doho.

■ *On all other nights we eat either leavened bread or matzah; on this night only matzah.*

Kila loshiko tolelya matwajo na miji mikale ja aina josee; obushiko bwa lelo tolelya matwajo na miji mikale doho.

■ *On all other nights we eat all kinds of herbs; on this night only bitter herbs.*

Kila loshiko tutokojaga nolo kamo; obushiko obo tutokojaga kabele.

■ *On all other nights we do not dip even once; on this night we dip twice.*

Kila loshiko tokolyaga twishaga nolo twasendemaga; obushiko obo tokalyaga twasendamaga doho.

■ *On all other nights we eat either sitting up or reclining; on this night we recline.*

Kila loshiko tukulyaga mubutungelija; obushiko bwa lelo tokolya na buyege bose.

■ *On all other nights we eat in an ordinary manner; on this night we dine with special ceremony.*

ABOUT THE LANGUAGE:

Sukuma

Number of speakers: 5,430,000
Rank: 127

Sukuma is spoken in northwest Tanzania, between Lake Victoria and Lake Rukwa, Shinyanga to the Serengeti Plain, and in Mwanza. Very few people in the major cities speak the language. It is called Kisukuma by its speakers.

ABOUT THE SPEAKER:

Joanita Ngaiza

Age: 38   Recorded: 2010
Town: Dar es Salaam, Tanzania

Joanita is a native speaker of Kihaya, fluent in Kihehe, and can read and write Sukuma and the other languages she recorded. Born in Dar es Salaam, during her early education she lived in Iringa, Lushoto Tanga, Korogwe and Tabora. She worked as Senior Library Assistant at International School of Tanganyika, and recently went back to school as a history major at the Open University of Tanzania, with a minor in Linguistics. Joanita has traveled to 22 of Tanzania's 26 regions. All her siblings have advanced degrees (Masters in Law, Land Management and Communications).

Photo by Ilana Locker

Tanzania's beautiful Zanzibar Island

ABOUT THE TRANSLATOR:

Esther Kasenga

Age: 45   Translated: 2009
Towns: Kwimba Mwanza / Dar es Salaam, Tanzania

Native speaker Esther runs her own tailoring and handcraft business. She travels internationally for marketing and sales.

Sranan

Fu san ede a neti disi de difrenti fu tra neti?

■ *Why is this night different from all other nights?*

**Na ala tra neti, wi e nyan srudeki brede noso mason brede.
Tapu a neti disi, soso mason brede.**

■ *On all other nights we eat either leavened bread or matzah;
on this night only matzah.*

**Na ala tra neti, wi e nyan ala sortu gruntu.
Tapu a neti disi, soso bita gruntu.**

■ *On all other nights we eat all kinds of herbs;
on this night only bitter herbs.*

**Na ala tra neti, wi no e dopu no wan leysi.
Tapu a neti disi, wi e dopu tu leysi.**

■ *On all other nights we do not dip even once;
on this night we dip twice.*

**Na ala tra neti, wi e sidon nyan efu tanapu skoynsi.
Tapu a neti disi, wi e tanapu rostu un baka.**

■ *On all other nights we eat either sitting up or reclining;
on this night we recline.*

**Na ala tra neti, wi e nyan na ala sortu fasi.
Tapu a neti disi, wi e nyan na wan respeki fasi.**

■ *On all other nights we eat in an ordinary manner;
on this night we dine with special ceremony.*

ABOUT THE TRANSLATOR AND SPEAKER:

Dr. Harold Charles Slengard

Age: Unavailable   Recorded: 1996
Town: Zoetemeer, Netherlands

Dr. Slengard, a native speaker of Sranan Toto, teaches the language
and has written course books and recorded many Sranan texts. A
professional translator, Harold holds the title of "Sworn-in Translator",
working for the Court of Justice in Rotterdam and The Hague and for the
Ministries of Education and Justice. Harold is a member of a commission
to increase the use of the language. He took great care to ensure the
translation was proper in accordance with the Surinamese Jews in
Paramaribo. Harold lives in Zoetermeer, a suburb of The Hague.

ABOUT THE LANGUAGE:

Sranan

Number of speakers: 126,400
Rank: 1,095

Sranan, also called Sranan Togo,
is the primary language spoken in
Suriname – mainly in Paramaribo
and along the coast. It is also
spoken in Aruba, Netherlands and
the Netherlands Antilles.

Suriname has one of the oldest
Jewish populations on the
American continent.

Photo by Bcris Kester

**St. Peter & Paul Cathedral in
Surinam's capital, Paramaribo,
claimed to be the largest wooden
building in South America**

Spanish

¿Por qué es diferente esta noche de todas las otras noches?

■ *Why is this night different from all other nights?*

En todas las otras noches comemos pan hecho con levadura o pan ázimo; en esta noche solamente matzah.

■ *On all other nights we eat either leavened bread or matzah;*
on this night only matzah.

En todas las otras noches comemos toda clase de hierbas; en esta noche comemos hierbas amargas.

■ *On all other nights we eat all kinds of herbs;*
on this night only bitter herbs.

En todas las otras noches no sumergimos las hierbas de ninguna manera; en esta noche las sumergimos dos veces.

■ *On all other nights we do not dip even once;*
on this night we dip twice.

En todas las otras noches comemos sentados rectos o inclinados; en esta noche nos sentamos inclinados.

■ *On all other nights we eat either sitting up or reclining;*
on this night we recline.

En todas las otras noches comemos de manera ordinaria; en esta noche comemos con ceremonia especial.

■ *On all other nights we eat in an ordinary manner;*
on this night we dine with special ceremony.

It was the authors' choice to represent Spanish from the Western Hemisphere, as opposed to Castilian Spanish.

ABOUT THE LANGUAGE:

Spanish

Number of speakers: 328,518,810
Rank: 2

Spanish, also called Español, is a language of central and southern Spain that has a major number of speakers in 43 other countries. Spanish's population centers are in Argentina, Bolivia, Chile, Colombia, Cuba, Dominican Republic, Ecuador, El Salvador, Guatemala, Honduras, Mexico, Nicaragua, Peru, USA (where it is spoken by 9% of the population) and Venezuela.

ABOUT THE TRANSLATOR AND SPEAKER:

Edna Alex

Age: 50s   Recorded: 2001
Towns: Puerto Rico / East Brunswick, NJ

Edna was educated in Puerto Rico. She converted to Judaism and currently lives in East Brunswick, NJ. Spanish translations were also created by **Zobeida B. Roitstein** (from Havana, Cuba), **Maria J. Machuca** (from Oviedo, Spain) and **Peter Salamon**.

The Inn of Juderia (Jewish district) in Spain's Cordoba, where Maimonides was born

Sotho

Hobaneng bosiu bona bo fapana le masiu a mang ohle?
■ Why night this it differs nights others all?

Ka masiu ohle, re ja bohobe bonang le tomoso kapa bo se nang tomoso; ka bosiu bona, bo se nang tomoso feela.
■ On nights other, we eat bread that has yeast or bread that do not have yeast; on night this, bread that have yeast only.

Ka masiu ohle, re ja mefuta kaofela ya dinoko; ka bosiu bona, dinoko tse babang feela.
■ On nights other, we eat all kinds of herbs; on night this, herbs that have of bitter only.

Ka masiu ohle, ha ja qopetse leha ele ha nngwe; ka bosiu bona, re qopetsa ha bedi.
■ On nights other, not we dip even one time; on night this, we dip two times.

Ka masiu ohle, re ja re dutse re otlolohile kapa re kobehile; ka bosiu bona, re kobehile.
■ On nights other, we eat we are sitting we straight or we are bent; on night this, we are bent.

Ka masiu ohle, re ja ka mokgwa o tlwaelehileng; ka bosiu bona, re ja ka mokgwa o kgethehileng.
■ On nights other, eat with manner of ordinary; on night this, we eat with manner of special.

Photo by Stephanie Goldhuber

Traveling in a *Makoro* boat in Botswana's Okavango Delta

ABOUT THE LANGUAGE:

Southern Sotho

Number of speakers: 6,024,000
Rank: 117

Southern Sotho, called Sesotho by its speakers, is the national language of Lesotho. It is also spoken in Botswana and South Africa.

ABOUT THE TRANSLATOR:

Jocobus Alwyn Kruger Olivier

Age: Unavailable   Translated: 1998
Towns: Heilbron / Sasolburg, South Africa

Jako was born and raised in Heilbron, Free State Province, South Africa. At the time of the translation, he was a student with a keen interest in languages and South African cultures, living in Sasolburg. Jako's mother tongue is Afrikaans; Sesotho, his third language, was learned in school. He planned further studies at Potchefstroom University in the languages of Sesotho and Afrikaans-Dutch.

Jako has worked as a tutor in South African cultures and languages, at Virtual University (www.vu.org), and has done freelance translation work for several companies and individuals over the Internet.

Several years after doing the Sotho translation for our collection, Jako assembled a collection of his own: Silent Night in over 100 languages!

ABOUT THE SPEAKER:

Phuzile Eveline Ntshumayelo

Age: Unavailable   Recorded: 1998
Towns: Heilbron / Sasolburg, South Africa

Phuzile was also born in Heilbron, Free State Province, South Africa. Her mother tongue is Zulu; she learned Sesotho in school. She graduated grade 12 with Sesotho subject matter as the first language.

Phuzile speaks Afrikaans and English with near fluency and understands the speech of Xhosa, Sepedi and Setswana. She has a keen interest in Sesotho novels. She is employed as a domestic worker in Sasolburg, South Africa.

Sorbian

Čehodla je tuta nóc hinaša hač wšě tamne nocy?

■ *Why is this night different from all other nights?*

We wšěch tamnych nocach jěmy pak ze zakisom pječeny chlěb pak njekisany chlěb;
w tutej nocy pak jenož njekisany chlěb.

■ *On all other nights we eat either leavened bread or matzah;*
on this night only matzah.

We wšěch tamnych nocach jěmy wšě móžne zela;
w tutej nocy pak jenož hórke zela.

■ *On all other nights we eat all kinds of herbs;*
on this night only bitter herbs.

We wšěch tamnych nocach njetunkamy ani jónu;
w tutej nocy pak tunkamy dwójce.

■ *On all other nights we do not dip even once;*
on this night we dip twice.

We wšěch tamnych nocach jěmy zruna sedźo abo na bok zlehnjeni;
w tutej nocy pak so na bok zlehnjemy.

■ *On all other nights we eat either sitting up or reclining;*
on this night we recline.

We wšěch tamnych nocach jěmy na wšědne wašnje;
w tutej nocy pak wječerjamy na wosebite wašnje.

■ *On all other nights we eat in an ordinary manner;*
on this night we dine with special ceremony.

The term *chlěb* normally means "leavened bread" and it is not necessary to add *ze zakisom pječeny* "made with yeast". Only in case of unleavened bread known from other cultures (e.g., from the Bible) we would need the qualifying expression *njekisany*. In these sentences, which refer to both kinds of bread, it is better to express it as above. *pak* "but" is not necessary but sounds better in this context. *na wšědne wašnje* means: "in an ordinary / usual way / manner". *na wosebite wašnje* means: "in a special / unusual way / manner".

ABOUT THE LANGUAGE:

Upper Sorbian

Number of speakers: 18,240
Rank: 2,514

Upper Sorbian, also called Obersorbisch and Wendish, is spoken in Germany – upper Saxony and eastern Germany; the principal towns where Sorbian is spoken are Bautzen and Kamenz. There are reported to be a few speakers in Texas.

ABOUT THE TRANSLATOR AND SPEAKER:

Dr. Hync Richter

Age: Unavailable   Recorded: 1998
Towns: Schleife / Slepo / Leipsig, Germany

Dr. Richter is a linguist at the Institute for Sorabistik, at the University of Leipzig. Hync ("Heinz") grew up in Schleife/Slepo, which is in the middle part of Sorbian Lausitz the first 18 years of his life.

Rabbis seated around the Seder table; the Erna Michael Haggadah, from the Middle Rhine, ca. 1400

Somali

Habeenkani muxuu kaga duwanyahay habeennada kale oo dhan?
- *Why is this night different from all other nights?*

Habeennada kale oo dhan, ama roodhi la khamiiriyey baannu cunnaa ama Matzah; habeenkanise Matzah qudha.
- *On all other nights we eat either leavened bread or matzah; on this night only matzah.*

Habeennada kale oo dhan, cagaar jaadwalba waannu cunnaa; habeenkanise dhir-reerood baannu si gaar ah u cunnaa.
- *On all other nights we eat all kinds of herbs; on this night only bitter herbs.*

Habeennada kale oo dhan, habayaraatee, waxba cagaarka kuma dhuuqno; habeenkanise laba jeer baannu wax ku dhuuqnaa.
- *On all other nights we do not dip even once; on this night we dip twice.*

Habeennada kale oo dhan, si caadi ah baannu wax u cunnaa; caawase dammaashaad baannu ku daraynaa.
- *On all other nights we eat either sitting up or reclining; on this night we recline.*

Habeennada kale oo dhan, kuudud ama jiqlaysi baannu wax ku cunnaa; habeenkanise waannu jiqlaysannaa.
- *On all other nights we eat in an ordinary manner; on this night we dine with special ceremony.*

ABOUT THE TRANSLATOR AND SPEAKER:

Abdirahman A Farah Barwaqo Hargeisa

Age: Unavailable   Recorded: 1996
Town: Hargeisa, Somalia / Canada

Abdirahman, a Somalian living in Canada, calls Hargeisa, Somalia his home.

ABOUT THE LANGUAGE:

Somali

Number of speakers: 13,871,700
Rank: 62

Somali is the national language of Somalia. There are a significant number of speakers in Ethiopia, Kenya and Djibouti, with some speakers in at least 8 other countries.

Sheikh Uweys of the Confraternity Qadiriyyah (died 1909) devised an Arabic-based alphabet for Somali, but this was replaced by the Somali alphabet (Osmanya) created in the early 1920s by the brother of the Sultan of Obbia. By 1961, both Latin and Osmanya scripts were used for Somali, with the sole adoption of Latin by the government in 1972.

Courtesy of flagspot.net

The Somali national flag: the blue color stands for the UN, which helped attain Somali independence; white means peace and prosperity; and the star's points show the five regions of the Somali people

Z Y X W V U T S R Q P O N M L K J I H G F E D C B A

Slovenian

Zakaj je ta noč drugačna od vseh drugih noči?

■ *Why is this night different from all other nights?*

Ob vseh drugih nočeh jemo ali kvašen ali nekvašen kruh; nocoj le nekvašenega.

■ *On all other nights we eat either leavened bread or matzah; on this night only matzah.*

Ob vseh drugih nočeh jemo vse vrste zeli; nocoj le grenke.

■ *On all other nights we eat all kinds of herbs; on this night only bitter herbs.*

Ob vseh drugih nočeh ne pomočimo niti enkrat; nocoj pomakamo dvakrat.

■ *On all other nights we do not dip even once; on this night we dip twice.*

Ob vseh drugih nočeh jemo bodisi vzravnani bodisi naslonjeni; nocoj se naslanjamo.

■ *On all other nights we eat either sitting up or reclining; on this night we recline.*

Ob vseh drugih nočeh jemo običajno; nocoj večerjamo s posebnim obredom.

■ *On all other nights we eat in an ordinary manner; on this night we dine with special ceremony.*

ABOUT THE LANGUAGE:

Slovenian

Number of speakers: 1,909,050
Rank: 245

Slovenian (Slovene) is the national language of Slovenia and is primarily spoken in Carniola and southern parts of Styria and Carinthia; lower Carniola in Dolenjsko, upper Carniola in Gorenjska, Primorski in west Slovenia and Stajerski in Styria. There are also speakers in Argentina, Australia, Austria, Canada, Croatia, Hungary, Italy, Serbia and Montenegro and the USA.

Publishing in Slovenian began in 1551 with a catechism and an alphabet book. The first Slovenian Bible translation was published in 1584. In 1811, Slovenian was adopted as the language of education, administration and media; later it was declared the official language of Slovenia.

ABOUT THE TRANSLATOR AND SPEAKER:

Jaro and Andrej Lajovic

Age: Unavailable   Recorded: 1996
Town: Ljubljana, Slovenia

Andrej and Jaro live in Ljubljana. Dr. Jaro Lajovic is on the faculty of the University of Ljubljana. Jaro corrected an earlier translation by non-native speaker **Aaron Vaughn**, a student at Brigham Young University. Native speaker Andrej recorded the text.

Photo © Barry Hantman

Ljubljana, capital of Slovenia

Slovak

Prečo je vyznačená táto noc zo všetkých noci?
- *Why is this night different from all other nights?*

**V každej inej noci smieme jest kvasené i nekvasené;
v tejto noci len nekvasené.**
- *On all other nights we eat either leavened bread or matzah;
on this night only matzah.*

**V každej inej noci smieme jest všetky druhy bylin;
v tejto noci len horké byliny.**
- *On all other nights we eat all kinds of herbs;
on this night only bitter herbs.*

**V každej inej noci jedenkrát nenamáčame;
v tejto noci dvakrát.**
- *On all other nights we do not dip even once;
on this night we dip twice.*

**V každej inej noci smieme jest sediac rovno alebo súc opreni;
v tejto noci len súc opreni.**
- *On all other nights we eat either sitting up or reclining;
on this night we recline.*

**V každej inej noci smieme jest obyčajnym spôsobom;
v tejto noci sa hostime podľa zvláštneho obradu.**
- *On all other nights we eat in an ordinary manner;
on this night we dine with special ceremony.*

Grand Praha hotel, built in 1903-1905, situated
at the foot of Slovakia's Tatra Mountains

In the recordings: Only the first four questions are read.

ABOUT THE LANGUAGE:

Slovak

Number of speakers: 5,019,950
Rank: 129

Slovak, or Slovakian, is the national language of Slovakia,
spoken primarily in the western upland country around
Bratislava. There are also speakers in Canada, Hungary,
Poland, Romania, Serbia and Montenegro, Ukraine and the
USA. Most Slovak dialects are inherently intelligible with
Czech; were it not for political and social divisions, many
linguists would classify Slovak and Czech as a single language.

Documents in Slovak appeared in the 15th C; however, a widely
accepted literary standard for Slovak did not emerge until the
19th C. Slovak literature flourished between 1918 and 1938
when the Slovak-speaking area became part of Czechoslovakia.

ABOUT THE TRANSLATOR AND SPEAKER:

Eva Vogel

Age: Unavailable   Recorded: 1996
Towns: Košice, Slovakia / NJ

Dr. Vogel was raised in Košice but moved around due to political purges when she
was young. She is a research scientist, working on glass and ceramic materials and
fiber-optic components for telecommunications. The first four questions were taken
from a Slovak Haggadah faxed from Bratislava; Eva translated the final question.

Sinhala

අනෙක් සියලුම රාත්‍රීවලට වඩා මෙ රාත්‍රීය වෙනස් ඇයි?

■ Anek siyaluma rathrivalata vadaa mei rathriya venas ai?

■ *Why is this night different from all other nights?*

අනෙක් සියලුම රාත්‍රීවල රොටී හෝ පාන් කන අපි,
අද රෑට පාන් පමනක් කමු.

■ Anek siyaluma rathrivala rotee ho pan kana api;
adha raata pan pamanuk kamu.

■ *On all other nights we eat either leavened bread or matzah;
on this night only matzah.*

අනෙක් සියලුම රාත්‍රීවල නොයෙක් වර්ගයේ පලා කන අපි,
අද රෑට තිත්ත පලා පමනක් කමු.

■ Anek siyaluma rathrivala noyek vargayeh palaa kana api;
adha raata thiththa palaa pamanuk kamu.

■ *On all other nights we eat all kinds of herbs;
on this night only bitter herbs.*

අනෙක් සියලුම රාත්‍රීවල එක වරක්වත් නොපොසුවන අපි,
අද රෑට දෙවරක් පොසුවමු.

■ Anek siyaluma rathrivala ek varakwath nopongawana api;
adha raata dewarak pongawamu.

■ *On all other nights we do not dip even once;
on this night we dip twice.*

අනෙක් සියලුම රාත්‍රීවල තැගිටගන හෝ වාඩිවී කෑමකන අපි,
අද රෑට වාඩිවී කමු.

■ Anek siyaluma rathrivala nagitagena ho vadivee kaamakana api;
adha raata vadivee kamu.

■ *On all other nights we eat either sitting up or reclining;
on this night we recline.*

අනෙක් සියලුම රාත්‍රීවල සුපුරුදු ලෙස කෑමකන අපි,
අද රෑට විශේෂ උත්සවයක් වගේ ආහාර ගනිමු.

■ Anek siyaluma rathrivala supurudhulesa kaamakana api;
adha raata vishesha uthsavayuk vage aahaara ganimu.

■ *On all other nights we eat in an ordinary manner;
on this night we dine with special ceremony.*

* For additional information, see
"*Focus on ... pages.pdf*" on the DVD.

ABOUT THE LANGUAGE:

Sinhala *

Number of speakers: 15,568,750
Rank: 58

Sinhala is the national language of Sri Lanka and is spoken throughout the country except some districts in the south, east and center. Sinhala is also spoken in Canada, Maldives, Midway Islands, Singapore, Thailand and the United Arab Emirates.

Sinhala's alphabet, a descendent of the *Brahmi* script, started to appear in inscriptions during the 3rd and 2nd centuries BCE. The earliest surviving literature in Sinhala dates from the 9th C CE.

ABOUT THE TRANSLATOR AND SPEAKER:

Samarada Weerahandi

Age: 40s   Recorded: 1996
Towns: Rathgama, Sri Lanka / NJ

Dr. Weerahandi was born in Rathgama, a fishing village near town of Galle. After college, Sam lived in Colombo, the capital of Sri Lanka where he was a Professor. He moved to the USA in his 20s. Sam is a world-renowned statistician researcher.

The first draft of the translation was prepared by **Tariq Zawahir**. Tariq was born in Sri Lanka and lived in Bangladesh and Egypt. He is at the Computer Science Department of Northwestern University. Tariq's father was a diplomat of Sri Lanka.

Scenes from Dambulla Rock Temple built in the 1st C by King Walagambahu

Photos by Stephanie Goldhuber

Sindhi

اجو کی رات بین راتین کان فرق چو آهی

■ *Why is this night different from all other nights?*

بین سپنی راتین راسین دیل روٹی یان ماٹزا کائیدا آھیون
اجو کی رات تی رگو ماٹزا کائیندا آھیون

■ *On all other nights we eat either leavened bread or matzah;*
on this night only matzah.

بین سپنی راتین تی اسین سپنی قسمن جون پوٹھیون کائیندا آھیون
اجو کی رات رگو یحوزیون پوٹھیون کائیدا آھیون

■ *On all other nights we eat all kinds of herbs;*
on this night only bitter herbs.

بین سپنی راتین تی ھک دفعو پوزیندا آھیون
اجو کی رات اسین ٢ دفعا پوزیندا آھیون

■ *On all other nights we do not dip even once;*
on this night we dip twice.

بین سپنی راتین تی ویھی یان آرام سان کائیندا آھیون
اجو کی رات جو اسین آرام سان کائیندا آھیون

■ *On all other nights we eat either sitting up or reclining;*
on this night we recline.

بین سپنی راتین تی اسین انئیئی کائیندا آھیون
اجو کی رات جو اسین حاٰم نمونی ملا ھیندا آھیون

■ *On all other nights we eat in an ordinary manner;*
on this night we dine with special ceremony.

---

* For additional information, see
"Focus on ... pages.pdf" on the DVD.

ABOUT THE LANGUAGE:

Sindhi *

Number of speakers: 21,382,120
Rank: 48

Sindhi is spoken in the Sindh region of Pakistan. There are many speakers in India and more in Oman, Philippines, Singapore, United Kingdom and the USA. There are a number of dialects, such as Kachchi, Lari, Lasi, Thareli and Vicholo. 100,000 speakers in rural Sindh came originally from the Kathiawar Peninsula in India. They are now almost fully assimilated with the Sindhi people.

ABOUT THE TRANSLATOR AND SPEAKER:

Veena Motwani

Age: Unavailable   Recorded: 1997
Towns: Pakistan / Freehold, NJ

Veena Motwani was raised in Pakistan and now lives in Freehold, NJ. The text was typed by **Ahsan Hundal** of Pakistan and was checked by a Sindhi-speaking friend of Ahsan's.

Photo by Affan A Syed

The modern Faisal Mosque is located in Islamabad, Pakistan

Signed English

The accompanying DVD contains a video of Danielle Marin signing the Four Questions in Signed English.

ABOUT THE LANGUAGE:

Signed English

Number of users: Unavailable
Rank: N/A

Signed English, sometimes called Pidgin Signed English, is used to teach English spelling and the structure of English to deaf and hearing-impaired persons. Many teachers use Signed English. Its vocabulary (signs) is drawn from American Sign Language (ASL) but follows English word order. Signed English is not considered a language of the deaf like the other Sign languages in this collection and the more than 120 Sign languages used by deaf communities around the world.

ABOUT THE TRANSLATOR AND SIGNER:

Danielle Marin

Age: Unavailable   Recorded: 1997
Town: Lawrenceville, NJ

Danielle Marin has 6 years experience as a teacher of deaf and hearing impaired children. She verified the translation with Rabbi Daniel Grossman of Lawrenceville, NJ. Rabbi Grossman is hearing-impaired and works with the Deaf community.

Sicilian

Cchi cc'è d'autru a sta sira ccu l'autri siri?

■ *Why is this night different from all other nights?*

**Ca tutti l'autri siri, mangiamu pani allivitatu e pani lisu;
mentri a sta sira, mangiamu sulu pani lisu.**

■ *On all other nights we eat either leavened bread or matzah;
on this night only matzah.*

**Ca tutti l'autri siri, mangiamu quali virdura sia;
mentri a sta sira, sulu erva amàra.**

■ *On all other nights we eat all kinds of herbs;
on this night only bitter herbs.*

**Ca tutti l'autri siri, nun ni spunzamu a virdura mancu na vota;
mentri a sta sira, n'a spunzamu du voti.**

■ *On all other nights we do not dip even once;
on this night we dip twice.*

**Ca tutti l'autri siri, mangiamu assittati comu apparteni o stinnicchiati;
mentri a sta sira, siemu tutti stinnicchiati.**

■ *On all other nights we eat either sitting up or reclining;
on this night we recline.*

**Ca tutti l'autri siri, mangiamu com'ô sòlitu;
mentri a sta sira, ni trattamu cu na cirimònia spiciali.**

■ *On all other nights we eat in an ordinary manner;
on this night we dine with special ceremony.*

Pronunciation notes:
o, e: always open
ò: long and open
i, u: as in English fill and bull
cchi+vowel: velar tongue-tip curled back (e.g. retroflex)
initial b: in some cases alternates with v, but never a bilabial fricative
cia, cio, ciu, gia, gio, giu: the "i" is never pronounced
p, t, c: voiceless stops weakly articulated
initial r: retroflex tongue-tip in many dialects found on mainland
s: never voiced, always voiceless but weakly articulated
tr: retroflex tongue-tip, almost like English train
st, sp: pronounced in Tuscan or even Naples fashion

ABOUT THE LANGUAGE:

Sicilian

Number of speakers: 4,830,000
Rank: 137

Sicilian, also called Calabro-Sicilian and Sicilianu, is the language of
Sicily, an island off the southern mainland of Italy. The language shows
some influence from French.

ABOUT THE TRANSLATOR AND SPEAKER:

Sebastiano Trigilla

Age: 46   Recorded: 2001
Town: near Siracusa, Italy

Sebastiano was born and raised in a village near Siracusa. To people who
know only standard Italian, Sebastiano's speech is largely unintelligible.

A translation was also developed by **Fiorello Cicala**, who grew up in
Fiumedinisi in the province of Messina and left for the USA at age 20.

Cover of an Italian Haggadah

Shona

Sei manheru anhasi akasiyana nemamwe manheru?

■ *Why is this night different from all other nights?*

**Mamwe manheru, tinodya chingwa chisina matzah;
Manheru anhasi, matzah chete.**

■ *On all other nights we eat either leavened bread or matzah;
on this night only matzah.*

**Mamwe manheru, tinodya miriwo yese;
Manheru anhasi, miriwo inovava chete.**

■ *On all other nights we eat all kinds of herbs;
on this night only bitter herbs.*

**Mamwe manheru, tinoseva kamwechete;
Manheru anhasi, wenoseva kaviri.**

■ *On all other nights we do not dip even once;
on this night we dip twice.*

**Mamwe manheru, tinodya takagara kana kuti takavhumbama;
Manheru anhasi, tinodya takavhumbama chete.**

■ *On all other nights we eat either sitting up or reclining;
on this night we recline.*

**Mamwe manheru, tinodya semazuva ese;
Manheru anhasi, tonodya mabiko anokosa.**

■ *On all other nights we eat in an ordinary manner;
on this night we dine with special ceremony.*

ABOUT THE LANGUAGE:

Shona

Number of speakers: 10,759,200
Rank: 75

Shona, also called Chishona, is a language of Zimbabwe understood nearly everywhere in the country. There are also considerable numbers of Shona speakers in Zambia and a few more in Botswana and Malawi.

The written language of Shona is based chiefly on the African languages of Karanga and Zezuru with some words originally found in Manyika and Korekore.

ABOUT THE TRANSLATOR AND SPEAKER:

Masimba Tafirenyika

Age: Unavailable   Recorded: 1997
Towns: Harare, Zimbabwe / Queens, NY

Masimba was born and raised in Zimbabwe's capital, Harare. He works at the United Nations in Peace Keeping operations.

Photo by Stephanie Goldhuber

Victoria Falls, the widest waterfall in the world, is near the border of Zimbabwe and Zambia

Sherpa

Wgaring nup ti chila nup yanmba taan michikpu yin?

■ *Why is this night different from all other nights?*

Nup yanmbala waare phaap lüwu kur yangni matzah soawin; wgaring nupla matzah tirang.

■ *On all other nights we eat either leavened bread or matzah; on this night only matzah.*

Nup yanmbala waareki lüm namba gangbu saewi; wgaring nuplati lüm khakti tirang saache yin.

■ *On all other nights we eat all kinds of herbs; on this night only bitter herbs.*

Nup yanmbala waareki lüm kaanni mabangbi; wgaring nembi tila khepnyi bangiwi.

■ *On all other nights we do not dip even once; on this night we dip twice.*

Nup yanmbala waare kichokpa deni yinsinang nyalni yinsinang saewi; wgaring nupti waarung nyalgiwi.

■ *On all other nights we eat either sitting up or reclining; on this night we recline.*

Nup gaangbula waareki naangzung kheni saama saewi; wgaring nuplati thaangdi kheni kiki tangni saewi.

■ *On all other nights we eat in an ordinary manner; on this night we dine with special ceremony.*

Translator's notes: *Wgaring Nup* = This night; *Nup Yanmba* = Other nights; *Michikpu* = Different; *Phapp* = Yeast; *Chherma* = Green vegetable (green leaves); *Lüm* = Weeds (also gives close meaning for herbs); *Khakti* = Bitter; *Kiki Tangni* = With joy. Sherpa has no common word for herbs; there are particular words for each herb. Leaning or reclining while eating is not good manners in our culture.

Photo by Jeff Spiegel

Annapurna mountain range of the Himalayas, Gorka region of Nepal

ABOUT THE LANGUAGE:

Sherpa

Number of speakers: 86,200
Rank: 1,325

Sherpa is spoken in Nepal: Solu Khumbu District; northern mountains; north of Namche Bazaar; villages of Gumdi, Sete, Junbesi, Phaplu and Saller; around Rolwaling, Taplejung and in Kathmandu. There are also Sherpa speakers in Bhutan, China, India, South Korea and the USA. As opposed to Nepali, which is spoken by nearly 60% of the Nepalese population, Sherpa is spoken by less than 0.2% of the population.

ABOUT THE TRANSLATOR AND SPEAKER:

Ngawang Norbu Sherpa

Age: 42   Recorded: 1999
Towns: Sdokhumbu, Nepal / Jackson Heights, NY

Ngawang (called Dawa) was raised in the mountain village of Sdokhumbu (altitude 9,300 ft). At age 15, Dawa moved to the capital, Kathmandu; at 41 he moved to the USA. The translation was also worked on by **Ang Chokpa Sherpa**, in Flemington, NJ.

Some excerpts from Dawa's 7-page letter about his culture and bio: "Sherpas are from the Mongolian tribe that migrated approximately 4-5 centuries [ago] from Tibet and settled in the northeastern part of Nepal. The word Sherpa actually means The Easterners. Sherpas have some 12 different sub-castes. We cannot marry with one of our own sub-caste, because sub-castes are [like] a relationship of brother or sister. My sub-caste is Salaka, so in reality my name is Dawa Norbu Serpa (Salaka).

We Sherpas are followers of Tibetan Buddhism; our culture is influenced by Tibetan culture. Most Sherpas grow up in our very high altitude land in the Great Himalayan Ranges. [T]he first conqueror on the world's highest peak, Mt. Everest, was Tenzing Norgay Sherpa with Sir Edmund Hillary. In Nepal, tourism has been a major profession of the Sherpas. Sherpas are hired to bring all [the] gear and supplies for the expedition team[s] to the high mountains.

I am interested in doing social works [and] have done many in our villages. My first priority was education [for] the poor and helpless children in the villages. I requested [support from the] German Embassy [in] Nepal and they gave us ~20,000 DM for the school project. In 1983 I made suspension bridges, health posts, flood-affected relief programs and many other social activities.

My childhood was a pleasant life with my beloved parents. Due to far-distanced school, I could not join school in time. At 9 years, I [attended a] primary school established by Sir Edmund Hillary. At 10, my father admitted me to a school associated with the very famous Buddhist monastery, Tengboche Monastery. Unfortunately, my father was killed in an expedition with an American climbing team to Mt. Dhaulagiri (about 8000 meters high). I cannot forget the painful feeling and life after the death of my father. Although it was a hard time for my mother, she continued my education for another 4 years at the monastery. But I could not keep on looking to the hard life of my mother. So I left school and helped my mother in the village, because my 2 brothers and 2 sisters were too young. This situation happens to many young Sherpa families.

[When I was] 15, a kind German doctor came trekking [at] the Everest base camp. He decided to finance my education and give me a better education. He brought me to Kathmandu for study, [where I studied] until high school. After high school, I worked 10 years (1980-1990) with German[s] in Kathmandu at a waste management project. After that I [went into] business [for myself, and later came to the US]."

Serbian

Zašto je ova noć različita od svih ostalih noći?

■ *Why is this night different from all other nights?*

Svih ostalih noći, jedemo ili hleb sa kvascem ili maco; ove noći, samo maco.

■ *On all other nights we eat either leavened bread or matzah; on this night only matzah.*

Svih ostalih noći, jedemo sve vrste zeleniša; ove noći, samo gorki zeleniš.

■ *On all other nights we eat all kinds of herbs; on this night only bitter herbs.*

Svih ostalih noći, ne umačemo zelenis ni jednom; ove noći, umačemo ih dva puta.

■ *On all other nights we do not dip even once; on this night we dip twice.*

Svih ostalih noći, jedemo sedeći ispravljeni ili opušteni; ove noći, opušteni.

■ *On all other nights we eat either sitting up or reclining; on this night we recline.*

Svih ostalih noći, jedemo na bilo koji običan način; ove noći, večeramo uz svečanu ceremoniju.

■ *On all other nights we eat in an ordinary manner; on this night we dine with special ceremony.*

ABOUT THE TRANSLATOR AND SPEAKER:

Ljiljana Trajkovic

Age: Unavailable   Recorded: 1998
Towns: Priština, Yugoslavia / NJ / CA / Burnaby, BC

Dr. Trajkovic was raised in Priština, Yugoslavia. She is now Professor of Engineering and Computing Science at Simon Fraser University.

ABOUT THE LANGUAGE:

Serbian

Number of speakers: 17,020,550
Rank: 106

Serbian is spoken in Serbia, Montenegro and the former Yugoslavian Republics, currently Macedonia, Bosnia and Herzegovina. It is also spoken in a dozen other countries, with the most speakers in Turkey. Serbian is closely related to Croatian and Bosnian; some linguists would classify Serbo-Croatian as a single language, were it not for the political and social divisions between their peoples.

The division between Croats and Serbs originated in the 11th C, when both groups converted to Christianity. The Serbs aligned themselves with Constantinople and the Eastern Orthodox church and adopted the Cyrillic alphabet (though also using the Latin alphabet); the Croats favored the Roman Catholic church and the Glagolitic alphabet, later converting to the Latin alphabet. Presently, Croatian uses the Latin alphabet exclusively, while Serbian uses both the Latin and Cyrillic alphabets.

Зашто је ова ноћ различита од свих осталих ноћи?

Свих осталих ноћи, једемо или клеб са квасцем или мацо.

Ове ноћи, само мацо.

Свих осталих ноћи, једемо ове врсте зелениша;

Ове ноћи, само горки зелениш.

Свих осталих ноћи, не умачемо ни једном;

Ове ноћи, умачемо два пута.

Свих осталих ноћи, једемо седећи исправљени или опуштени;

Ове ноћи, опуштени.

Serbian translation in Cyrillic script

Secoya

Translated from Spanish

Meyoquë coaquenì ịye ñami cuine yaquë ñami?
- ¿Por qué es diferente esta noche de todas las otras noches?

**Sia ye'quë ñamiña a̱ñu'u a̱'ojojo' cojo*;
ịye ñami a̱'orepase'e.**
- *En todas las otras noches comemos pan hecho con levadura o pan ázimo;
en esta noche solamente matzah.*

**Sia ye'quë ñamiña a̱ñu'u coasia taya;
ịye ñami taya sijẹñe.**
- *En todas las otras noches comemos toda clase de hierbas;
en esta noche comemos hierbas amargas.*

**Sia ye'quë ñamiña a̱ñu'u oco neñe pañu'u yeja y̱eque yo oye pañu'u;
ịye ñami s̱asuñu'u ocona cayaye pa'ye.**
- *En todas las otras noches no sumergimos las hierbas de ninguna manera;
en esta noche las sumergimos dos veces.*

**Sia ye'quë ñamiña a̱ñu'u jaruni nuiñe o quëruhuë;
ịye ñami pañu'u ja'ruye quëruhuë.**
- *En todas las otras noches comemos sentados rectos o inclinados;
en esta noche nos sentamos inclinados.*

**Sia ye'quë ñamiña a̱ñu'u sia yëquë maca;
ịye ñami s̱ịa huai deoyecuachajë.**
- *En todas las otras noches comemos de manera ordinaria;
en esta noche comemos con ceremonia especial.*

* *Cojo* **was added when the text was spoken.**

ABOUT THE LANGUAGE:

Secoya

Number of speakers: 690
Rank: 5,361

Secoya is spoken in the northeastern jungle Aguarico, Cuyabeno and Eno rivers, all near the Colombian border. Secoya is also spoken in Peru.

ABOUT THE TRANSLATOR AND SPEAKER:

Guillermo Payahuaje

Age: 46   Recorded: 2000
Town: San Pablo De Kantesteya, Ecuador

Guillermo lives in San Pablo De Kantesteya, a village of 180 people in El Oriente on the Aguarico River in Ecuardor's northern jungle. He works as the mechanic for Aguarico area and the Orientgal Agency.

**Boating on the Aguarico River
in Ecuador's Jungle**

Scots

Fit wy is the nicht nae the same as a the ithers?

■ *Why is this night different from all other nights?*

**Oan a ither nichts, we hae oor fill o' a pan loaf or oatcakes;
The nicht, jist oatcakes.**

■ *On all other nights we eat either leavened bread or matzah;
on this night only matzah.*

**Oan a ither nichts, we hae oor fill o' a kinds o' herbs;
The nicht, jist soor yins.**

■ *On all other nights we eat all kinds of herbs;
on this night only bitter herbs.*

**Oan a ither nichts, we dinnae dook even eence;
The nicht, we dook twa times.**

■ *On all other nights we do not dip even once;
on this night we dip twice.*

**Oan a ither nichts, we hae oor fill at the taible or lyin doon;
The nicht, wur lyin doon.**

■ *On all other nights we eat either sitting up or reclining;
on this night we recline.*

**Oan a ither nichts, we hae oor fill per the usual;
The nicht, wur haein a perty.**

■ *On all other nights we eat in an ordinary manner;
on this night we dine with special ceremony.*

ABOUT THE LANGUAGE:

Scots

Number of speakers: 200,000 (some estimates much higher)
Rank: 895

Scots is spoken throughout Scotland, except highlands and Aberdeen to Ayrshire in the lowlands. Scots is closest to English and Frisian. It is also spoken in Ireland. Intelligibility is difficult between the dialects (Northern Scots, Southern Scots, Ulster) and some linguists consider Northern Scots on the Scottish Islands to be a different language. Fewer people speak Scottish (Scottish Gaelic).

Scots was originally known as 'Inglis' and has been influenced by Gaelic, Norse, Latin, Dutch, Norman French, Standard French and English. By the 14th C, Scots was the main language of Scotland.

During the 19th and early 20th century efforts were made to eradicate Scots, mainly by punishing schoolchildren. Attitudes began to change in the 1980s and 1990s and there is now some use of Scots in education, media and literature.

Before laughing at the use of oatcakes in this translation, recall that the Passover Haggadah states "They baked unleavened *cakes* of the dough ..."

ABOUT THE TRANSLATOR AND SPEAKER:

Graeme W Smith

Age: 34   Recorded: 1996
Towns: Arbroath / Edinburgh, Scotland / Boston, MA

Dr. Smith, a speech researcher, was born in Arbroath, Scotland; at age 22 he left Scotland to work in England, at 26 he went back to Edinburgh and moved to the USA at 29.

He writes about his birthplace: "Arbroath is a small fishing town of around 25,000 people, also boasts a productive farming community in the outlying villages. Arbroath is perhaps most remembered for the signing of the Scottish Declaration of Independence that was sent to the Pope in 1320. The document was written at Arbroath Abbey (the ruins are now a tourist attraction and you can drive through the main dining hall!) on 6th April 1320 and delivered to the Pope in Avignon. The Pope wrote to Edward II urging him to make peace, although it was not until 1324 that the Pope addressed Robert Bruce as King."

Photo by Joan Hantman

The mother church of Presbyterians, Edinburgh Cathedral, properly called St. Giles' Cathedral, was founded in 1120. The first of many rebuildings followed a fire in 1385. The cathedral's stained glass windows date from 1870 onward

Sardinian

Ghitte b' à de diversu custu sero dae tottu sos àtteros seros?

■ *Why is this night different from all other nights?*

**ca tottu sos àtteros seros, mandicamus e pane pesàu e pane chene madriche;
custu sero, imbéttses, solus pane chene madriche.**

■ *On all other nights we eat either leavened bread or matzah;
on this night only matzah.*

**ca tottu sos àtteros seros, mandicamus cada zenìa de ortalìssia;
custu sero, imbéttses, solus erba rànchia.**

■ *On all other nights we eat all kinds of herbs;
on this night only bitter herbs.*

**ca tottu sos àtteros seros, nois no intinghimus s' ortalissia nemmancu una 'orta;
custu sero, imbéttses, la intinghimus duar vortas.**

■ *On all other nights we do not dip even once;
on this night we dip twice.*

**ca tottu sos àtteros seros, mandicamus séttios o imbaràos;
custu sero, imbéttses, semus tottus imbaràos.**

■ *On all other nights we eat either sitting up or reclining;
on this night we recline.*

**ca tottu sos àtteros seros, mandicamus comente a sémpere;
custu sero, imbéttses, chenamus chi nd' una tsilimona rara.**

■ *On all other nights we eat in an ordinary manner;
on this night we dine with special ceremony.*

ABOUT THE LANGUAGE:

Sardinian

Number of speakers: 500,000
Rank: 548

Sardinian (also called Sard, Sardarese, Logudorese) is spoken in Italy's central Sardinian region. There is no standard form of Sardinian for literary purposes. Farmers and housewives over 35 use almost no Italian.

ABOUT THE TRANSLATOR AND SPEAKER:

Luisa Selis

Age: Unavailable   Recorded: 1996
Town: Sassari, Sardinia, Italy

Luisa grew up in Sassari in Sardinia. She is an Ethnologist of Sardinian culture. She has been collecting traditional Sardinian lexicons and was involved in a project to collect and classify published and unpublished materials of the Sardinian anthropologist Raffaello Marchi.

Florence's Basilica, world's largest
Franciscan church, with its prominent
Star of David, was designed by
Jewish architect Niccolo Matas

Sanskrit

कूतः एषाः रात्री सर्वान्यरात्रीभ्यः भिद्यते

- kutaḥ eṣā rātī sarvānyatrībyaḥ bhidyate?
- *Why is this night different from all other nights?*

सर्वान्यरात्रीषु दूषितापूपं वादूषितापूपं वा भूञ्जामः ।
एतस्यां रात्र्यां अदूषितापूपमेव भूञ्जामः ॥

- sarvānyarātrīṣu dūṣitāpūpaṁ vādūṣitāpūpaṁ vā bhuñjāmaḥ;
  etasyāṁ rātryāṁ adūṣitāpūpameva bhuñjāmaḥ.
- *On all other nights we eat either leavened bread or matzah;
  on this night only matzah.*

सर्वान्यरात्रीषु सर्वश्चित् हरितपत्रानि भूञ्जामः ।
एतस्यां रात्र्यां तिक्तहरितपत्रान्येव भूञ्जामः ॥

- sarvānyarātrīṣu sarvāms'cit haritapatrāni bhuñjāmaḥ;
  etasyāṁ rātryāṁ tiktaharitapatrānyeva bhuñjāmaḥ.
- *On all other nights we eat all kinds of herbs;
  on this night only bitter herbs.*

स्वान्यरात्रीषु एक वारमपि नाप्लवाम ।
एतस्यां रात्र्यां द्विवारं आप्लवाम ॥

- sarvānyarātrīṣu ekavāramapi nāplavāmaḥ;
  etasyāṁ rātryāṁ dvivāraṁ āplavāmaḥ.
- *On all other nights we do not dip even once;
  on this night we dip twice.*

स्वान्यरात्रीषु आसानाः वा शेमानास्वा भूञ्जामः ।
एतस्यां रात्र्यां शेमहः ॥

- sarvānyarātrīṣu āsānāḥ vā śemānāsvā bhuñjāmaḥ;
  etasyāṁ rātryāṁ śemahe.
- *On all other nights we eat either sitting up or reclining;
  on this night we recline.*

स्वान्यरात्रीषु लौकिकं भूञ्जामः ।
एतस्यां रात्र्यां विशेषविधिना भूञ्जामः ॥

- sarvānyarātrīṣu laukikaṁ bhuñjāmaḥ;
  etasyāṁ rātryāṁ vis'eṣavidhinā bhuñjāmaḥ.
- *On all other nights we eat in an ordinary manner;
  on this night we dine with special ceremony.*

ABOUT THE LANGUAGE:

Sanskrit

Number of speakers: 2,950
Rank: 4,252

Sanskrit is an ancient classical Indian language, the oldest parent of all Indo-European family of languages. Sanskrit is still used as a literary and liturgical language by about 200,000 people. Efforts are currently underway to revive it as a spoken language.

ABOUT THE TRANSLATOR AND SPEAKER:

Manasi Tirodkar

Age: 20s   Recorded: 1998
Towns: Maharashtra, India / British Columbia, Canada

Manasi was born in Maharashtra, India, and now lives in British Columbia. He is a native speaker of English, fairly fluent in Marathi and knows some Hindi and Sanskrit. The translation was assisted by **Nathan Ryan** of Dartmouth College's Math Department.

ABOUT THE TRANSLATION:

Words selected for leavened and unleavened bread were *duusitaapuupan* and *aduusitaapuupan*. As in English, the only difference is the prefix. In English, 'leavened' is a past passive particle meaning 'was caused to rise'. In Sanskrit there is a verbal form, the causative, which means 'to cause to X', where X is a verb root. The Sanskrit word *duusita* is the past passive participle of the causative of the root *dus* and thus means 'was caused to rise'. The basic word for bread *aapuupan* was taken from Monier William's Sanskrit-English dictionary, and literally means a type of cake made with flour.

The word *laukikam* means mundane, or earthly (as opposed to divine) and was used to describe an ordinary way of eating.

The compound *haritapatraani*, meaning "green-leaved", was used for herbs.

Mysore Palace at night

Photo by Tony DeJoie

Pronunciation notes:
The Romanization shown is typically used by Sanskritists. A letter with a dot beneath it means the sound is guttural. An 's' with accent (ś) is 'sh'. (The s's with a dot below sound like 'sh' also.) The 'n' with a tilde (ñ) is a palatal n. Bars over vowels indicate a longer length.

Samoan

Aiseā ue tulaga ese ai lenei pō, mai isi po?

■ *Why is this night different from all other nights?*

O isi pō, tatou te aai ai a lē o falaoa ua faafefeteina o falava e lei faafefeteina;
O le pō lenei, na o falava e lē faafefeteina.

■ *On all other nights we eat either leavened bread or matzah;*
on this night only matzah.

O isi pō, tatou te āai ai i laau ōōna;
O le pō lenei, ua na o vine vao.

■ *On all other nights we eat all kinds of herbs;*
on this night only bitter herbs.

O isi pō, tatou te aai ai fufuiina lava se mea āi ise suavai oona;
O le pō lenei, e faalua ona fufui a tatou mea āi i le suavai oona.

■ *On all other nights we do not dip even once;*
on this night we dip twice.

O isi pō, tatou te aai ai a le ose nofo sao, poo le taooto faatatafa;
O le pō lenei, tatou te taooto faatatafa.

■ *On all other nights we eat either sitting up or reclining;*
on this night we recline.

O isi pō, tatou te aai ai lava e pei ona masani ai;
O le pō lenei, tatou te aai ai i le sauniga faapitoa.

■ *On all other nights we eat in an ordinary manner;*
on this night we dine with special ceremony.

The third question was read as: "O isi po, ele fufuiina lava se mea āi ise suavai oona ..."

As we lost contact with the translator, we attempted to reconcile inconsistencies in the hand-written text. Some we were unable to determine:
- *ue* in the first phrase might be *ua*
- *falava* in the first question might be *falaua* or *falaoa*.
- *faafefeteina* in the first question might be *fa'afefeteina*.
- *oona* in the third question might be *ōōna* (as in the second).

ABOUT THE LANGUAGE:

Samoan

Number of speakers: 369,957
Rank: 642

Samoan is spoken in Western Samoa. There are also speakers in American Samoa, Fiji, New Zealand, Tonga and the USA.

ABOUT THE TRANSLATOR AND SPEAKER:

Reverend Fàafili Tusani

Age: Unavailable   Recorded: 1996
Town: Apia, Western Samoa

Reverend Tusani is the pastor at the Congregational Christian Church in Sàaga Siumu.

An open-sided community assembly hall in the center of Apia, Western Samoa's capital. Common to every village in Samoa, much of what is social is carried out in these halls

Photos by Barnard Cloutier (berclo.net)

A traditional Samoan house (*fale*) at Tanu Beach on the shore of Savai'i. *Fales* are open to the cool breeze with palm-frond blinds that can be lowered at night. Most Samoans maintain *fales* next to a closed-in house where their household appliances and belongings are kept

Sambal, Tina

Angket hawanin yabi laloma ha halban yabin nakalaba?

■ *Why is this night different from all other nights?*

Hin yaw yabin nakalaba, nangan tamon nin tinapay tan matza; hawanin yabi, matza bungat.

■ *On all other nights we eat either leavened bread or matzah; on this night only matzah.*

Hin yaw yabin nakalaba, kinan tamoy halban klasin kakanin; hawanin yabi, mapait bungat.

■ *On all other nights we eat all kinds of herbs; on this night only bitter herbs.*

Hin yaw yabin nakalaba, kay tamo na misawsaw; hawanin yabi, nagsawsaw tamo nin luway beses.

■ *On all other nights we do not dip even once; on this night we dip twice.*

Hin yaw yabin nakalaba, ampangan tamon ampikno tan ampeQreng; hawanin yabi, ampeQreng bungat.

■ *On all other nights we eat either sitting up or reclining; on this night we recline.*

Hin yaw yabin nakalaba, nangan tamon nin ordinaryong paQmangan; hawanin yabi, mapangan tamon espesyal.

■ *On all other nights we eat in an ordinary manner; on this night we dine with special ceremony.*

Translation note: The Q indicates a glottal stop. Glottal stops are phonemic in most Philippine languages. There is minor variation in sentence structure between the written and the oral version of the text, but semantically they're the same.

ABOUT THE LANGUAGE:

Sambal, Tina

Number of speakers: 70,000
Rank: 1,445

Tina Sambal is spoken in the Philippines, specifically Luzon in the northern Zambales Province.

ABOUT THE TRANSLATOR AND SPEAKER:

Helen Diaz

Age: 62   Recorded: 1998
Towns: Iba, Sambales / Quezon City, Phillipines

Helen is a native speaker of Sambal. She was rasied in Iba, Zambales but now lives in Quezon City. She continues to travel back to Iba twice monthly to attend to her farm.

Photo by Rody Torres

Children's choir in Tondo, Manila. Contribution boxes show month of birthday

Saami, North

Manne lea dát idja earálágán go buot eará ijat?

■ *Why is this night different from all other nights?*

Buot eará ijaid borrat mii juogo suvrutkeahtes láibbi dahje matzah; dán ija dušše matzah.

■ *On all other nights we eat either leavened bread or matzah; on this night only matzah.*

Buot eará ijaid borrat mii juohkelágán dálkkasšattuid; dán ija dušsše bahča dálkkasšattuid.

■ *On all other nights we eat all kinds of herbs; on this night only bitter herbs.*

Buot eará ijaid mii eat buonjo okte ge; dán ija mii buotnjut guktii.

■ *On all other nights we do not dip even once; on this night we dip twice.*

Buot eará ijaid mii borrat čohkkut dahje mieigu; dán ija mieigut.

■ *On all other nights we eat either sitting up or reclining; on this night we recline.*

Buot eará ijaid mii borrat buot eará dábálaš vugiid mielde; dán ija mii boradit árvvuin.

■ *On all other nights we eat in an ordinary manner; on this night we dine with special ceremony.*

Written and recorded versions use *borrat* inconsistently. This represents natural variation in how sentences would be spoken in Saami.

ABOUT THE LANGUAGE:

North Saami

Number of speakers: 20,700
Rank: 2,359

North Saami, also called Northern Lappish, is spoken in Norway's Finnmark, Troms, Nordland and Ofoten regions. Saami is also spoken in Sweden and Finland.

The Saami people live in Arctic regions on all continents: northern Norway, Finland, Canada, Siberia, Alaska, etc. The Saami consider the term Lapp to be derogatory.

ABOUT THE TRANSLATOR AND SPEAKER:

Mai Britt Utsi

Age: Unavailable   Recorded: 1997
Town: Guovdageaidnu, Norway

Mai, a native Saami, lives in Guovdageaidnu, Norway. The Norwegian name for the town is Kautokeino. It is located on the Finnmark plateau, about 200 miles north of the Arctic Circle. The main industry in the area is reindeer herding. The Saami translation was obtained by **Lloyd Binder**, the former Vice President of the Saami Association of North America.

Narvik Norway, the nothern-most spot served by regular rail service anywhere in the world, is 1500 miles from the North Pole and about 175 miles north of the Arctic Circle

Saamia

Eshichira eshiro shino nishiahukhaane nende ebindi biosi nishiina?
- *Why is this night different from all other nights?*

**Mubutukhu bundi bwosi, Khuliitsanga omukaate kubulamwo limera kata matsa;
Mushiro shia leero, eliani lilulu lionyene.**
- *On all other nights we eat either leavened bread or matzah;
on this night only matzah.*

**Mubutukhu bundi bwosi, shikhutonganga kata lulala;
Mushiro shia leero, khutonga khabili.**

**Mubutukhu bundi bwosi, khuliitsanga nikhweemire noho nikhuyeeshire;
Mushiro shia leero, Khuhuluukha.**

**Mubutukhu bundi bwosi, khuliitsanga shinga buli lwosi;
Mushiro shia leero, khwishiera nende lisabo liahukhaane.**

ABOUT THE LANGUAGE:

Saamia

Number of speakers: 335,000
Rank: 670

Saamia (also called Luyia and Luhya) is spoken in the Lake Victoria areas of Kenya and Uganda. The people are called the *Abaluyia*.

ABOUT THE TRANSLATOR AND SPEAKER:

Daniel Wemali

Age: Unavailable   Recorded: 1999
Town: Nairobi, Kenya

Daniel is a language instructor at the ACK Language School in Nairobi. He is a fluent speaker of Saamia.

Photo © Susan Hantman

The translation is incomplete. It is not known which of the last 4 questions is missing. The "b" sound in Saamia is pronounced as "bh" – that is, the speaker should ensure the lips do not meet when making the consonant.

A giraffe in Tsavo National Park, Kenya's largest, and one of the world's largest parks

Russian

Чем отличается эта ночь от всех других ночей?
- Chem otlichayetsya eta noch ot v'sekh drugikh nochay?
- *Why is this night different from all other nights?*

Во все другие ночи мы едим либо квашеный хлеб либо мацу;
а в эту ночь-только мацу.
- Vo v'seh drugiyeh nochi, m'yedim libo kvashenih khleb libo matzu;
  A v'etu noch, tolko matzu.
- *On all other nights we eat either leavened bread or matzah;
  on this night only matzah.*

Во все другие ночи мы едим любую зелень;
а в эту ночь-только горькую.
- Vo v'seh drugiyeh nochi, m'yedim lubuyu zelen;
  A v'etu noch, tolko gorkuyu.
- *On all other nights we eat all kinds of herbs;
  on this night only bitter herbs.*

Во все другие ночи мы вообще не обмакиваем зелени;
а в эту ночь-обмакиваем ее дважды.
- Vo v'seh drugiyeh nochi, m'vobshche ne obmakivaem zelen;
  A v'etu noch, obmakivaem yeyo d'vazhdih.
- *On all other nights we do not dip even once;
  on this night we dip twice.*

Во все другие ночи мы едим сидя или возлегая;
а в эту ночь-возлегая.
- Vo v'seh drugiyeh nochi, m'yedim sidya ili vozlegaya;
  A v'etu noch, vozlegaya.
- *On all other nights we eat either sitting up or reclining;
  on this night we recline.*

Во все другие ночи мы едим обыденно;
а в эту ночь-у нас ритуальная трапеза.
- Vo v'seh drugiyeh nochi, m'yedim obidenno;
  A v'etu noch, u nas rityualihnaya trapeza.
- *On all other nights we eat in an ordinary manner;
  on this night we dine with special ceremony.*

The recording is somewhat different from this text.

ABOUT THE LANGUAGE:

Russian

Number of speakers: 143,553,950
Rank: 8

Russian is spoken throughout the former republics of the USSR and in over 30 other countries.

Until the 17th C, the only written language in Russia was (Old) Church Slavonic. Russian started appearing in writing during the reign of Peter the Great (1672-1725) who introduced a revised Cyrillic alphabet still used today.

ABOUT THE TRANSLATOR AND SPEAKER:

Alex Gelman

Age: 50s   Recorded: 1996
Towns: Chernovtsy, Ukraine / Brooklyn, NY

Dr. Gelman was born in Chernovtsy, western Ukraine, northern Bukovina. He is a world-renowned communications engineer. Alex is Vice President of the Communication Society of IEEE. Most of the translation text is traditional. **Helen Blum, Valerie Rose Grier** and **Liliya Krasner** made corrections.

Photo © Barry Hantman

St. Petersburg's famous Hermitage Art Museum – home to 3 million works of art

Romansch

Pertgei ei questa notg differenta da tut las autras notgs?

■ *Why is this night different from all other nights?*

Tut las autras notgs magliein nus paun cun levon u matzah; questa notg mo matzah.

■ *On all other nights we eat either leavened bread or matzah; on this night only matzah.*

Tut las autras notgs magliein nus tuttas sorts jarvas; questa notg specialmein jarvas petras.

■ *On all other nights we eat all kinds of herbs; on this night only bitter herbs.*

Tut las autras notgs bugnein nus buca las jarvas; questa notg bugnein nus ellas duas ga.

■ *On all other nights we do not dip even once; on this night we dip twice.*

Tut las autras notgs magliein nus sesond sidretg u sepusond; questa notg sepusein nus.

■ *On all other nights we eat either sitting up or reclining; on this night we recline.*

Tut las autras notgs magliein nus en maniera ordinaria; questa notg tschenein nus cun ceremonia speciala.

■ *On all other nights we eat in an ordinary manner; on this night we dine with special ceremony.*

ABOUT THE LANGUAGE:

Romansch

Number of speakers: 35,100
Rank: 1,916

Romansch, also called Rheto-Romance, is spoken near the common borders of Switzerland, Austria and Italy. Within Switzerland, Romansch is located in Graubünden Canton, Grisons valley of Surselva, valley of Voderrhein, Engadin and Val Mustair in southeast Switzerland.

Rheto-Romance (Rhaeto-Romanic) is a collective term for 3 languages in the Romance family spoken in northeast Italy and southeast Switzerland. In Switzerland, it is known as Romontsch and is one of the 4 official languages of the country. In Italy it is considered a patois and has no official status (the Italian variants are called Friulian and Ladin).

Photo © Susan Hantman

The 16th C *Zytgloggeturm* (clock tower) in Bern, Switzerland features a clockwork display including a jester ringing bells and a procession of bears

ABOUT THE TRANSLATOR AND SPEAKER:

Frank Roos

Age: Unavailable   Recorded: 1996
Town: Zürich, Switzerland

Frank speaks the Sursilvan dialect, one of the varieties of Romansch.

Romanian

De ce este aceastã noapte diferitã de toate noptile?
- de ce este a:tʃe'astə: ŋoa:'pte di:feri'tə de twa:'te 'ŋoptzile?
- *Why is this night different from all other nights?*

In toate nopţile, mâncãm fie pâine, fie pitã.
In aceastã noapte, mâncãm numai pitã.
- ən twa:'te 'ŋop'tzile, məŋ'kə:m fi:e 'pə:iŋe fi:e pitə
  ən a:tʃe'astə: nwa:pte məŋ'kə:m nou:mai pitə
- *On all other nights we eat either leavened bread or matzah; on this night only matzah.*

In toate nopţile, mâncãm tot felul de ierburi.
in aceastã noapte, mâncãm numai ierburi tãmãduitoare.
- ən twa:'te 'ŋop'tzile, məŋ'kə:m to:t fʲeəlul de iərbu:ri
  ən a:tʃe'astə: nwa:pte, məŋ'kə:m nou:mai iərbu:ri t'ə:mə:du'itoa:re
- *On all other nights we eat all kinds of herbs; on this night only bitter herbs.*

In toate nopţile, nu dumicãm nici mãcar odatã.
în aceastã noapte, ne-am sãturat.
- ən twa:'te 'ŋop'tzile, nu du:mikəm nitʃi məŋcəm odat
  ən a:tʃe'astə: nwa:pte, ne'am səturat
- *On all other nights we do not dip even once; on this night we dip twice.*

In toate nopţile, mâncãm fie stând în picioare fie stând jos.
în aceasta noapte, mâncãm stând pe scaune.
- ən twa:'te 'ŋop'tzile, məŋ'kə:m fi:e stəŋd ən pitʃwa:re fi:e stəŋd djoθ
  ən a:tʃe'astə: nwa:pte, məŋ'kə:m stəŋd pe scaune
- *On all other nights we eat either sitting up or reclining; on this night we recline.*

In toate nopţile, mâncãm într-o manierã urâtã.
în aceastã noapte, cinãm festiv.
- ən twa:'te 'ŋop'tzile, məŋ'kə:m əntr-o: manierə urətə:
  ən a:tʃe'astə: nwa:pte, tʃinəm festiv
- *On all other nights we eat in an ordinary manner; on this night we dine with special ceremony.*

Dracula's Castle
(*Cetatea Poienari*)

ABOUT THE LANGUAGE:

Romanian

Number of speakers: 23,351,080
Rank: 45

Romanian is the national language of Romania. Other countries with major populations speaking Romanian are Moldova, Ukraine, Yugoslavia, Israel and Hungary. Romanian has considerable vocabulary with Italian, French, Sardinian, Catalan, Portuguese, Rheto-Romance and Spanish.

ABOUT THE TRANSLATOR AND SPEAKER:

Valeriu Rusu

Age: 61   Recorded: 1996
Towns: Mihaileanca-Hotin / Bucharest, Romania / Aix-en-Provence, France

Dr. Valeriu Rusu was born in Mihaileanca-Hotin, lived and worked in Bucharest until, at age 48, he left for France as a political refugee. He was a Professor of Romanian (currently Professor Emeritus) at the University of Provence. The transcription uses the IPA (International Phonetic Alphabet); explanations of IPA are available on many web pages.

Brasov Synagogue, built in 1901

Photos © Barry Hantman

Romani

Anda soste či mjazol e rjat e kadja sa'l aver rjat?
- *Why is this night different from all other nights?*

Pe sa'l aver rjat, xas amenge vaj manrro vaj bokoli;
Pe kadja rjat, numaj e bokoli xas.
- *On all other nights we eat either leavened bread or matzah;*
  on this night only matzah.

Pe sa'l aver rjat, sa fjalurja zelenimata xas amenge;
Pe kadja rjat, ferdi e kerke patrinja.
- *On all other nights we eat all kinds of herbs;*
  on this night only bitter herbs.

Pe sa'l aver rjat, daži či boldas and'o lon jekhvar;
Pe kadja rjat, duvar boldas ame.
- *On all other nights we do not dip even once;*
  on this night we dip twice.

Pe sa'l aver rjat, šaj bešas te pravaras amenge, vaj pašljovas;
Pe kadja rjat, pašljovas ame.
- *On all other nights we eat either sitting up or reclining;*
  on this night we recline.

Pe sa'l aver rjat, prostones xas amenge;
Pe kadja rjat, rajalo kidipe si.
- *On all other nights we eat in an ordinary manner;*
  on this night we dine with special ceremony.

ABOUT THE TRANSLATOR AND SPEAKER:

Ian Hancock

Age: Unavailable   Recorded: 1996
Towns: London, England / Austin, TX

Dr. Hancock is Professor of English and Linguistics at the University of Texas. A native Rom and native speaker of Vlax Romani, Ian was the United Nations representative for Roma. He also has been an activist in the local Romani/Jewish alliance as well as many other human rights organizations. His father's family were Hungarian Roma; his mother's family were Romanichal.

Roma woman
in Târgu Mureș,
Romania

ABOUT THE LANGUAGE:

Romani, Vlax

Number of speakers: 885,970
Rank: 393

Romani is the language of the Rom or Roma people, originating from Romania. (Gypsy is now considered a derogatory term.) Romani is spoken in 27 countries, with the largest numbers in Albania, Colombia, France, Russia, Germany, Poland and Italy. Vlax developed from the Romani spoken when they were slaves in Romania for 500 years. There were migrations out of Romania from the mid-14th to mid-19th centuries. Those who left earlier have less Romanian influence in their dialects. Each of the 20 or so dialects share lexical similarities with the dominant language, e.g. Kalderash and Russian, Lovari and Hungarian, Grekurja and Turkish.

Traditionally, the Roma were isolated peoples, experienced in music and arts, viewed as being somewhat mystical and different. The Roma were persecuted and slaughtered along with the Jews by the Nazis during World War II.

Spread across the world from India to the British Isles, the Roma united the first time at an International Romani conference in 1971. There the Roma adopted a flag and an anthem. They have been credited with the origins of Klezmer, Flamenco and Django music.

Quechua, South Bolivian

Translated from Spanish

Imaj key tuta mana shaq'ay wakin tutas jinachu?

■ *¿Por qué es diferente esta noche de todas las otras noches?*

Sapa tuta centenumanta th'antata miq'unchaj; cunan tutaq'a matzahllata.

■ *En todas las otras noches comemos pan hecho con levadura o pan ázimo; en esta noche solamente matzah.*

Sapa tuta imasta miqh'unchaj; cunan tutaq'a jaya qh'opallata.

■ *En todas las otras noches comemos todas clases de hierbas; en esta noche comemos hierbas amargas.*

Sapa tuta mana chulluchinchajchu qh'opataqa; cunan tutaq'a chulluchisunchaj iscay qutimanta.

■ *En todas las otras noches no sumergimos las hierbas de ninguna manera; en esta noche las sumergimos dos veces.*

Sapa tuta tiyaspa sirispa miqh'unchaj; cunan tutaq'a tucuy sirispalla kash'anchaj.

■ *En todas las otras noches comemos sentados rectos o inclinados; en esta noche nos sentamos inclinados.*

Sapa tuta miqh'unchaj imatapis; keytutaq'a jain Pachajpaj jina miqh'usunchaj.

■ *En todas las otras noches comemos de manera ordinaria; en esta noche comemos con ceremonia especial.*

ABOUT THE LANGUAGE:

Quechua, South Bolivian

Number of speakers: 3,635,000
Rank: 163

South Bolivian Quechua, an official language of Bolivia, is spoken through the highland and lowland regions except around Apolo. It is also spoken in Buenos Aires and Salta Province in Argentina.

Quechua Bolivians near the border with Peru playing music

Photo by Stephanie Goldhuber

ABOUT THE TRANSLATOR AND SPEAKER:

Desiderio Arce

Age: Unknown   Recorded: 1996
Town: Salta, Argentina

Desiderio was reached through his son, **Antonio Arce** in Provo, UT and **Brenda Francis** in Orem, UT. A translation was also worked on by **Roger Jefferson** of Columbia, OH.

Quechua, Napo Lowland

Translated from Spanish

Imarasha cay tuta shutuno tucun mana maican tuta cuenta?

■ *¿Por qué es diferente esta noche de todas las otras noches?*

Tucui shutu ta micunchi tandara o lumo palara;
cay tutai cailliara micunchi lumo palara.

■ *En todas las otras noches comemos pan hecho con levadura o pan ázimo;*
en esta noche solamente matzah.

Tucui shutu ta micunchi tucui panga cunara;
cay tutai cailliara micunchi ayag quihuara.

■ *En todas las otras noches comemos todas clases de hierbas;*
en esta noche comemos hierbas amargas.

Tucui shutu ta micunchi mana munanchicho mana shuguio quihua cunara;
cay tutai cailliara micunchi yacuma saguinche isgui cuti.

■ *En todas las otras noches no sumergimos las hierbas de ninguna manera;*
en esta noche las sumergimos dos veces.

Tucui shutu ta micunchi tiarisha recto o quimirisha;
cay tutai cailliara micunchi tiarisha quimirisha.

■ *En todas las otras noches comemos sentados rectos o inclinados;*
en esta noche nos sentamos inclinados.

Tucui shutu ta micunchi ima mumashcaros icuna ima shituaras;
cay tutai cailliara micunchi ashca valig cunara.

■ *En todas las otras noches comemos de manera ordinaria;*
en esta noche comemos con ceremonia especial.

ABOUT THE LANGUAGE:

Napo Lowland Quechua

Number of speakers: 14,000
Rank: 2,745

Napo Lowland Quechua is spoken in Ecuador's
Napo River Region and on the Putumayo river.
Some speakers were moved to Madre de Dios.
Napo Lowland Quechua is also spoken in
Colombia and Ecuador.

ABOUT THE TRANSLATOR AND SPEAKER:

Venancio Chimbo

Age: 43   Recorded: 2000
Town: San Pablo De Kantesteya, Ecuador

Venancio was born and raised in San Pablo De Kantesteya, a
village on Aguarico River in El Oriente (Ecuador's Jungle region).
Venancio works as an indigenous jungle guide for the Orientgal
Agency. The text was written phonetically by **Neiser**, tour leader
for Orientgal, with translation guidance from **Jim Weintraub**.

**Venancio Chimbo (in green shirt) translating text
with Neiser in hut located in Ecuador's El Oriente**

Quechua, Huanca

¿Imapiqmi kay tuta mana llapa tutakunanawllachu?

■ *Why is this night different from all other nights?*

Wakin tutakuna, qunchuchashqa tantakta ichaqa mana qunchuchashqa tantaktam mikunchik;
kanan tutañatak mana qunchuchashqa tantallakta.

■ *On all other nights we eat either leavened bread or matzah;*
on this night only matzah.

Wakin tutakuna, llapa lichka mishki ashnaniyuq qulakunaktam mikunchik;
kanan tutañatak trakta qulakunallakta.

■ *On all other nights we eat all kinds of herbs;*
on this night only bitter herbs.

Wakin tutakuna, manam huk kutillaktapis shatilkul pushkaykachinchikchu;
kanan tutañatak ishkay kutikta.

■ *On all other nights we do not dip even once;*
on this night we dip twice.

Wakin tutakuna, umanchik pallakushqa, tikshuypa tikshushqa taakukulmI mikunchik;
kanan tutañatak tikshuypa tikshushqalla taakukunchik.

■ *On all other nights we eat either sitting up or reclining;*
on this night we recline.

Wakin tutakuna, imanawllappis mikunchik;
kay tutañatak Mama Pachakta mañakushtinnilaq mikunchik.

■ *On all other nights we eat in an ordinary manner;*
on this night we dine with special ceremony.

ABOUT THE TRANSLATOR AND SPEAKER:

Serafín Coronel-Molina

Age: Unknown   Recorded: 1996
Locations: Huancayo/ Lima, Peru / Claremont, CA / Drexel Hill, PA

Serafín's mother tongue was Huanca, the language of his hometown.
He was educated at the University of Pennsylvania's Doctoral
program in Educational Linguistics.

ABOUT THE LANGUAGE:

Quechua, Huanca

Number of speakers: 250,000
Rank: 791

Huanca Quechua, also called Huaylla
Wanca Quechua, is spoken in Peru's
southern Junín Department, Huancayo
and Concepción provinces. It is an
official language of Peru.

Street scene in Pisac, Peru

Photo by Tom Judd

Quechua, Cuzco

Translated from Spanish

Imanaqtinmi kay tuta wakin tutakunamanta huk niray?

■ *Por que es esta noche diferente a todas las otras noches?*

Wakin tutakunaqa ta`tanta (matsahta) mikhunchis;
kay tutataq matsahllata.

■ *Todas las otras noches comemos pan con levadura o matzah;*
esta noche solo matzah.

Wakin tutakunaqa imaymana qurakunata mihunchis;
kunan tutataq haya qurakunallata.

■ *Todas las otras noches comemos todo tipo de hierbas;*
esta noche solo hierbas amargas.

Sapa tutakunan mihunata mana unuman challpuspa mikhunchis;
kunan tutaqa iskay kutitan ruranchis.

■ *Todas las otras noches no sumerjimos la comida en agua;*
esta noche lo hacemos dos veces.

Sapa tutakunan tiyaspa mana hinaqa qunqurisqa mikhunchis;
kunan tutaqa qunqurchasqa.

■ *Todas las otras noches comemos sentados o reclinados;*
esta noche lo hacemos reclinados.

Wakin tutakunaqa imayna mikhunallanchistan mikhunchis;
kay tutaqa saminchasqa huñunakuypin mikhunchis.

■ *Todas las otras noches comemos de manera comun;*
esta noche comemos con una ceremonia especial.

ABOUT THE LANGUAGE:

Cuzco Quechua

Number of speakers: 1,500,000
Rank: 280

One of the official languages of Peru, Cuzco Quechua (also called Cusco Quechua) is spoken in the Departments of Cusco, half of Puno, and northeast Arequipa. As one of the official languages of Peru, Cuzco is taught in the schools.

ABOUT THE TRANSLATOR AND SPEAKER:

Hipolito Peralta Ccama

Age: Unavailable   Recorded: 2010
Town: Cuzco, Peru

Hipolito lives in Cuzco.

Photo by Christophe Meneboeuf.
Provided under Creative Commons Attribution-Share Alike 2.5 Generic License

The main square of Cuzco - this location marked the very center of the Incan Empire

Quechua, Ayacucho

¿Imanasqataq kay tuta mana tukuy tutakuna hinallachu?
- *Why is this night different from all other nights?*

Wakin tutakuna, qunchuchasqa tantata ichaqa mana qunchuchasqa tantatam mikunchik;
kunan tutañataq mana qunchuchasqa tantallata.
- *On all other nights we eat either leavened bread or matzah;*
  on this night only matzah.

Wakin tutakuna, imaymana miski asnaniyuq qurakunata mikunchik;
kunan tutañataq haya qurakunallata.
- *On all other nights we eat all kinds of herbs;*
  on this night only bitter herbs.

Wakin tutakuna, manam huk kutillatapis chulluykachinchikchu;
kunan tutañataq iskay kutita.
- *On all other nights we do not dip even once;*
  on this night we dip twice.

Wakin tutakuna, umanchik pallakusqapas, wikchusqa tiyaspapas mikunchik;
kunan tutañataq wikchusqa tiyaspalla.
- *On all other nights we eat either sitting up or reclining;*
  on this night we recline.

Wakin tutakuna, imallatapas mikunchik;
kunan tutañataq Mama Pachata mañakustin hina mikunchik.
- *On all other nights we eat in an ordinary manner;*
  on this night we dine with special ceremony.

ABOUT THE LANGUAGE:

Quechua, Ayacucho

Number of speakers: 900,000
Rank: 389

Ayacucho Quechua, an official language of Peru, is spoken in the southwestern Ayacucho Region and in Lima. It is sometimes called Runasimi or Chanka by its speakers.

ABOUT THE TRANSLATOR AND SPEAKER:

Serafin Coronel-Molina

Age: Unknown   Recorded: 1996
Towns: Huancayo/ Lima, Peru / Claremont, CA / Drexel Hill, PA

Serafin was educated at the University of Pennsylvania's Doctoral program in Educational Linguistics. Although Serafin's mother tongue was Huanca, when he lived in Lima (from age 10 until college age), he learned Ayacucho from friends who had lived there. He also studied it at the University for one year and considers that he has native fluency.

Photo by Tom Judd

Native villagers in Willoq, Peru

Q'eqchi'

Cau't na'ak he coutink hain ha'la'n tchi pu xunil leb xcomon?

■ *Why is this night different from all other nights?*

Chiru xunil coutink na ka cua'k cau cuank xtubil;
ha coutink ha'in k'a cua'k maka xtubil.

■ *On all other nights we eat either leavened bread or matzah;*
on this night only matzah.

Xunileb coutink na ka cuak he'b yalak chank ru pim;
ha coutink ha'in cahwi ca'ah pim.

■ *On all other nights we eat all kinds of herbs;*
on this night only bitter herbs.

Xunileb coutink no co tzahok ma hun sut;
ha coutink ha'in nabal sut no co'h tzahok.

■ *On all other nights we do not dip even once;*
on this night we dip twice.

Xunileb coutink no co cua se'xtalalil;
ha coutink ha'in no co cua chi ty'octyo.

■ *On all other nights we eat either sitting up or reclining;*
on this night we recline.

Xunileb coutink no co cua cama na ca' banu rahlal;
ha coutink ha'in no co cua se nim xcuanki.

■ *On all other nights we eat in an ordinary manner;*
on this night we dine with special ceremony.

ABOUT THE LANGUAGE:

Q'eqchi'

Number of speakers: 423,500
Rank: 591

Q'eqchi', also called Kekchi, Quecchí and
Cacché, is spoken in Guatemala and Belize.
Most speakers in Guatemala are in northern
Alta Verapaz and southern Petén departments.
There are also some speakers in El Salvador.

ABOUT THE TRANSLATOR AND SPEAKER:

Justo Kib

Age: 22   Recorded: 1999
Town: Maya Center, Belize

Justo is fluent in Q'eqchi', Mopan, Spanish and
knows some English. He is a waiter at the
Sand Box, a well known restaurant in Caye
Caulker, Belize.

1988 map of Q'eqchi' and Mopan
villages in Belize, compiled by R
Wik and M Chapin (Care of Cultural
Survival Quarterly, Summer 1995)

Q'eqchi' speakers in Sayache, Guatemala

Photo by Don Kissil

Built in 1552, La Merced (Lady of Mercy
Church) in Antigua, Guatemala is a
striking example of colonial architecture.
The *churrigueresque* decoration (an
exuberantly ornamental phase of
Spanish decoration) was applied in the
19th C and includes massive columns
and statues of saints in its niches

Pulaar

Translated from French

Ko hondun sindi o djemma e dhiya dyemmadyi?

■ *Pourquoi cette soirée se distingue-t-elle des autres soirées?*

Dhiya dyemmadyi *fow*, hidhen gnama bireedi wondhudhun e ewen,
si wanadhum, bireedi ko aldaa e lewen;
o dyemma, ko gnametin, ko bireedi mo aldaa e lewen.

■ *Tous les autres soirs nous pouvons manger du pain levé ou du pain azyme;*
ce soir seulement du pain azyme.

Dhiya dyemmadyi *fow*, hidhen gnama kudhi none ma e none;
o dyemma, en gnami wo kudhi hadhudi.

■ *Tous les autres soirs nous pouvons manger toutes sortes d'herbes;*
ce soir seulement des herbes amères.

Dhiya dyemmadyi *fow*, haye en bhubhinta nde wootere;
o dyemma, en bhubinay labhi dhidhi.

■ *Tous les autres soirs nous ne trempons pas la nourriture même pas une fois;*
ce soir nous trempons deux fois.

Dhiya dyemmadyi *fow*, en gnamay hidhen dyodhi ma hara hidhen fottyi;
o dyemma, en fotyoto.

■ *Tous les autres soirs nous mangeons assis droit ou accoudés;*
ce soir accoudés seulement.

Dhiya dyemmadyi *fow*, hidhen gnama no wowirnodhen non;
o dyemma, en hirtoto wasiko haadyu keldhudho.

■ *Tous les autres soirs nous mangeons de manière ordinaire;*
ce soir nous mangeons de manière spéciale.

Translation notes: Rebecca capitalized *fow* to show the word's emphasis, as in ON EVERY OTHER NIGHT WITHOUT EXCEPTION EVER. The authors chose to use italics to accomplish the same thing.

Soulymane ends his recording with his name and the name of the language, spoken in Pulaar and French.

ABOUT THE LANGUAGE:

Pulaar

Number of speakers: 3,691,000
Rank: 161

Pulaar (also called Fulfulde and Fuuta Jalon) is a language of Senegal. It is spoken in the Senegal River Valley and Mauritania, Upper Casamance Region, from 40 miles west of Kolda to the headwaters of the Gambia River in the east, from the southern border of Senegal in the south to the Gambian border in the north. It is also spoken in Gambia, Guinea, Guinea-Bissau, Mali and Mauritania.

Pulaar does not have a standardized spelling system.

ABOUT THE TRANSLATOR AND SPEAKER:

Souleymane Bah

Age: Unavailable   Recorded: 2000
Towns: Pita / Conakry, Guinea

Souleymane is a native speaker of Pulaar. He was born and raised in Pita and now lives in the capital city, Conakry. The translation was modified slightly by linguist **Rebecca Camara**.

Photo by Boris Kester

The beautiful island of Gorée, near Dakar Senegal

Provençal

Per que aquesto serado es diferento dis autri serado?

■ *Why is this night different from all other nights?*

Touti lis autri sero pouden manja de pan leva o de pan azime; aquest sero soulament de pan azime.

■ *On all other nights we eat either leavened bread or matzah; on this night only matzah.*

Touti lis autri sero pouden manja touto meno d'erbo; aquest sero soulament d'erbo amaro.

■ *On all other nights we eat all kinds of herbs; on this night only bitter herbs.*

Touti lis autri sero bagnan pas lou manja, pas manco un copi; aquest sero bagnan dous cop.

■ *On all other nights we do not dip even once; on this night we dip twice.*

Touti lis autri sero manjan asseta, dre o acouida; aquest sero acouida soulament.

■ *On all other nights we eat either sitting up or reclining; on this night we recline.*

Touti lis autri sero manjan d'un biais simple; aquest sero fasen uno ceremòni especialo.

■ *On all other nights we eat in an ordinary manner; on this night we dine with special ceremony.*

Illustrated Order of the Seder from the *Machanayim* Haggadah, based on the Avignon Haggadah. Avignon is the heart of France's Provence region

ABOUT THE LANGUAGE:

Provençal

Number of speakers: 147,000
Rank: 1,033

Provençal (Franco-Proveçal) is spoken in southeastern France, province of Provence, south of Dauphiné and the region of Nimes in Languedoc. It is also spoken in Italy and Monaco. There are many dialects, none of which are universally accepted as the standard form. Some linguists feel Provençal is a dialect of Occitan, while others classify them as separate languages.

Occitan began to appear in writing during the 10th C and was used particularly to write the poetry of troubadours. When France was unified in the 15th C, Occitan and other regional languages went into decline. Its revival is largely credited to the Provençal poet Frédéric Mistal (1830-1914), who was awarded the Nobel Prize for Literature.

ABOUT THE TRANSLATOR AND SPEAKER:

Claude Mauron

Age: Unavailable   Recorded: 1996
Town: Aix-en-Provence, France

Dr. Mauron is Professor of Linguistics at l'Université de Provence, Aix-en-Provence. He received his doctorate in Linguistics in 1989 at the Sorbonne in Paris. Claude's area of expertise is the language of literature of Provençal.

Photo by Gheorghe Alexe

The coast of Provence

Portuguese

Porque é esta noite diferente de todas as outras noites?

■ *Why is this night different from all other nights?*

Em todas as outras noites comemos paõ fermentado e matzah; nesta noite só comemos matzah.

■ *On all other nights we eat either leavened bread or matzah; on this night only matzah.*

Em todas as outras noites comemos ervas de todo tipo; nesta noite só comemos ervas amargas.

■ *On all other nights we eat all kinds of herbs; on this night only bitter herbs.*

Em todas as outras noites naõ imergimos nem uma vez; nesta noite imergimos duas vezês.

■ *On all other nights we do not dip even once; on this night we dip twice.*

Em todas as outras noites comemos sentados ou reclinados; nesta noite estamos todos reclinados.

■ *On all other nights we eat either sitting up or reclining; on this night we recline.*

Em todas as outras noites comemos de manera ordinario; nesta noite comemos con ceremonia especial.

■ *On all other nights we eat in an ordinary manner; on this night we dine with special ceremony.*

> The recorded version differs somewhat from the text shown here.

Photo by Tom Judd

Fishing boats in Trafaria, Portugal

ABOUT THE TRANSLATOR AND SPEAKER:

Chaim Litewski

Age: Unavailable   Recorded: 1999
Towns: Rio de Janeiro, Brazil / New York, NY

Chaim was raised in Rio De Janeiro. He moved to New York and works at the United Nations. Another version was worked on by an Israeli named **Issar** who lived in Brazil for many years.

ABOUT THE LANGUAGE:

Portuguese

Number of speakers: 163,000,000
Rank: 7

Portuguese is the national language of Portugal (primarily spoken in Iberia, Azores and Madeira) and is the language of Brazil. It is also the official language of Angola, Cape Verde Islands, East Timor, Guinea-Bissau, Mozambique and São Tomé. There are significant numbers of speakers in France and two dozen other countries.

The common ancestor of Portuguese and Galician first appeared in writing in the late 12th C. The two began to grow apart in the 14th C. By the 16th C, Portuguese probably sounded very much as it does today. Spelling reforms in Portugal (1916) and Brazil (1943 and 1970) brought Portuguese's spelling into closer conformance with its pronunciation.

Pontic Greek

Translated from Greek

Για τόπιον αβούτο η νύχτα εν αλλοιώτικον ας όλε τ'άλλα νύχτας;
- Γιατί αυτή η νύχτα είναι διαφορετική από όλες τις άλλες νύχτες;

Όλε τ'άλλα νύχτας τρώμε ζυμωμένον ψωμίν ή "μάτσα"·
αβούτο τη νύχταν μόνον "μάτσα".
- Όλες τις άλλες νύχτες τρώμε ξυμωμένο ψωμί ή "μάτσα"·
αυτή τη νύχτα μόνο μάτσα.

Όλε τ'άλλα νύχτας τρώμε όλων των λογιών μυρωδικά·
αβούτο τη νύχταν μόνον πικρά μυρωδικά.
- Όλες τις άλλες νύχτες τρώμε κάθε λογής μυρωδικά·
αυτή τη νύχτα μόνο πικρά μυρωδικά.

Όλε τ'άλλα νύχτας κι βουτούμε·
αβούτο τη νύχταν βουτούμε δύο φοράς.
- Όλες τις άλλες νύχτες δεν βουτάμε·
αυτή τη νύχτα βουτάμε δύο φορές.

Όλε τ'άλλα νύχτας τρώμε ίσα ή γερτά·
αβούτο τη νύχταν μόνο γερτά.
- Όλες τις άλλες νύχτες τρώμε ίσια ή γυρτά·
αυτή τη νύχτα μόνο γυρτά.

ABOUT THE LANGUAGE:

Pontic Greek

Number of speakers: 324,540
Rank: 680

Pontic is spoken in Greece, primarily in Salonica and the rest of Macedonia in Greece. Pontic is also spoken in Azerbaijan, Canada, Georgia, Kazakhstan, USA and perhaps Turkey's Black Sea coast. Speakers in the USA are reputed to hold onto their language even more zealously than those in Greece. Pontic was brought to Greece by immigrants from the Black Sea coast in the 1920s and 1930s.

ABOUT THE TRANSLATOR AND SPEAKER:

Elisavet Pliakas

Age: 55   Recorded: 2004
Towns: Thessaloniki, Greece / Astoria, Queens, NY

Elisavet was born in Thessaloniki (Salonica), Greece. Pontic is her first language.

In the recordings: Elisavet ends her recording with her name and the name of the language, spoken in Pontic. The punctuation is correct: Greek uses a semicolon to represent a question mark and a raised dot for commas.

Pontic costumes from the Black Sea and Asia Minor areas.
Photos courtesy of Yiannis Amarantidis, who is shown seated on the left

Polish

Dlaczego ta noc jest inna od każdej nocy?
- Dlachego ta nots yest inna od kazhday notsih?
- *Why is this night different from all other nights?*

**W każdą inną noc jemy dozwolny chleb lub macę;
w tą noc jemy tylko macę.**
- Fkazhdõ innõ nots yemih dozvolnih Hlep loop matseh;
ftõ nots yemih tilko matseh.
- *On all other nights we eat either leavened bread or matzah;
on this night only matzah.*

**W każdą inną noc jemy różne zioła;
ale w tą noc jemy tylko gorzkie zioła.**
- Fkazhdõ innõ nots yemih roozhneh zyowa;
aleh ftõ nots yemih tilko gozhkyeh zyowa.
- *On all other nights we eat all kinds of herbs;
on this night only bitter herbs.*

**W każdą inną noc my nie niezanurzamy nawet jeden raz;
ale w tą noc zanurzamy dwa razy.**
- Fkazhdõ innõ nots may nyeh nyehzanoozhamih navet yeden raz;
aleh ftõ nots zanoozhamih dva razih.
- *On all other nights we do not dip even once;
on this night we dip twice.*

**W każdą inną noc jemy siedząc prosto albo się pochylamy;
ale w tą noc pochylamy się.**
- Fkazhdõ innõ nots yemih syedõts prosto albo syeh poHilamih;
aleh ftõ nots poHilamih syeh.
- *On all other nights we eat either sitting up or reclining;
on this night we recline.*

**W każdą inną noc jemy w sposób zwyczajny;
ale w tą noc jemy ze specjalną ceremonią.**
- Fkazhdõ innõ nots yemih fsposoop zvichĩnih;
aleh ftõ nots yemih ze spetsyalnõ tseremoniõ.
- *On all other nights we eat in an ordinary manner;
on this night we dine with special ceremony.*

Note: The recording differs considerably from the translation shown here, for instance using the word for evening rather than for night.

Z Y X W V U T S R Q **P** O N M L K J I H G F E D C B A

ABOUT THE LANGUAGE:

Polish

Number of speakers: 39,990,670
Rank: 27

Polish, called Polski by its speakers, is the national language of Poland. It is also spoken in 20 other countries, primarily Germany, Israel, Czech Republic, Slovakia and Romania.

Polish first appeared in writing in 1136 in the *"Gniezno papal bull"*, which included 410 Polish names. The first Polish sentence appeared in *Ksiega henrykowska* in 1270.

Pronunciation notes: All consonants pronounced, even in clusters like *ftsaleh*. Stress is always on the next-to-last syllable.
a: as in "father"
ay: as in "day"
e, eh: e of "bet" (eh used at end of word for clarity)
i, ih: i of "bit" (ih used at end of word for clarity)
ĩ: long i, as in "my"
o: short, pure "oh", similar to 'o' in "more" without the "r" sound
oo: between "boot" and "book"
õ: nasal vowel, as in French
ch: as in "church"
H: strong h, close to German 'ch' (as in Bach)
y: always as in "yes", even after consonants (*gozhkyeh, syeh*)
zh: s in "treasure"

ABOUT THE SPEAKER:

Anna Janowska

Age: Unavailable   Recorded: 1999
Towns: Warsaw, Poland / New York, NY

Anna grew up in Warsaw. She currently lives in New York City and works at the United Nations. Translations or corrections were provided by **Maria Tokarz, Malgorzata Wojtaszek Legnica** and **Ruth Manor**. The transliteration was created by linguist **Dan Kahn** from rudimentary knowledge of Polish.

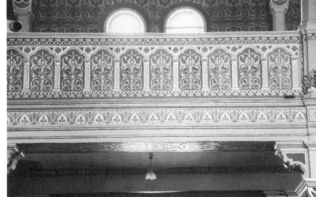

Detail of Synagogue balcony in Krakow's *Kazimierz* district

Pitcairn

Footay night nor semes hem other one?

■ *Why is this night different from all other nights?*

Hem odder night we una eat leavened bread or matzawa bread;
On dis night, only matzawa.

■ *On all other nights we eat either leavened bread or matzah;*
  on this night only matzah.

Hem odder night we eat em odder kinds o herbs too;
On dis night, we una eat hem bitter kine.

■ *On all other nights we eat all kinds of herbs;*
  on this night only bitter herbs.

Hem odder night we no dip any;
Dis night, we una dip two time.

■ *On all other nights we do not dip even once;*
  on this night we dip twice.

Hem odder night we una eat sittin up;
Des time, we lay down.

■ *On all other nights we eat either sitting up or reclining;*
  on this night we recline.

Hem odder night we eat same as all dem odder time;
On dis night, we eat samaza big bug.

■ we eat all dressed up.

■ *On all other nights we eat in an ordinary manner;*
  on this night we dine with special ceremony.

Ray Young (left) at Christian's Cave on Pitcairn Island,
where Fletcher Christian went when he wanted solitude

Used with perminssion of Amanda Young

ABOUT THE LANGUAGE:

Pitcairn

Number of speakers: 436
Rank: 5,611

Pitcairn (also called Pitcairn-Norfolk) is spoken in Pitcairn and Norfolk Islands, in Australia and New Zealand. Pitcairn arose from the Pidgin English the sailors on the HMS Bounty developed to communicate with the Tahitian peoples. After their mutiny from Captain Bligh's command, the sailors' primary mode of communication with the Tahitians was the Pidgin language. After the landing on Pitcairn in 1790, this pidgin developed into the Pitkern Language (later spelled Pitcairn) spoken today. While the primary language of Pitcairn is English, Pitcairn is commonly used in informal conversation among the Pitcairners.

The sailors chose the island to hide because it had been charted incorrectly by other sailors several years earlier. The island was so remote it took 18 years for a ship to discover their hideout. To this day, Pitcairn has no paved roads, no sewage system and no land-line telephones.

ABOUT THE TRANSLATOR AND SPEAKER:

Ray Young

Age: 81   Recorded: 1998
Towns: Pitcairn Island / Tauranga, New Zealand.

Ray was born on Pitcairn Island and joined the Merchant Navy between the ages of 18 and 20. At the time of the translation, Ray lived in Tauranga, New Zealand. There is no official written form of the language, as it is used only for informal communication. The recording was transcribed by Ray's granddaughter, **Amanda Young Gay**. She said all translations are quite inexact, since the language consists mostly of slang phrases. Ray is a direct descendant of Edward Young, who along with Fletcher Christian, was one of the two main HMS Bounty mutineers. Ray died a few years after doing the translation.

Pipil

Translated from Hebrew and English

Taika te kenha ini tayua ken muchi ne tajtayua?

■ Why is this night not the same as all the nights?

■ מַה נִּשְׁתַּנָּה הַלַּיְלָה הַזֶּה מִכָּל הַלֵּילוֹת?

Ka muchi ne tajtayua tejemet tikwat pan wan matzaj;
tik ini tayua muchi matzaj.

■ For all the nights we eat "pan" and matzah;
on this night all matzah.

■ שֶׁבְּכָל הַלֵּילוֹת אָנוּ אוֹכְלִין חָמֵץ וּמַצָּה.
הַלַּיְלָה הַזֶּה כֻּלּוֹ מַצָּה:

Ka muchi ne tajtayua tejemet tikwat muchi ne kijkilit;
tik ini tayua, chichik.

■ For all the nights we eat all the greens;
on this night, bitter.

■ שֶׁבְּכָל הַלֵּילוֹת אָנוּ אוֹכְלִין שְׁאָר יְרָקוֹת.
הַלַּיְלָה הַזֶּה מָרוֹר:

Ka muchi ne tajtayua inte titajwiliat nian se wipta;
tik ini tayua ume wipta.

■ For all the nights we do not dip/wet not even one time;
on this night two times.

■ שֶׁבְּכָל הַלֵּילוֹת אֵין אָנוּ מַטְבִּילִין אֲפִילוּ פַּעַם אֶחָת.
הַלַּיְלָה הַזֶּה שְׁתֵּי פְעָמִים:

Ka muchi ne tajtayua tejemet titakwat muetztuk o timunekwiluat;
tik ini tayua muchi timunekwiluat.

■ For all the nights we eat sitting or we lean;
on this night we all lean.

■ שֶׁבְּכָל הַלֵּילוֹת אָנוּ אוֹכְלִין בֵּין יוֹשְׁבִין וּבֵין מְסֻבִּין.
הַלַּיְלָה הַזֶּה כֻּלָּנוּ מְסֻבִּין:

Ka muchi ne tajtayua tejemet titakwat ken senpa;
tik ini tayua tikchiwat te kenha.

■ For all the nights we eat as always;
on this night we do it different.

■ *On all other nights we eat in an ordinary manner;*
on this night we dine with special ceremony.

Translation notes: Alan preferred the Hebrew version whenever it resulted in a Nawat phrase that was at least as natural-sounding than staying closely to the English (eg: *kulo matzah* = all matza; *kulanu mesubin* = we all recline, etc). He used *pan* rather than "bread" for two reasons. First, bread is a semi-exotic concept. Also, whereas the starch staple in Central America, the tortilla, has no leavening, all *pan* is made with yeast. Thus, in the Nawat's context, pan means leavened bread.

ABOUT THE LANGUAGE:

Pipil / Nahuat

Number of speakers: 20-200
Rank: 6,415

Pipil, also called Nahuat and Nawat, is spoken in El Salvador, in the Municipio of Dolores, Ocotepeque Department, near the southwestern border of El Salvador.

A nearly extinct language, Pipil was formerly spoken quite widely in western and central El Salvador, but its speakers were persecuted and forced to abandon their traditional dress and language in the early 20th C. Today only a few elderly people can still speak it. As El Salvador has a large diaspora, there may be a few speakers elsewhere, particularly in the USA.

ABOUT THE TRANSLATOR:

Alan R King

Age: 54   Translated: 2010
Locations: England / CA / Catalonia / Wales / El Salvador / Basque Country

Alan is a qualified linguist and professional translator, with a special interest in minority languages and experience in Bible translation. He received degrees from the University of California and University of London. He is married to a Salvadorean and worked on the Nawat language for over two years amongst its speakers. He currently lives in the Basque Country.

Photo by Werner Hernández

A typical house in the Pipil area of El Salvador

Piemontese

Translated from Italian

Përché costa neuit a l'é diversa da j'àutre neuit?

■ *Perchè è diversa questa notte dalle altre notti dell'anno?*

J'àutre neuit ëd l'ani i mangioma ël pan alvà o sensa alvà; sta neuit sì i mangioma màch pan sensa alvà.

■ *Le altre notti dell'anno, mangiamo o pane lievitito o slievitato; questa notte, mangiamo solamente pane slievitato.*

J'àutre neuit ëd l'ani i mangioma tuti i géner d'erba; sta neuit sì i mangioma màch erbe amère.

■ *Le altre notti dell'anno, mangiamo ogni tipo d'erba; questa notte, mangiamo solamente le erbe espressamente amare.*

J'àutre neuit ëd l'ani i pocioma j'erbe an gnente; sta neuit sì i pocioma doe vòlte.

■ *Le altre notti dell'anno, non immergiamo le erbe in niente; questa notte, le immergiamo due volte.*

J'àutre neuit ëd l'ani i mangioma da setà, da 'n pé ò chinà; sta neuit sì i mangioma piegà an giù.

■ *Le altre notti dell'anno, mangiamo seduti dritti o reclinati; questa notte, mangiamo reclinati.*

J'àutre neuit ëd l'ani i mangioma an manera ordinaria; sta neuit sì i mangioma con gradiosa sirimònia.

■ *Le altre notti dell'anno, mangiamo in modo ordinario; questa notte, mangiamo con gran cerimonia.*

Translation note: Guido had used both *ij* and *i* in his translation. These were regularized to *i*, the more frequently used spelling. Roberto said both spellings were 'correct'.

ABOUT THE LANGUAGE:

Piemontese

Number of speakers: 3,110,000
Rank: 184

Piemontese is spoken in the regions of northwest Italy, around Turin, near the border with France. It shows considerable influence from French. There are also speakers in Australia and the USA.

The Jewish community in Piedmont can be traced to the 5th C. Jews were active in the region's *Risorgimento* (unification movement) in the mid-1800s. The symbol of Turin, *Mole Antonelliana*, was originally designed as a Synagogue for the community.

ABOUT THE TRANSLATOR:

Guido Bosco

Age: ~78   Translated: 2002
Village: Castagnole Monferrato, Italy

Guido was born in Castagnole, worked in Turin (Torino), and lived in Butiglierra Alta (Turin's suburb west toward the French Alps) and Castagnole (east of Turin in the hilly grape-growing region).

He wrote historical stories, many of them in Piemontese and some even in Castagnolese, the dialect specific to his village.

ABOUT THE SPEAKER:

Roberto Bosco

Age: 51   Recorded: 2005
Towns: Torino / Rosta, Italy

Roberto, Guido's son, was born and raised in Turin (Torino). At age 49 he moved to Rosta, a small village near Turin.

Guido created beautiful copper-plate etchings showing scenes of his village

Pashto, Northern

ABOUT THE LANGUAGE:

Northern Pashto *

Number of speakers: 9,720,700
Rank: 81

Pashto is spoken in Pakistan, and in Afghanistan (where it is a national language), India, United Arab Emirates and the United Kingdom. In Pakistan, the Powinda are a nomadic Pashto-speaking group; in Afghanistan, Pashto speakers are called the Pakhtoon and Pashtoon, who use a modified Perso-Arabic script; and in the United Arab Emirates they are called the Pathans, who use a modified Urdu script.

Pashto first appeared in writing during the 16th C in an account of Shekh Mali's conquest of Swat. It is written in a version of the Arabic script.

ABOUT THE TRANSLATOR AND SPEAKER:

Fareed Shirzai Wardak

Age: 32   Recorded: 2002
Towns: Khoshal-Khan Mina, Afghanistan / Livermore, CA

Fareed was born in Wardak Province west of Kabul, but from infancy through late teens he was raised in the town Khoshal-Khan Mina in Kabul, Afghanistan. He attended one year of Medical school at the Kabul Medical Institute and was forced to move to Pakistan for a year and a half; at the age of 19, Fareed moved to the USA. Both Dari and Pashto are his native languages. Fareed's Arabic script was typed by **Faramak Vakil**.

Photo by Jim Weintraub

A Pakistani snake charmer near Karachi

چرا این شب با شب های دیگر فرق دارد ؟

■ Wali da shpa la nuro shpo chkha farq laree?

■ *Why is this night different from all other nights?*

در همه شب های دیگر ، ما نان خمیر ویا فطیر میخوریم
در این شب صرف نان فطیر

■ Pa tolo nuro shpo ke mong khamira ya fatira dodai khwarala;
Kho pa-de shpa yawazi fatira.

■ *On all other nights we eat either leavened bread or matzah; on this night only matzah.*

در همه شب های دیگر ، ما هر نوع سبزیجات میخوریم
در این شب صرف سبزیجات تند

■ Pa tolo nuro shpo ke mong har dawl sabzijat khwaral;
Kho pa-de shpa yawazi tarkha sabzijat.

■ *On all other nights we eat all kinds of herbs; on this night only bitter herbs.*

در همه شب های دیگر ، ما حتی یکمرتبه هم نان تر نکردیم
در این شب ما ، دو مرتبه نان تر کردیم

■ Pa tolo nuro shpo ke mong yaw zal ham dodai na-londawala;
Pa-de shpa mong dewa zali landa kra.

■ *On all other nights we do not dip even once; on this night we dip twice.*

در همه شب های دیگر ، ما نشسته یا تکیه کرده نان میخوریم
در این شب ما تکیه کرده ایم

■ Pa tolo nuro shpo ke mong pa nasta aaw ya pa takya dodai khwarala;
Kho pa-de shpa mong takya karida.

■ *On all other nights we eat either sitting up or reclining; on this night we recline.*

در همه شب های دیگر ، ما بشکل معمولی نان میخوریم
در این شب ما با مراسم خاص نان میخوریم

■ Pa tolo nuro shpo ke mong pa aadee dawal dodai khwarala;
Pa-de shpa mong pa khaso dodoono sara dodai khwro.

■ *On all other nights we eat in an ordinary manner; on this night we dine with special ceremony.*

* For additional information, see *"Focus on ... pages.pdf"* on the DVD.

Papiamentu

Dikon e anochi aki ta otro for di tur e otro anochinan?

■ *Why is this night different from all other nights?*

**Tur e otro anochinan nos ta kome sea pan òf matso;
E anochi aki, nos ta kome matso so.**

■ *On all other nights we eat either leavened bread or matzah;
on this night only matzah.*

**Tur e otro anochinan nos ta kome yen sorto di bèrdura;
E anochi aki, nos ta kome un bèrdura stinki so.**

■ *On all other nights we eat all kinds of herbs;
on this night only bitter herbs.*

**Tur e otro anochinan nos no ta dòp ningun biaha;
E anochi aki, nos ta dòp dos biaha.**

■ *On all other nights we do not dip even once;
on this night we dip twice.*

**Tur e otro anochinan nos ta kome sea sintá òf nos ta lèn kome;
E anochi aki, nos ta lèn.**

■ *On all other nights we eat either sitting up or reclining;
on this night we recline.*

**Tur e otro anochinan nos ta kome kualke manera komun;
E anochi aki, nos ta kome yen di seremonia.**

■ *On all other nights we eat in an ordinary manner;
on this night we dine with special ceremony.*

ABOUT THE SPEAKERS:

Hetty Kook and Felicia Emerencia Baran

Ages: Unavailable   Recorded: 1996
Locations: Curaçao and Bonaire Islands / Newark, NJ

Hetty Kook speaks the dialect used in Curaçao. Felicia was born and raised on Bonaire Island and currently lives in Newark, NJ.

ABOUT THE LANGUAGE:

Papiamentu

Number of speakers: 320,200
Rank: 686

Papiamentu is spoken in the Netherlands Antilles islands of Curaçao, St. Maarten and Bonaire off the Venezuela coast and in islands off Nicaragua. It is also spoken in Aruba, Netherlands, Puerto Rico and the US Virgin Islands. Papiamentu is taught in first 2 years of primary school on Curaçao and Bonaire.

The importance of the language is different on each island: it is not used widely on St. Maarten. Most Papiamentu speakers on Curaçao and Bonaire use Dutch at school, Spanish with Spanish-speaking persons and English and Dutch with tourists. The language is becoming more like Spanish, which is considered more prestigious.

ABOUT THE TRANSLATOR:

Hetty Kook

Age: Unavailable   Translated: 1996
Towns: Curaçao, Netherlands Antilles / Leiden, Netherlands

Hetty was born and raised on the island of Curaçao. She left at age 20 and now lives in Leiden, the Netherlands.

Photo by Joan Hantman

**Aruba Beach, Aruba,
Netherlands Antilles**

Panjabi

ਇਹ ਰਾਤ ਦੂਜੀ ਰਾਤਾਂ ਤੋਂ ਅਲਗ ਕਿਉਂ ਹੈ?

- Eh raat dooji raatan ton alag kyoun hai?

- *Why is this night different from all other nights?*

ਦੂਜੀ ਰਾਤਾਂ ਤੇ ਅਸੀ ਰੋਟੀ ਯਾ ਮਾਤਜ਼ਾ ਖਾਂਦੇ ਹਾਂ,
ਇਸ ਰਾਤ ਤੇ ਸਿਰਫ ਮਾਤਜ਼ਾ ।

- Dooji raatan te assi roti ya matzah khandi haan;
  is raat te sirf matzah.

- *On all other nights we eat either leavened bread or matzah;
  on this night only matzah.*

ਦੂਜੀ ਰਾਤਾਂ ਤੇ ਅਸੀ ਹਰ ਕਿਸਮ ਦੇ ਮਸਾਲੇ ਖਾਂਦੇ ਹਾਂ,
ਇਸ ਰਾਤ ਤੇ ਸਿਰਫ ਕੜਵੇ ਮਸਾਲੇ ਖਾਂਦੇ ਹਾਂ ।

- Dooji rratan te assi har kisam di masaale khande haan;
  is raat te sirf karve masaale khande haan.

- *On all other nights we eat all kinds of herbs;
  on this night only bitter herbs.*

ਦੂਜੀ ਰਾਤਾਂ ਤੇ ਅਸੀ ਡਬੋਂਦੇ ਨ੍ਹੀ,
ਇਸ ਰਾਤ ਤੇ ਬਾਰ ਬਾਰ ਡਬੋਂਦੇ ਹਾਂ ।

- Dooji raatan te assi dubonde nahin;
  is raat te baar baar dubonde haan.

- *On all other nights we do not dip even once;
  on this night we dip twice.*

ਦੂਜੀ ਰਾਤਾਂ ਤੇ ਅਸੀ ਬੈਠ ਕੇ ਯਾ ਲੇਟ ਕੇ ਖਾਂਦੇ ਹਾਂ,
ਇਸ ਰਾਤ ਤੇ ਸਿਰਫ ਲੇਟ ਕੇ ਖਾਂਦੇ ਹਾਂ ।

- Dooji raatan te assi baith ke ya let ke khande haan;
  is raat te sirf let ke khande haan.

- *On all other nights we eat either sitting up or reclining;
  on this night we recline.*

ਦੂਜੀ ਰਾਤਾਂ ਤੇ ਅਸੀ ਰੋਜ਼ ਜਿਵੇਂ ਖਾਂਦੇ ਹਾਂ,
ਇਸ ਰਾਤ ਤੇ ਅਸੀ ਖੁਸ਼ਿਆਂ ਮਨਾਂਦੇ ਹਾਂ ॥

- Dooji raatan te assi roz jiven khande haan;
  is raat te assi khushiyaan manande haan.

- *On all other nights we eat in an ordinary manner;
  on this night we dine with special ceremony.*

* For additional information, see
"Focus on ... pages.pdf" on the DVD.

ABOUT THE LANGUAGE:

Eastern Panjabi *

Number of speakers: 28,163,600
Rank: 40

Eastern Panjabi (somtimes spelled Punjabi) is spoken in India's northern region of Punjab, Majhi in the Gurdaspur and Amritsar districts; Bhatyiana in South Firozpur District; Rajasthan, Bhatyiana in north Ganganagar District; Haryana; Delhi; and the states of Jammu and Kashmir. There is a continuum of varieties between Eastern and Western Panjabi, spoken in the Punjab area of Pakistan.

Ancient temple in the Belur-Halebid area near Bangalore

Photo by Tony DeJoie

ABOUT THE TRANSLATOR:

Kamal Chadha

Age: 20s   Translated: 1995

Towns: New Delhi / Dehra Dun, India / NJ / PA

Kamal was raised in Geneva and New Delhi. Like her sister, Rita, she attended a residential school in Dehra Dun. She attended the University of Delhi and later obtained Masters degrees in Computer Science and Technology Management in NJ and PA.

ABOUT THE SPEAKER:

Ritu Chadha

Age: 30s   Recorded: 1995

Towns: New Delhi / Dehra Dun, India / NY / Amman / Brussels / Geneva / NJ

Dr. Chadha was born in New Delhi and raised in many major cities. As an undergraduate, she held the record for highest aggregate grades ever obtained in Delhi University's honors Bachelors program. She has a PhD in Computer Science and does research in networking for telecommunications and the US Government.

Z Y X W V U T S R Q P O N M L K J I H G F E D C B A

Panjabi Transliteration

ਮਾ ਨੀਸ਼ਟਾਨਾ ਹਾਲਇਲਾ ਹਾਜ਼ੇ ਮੀਖੋਲ ਹਾਲੇਲੋਟ?

■ mah neesh-tah-nah hah-lai-lah hah-zeh mee-kol hah-leh-lot?

ਸ਼ੇਬਿਖੋਲ ਹਾਲੇਲੋਟ ਆਨੂ ਓਖਲੀਨ ਖ਼ਾਮੇਟਸ ਉਮਾਟਸਾ
ਹਾਲਇਲਾ ਹਾਜ਼ੇ ਕੁਲੋ ਮਾਟਸਾ ।

■ sheh-bih-khol ha-leh-lot ah-nu okh-leen khah-meht-es u-mah-tsah;
hah-lai-lah hah-zeh ku-lo mah-tsah.

ਸ਼ੇਬਿਖੋਲ ਹਾਲੇਲੋਟ ਆਨੂ ਓਖਲੀਨ ਸ਼ਆਰ ਯਿਰਾਖੋਟ
ਹਾਲਇਲਾ ਹਾਜ਼ੇ ਮਾਰੋਰ ।

■ sheh-bih-khol ha-leh-lot ah-nu okh-leen sh-ar yih-rah-kot;
hah-lai-lah hah-zeh mah-ror.

ਸ਼ੇਬਿਖੋਲ ਹਾਲੇਲੋਟ ਐਨ ਆਨੂ ਮਾਟਬੀਲੀਨ ਆਫ਼ੀਲੂ ਪਾਆਮ ਆਖ਼ਾਟ
ਹਾਲਇਲਾ ਹਾਜ਼ੇ ਸ਼ਟੇ ਪਿਆਮੀਮ ।

■ sheh-bih-khol ha-leh-lot ehn ah-nu mat-bee-leen ah-fee-lu pah-ahm ah-khat;
hah-lai-lah hah-zeh sh-teh pih-ah-meem.

ਸ਼ੇਬਿਖੋਲ ਹਾਲੇਲੋਟ ਆਨੂ ਓਖਲੀਮ ਬੇਨ ਯੋਸ਼ਵੀਨ ਉਵੇਨ ਮਿਸੁਬੀਨ
ਹਾਲਇਲਾ ਹਾਜ਼ੇ ਕੁਲਾਨੂ ਮਿਸੁਬੀਨ ॥

■ sheh-bih-khol ha-leh-lot ah-nu okh-leen behn yosh-veen u-vehn mih-su-been;
hah-lai-lah hah-zeh ku-lah-nu mih-su-been.

ABOUT THE TRANSLATORS AND SPEAKER:

Tarun Singh and Ilan Caplan

Ages: 18 (Tarun) 20 (Ilan)   Recorded: 2007
Towns: Patiala, India / Santa Maria, CA / Cambridge, MA (Tarun)
Caldwell, NJ / Cambridge, MA (Ilan)

Tarun is a Harvard undergraduate in the College of Arts and Sciences. Tarun moved from Patiala, India, when he was two years old. He is a religious Sikh heavily interested in politics. Panjabi is his first language, and he still speaks both Panjabi and English at home. He never heard the *Ma Nishtana* before now, but is now slowly becoming acquainted with the Hebrew alphabet. That's Tarun reading the ਮਾ ਨੀਸ਼ਟਾਨਾ (*Ma Nishtana*) in the recordings.

Ilan is Tarun Singh's roommate at Harvard. That is his main claim to fame, besides being Jewish. He has listened to his younger sisters and cousins recite the *Ma Nishtana* for many years, and in his early years was given the honor of reading it once or twice as well (or so he is told ...). The son of a Cantor, Ilan is slowly trying to learn to read Panjabi, and at the same time trying to get Tarun to read Hebrew.

Drawing by Emily Seltzer,
5th grade, Livingston, NJ

**The plagues sent down
to the Egyptians**

Pampangan

Bauit ing beñing ini aliroa ya kareng milabasan a beñgi?

■ *Why is this night different from all other nights?*

**Ating beñging ma mañgnan tamung tinape o matzah;
pero ngening beñgi matzah niu.**

■ *On all other nights we eat either leavened bread or matzah;
on this night only matzah.*

**Ating beñging ing kakanan tamu milimang clasing herbo;
dapot ñgening beñgi mamañgan tamung mapait herbo.**

■ *On all other nights we eat all kinds of herbs;
on this night only bitter herbs.*

**Ating beñging eta ya susoso ing herbo;
pero ñgening beñgi mekatadiva tayang gewa ini.**

■ *On all other nights we do not dip even once;
on this night we dip twice.*

**Kareng anggang beñgi mamañgan tamung maka lukluk matulil o makapandal;
dapot ñgening beñgi makasandal tamu.**

■ *On all other nights we eat either sitting up or reclining;
on this night we recline.*

**Kareng beñging beñgi mamañgan tamung ordinaryo;
pero ñgening beñgi tit aluvaz ya at spesyal.**

■ *On all other nights we eat in an ordinary manner;
on this night we dine with special ceremony.*

ABOUT THE LANGUAGE:

Pampangan

Number of speakers: 1,905,550
Rank: 246

Pampangan (also called Pampango and Pampangueño) is spoken in the Pampanga, Tarlac and Bataan provinces of the Philippines.

ABOUT THE TRANSLATOR AND SPEAKER:

Pastor Allan Luna

Age: Unavailable   Recorded: 1999
Town: Quezon City, Philippines

Pastor Luna is the priest for the Church of the Risen Lord, at the University of the Philippines in Quezon City. He is a native Pampangan speaker.

In the recordings: There are minor variations in the sentence structure between the written and oral versions, but semantically they're the same.

Photo by Rody Torres

Rice fields and Plantation in Pampanga, the Philippines

Z Y X W V U T S R Q P O N M L K J I H G F E D C B A

Oromo

Halkan kun, halkan biroo hunda irraa maaliif garaagara tahee?
- *Why is this night different from all other nights?*

Halkan biroo hunda, cumboo [bukaawe] nyaanna; halkan kana, maxinoo nyaanna.
- *On all other nights we eat either leavened bread or matzah; on this night only matzah.*

Halkan biroo hunda, hebela halle nyaanna; halkan kana, hebela hadhaawaa nyaanna.
- *On all other nights we eat all kinds of herbs; on this night only bitter herbs.*

Halkan biroo hunda, ala takkallee hincuubannu; halkan kana, ala lama cuubanna.
- *On all other nights we do not dip even once; on this night we dip twice.*

Halkan biroo hunda, teenyee yookiis hirkannee nyaanna; halkan kana, nihirkanna.
- *On all other nights we eat either sitting up or reclining; on this night we recline.*

Halkan biroo hunda, ayyaaneffata malee nyaanna; halkan kana, ayyaaneffata addaatiin dhiyaana.
- *On all other nights we eat in an ordinary manner; on this night we dine with special ceremony.*

Pronunciation notes: c in such as *cumboo, hinccubannu* and *cuubanna* is pronounced as an explosive 'ch'. dh in *hadhaawaa* is an explosive 'd' (unique to Oromo). ny in *nyaanna* is pronounced as in French 'gn'.

Translation notes: Dabala writes "Our speech is basically of the West Oromia dialect, but we have been sensitized to the variations in the language as a result of having lived or worked with people from other regions. This translation is as standardized as it gets at present. With the probable exception of two words, Oromos will have no difficulty with it. You may find Oromos who use the word *daabboo* (Amharic word for 'bread') rather than *cumboo*, which I have used here. The word *hebela* (herbs) is also a result of our search for a one-word equivalent.

"You may want to note the following expressions: *ayyaaneffata malee* ('without ceremony', actually, 'ceremony without'); *ayyaaneffata addaan* ('with special ceremony', literally 'ceremony special with'). I put the word *bukaawe* (leavened) in brackets because by definition *cumboo* is leavened."

Photo by Bernard Cloutier (berclo.net)

Religious gathering near the village of Gewane, Ethiopia

Oriya

Translated from Hindi

ଏ ରାତି ଅନ୍ୟ ରାତି ଠୁ ଅଲଗା କାହିଁକି ?

■ ये रात दूसरी रातों से आलग क्यों है ?

ଅନ୍ୟ ରାତିରେ ଆମେ ଖମରି ରୋଟି କିମ୍ବା ମଜ୍ଜା ଖାଉ ଏ ରାତି ରେ କେବଲ ମଜ୍ଜା ।
ଏ ରାତି କେବଲ ମଜ୍ଜା ।

■ दूसरी रातों को हम ख़मीरी रोटी या मात्तज़ा खाते हैं ।
इस रात सिर्फ़ मत्तज़ा ।

ଅନ୍ୟ ରାତିରେ ଆମେ ସବୁ ପ୍ରକାର ଶସ୍ୟ ଖାଉ ।
ଏ ରାତିରେ ଆମେ କେବଲ ପିତା ଶସ୍ୟ ଖାଉ ।

■ दूसरी रातों को हम हर तरह की हर्ब खाते हैं ।
इस रात हम सिर्फ़ कड़वी हर्ब खाते हैं ।

ଅନ୍ୟ ରାତିରେ ଆମେ ଥରେ ମଧ୍ୟ ବୁଡ଼ାଉ ନାହୁଁ ।
ଏ ରାତିରେ ଆମେ ଦୁଇଥର ବୁଡ଼ାଉ ।

■ दूसरी रातों को हम एक बार भी डुबोते नहीं ह ।
इस रात हम दो बार डुबोते हैं ।

ଅନ୍ୟ ରାତିରେ ଆମେ ବସିକରି କିମ୍ବା ଟେରି ହୋଇ ଖାଉ ।
ଏ ରାତିରେ ଆମେ ଟେରି ହୋଇ ଖାଉ ।

■ दूसरी रातों को हम या तो बैठ कर या टेक लगा कर खाते हैं ।
इस रात हम टेक लगा कर खाते हैं ।

ଅନ୍ୟ ରାତିରେ ଆମେ ନିତିଦିନ ପରି ଖାଉ ।
କିନ୍ତୁ ଏ ରାତିରେ ଆମେ ମଉଜ ଉଘ୍ରବ କରି ଖାଉ ।

■ दूसरी रातों को हम रोज़ की तरह खाते हैं ।
लेकिन इस रात हम उत्सव मना के खाते हैं ।

The Oriya Script:
The curved appearance of the Oriya script is a result of writing on palm leaves, which tear if too many straight lines are used.

* For additional Information, see
"Focus on ... pages.pdf" on the DVD.

ABOUT THE LANGUAGE:

Oriya *

Number of speakers: 31,732,500
Rank: 37

Oriya is chiefly spoken in the Indian state of Orissa, but speakers also live in the states of Bihar, West Bengal, Assam, Andhra Pradesh, as well as Bangladesh.

Oriya's script developed from the *Kalinga* script, one of the many descendents of ancient India's *Brahmi* script. The earliest known inscription in Oriya date from 1051; these use the *Kalinga* script.

In Oriya's syllabic alphabet, all consonants have an inherent vowel. Diacritics – above, below, before or after the consonant they belong to – change the inherent vowel.

ABOUT THE TRANSLATOR:

Gurpreet Singh

Age: Unavailable   Translated: 2004
Towns: Punjab, India / Edison, NJ

Gurpreet's first language was Oriya. He was born in Punjab and now lives in NJ.

ABOUT THE SPEAKER:

Bikash Sabata

Age: Unavailable   Recorded: 2005
Town: Bombay, India / NJ

Gurpreet's translation was typed in and recorded by Bikash, a native of Bombay.

Illustration by Alysa Lerman

Hundru Falls in Bihar; the Subarnrekha river cascades down from an altitude of 320 feet

Oneida

Na'hte? aoli:wa   Tsi? tekyatih^́   ka?i:k^   wasuta:te: Tsi?ni:yot   oya:shu?   wasuta:te?

■   Why is it   that it's different   this   night   the way it is   other   nights?

Oya:shu?   wasuta:te: wattu?kwa'htu   kana:talo'k   tathu'ni   Tsi?ka:y^:   yatye?wati'   wattukwa'tu   kana:talok   h^twak

■ Other   nights   yeast   bread   or   just   (without the yeast)   bread   we eat;

K^h   wasutá:te: kwah   noktsi   kanata'lok   ^twa'ke?.

■ This night   just   bread   we will eat.

Oya:shu?   wasuta:te: kwahtsyo'k   hi:yo't   oh^te?shu'ha   I?twa'ks

■ Other   nights   all kinds of   herbs   we eat;

K^h   wasuta:té: nok   Tsi?kay^́   teyotska:la':t   ^twa'k.

■ This night   just the kind   that's bitter   we eat.

Oya:shu?   wasutá:te: swatye:l^   tw^tsko':te?   tathu'ni   twaya?takal^'le?   n^   ^twatekhu:ni

■ Other   nights   sometimes   sit up   or   recline   when   we eat;

K^h   wasutá:te: twaya?takal^'le?.

■ This night   reclining.

Oya:shu?   wasuta:te: twi?nityukwal^nha':u   tsi?   ni:yot   Tsi?   atwatekhu:ni

■ Other   nights   natural   the way   that we will eat;

K^h   wasuta:te: wat^:nyote?   tsi?   ^twatekhu:ni.

■ This night   a feast   the way   that we will eat.

In the recordings: Norma ends with the name of the language, spoken in Oneida.

Translation notes: ? is a glottal stop. Because accents were used inconsistently, the authors were unable to correct them on *watsuta:te:* (night/nights) and *kana:talok* (bread). The third phrase (dipping) was not translated.

ABOUT THE TRANSLATOR AND SPEAKER:

Norma Kennedy

Age: Unavailable   Recorded: 1997
Town: Oneida, NY

Oneida was Norma's first language as a little girl in Oneida Reserve, located 19 miles west of London, Ontario. She left the language as an adult, but later relearned it in courses she took at the University in London, Ontario. During the mid-1990s, Norma was a teacher at the Oneida Nation Territory, Oneida, NY.

ABOUT THE LANGUAGE:

Oneida

Number of speakers: 250
Rank: 5,908

Oneida is spoken by some of the older adults in the Six Nations Reserve of southern Ontario, Canada. There are only a few dozen speakers in central New York and eastern Wisconsin.

Miriam and her tambourine.
Drawing by Zoe Elfenbein, Age 10, N Caldwell, NJ

Okinawan

ぬん　　　　ちゅう　ゆろー　　びち　ゆる　　か
何でぃいちー　今日ぬ夜　　別ぬ夜とぅ　変わとぅびいがやー？

■ Nundichi- chu-nu yuro- bichinu yurutu kawatoubi-gaya- ?

■ *Why is this night different from all other nights?*

ちに　　　　　　わったぁー
常ひいじいや、私達や　　パン又やマッツアードぅ　かまびーしが；
ちゅう　　　　　　　ゆろー
今日 ぬ 夜、マッツアーばけー やいーんびん。

■ Chinihi-ji-ya, wattaha-ya pan mataya matsa du kamabi-shiga;
chu-nu yuro-, matsa bake- yai-in bin.

■ *On all other nights we eat either leavened bread or matzah;*
on this night only matzah.

ちに　　　　　わったぁー　　くすいやーせー　　いるかじ
常ひいじいや、私達や　　薬野菜ぬ　　色数　　かどうびーしが；
ちゅう　　ゆろー　んじゃ　くすいやーせー
今日ぬ　夜、苦さぬ 薬野菜　　ばけー やいーんびん。

■ Chinihi-ji-ya, wattaha-ya kusui-ya-se- nu irukaji kado-bi-shiga;
chu-nu yuro-, njasanu kusui-ya-se- bake- yai- in bin.

■ *On all other nights we eat all kinds of herbs; on this night only bitter herbs.*

ちに　　　　　わったぁー
常ひいじいや、私達や　ちゅけーんぬん　ちきやびらんしが；
ちゅう　　　　　　　ゆろー　　　　　　わったぁー
今日ぬ 夜, 私達 や　　たけーん ちきやーびん。

■ Chinihi-ji-ya, wattaha-ya chuke-nun chikiyabiranshiga;
chu-nu yuro-, wattaha-ya take-n chikiya-bin.

■ *On all other nights we do not dip even once; on this night we dip twice.*

ちに　　　　　わったぁー
常ひいじいや、私達や　まっとぅーば 又や　うちゃかてぃ　いちょうびいーしが；
ちゅう　　　　　　ゆろー　わったぁー
今日ぬ　夜、　私達や うちゃかてぃ　いちょうびん。

■ Chinihi-ji-ya, wattaha-ya mattou-ba mataya uchakati ichoubi-shiga;
chu-nu yuro-, wattaha-ya uchakati ichoubin.

■ *On all other nights we eat either sitting up or reclining; on this night we recline.*

ちに　　　　　わったぁー　ひーじー
常ひいじいや、私達や　　平生 どぅーい　　むのー　かどうびーしが；
ちゅう　　　　　ゆろー　わったぁー　　とぅく
今日 ぬ 夜、　私達や　特に　しちびどぅーい　　むのー　かどうびん。

■ Chinihi-ji-ya, wattaha-ya hi-jidu-yi muno- kado-bi-shiga;
chu-nu yuro-, tukuni shichibidu-i muno- kado-bin.

■ *On all other nights we eat in an ordinary manner;*
on this night we dine with special ceremony.

Hyphens in the transliteration indicate lengthened vowels. The *Hiragana* phonetic pronunciation is shown above the *Kanji* translation.

ABOUT THE LANGUAGE:

Okinawan, Central

Number of speakers: 984,000
Rank: 375

Okinawan is spoken primarily on the island of Okinawa, Japan. It is also spoken on the Kerama, Kume-jima, Tonaki and Aguna islands, and islands east of Okinawa Island. In general, there is little intelligibility between Okinawan and Japanese.

See Japanese entry for description of the different scripts (*Kanji*, *Hiragana* and *Katagana*).

ABOUT THE TRANSLATOR AND SPEAKER:

Teiko Yohana-Tursi

Age: 61　　　　Recorded: 2000
Towns: Nago City, Japan / Berlin, NJ

Teiko was born Nago City, Kunigami, on the northern part of Okinawa Island. She arrived in the USA at age 22. Teiko is President of the New York area Okinawan Organization. She is a reporter, social worker and amateur anthropologist. She has attended several Passover Seders as she had a Jewish son-in-law.

Woven textiles of Okinawa using traditional *Shuri* textile techniques: Classical Dancers (right) and Shuri Castle in Okinawa (below)

Book by Teiko Yohana-Tursi

Nzema

Duzu ati yɛ nosulɛ ɛhye li ngahyele tɛla nosulɛ muala ɛ?

■ *Why is this night different from all other nights?*

Nosulɛ biala yɛdi pano mɔ lest ɛne nula anakɛ maasa; nosulɛ ye yɛlile maasa.

■ *On all other nights we eat either leavened bread or matzah; on this night only matzah.*

Nosulɛ biala ɛdi nya biala; Nosulɛ ehye ɛdiɛ ɛdi nyaɛnwunle.

■ *On all other nights we eat all kinds of herbs; on this night only bitter herbs.*

Nosulɛ yɛni aliɛ ko bɔbɔ; nosulɛ ɛhyeɛdiɛ yɛli debia nyiɔ.

■ *On all other nights we do not dip even once; on this night we dip twice.*

Nosulɛ biala yɛtenla aze yɛdi debie; nosulɛ ɛhyeɛdiɛ yɛhisa ɛkɛ.

■ *On all other nights we eat either sitting up or reclining; on this night we recline.*

Nosulɛ biala ɛdi aliɛ biala; nosulɛ ɛhye ɛdiɛ yɛdi aliɛ ngahyile wɔ nyanu.

■ *On all other nights we eat in an ordinary manner; on this night we dine with special ceremony.*

ABOUT THE LANGUAGE:

Nzema

Number of speakers: 328,700
Rank: 675

Nzema, also called Nzima and Appolo, is spoken in the southwest corner of Ghana and into neighboring areas of the Ivory Coast.

ABOUT THE TRANSLATOR AND SPEAKER:

Victoria Blay

Age: Unavailable   Recorded: 2002
Town: Tema, Ghana

Victoria Blay, a native speaker of Nzema, lives in Tema, Ghana.

A typically colorful scene at the Makola Market in Accra, Ghana

Photo by Ayeley Mills-Tettey

Nynorsk

Kvifor er denne kvelden ulik alle andre kveldar?
- *Why is this night different from all other nights?*

På alle andre kveldar et vi gjærbakst eller usyra brød;
på denne kvelden et vi berre usyra brød.
- *On all other nights we eat either leavened bread or matzah;*
  on this night only matzah.

På alle andre kveldar et vi alle slags urter;
på denne kvelden et vi berre beiske urter.
- *On all other nights we eat all kinds of herbs;*
  on this night only bitter herbs.

På alle andre kveldar duppar vi aldri;
på denne kvelden duppar vi to gonger.
- *On all other nights we do not dip even once;*
  on this night we dip twice.

På alle andre kveldar et vi medan vi sit rett eller halvt liggjande;
på denne kvelden et vi i halvt liggjande stilling.
- *On all other nights we eat either sitting up or reclining;*
  on this night we recline.

På alle andre kveldar et vi på daglegdags vis;
på denne kvelden et vi som ein lekk i ein særskild seremoni.
- *On all other nights we eat in an ordinary manner;*
  on this night we dine with special ceremony.

ABOUT THE TRANSLATOR AND SPEAKER:

Leonard Løvoll

Age: Unavailable   Recorded: 1999
Towns: Eisdal / Ålesund, Norway

Leonard Løvoll writes and speaks Nynorsk every day in his work as a reporter. He was born in Eisdal, approximately 12km from Geiranger and currenty lives in Ålesund. He writes "There is not much difference between Bokmål Norwegian and Nynorsk. Nynorsk has many words, that have been forgotten by ordinary people. Nynorsk has more words from the old times, dialects and even Swedish. In Iceland they talk more like they talked in Norway 1000 years ago and you will find many more similar words in Iceland to Nynorsk than to Bokmål or Danish." A translation was also developed by **Thor Soreland**, who works at the Norway Times in New York City.

ABOUT THE LANGUAGE:

Nynorsk

Number of speakers: Unknown
Rank: N/A

Nynorsk is one of the official languages of Norway. In an odd perversity of history, Nynorsk (New Norse) is in some senses older than Norwegian. In the 1830s, a movement began to create a new national language, because written Danish differed greatly from the spoken Norwegian. Two languages arose from this effort: *Landsmål* (language of the country) [now called *Nynorsk*], founded by linguist Ivar Aasen, was based on regional dialects and Old Norse, in an attempt to reconstruct the original, older Norwegian. *Riksmål* (national language) [now called *Bokmål*] *is* based on selected dialects purged of foreign borrowings and resembles modern written Danish.

In the recordings: Leonard ends his recording with *Mange takk, som vi seier på Nunorsk* (Thank you very much, as we say in Nynorsk).

Rock outcropping overlooking Geiranger Fjord

Z Y X W V U T S R Q P O **N** M L K J I H G F E D C B A

Nyanja

Chifukwa usiku uyu usiyana ndi masiku onse?

■ *Why is this night different from all other nights?*

Masiku ena onse, timadya mkhate wa "leavened bread" olo "matzah"; uyu usiku ni "matzah" chabe.

■ *On all other nights we eat either leavened bread or matzah; on this night only matzah.*

Masiku ena onse, timadya masamba osiyana siyana; uyu usiku ni nimasamba olula okha.

■ *On all other nights we eat all kinds of herbs; on this night only bitter herbs.*

Masiku ena onse, sititowela olo kamozi; uyu usiku titowela kawiri.

■ *On all other nights we do not dip even once; on this night we dip twice.*

Masiku ena onse, timadya tilikhale olo tiligone; uyu usiku tiwelama.

■ *On all other nights we eat either sitting up or reclining; on this night we recline.*

Masiku ena onse, timadya popanda mwambo; uyu usiku timady mwamwambo.

■ *On all other nights we eat in an ordinary manner; on this night we dine with special ceremony.*

ABOUT THE LANGUAGE:

Nyanja

Number of speakers: 8,659,700
Rank: 91

Nyanja is the official language of Malawi (with 7 million speakers) and is widely spoken in several neighboring countries.

ABOUT THE TRANSLATOR:

Zilore Mumba

Age: Unavailable   Translated: 2010
Town: Lusaka, Zambia

Zilore Mumba was born and raised in Zambia's capital city, Lusaka. He speaks both Nyanja and Bemba. Zilore is head of the weather forecasting division of ACMAD, an Africa-wide company that supports sustainable development in Africa via weather forecasting and training of African meteorologists.

Photo by Bernard Cloutier (berclo.net)

The quiet African village of Cape McLear borders beautiful Kasankha Bay in Malawi

Nyamwezi

Kunguno wuzighu walero na wigolo zeli kira?

■ *Why is this night different from all other nights?*

Ishiku joose tulilyaga mghaate kotetela hamira au bolegele amira; uziku bhunubhu tukulya mghaate bolegele amira doho.

■ *On all other nights we eat either leavened bread or matzah; on this night only matzah.*

Ishiku joose tukulya mbiu na mizi joose; guzighu walelo tukulya mbiu na mizi milulu.

■ *On all other nights we eat all kinds of herbs; on this night only bitter herbs.*

Shiku joose tukavile kukoja kamo; guzighu walelo tulikoja tuwili.

■ *On all other nights we do not dip even once; on this night we dip twice.*

Shiku joose guzighu tulilya tuwikala au tulesengema; guzighu walelo tulisengema doho.

■ *On all other nights we eat either sitting up or reclining; on this night we recline.*

Ishiku joose tulilya nakwikomeleja; guzighu walelo tulilya na wenga.

■ *On all other nights we eat in an ordinary manner; on this night we dine with special ceremony.*

ABOUT THE TRANSLATOR:

James Chambala

Age: 54   Translated: 2009
Towns: Shinyanga / Dar es Salaam, Tanzania

James, a native speaker of Nyamwezi, works at a copy center in Dar es Salaam. His interests are singing and politics.

ABOUT THE LANGUAGE:

Nyamwezi

Number of speakers: 980,000
Rank: 376

Nyamwezi is spoken in northwest central Tanzania and between Lakes Victoria and Rukwa in the Tabora region, as well as other regions.

ABOUT THE SPEAKER:

Joanita Ngaiza

Age: 38   Recorded: 2010
Town: Dar es Salaam, Tanzania

Joanita is a native speaker of Kihaya, fluent in Kihehe, and can read and write Nyamwezi and the other languages she recorded. Her full biography is on the Sukuma page.

Photo by Ilana Locker

A beautiful sunset in Zanzibar

Z Y X W V U T S R Q P O N M L K J I H G F E D C B A

Nyakyusa-Ngonde

Papo fiki ikilo kya lino kikindene ne'kilo kya masiku agangi gosa?
- *Why is this night different from all other nights?*

Amasiku gosa tukulya umukate ugubakile hamira rumo tukulya ugu gukanamira;
pa kilo hiki tukulya umukate ugukaanajo hamira.
- *On all other nights we eat either leavened bread or matzah;*
  on this night only matzah.

Amasiku gosa tukulya iseke rumo ilisu fyosa pamopene;
isiku lya lino tukulya iseke ne ilisu ikali.
- *On all other nights we eat all kinds of herbs;*
  on this night only bitter herbs.

Amasiku gosa titukutobela na kamo;
pa kilo ikya leno tukutobela kavili.
- *On all other nights we do not dip even once;*
  on this night we dip twice.

Amasiku gosa tukulya botwitugele rumo tukulya bo twimile;
pa kilo ikya leno tukulya bo twimile.
- *On all other nights we eat either sitting up or reclining;*
  on this night we recline.

Amasiku gosa tukulya nipyana;
pa kilo kwa mwisyugu tukulya no lusekelo losa.
- *On all other nights we eat in an ordinary manner;*
  on this night we dine with special ceremony.

ABOUT THE LANGUAGE:

Nyakyusa-Ngonde

Number of speakers: 1,105,000
Rank: 335

Nyakyusa-Ngonde is spoken in various areas of Tanzania: Mbeya and Iringa regions, Lake Malawi and the Makete District. There are over 300,000 speakers in Malawi.

ABOUT THE TRANSLATOR:

Oswand Mwitika

Age: 53   Translated: 2009
Towns: Mbeya / Dar es Salaam, Tanzania

A native speaker of Nyakyusa, Osward is a gardener in Dar es Salaam, and loves sports.

Photo by Ilana Locker

A baboon enjoying the view from a tree in Mkumi National Park, Tanzania

ABOUT THE SPEAKER:

Joanita Ngaiza

Age: 38   Recorded: 2010
Town: Dar es Salaam, Tanzania

Joanita is a native speaker of Kihaya, fluent in Kihehe, and can read and write Nyakyusa and the other languages she recorded. Her full biography is on the Sukuma page.

Norwegian

Hvorfor er denne kvelden forskjellig fra alle andre kvelder?

■ *Why is this night different from all other nights?*

**På alle andre kvelder spiser vi gjærbakst eller usyret brød;
på denne kvelden spiser vi bare usyret brød.**

■ *On all other nights we eat either leavened bread or matzah;
on this night only matzah.*

**På alle andre kvelder spiser vi alle slags urter;
på denne kvelden spiser vi bare bitre urter.**

■ *On all other nights we eat all kinds of herbs;
on this night only bitter herbs.*

**På alle andre kvelder dypper vi aldri;
på denne kvelden dypper vi to ganger.**

■ *On all other nights we do not dip even once;
on this night we dip twice.*

**På alle andre kvelder spiser vi i rettsittende eller i tilbakelent stilling;
på denne kvelden spiser vi alltid i tilbakelent stilling.**

■ *On all other nights we eat either sitting up or reclining;
on this night we recline.*

**På alle andre kvelder spiser vi pa dagligdags vis;
på denne kvelden spiser vi ved en spesiell seremoni.**

■ *On all other nights we eat in an ordinary manner;
on this night we dine with special ceremony.*

ABOUT THE LANGUAGE:

Bokmål Norwegian

Number of speakers: 4,640,000
Rank: 139

Bokmål (book language) Norwegian is the national language of Norway. Its written version draws words and syntax from both west and east Scandinavian languages. It is a constructed language that replaced *Riksmål* as the official national language in 1938.

The first known written language of Scandinavia was Old Norse or the *Dansk tunga* (Danish tongue), which appeared in Runic inscriptions from about 700 CE onwards.

Early Norwegian literature was written in West Norse and flourished between the 9th and 14th centuries. After that, Norway came under Swedish and then Danish rule. Norwegian continued to be spoken but Danish was used for official purposes. A movement to create a new national language emerged in the 1830s, because written Danish differed greatly from the spoken Norwegian. From these efforts were developed *Riksmål* (national language) which became *Bokmål*.

ABOUT THE TRANSLATOR AND SPEAKER:

Liv Svendsen

Age: Unavailable   Recorded: 1998
Towns: Norway / Point Pleasant, NJ

Liv is a native of Norway, currently living in Point Pleasant, NJ. She is an officer of the Sons of Norway Lodge in NJ. The translation was also worked on by **Melvin Klassen** of the University of Victoria in British Columbia, Canada and **Leonard Løvoll** of Ålesund, Norway.

Vigeland Sculpture Park, dedicated to Norway's most celebrated sculptor, Gustav Vigeland (1869-1943)

Z Y X W V U T S R Q P O N M L K J I H G F E D C B A

Newari

थौया चा न्ह्याबले स्वया छ्रय् फरक जुगु?
- Thauyaa chaa nhyaabalé swoyaa chhaaw pharak ju:gu?
- *Why is this night different from all other nights?*

मेमेबलय् चाकु सवाः दूगु मरी वा माट्स
नयेगु तर थौ चानय् माट्स जक नयेगु।
- Maymaybalay chaaku sawaa: dugu mari wa matzah;
  nayegu thaü chaanay matzah jaka nayegu.
- *On all other nights we eat either leavened bread or matzah;
  on this night only matzah.*

मेमेबलय् वाउंगु साः गु तरकारी
नयेगु तर थौ चानय् खायूगु तरकारी जक नयेगु।
- Maymaybalay waaügu saa:gu tarakaari;
  nayegu tara thaü chaanay khaayuugu tarakaari jaka nayegu.
- *On all other nights we eat all kinds of herbs;
  on this night only bitter herbs.*

मेमेबलय् तरकारी मथुंसेः
नयेगु तर थौ चानय् निकः थुनाः नयेगु।
- Maymaybalay tarakaari mathüse;
  nayegu tara thaü chaanay nika: thunaa nayegu.
- *On all other nights we do not dip even once;
  on this night we dip twice.*

मेमेबलय् आराम यानाः फयतुनाः
नयेगु तर थौ चानयु लिधनाः नयेगु।
- Maymaybalay aaraam yaanaa: phytunaa;
  nayegu tara thaü chaanay lidhanaa: nayegu.
- *On all other nights we eat either sitting up or reclining;
  on this night we recline.*

मेमेबलय् साधारण किसिमंः
नयेगु तर थौ चानय् झीपिं बिशेष समारोह हनाः नयेगु ॥
- Maymaybalay saadhaaran kisimã;
  nayegu tara thaü chaanay jhi:pî bishesh samaaroha hanaa: nayegu.
- *On all other nights we eat in an ordinary manner;
  on this night we dine with special ceremony.*

Transliteration notes:
a = as in c<u>o</u>me
aa = as in c<u>a</u>lm
ã é ü = nasal vowels
Colon [:] indicates long vowels

ABOUT THE LANGUAGE:

Newari

Number of speakers: 839,000
Rank: 408

Newari, also called Newar and Nepal Bhasha, is spoken in Kathmandu Valley and in all towns and larger villages throughout Nepal. It is also spoken in India.

Newari is written using the *Devanagari* script, used for many of the Indian languages.

ABOUT THE TRANSLATOR AND SPEAKER:

Daya R Shakya

Age: Unavailable   Recorded: 1998
Towns: Kathmandu, Nepal / Portland, OR

Daya is a linguist and teacher of Newar. He was born in Kathmandu, the capital of Nepal. At the time of the recording, Daya had lived in the USA for 10 years.

Traditional Nepal dancers at the Nepa Friendship Festival, Washington, DC

Courtesy of Daya Shakya

Nepali

आजको रात अरू रात भन्दा किन भिन्न छ ?
- Aajako raat aru raat bhandaa kina bhinna chha?
- This night other nights than why different is?

अरू रातमा हामी खमीर हालेको रोटी अथवा माट्स खान्छौ
तर आज राती हामी माट्स मात्रै खान्छौ ।
- Aru raatma haami khamir haaleko roTi athwaa maatsa khaanchhaü;
  tara aaja raati naami maatsa maatrai khaanchhaü.
- Other nights we yeast put bread or matzah eat;
  but this night matzah only.

अरू रातमा बिभिन्न किसिमको हरियो साग पात खान्छौ
तर आज राती हामी तितो झार मात्रै खान्छौ ।
- Aru raatmaa bibhinna kisimko hariyo saagpaata tarkaari khaancchaü;
  tara aaja raati haami teetay jhaar maatrai khaancchaü.
- Other nights we different types of green vegetables eat;
  but this night bitter green only.

अरू रातमा हामीले हरियो सागपातलाई एक चोटी पनि चोपेनौ
तर आज राती हामी द्‌ईचोटी चोप्छौं ।
- Aru raatmaa haamile hariyo saagpaaltaai ekchoTi pani chopdainaü;
  tara aaja raati haamidui choTi chopchhaü.
- Other nights we one time even dip;
  but this night two times dip.

अरू रातमा हामी आराम साथ बसेर खान्छौ
तर आज राती हामी ढल्केर खान्छौ ।
- Aru raatmaa haami aaraam saath basera khaanchhaü;
  tara aaja raati haami Dhalkera khaanchhaü.
- Other nights we (by) sitting or reclining eat;
  but this night we recline eat.

अरू रातमा हामी साधारण किसिमले खान्छौ
तर आज राती हामी बिशेष समारोह साथ खान्छौ ।
- Aru raatmaa haami saadhaaran kisimle khaanchhaü;
  tara aaja raati haami bishesh samaaroha saath khaanchhaü.
- Other nights we ordinary manner (with) eat;
  but this night we special ceremony with eat.

Transliteration notes: a = c<u>o</u>me • aa = c<u>a</u>lm
t/d = regular • T/D = retroflex

ABOUT THE LANGUAGE:

Nepali *
Number of speakers: 13,875,700
Rank: 61

Nepali is the national language of Nepal, primarily spoken in the eastern region and adjacent south-central region. Nepali is also spoken in Bhutan, Brunei and India.

ABOUT THE TRANSLATOR AND SPEAKER:

Daya R Shakya
Age: Unavailable   Recorded: 1998
Towns: Kathmandu, Nepal / Portland, OR

Daya is a native speaker of Nepali. She is a linguist and teacher of Newar in Portland. She was born in Kathmandu and has lived in the USA since 1988. The translation was also worked on by **Anju Bhattrai** of Muncie, IN and typed by **Shobha Erramilli**.

Children in Annapurna playing *Bang Chal* ("Tiger Moves"), a strategy game played in Nepal for over 1000 years

Photo by Stephanie Goldhuber

* **For additional information, see *"Focus on ... pages.pdf"* on the DVD.**

Z Y X W V U T S R Q P O N M L K J I H G F E D C B A

Nenets

Тюку пзвсюмбы няхатата ӈамгэ яӈга?
- ■ Tyuku° pæw°syumpi nyax°tøta ngømke° yønkø°?
- ■ This darktime from-others why differs?

Хурина пзвсюмбыӈз няньм', лескам' ӈаворӈава";
тюку пзвсюмбы' няня лескарим'.
- ■ Xuryina pæw°syumpingæ nyany°m, lyes°kam ngøworngawaq;
  tyuku° pæw°syumpih nyana lyes°karyim.
- ■ Generally for-darktime bread [or] unleavened-bread we-eat;
  this darktime at unleavened-bread-only.

Хурина пзвсюмбыӈз тодо' тзнз ӈамдздо ӈаворӈава";
тюку пзвсюмбы' няня ибцьда ӈамдз"ли.
- ■ Xuryina pæw°syumpingæ todoh tenc° ngømtedo ngøworngawaq;
  tyuku° pæw°syumpih nyana yibcy°da ngømteqlyi.
- ■ Generally for-darktime any sort plants we-eat;
  this darktime at bitter plants-only.

Хурина пзвсюмбы' няня ӈобкарт' нина" палабтамбю";
тюку пзвсюмбы' няня сидя' палабтамбина".
- ■ Xuryina pæw°syumpih nyana ngobkørt°h nyínaq pøl°btampyuq;
  tyuku° pæw°syumpih nyana syidyah pøl°btampyinaq.
- ■ Generally darktime at not-once we-do-not-them dip;
  this darktime at twice we-dip-them.

Хурина пзвсюмбы' няня ӈамдё, саликадё ӈаворӈава";
тюку пзвсюмбы' няня саликадыва".
- ■ Xuryina pæw°syumpih nyana ngamtyo°, sølyikødyo° ngøworngawaq;
  tyuku° pæw°syumpih nyana sølyikødiwaq.
- ■ Generally darktime at sitting [or] leaning we-eat;
  this darktime at we-lean.

Хурина пзвсюмбы' няня тзри ӈаворӈава";
тюку пзвсюмбы' няня хаӈорондава".
- ■ Xuryina pæw°syumpih nyana tæryi ngøworngawaq;
  tyuku° pæw°syumpih nyana xangorontø°waq.
- ■ Generally darktime at just we-eat;
  this darktime at we-eat-ceremonially.

The phonetic transcription is shown. The single and double apostrophes, letters of the Tundra Nenets alphabet, refer to two glottal stop sounds.

In the recordings: Anastasia ends her recording with "Hello there! (*Nganyih torowa!*). This is Anastasia Lapsui speaking to you," spoken in Nenets.

ABOUT THE LANGUAGE:

Nenets

Number of speakers: 31,300
Rank: 1,995

Nenets is spoken in northwest Siberia; tundra area from the mouth of the northern Dvina River in northeastern Europe to the delta of the Yenisei in Asia; also a scattering on the Kola Peninsula; as well in the Nenets, Yamalo-Nenets and Taimyr national *okrugs*.

The Nenets are mainly nomadic reindeer herdsmen. The area has snow and freezing temperatures 260 days of the year.

ABOUT THE TRANSLATOR AND SPEAKER:

Anastasia Lapsui

Age: 52   Recorded: 1998
Towns: Nyda / Salekhard, Yamalo-Nenets District, Siberia

Anastasia (who also uses Anastasia Timofeevna) was born in Nyda, some 1,000 km east of the northernmost Ural mountains. She lived mostly in Salekhard, the center of the Yamalo-Nenets District, where she is a journalist and responsible for Nenets language broadcasting. We were astounded by Judaic connections at this remote location: Anastasia's brother-in-law, a well-known Moscovite musicologist, is Jewish.

A Jewish friend told Anastasia not to refer to a traditional Nenets bread that is flat and unleavened. When we discovered the reasoning – "лескам' is round but matzah *must* be square" – we told her traditional matzah ('*shmura matzah*') is also round, and that referencing the Nenets bread would be culturally appropriate.

Photo courtesy of Tjeerd de Graaf

Nenets children in a reindeer sled

Ndonga

Omolwashike ongulohi ndjika ya yooloka koongulohi oonkwawo dhilwe adhihe?

■ *Why is this night different from all other nights?*

Oongulohi oonkwawo dhilwe adhihe, ohatu li omboloto yefulika nenge omatzaha;
mongulohi ndjika, otatu li ashike omatzaha ageke.

■ *On all other nights we eat either leavened bread or matzah;*
on this night only matzah.

Oongulohi oonkwawo dhilwe adhihe, ohatu li omaludhi agehe giigwanga;
mongulohi ndjika, otatu li ashike iigwanga iilulu.

■ *On all other nights we eat all kinds of herbs;*
on this night only bitter herbs.

Oongulohi oonkwawo dhilwe adhihe, inatu lya nando olumwe;
mongulohi ndjika, otwa li lwaali.

■ *On all other nights we do not dip even once;*
on this night we dip twice.

Oongulohi oonkwawo dhilwe adhihe, otwa kala tatu li twa kuutumba nenge twe egamena;
mongulohi ndjika, otwe egamena owala.

■ *On all other nights we eat either sitting up or reclining;*
on this night we recline.

Oongulohi oonkwawo dhilwe adhihe, ohatu li tatu li pamukalo gwoshito;
mongulohi ndjika, otatu li tu na oshituthi showina.

■ *On all other nights we eat in an ordinary manner;*
on this night we dine with special ceremony.

ABOUT THE LANGUAGE:

Ndonga

Number of speakers: 1,070,000
Rank: 339

Ndonga, called Oshindonga, Otjiwambo and Owambo by its speakers, is spoken in Namibia's Ovamboland, as well as in Angola.

ABOUT THE TRANSLATOR AND SPEAKER:

Loide Mbenzi

Age: Unavailable   Recorded: 1998
Town: Ndonga, Namibia

Loide, a native speaker of Ndonga, was born and raised in Ndonga, Namibia. The text was also translated by **Desiewaar (Desie) D.N. Heita**, age 19 (1998). Desie grew up in the mixed-language community of Ondangwa. Since Desie's experience with Ndonga was limited to studies in school, we've used native-speaker Loide's translation. The two translations differed slightly for some phrases.

Photo by Boris Kester

Kolmanskop, Namibia was erected in the early 1910s when diamonds were discovered, some lying directly on the sand dunes. The ensuing diamond rush led to an elegant town with a casino, theater, lemonade plant, swimming pool and hospital with the Southern Hemisphere's first X-ray machine. In 4 years, one ton of diamonds (5 million carats) were found. 300 German adults and 800 Owambo workers lived in the town at its peak. Completely abandoned after a diamond slump in 1956, Kolmanskop is now a ghost town overrun by sand dunes

Ndebele

Kungani lobu ubusuku behlulekile kobunye ubusubu?

■ *Why is this night different from all other nights?*

**Kobunye ubusuku bonke, sidla isinkwa esile mvubelo kumbe z"imatzah";
Kulobu ubusuku "imatzah" kuphela.**

■ *On all other nights we eat either leavened bread or matzah;
on this night only matzah.*

**Kobunye ubusuku bonke, sidla imihlobo yonke yezihlahlakazana;
Kulobu ubusuku sidla izihlahlakazana ezibabayo kuphela.**

■ *On all other nights we eat all kinds of herbs;
on this night only bitter herbs.*

**Kobunye ubusuku bonke, kasizi tshebi ngitsho izihlahlakazana;
Kulobu ubusuku sizitsheba kabili.**

■ *On all other nights we do not dip even once;
on this night we dip twice.*

**Kobunye ubusuku bonke, sidla sihlezi siqondile kumbe sibambelele;
Kulobu ubusuku siyabambelela.**

■ *On all other nights we eat either sitting up or reclining;
on this night we recline.*

**Kobunye ubusuku bonke, sidla ngendlela ejayelekileyo;
Kulobu ubusuku bonke sidla ngendlela etshengisela ukuthi kulolutho oluthakazelelwayo.**

■ *On all other nights we eat in an ordinary manner;
on this night we dine with special ceremony.*

ABOUT THE LANGUAGE:

Ndebele

Number of speakers: 1,572,800
Rank: 270

Ndebele (also called Tabele) is spoken in Matabeleland in Zimbabwe, near Bulawayo. It is also spoken in Botswana.

Ndebele is quite close to Zulu – several of the phrases in this translation are similar. This is akin to Swedish and Norwegian, mutually intelligible languages that have different syntax and grammars.

ABOUT THE TRANSLATOR AND SPEAKER:

Sue Nyoni

Age: 22   Recorded: 1998
Towns: Bulawayo, Zimbabwe / England / Morristown, NJ

Sue's first language is Ndebele. She was born in Bulawayo, Zimbabwe, moved to England at age 4, then back to Zimbabwe at age 8. At 18, she left for the USA where she attended college for 4 years. The translation's text was clarified with help from her mother, still in Zimbabwe.

Photo by Stephanie Goldhuber

Spirit bird dancer in Zimbabwe

Navajo

Haash yit'éego díí tł'éé' ígíí t'éiyá łahgo áhóhoot'eego bee nihoot'ą́?

■ *Why is this night different from all other nights?*

T'áá 'ákwíí tł'ee' éí bááh bił ál'íní t'áágééd ályaa' deidą́; díí tł'éé' matzah t'éiyá dabi'niidą́ą́.

■ *On all other nights we eat either leavened bread or matzah; on this night only matzah.*

T'áá 'ákwíí tł'éé' éí ch'il azee' ał'ą́ą́ ádaat'éhígíí deidą́; díí tł'éé' éí ch'il dich'íí'ígíí t'éiyá dabi'niidą́ą́.

■ *On all other nights we eat all kinds of herbs; on this night only bitter herbs.*

T'áá 'ákwíí tł'éé' éí doo hááda'iikáah da nít'ę́ę́; díí tł'éé' éí naakidi háádadiikááł.

■ *On all other nights we do not dip even once; on this night we dip twice.*

T'áá 'ákwíí tł'éé' éí dahjisjíídk'ehgo nahásíitą́ą́ nít'ę́ę́ doodaii nát'ą́ą́' nidasiidáago nída'iidíjíh nít'ę́ę́; díí tł'éé' éí nát'ą́ą́' nidasiidáago da'diidíjíł.

■ *On all other nights we eat either sitting up or reclining; on this night we recline.*

T'áá 'ákwíí tł'éé' éí t'áá da'jiyánígi át'éego nída'iidíjíh nít'ę́ę́; díí tł'éé' éí dahodííníilzingo da'diidíjíł.

■ *On all other nights we eat in an ordinary manner; on this night we dine with special ceremony.*

In the recordings: Roseann ends her recording with the name of the language, *Dine Bizaad*, in Navajo.

Navajo Code Talkers   The idea of using Navajo for secure wartime communications in World War II came from Philip Johnston, the son of a missionary to the Navajos and one of the few non-Navajos who spoke their language fluently. Navajo code talkers took part in every assault the U.S. Marines conducted in the Pacific from 1942 to 1945. They served in all six Marine divisions, Marine Raider battalions and Marine parachute units, transmitting messages by telephone and radio in their native language: it was a code the Japanese never broke.

Johnston, reared on the Navajo reservation, knew the military was searching for a code that could withstand attempts to decipher it. He also knew Native American languages, particularly Choctaw, had been used in World War I to encode messages. In all, 375 to 420 Navajos served as code talkers.

They were praised for their skill, speed and accuracy. Major Howard Connor declared, "*Were it not for the Navajos, the Marines would never have taken Iwo Jima.*" Connor had six Navajo code talkers working around the clock during the first two days of the battle. Those six sent and received over 800 messages, all without error. The Navajo code talker exhibit is a regular stop on the Pentagon tour. Read additional information at: www.history.navy.mil/faqs/faq61-2.htm

---

ABOUT THE LANGUAGE:

Navajo

Number of speakers: 149,000
Rank: 1,025

Navajo, called *Diné* by its speakers, is spoken in Arizona, New Mexico and Utah. It is closely related only to Apache and no other Native American language. A Navajo word list was first written in 1849. Missionaries writing religious texts in Navajo during the early 20th C each developed their own spelling systems. The modern system was originally developed in 1939 by John Collier, head of Indian Affairs. Originally disliked by the tribe for political reasons, the alphabet has undergone a recent revival of interest and learning.

ABOUT THE TRANSLATOR AND SPEAKER:

Roseann Willink

Age: Unavailable   Recorded: 2004
Town: Corrales, NM

Roseann's first language is Navajo. She holds a position equivalent to dean of college-level Navajo teachers, and has been an instructor at the University of New Mexico for nearly 35 years. Roseann is also an interpreter for the court, medical and museum communities.

Roseann has a reputation for being a very caring, supportive teacher of native-speaking Navajos learning to read and write their language, and an extremely effective teacher of that difficult language to non-Navajos. She is also active in linguistic circles where an effort is being made to preserve indigenous languages, not only across North America, but world-wide. In short, she is a venerable presence in the teaching of Navajo and in the movement to preserve other Native American languages. (Words by close colleague, **Paul Zolbrod**.)

Photo by Jim Weintraub

Navajo demonstration at the reservation near Navajoland's Monument Valley

Nahautl, Eastern Huasteca

Translated from Spanish

¿Quenque axcanah cencah ni yahualli tlen nochin nopa cequinoc yahualli?

■ ¿Por qué es diferente esta noche de todas las otras noches?

Nochin nopa cequinoc yahualli ticcuah pantzin ica levadura, o *matsah*; pan ni yahualli zan *matsah*.

■ En todas las otras noches comemos pan hecho con levadura o pan ázimo; en esta noche solamente matzah.

Nochin nopa cequinoc yahualli ticcuah miyac tlamantli xihuitl; pan ni yahualli ticcuazceh chichic xihuitl.

■ En todas las otras noches comemos toda clase de hierbas; en esta noche comemos hierbas amargas.

Nochin nopa cequinoc yahualli axcanah ticcacalaquiah yon ce hueltah; pan ni yahualli ticcacalaquizceh ome hueltah.

■ En todas las otras noches no sumergimos las hierbas de ninguna manera; en esta noche las sumergimos dos veces.

Nochin nopa cequinoc yahualli, titlacuah timocehuihtoqueh xitlahuac o timopantetonihtoqueh; pan ni yahualli titlacuazceh timopantetonihtoqueh.

■ En todas las otras noches comemos sentados rectos o inclinados; en esta noche nos sentamos inclinados.

Nochin nopa cequinoc yahualli titlacuah cencah mohmoztla; pan ni yahualli titlacuazceh ica ce hueyi campeca.

■ En todas las otras noches comemos de manera ordinaria; en esta noche comemos con ceremonia especial.

Seralina Maximino Santos, living in a village near Puerto Vallarta, earns income selling her beaded anklets and silver necklaces to tourists

ABOUT THE LANGUAGE:

Nahuatl, Eastern Huasteca

Number of speakers: 410,000
Rank: 602

Nahuatl (also written Náhuatl) is a group of Aztec languages spoken by the indigenous peoples of Central Mexico. All modern variants show influence of Spanish and are not identical to Classical Nahuatl, the language of the Aztec empire. Classical Nahuatl was spoken throughout Mesoamerica from the 12th C (some sources say as early as the 7th C) until the 16th C.

Eastern Huasteca has the most speakers of Nahuatl varieties. It is spoken in 1,500 villages, primarily around Huautla, Hidalgo, but also in Puebla and Veracruz.

Nahuatl was originally written with a pictographic script that was not a full writing system, but instead served as a mnemonic to remind readers of texts they had learned orally. The Spanish introduced the Latin alphabet in the 16th and 17th C for writing Nahuatl. Many examples of the original pictographic script, which appeared in inscriptions carved in stone and in picture books, were destroyed during the Spanish conquest.

ABOUT THE TRANSLATOR AND SPEAKER:

Victoriano de la Cruz Cruz

Age: 25   Recorded: 2007
Towns: Tepoxteco, Chicontepec, Veracruz / Zacatecas, Mexico

Victoriano is a recent graduate of the School of Administration and Accounting at the State University of Zacatecas, and a Masters student in Indoamerican Linguistics at the Center for Research and Advanced Studies in Social Anthropology, Mexico City.

He was born in the village of Tepoxteco, municipality of Chicontepec, state of Veracruz, in Mexico.

This translation was developed with the assistance of **Dr. John Sullivan**, Professor of Nahua Language and Culture at the Zacatecas Institute. Dr. Sullivan is the recipient of a Guggenheim Fellowship for his work on Huastecan Nahuatl.

Mungaka

A ye kue jemole kuepti ni gong fiyum meh me.
■ *Why is this night different from all other nights?*

Bu ni kwet bled ni gong fiyum meh;
la bu kwet bo maatzah ndi.
■ *On all other nights we eat either leavened bread or matzah;*
on this night only matzah.

Bu ni kwet sanjap ni gong finyum meh;
la bu kwet bue voup ndi.
■ *On all other nights we eat all kinds of herbs;*
on this night only bitter herbs.

Bu du mu kwet ni ntoe ngong fiyum meh bo;
la bu kwet ni san jap nka-iba ndi.
■ *On all other nights we do not dip even once;*
on this night we dip twice.

Bu ni nchini kutie nchiniket ni gong fiyum meh ma jee;
la ndi bu bolie ma keing ku bo kusi boh.
■ *On all other nights we eat either sitting up or reclining;*
on this night we recline.

Ni gong fiyum meh, bu ni jee ni ngong bom manjie bu kong ahh;
la ni fiyum o le bu jee kwah ni nooh.
■ *On all other nights we eat in an ordinary manner;*
on this night we dine with special ceremony.

In the recordings: Richard ends his recording with *Njika, nchu bo ni chu bani* (Thank you, I spoke in Bali).

ABOUT THE LANGUAGE:

Mungaka / Bali

Number of speakers: 50,100
Rank: 1,628

Mungaka (called Bali by some of its speakers) is spoken in Cameroon's North West Province, Mezam Division, Bali Subdivision; West Province, Bamboutos Division, southeastern Galim Subdivision and Mifi Division, northern Bafoussam Subdivision. The speakers of Mungaka are called the 'Bali' people.

ABOUT THE TRANSLATOR AND SPEAKER:

Richard Gwananji

Age: Unavailable   Recorded: 1997
Locations: Camaroon / CA

Richard was born and raised in Cameroon. He works as a lawyer in San Jose, CA.

Photo by Sister Mary Lynne, St. John the Baptist Convent

Church women dancing in honor of a deceased grandmother in Bamenda, Cameroon

Mopán Maya

Cu'cajaj a acu' a daja jumpaj tuwich īulacal a acu'oo?

■ *Why is this night different from all other nights?*

īulacal a acu', īi janta a pana yīzican;
īi'i a acu' adaj jadi īzi'can.

■ *On all other nights we eat either leavened bread or matzah;*
on this night only matzah.

īulacal a acu', īi janta a jumpaj p'ooche;
īi'i a acu' adaj jadi a cuj' p'ooche.

■ *On all other nights we eat all kinds of herbs;*
on this night only bitter herbs.

īulacal a acu', ha īi īzhaj ma'ax jun suc'j;
īi'i a acu' adaj, ca' sucī īi īz maj.

■ *On all other nights we do not dip even once;*
on this night we dip twice.

īulacal a acu', janoon īi īinaanoon y īi cu'yaanoon;
īi'i a acu' adaj cu'lajoon.

■ *On all other nights we eat either sitting up or reclining;*
on this night we recline.

īulacal a acu', janoon;
īi'i a acu' adaj, janoon etel u yanil.

■ *On all other nights we eat in an ordinary manner;*
on this night we dine with special ceremony.

ABOUT THE LANGUAGE:

Mopán Maya

Number of speakers: 11,800
Rank: 2,889

Mopán Maya is spoken in Toledo, Stann Creek, and Cayo districts of Belize and the Petén Department of Guatemala. Mopan is one of several Mayan languages. (See more details about the ancient Mayan culture and its logographic/syllabary on the Yucateco Maya page.)

ABOUT THE TRANSLATOR AND SPEAKER:

Ernesto Saqui

Age: 39   Recorded: 1998
Town: Maya Center, Belize

Ernesto was educated in Belize, including teacher's training at Ecumenical College in Dangriga, Belize. In the year surrounding the time of the translation, he served in the new position of Park Director for the Cockscomb Basin Wildlife Sanctuary. Ernesto is a sought-after leader of his community and the Stann Creek region. He lives with his wife Aurora (translator for Yucateco) and 2 sons in Maya Center, Belize.

Belize's Lamanai Mayan site has the world's largest sculpted jade: the 10 pound mask of the Sun God, *Kinich Ahau*

Mongolian

Юугаараа ϕнϕϕ шϕнϕ ьусад бух шϕнϕϕс ялгаатай вз?

■ Jugaaraa önöö shönö busad büch shönöös jalgaatai ve?

■ *Why is this night different from all other nights?*

Фмнϕ нь бид хϕϕлгϕсϕн талх юмуу маатса иддэг байсан бол;
ϕнϕϕ шϕнϕ эϕвхϕн маатса иднэ.

■ Ömnö ni bid höölgösön talh jumuu maatsuh iddeg baisan bol;
önöö shönö zövhön maatsuh idne.

■ *On all other nights we eat either leavened bread or matzah;
on this night only matzah.*

Фмнϕ нь бид янэ бурийн ур тариа иддэг байсан бол;
ϕнϕϕ шϕнϕ эϕвхϕн гашуунаас нь иднэ.

■ Ömnö ni bid jianz buriin ÿr taria iddeg baisan bol;
önöö shönö zövhön gashuunaas ni idne.

■ *On all other nights we eat all kinds of herbs;
on this night only bitter herbs.*

Фмнϕ нь бид давстай усанд нэг ч удаа дурэлгуй иддэг байсан бол;
ϕнϕϕ шϕнϕ хоёр удаа дурж иднэ.

■ Ömnö ni bid davstai usand neg cīhī udaa durelgui iddeg baisan bol;
önöö shönö zövhön höyör udaa durj idne.

■ *On all other nights we do not dip even once;
on this night we dip twice.*

Фмнϕ нь бид цэх сууж юмуу хажуулдаж иддэг байсан бол;
ϕнϕϕ шϕнϕ эϕвхϕн хажуулдаж иднэ.

■ Ömnö ni bid tseh suujī jīumuu hajīuuldajī iddeg baisan bol;
önöö shönö zövhön hajuuldaj idne.

■ *On all other nights we eat either sitting up or reclining;
on this night we recline.*

Фмнϕ нь бид ердийн байдлаар хооллодог
байсан бол;
ϕнϕϕ шϕнϕ хундэтгэлтэйгээр эооглоно.

■ Ömnö ni bid erdiin baidlaar hoollodog baisan bol;
önöä shönö hundetgelteigeer zooglono.

■ *On all other nights we eat in an ordinary manner;
on this night we dine with special ceremony.*

ABOUT THE LANGUAGE:

Mongolian

Number of speakers: 2,341,240
Rank: 211

Mongolian, also called Halh, is the national language of Mongolia. There are also speakers in Russia, Kyrgyzstan and Taiwan.

As a result of pressure from the Soviet Union, Mongolia adopted the Latin alphabet in 1931, and in 1937 the Cyrillic alphabet shown here. In 1941 the Mongolian government passed a law to abolish the ancient Mongolian alphabet, but there is a resurgence of interest and it is now taught in schools.

ABOUT THE TRANSLATOR AND SPEAKER:

Banzragchiin Khurelbat

Age: Unavailable   Recorded: 1997
Towns: Ulaanbaatar, Mongolia / Bloomington, IN

Professor Khurelbat was born in the capital of Mongolia, Ulaanbaatar. He is a Mongolian linguist, receiving a Masters degree from Mongolian State Unversity. Banzragchiin was a linguistics teacher for five years at Mongolian State Pedagogical University, held the position of Visiting Professor four years at Jawaharlal Nehru University, and taught at Indiana University several more years. He also was a language instructor for the Peace Corps in Mongolia.

Photos by Bernard Cloutier (berclo.net)

Women in traditional dress are still frequently seen
in Mongolia's capital, Ulaan Baatar

The photographer in front of the luxurious *gers*
(traditional tent dwelling) of the Mongol Khans
and nobles

Mohawk

Nahò:ten tekiattíhen nón:wa tsi wahsontá:te?

■ What difference right now this night?

Thikawenní:io kátke teniakwatská:hon, kanà:taro tówani kana'tarokhón:we;
ón:wa wahsontá:te nék ne kana'tarokhón:we.

■ Generally when we are eating, bread or unleavened bread;
right now this night only the unleavened bread we eat.

Thikawenní:io kátke teionkwatskà:hon nia'teiotikióhkwake nohtehra'shón:'a iákwaks;
ki wahshontá:te nék ne iotská:ra ohtehra'shón:'a iákwaks.

■ Generally when we are eating, many kinds of roots we eat;
this night only bitter roots we eat.

Thikawennió:io kátke thaó:ten khieiakotsiénhtha;
ki wahsontá:te tékeni ia'teniakótsienhte.

■ Generally when never do we dip;
this night twice we dip.

Thikawennió:io kátke nó:nen teionkwatskà:hon, ionkwattakwaríhshion tsi iakwéntskote tówani ieiakwaswarákaren;
ki wahshontá:te nék ne ieiakwaswarákaren.

■ Generally when right now we are eating, we are straight seated or reclining;
this night only, we recline.

Thikawennió:io kátke, thikawennió:io nahò:ten eniákweke ne teionkwatskà:hon;
ki wahsontá:te kwáh tenkén tsi ionkwa'nikonhrahsa'áhton tánon ionkwatonhnháhere tsi teionkwatskà:hon.

■ Generally when, generally we will eat whatever while eating;
this night in earnest with all our minds and with good feeling do we eat.

ABOUT THE LANGUAGE:

Mohawk

Number of speakers: 3,760
Rank: 4,001

Mohawk is spoken in southwestern Quebec and southern Ontario and in the USA. It is called Kanien'kéha by the Mohawk tribe.

ABOUT THE TRANSLATOR AND SPEAKER:

Lawrence H Francis

Age: 50s   Recorded: 1997
Town: Ahkwesasne Mohawk Reserve, Rooseveltown, NY

Lawrence is the official Court translator for Ontario Province and for many years headed the government at Ahkwesahsne (also called the St. Regis Mohawk Reserve), which straddles New York and Ontario. Kanien'kéha is his native tongue.

The audio recording was transcribed by **Daniel Thompson**, Director of the Ahkwesahsne Mohawk Language Program. Daniel also learned Kanien'kéha as his first language, learning it from his mother before he learned to read English from his sisters.

Daniel writes: "The only thing to read in Kanien'kéha in those days was the bible. By the time I got to school at age four, I could speak and read both Kanien'kéha and English. It was the policy of the government around that time to eradicate the Kanien'kéha language. It was forbidden on the school grounds on the threat of a severe beating if you were caught speaking it. Officially this policy was supposed to have been rescinded by the time I got to school but I still have scars just for being left handed. The kind of abuse I saw and experienced is not tolerated today. I don't like to remember those days much."

Daniel is one of the few people who are well versed in the recently standardized form of writing. For many years in the 17th and 18th centuries, a form of phonetic writing based on French was used by most people. Without a standard form, the writing varied widely between communities and individuals. Within the 1990s, a standard form of this old system was adopted by consensus during a series of conferences sponsored by the Canadian government. Daniel spearheaded the translation and production of the final report from this project.

Lawrence was helped by his fiancé, **Christine Zachary Deom**, who has several Jewish friends and has attended Passover Seders with them.

Mirandese

Translated from Spanish

¿Porquei esta nuite ye diferente de todas las outras nuites?

■ *¿Por qué es diferente esta noche de todas las otras noches?*

An todas las outras nuites comemos pan cum formiento ou pan azedo; esta nuite solo comemos pan azedo.

■ *En todas las otras noches comemos pan hecho con levadura o pan ázimo; en esta noche solamente matzah.*

An todas las outras nuites comemos yerbas de todos ls feitios; esta nuite solo comemos yerbas azedas.

■ *En todas las otras noches comemos todas clases de hierbas; en esta noche comemos hierbas amargas.*

An todas las outras nuites nun molhemos la comida ua sola beç; esta nuite molhamos-la dues bezes.

■ *En todas las otras noches no sumergimos las hierbas de ninguna manera; en esta noche las sumergimos dos veces.*

An todas las outras nuites comemos sentados, dreitos ou ancuostados; esta nuite solo mos ancuostamos.

■ *En todas las otras noches comemos sentados rectos o inclinados; en esta noche nos sentamos inclinados.*

An todas las outras nuites comemos cumo siempre; esta nuite comemos de maneira special.

■ *En todas las otras noches comemos de manera ordinaria; en esta noche comemos con ceremonia especial.*

ABOUT THE LANGUAGE:

Mirandese

Number of speakers: 15,000
Rank: 2,673

Mirandese, also called Mirandés and Mirandesa, is spoken on the border of Portugal near Spain, near the city of Miranda.

Mirandese shows superficial relationships with both Spanish and Portuguese; it is more closely related to the languages of Asturian and Leonés. The speakers are thought to have separated from them at the time of the invasion of the Moors.

ABOUT THE TRANSLATOR AND SPEAKER:

António Bárbolo Alves

Age: 38   Recorded: 2002
Towns: Picote, Portugal / Nice, France

António was born in the village of Picote, near Miranda do Douro, in the district of Braganga. He learned Mirandese from his family. António lived in the region until age 24.

António is an internationally recognized linguist for Mirandese; he currently holds the position of Reader of Portuguese Language and Culture at the University of Nice.

Photos by Jim Waintraub

Two views of Portugal near the border with Spain:
(Left) Marvao Castle built in the 1300s for defense
(Right) The picturesque border town of Monsaraz

Mingrelian

ათე სერი არძო შხვა სერეფ(ი)შე მუთ(უ) ვაგუ?
- ate seri arjo šxva serep(i)še mut(u) vagu?
- *Why is this night different from all other nights?*

არძო შხვა სეთე(ი)ს ჩქი ვარა ქობალს ბჭკომუნთ
ვარა ჭკიდ(ი)ს;
ამუსერი ჭკიდს ბჭკომუნთ.
- arjo šxva serep(i)s čki vara kobals bč'Íomunt vara č'Íid(i)s; amuseri č'Íids bč'Íomunt.
- *On all other nights we eat either leavened bread or matzah;*
  on this night only matzah.

არძო შხვა სერეფ(ი)ს ჩქი შხვადოშხვა სუნელეფს ბჭკომუნთ;
ამუსერი ხვალე ნწარეს ბჭკომუნთ.
- arjo šxva serep(i)s čki šxvadošxva suneleps bč'k'omunt; amuseri xvale nc'ares bč'k'omunt.
- *On all other nights we eat all kinds of herbs;*
  on this night only bitter herbs.

არძო შხვა სერთე(ი)ს ჩქი ართიშა(ხ) ხოლო ვავუწაწუანთ;
ამუსერი ჩირიშა(ხ) ხოლო ვუწაწუანთ.
- arjo šxva serep(i)s čki artiša(x) xolo vavuc'ac'uant; amuseri čiriša(x) xolo vuc'ac'uant.
- *On all other nights we do not dip even once;*
  on this night we dip twice.

არძო შხვა სერეფ(ი)ს ჩქი ვარა დოხუნელო ვარა
დონჯირელო ბჭკომუნთ;
ამუსერი დონჯირელო ბჭკომუნთ.
- arjo šxva serep(i)s čki vara doxunelo vara donjirelo bč'k'omunt; amuseri donjirelo bč'k'omunt.
- *On all other nights we eat either sitting up or reclining;*
  on this night we recline.

არძო შხვა სერეფ(ი)ს ჩქი თეშ ბჭკომუნთ;
ამუსერი ჩქი უმოსო/ჯალამი მონდომებულო ბჭკომუნთ.
- arjo šxva serep(i)s čki teš bč'k'omunt; amuseri čki umoso/jalami mondomebulo bč'k'omunt.
- *On all other nights we eat in an ordinary manner;*
  on this night we dine with special ceremony.

ABOUT THE LANGUAGE:

Mingrelian

Number of speakers: 500,000
Rank: 545

Mingrelian, also called Margaluri, is spoken in the lowlands of western Georgia.

The *Mkhedruli* alphabet developed from an older Georgian alphabet known as *Nuskha-khucuri* between the 11th and 13th centuries. The first material in the Georgian language using the *Mkhedruli* alphabet was published in 1669. Since then the alphabet has changed very little; some letters were added in the 18th C and a few were dropped in reforms during the 1860s.

ABOUT THE TRANSLATOR AND SPEAKER:

Zaira Khiba

Age: Unavailable   Recorded: 1997
Towns: Ochamchira, Abkhazia / London, England

Dr. Zaira Hewitt Khiba was born and raised in Ochamchira, Abkhazia. She learned Mingrelian through conversations with neighbors as a child. She learned Russian in school; knows German, which she learned at the Sukhum Pedagogical Institute; Georgian, from living in Tbilisi; and English, via her current residence in London. Her postgraduate research was on consonant-complexes in Abkhaz. At the time of recording, she had lived in England 21 years.

Zaira is married to Dr. George Hewitt, Professor of Caucasian Languages, at the University of London's School of Oriental and African Languages.

Photo by Boris Kester

A street vendor in Tbilisi, Georgia

Transliteration key:
j = dz
š = "sh"
č = t + "sh" ("ch")
ǰ = d + zh of "azure"
c' = ts'
č' = t + sh'

Mende

Gbei kpškši ngi gba kpškc kpeema?

■ *Why is this night different from all other nights?*

**Kpškš gbi, ma lewei mon gši lo meh;
keh kpškši ngi, matsui lea mia.**

■ *On all other nights we eat either leavened bread or matzah;
on this night only matzah.*

**Kpškš gbi, ma tifae yea lasi gbi lš meh;
keh kpškši ngi, yea honagši lae mia.**

■ *On all other nights we eat all kinds of herbs;
on this night only bitter herbs.*

**Kpškš gbi, mši kpujahun yila;
keh kpškši ngi, mu kpujeihun felei.**

■ *On all other nights we do not dip even once;
on this night we dip twice.*

**Kpškš gbi, ma mehe meh ndihe hunlš;
keh kpškši ngi, mu mei lahahunlš.**

■ *On all other nights we eat either sitting up or reclining;
on this night we recline.*

**Kpškš gbi, ma mehe meh lea gbama;
keh kpškši ngi, mu mei n'konehun lš.**

■ *On all other nights we eat in an ordinary manner;
on this night we dine with special ceremony.*

About the Language:

Mende

Number of speakers: 1,499,700
Rank: 283

Mende is spoken in south-central areas of Sierra Leone and towards the coast. Mende is also spoken in Liberia.

An indigenous syllabary (one symbol per syllable) called *Kikaku* was invented in 1921 by Kisimi Kamala for writing Mende. Through the 1920s and 1930s, it was a popular method for keeping records and writing letters. *Kikaku* is still used, but has been largely replaced by the Latin-letter version seen here.

About the Translator and Speaker:

Ahmed Munda Smart

Age: 48   Recorded: 2004
Towns: Tikonko-Bo District, Sierra Leone / Bronx, NY

Ahmed was born in the Tikonko-Bo District, Sierra Leone Mission. He now lives in the Bronx, NY. Ahmed arrived in the USA at age 36.

Photo by Boris Kester

The market in Freetown, Sierre Leone

Mbukushu

Pashanye ghuna kutjakera oghu ghuthiku pithagho kughanekera no maghuthiku ghomalheya?

■ *Why is this night different from all other nights?*

Maghuthiku gho maheya ne, atwe ne kudya ghuroto gho ghuhahu endi ghuroto gho kupira ghuhahu;
Ghuthiku gho dyarero ne, ghureto go kupira ghuhahu.

■ *On all other nights we eat either leavened bread or matzah;*
on this night only matzah.

Maghuthiku gho maheya ne, atwe ne kudya mahako gho kukutjaka;
Ghuthiku gho dyarero ne, mahako gho maruru ngenyu.

■ *On all other nights we eat all kinds of herbs;*
on this night only bitter herbs.

Maghuthiku gho maheya ne, atwe ne mgadi twa vereranga norofotji temba;
Ghuthiku gho dyarero ne, ruwadi tuna kuverera.

■ *On all other nights we do not dip even once;*
on this night we dip twice.

Maghuthiku gho maheya ne, twa dya nga ghu hungumano endi ghu nyongameno;
Ghuthiku gho dyarero ne, tuna nyongama.

■ *On all other nights we eat either sitting up or reclining;*
on this night we recline.

Maghuthiku gho maheya ne, atwe ne kudya pa muhingo mwene;
Ghuthiku gho dyarero ne, kuna kudya pa muhingo gho pa difeste.

■ *On all other nights we eat in an ordinary manner;*
on this night we dine with special ceremony.

ABOUT THE LANGUAGE:

Mbukushu

Number of speakers: 35,100
Rank: 1,915

Mbukushu (also called Mambukush, Thimbukushu, Gova, Kusso among other alternate names) is spoken in Namibia's Ovambo and northeast Okavango areas and in Andara. Mbukushu is also spoken in Angola, Botswana and Zambia. It is a national language of Namibia and Zambia.

ABOUT THE SPEAKER:

Andrew Matjila

Age: Unavailable   Recorded: 1998
Locations: South Africa / Namibia

Mr. Matjila lives near Windhoek, Namibia. Andrew grew up in a Setswana-speaking community in South Africa.

ABOUT THE TRANSLATOR:

Mr. Twela

Age: Unavailable   Recorded: 1998
Location: Namibia

Mr. Twela lives near Windhoek, Namibia. Thimbukushu is his first language.

Photo by Boris Kester

Elephants enjoying a sunset in Etosha National Park, Namibia

Masalit

Go kosang gi kosanta to malak khas te?
■ Why night these nights other from special?

**Kosanta tum me kisereta walla masa minye;
amin kosan masade minye.**
■ Nights other breads or matzah eat;
now night matza-only eat.

**Kosanta tum habutu genim malak ningarao minye;
amin kosan so ginda ningde minye.**
■ Nights other something earth from grow eat;
now night ginda-herb of-only eat.

**Kosanta tum ganu tilo koi motunyende;
amin kosan jo mbara motunye.**
■ Nights other one even no-dip;
now night times two dip.

**Kosanta tum nyung aw fi minye;
amin kosan fi minye.**
■ Nights other sit or recline eat;
now night recline eat.

**Kosanta tum ale migenungde ke minye;
amin kosan minta ambo manyen tiren nyo minde.**
■ Nights other-way before-only like eat;
now night with happiness gather sit eat.

> **Translation note:** Ginda is a leaf used for soup but must be treated before it is edible due to its bitterness.

ABOUT THE LANGUAGE:

Masalit
Number of speakers: 60,900
Rank: 1,506

Masalit (Massaleit) is spoken throughout Sudan, especially Darfur province. Due to the war in Darfur, many have fled to Chad, where 60,000 speakers now reside, and to the USA. Its speakers also call the language Jwisince and Kaana Masala.

ABOUT THE TRANSLATOR AND SPEAKER:

Daowd Ibrahim Salih

Age: 45   Recorded: 2010
Towns: Darfur / New York, NY

Daowd Ibrahim Salih was raised in Darfur, but was forced to leave Sudan in 2000 due to his advocacy work on behalf of the Massaleit and other Darfurian ethnic groups. In Sudan, Daowd was an assistant field officer for the German and Swiss Red Crosses and the Sudanese Red Crescent before he came to the USA as a refugee in exile.

Mr. Salih was among the first activists to focus global attention on the genocide in Darfur. He is a founding member and Board President of the Damanga Coalition for Freedom and Democracy. His reports have been referenced by the UN General Assembly, Human Rights Watch and Amnesty International.

Photo by US Agency for Internal Development (USAID)

Refugee camp south of Darfur. People displaced by the conflict in Darfur construct shelters from sticks, straw and scraps of plastic to protect against the hot Sudan climate

Masaba

Lwakyina kyiro kyekyalero kyenjawulo kubiro byabukyere?

■ *Why is this night different from all other nights?*

**Biro byabukyere kulya migati izilimo kyizukisa;
kyiro kyekyalero kulya matzah yenyene.**

■ *On all other nights we eat either leavened bread or matzah;
on this night only matzah.*

**Biro byabukyere kunyala kulya kuzinyinyi zezisa-mbo zosizana;
kyiro kyekyalero kulya zinyinyi ziluluwa zonyene.**

■ *On all other nights we eat all kinds of herbs;
on this night only bitter herbs.*

**Biro byabukyere kekukoza zinyinyi nakajekye;
kyiro kyekyalero kukoza mirundi gibiri.**

■ *On all other nights we do not dip even once;
on this night we dip twice.*

**Biro byabukyere kunyala kulya nga kwikare busimba nalundi nga nwidiire;
kyiro kyekyalero kuli nikukwidira kwonyene.**

■ *On all other nights we eat either sitting up or reclining;
on this night we recline.*

**Biro byabukyere kulya musambo iyabukyere;
kyiro kyekyalero kulya musambo iyenjauro.**

■ *On all other nights we eat in an ordinary manner;
on this night we dine with special ceremony.*

> **Bonus in the recordings:** The DVD contains the remarkable story of the Abayudaya Jews.

ABOUT THE LANGUAGE:

Masaba

Number of speakers: 1,120,000
Rank: 333

Masaba, also known as Lugisu and Lumasaba, is spoken in Uganda, by the Bagisu, primarily in Mbale (formerly called Bugisu) Province and in eastern areas south of the Kupsabiny.

ABOUT THE TRANSLATOR AND SPEAKER:

Joab Jonadab Keki

Age: Unavailable   Recorded: 1999
Towns: Mbale / Nabugoye, Uganda

Joab, known as "JJ", is ex-chairman of Abayudaya Congregation, the congregation of Ugandan Jews located near Mbale. JJ was born in Mbale to a Mugisu mother; Masaba is his mother tongue.

In 2003, JJ was elected to be Chairperson of the Local Council III in the Namanyonyi sub-county, comprising 30 villages with 30,000 Ugandans. He is the first Jewish person to hold office in Uganda.

Photo by Abby Meth Kanter

JJ Keki during a visit to the USA

Marwari

या रात दूजी रातासू न्यारी क्यूँ?

- Ya raat dooji ratasu nyari kyŭ?

- *Why is this night different from all other nights?*

सब राता तो म्हे जीमा रोटी या डबल रोटी;
पच्छे आज केवल रोटी क्यूँ?

- Sab rata to mhe jeema roti ya doublerot;
  Pacche aaj kewal roti kyŭ?

- *On all other nights we eat either leavened bread or matzah;
  On this night only matzah.*

सब राता तो म्हे जीमा तरहा तरहाकी सागा;
पच्छे आज केवल कड़वी साग क्यूँ?

- Sab rata to mhe jeema tarha tarhaki saga;
  Pacche aaj kewalkadwi saag kyŭ?

- *On all other nights we eat all kinds of herbs;
  on this night only bitter herbs.*

सब राता तो म्हे जीमा इ॒ बाया बिना;
पच्छे आज द॒ बारा इ॒ बावा क्यूँ?

- Sab rata to mhe jeema dubaya bina;
  Pacche aaj dubara dubawa i kyŭ?

- *On all other nights we do not dip even once;
  on this night we dip twice.*

सब राता तो म्हे जीमा सीधी बैठके या झ॒ कके;
पच्छे आज जीमा केवल झ॒ कके क्यूँ?

- Sab rata to mhe jeema sidho baithke ya jhukke;
  Pacche aaj jeema kewal jhukke kyŭ?

- *On all other nights we eat either sitting up or reclining;
  on this night we recline.*

सब राता तो म्हे जीमा प॒ जा करया बिना;
पच्छे आज यो प॒ जारो ठाठ क्यूँ?

- Sab rata to mhe jeema pooja karya bina;
  Pacche aaj yo poojaro thath kyŭ?

- *On all other nights we eat in an ordinary manner;
  on this night we dine with special ceremony.*

In the recordings: The instrument playing is a *Tanpura*, used as a background drone in all India musical performances. Common to all Indian music, it serves as a reference note for the musicians.

ABOUT THE LANGUAGE:

Marwari

Number of speakers: 5,622,600
Rank: 123

Marwari (also called Rajisthani) is spoken in many districts of India (Rajasthan, Jodhpur, Jaisalmer, Barmer, Bikaner, Churu, Pali, Jalore districts; Gujarat; Madhya Pradesh; Punjab; Delhi; Haryana; Uttar Pradesh) as well as Nepal and Pakistan. The major dialects are Barmeri, Bikaneri, Jaisalmeri and Jodhpuri.

ABOUT THE TRANSLATOR AND SPEAKER:

Dr. Bhagawandas P Lathi

Age: 72   Recorded: 1996 and 2006
Towns: Rajistan, India / Carmichael, CA

Bhagawandas ("Das") lives in California and was raised in the Rajistan area of India. He came to the USA at age 23. Das, recipient of a PhD in Electrical Engineering, is the author of eight books in Signal Processing, three of which were published by Oxford University Press. He is currently Professor Emeritus from California State University at Sacramento. The text was typed by **Chetan** and **Akshar Narain**.

Photo by Jignesh Patel

Swaminarayan Temple in Gadhada, Gujarat

Marshallese

Etke eoktak buṇunin jān aolepān boñōn ko jet?

■ *Why is this night different from all other nights?*

Aolepān boñōn ko jet, jej ṃōñā ñe jab pilawā ej jab kauwe ekwe matzah; buṇinin-matzah wōt.

■ *On all other nights we eat either leavened bread or matzah; on this night only matzah.*

Aolepān boñōn ko jet, jej ṃōñā aolep kain ine; buṇunin eḷap wōt ad ṃōñā ine ko rōmeọ.

■ *On all other nights we eat all kinds of herbs; on this night only bitter herbs.*

Aolepān boñōn ko jet, jej jab kattu ine ñan jidik; buṇinin ruo alen ad kattu ine.

■ *On all other nights we do not dip even once; on this night we dip twice.*

Aolepān boñōn ko jet, jej jijet im ṃōñā ak ñe jab ekwe jej atōrak; buṇinin jej atōrak.

■ *On all other nights we eat either sitting up or reclining; on this night we recline.*

Aolepān boñōn ko jet, jabdetakwōt kilen ad ṃōñā; buṇinin jej kōjota ilo juon wāween ejenolọk.

■ *On all other nights we eat in an ordinary manner; on this night we dine with special ceremony.*

ABOUT THE LANGUAGE:

Marshallese

Number of speakers: 49,550
Rank: 1,693

Marshallese is the official language of the Marshall Islands. There are two major dialects in the Marshalls, correlating to the two chains of atolls: Ralik and Ratak. There have been several recent attempts at spelling reform; the spelling shown here is used in Dr. Capelle's Marshallese-English dictionary.

The traditional Marshallese greeting *Yok we yuk* means 'Love to you'.

ABOUT THE TRANSLATOR AND SPEAKER:

Alfred Capelle

Age: Unavailable   Recorded: 1996
Town: Majuro, Marshall Islands

Dr. Capelle is a native Marshallese. He is the former President of the College of the Marshall Islands and the current Representative of the Marshall Islands to the United Nations. He studied linguistics in 1971-1976 with Dr. Byron Bender at the University of Hawaii and co-authored a widely used Marshallese-English dictionary.

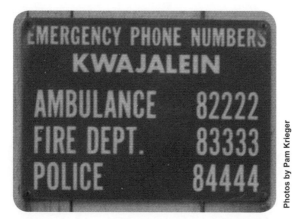

Photos by Pam Krieger

Early pictures of Kwajalein Atol, in the Marshall Islands

Marathi

सर्व रात्री पेक्षा आजची रात्र कशामळे निराळी आहे ?

- Sarva rathripeqsha aajchi rathra kashamule nirali aahe?
- Why is this night so special compared to other nights?

दुस्या सर्व रात्री आपण एक वेळही बुडवून खात नाही ,

परंतु या रात्री दोन वेळा बुडवून खातो. (हे का ?)

- Dusrya sarva rathri aapan ek velhi budvun kath nahi;
  paranthu ya rathri don vela budvun katho. (he ka?)
- In the other nights we do not dip* even once;
  but this night we eat by dipping twice. (Why?)

दुस्या सर्व रात्री आपण फुगलेली व न फुगलेली भाकर खात असतो ,

परंतु या रात्री न फुगलेली भाकरच (मास्सा) मात्र खातो. (हे का ?)

- Dusrya sarva rathri aapan phugleli va na phugleli bhakar kath aastho;
  paranthu ya rathri na phugleli bhakarats (massa) mathra katho. (he ka?)
- In the other nights we eat bread that rises or not:
  but this night we only have flat bread (massa). (Why?)

दुस्या सर्व रात्री आपण इतर सर्व भज्या खात असतो ,

परंतु या रात्री मारोर (कडवट भाजी) मात्र खातो. (हे का ?)

- Dusrya sarva rathri aapan ithr sarva bhajya kath aastho;
  paranthu ya rathri maror (kadvat bhaji) mathra katho. (he ka?)
- In the other nights we eat all kinds of vegetables;
  but this night we only eat maror (bitter vegetables). (Why?)

दुस्या सर्व रात्री आपण बसून अथवा टेकून खात पित असतो ,

परंतु या रात्री टेकूनच खातो पितो. (हे का ?)

- Dusrya sarva rathri aapan basun athva tekun kath pith aastho;
  paranthu ya rathri tekunuts katho pitho. (he ka?)
- In the other nights we sit [normally] or sit comfortably when we eat/drink;
  but this night we only eat/drink comfortably. (Why?)

Pronunciation notes: a: a as in father • aa:
longer than single a • a at end of word: uh • e:
long a as in say • i: long ee as in bee • u: as in oo

---

* Kirthika Parmeswaran, who provided the gloss
and typed the text, said speaking of dipping
foods in Marathi (and only in Marathi) colloquially
represents a sumptuous meal.

---

* For additional information, see
"*Focus on ... pages.pdf*" on the DVD.

ABOUT THE SPEAKER:

Sarvar Patel

Age: Unavailable   Recorded: 1995
Towns: Bhiwandi, India / Edison, NJ

Sarvar Patel grew up in Bhiwandi, in
Maharashtra State, India; he currently
lives in NJ.

ABOUT THE LANGUAGE:

Marathi *

Number of speakers: 68,061,130
Rank: 15

Marathi is spoken in India, in Maharashtra State and adjacent states. Marathi is also
spoken by about 8,000 speakers in Israel and by about 12,000 speakers in Mauritius. The
Bene Israel are a Marathi-speaking Jewish group living in Bombay.

Throughout the greater Marathi-speaking area, the dialect situation is complex because
dialects bordering other major language areas share many features with those languages.

Marathi is thought to be a descendent of Maharashtri, one of the *Prakrit* languages which
developed from Sanskrit. Marathi first appeared in writing during the 11th C in the form
of inscriptions on stones and copper plates. From the 13th through mid-20th centuries,
it was written with the *Modi* alphabet. Since 1950 it has been written with the *Devanagari*
alphabet.

ABOUT THE TRANSLATOR:

Abdul Mateen Patel

Age: Unavailable   Translated: 1994
Location: India

Abdul was raised and currently lives in Maharashtra State, India; his translation was
based on usage within the Jewish community. Note the text explicitly asks 'Why?' after
each statement. The text was typed by **Kirthika Parmeswaran**.

Page from a Marathi Haggadah

Mapudungun

Translated from Spanish

Chumngelu cangechiley tfachi pun ka dom kake pun meu?

■ *¿Por qué es diferente esta noche de todas las otras noches?*

Kom keke pun meu ikeyi faym cofke o kofke seumakeyi; tfachi pun solamente kofke mten deumakeyi.

■ *En todas las otras noches comemos pan hecho con levadura o pan ázimo; en esta noche solamente matzah.*

Kom kake pun ikeyi kom chemkn llerfa; fey tfachi pun ikeyi frechi llerfa.

■ *En todas las otras noches comemos todas clases de hierbas; en esta noche comemos hierbas amargas.*

Kom kake pun ichu mnchentukukeyu kie no rume; tfachi pun mnchentukukeyu epu nau meu.

■ *En todas las otras noches no sumergimos las hierbas de ninguna manera; en esta noche las sumergimos dos veces.*

Kom kake pun ikeyi kme anlen ka kiekemu lloyilen; tfachi pun ankeyi lloyilen.

■ *En todas las otras noches comemos sentados rectos o inclinados; en esta noche nos sentamos inclinados.*

Kom kake pun rume weda ikeyi; tfachi pun ikeyi kme ngillatunmeu.

■ *En todas las otras noches comemos de manera ordinaria; en esta noche comemos con una ceremonia especial.*

ABOUT THE LANGUAGE:

Mapudungun

Number of speakers: 300,039
Rank: 710

Mapudungun is spoken in Chile, between the Itata and Tolten rivers, east of the port town of Concapcion. Those who speak Mapudungun are the Mapuche (mapu = earth, che = people) native Americans. Mapudungun speakers also live in Argentina.

ABOUT THE TRANSLATOR:

Cristian Carrillan Anton

Age: Unavailable   Translated: 2005
Town: Temuco, Chile

Cristian was born, raised and has always lived in Temuco. His mother tongue is Mapudungun, dialect: Nguluche. Cristian learned Mapudungun from his mother, not at school. Cristian is working with Carnegie-Mellon University researchers interested in developing speech technology for resource-poor (minority) languages.

Photo by Ralf Brown

Mapudungun speakers, with their teacher, in a class for setting up their own business

Mapuche Ceremonies:

In several mapuche rituals, the compensation of the forces of good (*Ngnechen*) by those of evil (*weküfe*) is pursued. Major prayer rituals are: *nguillatun*, a ceremony of prayer, *machitun*, a healing ritual, and *wentripantu*, a celebration of the New Year, on the Winter solstice.

The *nguillatun* requires a place specially designated for the ceremony. The *rewe* is installed at the center and participants gather around. It lasts a minimum of two days and a maximum of four. In certain zones of the Araucania they were held each two, three or four years, as needed. The public prayer is held for various motives: the weather, the crops, to avoid illness or for plenty of food. During the ceremony there is dancing accompanied by different prayers. An animal is sacrificed, generally a lamb for the *ngepin*, who directs the rite. The animal's blood is sprinkled or distributed among the guests, and the ritual drink *mudai* (fermented grain) is offered to participants. The dead animal's body may be completely burned in a bonfire and eaten.

In this ceremony, the *machi* acts as the celebrant's assistant and, between the sound of her *kultrung*, she sings: "We pray that it rains so that the crops may prosper and we may have animals. "Let it rain," say you, Big Man With Golden Head, and you, Big Woman, we pray to both big and old persons." (Based on University of Chile, School of Arts exhibit on Mapuche culture.)

Māori

He aha te take i rerekē ai tēnei pō i ētahi atu?

■ *Why is this night different from all other nights?*

**I ēra atu pō ka kai tātou i te pātraoa rēwena i te Mataka rānei;
i tēnei pō e kai ai tāttou i te Mataka anake.**

■ *On all other nights we eat either leavened bread or matzah;
on this night only matzah.*

**I ēra atu pō ka kai tātou i ngā momo otaota katoa;
ko tēnei anake pō e kai ai tātou i te otaota kawa.**

■ *On all other nights we eat all kinds of herbs;
on this night only bitter herbs.*

**I ēra atu kāore tātou e tou i a tātou otaota;
engari i tēnei pō ka toua tuaratia e tātou.**

■ *On all other nights we do not dip even once;
on this night we dip twice.*

**I ēra atu pō i te wa e kai ana tātou ka noho tika tātou ka kai
noho whakataretare rānei;
ko tēnei anake pō e kai whakataretare ai tātou.**

■ *On all other nights we eat either sitting up or reclining;
on this night we recline.*

**I ēra atu pō ka kai tātou;
engari i tēnei pō ka hākari tātou.**

■ *On all other nights we eat in an ordinary manner;
on this night we dine with special ceremony.*

The translation's language embodies the viewpoint of a person within a community speaking both *about* its own members and *to* its own members.

Page border shows *Patiki*, a traditional Māori pattern representing hospitality from Pare Hauraki.

ABOUT THE LANGUAGE:

Māori

Number of speakers: 60,260
Rank: 1,508

Māori is primarily spoken in New Zealand's North Island. Māori is fairly closely related to other Polynesian languages such as Hawaiian and Samoan.

The first printed Māori book was Thomas Kendall's 1815 reader called *E korao no New Zealand* ("Talk from New Zealand"). By 1900, more than a thousand publications in Māori had appeared.

ABOUT THE TRANSLATOR:

Colonel R N Grove

Age: Unavailable   Translated: 1997
Town: Wellington, New Zealand

Colonel Grove studied the Māori language at the doctoral level at Victoria University in Wellington, New Zealand. Another version of the translation was provided by an unnamed teacher in a high school in Wellington. The translation and recording used was further corrected and approved by Panui and others at maori.org.nz.

ABOUT THE SPEAKER:

Matua Moeke

Age: 14   Recorded: 1997
Towns: Hawkes Bay / Pukerua Bay, New Zealand

Matua Moeke, of the *Iwi* (tribe) *Ngati Koru*, was born in Hawkes Bay on the east coast of North Island and moved to Pukerua Bay at age 7. Māori is his second language, learned from his father and in school.

Photo courtesy of maori.org.nz, the main Maori site on the Net

Rerenga Wairua, known as The Departing Place of Spirits for the Māori; situated at Cape Reinga, northern-most accessible place in Aotearoa, North Island, New Zealand

Maltese

Għaliex dan il-lejl m'hux bħall-iljieli l-oħra kollha?

■ *Why is this night different from all other nights?*

Fl-iljieli l-oħra kollha, aħna nieklu ħobż magħġun bil-ħmira jew matzah; f'dan il-lejl matzah biss.

■ *On all other nights we eat either leavened bread or matzah; on this night only matzah.*

Fl-iljieli l-oħra kollha, nieklu kull xorta ta' ħxejjex; f'dan il-lejl ħxejjex morr biss.

■ *On all other nights we eat all kinds of greens (herbs); on this night only bitter herbs.*

Fl-iljieli l-oħra kollha, anqas inbillu darba waħda biss; f'dan il-lejl inbillu darbtejn.

■ *On all other nights we do not dip even once; on this night we dip twice.*

Fl-iljieli l-oħra kollha, nieklu jew bil-qiegħda dritti jew baxxuti; f'dan il-lejl inpoġġu la ġenb.

■ *On all other nights we eat either sitting or bending (sitting up or reclining); on this night we sit comfortably sideways (recline).*

Fl-iljieli l-oħra kollha, nieklu b'mod ordinarju; f'dan il-lejl nieklu f'ċerimonja speċjali.

■ *On all other nights we eat in an ordinary manner; on this night we dine with special ceremony.*

ABOUT THE TRANSLATOR AND SPEAKER:

Grazio Falzon

Age: Unavailable   Recorded: 1996
Towns: Zejtun, Malta / CA / OR / Sandusky, OH

Grazio was raised in the Republic of Zejtun, about 5 miles southeast of Valletta, the capital of Malta. He taught romance languages at Pepperdine and Pacific Universities. A translation was also developed by **Anna** at Westgate Internet, a London-based site for Maltese real estate.

ABOUT THE LANGUAGE:

Maltese

Number of speakers: 387,270
Rank: 631

Maltese (also called Malti) is the official language of the Maltese Islands. It is also spoken in Australia, Canada, Italy, Tunisia, United Kingdom and the USA.

The Maltese language developed from the Arabic spoken by Arabs who invaded and occupied Malta in 870 CE, hence it is a Semitic language. The first known Maltese text, *Il Cantilena*, appeared during the 15th C.

Photo by Boris Kester

The harbor of Malta

Malinke

About the Translators:

Fodé S Camera and Rebecca Rhodes

Age: Unavailable   Translated: 2000
Towns: Guinea / Takoma Park, MD

Fodé was interested in translating this text because his first visit to the USA involved flying 14 hours from Guinea to Newark Airport and driving directly to a Passover Seder in Princeton.

About the Language:

Malinke / N'ko

Number of speakers: 525,300
Rank: 525

Malinke is spoken on the border of Mali and Guinea, as well as Guinea-Bissau, Gambia and Senegal. The written version is called N'ko.

Malinke is spoken all over the area that was once the Mali empire; it is the principal Mandingo language. It was the native language of many Africans taken as slaves to the USA in the 18th and 19th centuries. Interestingly, it has many words identical to their Hebrew equivalents. As a Moslem culture, the influence of Arabic added many Semitic roots to the language. The Malinke word for blessing is *baraka* and the word for charity is a close approximation to *tzaddaka*.

Photo by Boris Kester

The deeply rutted highway in Guinea's jungle near Macenta

ma lu to su bo min su ka ne mu ■

■ *Why is this night different from all other nights?*

tan leben buru te wo ni damuna ne ma leben buru an'darini - be lu to su ■
damuna ne tan leben buru n'ato an ,men su bani

■ *On all other nights we eat either leavened bread or matzah; on this night only matzah.*

damuna le be su bin an'darini - be lu to su ■
damuna ne kumun bi n'ato an ,men su bani

■ *On all other nights we eat all kinds of herbs; on this night only bitter herbs.*

kelen ko hali dhjiro la se te an'darini - be lu to su ■
fila ko sumala an n'ato an ,men su bani

■ *On all other nights we do not dip even once; on this night we dip twice.*

samanin na an ,te wo ni sini an damunekela an'darini - be lu to su ■
samanale do an n'ato an ,men su bani

■ *On all other nights we eat either sitting up or reclining; on this night we recline.*

la le koro andarina damunekela ye an ,be lu to su ■
lero la wasanin djamarola damunekela n'ato an ,men su bani

■ *On all other nights we eat in an ordinary manner; on this night we dine with special ceremony.*

About the Speaker:

Daye Mara

Age: Unavailable   Recorded: 2000
Towns: Kissidougou / Conakry, Guinea

Daye Mara is a native of Kissidougou, Guinea. He now lives in the capital city, Conakry.

In the recordings: Daya ends his recording with his name and the name of the language, spoken in French.

Malayalam

ഈ രാത്രി മറ്റുള്ള രാത്രികളിൽ നിന്ന് എന്തുകൊണ്ടു് വ്യത്യാസമായിരിക്കുന്നു?

■ Ee raathri mattulla raathrikalilninnu enthukontu vyathyaasamaayirikkunnu?

■ **Why is this night different from all other nights?**

മറ്റുള്ള രാത്രികളിൽ നമ്മൾ കഴിക്കാറുള്ള അ പ്പം പുളിപ്പിച്ചതോ അല്ലെങ്കിൽ
പുളിപ്പിക്കാത്തതോ ആകാം;
ഈ രാത്രിയിൽ പുളിപ്പിക്കാത്ത അ പ്പം മാത്രം കഴിക്കും.

■ Mattulla raathrikalil nammal kazhikkaarulla appam pulipichatho allenkil
pulippikkaathatho aakam;
ee raathriyil, pulipikkaatha appam maathran kazhikkum.

■ On all other nights we eat either leavened bread (bread with yeast)
or matzah bread without yeast;
on this night only matzah (bread without yeast).

മറ്റുള്ള രാത്രികളിൽ നമ്മൾ എല്ലാ വിധത്തിലും ഉള്ള പ ച്ച ഇലകൾ കഴിക്കും;
ഈ രാത്രിയിൽ കയ്പ്പുള്ള ഇലകൾ മാത്രം കഴിക്കും.

■ Mattulla raathrikalil nammal *kazhikkaarulla appam pulippichatho allenkil
pulippikkaathatho aakam;
ee raathriyil, pulippikkaatha appam maathram kazhikkum.

■ *On all other nights we eat all kinds of herbs* (greens or spices);
on this night only bitter herbs.

മറ്റുള്ള രാത്രികളിൽ നമ്മൾ ഒരിക്കൽ പോലും മുക്കാതെ കഴിക്കും;
ഈ രാത്രിയിൽ നമ്മൾ രണ്ടു പ്രാവശ്യം മുക്കി കഴിക്കും.

■ Mattulla raathrikalil nammal ellaa *vidhathilum ulla pacha elakal kazhikkum;
ee raathriyil kayappulla elakal maathram kazhikkum.

■ **On all other nights we do not dip even once;**
on this night we dip twice.

മറ്റുള്ള രാത്രികളിൽ നമ്മൾ നേരേ ഇരുന്നോ അ ല്ലെങ്കിൽ ചരിഞ്ഞ് ഇരുന്നോ കഴിക്കും;
ഈ രാത്രിയിൽ നമ്മൾ ചരിഞ്ഞ് ഇരുന്നു മാത്രം കഴിക്കും.

■ Mattulla raathrikalil nammal orikkal polum mukkaathe kazhikkum;
ee raathriyil nammal randu praavashyam *mukki kazhikkum.

■ *On all other nights we eat either sitting up or reclining;*
on this night we recline.

മറ്റുള്ള രാത്രികളിൽ നമ്മൾ സാധാരണ രീതിയിൽ കഴിക്കും;
ഈ രാത്രിയിൽ വിശേഷമായ ഊണ് ആയിരിക്കും.

■ Mattulla raathrikalil nammal saadhaarana reethiyil kazhikkum;
ee raathriyil vishaeshamaaya oonu aayirikkum.

■ *On all other nights we eat in an ordinary manner;*
on this night we dine with special ceremony.

---

* Asterisks indicate words not in the recording
(text was modified later by other translators).

> *** For additional information, see**
> **"*Focus on ... pages.pdf*" on the DVD.**

ABOUT THE LANGUAGE:

Malayalam *

Number of speakers: 35,893,990
Rank: 32

Malayalam is chiefly spoken in India's southern state of Kerala, as well
as the Laccadive Islands and states neighboring Kerala. The largest
population of speakers outside of India are in Singapore. The Jews
of Cochin, who speak Malayalam, are an ancient community with
claims of being one of the Lost Tribes of Israel's exiles from the time
of Nebuchadnezzar. In Cochin's Synagogue, built in the 16th C, are
documents (on copper plates) written around the 8th C by the king
offering protection to the Jewish community. About a dozen elderly
Jews remain in Cochin; most of the community now lives in Israel.

Malayalam first appeared in the *Vazhappalli* inscription, dating from
about 830 CE. In the 13th C Malayalam script developed from a script
known as *Vattezhuthu* (round writing). A simplified version of the
script was introduced in the 1970s and 1980s, where consonants and
diacritics are written separately rather than as complex characters.

ABOUT THE TRANSLATOR AND SPEAKER:

Nessy Jayakumar

Age: Unavailable   Recorded: 1996
Towns: Kerala, India / Somerset, NJ

Nessy was born and raised in the state of Kerala, India. She is a
native speaker of Malayalam.
Her translation was guided
by earlier translations by **Mor
Nicholovos Zachariah** (New
York), **M. Krishnakumar**;
Nessy's translation was further
refined by **Gopal Meempat**
(New Jersey) and an unnamed
associate of **Nathan Katz**
(Florida). The text was typed
in by native Malayalam speaker
Issac Mathew (New Jersey).

From the private collection of Dr. K V Rao

भारत INDIA
20
कोचीन सिनागोग
COCHIN SYNAGOGUE
• 1568-1968 •

> **Bonus on the DVD:** Chants
> for the *Ma Nishtana*, *Kiddush*
> and other prayers used by
> the Jews of Cochin, India.

Malay

Kenapa malam ini berbeza daripada malam-malam yang lain?

■ *Why is this night different from all other nights?*

**Pada malam-malam yang lain, kami memakan samada roti yang tidak berkembang atau matzah;
pada malam ini cuma matzah.**

■ *On all other nights we eat either leavened bread or matzah;
on this night only matzah.*

**Pada malam lain, kami makan berbagai jenis herba;
pada malam ini cuma herba pahit.**

■ *On all other nights we eat all kinds of herbs;
on this night only bitter herbs.*

**Pada malam-malam lain, kami tidak mencecah herba sama sekali;
pada malam ini kami mencecah herba dua kali.**

■ *On all other nights we do not dip even once;
on this night we dip twice.*

**Pada malam lain, kami makan berdiri tegak atau membongkok ke hadapan;
pada malam ini kami membongkok ke hadapan.**

■ *On all other nights we eat either sitting up or reclining;
on this night we recline.*

**Pada setiap malam lain, kami makan dengan cara biasa;
malam ini kita makan kenduri.**

■ *On all other nights we eat in an ordinary manner;
on this night we dine with special ceremony.*

Translation notes: Many Malay words are taken from English. For instance, the Malay word for herbs is *herba*. The 5th question is not contained in the recordings.

ABOUT THE LANGUAGE:

Malay

Number of speakers: 10,296,000
Rank: 80

Malay, the official language of Malaysia, is spoken in all districts of Peninsular Malaysia, Sabah and Sarawak. There are also Malay speakers in Brunei, Sumatra, Myanmar, Singapore, Thailand, United Arab Emirates and the USA.

ABOUT THE TRANSLATOR:

Eugene Kang

Age: Unavailable   Translated: 1995
Town: Kuala Lumpur, Malaysia

Eugene was born and raised in Malaysia's capital, Kuala Lumpur.

ABOUT THE SPEAKER:

Hui Mian Tay

Age: Unavailable   Recorded: 1995
Town: Kuala Lumpur, Malaysia

Hui's family moved around a lot because her father was in the Malaysian military. She considers herself to be from Kuala Lumpur.

Kuala Lumpur's Sultan Abdul Samed Building, home of Malaysia's Supreme Court. This example of Victorian Moorish architecture was built in the 19th C

Malagasy

Fa nahoana ity alina ity no hafa noho ny alina rehetra?

■ *Why is this night different from all other nights?*

Tamin'ireo alina hafa rehetra isika dia nihinana mofo nisy na tsy nisy masirasira; fa ity alina ity kosa dia mofo tsy misy masirasira ihany.

■ *On all other nights we eat either leavened bread or matzah; on this night only matzah.*

Tamin'ireo alina hafa rehetra dia nihinana ireo karazan' anana rehetra isika; fa ity alina ity kosa dia toa ny anana masiaka ihany.

■ *On all other nights we eat all kinds of herbs; on this night only bitter herbs.*

Tamin'ireo alina hafa rehetra dia tsy niondrika isika raha nitango anana na indray mandeha aza; fa amin' izao alina izao kosa dia indroa isika no miondrika mitango azy ireo.

■ *On all other nights we do not dip even once; on this night we dip twice.*

Tamin'ireo alina hafa rehetra isika rehefa nisakafo dia nipetraka na nitsilany; fa amin'izao alina izao kosa dia toa mitsilany ihany.

■ *On all other nights we eat either sitting up or reclining; on this night we recline.*

Tamin'ireo alina hafa rehetra dia nisakafo amin' ny fomba nahazatra isika; fa ity alina ity kosa dia misakafo amin' ny fomba manetriketrika.

■ *On all other nights we eat in an ordinary manner; on this night we dine with special ceremony.*

> **Bonus in the recordings:** Samples of typical Malagasy music were provided by the translators: the album Barikavily by Erick Manana and Akory Kabaro by Mily Clement.

ABOUT THE LANGUAGE:

Plateau Malagasy

Number of speakers: 7,528,900
Rank: 101

Plateau Malagasy is the most common language spoken in Madagascar, within the capital and central parts of the Island. There are also some speakers in Comoros, Réunion.

ABOUT THE TRANSLATOR AND SPEAKER:

Jonah Ratsimbazafy and Vololontiana (Tiana) Razafindratsita

Ages: Unavailable   Recorded: 1996
Towns: Antananarivo, Madagascar / Stony Brook, NY

Both Jonah and Tiana were born and raised in Antananarivo, Madagascar. As college students, they moved to the USA to study at SUNY Stony Brook. Their recording is unique in this collection, as they jointly read the Malagasy translation.

Photo by Stephanie Goldhuber

The Malagasy people playing traditional instruments

Makonde

Kwa chini chilo cha nelo chinitindana na chilo cha jisiku jingi?

■ *Why is this night different from all other nights?*

Jisiku jahijohe chilo tulya mkate uvatandile hamira au uvakatandile hamira; kwa chilo cha nelo tulambela kulya mkate uvakatandile hamira.

■ *On all other nights we eat either leavened bread or matzah; on this night only matzah.*

Jisiku jahijohe tulya milandi na jinyia; jahijohe chilo cha nelo tulambelulya jinyia jakukalala weka.

■ *On all other nights we eat all kinds of herbs; on this night only bitter herbs.*

Jisiku jahijohe chilo tukachuvika wala mwanda umo; chilo cha nelo tukambeka kuchuvika mindamivili.

■ *On all other nights we do not dip even once; on this night we dip twice.*

Jisiku jahijohe chilo tulya tuikele au tuyamile; lakini chilo chinu tulambekulya tuyamile.

■ *On all other nights we eat either sitting up or reclining; on this night we recline.*

Jisiku jahijohe chilo tulya kwa utulivu chihi lakini chilo cha nelo; tulambekulya kwa kuyangala nawene.

■ *On all other nights we eat in an ordinary manner; on this night we dine with special ceremony.*

ABOUT THE LANGUAGE:

Makonde

Number of speakers: 1,340,000
Rank: 302

Makonde is spoken in the Mtwara region of Tanzania, primarily the districts of Mtwara Urban, Mtwara Rural, Tandahomba and Newala. There are also several hundred thousand speakers in Mozambique.

ABOUT THE TRANSLATOR:

Nurdin Nayopa

Age: 40   Translated: 2009
Town: Dar es Salaam, Tanzania

Nurdin works as a gardener and his interests are centered on sports. He is a native speaker of Makonde.

ABOUT THE SPEAKER:

Joanita Ngaiza

Age: 38   Recorded: 2010
Town: Dar es Salaam, Tanzania

Joanita is a native speaker of Kihaya, fluent in Kihehe, and can read and write Makonde and the other languages she recorded. Her full biography is on the Sukuma page.

Photo by Ilana Locker

Zanzibar's Ngalawa boats are the precursors of the modern hydrofoil. These traditional boats are flanked by a form of water skis, which provide stability and lift

Makhuwa

Sheny ohiyu ula wilikana ni ohiyu sikina?
- ShayNEE ohiyu uLA WILikana n' ohiyu sikina?
- *Why is this night different from all other nights?*

Wakunla ohiyu, ninja epophoro yoloka, walaa yohikhalana eferemento;
Ohiyu ula, eriy yohikhalana eferemento paahi.
- Wakunla ohiyu, ninJA aypop'hoRO YOloka, waLAA yohiKHAlana efeREMenTO;
  Ohiyu uLA, ayrYI yohiKHAlana eferemento pa'ahi.
- *On all other nights we eat either leavened bread or matzah;*
  on this night only matzah.

Ohiyu sikina ninja mathapa manjene ohilikana;
Ohiyu ula, ariy mathapa owawa paahi.
- Ohiyu sikina ninJA mat'HApa manjAYnay OHiliKAna;
  Ohiyu uLA, aRIY mat'HApa Owawa pa'Ahi.
- *On all other nights we eat all kinds of herbs;*
  on this night only bitter herbs.

Wakunla ohiyu, khannatthi ovelavela nnakhala vamosa;
Ohiyu ula, ni ovelavela emara pili.
- Wakunla ohiyu, khaNAT'hi ovelavela nakhala vamoSAH;
  Ohiyu uLA, n' ovelavela emara piLI.
- *On all other nights we do not dip even once;*
  on this night we dip twice.

Wakunla ohiyu, ninja moota ontthuna ahum;
Ohiyu ula, ni nomurama.
- Wakunla ohiyu, ninJA mo'oTA ont'huna aHUM;
  Ohiyu uLA, n' nomurama.
- *On all other nights we eat either sitting up or reclining;*
  on this night we recline.

Wakunla ohiyu, ninja moota sana;
Ohiyu ula, ninja moota wottitthimiha.
- Wakunla ohiyu, ninJA mo'oTA sana;
  Ohiyu uLA, ninJA mo'ota wotit'himiHAH.
- *On all other nights we eat in an ordinary manner;*
  on this night we dine with special ceremony.

Translation notes: th is very strongly aspirated t, same for kh. The next-to-last syllable has primary stress unless otherwise marked.

ABOUT THE LANGUAGE:

Makhuwa

Number of speakers: 3,090,000
Rank: 186

Makhuwa, called Makhuwa-Metto or Emakhuwa by its speakers, is spoken in Mozambique's Nampula province, south of the area of Meeto.

ABOUT THE TRANSLATOR AND SPEAKER:

Loubato Maria Pinto

Age: 25   Translated: 1995
Towns: Nampula Province, Mazambique / Odivelas, Portugal

Loubato was born and raised in Mozambique's Nampula province, where his first language was Makhuwa. At age 19, he moved to Portugal for studies and now works for the Portuguese-African Institute for Scientific and Technological Cooperation (*Instituto Luso Africano para a Cooperação Científica e Tecnológica*) in Amadora, Portugal and also does part-time teaching of the language and culture of the Makhuwa people. Loubato worked with **Joao Gabriel de Barros** on the translation.

Photo by Bernard Cloutier (berclo.net)

The 1900s-era railroad station in Mozambique's capital, Maputo, was designed by Gustave Eiffel

Macedonian

Zošto e ovaa večer drugčija od drugite večeri?

■ *Why is this night different from all other nights?*

Na site drugi večeri, nie jademe običen leb ili bez dvasec; ovaa večer samo bez kvasec.

■ *On all other nights we eat either leavened bread or matzah; on this night only matzah.*

Na site drugi večeri, nie jademe bilo kakvi rastenija; ovaa večer samo gorčlivi rastenija.

■ *On all other nights we eat all kinds of herbs; on this night only bitter herbs.*

Na site drugi večeri, nie ne namaknuvame nitu ednaš; ovaa večer nie namaknuvame dvapati.

■ *On all other nights we do not dip even once; on this night we dip twice.*

Na site drugi večeri, nie jademe sedejki ili ležejki; ovaa večer ležejki.

■ *On all other nights we eat either sitting up or reclining; on this night we recline.*

ABOUT THE LANGUAGE:

Macedonian

Number of speakers: 2,113,170
Rank: 222

Macedonian (also called Makedonski and Slavic) is the national language of Macedonia. The northern dialect is in Kumanovo-Kratovo Region; the southeastern dialect around Gevgelija, Strumica and Lake Dojran; western dialects are in the Veles, Prilep, Kichevo and Bitola regions and another in the Debar-Galchnik region. There are significant numbers of speakers in Greece, Albania and Bulgaria.

ABOUT THE TRANSLATOR AND SPEAKER:

George Tomov

Age: 62   Recorded: 1995
Towns: Strumica, Macedonia / Queens, NY

George was born and raised in Strumica, Macedonia. He is a world-renowned folk-dance teacher. George had an unprecedented 16-year tenure as a solo dancer with two national ensembles in Yugoslavia. He is a noted authority on the music, dance and culture of the ethnic regions comprising the former Yugoslavia. He emigrated to the USA at age 36.

George Tomov, feted at his 70th birthday, celebrating 50 years of professional folkdance

Maasai

Kainyoo pee epaasha ena miso (kewarie) alang' nkulie misoi (kewarieitin) pooki?

■ *Why is this night different from all other nights?*

Kore too nkulie misoi pookin, naa kinosh (kinya) emukate naisuijo arashu Matzah;
Kake kore tena miso naa kinos Matzah ake.

■ *On all other nights we eat either leavened bread or matzah;*
on this night only matzah.

Kore too nkulie misoi pookin, naa kinos mpukunut kumok o' mbenek;
kake kore tena miso naa kinos mbenek naa' dua ake.

■ *On all other nights we eat all kinds of herbs;*
on this night only bitter herbs.

Kore too nkulie misoi pookin, naa mikilopilopie hata kata nabo;
kake kore tena miso naa kilopilopie katitin are.

■ *On all other nights we do not dip even once;*
on this night we dip twice.

Kore too nkulie misoi pookin, naa kidaa kintashe arashu kimperipera;
kake kore tena miso naa kidaa kimperipera aka.

■ *On all other nights we eat either sitting up or reclining;*
on this night we recline.

Kore too nkulie misoi pookin, naa kidaa kintashe arashu kimperipera;
kake kore tena miso naa kidaa kimperipera aka.

■ *On all other nights we eat in an ordinary manner;*
on this night we dine with special ceremony.

Photo © Susan Hantman

An elderly Maasai in warrior dress

Translation notes: The parenthesized words are terms specific to Kimeli's local community, e.g. for "night". Unparenthesized words are those more commonly used in Maasai. The word for leavened bread used in the Maasai Bible is a Swahili word; he also used the Swahili word for spices (herbs) and the Hebrew loan word for Matzah.

ABOUT THE TRANSLATOR AND SPEAKER:

Kimeli Willson Naiyomah

Age: 25   Recorded: 2002
Towns: Enoosaen, Kenya / Stanford, CA

Kimeli is a junior Maasai warrior. He was raised in Enoosaen, a village 10 miles from the Kenyan Game Reserve. Maasai is his native tongue: his father is Maasai and his mother speaks Kalenjin. He also speaks Kiswahili.

Kimeli was in the national news because of a donation of sacred cows. This Maasai warrior was in New York City during the attacks of September 11, 2001, on the World Trade Center. When he told his community in West Kenya about the attacks, the community elders wanted to donate sacred cows to America – a traditional Maasai symbol of consolation. (The cows couldn't be sent to the USA, so Kenyan crafts were later sent.)

He is currently writing a dictionary of Maasai and pursuing a pre-med program.

ABOUT THE LANGUAGE:

Maasai

Number of speakers: 1,045,000
Rank: 348

Maasai (called Maa by its speakers) is spoken in Kenya's Kajiado and Narok districts in the Rift Valley Province. There are also speakers in Tanzania.

Luxembourgish

Waat mecht dest nuecht aanecht vun all di aner nuechten?

■ *Why is this night different from all other nights?*

Di aner nuechten zappen mer eisen Brout mol net eng keier; mee dest nuecht zappen mer et zwee mol.

■ *On all other nights we eat either leavened bread or matzah; on this night only matzah.*

Di aner nuechten iessen mer entweder Chametz (Broud met Hief gebaakt) oder Matza (Broud ouni Hief); mee dest nuecht nemmen Matza.

■ *On all other nights we eat all kinds of herbs; on this night only bitter herbs.*

Di aner nuechten iessen mer all sort vun Gemeis; mee dest nuecht nemmen Maror (batter Gemeiss).

■ *On all other nights we do not dip even once; on this night we dip twice.*

Di aner nuechten iessen mer am setzen oder gesteip; mee dest nuecht iessen mer just gesteipt.

■ *On all other nights we eat either sitting up or reclining; on this night we recline.*

Di aner nuechten iessen mer op enger normaler manneiere; mee dest nuecht iessen mer wei an engem Fest.

■ *On all other nights we eat in an ordinary manner; on this night we dine with special ceremony.*

ABOUT THE LANGUAGE:

Luxembourgish

Number of speakers: 320,830
Rank: 685

Luxembourgish is the national language of Luxembourg. It is as distinct from Standard German as is Dutch.

ABOUT THE TRANSLATOR AND SPEAKER:

Fabien Malouin

Age: 22   Recorded: 2010
Towns: Luxembourg / Ottawa, Canada

Fabien Malouin is an undergraduate undergoing conversion to Orthodox Judaism in Ottawa. A native of the capital city of Luxembourg for most of his life, Fabien speaks 6 languages. His strongest interests are language and culture.

Fabien provided translations of Luxembourgish from English as well as a Yiddish-to-Luxembourgish version, which for his choice of Sephardic traditions, has a different question order.

Luxembourgish translation from Fabien's Yiddish version:

Waat ass anecht un dest Nuecht vun all di aner nuechten vum ganzen joer?

■ וואָס איז אַנדערעש פֿון דער נאַכט פֿון פּסח פֿון אַלע נעכט פֿון אַ גאַנץ יאָר?

All nuecht vum ganzen joer zappen mer net cmol eng keier, mee haut op der Nuecht vun Pesach (Passafest), zappen mir, een, zwee mol – een mol den karpas am Salzwaasser, dann den zweete mol marror am charoses.

■ אַלע נעכט פֿון אַ גאַנץ יאָר טונקען מיר נישט איין אַפֿילע איין מאָל; אָבער די נאַכט פֿון פּייסאַך, טונקען מיר איין צוויי מאָל – איין מאָל קאַרפּאַס אין זאַלץ וואַסער, די צוויטע מאָל מאַראָר אין חאַראָסעף.

All nuecht vum ganzen joer, iessen mer chometz oder Matza; mee op der Nuecht vun Pesach, iessen mer nemmen Matza.

■ אַלע נעכט פֿון אַ גאַנץ יאָר עפֿן מיר חאָמעטץ אָבער מאַטסעה, אָבער די נאַכט פֿון פּייסאַך, עפֿן מיר נאָר מאַטסעה.

All nuecht vum ganzen joer, iessen mer all sort vun Gemeiss; mee op der Nuecht vun Pesach, iessen mer nemmen batter Gemeiss.

■ אַלע נעכט פֿון אַ גאַנץ יאָר עפֿן מיר אַלערלײַ גרינטסן, אָבער די נאַכט פֿון פּייסאַך, עפֿן מיר נאָר ביטערע גרינטסן.

All nuecht vum ganzen joer, iessen mer mer am setzen oder am steipen; mee op der Nuecht vun Pesach, iessen mer nemmen am steipen.

■ אַלע נעכט פֿון אַ גאַנץ יאָר עפֿן מיר סײַ זיטסנדיקערהייט און סײַ אָנגעלײנטערהייט; אָבער די נאַכט פֿון פּייסאַך, עפֿן מיר נאָר אָנגעלײנטערהייט.

Tate, ich hun dir elo di veier kashes gestallt, elo geff mer eng aentwert.

■ טאַטע, איך האָב בײַ דיר געפֿרעגט די די פֿיר קאַשעף יעצט גיב מיר אַ טערעץ.

The synagogue in Luxembourg City, rebuilt after the Second World War

Luo

Ang'o momiyo otieno ni opogore gi otieno mamoko?

■ *Why is this night different from all other nights?*

Otieno mamoko duto wachamo kuon moyieny; otienoni to mana kuon ma okoyieny.

■ *On all other nights we eat either leavened bread or matzah; orn this night only matzah.*

Otieno mamoko duto wachamo alote duto; otienoni to mana alote makech.

■ *On all other nights we eat all kinds of herbs; on this night only bitter herbs.*

Otieno mamoko duto okwayuthi kata dichiel; otienoni to wayutho diriyo.

■ *On all other nights we do not dip even once; on this night we dip twice.*

Otieno mamoko duto wachiemo kawabet tir kata kawayiengore; otienoni to mana kawabet tir.

■ *On all other nights we eat either sitting up or reclining; on this night we recline.*

Otieno mamoko wachiemo kapile; otienoni to wagago gi nyasi makende.

■ *On all other nights we eat in an ordinary manner; on this night we dine with special ceremony.*

The recordings speak the first translation we received (below). Because it is different from the one above, we do not know which question is missing.

Ang'o mumiyo otieno makawuono ni opogore gimamuko?
Otieno mamokogo wachamo kuon mobagi gi thome kata matzah;
  Otieno makawuono ni to wachamo mana manyasi makech.
Otieno mamokogo te, ok waluti katamana dicheil;
  To Otieno makawuono ni, to waluto diriyo.
Otieno mamokogo te, wachiemo mana kawachung'o kata kawayiengore;
  wayiengore.
Otieno mamokogo duto te, wachiemo mana kaka pile;
  Otieno ni, to wachiemo mana gi nyasi.

ABOUT THE LANGUAGE:

Luo

Number of speakers: 4,410,000
Rank: 145

Luo, called Dholuo by its speakers, is spoken in Kenya's Nyanza Province. There are also a significant number of speakers in Tanzania.

ABOUT THE TRANSLATOR AND SPEAKER:

Timon Onjero Maingi

Age: Unavailable   Recorded: 1999
Town: Nairobi, Kenya

Timon is a language instructor in Nairobi, Kenya, and a fluent speaker of Luo.

Photo © Niko Lipsanen

A view of Kibera, a poor area near Nairobi, Kenya

Luiseño

Híyngay su `iví´ túukumit `awóonganwish chóo´onngay túukumingay `awóongay?

■ *Why is this night different from all other nights?*

Chóo´onnga túukuminga `awóongacha qwá´ma şáawokish havúşşilatal mán
şáawokish qáy havúşşilatal;
Pitóo túkva po'éek şáawokish qáy havúşşilatal.

■ *On all other nights we eat either leavened bread or matzah; on this night only matzah.*

Chóo´onnga túukuminga `awóongacha qwá´ma chóo´on michát `ánkichi túu´qati;
Pitóo túkva po'éek túu´qati chíivuti.

■ *On all other nights we eat all kinds of herbs; on this night only bitter herbs.*

Chóo´onnga túukuminga `awóongacha qáy súplish yú´chima;
Pitóo túkvacha yú´chiwun wéhkun.

■ *On all other nights we do not dip even once; on this night we dip twice.*

Chóo´onnga túukuminga `awóongacha qwá´ma tavá´ `anik mán máşşanik;
Pitóo túkvacha máşşaan.

■ *On all other nights we eat either sitting up or reclining; on this night we recline.*

Chóo´onnga túukuminga `awóongacha qwá´ma michá´ `axánninik mímchapan;
Pitóo túkvacha náachaxanwun tóşngush nónminik.

■ *On all other nights we eat in an ordinary manner; on this night we dine with special ceremony.*

Recording ends with: `ivíp Eric Elliott
`atáaxum pomtéelangax téetilaqat
("This is Eric Elliott speaking Luiseño").

ABOUT THE LANGUAGE:

Luiseño

Number of speakers: 35
Rank: 6,336

Luiseño is spoken in southern California by the San Juan Capistrano Indians. The name of the language is taken from the nearest Spanish mission (Mission San Luis Rey).

ABOUT THE TRANSLATOR AND SPEAKER:

Eric Elliott

Age: 40s   Recorded: 2004
Location: Southern California

Eric Elliott studied linguistics in college (UCLA at Irvine) and learned Luiseño from fluent speaker Villiana Hyde of the Rincón Indian Reservation. Eric documented the language and has been a leading expert in the Uto-Aztecan languages.

He was born in Los Angeles and raised in California's Coachella Valley. He currently teaches Luiseño on the Pechanga and Pauma reservations.

Z Y X W V U T S R Q P O N M L K J I H G F E D C B A

Photo by Tom Judd

California's Golden Gate Bridge, built 1933-1937, is named after the Golden Gate Strait entrance of the San Francisco Bay

Lozi

Kiñi busihu bo ha bu fapana ni masihu a mañwi?

■ *Why is this night different from all other nights?*

Masihu Kaufela, lu ca sinkwa se se si beilwe mumela Kapa matzah; mwa busihu bo, ki matzah fela.

■ *On all other nights we eat either leavened bread or matzah; on this night only matzah.*

Mwa masihu Kaufela, lu ca mifuta kaufela ya milyani; mwa busihu bo, milyani ye baba fela.

■ *On all other nights we eat all kinds of herbs; on this night only bitter herbs.*

Mwa masihu Kaufela, ha lu sunsi ni haiba hañwi; mwa busihu bo, lu sunsa habeli.

■ *On all other nights we do not dip even once; on this night we dip twice.*

Mwa masihu Kaufela, lu ca lu inzi lu otolohile Kapa lu endami; mwa busihu bo, lwa endama.

■ *On all other nights we eat either sitting up or reclining; on this night we recline.*

Mwa masihu Kaufela, lu ca Ka mukwa wa ku twaela; mwa busihu bo, lu ca ka mukwa wa sebelezo ye ketilwe.

■ *On all other nights we eat in an ordinary manner; on this night we dine with special ceremony.*

ABOUT THE LANGUAGE:

Lozi

Number of speakers: 722,600
Rank: 446

Lozi (called Silozi by its speakers) is spoken in Zambia's Barotseland, Western Province and Southern Province near Livingstone. It is also spoken in Botswana, Namibia and Zimbabwe.

ABOUT THE TRANSLATOR AND SPEAKER:

Andrew Matjila

Age: Unavailable   Recorded: 1998
Towns: South Africa / Caprivi, Namibia

Andrew grew up in South Africa and partly in Caprivi, Namibia, where most people speak Lozi. He is a fluent speaker of the language.

Photo by Stephanie Goldhuber

Wood-carvings by a native of Mukuni, Zambia

Lithuanian

Kuo ši naktis skiriasi nuo visų kitų naktų?
- Koo-o shee nahtees skeer'ahsee noo-o veesoo keetoo nahktoo?
- *Why is this night different from all other nights?*

Visomis kitomis naktimis mes valgome duoną ir matzus; o šią naktį - tik matzus.
- Veesomess keetomees nahkteemees møs vahlgomø doo-onah eer mahtzoos; o sheeah nahktee teek mahtzoos.
- *On all other nights we eat either leavened bread or matzah; on this night only matzah.*

Visomis kitomis naktimis mes valgome įvairius žalumynus; o šią naktį - tik karčias žoles.
- Veesomess keetomees nahkteemees møs vahlgomø eeviroo zhahloomeehnoos; o sheeah nahktee teek :kahrchahs zholøs.
- *On all other nights we eat all kinds of herbs; on this night only bitter herbs.*

Visomis kitomis naktimis mes nepasidažome nei vieno karto; o šią naktį - net du kartus.
- Veesomess keetomees nahkteemees møs nøpahseedahzhomø nøee vee'øno kahrto; o sheeah nahktee nøt doo kahrtoos.
- *On all other nights we do not dip even once; on this night we dip twice.*

Visomis kitomis naktimis mes sėdime tiesiai arba pasvirę; o šią naktį - tik pasvirę.
- Veesomess keetomees nahkteemees møs søndeemø teeøseei ahrbah pahsveerøh; o sheeah nahktee teek pahsveerøh.
- *On all other nights we eat either sitting up or reclining; on this night we recline.*

Visomis kitomis naktimis mes valgome įprastai; o šią naktį mes pietaujame iškilmingai.
- Veesomess keetomees nahkteemees møs vahlgomø eeprahsti'; o sheeah nahktee møs peeøto'uyahmø eeshkeelmee'ngi.
- *On all other nights we eat in an ordinary manner; on this night we dine with special ceremony.*

Translation notes: The word for "night" *naktį* was used for a more literal translation, although in Lithuanian the word is specifically used for the time after midnight (e.g. activities like this would not normally occur at night).
ø in the transliteration indicates a vowel like 'a' in bat, but more open.

ABOUT THE LANGUAGE:

Lithuanian
Number of speakers: 3,154,180
Rank: 179

Lithuanian is the national language of Lithuania. There are speakers in 18 other countries, from Argentina to Uzbekistan.

Lithuanian is considered to be the oldest surviving Indo-European language and is thought to retain features of Proto-Indo-European, such as pitch-accent and a complex inflexional case system. Some words in Lithuanian resemble words in Sanskrit and Latin.

Lithuanian first appeared in print in the form of a catechism in 1547. The first Lithuanian dictionary was printed during the 17th C. Between 1864 and 1904 the printing and teaching of Lithuanian was banned - Russian, Polish, Belarussian or Latin had to be used instead. When the ban was lifted in 1904, there was a resurgence of Lithuanian literature.

ABOUT THE TRANSLATOR AND SPEAKER:

Dr. Virginia Vaitekonis Obando
Age: Unavailable   Recorded: 1996
Towns: Radviliskis, Lithuania / Elizabeth, NJ

Dr. Obando was Professor of Linguistics at Vilnius University. She emigrated to the USA and now sits on the Supreme Council of the National Knights of Lithuania.

Photos by Karen and Ed Kaplan

Views of the Jewish district in Vilnius (Vilna), which dates before 1568. East European Jewry called it the "Jerusalem of Lithuania"

Lingala

Buto oyo eza kesena na butu nyoso pona-nini?

■ *Why is this night different from all other nights?*

**Na butu mosuzu nyoso toliaka napa to matzah;
na butu oyo toliaka kaka matzah.**

■ *On all other nights we eat either leavened bread or matzah;
on this night only matzah.*

**Na butu mosuzu nyoso toliaka nkasa nyoso;
na butu oyo toliaka nkasa bololo.**

■ *On all other nights we eat all kinds of herbs;
on this night only bitter herbs.*

**Na butu mosuzu nyoso tosukolaka nkusote;
na butu oyo tosukolaka nkasa mobule.**

■ *On all other nights we do not dip even once;
on this night we dip twice.*

**Na butu mosuzu nyoso toliaka;
na butu oyo toliaka malamu.**

■ *On all other nights we eat either sitting up or reclining;
on this night we recline.*

**Na butu mosuzu nyoso tofandaka semba tompemba;
na butu oyo topemaka.**

■ *On all other nights we eat in an ordinary manner;
on this night we dine with special ceremony.*

ABOUT THE LANGUAGE:

Lingala

Number of speakers: 2,141,300
Rank: 219

Lingala, also called Ngala, is spoken in the Democratic Republic of the Congo as well as Congo. It is widely used in Bandundu, Equateur and Orientale provinces.

ABOUT THE TRANSLATOR AND SPEAKER:

Kimfuemina Luvuma

Age: Unavailable   Recorded: 1998
Locations: Democratic Republic of the Congo / PA

Kimfuemina (pronounced "Kimvuemina") indicated there are two major types of Lingala. The one shown here is a classic or archaic form. She was a student at the University of Pennsylvania when she did the translation. An earlier translation was worked on by **Larry** in NJ.

Photo by Elise Korn

Gorillas in the Virunga Mountains of the Democratic Republic of the Congo

Leti

Translated from Indonesian

Unne siapo mèldi ta emmèka mèlduma?
- ■ reason what.then night.now not like night.some?
- ■ *Mengapa malam ini berbeda dari malam-malam sebelumnya?*

Mèldumpo tòòne kuksi duma mats;
Mèldi di matsa mèko.
Mèldumpo tòòne avièrsa-vètra; mèldi di, avièrasmèke.
- ■ night.some.then we.eat bread or matzah;
  night.now now matzah only.
  night.some.then we.eat rice-maize; night.now now rice-only.
- ■ *Malam-malam sebelumnya, kita makan roti atau matsa;
  malam ini, hanya matsa.*

Mèldumpo tòòne ortavi-atiavi;
mèldi di ortappiapiaitmèke.
- ■ night.some.then we.eat bamboo.leaf-tree.leaf;
  night.now now bamboo.leaf.bitter.only.
- ■ *Malam-malam sebelumnya, kita makan berbagai jamu;
  malam ini, hanya jamu pahit.*

Mèldumpo ittounde reeni idtawali;
mèldi di ittounde reeni voruo.
- ■ night.some.then we.dip.once times one.not.also;
  night.now now we.dip.once times two.
- ■ *Malam-malam sebelumnya, sekalipun kita tidak mencelupkan;
  malam ini, kita mencelupkan dua kali.*

Mèldumpo tòande tamtiètna ka tasrièi ka;
mèldi di tasriemianmano.
Mèldumpo tamtiètna-taprirpio tòan; mèldi di taprirmianmano.
- ■ night.some.then we.sit or we.lean or;
  night.now now we.lean.continuous.
  night.some.then we.sit-we.stand.then we.eat; night.now now we.stand.continuous.
- ■ *Malam-malam sebelumnya, kita makan sambil duduk atau bersandar santai;
  malam ini, kita bersandar santai.*

Mèldumpo tòande emso mèko;
mèldi di tòande todi sniolmiòkmòklawarresio.
Mèldumpo todi snioli-ièvsa mnniniru-mnanapambo tòan;
mèldi di todi snioli-liète po tòan.
- ■ night.some.then we.eat.once like.that only;
  night.now now we.eat.once behavior.good.very.
  night.some.then we.carry behavior-conduct silent-soft.then we.eat;
  night.now now we.carry behavior-tradition then we.eat.
- ■ *Malam-malam sebelumnya, kita makan secara biasa;
  malam ini, kita santap dengan upacara khusus.*

ABOUT THE LANGUAGE:

Leti

Number of speakers: 7,500
Rank: 3,323

Leti is spoken on Leti Island in Indonesia.

Photo by Aone van Engelenhoven

The coastline of the Indonesian island of Leti

ABOUT THE TRANSLATOR AND SPEAKER:

Dr. Aone Th. P G van Engelenhoven

Age: 36   Recorded: 1998
Towns: Halsteren / Leiden, Netherlands

Dr. van Engelenhoven is an Astronesian linguistics professor in Leiden University's Department of Languages & Culture Southeast Asia & Oceania. Aone is of mixed Letinese and Dutch descent, and is bilingual in Dutch and Malay (Indonesian). He has been in contact with Leti since childhood, has spoken it often and studied the language as an undergraduate and in his post-doctoral professional career.

Aone reports the text was vaguely familiar because very remote Jewish relatives mentioned the ritual of Passover to him. The Leti translation was developed primarily from the Indonesian translation (with reference to the English as well).

In the recordings: Unaccountably, the recording received was missing most of the 1st question. The reading differs slightly from both the linguistic and cultural versions for most questions. In question 4, there is a significant difference; question 5 appears to be based on the cultural translation.

Translation notes: The translation shows two versions – a linguistic translation (rendering the exact text into Leti) and a looser cultural translation (using concepts more familiar to the Letinese). Just as the cultural translation (referring to maize or rise and standing continuously) appears strange to us, the linguistic translation would appear strange to the Letinese.

A/E
Z Y X W V U T S R Q P O N M L K J I H G F E D C B A

Lenape

Kweekw ha kway wunj-yoon piiskeew paliiw wunj-ktakan piiskeewal.

■ *Why is this night different from all other nights?*

**Weemu ktakan piiskeewal numiichihna paasapwaan ii-na waak matzah;
Kway yoon piiskeew shukehla matzah.**

■ Paasapwaan (a Lenape bread that rises)

■ *On all other nights we eat either leavened bread or matzah;
on this night only matzah.*

**Weemu ktakan piiskeewal numiichihna kaahaniipakwal;
Kway yoon piiskeew shukehla laxkeetkweekal.**

■ Laxkeetkweekal "bitter greens" is a derivation of laxkiipookwun
(bitter to taste) and askiixaskwal (green/raw grass)

■ *On all other nights we eat all kinds of herbs;
on this night only bitter herbs.*

**Weemu ktakan piiskeewal mah ngwutun namukwunumihna;
Kway yoon piiskeew niishun namukwunumihna.**

■ *On all other nights we do not dip even once;
on this night we dip twice.*

**Weemu ktakan piiskeewal nzhaaxkohkweepihna ii-na waak
mbumiitohkweepihna miitsiiyeengwa;
Kway yoon piiskeew mbumiitohkweepihna.**

■ *On all other nights we eat either sitting up or reclining;
on this night we recline.*

**Weemu ktakan piiskeewal lunii-numiitsihna;
Kway yoon piiskeew weelihk ndakwiipwihna.**

■ Weelihk (special feast)

■ *On all other nights we eat in an ordinary manner;
on this night we dine with special ceremony.*

> **In the recordings:** Dianne ends her recording with *Anushiik*
> "anisheek" (Thank you) spoken in Lenape. The name of
> the language is spoken by Nora Thompson Dean (Touching
> Leaves Woman), 1907-1964.

> *** For additional information, see**
> **"*Focus on ... pages.pdf*" on the DVD.**

ABOUT THE LANGUAGE:

Lenape *

Number of speakers: 6
Rank: 6,547

Lenape, also called Munsee, Delaware and Unami, was originally
spoken by native Americans living in current areas of New York and
New Jersey. Many geographic names are derived from Lenape; for
instance, 'Manhattan' is a Lenape word. Around 1750, some of the tribe
moved to Ontario and the rest to Kansas, then to Oklahoma. Although
the tribes remain in both areas, Lenape speakers survive only in
Ontario. (The last speaker of the Oklahoma dialect died in 2002.)

Lenape is the rarest living language in this collection.

ABOUT THE TRANSLATOR AND SPEAKER:

Dianne Snake

Age: 61   Recorded: 2003
Town: Moraviantown, Ontario

Dianne is the youngest of the 6 surviving native speakers of Lenape,
and its most fluent speaker. She is involved in many language
preservation efforts in Moraviantown.

Photo by Jerry McCrea © NJ Star Ledger

In a language exercise, Dianne
Snake whispers a Delaware
phrase to a fellow Lenape

Latvian

Kāpēc šīnakts atšķiras no visām citām naktīm?

■ *Why is this night different from all other nights?*

Visās citās naktīs mēs ēdam vai nu raudzētu maizi vai neraudzētu maizi;
Šai naktī, tikai neraudzētu maizi.

■ *On all other nights we eat either leavened bread or matzah;*
on this night only matzah.

Visās citās naktīs mēs ēdam dažādus augus;
Šai naktī, tikai rūgtus augus.

■ *On all other nights we eat all kinds of herbs;*
on this night only bitter herbs.

Visās citās naktīs mēs neiemērcam pat vienreiz;
Šai naktī, mēs iemērcam divas reizes.

■ *On all other nights we do not dip even once;*
on this night we dip twice.

Visās citās naktīs mēs ēdam vai nu sežot vai atlaižoties;
Šai naktī, mēs atlaižamies.

■ *On all other nights we eat either sitting up or reclining;*
on this night we recline.

Visās citās naktīs mēs ēdam parastā veidā;
Šai naktī, mēs ar īpašu cermoniju mielojamies.

■ *On all other nights we eat in an ordinary manner;*
on this night we dine with special ceremony.

ABOUT THE LANGUAGE:

Latvian

Number of speakers: 1,504,880
Rank: 275

Latvian is the national language of Latvia. There are also speakers in 14 other countries from Australia to Venezuela. The first publication in Latvian was a catechism in 1585. The first Latvian dictionary was compiled in 1638. Until 1930, Latvian was written with the *Fractur* alphabet, which was derived from German. Afterwards, the modified Latin alphabet seen here was adopted.

ABOUT THE TRANSLATOR AND SPEAKER:

Ināra Āboliņš

Age: Unavailable   Recorded: 1997
Towns: Latvia / Germany / Kenton, Middlesex, England

Ināra, a native speaker of Latvian, went to a Displaced Persons' Camp in Germany. At age 10, after WW II she arrived as a refugee to England where she now lives. The translation was also worked on by her son, **Inta Batsman** and her husband, **Ziedonis Āboliņš**. As Inara's husband Ziedonis is Jewish, the text was familiar and helped provide insight in translating the text.

Photo © Niko Lipsanen

The medieval Dome Cathedral in Riga, Latvia, founded in 1212, is the largest church in the Baltics. It contains an organ with 6,718 pipes, which was the world's largest when it was installed in 1884

Lao

ເປັນຫຍັງຄືນນີ້ຈິ່ງແຕກຕ່າງກັບຄືນອື່ນ ໆ ທັງໝົດ
- ■ Pen yang khun-ni jung taek tang kab khun-un-un thangmod?
- *■ Why is this night different from all other nights?*

ໃນຄືນອື່ນ ໆ ເຮົາກິນເຂົ້າຈີໃສ່ເຊື້ອມັກໃຫ້ຟູ ຫຼືເຂົ້າຈີບໍ່ໃສ່ເຊື້ອ

ແຕ່ໃນຄືນນີ້ເຮົາກິນເຂົ້າຈີບໍ່ໃສ່ເຊື້ອເທົ່ານັ້ນ
- ■ Nai khun un-un rao kin khao-ji sia sua mak hai fun lu khao-ji bo sai sua;
  tae khun-ni rao kin khao-ji bo sai sua thao-nan.
- *■ On all other nights we eat either leavened bread or matzah;*
  on this night only matzah.

ໃນຄືນອື່ນ ໆ ເຮົາກິນຜັກຂຽວ ແຕ່ໃນຄືນນີ້ເຮົາກິນຜັກຂົມເທົ່ານັ້ນ
- ■ Nai khun un-un rao kin phak-khiao;
  tae khun-ni rao kin phak-khom thao-nan.
- *■ On all other nights we eat all kinds of herbs;*
  on this night only bitter herbs.

ໃນຄືນອື່ນ ໆ ທັງໝົດບໍ່ໄດ້ຈຸ່ມຜັກຂຽວໃສ່ນ້ຳເຄື່ອ ແຕ່ໃນຄືນນີ້ເຮົາຈຸ່ມສອງເທື່ອ
- ■ Nai khun un-un thang-mod bo dai jum phak nai nam-kua;
  tae khun-ni rao jum song thua.
- *■ On all other nights we do not dip even once;*
  on this night we dip twice.

ໃນຄືນອື່ນ ໆ ເຮົານັ່ງກິນຫຼືນອນກິນ ແຕ່ໃນຄືນນີ້ເຮົານອນກິນ
- ■ Nai khun un-un rao nang kin lu non kin;
  tae nai khun-ni rao non kin.
- *■ On all other nights we eat either sitting up or reclining;*
  on this night we recline.

ໃນຄືນອື່ນ ໆ ເຮົາກິນແບບປົກະຕິທັມະດາ ແຕ່ໃນຄືນນີ້ເຮົາກິນດ້ວຍພິທີພິເສດ
- ■ Nai khun un-un rao kin baeb pokgati thammada;
  tae nai khun-ni rao kin duay phithii phiset.
- *■ On all other nights we eat in an ordinary manner;*
  on this night we dine with special ceremony.

ABOUT THE LANGUAGE:

Lao

Number of speakers: 3,184,500
Rank: 178

Lao, a tonal language with 6 tones, is the national language of Laos. It is spoken in the Mekong River Valley from Luang Prabang south to the Cambodian border. Lao is also spoken in Vietnam, Thailand, Cambodia, Canada and the USA.

Lao is closely related to Thailand's Northern Thai (Lao is sometimes called Laotian Thai).

After unification of Lao principalities in the 14th C, Lan Xang monarchs asked their scholars to create a new script for Lao. The scholars adapted an early version of the Thai script, itself based on Old Khmer. Modern Lao retains many aspects of the early Thai script that have disappeared in modern Thai.

Syllables are based on consonants; vowels appear as diacritics appearing above, below or to the side of consonants.

ABOUT THE TRANSLATOR AND SPEAKER:

Suvan Sitibong

Age: Unavailable   Recorded: 1996
Location: Laos

Suvan works for the Asian Translation Service in Midvale, UT. Translation kindly provided by ATS.

Photo by Elise Korn

Richly colored figures in a Buddhist Temple in Vientiane, Laos' capital

Lakota

Takuwe ċa haŋheṗi ki le, haŋheṗi uŋma ki heŋa iyuha itokeċa huwo?

■ *Why is this night different from all other nights?*

Haŋheṗi uŋma ki iyuha aguyaṗi ṅapohyaṗi ŋa iŋṡ aġuyapi ikċeḱa uŋyutaṗi;
eyaṡ le haŋheṗi ki aġuyaṗi ŋaṗohyaṗi eċela uŋyutaṗelo.

■ *On all other nights we eat either leavened bread or matzah;*
on this night only matzah.

Haŋheṗi uŋma ki wahṗe toḱeċa uŋyataṗi;
eyaṡ le haŋheṗi ki wahṗe ṗa eċela uŋyutaṗelo.

■ *On all other nights we eat all kinds of herbs;*
on this night only bitter herbs.

Haŋheṗi uŋma ki wanji ŋaku uŋḱoputḱaŋpi ṡni;
eyaṡ le haŋheṗi ki kuṗa kigle uŋḱoṗutḱaŋ pelo.

■ *On all other nights we do not dip even once;*
on this night we dip twice.

Haŋheṗi uŋma ki atalya woslaya uŋyaŋḱaṗi ŋa iŋṡ hokul hṗaya wauŋtaṗi;
eyaṡ le haŋheṗi ki hokul uŋhṗaya pelo.

■ *On all other nights we eat either sitting up or reclining;*
on this night we recline.

Haŋheṗi uŋma ki iyuha ikċeya wauŋtaṗi;
eyaṡ le haŋheṗi ki wiċohaŋ wakatuya waŋ ogŋa wauŋtaṗelo.

■ *On all other nights we eat in an ordinary manner;*
on this night we dine with special ceremony.

ABOUT THE LANGUAGE:

Lakota

Number of speakers: 6,390
Rank: 3,473

Lakota, the language of the Sioux tribe, is spoken in northern Nebraska, southern Minnesota, North and South Dakota and northeastern Montana, as well as in Canada.

Lakota's first alphabet was known as Riggs. It was devised in 1834 by several missionaries led by Stephen Return Riggs. It has been modified several times over the years.

This translation uses a system developed by Sinte Gleska University. Duane writes: "We do not follow any linguist's recorded writings of the past or even of today. My elders believe that what has been written in the past does not do justice to our language and therefore we, as educators, are now using a writing system that has been developed by one of our own staff members at Sinte Gleska University. And of course, this being our own language, we feel we should be the people deciding on how our language should be pronounced and written."

ABOUT THE TRANSLATOR AND SPEAKER:

Duane Hollow Horn Bear

Age: Unavailable   Recorded: 1998
Town: Mission, SD

Duane, a native speaker of Lakota, is a teacher in the Lakota Studies Department of Sinte Gleska University in Mission, SD. The translation was first created by a "Lakota language enthusiast," linguist **Dr. Bruce Ingham**, Reader in Arabic Linguistic Studies at the University of London's School of Oriental and African Studies.

MORE INFORMATION:

The Lakota people (Sioux) experienced the 1890 massacre at Wounded Knee Creek. The massacre at Wounded Knee is considered the last battle between white soldiers and Native Americans, and has been used as a symbol of their treatment by the US Government.

The Lakota language was featured in Kevin Kostner's 1990 film *Dances With Wolves*.

Lakota Chief Sitting Bull (1831-1890).
"Each man is good in the sight of the Great Spirit"
Above: A logo used by Sinte Gleska University

Lak

Циванни ва хьхьу личӀисса цаймминнуя?

■ *Why is this night different from all other nights?*

**Гьарца хьхьуну жува букару личӀи-личисса ччатӀ кӀяла ччатӀ ва бившу ччатӀ;
ва хьхьуну амма бившу ччатӀ.**

■ *On all other nights we eat either leavened bread or matzah;
on this night only matzah.*

**Гьарца хьхьуну жува дукару
личӀи-личӀисса уртту-шин;
ва хьхьуну амма кьурчӀисса уртту.**

■ *On all other nights we eat all kinds of herbs;
on this night only bitter herbs.*

**Гьарца хьхьуну жува чак бару цал;
ва хьхьуну кӀилла.**

■ *On all other nights we do not dip even once;
on this night we dip twice.*

**Гьарца хьхьуну жува за дукару шя
бивкӀун ягу кьис бивкӀун;
ва хьхьуну кьис бивкӀун.**

■ *On all other nights we eat either sitting up or reclining;
on this night we recline.*

**Гьарца хьхьуну жува за дукару паракьатну;
ва хьхьуну аьдатрайн бувну.**

■ *On all other nights we eat in an ordinary manner;
on this night we dine with special ceremony.*

Pronunciation notes:
Ӏ after consonant makes consonant harder;
Ӏ before vowel adds a glottal stop

In the recordings: Zakir ends his
recording with his name and the name of
the language, spoken in Lak.

ABOUT THE LANGUAGE:

Lak

Number of speakers: 164,420
Rank: 971

Lak, also called Laki and Kazikumukhtsy, is spoken in southern Dagestan in Russia. There are also speakers in Azerbaijan, Georgia, Kazakhstan, Kyrgyzstan, Tajikistan, Turkey, Turkmenistan, Ukraine and Uzbekistan.

ABOUT THE TRANSLATOR AND SPEAKER:

Zakir Omarov

Age: Unavailable   Recorded: 1998
Towns: Kumoch, Daghestan / Miami Beach, FL

Zakir is a native speaker of Lak. He was born in Kumoch, Daghastan, which according to Zakir, is a village that speaks one of the purest forms of Lak. Zakir says there is considerable variation and influence from neighboring languages in the other locations where Lak is spoken.

Photo © Barry Hantman

**Moscow's colorful St. Basil Cathedral
on the edge of Red Square was built
between 1555 and 1561**

Ladino

¿Cuanto fue demudada la noche la esta mas que todas las noches?

■ How much is this night different more than all the other nights?

■ קוֹאַנְטוֹ פֿוּאֶי דֵימוּדָאדָה לָה נוֹגִ׳י לָה אֶיסְטָה מָס קִי טוֹדָאס לָאס נוֹגִ׳יס?

Que en todas las noches non mos entinientes afilu vez una;
y la noche la esta dos vezes.

■ That in all the other nights we don't even dip once;
and this night we dip twice.

■ קִי אֶין טוֹדָאס לָאס נוֹגִ׳יס, נוֹן מוֹס אִינְטִינְיֶינְטֶיס אַפֿילוּ בֶּין אוּנָה:
אִי לָה נוֹגִ׳י לָה אֶיסְטָה דוֹס בֶּ׳זִים.

Que en todas las noches mos comientes hametz o matzah;
y la noche la esta todo el matzah.

■ That in all the other nights we eat leavened bread or matzah;
and this night we only eat matzah.

■ קִי אֶין טוֹדָאס לָאס נוֹגִ׳יס, נוֹן מוֹס קוֹמְיֶינְטֶיס חָמֶץ אוֹ מַצָה:
אִי לָה נוֹגִ׳י לָה אֶיסְטָה טוֹדוֹ אֶיל מַצָה.

Que en todas las nochas mos comientes risto de vidruras;
y la noche la esta lechuga.

■ That in all the other nights we eat any species of greens;
and this night we only eat bitter herbs.

■ קִי אֶין טוֹדָאס לָאס נוֹגִ׳יס, מוֹס רֵיסְטוֹ דֵי וִידְרוּרָאס:
אִי לָה נוֹגִ׳י לָה אֶיסְטָה לִיגֻ׳וּנָה.

Que en todas las noches mos comientes y bevientes quien
asentados y quien ariscovdados;
y la noche la esta todos mos ariscovdados.

■ That in all the other nights we eat and drink some seated and some reclining;
and this night we all recline.

■ קִי אֶין טוֹדָאס לָאס נוֹגִ׳יס, מוֹס קוֹמְיֶינְטֶיס אִי בֶּ׳יבְּיֶינְטֶיס, קֵן אַסֵינְטָאדוֹס אִי קֵן אַרִיסְקוֹבֿ׳דָאדוֹס:
אִי לָה נוֹגִ׳י לָה אֶיסְטָה טוֹדוֹס מוֹס אַרִיסְקוֹבֿ׳דָאדוֹס.

Que en todas las noches mos comientes en manera comun;
y la noche de esta todos mos comientes con ceremonia especial.

■ That in all the other nights we eat in an ordinary manner;
and this night we all eat with special ceremony.

■ קִי אֶין טוֹדָאס לָאס נוֹגִ׳יס, מוֹס קוֹמְיֶינְטֶיס אֶין מַנֵירָה קוֹמוּן:
אִי לָה נוֹגִ׳י דֵי אֶיסְטָה טוֹדוֹס מוֹס קוֹמְיֶינְטֶיס קוֹן סֵירֵמוֹנִי אֶסְפֶּסְיָאל.

ABOUT THE LANGUAGE:

Ladino

Number of speakers: 110,310
Rank: 1,156

Ladino, also called Judeo-Spanish, Sefardi and several other names, including Judezmo used by some linguists, is primarily spoken in Israel now. There are also speakers in Turkey, Salonica and other areas of Greece; Sofia, Bulgaria; Puerto Rico; the USA; and formerly Morocco.

Ladino is derived from medieval Castilian Spanish. It is spoken by the descendants of the Sefardim, Jews who were expelled from Spain in 1492. The translation in Hebrew characters is shown last.

ABOUT THE TRANSLATOR AND SPEAKER:

Murray Hasson

Age: 68   Recorded: 1994
Towns: New York, NY / Randolph, NJ

Murray learned Ladino from his father, aunt and uncle, who all grew up in Rhodes, Greece. Although the paternal side of the family all knew Ladino, Murray is the last person in his family to speak it.

Ladino speaker Murray Hasson

Ladin

¿Parčie sta not e differente de thute le autre not?

■ *Why is this night different from all other nights?*

Thute le autre not, noi mañon o al pan leva o matzah;
kesta not, sol matzah.

■ *On all other nights we eat either leavened bread or matzah;*
on this night only matzah.

Thute le autre not, se maña thute sort de arbe;
kesta not, noi mañon arbe agre.

■ *On all other nights we eat all kinds of herbs;*
on this night only bitter herbs.

Thute le autre not, noi no si bañe le arbe par nia;
kesta not, noi le bañon doi ote.

■ *On all other nights we do not dip even once;*
on this night we dip twice.

Thute le autre not, se maña sentai su derč o cuffai;
kesta not, cuffai.

■ *On all other nights we eat either sitting up or reclining;*
on this night we recline.

Thute le autre not, noi mañon com el solito;
kesta not, noi mañon con propio ceremonia.

■ *On all other nights we eat in an ordinary manner;*
on this night we dine with special ceremony.

In the recordings: The word *noi* is missing from the phrases *noi le bañon doi ote* and *noi mañon com el solito*.

ABOUT THE LANGUAGE:

Ladin

Number of speakers: 30,000
Rank: 2,040

Ladin, also called Dolomite, is spoken in regions bordering Italy and Germany: the autonomous province of Bolzano / southern Tyrol (Italian: *Alto Adige*, German: *Südtirol*), the valleys of Gherdëina (Italian: *Val Gardena*, German: *Grödnertal*) and of Badia (Italian: *Val Badia*, German: *Gadertal*); the autonomous province of Trento (*Trient*) or Trentino, the valley of Fascia (Italian: *Val di Fassa*, German: *Fassatal*), the province of Belluno in Fodom (Italian: *Livinallongo*, German: *Buchenstein*) and Anpezo (Italian: *Ampezzo*, near *Cortina d'Ampezzo*).

ABOUT THE TRANSLATOR AND SPEAKER:

Adele Gerace

Age: Unavailable   Translated: 1997
Town: Perth, Australia

Adele's first language is Ladin, but she only speaks it with her father and people of his generation. Most of the time, she uses standard Italian, which she learned at school in Australia. She is a cousin of Aristide Bonifacio, a Ladin author.

Opening text of the Seder from the 15th C Joel Ben Simeon Haggadah, from northern Italy and Germany

Kwanyama

Omolwashike oufiku wonena inau fa omaufiku makwao aeshe?
- *Why is this night different from all other nights?*

Omaufiku makwao aeshe ohatu li omboloto ya tumba (ya ya efulika) ile tu lye omatazo;
ndele oufiku wonena ohatu li ahike omatzah.
- *On all other nights we eat either leavened bread or matzah;*
  on this night only matzah.

Omaufiku makwao aeshe ohatu li oimbodi yomaludi aeshe;
ndele oufiku wonena ohatu li ashike oimbodi ilula.
- *On all other nights we eat all kinds of herbs;*
  on this night only bitter herbs.

Omaufiku makwao aeshe ihatu velele nande olumwe;
ndele oufiku wonena ou ohatu velele luvali.
- *On all other nights we do not dip even once;*
  on this night we dip twice.

Omaufiku makwao aeshe ohatu li tu li omutumba twa yukilila ile twa endeka;
ndele oufiku wonena ohatu li ashike twa endeka.
- *On all other nights we eat either sitting up or reclining;*
  on this night we recline.

Omaufiku makwao aeshe ohatu li ngaashi hatu li shito;
ndele oufiku wonena ohatu lile melongelokalunga lowina.
- *On all other nights we eat in an ordinary manner;*
  on this night we dine with special ceremony.

ABOUT THE LANGUAGE:

Kwanyama

Number of speakers: 668,000
Rank: 462

Kwanyama (called Oshikwanyama, Otjiwambo, Owambo and Ovambo by its speakers) is a national language of Angola and Namibia. It is spoken in south-central Angola and in northern Okavangoland, Namibia

ABOUT THE TRANSLATOR AND SPEAKER:

Paavo Hasheela

Age: Unavailable   Translated: 1998
Towns: Oukwanyama / Windhoek, Namibia

Mr. Hasheela was born and raised in Oukwanyama, which is near the border with Angola, where he was a teacher for 10 years. Paavo moved to Windhoek and worked as announcer in the Namibian Broadcasting Corporation for 5 years. For 21 years he has been the language official/planner in Namibia's Ministry of Education and Culture. Paavo is a native speaker of the language, which he calls Oshikwanyama.

We simultaneously received a translation from **Desiewaar (Desie) D.N. Heita**, age 19, a native speaker who grew up in the mixed language community of Ondangwa. In some places the two translations differ by very small amounts, indicating either regional differences in spelling or a sound-oriented spelling.

Photo by Boris Kester

Wildebeest in Etosha National Park, Namibia

Kwangali

Morwasinke masiku aga gana lisigi komasiku makwawo nagenye?

■ *Why is this night different from all other nights?*

Masiku makwawo nagenye ose pamwe kulya mboroto zoyifuliso ndi matzah;
Masiku aga matzah gelike.

■ *On all other nights we eat either leavened bread or matzah;*
on this night only matzah.

Masiku makwawo nagenye ose kulya marudi nagenye geidi;
Masiku aga eidi lyoururu lyelike.

■ *On all other nights we eat all kinds of herbs;*
on this night only bitter herbs.

Masiku makwawo nagenye ose kapi atu vereda nampili mumwe tupu;
Masiku aga ose kuna vereda ruvali.

■ *On all other nights we do not dip even once;*
on this night we dip twice.

Masiku makwawo nagenye ose pamwe kulya oku kuna hingire kuvyukilira ndi
kuhingilisa konyonga;
Masiku aga ose kuna hingilisa konyonga.

■ *On all other nights we eat either sitting up or reclining;*
on this night we recline.

Masiku makwawo nagenye ose kulya pankedi ezi za hwa nkenye apa;
Masiku aga ose kuna kulya murarero mezumbu lyokulikarera.

■ *On all other nights we eat in an ordinary manner;*
on this night we dine with special ceremony.

ABOUT THE LANGUAGE:

Kwangali

Number of speakers: 84,000
Rank: 1,343

Kwangali, also called Sikwangali, Rukwangali or Kwangari by its speakers, is one of the national languages of Namibia. It is spoken in the Okavango region and also has a significant population of speakers in south-central Angola.

ABOUT THE SPEAKER:

Hermien Nakare

Age: Unavailable   Translated: 1998
Towns: Todoro Rundu / Windhoek, Namibia

Hermien was born in Todoro Rundu, which is in the Okavango region. She grew up in Windhoek where she now lives. Hermien is a native speaker and calls her language Rukwangali.

ABOUT THE TRANSLATOR:

Lazarus Issala

Age: Unavailable   Translated: 1998
Town: near Windhoek, Namibia

We are thankful to Lazarus Issala for translating the text; unfortunately, we know nothing more about him.

Photo by Boris Kester

The Sossusvlei dunes, in the Namib desert, one of the driest places on Earth

Krio

Na wetin mɛk dis nɛt kin difa frɔm ɔl dɛn ɔda nɛt?

■ *Why is this night different from all other nights?*

Pan ɔl dɛn ɔda nɛt, aida wi blant de yit raizin-bred ɔ matsɔ;
Pan dis nɛt ya so, na matsɔ nɔmɔ wi de yit.

■ *On all other nights we eat either leavened bread or matzah;
on this night only matzah.*

Pan ɔl dɛn ɔda nɛt, wi kin yit ɔl kanaba grins;
Pan dis nɛt, na soso bitas.

■ *On all other nights we eat all kinds of herbs;
on this night only bitter herbs.*

Pan ɔl dɛn ɔda nɛt, wi nɔ de dɔk am na di sɔl wan tɛm sɛf;
Pan dis nɛt, na tu tɛm wi kin dɔk am.

■ *On all other nights we do not dip even once;
on this night we dip twice.*

Pan ɔl dɛn ɔda nɛt, we wi de yit wi kin de sidɔm ɔ ling lusbɔdi;
Pan dis nɛt, na ling wi kin ling nɔmɔ.

■ *On all other nights we eat either sitting up or reclining;
on this night we recline.*

Pan ɔl dɛn ɔda nɛt, wi blant de yit kɔmɔn fashin;
Pan dis nɛt, ne spɛshal sɛrɛmoni.

■ *On all other nights we eat in an ordinary manner;
on this night we dine with special ceremony.*

ABOUT THE LANGUAGE:

Krio

Number of speakers: 493,470
Rank: 552

Krio is a language of Sierra Leone, spoken primarily in some communities in Freetown, on the Peninsula, on the Banana Islands, York Island, in Bonthe, and by the de-tribalized Sierra. Krio is also spoken in Gambia, Guinea and Senegal. It is also known as Creole and Patois.

ABOUT THE TRANSLATOR AND SPEAKER:

Ian Hancock

Age: Unavailable   Recorded: 1996
Towns: London, England / Austin, TX

Dr. Hancock is Professor of English and Linguistics at the University of Texas. Ian is a native Rom, raised in London. He is a UN representative for the Roma and an activist with the local Romani/Jewish Alliance in Texas.

Although not a native speaker, he has studied and published articles about the Krio language.

Photo by Boris Kester

Spontaneous smiles in a wooden hut in Freetown, Sierra Leone

Z Y X W V U T S R Q P O N M L K J I H G F E D C B A

Korean

왜 오늘밤은 다른 여느날 밤들과 다릅니까 ?

- (wae) (oh nihl bomb yhin) (da reun) (yuh nuh nal) (bomb dihl gua) (da ruem ni ga)?
- Why is tonight different from any other nights?

다른날들은 발효된 빵이나 발효안된 맏사빵들을 먹지만;
오늘밤은 맏사빵들만 먹습니다.

- (Da ruen nal deul yhin) (bal hyo dwen) (bahang eena) (bal hyo aan dwen) (bahang matsa deul ul) (muk ji mahn);
  (oh neul bomb yhin) (matsa bahang mahn ul) (muk suhm ni da)
- In other days we eat fermented (leavened) or non-fermented (unleavened) bread;
  but tonight we only eat matsa bread.

다른날들은 모들 종류의 상추를 먹지만;
오늘밤은 오직 쓴 상추만을 먹습니다.

- (Da ruen nal deul yhin) (mo duhn) (jong ryu oi) (saang choo rehl) (muk ji mahn);
  (oh neul bomb yhin) (oh jick) (ssyhin) (saang choo mahn ul) (muk sseum ni da).
- In other days we eat all kinds of lettuce (greens);
  but tonight we only eat bitter/sour greens.

다른날들은 상추를 한번도 찍어먹지 않지만;
오늘밤은 두번 찍어 먹습니다.

- (Da ruen nal deul yhin) (saang choo reul) (han bun do) (jjick oh muk ji) (ahn ji mahn);
  (oh neul bomb yhin) (doo bun) (jjick oh) (muk sihm ni da).
- In other days we eat without dipping;
  but tonight we eat by dipping twice.

모든 다른날들은 바로앉거나 편안히 기대어 앉아 식사하지만;
오늘밤은 편안히 기대어 앉아 식사합니다.

- (Mo duhn) (da reun nal deul yhin) (ba ro ahn gaw na) (pyuhn an hee) (gi dae awh) (an ja) (shik sa ha ji mahn);
  (oh nuel bomb yhin) (pyuhn ahn hee) (gi dae awh) (an ja) (shik sa hahm ni da).
- In other days we eat sitting upright or leaning;
  but tonight we eat while comfortably leaning.

다른날들은 보통식으로 식사를 합니다만;
오늘밤은 특별식으로 합니다.

- (Da ruen nal deul yhin) (bo tong shik uro) (shik sa reul) (hap ni da mahn);
  (oh neul bomb yhin) (tuhk byul shik uro) (hamm ni da).
- In other days we eat in regular ways.
  but tonight we eat in a special way.

ABOUT THE LANGUAGE:

Korean

Number of speakers: 66,305,890
Rank: 17

Korean is spoken in North and South Korea, as well as nearly 30 other countries from Australia and Belize to the USA and Uzbekistan. There is a difference of opinion among scholars as to whether Korean is related to Japanese. Some scholars suggest both are distantly related to the language family called Altaic, which includes Mongolian and Turkic languages.

Chinese writing has been known in Korea for over 2,000 years. By the 5th C BCE, Koreans started to write in Classical Chinese. They later devised three different systems for writing Korean with Chinese characters: *Hyangchal*, *Gukyeol* and *Idu*. These systems were similar to those developed in Japan and were probably used as models by the Japanese. A strictly Korean alphabet, now called *Hangeul* was invented in 1444. Beginning in the 19th C, a mixed writing system was used which combines *Hanja* (Chinese characters) and *Hangeul*. High school children in both North and South Korea are expected to know upwards of 2000 *Hanja*, even though they are rarely used in literature and informal writing. Korean can be written in vertical columns or left to right in horizontal lines (as shown here).

ABOUT THE TRANSLATOR AND SPEAKER:

Mark Yun

Age: Unavailable   Recorded: 1995
Towns: Seoul, Korea / Queens, NY

Mark Yun, grew up Seoul, Korea. At the time of recording, he worked at the United Nations. **Hyong Sop Shim** typed the text and provided the gloss.

Photo © Susan Hantman

Seoul's Poshin-gak bell, first cast in 1468, originally signaled the daily opening and closing of the city gates. Now, it rings in the New Year

Koongo

Bwe bwenina bobo vo mâsika mpila mu mpila konso fuku ankaka ê?

■ How does it happen that this night is different from all other nights?

Kiamene mene, twadianga ndimpa funisa vo ndimpa ka funisa ko; kasi nkokila twadianga ampivi ndimpa ka funisa ko.

■ A normal thing that happens all the time, repeatedly, we eat leavened bread or bread that is not leavened; but this night we eat only bread that is not leavened.

Kiamene mene, twadianga kintintikidi mawa mawa; kasi nkokila twadianga ampivi kintintikidi lula.

■ A normal thing that happens all the time, repeatedly, we eat little bushes; but this night we eat only little bushes [which are] bitter.

Kiamene mene, ka vûngila ko; kasi nkokila vûngila nkumbu zoôli.

■ A normal thing that happens all the time, repeatedly, we do not dip; but this night we dip two times.

Kiamene mene, twadianga mu vumbuka vo mu lambalala; kasi nkokila twalambalalanga.

■ A normal thing that happens all the time, repeatedly, we eat sitting up or reclining; but this night we are (in the act of) reclining.

Kiamene mene, twadianga keti kalakala; kasi nkokila twadianga kwa fuka kiakingi.

■ A normal thing that happens all the time, repeatedly, we eat as from the beginning, but this night we eat with much ceremony.

Translation notes: Although *kintintidi* means "little bushes", it is the usual word used for herbs and natural medicines among the Kikongo.

Kikongo is rarely written being primarily a spoken language. In the multilingual circumstances in which it exists, usually other closely related languages (Lingala, Kituba, Kikoongo ya leta, Kimbundu) or one of several European languages serve as the language of business or official documents. The translation attempted to remain close to the original. Although some common Kikongo phrases have an identical meaning to the text, literally translated they sound quite foreign to the Kikongo ear. Therefore, some colloquialisms were used to make the translation flow more poetically, as appropriate for a religious occasion.

ABOUT THE LANGUAGE:

Koongo

Number of speakers: 5,000,000
Rank: 131

Koongo (called Kikongo by its speakers) is spoken in Democratic Republic of the Congo, in the Bas-Congo Province. Kongo is also spoken in Angola and Congo.

ABOUT THE TRANSLATOR AND SPEAKER:

Eoghan C Ballard

Age: 42   Recorded: 1998
Towns: Newton, NJ / Ireland / Philadelphia, PA

Eoghan was born in NJ and has lived in the USA and Ireland. He is multilingual (French, English, Kikongo, Lingala and Kituba) and pursued a degree in French Literature. He studied Kikongo a year with **Kimfuemina Luvuma**, a native of Mbanza Ngungu in the Democratic Republic of the Congo who helped with this translation. Although Eoghan's speech is nonnative, Kimfuemina certified him as an intermediate speaker.

Photo by Elise Korn

Village children in the Democratic Republic of the Congo's Virunga Mountains

Kodava

ವಿನ್ನೆಂಗ್ ಇಂದ್ ಬ್ಯೆಟ ಬೋರೆಲ್ಲ ಬ್ಯೆತೆರನೆಕೆ ಇಲ್ಲ?

■ *Why is this night different from all other nights?*

ಬೋರೆಲ್ಲ ಬ್ಯೆಟ ನಂಗ ತೆ ಎತ್ ಉಳ್ಳ್ ಒಟ್ಟೆ ತಿಂಬ.
ಇಂದ್ ಬ್ಯೆಟ ನಂಗ ತೆ ಎತ್ ಇಲ್ಲ ತ್ ಒಟ್ಟೆ ತಿಂಬ.

■ *On all other nights we eat either leavened bread or matzah;*
on this night only matzah.

ಬೋರೆಲ್ಲ ಬ್ಯೆಟ ನಂಗ ಎಲ್ಲಿ ತರತರ ತೆ ಒಪ್ಪೆ ತಿಂಬ.
ಇಂದ್ ಬ್ಯೆಟ ನಂಗ ಕ್ರಿಪ ತೆ ಒಪ್ಪೆ ವೆ ನಾತ್ರ ತಿಂಬ.

■ *On all other nights we eat all kinds of herbs;*
on this night only bitter herbs.

ಬೋರೆಲ್ಲ ಬ್ಯೆಟ ನಂಗ ತೆ ಒಪ್ಪ ವುಂಕ್ಕಿತ್ ತಿಂಬ.
ಇಂದ್ ಬ್ಯೆಟ ನಂಗ ದೆಂಡ್ ಕ ರಿ ವುಂಕ್ಕಿತ್ ತಿಂಬ.

■ *On all other nights we do not dip even once;*
on this night we dip twice.

ಬೋರೆಲ್ಲ ಬ್ಯೆಟ ನಂಗ ನೋ ರೆ ಅಳ್ ತೆಂಡೆ ಇಲ್ಲಿಂಗಿ
ಆರಾವೆ ಎಲ್ ತಾಂಗಿಯೆ ಎಂಡ್ ತಿಂಬ.
ಇಂದ್ ಬ್ಯೆಟ ನಂಗ ಆರಾವೆ ಎಲ್ ತಾಂಗಿಯೆ ಎವ.

■ *On all other nights we eat either sitting up or reclining;*
on this night we recline.

ಬೋರೆಲ್ಲ ಬ್ಯೆಟ ನಂಗ ವೆ ನಾವೆ ಎ ಎಲ್ ರೀ ತಿಲ್ ಉರಿಬ.
ಇಂದ್ ಬ್ಯೆಟ ನಂಗ ನವೆ ಎ ರ ತರತ್ ಲ್ ಉಂಬ.

■ *On all other nights we eat in an ordinary manner;*
on this night we dine with special ceremony.

ABOUT THE LANGUAGE:

Kodava

Number of speakers: 241,000
Rank: 809

Kodava, also called Coorge, is spoken in India's Karnataka, Coorg (Kodagu) District, around Mercara and bordering on Malayalam to the south. It is the first language of the Airi, Male-Kudiya, Meda, Kembatti, Kapal, Maringi, Heggade, Kavadi, Kolla, Thatta, Koleya, Koyava, Banna, Golla, Kanya, Ganiga and Malaya peoples. Linguists are not certain if various dialects may constitute separate languages. Kodava uses the *Kannada* script.

ABOUT THE TRANSLATOR AND SPEAKER:

C M Sunita

Age: Unavailable   Recorded: 2001
Towns: Madikeri / Bangalore, India

C M Sunita, a native speaker of Kodava, was born in Madikeri. She now lives in Bangalore/Bengaluru, India. The first sentence was spoken by **Meenakshi G Bhat**, who also was born in Madikeri. He is fluent in Kodagu, but not a native speaker. The text was typed in by **Maya Yajnik** with help from **Chetna Cariapa**.

Photo by Tony DeJoie

Karnataka's High Court

Kisar

Translated from Indonesian

Alhi`ihepe alam eni noro alam namehin ka ramnehe?
- Why night this with night different no similar?
- *Mengapa malam ini berbeda dari malam-malam sebelumnya?*

Alam namehini, ka`an kukis me matsa;
Alam enienie, matsa mamani.
- Night different we.eat cookie or matza;
  night this matza continually.
- *Malam-malam sebelumnya, kita makan roti atau matsa;*
  malam ini, hanya matsa.

Alam namehini, ka`an kele`uuku aliwerhe;
Alam enienie, au kawi mermeru mamani.
- Night different we.eat maize rice;
  night this wood leaf bitter continually.
- *Malam-malam sebelumnya, kita makan berbagai jamu;*
  malam ini, hanya jamu pahit.

Alam namehini, i kak kuu`ul idewe me`e;
Alam enienie, ik ku`ul rewe ro`o.
- Night different we we.no dip once only;
  night this we dip time two.
- *Malam-malam sebelumnya, sekalipun kita tidak mencelupkan;*
  malam ini, kita mencelupkan dua kali.

Alam namehini, ka`ana, kamriri kaikoro me`e;
Alam enienie, kamriri mamani.
- Night different we.eat we.stand we.inc.sit alone;
  night this we.stand continually.
- *Malam-malam sebelumnya, kita makan sambil duduk atau bersandar santai;*
  malam ini, kita bersandar santal.

Alam namehini, ka`an o`onne me`e;
Alam enienie, ka`ana pak honoli wa`an narehi.
- Night different we.eat that alone;
  night this we.eat use tradition good win.
- *Malam-malam sebelumnya, kita makan secara biasa;*
  malam ini, kita santap dengan upacara khusus.

Translation notes: Apostrophes represent glottal stops. Asked why the 4th question was translated as "standing continually", quite the opposite of the meaning of "leaning because we are a free people", the linguist puzzlingly answered that the translator wanted to mold the text in parallel lines as they are used in their respective oral traditions.

ABOUT THE LANGUAGE:

Kisar

Number of speakers: 20,000
Rank: 2,424

Kisar, called Meher and Yotowawa by its speakers, is spoken in several islands northeast of Indonesia's Timor Island, specifically several villages on Kisar Island, the villages of Hila and Likagraha (Solath) on Roma Island, villages of Amau, Naumatan and Hi'ai on Wetar Island; there are several hundred speakers in Ambon city, Dili and Kupang.

Photos by Charles Katipana

Views of Kisar Island

ABOUT THE TRANSLATOR:

Godlief Adolf Katipana

Age: 71   Translated: 1999
Towns: Mesyapi, Kisar / De Bilt, The Netherlands

Godlief, a native speaker of Kisar, was born and raised in Mesyapi on Kisar Island. In his later years, he lived in De Bilt, near Utrecht, The Netherlands. He died 3 years after doing the translation.

A/Œ
Z Y X W V U T S R Q P O N M L **K** J I H G F E D C B A

Kinaray-A

Basi ang dya nga gabii iba kay sa tanan nga ibang gabii?

■ *Why is this night different from all other nights?*

Sa tanan mga ibang gabii, nagakaon kita it tinapay nga may lebadura kag matza;
kadya nga gabii, matza lang.

■ *On all other nights we eat either leavened bread or matzah;*
on this night only matzah.

Sa ibang mga gabii, nagakaon kita it tanan nga klase it dahon;
kadya nga gabii, pait lang nga dahon.

■ *On all other nights we eat all kinds of herbs;*
on this night only bitter herbs.

Sa ibang mga gabii, owa kita nagsawsaw maski isa ka beses;
kadya nga gabii, nagsawsaw kita it dalwa ka beses.

■ *On all other nights we do not dip even once;*
on this night we dip twice.

Sa ibang mga gabii, nagakaon kita nga nagapungko o nagasandig;
kadya nga gabii, nagasandig kita.

■ *On all other nights we eat either sitting up or reclining;*
on this night we recline.

Sa ibang mga gabii, gakaon kita it ordinaryo lang nga pagkaon;
kadya nga gabii, gakaon kita it espesyal.

■ *On all other nights we eat in an ordinary manner;*
on this night we dine with special ceremony.

ABOUT THE LANGUAGE:

Kinaray-A

Number of speakers: 378,000
Rank: 637

Kinaray-A is spoken in Iloilo and Antique provinces of western Panay in the Philippines.

ABOUT THE TRANSLATOR AND SPEAKER:

Joshibiah Gaa de Juan

Age: 24   Recorded: 1998
Towns: Looc, Romblon / Manila

Joshibiah is a student at College of Music at the University of the Philippines. A native speaker of Kinaray-A, he was born and raised in Looc, Romblon.

Photo by Rody Torres

The choir of St. Paul's United Methodist in Manila

In the recordings: The reading uses *kami* for 'we'. However, *kami* is the exclusive form; this was changed to *kita*, which is the inclusive form of the first person plural.

Kilivila

Avaka u'ula mabogina bogi ituali ituali kumwedona bogi igau?
■ What reason   this   night different different   all   night before?

Translation notes: Because of the ethnocentric nature of the text, Günter only translated the first line. The spelling follows orthography outlined in Günter's Kilivila grammar (*Kilivila – The Language of the Trobriand Islanders*. Berlin, New York, Amsterdam: Mouton de Gruyter, 1986.)

ABOUT THE LANGUAGE:

Kilivila

Number of speakers: 20,000
Rank: 2,422

Kilivila (also called Kiriwina) is spoken by the Trobriand Islanders who live in Milne Bay Province on Papua New Guinea.

The country of Papua New Guinea has the distinction of having more living languages (820) than any other country. The most commonly spoken language is Tok Pisin, with 4,121,000 first- and second-language speakers; the least is Laua, with 1 speaker. Indonesia is the next-most linguistically diverse country, with 742 living languages.

ABOUT THE TRANSLATOR:

Günter Senft

Age: Unavailable   Translated: 1997
Town: Nijmegen, The Netherlands

Dr. Senft is one of the leading linguists researching the language of the Trobriand Islanders. Günter has been studying and researching the Kilivila language since 1982.

One of many indigenous tribes in Papua New Guinea, the *Dani* tribesman live in the area of Irianjaya

Photos by Stephanie Goldhuber

Irianjaya natives from Papua New Guinea's Asmat region

Khoekhoegowab

Mati Ī os nē !oesa a !khara hoa !oete xu?

- *Why is this night different from all other nights?*

**Nau hoa !oedi ai da ge ‡habaperedi tamas ka io tsaopere-e gere ‡û;
Nē !oesa tsaopere-i |gui-e.**

- *On all other nights we eat either leavened bread or matzah;
on this night only matzah.*

**Nau hoa !oedi ai da ge !kharagagu khaohaina gere ‡û;
Nē !oes ai !gari khaohaib |guiba.**

- *On all other nights we eat all kinds of herbs;
on this night only bitter herbs.*

**Nau hoa !oedi ai da ge |gui !na-i tsîna ge |obe tama hâ i;
Nē !oes ai da ge |gam !nara ra |obe.**

- *On all other nights we do not dip even once;
on this night we dip twice.*

**Nau !oedi hoadi ai da ge ‡gose ‡nû tamas ka io !gîbasen hâse gere ‡û;
Nē !oes ai da ge !gîbasen hâ.**

- *On all other nights we eat either sitting up or reclining;
on this night we recline.*

**Nau hoa !oedi ai da ge ‖naectisa |gaub !nâ gere ‡û;
Nē !oes ai da ge !oe‡ûsa |ō-aisa ‖âudīb |kha ra di.**

- *On all other nights we eat in an ordinary manner;
on this night we dine with special ceremony.*

In the recordings: Reinhart Gaeb demonstrates the <u>four</u> different clicks that are used in the Khoekhoegowab language.

Pronunciation and translation notes: Macron (e.g. ē) indicates a lengthened vowel; circumflex (e.g. â) indicates a nasalized vowel. The symbols (! | ‖ ‡) represent the four different click sounds, which are used phonologically as consonants.

The word used for dip means "immerse".

ABOUT THE LANGUAGE:

Khoekhoegowab

Number of speakers: 251,100
Rank: 775

Khoekhoegowab, a language of Namibia, also goes by the names of Nama, Damara, Hottentot and Kakuya Bushman Nasie. (Our speaker used the name Khoekhoegowab.) The regions where its speakers live are south-central Namibia to the Orange River and the Great Namaland. There are also speakers in Botswana and South Africa.

The other click languages in this collection are Sotho, Xhosa and Zulu. However, none have as many different clicks (4) as Khoekhoegowab.

ABOUT THE TRANSLATOR AND SPEAKER:

Reinhart Gaeb

Age: 33   Recorded: 1998
Town: Windhoek, Namibia

Reinhart, a native speaker of Khoekhoegowab, was born and raised in Namibia's capital, Windhoek.

Reinhart's spelling was corrected by **Professor Wilfrid Haacke**, of the Linguistics Department of the University of Namibia.

This translation is one of many obtained through the kind and generous work of **Gamsberg Macmillan**, school-book publishers in Windhoek.

Photo by Boris Kester

Elephants in Namibia's Etosha National Park, called The Great White Place

Khmer

តើហេតុអ្វីបានជាយប់នេះខុសពីយប់ដទៃៗ?

■ *Why is this night different from all other nights?*

នៅពេលយប់ដទៃៗគ្នាយើងទទួលទានាន នំ ចាំងដែលមានមេស្រាបុ្រក៍ទទួលទានម៉ាតឡើ
នៅពេលយប់នេះយើងទទួលទានម៉ាតឡើ ។

■ *On all other nights we eat either leavened bread or matzah;*
on this night only matzah.

នៅពេលយប់ដទៃៗគ្នាយើងទទួលទានឆ្លី ជីត្រួប់មុខទាំងអស់
នៅពេលយប់នេះយើងទទួលទានតែជីដែលល្ងូង ។

■ *On all other nights we eat all kinds of herbs;*
on this night only bitter herbs.

នៅពេលយប់ដទៃៗគ្នាយើងតុក្តីដែលជ្រលក់សោះ
នៅពេលយប់នេះយើងជ្រលក់ពីរដង ។

■ *On all other nights we do not dip even once;*
on this night we dip twice.

នៅពេលយប់ដទៃៗគ្នាយើងទទួលទានដោយអង្គុយ
ត្រង់ឬអង្គុយដម្រេត នៅពេលយប់នេះ យើងអង្គុយម្រេត ។

■ *On all other nights we eat either sitting up or reclining;*
on this night we recline.

នៅពេលយប់ដទៃៗគ្នាយើងទទួលទានតាមរបៀបធម្មក្តា
នៅពេលយប់នេះយើងទទួលទានបាយកាមរបៀប ពិធីជាពិលេល ។

■ *On all other nights we eat in an ordinary manner;*
on this night we dine with special ceremony.

ABOUT THE TRANSLATOR AND SPEAKER:

Supharidh Hy

Age: Unavailable   Recorded: 1998
Towns: Phnom Penh, Cambodia / New York, NY

Supharidh grew up in Phnom Penh. He left Cambodia in 1968 and came to the USA in 1974. Supharidh works at the UN. He is a fluent speaker of Khmer, French and English.

ABOUT THE LANGUAGE:

Central Khmer

Number of speakers: 13,603,400
Rank: 64

Central Khmer (also known as Cambodian) is the official language of Cambodia. There are also speakers in Canada, China, France, Laos, USA and Vietnam.

The Khmer alphabet descended from the *Brahmi* script of ancient India by way of the *Pallava* script, which was used in southern India and southeast Asia during the 5th and 6th C CE. The oldest inscription in Khmer, found at Angkor Borei south of the capital, Phnom Penh, dates from 611.

The Khmer alphabet closely resembles the Thai and Lao alphabets, which were developed from it.

Angkor Watt, the temple built for King Suryavarman II in the early 12th C as his state temple and capital city

Photo by Elise Korn

Kei

Translated from Indonesian

Felbe de i waon inhaling inhov de lili'an?

■ How night this reason different with night diverse.other?

■ *Mengapa malam ini berbeda dari malam-malam sebelumnya?*

Nutun dede besa ta'an rot te matsa;
de i ta'an matsa mehe.

■ Each diverse.night all we.eat bread or matzah;
night this we.eat matzah alone

■ *Malam-malam sebelumnya, kita makan roti atau matsa;*
malam ini, hanya matsa.

Nutun dede besa ba'el ta'an siyor;
de i ta'an siyor kafefe.

■ Each diverse.night all just we.eat vegetable;
night this we.eat vegetable bitter

■ *Malam-malam sebelumnya, kita makan berbagai jamu;*
malam ini, hanya jamu pahit.

Nutun dede besa ita taan fa'a wuk waed;
de i ita taan fa'aru.

■ Each diverse.night all we dip once too not;
night this we dip twice

■ *Malam-malam sebelumnya, sekalipun kita tidak mencelupkan;*
malam ini, kita mencelupkan dua kali.

Nutun dede besa ta'an dokdok te tubtub;
de i ta'an tubtub mehe.

■ Each diverse.night all we.eat sitting sleeping;
night this we.eat sleeping alone

■ *Malam-malam sebelumnya, kita makan sambil duduk atau bersandar santai;*
malam ini, kita bersandar santai.

Nutun dede besa ta'an bias wa;
de i ta'an inhov ni adat wawaon.

■ Each diverse.night all we.eat normal just;
night this we.eat with tradition special

■ *Malam-malam sebelumnya, kita makan secara biasa;*
malam ini, kita santap dengan upacara khusus.

> **Translation notes:** Many languages distinguish between the inclusive and exclusive 'we'. This translation uses *ta'an* for the 1st person plural inclusive.

ABOUT THE LANGUAGE:

Kei

Number of speakers: 85,000
Rank: 1,334

Kei (also called Evav) is spoken in about 207 villages in the major part of 10 islands in Indonesia: Kei Kecil, Kei Besar, surrounding islands, the Kur Islands and southeast Maluku.

ABOUT THE TRANSLATOR AND SPEAKER:

Fera Ubro-Rahantoknam

Age: 38   Recorded: 1998
Towns: Kei Besar, Maluku, Indonesia / Zwolle,
          The Netherlands

Fera, a first-language speaker of Kei, was born and raised in Kei Besar (Tuturean), Maluku. She was a school teacher in Indonesia, when, at age 20, she married a Dutch citizen of Keiese descent and moved to the Netherlands. She currently lives in Zwolle (Overijssel). The translation was also worked on by **Ietje Rahakbauw-Rahanra**, a native-language speaker of Kei from Kei Besar also now living in Zwolle.

Photo by Aone van Engelenhoven

The Indonesian island of Kei from the surrounding ocean

Kazakh

Translated from Russian

Бугінгі туннің өзге туңдерден өзгешелігі неде?

■ Чем отличается эта ночь от всех других ночей?

Өзге тундердің бәрінде біз не ашыған нан не мацу жейміз;
ал бұл туні тек мацу ғана жейміз.

■ Во все другие ночи мы едим либо квашеный хлеб либо мацу;
а в эту ночь-только мацу.

Өзге тундердің бәрінде біз көк талғамайыз;
ал бұл туні оның тек ащысын ғана жейміз.

■ Во все другие ночи мы едим любую зелень;
а в эту-только горькую.

Өзге тундердің бәрінде біз көкті еш малмаймыз;
ал бұл туні оны екі рет маламыз.

■ Во все другие ночи мы вообще не обмакиваем зелени;
а в эту ночь-обмакиваем ее дважды.

Өзге тундердің бәрінде біз отырыш немесе жамбастап
жатып жейміз;
ал бұл туні жамбастап жатып жейміз.

■ Во все другие ночи мы едим сидя или возлегая;
а в эту ночь-возлегая.

Өзге тундердің бәрінде біз жайшылықтағыщай тамақтанамыз;
ал бугін асты бағштап жейміз.

■ Во все другие ночи мы едим как обыденно;
а сегодня у нас ритуадьная трапеза.

Translation story: A colleague (Alex Gelman) of one of the authors (Murray) approached Djafar Mynbaev, whose father was from Kazakhstan. Djafar's contacts reached Dr. Junisbekov, the translator. When the recording came back, Murray noticed the cassette had two languages. He gave it to Alex, who found the end held a message for Djafar. Djafar's father, a famous scientist, had started the Kazakhstan Academy of Sciences. The Kazakhstan scientific community was building a museum in memorial to Djafar's father. They were collecting money from the government and scientists, and were asking Djafar if he wanted to contribute.

Alex returned the tape to Djafar, telling him about the request. Djafar hadn't known about the museum dedicated to his father and cried when he heard the tape. (Surprisingly, the tape contained another message after the one for Djafar, this time for Alex.) It's amazing that the tape passed through 3 hands, each one unaware the end of the tape contained yet another message for someone else.

ABOUT THE LANGUAGE:

Kazakh

Number of speakers: 8,331,950
Rank: 93

Kazakh is primarily spoken in Kazakhstan, northern Soviet Middle Asia and western Siberia. It is also spoken in China, Kygyzstan and Mongolia.

Kazakh was first written in Arabic script during the 19th C. When many poets educated in Islam revolted against Russia, secular schools were set up by Russia to promote the Cyrillic alphabet. It was not widely accepted; by 1917 Arabic was reintroduced. Arabic was banned and the Latin alphabet was imposed when a Kazakh nationalist movement in 1927 was suppressed. Cyrillic replaced the Latin alphabet in 1940.

ABOUT THE TRANSLATOR:

Alimkhan Junisbekov

Age: Unavailable   Translated: 1997
Town: Almaty, Kazakhstan

Dr. Junisbekov, who lives in the pre-1997 capital of Kazakhstan, has the highest academic degree given in Russia, in the field of Philology (Linguistics). The translation was obtained via **Tetyana Sumarokova**, a Chemistry Professor in Almaty. Her Jewish husband, Michael Usanovish, is from a famous Russian family of nobles that has a document given by Catherine the Great.

ABOUT THE SPEAKER:

Akhmid Kali Jumajanula Alimbayev

Age: Unavailable   Recorded: 1997
Town: Almaty, Kazakhstan

Akhmid is the manager of Republic of Kazakhstan's Teleradio Channel. He lives in Almaty, Kazakhstan's largest city (and former capital).

Photo by Efrim Boritz

The Synagogue in the Bukharan community of Bishkek, Krygyzstan

Kashmiri

About the Language:

Kashmiri *

Number of speakers: 5,640,940
Rank: 122

Kashmiri is spoken in Jammu and Kashmir; Punjab, Uttar Pradesh, Delhi and the Kashmir Valley. Kashmiri is also spoken in Pakistan, the United Kingdom and the USA.

Kashmiri literature can be traced to the 1400s and poetry is very important. Although a national language of India, it is not used in primary education.

About the Translator:

Kuldeep Kapoor

Age: 70   Translated: 2004
Town: Jammu, Jammu Kashmir, India

Kuldeep is the father of Ajay Kapoor, the speaker.

The translation was typed in Urdu's Arabic script by **Dr. Rashid and Rasheeqa Ansari**, of Chicago, IL. Rashid is Professor of Electrical Engineering and Computer Science at the University of Chicago.

About the Speaker:

Ajay Kapoor

Age: 32   Recorded: 2004
Towns: Srinagar, Jammu Kashmir, India / Edison, NJ

Ajay Kapoor was born in Srinagar, in the state of Jammu Kashmir. He learned Kashmiri from friends at home and school. Ajay came to the USA at age 26. His dialect is Standard Kashmiri. He is a software engineer in the field of telecommunications.

Photo by Tony DeJoie

Ancient temple in the Belur-Halebid area near Bangalore

* For additional information, see "*Focus on ... pages.pdf*" on the DVD.

کیٔز چھ آز رات دوئٔ یمی راتوں خَط بَدَل؟

■ Kayz chuh aaz ich raat dooeemi raato khat badal?

■ *Why is this night different from all other nights?*

دوئٔ یمی راتوں چھ اَیٔیس قَمیر سۡرت یا مَتزا کھیواں؛
پَر آزچ رات چھ اَیٔیس متزا کھیواں.

■ Dooeemi raatoon chuh iss kamir sort ya matsah khawa; par azich raat chuh iss matsah khawa.

■ *On all other nights we eat either leavened bread or matzah; on this night only matzah.*

دوئٔ یمی راتوں چھ اَیٔیس قِسم قِسم کِ سِیٖن کھیواں؛
پَر آزچ رات چھ اَیٔیس ترّش سِیٖن کھیواں.

■ Dooeemi raatoon chuh iss kisim kismik syoon khawa; par azich raat chuh iss trush syoon khawa.

■ *On all other nights we eat all kinds of herbs; on this night only bitter herbs.*

دوئٔ یمی راتوں چھ اَیٔیس اِکلِ یَت سِیٖن چَلا؛
پَر آزچ رات چھ اَیٔیس دوئٔلِ یَت سِیٖن چَلا.

■ Dooeemi raatoon chuh iss eklet syoon chala; par azich raat chuh iss dyoilet syoon chala.

■ *On all other nights we do not dip even once; on this night we dip twice.*

دوئٔ یمی راتوں چھ اَیٔیس بِہِت اِئیا ڈَک دِت کھیواں؛
پر آزچ رات چھ اَیٔیس ڈَک دِت کھیواں.

■ Dooeemi raatoon chuh iss bihit eeya duk dit khawa; par azich raat chuh iss duk dit khawa.

■ *On all other nights we eat either sitting up or reclining; on this night we recline.*

دوئٔ یمی راتوں چھ اَیٔیس ساد پِٹ کھیواں؛
پَر آزچ رات چھ اَیٔیس داس پِٹ کھیواں.

■ Dooeemi raatoon chuh iss saad pit khawa; par azich raat chuh iss khas pit khawa.

■ *On all other nights we eat in an ordinary manner; on this night we dine with special ceremony.*

Kannada

ಈ ರಾತ್ರಿ ಮಿಕ್ಕೆಲ್ಲ ರಾತ್ರಿ ಗಳಂತಿಲ್ಲ – ಏಕೆ?

- Ee raathri mikkella raathrigalanthilla – éékay?

- This night all other not like nights – why?

ಮಿಕ್ಕೆಲ್ಲ ರಾತ್ರಿ ಗಳಲ್ಲಿ ಹುರುಗಿಸಿದ ರೊಟ್ಟಿ ತಿನ್ನುತ್ತೇವೆ,
ಈ ರಾತ್ರಿ ಹುರುಗಿಸಿಲ್ಲದ ರೊಟ್ಟಿ ತಿನ್ನುತ್ತೇವೆ.

- Mikkella raathrigalalli hudugisidha rotti thinnuthééway;
  ee raathri hudugisilladha rotti thinnuthééway.

- On all other nights leavened bread we eat;
  this night unleavened bread we eat.

ಮಿಕ್ಕೆಲ್ಲ ರಾತ್ರಿ ಗಳಲ್ಲಿ ಎಲಾ಼ಾ ತರಹದ ಸೊಪ್ಪು ಗಳನ್ನ ತಿನ್ನುತ್ತೇವೆ,
ಈ ರಾತ್ರಿ ಕ಼ಹಿ ಸೊಪ್ಪು ಗಳನ್ನ ತಿನ್ನುತ್ತೇವೆ.

- Mikkella raathrigalalli ellaatharahadha soppugalannu thinnuthééway;
  ee raathri kahĩ soppugalannu thinnuthééway.

- On all other nights all kinds of herbs we eat;
  this night bitter herbs we eat.

ಮಿಕ್ಕೆಲ್ಲ ರಾತ್ರಿ ಗಳಲ್ಲಿ ಸೊಪ್ಪು ಗಳನ್ನ ಸವರಿ ಕೊಳ್ಳದೆ ತಿನ್ನುತ್ತೇವೆ,
ಈ ರಾತ್ರಿ ಎರಡು ಬಾರಿ ಸವರಿ ಕೊಂಡು ತಿನ್ನುತ್ತೇವೆ.

- Mikkella raathrigalalli nettagé kulithu athawaa aaraamawaagi oragikondu naawu thinnuthééway;
  ee raathri naawu aaraamawaagi oraguthééway.

- On all other nights herbs without dipping we eat;
  this night two times dipping we eat.

ಮಿಕ್ಕೆಲ್ಲ ರಾತ್ರಿ ಗಳಲ್ಲಿ ಸಾವ಼ಾನ್ಯ ರೀತಿಯಲ್ಲಿ ಊಟ ಮಾಡುತ್ತೇವೆ,
ಈ ರಾತ್ರಿ ಸಂಬ್ರಮ ದಿಂದ ಓಟಣ ಮಾಡುತ್ತೇವೆ.

- Mikkella raathrigalalli saamaanya reethiyalli uuta maaduthééway;
  ee raathri sambrahmadhindha óóthana maaduthééway.

- On all other nights sitting up or reclining we eat;
  this night we recline._

ಮಿಕ್ಕೆಲ್ಲ ರಾತ್ರಿ ಗಳಲ್ಲಿ ನೆಟಗ಼ ಕುಲಿತು ಆದಿ಼ವ ಆರಾವುವಾಗಿ
ಒರಗಿಕೊಂಡು ನಾಮು ತಿನ್ನುತ್ತೇವೆ,
ಈ ರಾತ್ರಿ ನಾಮು ಆರಾವುವಾಗಿ ಒರಗುತ್ತೇವೆ.

- Mikkella raathrigalalli nettagé kulithu athawaa aaraamawaagi oragikondu naawu thinnuthééway;
  ee raathri naawu aaraamawaagi oraguthééway.

- On all other nights ordinary way dinner we have;
  this night celebrating (special) dinner we have.

Transliteration notes: Doubled consonants (kk and ll in *mikkella*) indicate extra stress • doubled vowels – aa (*raathri*) éé (*maaduthééway*) – indicate longer duration (éé is long ay sound; óó is long oh, not oo/u) • h softens the sound of d or t (dh, th) • i with tilde (kahĩ) is nasalized ee • the letters in bold (**l** and **n**) are retroflex: tongue starts bent backwards on the roof of the mouth and springs forward and straightens as the word is said.

ABOUT THE LANGUAGE:

Kannada

Number of speakers: 35,327,600
Rank: 33

Kannada is spoken in south India, in the states of Karnataka (where it is the official state language), Andhra Pradesh, Tamil Nadu and Maharashtra.

ABOUT THE TRANSLATOR AND SPEAKER:

Rajaram Bhat

Age: Unavailable   Recorded: 1996
Towns: Mercara / Mangalore / Madras / Bangalore,
       India / Middeltown, NJ

Rajaram was born in the small town Mercara in the Coorg (Kodagu) district of Karanataka State in south India. His very early years were spent in Mangalore and Madras; he grew up mostly in Bangalore. He moved to the USA when an adult. Earlier versions were developed by **Milton Tan**, a Harvard-PhD architect, currently Head of the School of Architecture in the National University of Singapore, **Yeshoda Bhat** and **Shanti Shashidhara**, of Princeton Junction, NJ. The text was typed in by **Bhagyavati**, born and raised in Bangalore.

Photo by Toby DeJoie

Inscription in the Kannada alphabet over LalBagh Park in Bangalore, the capital of the state of Karnataka

Kanjobal, Western

Translated from Spanish

¿Tzet yuu hun a'b'alilti' tx'oj yili ok tet maasanil wanxa a'b'al?

■ *¿Por qué es diferente esta noche de todas las otras noches?*

Maasanil wanxa a'b'al chi kulo' pan wa'xinaj yetoj yanil sulb'al yich ma pan k' am yich;
yet a'b'alilti' asan ixim pan man ey naoj yich.

■ *En todas las otras noches comemos pan hecho con levadura o pan ázimo; en esta noche solamente matzah.*

Maasanil wanxa a'b'al chi kuchi' ek'al tujan itaa k'achi';
yet a'b'alilti' hoj kuchi' k'a itaa.

■ *En todas las otras noches comemos todas clases de hierbas; en esta noche comemos hierbas amargas.*

Maasanil wanxa a'b'al maa kaoktoj huneloj;
yet a'b'alilti' hoj kaotoj kaeloj.

■ *En todas las otras noches no sumergimos las hierbas de ninguna manera; en esta noche las sumergimos dos veces.*

Maasanil wanxa a'b'al chotan linan, ma k'onan chun kulowi;
yet a'b'alilti' hoj kuey chotan k'onanoj.

■ *En todas las otras noches comemos sentados rectos o inclinados; en esta noche nos sentamos inclinados.*

Maasanil wanxa a'b'al chi ku komon lowi;
yet a'b'alilti' ti hoj kulo' txxaaeb'il lob'e.

■ [On this night] sacred foods that we are about to eat.

■ *En todas las otras noches comemos de manera ordinaria; en esta noche comemos con ceremonia especial.*

ABOUT THE SPEAKER:

Leonel Say

Age: Unavailable   Recorded: 1998
Towns: Menton, Guatemala / CA

Leonel works for Berlitz on behalf of the Immigration and Naturalization Service as a court translator for Kanjobal-speaking people. He grew up in the village of Menton, a few hours from San Miguel. Leonel came to the USA at age 14 and continues speaking Kanjobal with his parents and in his job.

ABOUT THE LANGUAGE:

Western Kanjobal

Number of speakers: 58,600
Rank: 1,557

Western Kanjobal (also called Akateko, San Miguel Acatán Kanjobal and Q'anjob'al) is spoken in Huehuetenango Department and San Miguel Acatán in northwestern Guatemala.

During Guatemala's civil war, the northwestern area was heavily targeted by the military – entire populations of some communities, including San Miguel Acatán, were either killed or displaced.

Although noted Mayan linguist Terry Kaufman classified in the 1970s the Kanjobal spoken in various communities as six distinctly different languages, a more recent movement among Mayan language promoters has advocated recombination for political and standardization reasons.

ABOUT THE TRANSLATOR:

José Juan

Age: 45   Translated: 1998
Towns: San Miguel Acatan, Guatemala / Mexico / Vancouver, Canada

José Juan grew up in San Miguel Acatan, Huehuetenango, Guatemala. He left for Mexico in his late 20s and spent 10 years there before obtaining political asylum in Canada.

Traditional musical instruments museum and store in Antigua, Guatemala

Kanjobal, Eastern

Translated from Spanish

¿Tzet yuj xan tx'oq yel jun aq'b'alti' yib'an janxa aq'b'al?

■ *¿Por qué es diferente esta noche de todas las otras noches?*

Yet masanil janxa aq'b'al tol chikolo' pat ma tx'ix;
yet jun aq'b'alti' asan tx'ix chikolo'.

■ *En todas las otras noches comemos pan hecho con levadura o pan ázimo;*
en esta noche solamente matzah.

Yet masanil janxa aq'b'al chikochi' k'al masanil jantaq itaj watx' sjab';
yet jun aq'b'alti' asan k'a itaj chikochi'.

■ *En todas las otras noches comemos todas clases de hierbas;*
en esta noche comemos hierbas amargas.

Yet masanil janxa aq'b'al k'am chikoteq koyal juneloq;
yet jun aq'b'alti' kayel chikoteq koyal.

■ *En todas las otras noches no sumergimos las hierbas de ninguna manera;*
en esta noche las sumergimos dos veces.

Yet masanil janxa aq'b'al tojol jay woqan kolowi ma tz'eyanhon;
yet jun aq'b'alti' tol tz'eyanhon.

■ *En todas las otras noches comemos sentados rectos o inclinados;*
en esta noche nos sentamos inclinados.

Yet masanil janxa aq'b'al komonk'al chiyun kolowi;
yet jun aq'b'alti' txajulk'al chiyun kolowi.

■ *En todas las otras noches comemos de manera ordinaria;*
en esta noche comemos con ceremonia especial.

Translation notes: In traditional Mayan culture, products made of dough ground from corn cooked in lime water are consumed as staples. *Pat* (tortilla) refers to the corn cake baked on the griddle and eaten at every meal – its presence defines the concept "meal". *Tx'ix* (tamal) is a steamed corn cake wrapped in corn husks or other leaves that is used for trips – because it has better qualities of preservation than tortillas – or for festive meals – because it takes more time to prepare and contains special ingredients. In other words, the *cultural* functions of these two types of bread correspond readily to the distinctions between bread and matzah.

The importance of corn in Mayan culture is signaled by the different verbs for eating. *Lo'* (*chikolo'* in the first question) refers to eating corn, while *chi'* (*chikochi'* in the second question) refers to eating other foods such as vegetables or meat.

ABOUT THE TRANSLATOR AND SPEAKER:

Gaspar Pedro González

Age: 50s   Recorded: 1996
Town: Guatemala City, Guatemala

Gaspar Pedro González (also known by his Mayan name, Kaxhin) is Professor of Mayan literature at the Mariano Galvez University in Guatemala City. He is a member of Academy of Mayan Languages of Guatemala, works in the Guatemalan Ministry of Culture and holds an influential position in the arena of indigenous affairs. Gaspar is an activist in the Mayan language preservation movement. His dialect is Eastern Kanjobal from San Pedro Soloma.

A poet and painter, Gaspar is best known as the first native Mayan novelist. His novel, *Sbeybal Jun Naq Maya Qanjobal* (The Road of a Mayan Kanjobal Man), was also published in Spanish as *La Otra Cara* (The Other Side/Face) and in English as *A Mayan Life*.

Photo by Don Kissil

Lake Atitlan, a natural wonder with its backdrop of three 10,000-foot volcanoes, was called by writer Aldous Huxley "the most beautiful in the world"

Kamba

Nĩkĩ ũtukũ ũũ wa ũmũnthi wĩ kivathukanio na motuku ala angi onthe ma mithenya ila ingi?

■ *Why is this night different from all other nights?*

Motukũ ala angi ma mĩthenya ĩla ĩngĩ tuĩsaa kimũtũ kimbye kana matzah; ũtukũ ũũ wa ũmunthĩ twĩya matzah vate kĩndũ kĩngĩ. *

■ Kimũtũ kimbye ('bread that has been made to grow big [by yeast]') represents *'leavened bread'*.
Vate kĩndũ kĩngĩ ('without anything else') represents *'only'*.

■ *On all other nights we eat either leavened bread or matzah; on this night only matzah.*

Motukũ ala angĩ onthe twisaa mithemba yonthe ye miti; ũtukũ ũũ wa ũmunthĩ no miti yi ũũ vate kĩndũ kĩngĩ.

■ Miti ('trees, vegetation') represents *'herbs'*.
Vate kĩndũ kĩngĩ ('without anything else') represents *'only'*.

■ *On all other nights we eat all kinds of herbs; on this night only bitter herbs.*

Motukũ ala angi onthe twivokethasyaa ona imwe; ũtukũ ũũ wa ũmunthĩ twivokethya maita elĩ.

■ *On all other nights we do not dip even once; on this night we dip twice.*

Motukũ ala angi onthe tuĩsaa tũilye nthĩ kana tũthũmũĩte nesa; ũtukũ ũũ wa ũmũnthĩ nituthumuite nesa.**

■ Tũthũmuĩte nesa ('when resting well, comfortably, nicely') represents *'reclining'*.

■ *On all other nights we eat either sitting up or reclining; on this night we recline.*

Motukũ ala angi onthe tuĩsaa ota tene; ũtukũ ũũ wa ũmũnthĩ twĩya kwa nzia ya mwanya yi kivathukanio na ila ingĩ.

■ *On all other nights we eat in an ordinary manner; on this night we dine with special ceremony.*

---

* Third line was recorded as *ũtukũ ũũ wa ũmunthgtwgya mgtgygũũ*.
The text shown here is more correct.
** At time of recording, the fourth question was not yet translated.

Photo © Niko Lipsanen

Uhuru Park, located near Nairobi's central business district

ABOUT THE LANGUAGE:

Kamba

Number of speakers: 3,960,000
Rank: 154

Kamba, also called Kikamba, is spoken in Kenya. The regions are South Central, Machakos and Kitui Districts and the Eastern Province. Fewer speakers are in Kwale District and the Coast Province.

ABOUT THE TRANSLATOR AND SPEAKER:

Mumo Kimanthi

Age: Unavailable   Recorded: 1999
Town: Nairobi, Kenya

Mumo is a language instructor in Nairobi.

Kabyle

Translated from French

Deg° acu iḍ agi yemxallaf si yak° uḍan nniḍen?

■ In what night this is_different from all nights other?

■ *Pourquoi cette soirée se distingue-t-elle des autres soirées?*

**Yak° uḍan nniḍen nezmer anečč tamtunt neγ aγum;
iḍ agi, ḥaca aγum.**

■ All nights other we_can we_eat galette (bread) or unleavened_bread;
night this, except (only) unleavened_bread.

■ *Tous les autres soirs nous pouvons manger du pain levé ou du pain azyme;
ce soir seulement du pain azyme.*

**Yak° uḍan nniḍen nezmer aneččkul leṣnaf n leḥcayec;
iḍ agi, ḥaca leḥcayec imerẓuga.**

■ All nights other we_can we_eat (food) all sorts of herbs;
night this, herbs bitter.

■ *Tous les autres soirs nous pouvons manger toutes sortes d'herbes;
ce soir seulement des herbes amères.*

**Yak° uḍan ur nessisin ara učči ula yiwet t-tikelt;
iḍ agi, sin iberdan anessisen.**

■ All nights other we_can not eat even one of-time;
night this, two times we_will dip.

■ *Tous les autres soirs nous ne trempons pas la nourriture même pas une fois;
ce soir nous trempons deux fois.*

**Yak° uḍan nniḍen nteṭ s iγimi, nqaad neγ nsenned;
iḍ agi, nteṭ ḥaca s usenned.**

■ All nights other we_eat with sitting, we_upright or we_on elbows;
night this, we_eat except (only) with elbows.

■ *Tous les autres soirs nous mangeons assis droit ou accoudés;
ce soir accoudés seulement.*

**Yak° uḍan nniḍen nteṭ menwala;
iḍ agi, nteṭ akken nniḍen.**

■ All nights other we_eat any thing (any way);
night this, we_eat as other (differently).

■ *Tous les autres soirs nous mangeons de manière ordinaire;
ce soir nous mangeons de manière spéciale.*

Translation notes: The Kabyle text is written using the Taqbaylit alphabet. *Agum* has been used for unleavened bread for some decades, but it is also used for ordinary baker's bread, even that containing yeast. Although the word-for-word gloss appears unstructured and haphazard, the Kabyle text is well structured.

ABOUT THE LANGUAGE:

Kabyle

Number of speakers: 3,126,000
Rank: 181

Kabyle, which is also called Taqbaylit and Tamazight, is a Berber language spoken in Algeria's Grande Kabylie Mountain range and western Kabylia. There are also speakers in Belgium and France. The name Kabyle is thought by some to derive from the Arabic word for 'tribesman'.

ABOUT THE TRANSLATOR AND SPEAKER:

Yazid At Yaagun

Age: 31   Recorded: 1998
Towns: Tizi Ibel, Algeria / Quebec, Canada

Yazid was born in Tizi Ibel (Tizi Hibel) in the Djurdjura mountains, 25 km from Tizi Ouzou, which is part of the city of At Aaysi in Algeria. At age 24, Yazid left for Canada, where he works as a computer scientist. The translation was also worked on by Yazid's sister, Kenza At Yaagun.

Yazid states that at the end of the 19th C during French colonization, France assigned arbitrary names for Kabyles, because at the time of a census, the Kabyle people did not have certain administrative paper work. His family was assigned Djerbib as a "last name". To make the name-creation task easier, the French used specific initials for each village. Most assigned family names in his village of Tizi Ibel start with C and D. One can tell a person's home village from the first letter of the family name.

The newly independent administration of Algeria "inherited" and retained the French work on family names. Although his official name is Yazid Djerbib, he sees it as an administrative artifact; Yazid prefers using his original last name, which is still used in his native village.

Photo by Bernard Cloutier (berclo.net)

Tebessa's original 6th C gate to the ancient Roman city of Theveste

Kabardian

ЛIо мы жещыр щIэщхьэхуэр?

■ *Why is this night different from all other nights?*

Адреи жэщхэм пщагъкIэ е пщагъэншэы щIа щIакхъуа дошх;
а жэщым пщагъэншэу щIа щIакхъуэщ тшхыр.

■ *On all other nights we eat either leavened bread or matzah;*
on this night only matzah.

Адреи жэщхэм удз лъэпкъуу щыIэр дошх;
а жэщым удз дыдж дошх.

■ *On all other nights we eat all kinds of herbs;*
on this night only bitter herbs.

Адреи жэщхэм шхыныр зэI шугъум хэдгъауэркъым;
а жэщым тIоней хыдогъауэ дошх.

■ *On all other nights we do not dip even once;*
on this night we dip twice.

Адреи жэщхэм е дыщысу е дыщылъу дошхэ;
а жэщым дыщулъу дошхэ.

■ *On all other nights we eat either sitting up or reclining;*
on this night we recline.

Адреи жэщхэм къызэрекIуэкIуу дошхэ;
а жэщым зэрышхэ хабзэм хуэдэу дошхэ.

■ *On all other nights we eat in an ordinary manner;*
on this night we dine with special ceremony.

ABOUT THE LANGUAGE:

Kabardian

Number of speakers: 1,632,500
Rank: 266

Kabardian, also called Beslenei and Upper or East Circassian, is spoken in the Russian regions of Kabardino-Balkaria and Karachai-Cherkessia. Kabardian also is spoken in Saudi Arabia, Turkey and the USA.

ABOUT THE TRANSLATOR AND SPEAKER:

Majdalin Hilmi

Age: Unavailable   Recorded: 1997
Towns: Jordan / New York, NY

Majdalin (Majida) was born and raised in Jordan. She is a Circassian princess and enjoys substantial standing in the Caucasian community. Majida is a native speaker of two forms of Circassian: Kabardian (East Circassian) and Adyghe (West Circassian, Bzhedukh dialect). The translation was also worked on by **Dr. Mikhail Alekseev**, a Daghestanian language specialist at the Institute of Linguistics Russian Academy of Sciences in Moscow.

Photo by Lorna Simon

In the recordings: The third question of Majida's spoken version does not end with **дошх**. The text was corrected after the recording.

World-famous Russian *Matryoshka* (nesting dolls) are symbols of motherhood, fertility and family life. The first came from a workshop near Moscow in 1890 and were inspired by a nesting Japanese doll

Juwri

Translated from Russian

Ə ħərəj imiṣəvi ṣ̣əv (jəħnim nisonu) nən i səvhojgə cy təfiħəti dəri?

■ Чем отличается эта ночь от всех других ночей?

Imu hər səv midanim xurdə nuniṣ̣ gogoliṣ̣;
omo imiṣəvi ṣəv xurdənim hə gogol.

■ Во все другие ночи мы едим либо квашеный хлеб либо мацу;
  а в эту ночь-только мацу.

I ṣ̣əvhojgə imu xurdənim hər ҫiro ħəvyҫ;
omo imiṣəvi ṣəv xurdənim təlħə ħəvyҫ.

■ Во все другие ночи мы едим любую зелень;
  а в эту-только горькую.

I ṣ̣əvhojgə imu ħəvyҫə ə ṣura ov dəzərə nəs xurdənim;
omo imiṣvi ṣəv urə dybo ə ṣura ov dəzərənim xurdə.

■ Во все другие ночи мы вообще не обмакиваем зелени;
  а в эту ночь-обмакиваем ее дважды.

I ṣ̣əvhojgə jə nyṣdənim, jə nebugə ə taraf cəp xurdənim cire;
omo i ṣəv ə zir gul imu bobuṣ dəṣəndə, jon gyrdə xyṣtərə ə taraf
cəp xurdənim cire.

■ Во все другие ночи мы едим сидя или возлегая;
  а в эту ночь-возлегая.

I ṣ̣əvhojgə cire xurdenim hemiṣəkirə xuno;
omo imburuz syfrə vokundənim ə dini ħədəthojmu giro.

■ Во все другие ночи мы едим как обыденно;
  а сегодня у нас ритуадьная трапеза.

In the recordings: Tereza ends her recording the phrase
"Language Juwri" spoken in Russian (*yazyk Juwri*).

ABOUT THE SPEAKER:

Tereza Elizarova

Age: Unavailable   Recorded: 2000
Towns: Azerbaijan / Brooklyn, NY

Tereza is the lead singer for "Ensemble Tereza",
a group promoting Juwri culture and music.

ABOUT THE LANGUAGE:

Juwri

Number of speakers: 70,000
Rank: 1,436

Juwri, also called Juhuri and Judeo-Tat, is primarily spoken in
Azerbaijan and Dagestan. It is now also spoken in Armenia,
Israel, Russia and the USA.

There may also be a Christian dialect. Speakers of Judeo-Tat
are called '*Bik*', a term they consider pejorative. They are called
'*Gorskiye Yevreyi*' ('Mountain Jews') in the Caucasus. Tradition
says that they have lived in the Caucasus since 722 BCE. Recent
literature uses Hebrew script; Cyrillic is still used in Russia.

ABOUT THE TRANSLATOR:

Raṣbil Ben Ṣamaj

Age: 67   Translated: 1998
Towns: Russia / Brooklyn, NY

Raṣbil (also known as Rashbil Shamayev) is a teacher of Judeo-
Tat throughout the New York area.

Photo by Daniel Rest

Tereza singing with her ensemble

Judeo-Greek / Romaniote

ABOUT THE CULTURE:

Romaniote / Yanioti

Romaniotes are Greek Jews, whose documented presence in Greece dates from approximately 300-250 BCE (the Hellenistic era), based on an inscription referring to "Moschos, son of Moschion the Jew". Oral tradition states the first Jews arrived in Ioannina soon after the destruction of the Second Temple (70 CE).

"Romaniote" derives from the old name for people in the Byzantine Empire, the ancient Romans. The Romaniotes (speaking Yevanic, a blend of Hebrew and Greek) are historically distinct from the Sephardim (speaking Ladino, a blend of Hebrew and Spanish), who came to Greece after the 1492 Inquisition. The customs of the Romaniotes were quite distinct from the Sephardic Jews.

Most Romaniote communitities were assimilated by the more numerous and prosperous Sephardim following their influx after the Inquisition. Small remnants of the community survive currently in Ioannina and Athens, in Greece, and in New York City.

ABOUT THE LANGUAGE:

Judeo-Greek / Romaniote / Yevanic

Number of speakers: 50
Rank: 6301

Judeo-Greek / Romaniote (called Yevanic by many linguists) is the nearly-extinct language of the Jews of Greece. Surviving speakers live in Israel, Turkey and the USA.

The term "Yevanic" stems from the Biblical word *yawan*, related to the word used for ancient Greeks and the lands they inhabited. It is also related to the name Ioannina.

ABOUT THE SINGER:

Sol Matsil

Age: 81   Recorded: 2010
Towns: Brooklyn / N Woodmere, NY

Sol is the youngest of the 10 children of Rabbi Matsliach Matsil, who was Ioannina's Rabbi, *Shochet* (kosher butcher) and *Mohel* until 1919 and thereafter in Brooklyn's Mapleton Synagogue. Sol learned the melodies of prayers and songs of the Romaniote community over many years from his father.

Photo by Sam Stein

> **In the recordings:** Sol sings the traditional chant used by the Romaniote Jews from Ioannina, Greece. In addition, he sings several other sections of the Seder, including the well-known "Who knows one?" in Judeo-Greek.

The only Romaniote synagogue operating in the Western Hemisphere, *Kehila Kedosha Janina*, was erected in 1927 in New York by Greek Jewish immigrants from Ioannina. Before WW II, there were three rabbis in the synagogue, with standing room only on the High Holidays. The building received landmark status in 2004

Photo © Harris Graber. Provided under Creative Commons Attribution 2.0 Generic License

The Romaniote synagogue in Ioannina

Javanese

Wonten menopo dalu puniko benten kaliyan dalu-dalu sanesipun?

■ *Why is this night different from all other nights?*

Wonten dalu-dalu sanesipun, kito nedo menawi mboten 'roti bolu' inggih 'matzah'; wonten dalu puniko, namung nedo 'matzah'.

■ *On all other nights we eat either leavened bread or matzah; on this night only matzah.*

Wonten dalu-dalu sanesipun, kito nedo sedoyo jenis 'ron-ron jejampian'; wonten dalu puniko, namung nedo 'ron-ron jejampian pahit'.

■ *On all other nights we eat all kinds of herbs; on this night only bitter herbs.*

Wonten dalu-dalu sanesipun, kito mboten nate nyelup; wonten dalu puniko, kito nyelup kaping kalih.

■ *On all other nights we do not dip even once; on this night we dip twice.*

Wonten dalu-dalu sanesipun, kito menawi mboten lenggahan inggih lelesehan; wonten dalu puniko, kito lelesehan.

■ *On all other nights we eat either sitting up or reclining; on this night we recline.*

Wonten dalu-dalu sanesipun, kito nedo nganggih coro samadyo; wonten dalu puniko kito, nedo dalu nganggih coro khusus.

■ *On all other nights we eat in an ordinary manner; on this night we dine with special ceremony.*

Translation note:
Quotation marks indicate phrases with loan words or text that was difficult to convey as Javenese concepts.

Photo courtesy of Tom Hoogervorst

Magelang, an area of central Java

Photo by Tom Judd

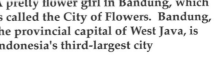

A pretty flower girl in Bandung, which is called the City of Flowers. Bandung, the provincial capital of West Java, is Indonesia's third-largest city

ABOUT THE LANGUAGE:

Javanese

Number of speakers: 84,608,470
Rank: 11

Javanese is spoken in Indonesia, primarily central Java, the eastern third of west Java, southwestern half of east Java. There are also resettlements in Papua, Sulawesi, Maluku, Kalimantan and Sumatra, and speakers in Malaysia, Netherlands and Singapore.

The earliest known Javanese writing dates from the 4th C, when it was written with the *Pallava* alphabet, which later developed into *Kawi*. By the 17th C, the Javanese alphabet had developed its current form. The alphabet was prohibited during the Japanese occupation of Indonesia (1942 to 1945). Since the 15th C, Javanese has also been written in a version of Arabic. The Latin alphabet has gradually supplanted the Javanese alphabet since the 19th C, when the Dutch introduced it to Indonesia.

ABOUT THE TRANSLATOR AND SPEAKER:

Priyono

Age: 30s   Recorded: 1996
Towns: Surabaya / Malang / Mataram, Java / Sydney, Australia

Priyono was born in Surabaya and moved to Malang at age 12 (both in East Java). He then moved to Mataram, Lombokat at age 26. At the time of the recording, Priyono was a postgraduate student majoring in Applied Linguistics at Macquarie University.

Many Indonesian people have only one name. Some people have two or more, but the last name does not necessarily represent the family name.

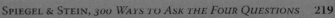

Japanese

どうして　今夜は他の夜と異なるのでしょうか？

■ Doushite konya wa hoka no yoru to kotonaruno deshouka?

■ *Why is this night different from all other nights?*

ふだんは、私達はパンかマッツァーを食べますが；
今夜はマッツァーだけです。

■ Fudanwa, watakushitachi wa pan ka matsa wo tabemasu ga;
konya wa, matsa dakedesu.

■ *On all other nights we eat either leavened bread or matzah;
on this night only matzah.*

ふだんは、私達はあらゆる種類のハーブを食べますが；
今夜は，苦いハーブだけです。

■ Fudanwa, watakushitachi wa arayuru ha-bu wo tabemasuga;
Konya wa, nigai ha-bu dakedesu.

■ *On all other nights we eat all kinds of herbs;
on this night only bitter herbs.*

ふだんは，私達は一度も　浸しては食べませんが；
今夜は，私達は　二回　浸して食べます。

■ Fudanwa, watakushitachi wa ichidomo hitashitewa tabemasenga;
konya wa, watakushitachi wa nikai hitashite tabemasu.

■ *On all other nights we do not dip even once;
on this night we dip twice.*

ふだんは，私達は真っ直ぐに座るか　或いは　寄り掛かって座りますが；
今夜は、私達は寄り掛かって座ります。

■ Fudanwa, watakushitachi wa massugu ni suwaru ka aruiwa yorikakkatte suwarimasu ga;
konya wa, watakushitachi wa yorikakkatte suwarimasu.

■ *On all other nights we eat either sitting up or reclining;
on this night we recline.*

ふだんは、私達はいつもの様に食べますが；
今夜は，私達は　特に儀式のとうり　食事をします。

■ Fudanwa, watakushitachi wa itsumo no youni tabemasuga;
konya wa, watakushitachi wa tokuni gishiki no touri shokuji wo shimasu.

■ *On all other nights we eat in an ordinary manner;
on this night we dine with special ceremony.*

ABOUT THE TRANSLATOR:

Teiko Yohana-Tursi

Age: 61   Translated: 2000
Towns: Nago city, Japan / Berlin, NJ

Teiko was born Nago city, Kunigami, on the northern part of Okinawa Island. She arrived in the USA at age 22. Teiko is President of the New York area Okinawan Organization.

ABOUT THE SPEAKER:

Yoko Yoshida

Age: Unavailable   Recorded: 2000
Towns: Tokyo, Japan / New York, NY

Yoko Yoshida grew up in Tokyo, the capital of Japan. She now works at the United Nations. The version of the text spoken by Yoko is slightly different from the one shown here, which is more accurate.

ABOUT THE LANGUAGE:

Japanese

Number of speakers: 122,080,100
Rank: 9

Japanese is the national language of Japan; it is also spoken in 26 other countries from Argentina and Australia to Mongolia, Peru and the Philippines.

Starting in the 4th C, the Japanese began to import and adapt the Chinese script (and Chinese culture), most likely via Korea.

Over time Chinese characters were used to write words borrowed from Chinese and Japanese words with similar meanings. Chinese characters were also used for their phonetic values to write grammar elements. The characters were simplified and eventually became two syllabic scripts, *hiragana* (sound-based phonetic writing, primarily for native Japanese words and word-endings) and *katagana* (sound-based phonetic writing for foreign words). Modern Japanese is primarily written with *kanji* (Chinese characters) mixed with *hiragana* and *katagana*. It may also include *rōmaji* (Roman letters), the standard way of writing Japanese in Latin letters. Japanese can be written in vertical columns or left to right in horizontal lines (as shown here).

Explanation of Seder Plate foods, from a Japanese Haggadah

過越祭の食事の準備

この夜の祭りのために食卓には別図のような6つの品が用意される。

1　מַצּוֹת（マツォト）
種入れぬパンが三重ねにしてあり、これらはそれぞれ祭司、レビ及びイスラエルを象徴する。

2　זְרוֹעַ（ズロア）
羊の前脚は古代イスラエルにおける過越の小羊の犠牲を象徴する。

3　בֵּיצָה（ベイツァー）
ゆで卵。これはエルサレム神殿における捧げ物を表し、また神殿破壊の嘆きを表す。

4　כַּרְפַּס（カルパス）
野菜であり、セロリーを用いる。これは元来は春先、地からとれる産物であったろう。これを塩水または酢に浸して食す。

5　מָרוֹר（マロール）
苦菜であり、わさびを用いる。エジプトにおける苦難を象徴する。

6　חֲרֹסֶת（ハロセット）
甘い果物のおろし汁に、くるみや干しぶどうを混ぜたもの。エジプトで作られた煉瓦の象徴とされる。

この他、各人に過越祭式次第（ハガダー）と酒杯、預言者エリヤのための酒杯が用意される。また主婦の祝祷によって燭台に火がともされる。

In the recordings: Yoko ends her recording with her name and the name of the language, spoken in Japanese.

Japanese Transliteration

マア　ニシュタナ　ハレイラア　ハゼア　ミコル　ハレイロツ?
- ma-a ni-shi-yu-ta-na ha-re-i-ra-a ha-ze-a mi-ko-ru ha-re-i-ro-tsu

シェヴェゴーゥ　ハレイロツ　アヌ　オクリン　カメツ　ウマツアー；
- shi-e-vu-e-go-ou ha-re-i-ro-tsu a-nu o-ku-rin ka-me-tsu u-ma-tsu-a-a

ハライラア　ハゼア　クロ　マツア
- ha-ra-i-ra-a ha-ze-a ku-ro ma-tsu-a

シェヴェゴーゥ　ハレイロツ　アヌ　オクリン　シアァ　ヤェラコツ；
- shi-e-vu-e-go-ou ha-re-i-ro-tsu a-nu o-ku-rin shi-a-a ya-i-ra-ko-tsu

ハライラア　ハゼア　マロア
- ha-ra-i-ra-a ha-ze-a ma-ro-a

シェヴェゴーゥ　ハレイロツ　アイン　アヌ　マツビリン　アフイル　パアム　エガツ；
- shi-e-vu-e-go-ou ha-re-i-ro-tsu a-i-n a-nu ma-tsu-bi-n a-fu-i-ru pa-a-mu e-ga-tsu

ハライラア　ハゼア　シュゼアイ　フェアミン
- ha-ra-i-ra-a ha-ze-a shi-yu-tsu-a-i fu-e-a-min

シェヴェゴーゥ　ハレイロツ　アヌ　オクリン　ベイン　ヨシュヴィン　ウヴェイン　メスビン；
- shi-e-vu-e-go-ou ha-re-i-ro-tsu a-nu o-ku-rin be-i-n yo-shi-yu-vo-i-n u-vo-e-i-n me-su-bi-n

ハライラア　ハゼア　クラヌ　メスビン
- ha-ra-i-ra-a ha-ze-a ku-ra-nu me-su-bin

ABOUT THE TRANSLATOR:

Miwako Kato

Age: 41   Translated: 2005
Towns: Kofu, Yamanashi Prefecture / Caldwell, NJ

Miwako was raised in Kofu, 80 miles from Tokyo. She came to the USA 9 years before working on the transliteration. As the mother of a Jewish household, Miwako knew the Hebrew text. Her recitation is titled "knowledgable" in the recording files.

ABOUT THE SPEAKERS:

Yuriko Ishihara and Rie Numata

Ages: 16   Recorded: 2005
Towns: Yawatahama city, Ehime Prefecture and Sanuki city, Kagawa Prefecture

Yuriko and Rie are both teenagers from Shikoku Island, the smallest of four islands comprising Japan. It is west-southwest of Tokyo. They had only a few years of English schooling; neither had seen or heard the Hebrew text.

Yuriko Ishihara

Rie Numata

Jamaican Creole

A wa mek disaya nait difren fram aal dem oda nait so?

■ *Why is this night different from all other nights?*

**Juurina aal dem oda nait, aida a iis bred wi a nyam aar a aad-tak;
bot pan dis nait ya so, a uongli di aad-tak wi a nyam.**

■ *On all other nights we eat either leavened bread or matzah;
on this night only matzah.*

**Juurina aal dem oda nait, wi a nyam aal kaina yaab;
bot pan dis nait ya so, a uongli dem bita yaab wi a nyam.**

■ *On all other nights we eat all kinds of herbs;
on this night only bitter herbs.*

**Juurina aal dem oda nait, wi na a dip iibm wan taim;
bot pan dis nait ya so, a tuu taim wi a dip.**

■ *On all other nights we do not dip even once;
on this night we dip twice.*

**Juurina aal dem oda nait, aida wi kuda sidong a nyam aar liin iizi so;
bot pan dis nait ya so, a liin wi a liin nomo.**

■ *On all other nights we eat either sitting up or reclining;
on this night we recline.*

**Juurina aal dem oda nait, wi kuda nyam eni-ou;
bot pan dis nait ya so, wi a iit laka se a speshal akiejan.**

■ *On all other nights we eat in an ordinary manner;
on this night we dine with special ceremony.*

ABOUT THE LANGUAGE:

Jamaican Creole

Number of speakers: 3,202,600
Rank: 176

Jamaican Creole (also known as Southwestern Caribbean Creole and Patois, Patwa, and Bongo Talk) is spoken throughout Jamaica, with additional speakers in Panama and Costa Rica, as well as others. Although Standard English is taught in schools, Jamaican Creole is the dominant language and gaining in prestige. (Most speakers believe they are speaking Standard English.) There are linguistic influences from several African languages, such as Akan and Bantu.

ABOUT THE TRANSLATOR AND SPEAKER:

Ian Hancock

Age: Unavailable   Recorded: 1996
Town: Austin, TX

Dr. Hancock is Professor of English and Linguistics at the University of Texas. A native Rom, Ian was the United Nations representative for Roma. As a linguist, he has researched and written about Jamaican Creole.

Photo by Andea and Steve Diamond

Jamaicans had long used bamboo rafts to transport bananas downriver. Decades ago actor Errol Flynn realized the rafts would make a good tourist attraction and millions of visitors have agreed

Italian

Perchè è diversa questa notte dalle altre notti dell'anno?
- *Why is this night different from all other nights?*

Le altre notti dell'anno, mangiamo o pane lievitito o slievitato; questa notte, mangiamo solamente pane slievitato.
- *On all other nights we eat either leavened bread or matzah; on this night only matzah.*

Le altre notti dell'anno, mangiamo ogni tipo d'erba; questa notte, mangiamo solamente le erbe amare.
- *On all other nights we eat all kinds of herbs; on this night only bitter herbs.*

Le altre notti dell'anno, non immergiamo le erbe in niente; questa notte, le immergiamo due volte.
- *On all other nights we do not dip even once; on this night we dip twice.*

Le altre notti dell'anno, mangiamo seduti dritti o reclinati; questa notte, mangiamo reclinati.
- *On all other nights we eat either sitting up or reclining; on this night we recline.*

Le altre notti dell'anno, mangiamo in modo ordinario; questa notte, mangiamo con gran cerimonia.
- *On all other nights we eat in an ordinary manner; on this night we dine with special ceremony.*

ABOUT THE TRANSLATOR AND SPEAKER:

Dominic Recchione

Age: 76   Recorded: 1997
Towns: Taranta Peligna, Italy / Largo, FL

Dominic's birthtown, Taranta Peligna, is in the province of Chieti, in the region of Abruzzi. He was raised in Rome from the ages of 7 to 17 after which he came to the USA.

ABOUT THE LANGUAGE:

Italian

Number of speakers: 61,696,677
Rank: 20

Italian is the national language of Italy, where it is called Italiano. It is also spoken in 29 other countries including Argentina, Australia, Belgium, Bosnia-Herzegovina, Brazil, Canada, Croatia, Egypt, Eritrea, France, Germany, Israel, Libya, Liechtenstein, Luxembourg, Paraguay, Philippines, Puerto Rico and San Marino.

Regional varieties coexist with the standard language; some are inherently unintelligible (Nida) to speakers of other varieties unless they've learned them. Aquilano, Molisano and Pugliese are very different from other Italian dialects. Piemontese and Sicilian (translations elsewhere in this book) are distinct enough to be separate languages. Venetian and Lombard are also very different. Neapolitan is reported to be unintelligible to speakers of Standard Italian. Northern varieties are closer to French and Occitan than to standard or southern varieties. There is considerable similarity in vocabulary with French, Spanish and Romanian. Most Italians use varieties along a continuum from standard to regional to local according to what is appropriate. Possibly nearly half the population may not use Standard Italian as their mother tongue.

**Majolica Seder plate
from Padua, Italy 1673**

Israeli Sign Language

The accompanying DVD contains a video of Ya'ara Brahm signing the Four Questions in Israeli Sign Language.

ABOUT THE TRANSLATOR AND SIGNER:

Ya'ara Brahm

Age: 28   Recorded: 1997
Towns: Tel Aviv, Israel / New York, NY

Ya'ara was born and raised in Tel Aviv. She moved to the USA at age 20, but continues to use Israeli Sign Language when visiting her friends in Israel.

ABOUT THE LANGUAGE:

Israeli Sign Language

Number of users: 5,000 primary users
Rank: 3,705

Israeli Sign Language is used by most (but not all) of the deaf in Israel. Israeli Sign Language is not derived from other sign languages and shows relatively little influence from other (sign) languages. There is a committee on national sign language and an organization for sign language teachers. The sign language used in classrooms is different from that used by deaf adults outside the school system. The first deaf school was established in Jerusalem in 1934. A fingerspelling system was developed in 1976.

ABOUT SIGN LANGUAGES:

Sign languages have developed among most deaf communities around the world. There are reported to be at least 120 different Sign languages.

Irish Gaelic

Cén ꝼaꞇh ʒo bhꝼuil an oíche ꝛeo éaʒꝛúil ꞇhaꝛ aon oíche eile?
- Kayen fhaw gu will un echah shah aghue-suel har aen echah ellah?
- *Why is this night different from all other nights?*

Chuile oíche eile, ioꝛann muꞃo aꝛán le ʒabháil nó aꝛán ʒan laibhín;
anochꞇ, ní ioꝛꝼaꞇh muꞃo ach aꝛán ʒan laibhín.
- Chuilla echah ellah, eason mwid ahraun le ga-wall neu ahraun gone lawbeen;
  annucht nee easa mwid och ahraun gone lawbeen.
- *On all other nights we eat either leavened bread or matzah;*
  on this night only matzah.

Chuile oíche eile, ioꝛan muꞃo luibh aꝛ biꞇh;
anochꞇ, ní bheꞇh aʒainn ach luibheanna ꝛeaꝛbh.
- Chuilla echah ellah, eason mwid luive err bih;
  anucht nee vei ainn och luiveanna sha-rov.
- *On all other nights we eat all kinds of herbs;*
  on this night only bitter herbs.

Chuile oíche eile, ní ꞇhumann muꞃo oiꞃeaꞇ iꞃ uaꝛ mháꝛ;
anochꞇ, ꞇumaꞇh muꞃo ꝼaoi ꝺhó.
- Chuilla echah ellah, nee thumb-en mwid ehred is uar awan;
  annucht thumben mwid fee dhoe.
- *On all other nights we do not dip even once;*
  on this night we dip twice.

Chuile oíche eile ioꝛann muꞃo ꝼa ꝛuí nó ꝛínꞇe;
anochꞇ, beꞇh muꞃo ꝛínꞇe.
- Chuilla echah ellah, eason mwid enna see no sheen-teh;
  annucht bei mwid shenn-teh.
- *On all other nights we eat either sitting up or reclining;*
  on this night we recline.

Chuile oíche eile, ioꝛann muꞃo aꝛ nóꝛ chuma liom;
anochꞇ, ioꝛꝼaꞇh muꞃo le ꝺeaꝛʒhnáꞇh.
- Chuilla echah ellah, eason mwid err nose chumba lum;
  annucht easa mwid le deasgnaw.
- *On all other nights we eat in an ordinary manner;*
  on this night we dine with special ceremony.

ABOUT THE LANGUAGE:

Irish Gaelic

Number of speakers: 391,470
Rank: 627

Irish, also called Gaelic and Erse, is spoken in many areas of Ireland, particularly, the western isles northwest and southwest coasts; the counties of Galway, Mayo, Kerry, Donegal, Meath, Cork and Waterford, in Scotland (Albain) and on the Isle of Man.

Irish first appeared in writing in Ogham inscriptions during the 3rd C CE. It has been written in Latin letters since the 5th C. Irish's uncial alphabet, a variant of the Latin, originated in medieval manuscripts.

ABOUT THE TRANSLATOR AND SPEAKER:

Pat Folan

Age: Unavailable   Recorded: 1996
Town: Connemara, Ireland

Pat is a native of Connemara, an area in County Galway in the west of Ireland. Munster is considered the standard Irish dialect; however, Connemara is the largest *Gaeltacht* (Gaelic-speaking) area in Ireland.

Bonus in the recordings: The recordings contain another dialect, Munster Irish. The translation developed from Munster is different than Connemara Irish.

Thatched roof cottage on the west coast of Ireland

Photo by Rick Morgan

Inuktitut, Eastern

ᓱᖕᒪᓄᓇ ᐅᓐᓅᔪᖅ ᐊᑦᔨᒋᔭᐅᙱᓚᖅ ᐅᓐᓄᔪᑦ ᐊᓯᖕᒋᓐᓂᑦ?

■ Sungmanuna unnuujuq atjigijaunngilaq unnuujut asinginnit?

■ ***Why is this night different from all other nights?***

ᐅᓐᓄᑕᒫᑦ ᐊᓯᖕᒋᓐᓂ, ᓂᕆᖅᑲᑦᑕᐳᒍᑦ ᓂᐊᖅᑰᔭᒥᒃ ᐳᕙᓪᓚᓴᐅᑎᖅᑲᖅᑐᒥᒃ ᐅᕝᕙᓗ ᒫᑦᔭᒥᒃ;
ᒫᓐᓇᓕ ᐅᓐᓄᒃ, ᒫᑦᔭᒥᒃ ᑭᓯᐊᓂ.

■ Unnutamaat asinginni, niriqattapugut niaquujamik puvallasautiqaqtumik uvvalu matjamik;
maannali unnuk, matjamik kisiani.

■ ***On all other nights we eat either leavened bread or matzah;***
on this night only matzah.

ᐅᓐᓄᑕᒫᑦ ᐊᓯᖕᒋᓐᓂ, ᓂᖅᑮᑦ ᐃᓚᐅᕈᑎᖕᒋᓐᓂᒃ ᓂᕆᖅᑲᑦᑕᓚᐅᖅᐳᒍᑦ;
ᒫᓐᓇᓕ ᐅᓐᓄᒃ, ᖃᓯᓕᓇᖅᑐᒥᒃ ᑭᓯᐊᓂ ᐃᓚᐅᕈᑎᑐᖅᐳᒍᑦ.

■ Unnutamaat asinginni, niqiit ilaurutinginnik niriqattalauqpugut;
maannali unnuk, qasilinaqtumik kisiani ilaurutituqpugut.

■ ***On all other nights we eat all kinds of herbs;***
on this night only bitter herbs.

ᐅᓐᓄᑕᒫᑦ ᐊᓯᖕᒋᓐᓂ, ᒥᓲᒃᑕᖅᑲᑦᑕᙱᓚᒍᑦ ᐊᑕᐅᓯᐊᖅᓗᑕᓘᓐᓃᑦ;
ᒫᓐᓇᓕ ᐅᓐᓄᒃ, ᒪᖅᑭᕕᒃᓯᑕ ᒥᓲᒃᑕᓕᖅᐳᒍᑦ.

■ Unnutamaat asinginni, misuuktaqattanngilagiut atausiaqlutaluunniit;
maannali unnuk, marruvisuta misuuktaliqpugut.

■ ***On all other nights we do not dip even once;***
on this night we dip twice.

ᐅᓐᓄᑕᒫᑦ ᐊᓯᖕᒋᓐᓂ, ᓂᕆᖅᑲᑦᑕᓚᐅᖅᐳᒍᑦ ᓂᑯᕕᖓᑦᓯᑕ ᐅᕝᕙᓗ ᐊᐅᖅᔪᖓᑦᓯᑕ;
ᒫᓐᓇᓕ ᐅᓐᓄᒃ, ᐊᐅᖅᔪᖓᕗᒍᑦ.

■ Unnutamaat asinginni, niriqattalauqpugut nikuvingatsuta uvvalu auqjungatsuta;
maannali unnuk, auqjungavugut.

■ ***On all other nights we eat either sitting up or reclining;***
on this night we recline.

ᐅᓐᓄᑕᒫᑦ ᐊᓯᖕᒋᓐᓂ, ᓂᕆᖅᑲᑦᑕᓚᐅᖅᐳᒍᑦ ᐱᐅᓯᑦᑎᓐᓂᒃ ᐊᑐᖅᓯᑕ;
ᒫᓐᓇᓕ ᐅᓐᓄᒃ, ᓂᕆᖅᑲᑎᒌᒃᐳᒍᑦ ᐊᑦᔨᐅᖕᒋᑦᑐᒥᒃ ᓇᓪᓕᐅᓐᓂᖅᓯᐅᖅᓯᑕ.

■ Unnutamaat asinginni, niriqattalauqpugut piusittinnik atuqsuta;
maannali unnuk, niriqatigiikpugut atjiungittumik nalliunniqsiuqsuta.

■ ***On all other nights we eat in an ordinary manner;***
on this night we dine with special ceremony.

About the Language:

Inuktitut / Eskimo

Number of speakers: 14,000
Rank: 2,736

Inuktitut (Eskimo) is spoken in Quebec (west of Hudson Bay and east through Baffin Island) and Labrador.

The Inuktitut syllabary was adapted from the Cree syllabary, itself adapted from the Ojibwe syllabary. Both the Ojibwe and Cree syllabaries were invented by James Evans, a Wesleyan missionary, between 1840 and 1860.

About the Translator and Speaker:

Bishop Ben Arreak

Age: 55 Recorded: 2003
Town: Kuujjuaq, Quebec

Bishop Benjamin Arreak is an Inuit Priest of the Catholic Church, serving the Inuit/Eskimo areas in far northern Quebec. Kuujjuaq is the unofficial capital of Ninavik, located at approximately 58° North parallel. The population of the town is approximately 1500 people.

Benjamin was born in Pond Inlet, Nunavik. He grew up in Pond and also Elsmer Island (called Alexander Fiord, Nunavek. He grew to adulthood in Clyde River, Nunavik, then moved back to Pond. He has been in Kuujjuaq, Nunavik since January 1996.

Benjamin was elected to Regional Bishop on May 2002 and consecrated in September, 2002. He serves the region of Nunavik, 15 communities including Nunavut Territories and Sanikiluaq, Nunavut in Hudson bay coast area, with a total Inuit population of approximately 15,000.

Since 1990, Ben was Coordinator and Translator for a team of four Bible translators. In 1991, they published an Inuktitut New Testament through the Canadian Bible Society. Since then, they have been working on the Old Testament. A first draft was completed in 2002.

Photo by Tom Judd

Windmill at Isle-aux-Coudre, Quebec

Indonesian

Mengapa malam ini berbeda dari malam-malam sebelumnya?

■ *Why is this night different from all other nights?*

Malam-malam sebelumnya, kita makan roti atau matsa; malam ini, hanya matsa.

■ *On all other nights we eat either leavened bread or matzah; on this night only matzah.*

Malam-malam sebelumnya, kita makan berbagai jamu; malam ini, hanya jamu pahit.

■ *On all other nights we eat all kinds of herbs; on this night only bitter herbs.*

Malam-malam sebelumnya, sekalipun kita tidak mencelupkan; malam ini, kita mencelupkan dua kali.

■ *On all other nights we do not dip even once; on this night we dip twice.*

Malam-malam sebelumnya, kita makan sambil duduk atau bersandar santai; malam ini, kita bersandar santai.

■ *On all other nights we eat either sitting up or reclining; on this night we recline.*

Malam-malam sebelumnya, kita makan secara biasa; malam ini, kita santap dengan upacara khusus.

■ *On all other nights we eat in an ordinary manner; on this night we dine with special ceremony.*

Culturally, the translation is very strange-sounding. Indonesians do not generally dip their foods into salt-water, sauces or spices. They also do not have *roti* (bread) during dinner; instead rice is their staple.

ABOUT THE LANGUAGE:

Indonesian

Number of speakers: 23,187,680
Rank: 46

Indonesian, also called Bahas Indonesia, is the official language and used in all regions of Indonesia. The regions of Indonesia are very linguistically diverse; although there are more native speakers of Javanese, Indonesian acts as the *lingua franca,* the language of wider commerce throughout the region.

As part of the independence movement in the 1930s, the Indonesian language was standardized (with many of its earlier Dutch spellings dropped) and Bahasa Indonesia was adopted as the language's name.

Indonesian is also spoken in the Netherlands, Philippines, Saudi Arabia, Singapore and the USA.

ABOUT THE TRANSLATOR AND SPEAKER:

I Wayan Arka

Age: Unavailable   Recorded: 1998
Towns: near Denpasar, Bali / Sydney, Australia / Stanford, CA

Wayan grew up in a village 8 km north of Denpasar, the capital city of Bali. He was a linguistics student at the University of Sydney. A native Balinese, Wayan was educated in Indonesian from age 6 and has used it over a quarter of century. He uses both Indonesian and Balinese in his family, and more recently, English with his daughter. Wayan considers he speaks Indonesian as well as other well-educated Indonesian speakers.

Photo by Tom Judd

Shy girls in an alleyway of Badang, West Java, Indonesia's third-largest city

Ilocano

Apay ta itatta nga rabii, ket saan nga agpada iti dadduma nga rabii?

■ *Why is this night different from all other nights?*

Iti dadduma nga rabii, ti kanen tayo ket tinapay wenno matsah; itatta nga rabii matsah laeng.

■ *On all other nights we eat either leavened bread or matzah; on this night only matzah.*

Iti dadduma nga rabii, kanen tayo amin nga naduma-duma nga ru-ut; itatta nga rabii diay napait laeng ru-ut.

■ *On all other nights we eat all kinds of herbs; on this night only bitter herbs.*

Iti dadduma nga rabii, saan-tayo nga agsaw-saw, uray no maminsan laeng; itatta nga rabii namindua tayo nga agsaw-saw.

■ *On all other nights we do not dip even once; on this night we dip twice.*

Iti dadduma nga rabii, mangan tayo nga nakatakder wenno nakailad; itatta nga rabii agilad tayo.

■ *On all other nights we eat either sitting up or reclining; on this night we recline.*

Iti dadduma nga rabii, mangan tayo ti ordinaryo nga pannangan; itatta nga rabii mangan tayo iti espesyal nga cermonia.

■ *On all other nights we eat in an ordinary manner; on this night we dine with special ceremony.*

Translation note: All 'o's are pronounced as 'u' in lute. Thus, the language name Ilocano is pronounced "ilucanu".

ABOUT THE LANGUAGE:

Ilocano

Number of speakers: 6,996,600
Rank: 107

Ilocano is spoken in The Philippines' northwestern Luzon, La Union and Ilocos provinces, Cagayan Valley, Babuyan, Mindoro and Mindanao. There are also many speakers in the USA.

ABOUT THE TRANSLATOR AND SPEAKER:

Miriam Schlauch

Age: Unavailable   Recorded: 1997
Towns: Santa Maria, Pangasinan, Luzon, Philippines /
        Minneapolis, MN

Miriam was born in Santa Maria, Pangasinan on the island of Luzon (the same island as Manila). Her parents are from the Ilocos Norte region. Ilocano is her first language.

Photo by Rody Torres

Typical department store in Manila

Igbo

Kedu ife Kpatalu anyasi a ji wee di iche n'anyasi ndi ọzọ?

■ *Why is this night different from all other nights?*

N'anyasi ndi ọzo, any n'ataa achicha ma ọbụ mgbodu ume; n'anyasi a sọ mgbodu ume.

■ *On all other nights we eat either leavened bread or matzah; on this night only matzah.*

N'anyasi ndi ọzo, anyi na eri akwụkwọ nri di iche iche; n'anyasi a sọ ụtazi.

■ *On all other nights we eat all kinds of herbs; on this night only bitter herbs.*

N'anyasi ndi ọzo, any anaro, esulu ma ọbu ofu ugbolo; n'anyasi a anyi sulu sọ ugbolu abụọ.

■ *On all other nights we do not dip even once; on this night we dip twice.*

N'anyasi ndi ọzo, any nonitelu enu ma obu dabelu adabe; n'anyasi a anyi dabelu adabe.

■ *On all other nights we eat either sitting up or reclining; on this night we recline.*

N'anyasi ndi ọzo, anyi na eri ife etu osi wee sọ anyi; n'anyasi a anyi na eri na ụsolo anyi ji eri oriri.

■ *On all other nights we eat in an ordinary manner; on this night we dine with special ceremony.*

Translation note: The written version used two instances of *anyi* and three of *any* (in 1st, 3rd and 4th questions). While these may be legitimate spelling variants, the latter were changed to *anyi* based on an analysis of the recording.

ABOUT THE LANGUAGE:

Igbo

Number of speakers: 18,000,000
Rank: 53

Igbo (pronounced "Ee-bo") is spoken in many areas of Nigeria. It is the official language of the southwest, and (where it is the majority language) is the main trade language of Abia, Anambra, Ebonyi, Enugu and Imo states. There are 30 dialects that vary in inherent intelligibility.

Many Igbo tribe members believe they are descendants of Israelites. They practiced circumcision on the eighth day, sat in mourning for a week and sounded a ram's horn long before they were exposed to the Bible by traders and missionaries. Many currently belong to Messianic congregations, while others are currently learning Hebrew and other aspects of traditional Judaism.

ABOUT THE TRANSLATOR AND SPEAKER:

Edward Chukwuerneke Okeke

Age: Unavailable   Recorded: 1998
Towns: Lagos, Nigeria / New York, NY

Edward Okeke was born, raised and educated in Lagos. He works at the United Nations' Administrative Law Unit.

Photos © Damilare Onajole

Nearly all kinds of foods and clothing are available at Oshodi market, the most popular market in Lagos, Nigeria. On the left, a woman sells the most common Nigerian food staples, *garri* (cassava grain) and *elubo* (yam flour)

Icelandic

Hvers vegna er Þetta kvöld öðruvísi en önnur kvöld?

■ *Why is this night different from all other nights?*

Öll önnur kvöld borðum við annað hvort sýrt brauð eða ósýrt brauð;
Þetta kvöld borðum við einungis ósýrt brauð.

■ *On all other nights we eat either leavened bread or matzah;*
on this night only matzah.

Öll önnur kvöld borðum við alls konar jurtir;
Þetta kvöld borðum við einungis bitrar jurtir.

■ *On all other nights we eat all kinds of herbs;*
on this night only bitter herbs.

Öll önnur kvöld dýfum við alls ekki jurtunum;
Þetta kvöld dýfum við Þeim tvisvar.

■ *On all other nights we do not dip even once;*
on this night we dip twice.

Öll önnur kvöld borðum við annað hvort sitjandi uÞÞrétt eða höllum okkur;
Þetta kvöld höllum við okkur.

■ *On all other nights we eat either sitting up or reclining;*
on this night we recline.

ABOUT THE LANGUAGE:

Icelandic

Number of speakers: 238,050
Rank: 810

Icelandic, called Íslenska by its speakers, is the national language of Iceland. There are also speakers in Canada and the USA. Icelandic is the closest of the existing Northern Germanic languages to Old Norse (prior to 14th C). When Iceland was governed by Norway (13th – 15th C) and later by the Danes, the official language was Norwegian, then Danish. When Iceland gained its independence from Denmark in 1944, Icelandic was revived as the country's official language.

Photo by Jacqueline Bernstein

ABOUT THE TRANSLATOR AND SPEAKER:

Sigrun Andradottir

Age: Unavailable   Recorded: 1995
Towns: Kopavogur, Iceland / Atlanta, GA

Sigrun grew up in Kopavogur, Iceland. She had lived in the USA 9 years at the time of the recording.

A UNESCO World Heritage site, Iceland's Þingvellir National Park is the site of the first parliament, where an open-air assembly representing the whole of Iceland was established in 930 and continued to meet until 1798

Ibanag

Natta yao nga gabi tanakwan ta ngamin nga gabi?

■ *Why is this night different from all other nights?*

Ta ngamin nga tanakwan nga gabi kuman tam ta pan o "matzah"; sangao nga gabi kuman tam ta "matzah" laman.

■ *On all other nights we eat either leavened bread or matzah; on this night only matzah.*

Ta ngamin nga tanakwan nga gabi kuman tam ta ngamin nga klase na gulay; sangao nga gabi kuman tam ta nappe nga gulay laman.

■ *On all other nights we eat all kinds of herbs; on this night only bitter herbs.*

Ta ngamin nga tanakwan nga gabi ari tam maddano maski mittan; sangao nga gabi mamiddwa tam nga maddano.

■ *On all other nights we do not dip even once; on this night we dip twice.*

Ta ngamin nga tanakwan nga gabi kaman tam nga nakatubang o nakagidda; sangao nga gabi nakagidda tam.

■ *On all other nights we eat either sitting up or reclining; on this night we recline.*

Ta ngamin nga tanakwan nga gabi ordinaryo laman y akakan tam; sangao nga gabi espesyal y klase na akakan tam.

■ *On all other nights we eat in an ordinary manner; on this night we dine with special ceremony.*

Translation notes: *gulay* means vegetable and *nakagidda* means lying down.

ABOUT THE LANGUAGE:

Ibanag

Number of speakers: 500,000
Rank: 541

Ibanag is spoken in the Philippine provinces of Isabela and Cagayan on the island of Luzon.

ABOUT THE TRANSLATOR AND SPEAKER:

Evelyn Caruncho

Age: Unavailable   Recorded: 2003
Towns: Tugwegarao, Cagayan, Philippines /
West Orange, NJ

Evelyn is a native speaker of Ibanag. She grew up in Tugwegarao, Cagayan, Philippines.

Photo by Rody Torres

Villa Escudero Resort in Batangas Province, Philippines. Guests eat on tables set over the cooling water

Hungarian

Miben különbözik ezen este a többi estéktöl?

■ *Why is this night different from all other nights?*

Máskor akármilyen kenyeret, kovászosat és kovásztalant is ehetünk;
ma azonban csak kovásztalant?

■ *On all other nights we eat either leavened bread or matzah;*
on this night only matzah.

Más estéken bármilyen zöldfélét ehetünk;
ma azonban csak keserüt?

■ *On all other nights we eat all kinds of herbs;*
on this night only bitter herbs.

Más estéken nem kell bemártanunk e zöldfélét egyszer sem;
ma pedig kétszer is?

■ *On all other nights we do not dip even once;*
on this night we dip twice.

Más estéken ehetünk akár ülve, akár támaszkodva;
ma azonban mindannyian csak támaszkodva?

■ *On all other nights we eat either sitting up or reclining;*
on this night we recline.

Máskor szokás szerint eszünk, de ezen az estén;
egy külön szertartást követve eszünk?

■ *On all other nights we eat in an ordinary manner;*
on this night we dine with special ceremony.

ABOUT THE LANGUAGE:

Hungarian

Number of speakers: 12,501,270
Rank: 73

Hungarian, also called Magyar, is the national language of Hungary. It is also spoken in Australia, Austria, Canada, Israel, Romania, Serbia and Montenegro, Slovakia, Slovenia, Ukraine and the USA. Hungarian is a highly inflected language in which nouns can have up to 238 possible forms.

The Hungarian language was influenced by Old Slavonic, medieval Latin and German, and also contains some Turkic loan words. Hungarian texts first appeared in the 13th C; the first book to be printed in Hungarian was published in Poland in 1527.

ABOUT THE TRANSLATOR AND SPEAKER:

Zoltan Herczegh

Age: Unavailable   Recorded: 1996
Towns: Funfkirchen / Pécs, Hungary / Sweden

Zoltan is a native Hungarian working in speech research in the laboratories of Telia, the Swedish telecommunications company. He was born and raised in Funfkirchen (now called Pécs). Pécs dates back to the 2nd C – at the time of the Roman Empire it was named Sopianae. The translation is traditional with additions by Zoltan.

A Hungarian translation was also worked on by **Rozi Kovesdi**.

Completed in 1859, Budapest's Great Synagogue is the second largest in the world. Its onion domes are Oriental-Byzantine and the brickwork patterns evoke ancient ruins of the Middle East. During WW II, the Synagogue was a ghetto; some 3,000 who died in the ghetto are buried in the Synagogue's courtyard

Huichol

Translated from Spanish

Naimetsie tukariku te pu teutikuaha naime yutxata te putikuaha tupiriya?

■ *¿Por qué es diferente esta noche de todas las otras noches?*

Naimetsie ipametsie tukariku teuteti kuaha pani wewiyatukaime iku ku.

■ *En todas las otras noches comemos pan hecho con levadura o pan ázimo;*
en esta noche solamente matzah.

Naimetsie tukariku te pu teutikuaha naime yutxata te putikuaha tupiriya.

■ *En todas las otras noches comemos toda cleses de hierbas.*

Naimetsie ipametsie tukariku te piti i nonoata tupiriya tsi kati a nemeku;
hiku tukariku hutaku tepiti hi nonuata.

■ *En todas las otras noches no somergimos las hierbas de ninguna manera;*
en esta noche las sumergimos dos veces.

Naimetsie ipametsie tukariku taputeutikua ha te hanukatetu heitserie hairruhanemeku;
ikutukariku tepanukayarre hairru hanemeku.

■ *En todas las otras noches comemos sentados rectos o inclinados;*
en esta noche nos sentamos inclinandos.

Naimetsie ipametsie tukariku te puteutikua ha yarreicua te mutei iweiya;
ikutukariku te pu teutikua ha te te ayerreiyatu airru hanemeku.

■ *En todas las otras noches comemos de manera ordinaria;*
en esta noche comemos con ceremonia especial.

Translation notes: The word *Naimetsie* was spelled *Naime tsie* in the next-to-last question and *Naimestie* in the last question. These were regularized, as they may be spelling variants or typographical errors. The translation may be missing some phrases, because the Spanish used by Hermenegildo (shown) was incomplete.

ABOUT THE LANGUAGE:

Huichol

Number of speakers: 20,000
Rank: 2,412

Huichol is spoken in northeastern Nayarit and northwestern Jalisco – states on the mid-western Pacific coast of Mexico. Huichols are well known for their fine violins and guitars, and their unique style of music.

ABOUT THE TRANSLATOR AND SPEAKER:

Hermenegildo Bautista Bautista

Age: 24   Recorded: 2007
Town: San Andrés Cohamiata, Jalisco, Mexico

Hermenegildo was born and raised in San Andrés Cohamiata, one of the main population centers where Huichol is spoken.

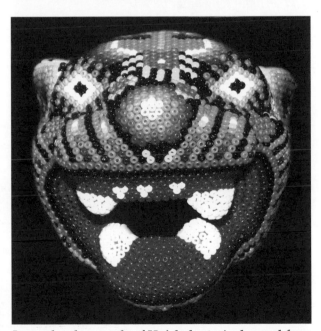

Hermenegildo working on the translation. On the table to his right is a form used for making beadwork figures

Jaguar head: example of Huichol art. A plywood form is covered with beeswax melted in the sun. To this is applied meticulous beadwork. Each figure, symbol and color has religious meaning. Traditional Huichol figures are not decoration but give expression to deep spiritual beliefs

Hopi

Sen pu' mihiqw apiy soosok mimhiqat amuupe hinta?
- *Why is this night different from all other nights?*

Aapiy mimhiqat ang itam pölavikit, ikis piqavikit nonvangwu; pu' mihiqw itam piqavikit sayani.
- pölavikit = native bread with yeast
  piqavikit = native tortilla without yeast
- *On all other nights we eat either leavened bread or matzah; on this night only matzah.*

Aapiy mimhiqat ang itam soosok hiita neevenit nonvangwu; pu' mihiqw itam kyasikyat neevenityani.
- neevenit = harvested wild green plants
  kyasikyat = very bitter/sour
- *On all other nights we eat all kinds of herbs; on this night only bitter herbs.*

Aapiy mimhiqat ang itam kasuus moroknayangwu: pu' mihiqw itam hapi löös moroknayani.
- *On all other nights we do not dip even once; on this night we dip twice.*

Aapiy mimhiqat ang itam yeeskyakyang, ikis taatsikiwkyakyang nonvangwu; pu' mihiqw itam tatsikiwkyang yungni.
- *On all other nights we eat either sitting up or reclining; on this night we recline.*

Aapiy mimhiqat ang itam yangkyakyang nonvangwu; pu' mihiqw itam pas pavan nonvani.
- *On all other nights we eat in an ordinary manner; on this night we dine with special ceremony.*

ABOUT HOPI RUNNERS:

Representing the USA in the 1908 and 1912 Olympic Games, Hopi Indian Louis Tewanima ran the 10,000-meter race. In 1912, Tewanima won a silver medal, establishing a USA record that stood for 52 years before it was broken by another Native American runner.

ABOUT THE LANGUAGE:

Hopi

Number of speakers: 5,260
Rank: 3,630

Hopi is spoken in several villages in northeast Arizona, with small numbers of speakers in Utah and New Mexico. With occupancy of Arizona since 500 BCE, the Hopi people have the longest authenticated occupation of a single area of any Native American tribe in the USA.

Like the Navajo, the Hopi people were involved with the WW II code talker projects.

ABOUT THE TRANSLATOR AND SPEAKER:

Marvin Lalo

Age: Unavailable   Recorded: 2004
Town: Kykotsmovi, AZ

Marvin is the Cultural Preservation Director of the Hopi Language Preservation Project. Marvin, a member of the Flute Clan, speaks the First Mesa dialect. His Hopi name, *Suhungwa*, means to come to an abrupt stop from a fast walk.

Saguaro National Park, near Tucson, AZ

Photo by Tom Judd

In the recordings: Marvin ends his recording with his name (*Suhungwa*) and the name of the language, spoken in Hopi.

Hindi

ये रात दूसरी रातों से आलग क्यों है?

■ Yeh raat doosri raatoun se alag kyoun hay?

■ *Why is this night different from all other nights?*

दूसरी रातों को हम ख़मीरी रोटी या मात्त्ज़ा खाते हैं।

इस रात सिर्फ़ मात्त्ज़ा।

■ Doosri ratoun ko hum khamiri roti ya matzah khate hain;
iss raat sirf matzah.

■ *On all other nights we eat either leavened bread or matzah;*
on this night only matzah.

दूसरी रातों को हम हर तरह की हर्ब खाते हैं।

इस रात हम सिर्फ़ कड़वी हर्ब खाते हैं।

■ Doosri ratoun ko hum har tarah ki herbs khate hain;
iss raat hum sirf kaevi herbs khate hain.

■ *On all other nights we eat all kinds of herbs;*
on this night only bitter herbs.

दूसरी रातों को हम एक बार भी डुबोते नहीं हैं।

इस रात हम दो बार डुबोते हैं।

■ Doosri ratoun ko hum ek baar bhi dubote nahin hain;
iss raat hum do baar dubote hain.

■ *On all other nights we do not dip even once;*
on this night we dip twice.

दूसरी रातों को हम या तो बैठ कर या टेक लगा कर खाते हैं।

इस रात हम टेक लगा कर खाते हैं।

■ Doosri ratoun ko hum ya tou baith kar ya tek laga kar khate hain;
iss raat hum tek lagakar khate hain.

■ *On all other nights we eat either sitting up or reclining;*
on this night we recline.

दूसरी रातों को हम रोज़ की तरह खाते हैं।

लेकिन इस रात हम उत्सव मना के खाते हैं।

■ Doosri ratoun ko hum roj ki tarah khate hain;
lekin iss raat hum utsav mana ke khate hain.

■ *On all other nights we eat in an ordinary manner;*
on this night we dine with special ceremony.

ABOUT THE LANGUAGE:

Hindi *

Number of speakers: 181,676,620
Rank: 5

Hindi is spoken throughout India, as well as in 16 other countries: Bangladesh, Belize, Botswana, Germany, Kenya, Nepal, New Zealand, Philippines, Singapore, South Africa, Uganda, United Arab Emirates, United Kingdom, USA, Yemen and Zambia.

Hindi's formal vocabulary is borrowed from Sanskrit, and has been de-Persianized and de-Arabicized. Hindi first started to be used in writing during the 4th C CE. It was originally written with the *Brahmi* script but since the 11th C has been written in the *Devanagari* alphabet. (Urdu, the main language of Pakistan, uses an Arabic script.) The first printed book in Hindi, published in 1796, was John Gilchrist's *Grammar of the Hindoostanee Language*.

The languages of Hindi, Hindustani and Urdu are sometimes considered co-dialects, but since they have important sociolinguistic differences, they are usually considered separate languages.

ABOUT THE TRANSLATOR AND SPEAKER:

Sanjai Narain

Age: 40   Recorded: 1995
Towns: several towns near New Delhi / Madison, NJ

Sanjai Narain received an MS from Syracuse University and a PhD from UCLA, both in Computer Science. He currently is Senior Research Scientist at Telcordia Technologies. Sanjai came to the USA at age 21. The translation was assisted by **Sudha Narain**, Sanjai's mother in New Delhi, India.

Photo by Stephanie Goldhumber

Taj Mahal, Agra, India

For additional information, see "*Focus on ... pages.pdf*" on the DVD.

Hiligaynon

Nga-a ang gab-i nga ini lain sa iban nga gab-i?

■ *Why is this night different from all other nights?*

Sa iban nga gab-i, ang aton ginakaon tinapay nga ginmasa ukon wala namasa; sa subong nga gab-i, ang indi lang namasa.

■ *On all other nights we eat either leavened bread or matzah; on this night only matzah.*

Sa iban nga gab-i, nagakaon kita sang tanan nga klase sang dahon-dahon; sa ini nga gab-i, mapait lang nga mga dahon-dahon.

■ *On all other nights we eat all kinds of herbs; on this night only bitter herbs.*

Sa iban nga gab-i, indi kita nagasawsaw maski kaisa; sa subong nga gab-i, nagasawsaw kita kaduwa ka beses.

■ *On all other nights we do not dip even once; on this night we dip twice.*

Sa iban nga gab-i, kon kita nagakaon kita ngapungko ukon nagahidag; sa subong nga gab-i, kita nagahidag.

■ *On all other nights we eat either sitting up or reclining; on this night we recline.*

Sa iban nga gab-i, kita nagakaon sa simple kag ordinaryo nga pamaagi; sa subong nga gab-i, magakaon kita nga may seremonya.

■ *On all other nights we eat in an ordinary manner; on this night we dine with special ceremony.*

ABOUT THE LANGUAGE:

Hiligaynon

Number of speakers: 5,770,000
Rank: 121

Hiligaynon, also called Ilonggo, is spoken in Iloilo and Capiz provinces, Panay, Negros Occidental and Visayas of the Philippines. There are also speakers in the USA.

ABOUT THE TRANSLATOR AND SPEAKER:

Rev. Barth Masa

Age: Unavailable   Recorded: 1998
Towns: Sibalom, Antique / Iloilo City / Diliman, Quezon City, Philippines

Reverend Masa is Christian Educational Director of the Church of the Risen Lord at the University of the Philippines. He was born in Sibalom and grew up in Iloilo City.

Photo by Rody Torres

Households throughout the Philippines roast a pig for hospitality during the Fiesta of their district's Patron Saint

Herero

Omena raṱjike ongurova ndji tji ya panguka kozongurova inḓa ozarwe?

■ *Why is this night different from all other nights?*

Mozongurova inḓa ozarwe azehe, tu rya kutja omboroto ndja worisiwa poo omatzah; ongurova ndjinondji, omatsah uriri.

■ *On all other nights we eat either leavened bread or matzah; on this night only matzah.*

Mozongurova inḓa ozarwe azehe, tu rya ovikurya vyokuti omihodo pekepeke; ongurova ndjinondji, omuti mbwi omururu uriri.

■ *On all other nights we eat all kinds of herbs; on this night only bitter herbs.*

Mozongurova inḓa ozarwe azehe, katu tjaveke nangarire rumwe; ongurova ndjinondji, matu tjaveke potuvari.

■ *On all other nights we do not dip even once; on this night we dip twice.*

Mozongurova inḓa ozarwe azehe, tu rya atwa haama osemba poo atu ri kotumbarambandja; ongurova ndjinondji, tu ri kotumbarambandja.

■ *On all other nights we eat either sitting up or reclining; on this night we recline.*

Mozongurova inḓa ozarwe azehe, tu rya otja komuano wetu mbu tu rya; ongurova ndjinondji, matu ri ape nondjoroka kaani.

■ *On all other nights we eat in an ordinary manner; on this night we dine with special ceremony.*

> **In the recordings:** Magdalena calls her language Otjiherero (sounds like "Oshiherero").

ABOUT THE SPEAKER:

Magdalena Tjiroze

Age: Unavailable   Recorded: 1998
Town: Otjinene, Namibia

Magdalena, a native speaker of Herero, was raised in Otjinene, Namibia.

ABOUT THE LANGUAGE:

Herero

Number of speakers: 237,000
Rank: 811

Herero, also called Ochiherero and Otjiherero, by its speakers, is spoken in Namibia, primarily in Damaraland, northwest Ovamboland territory and Kaokoveld. It is also spoken in Botswana by the Ovaherero people who came to Botswana as refugees in the early 1900s.

ABOUT THE TRANSLATOR:

Ella Kamaṱuka

Age: Unavailable   Translated: 1997
Location: Namibia

Ella, a native speaker of Herero, lives in Namibia.

This translation was obtained through the kind and generous work of **Gamsberg Macmillan**, school-book publishers in Windhoek, Namibia.

Photo by Boris Kester

Flamingoes flying over the sand dunes of Sandwich Harbor, Namibia

Hehe

Pede ndawuli ikilo iki pede kuliwungi na kilo cha ifilo ifingi?

- *Why is this night different from all other nights?*

**Ifilo mbefili pakilo twatwilya libumange;
neng'uni tukulya silihate visasanfu.**

- *On all other nights we eat either leavened bread or matzah;
  on this night only matzah.*

**Ifilo mbefili pakilo twatwilya ififyala na ndela ze ziwana mbezeli;
ikilo cha neng'uni twilya ifivyale na zindela ngali.**

- *On all other nights we eat all kinds of herbs;
  on this night only bitter herbs.*

**Ifilo mbefili pakilo sitwilovela sikumwi;
pakilo iki twiloveka lwa uvili.**

- *On all other nights we do not dip even once;
  on this night we dip twice.*

**Ifilo mbefili twilya tuteng'ime, ndauli tuhegavya;
pakilo ipa tulya tuhegavya hela.**

- *On all other nights we eat either sitting up or reclining;
  on this night we recline.*

**Ifilo mbefili twilya lwa ndolo lwa mbepaliiki;
cha namnyi twilya lwa kukela kunofu.**

- *On all other nights we eat in an ordinary manner;
  on this night we dine with special ceremony.*

ABOUT THE LANGUAGE:

Hehe

Number of speakers: 805,000
Rank: 418

Hehe is spoken in the Iringa region of Tanzania, south of Gogo. Hehe is called Kihehe by its speakers.

ABOUT THE TRANSLATOR:

Antery C Mswete

Age: 60   Translated: 2009
Towns: Iringa / Dar es Salaam, Tanzania

Antery works at a copy center in Tanzania, but his interests are in farming. He is a native speaker of Hehe.

ABOUT THE SPEAKER:

Joanita Ngaiza

Age: 38   Recorded: 2010
Town: Dar es Salaam, Tanzania

Joanita is a native speaker of Kihaya, fluent in Kihehe, and can read and write the other languages she recorded. Her full biography is on the Sukuma page.

Photos by Ilana Locker

Lions in Serengeti National Park

Tanzanians resting in the shade of a Baobab tree in Zanzibar

Hebrew

מַה נִּשְׁתַּנָּה הַלַּיְלָה הַזֶּה מִכָּל הַלֵּילוֹת?

שֶׁבְּכָל הַלֵּילוֹת אָנוּ אוֹכְלִין חָמֵץ וּמַצָּה.
הַלַּיְלָה הַזֶּה כֻּלּוֹ מַצָּה:

שֶׁבְּכָל הַלֵּילוֹת אָנוּ אוֹכְלִין שְׁאָר יְרָקוֹת.
הַלַּיְלָה הַזֶּה מָרוֹר:

שֶׁבְּכָל הַלֵּילוֹת אֵין אָנוּ מַטְבִּילִין אֲפִילוּ פַּעַם אֶחָת.
הַלַּיְלָה הַזֶּה שְׁתֵּי פְעָמִים:

שֶׁבְּכָל הַלֵּילוֹת אָנוּ אוֹכְלִין בֵּין יוֹשְׁבִין וּבֵין מְסֻבִּין.
הַלַּיְלָה הַזֶּה כֻּלָּנוּ מְסֻבִּין:

שֶׁבְּכָל הַלֵּילוֹת אָנוּ אוֹכְלִין בְּצוּרָה רְגִילָה.
הַלַּיְלָה הַזֶּה בְּרוֹב טְקָסִיּוֹת:

ABOUT THE LANGUAGE:

Hebrew

Number of speakers: 5,316,700
Rank: 128

Hebrew, called Ivrit by its speakers, is the national language of Israel. There are also major populations of speakers in Australia, Canada, Germany, Panama, United Kingdom and the USA.

Hebrew is one of the oldest languages, originating around 1200 BCE. Beginning in the late 1880s, Hebrew was successfully rescued from extinction when Eliezer Ben-Yehuda promoted Hebrew for daily use. Hebrew had not been a living, spoken language for as many as 1800 years. (It was slowly replaced by Aramaic, beginning 2,500 years ago.)

The earliest Hebrew script was derived from Phoenician. The modern Hebrew alphabet developed from early Aramaic script. Rashi script, used primarily for commentaries on texts, is named after Rashi, Rabbi Shlomo Yitzchaki (1040-1105 CE), one of the greatest medieval Jewish scholars and Bible commentators. Rashi did not use Rashi script for his commentaries but it is named in honor of him.

The third question is usually written with פַּעַם אֶחָת in most Ashkenazi Haggadahs and as פַּעַם אֶחָת in Sephardi Haggadahs. The two traditions also use a different order for the questions. Some melodies add כֻּלּוֹ מָרוֹר when the 4 Questions are sung. See the page for Arabic, Judeo-Iraqi and the main text for more examples of differences in the questions used by different communities.

The many faces of Moshiko

ABOUT THE SPEAKER:

Moshe Itzhak Halevy

Age: 64   Recorded: 1996
Towns: Jaffa / Tel Aviv, Israel

Moshe I. Halevy, known as Moshiko, is a renowned folkdance choreographer. Moshiko was originally a performer in *Inbalim*, Israel's renowned dance group. He is a very popular choreographer/composer/singer, with a career beginning in 1959 and spanning more than 40 years. He was born in Jaffa and lived most of his adult life in Tel Aviv.

The first Four Questions are traditional text, although their content and number have varied throughout history. The 5th question, based on English and Russian modernizations of the 4th question, was translated into Hebrew by **Rickey Stein** and native-born Israeli, **Leah Spiegel** (no relation to the author).

Haya

Kubaki obwire obu tinka bwa biro ebindi?

■ *Why is this night different from all other nights?*

Ebiro byona tuly'emikate eina ehamira anga etainamu hamira; kyonkai bwiro obu ntushohamu ogutaina hamira gwonkai.

■ *On all other nights we eat either leavened bread or matzah; on this night only matzah.*

Ebiro byona omukilo tulya ebishaka nemizi eya buli ngeli; obwire obu ntulya ebishaka nemizi elikushalila kusha.

■ *On all other nights we eat all kinds of herbs; on this night only bitter herbs.*

Ebiro byona titukoza na limoi; bwire obwa kileki tulakoza kabili.

■ *On all other nights we do not dip even once; on this night we dip twice.*

Ebiro byona tulya tushuntamile anga twegamile; kyonkai kileki tulalya twegamile.

■ *On all other nights we eat either sitting up or reclining; on this night we recline.*

Eboro byona tulya na makune; kyonkai kileki tulalya na obugenyi.

■ *On all other nights we eat in an ordinary manner; on this night we dine with special ceremony.*

ABOUT THE LANGUAGE:

Haya

Number of speakers: 1,300,000
Rank: 305

Haya is spoken in the Kagera region of Tanzania, mainly the Bukoba Urban and Bukoba Rural districts. Haya is also called Ekihaya, Kihaya, Ruhaya and Ziba by its speakers.

Tanzania's beautiful Zanzibar Island

ABOUT THE TRANSLATOR:

Vedasto Gasto Ngaiza

Age: 67 Translated: 2009
Towns: Bukoba / Dar es Salaam, Tanzania

Vedasto Gasto Ngaiza is a businessman in Dar es Salaam. A native speaker of Haya, he obtained an advanced degree in college. Through the success of Vedasto's business, he was able to send all seven of his children to universities in Tanzania. His interests are farming, traveling, reading and sports.

ABOUT THE SPEAKER:

Joanita Ngaiza

Age: 38 Recorded: 2010
Town: Dar es Salaam, Tanzania

Joanita is a native speaker of Kihaya, fluent in Kihehe, and can read and write the other languages she recorded. Her full biography is on the Sukuma page.

Zebra and wildebeest in Serengeti National Park

Hawaiian

He aha ka 'oko'a o keia pō mai na po 'e'e apau?
- *Why is this night different from all other nights?*

**I na pō 'e a'e apau pāina no makou i ka matzah;
i kēia pō matzah wale no.**
- *On all other nights we eat either leavened bread or matzah;
on this night only matzah.*

**I na pō 'e a'e apau 'ai mākou ika nāhelehele like 'ole;
kēia pō ai mākou i ka nāhelehele 'awa'awa wale no.**
- *On all other nights we eat all kinds of herbs;
on this night only bitter herbs.*

**I na pō 'e a'e apau 'a'ole mākou e ho'okomo wai ka nāhelehele;
kēia pō ho'opālua 'ia ka ho'okomo wai'ana.**
- *On all other nights we do not dip even once;
on this night we dip twice.*

**I na pō 'e a'e apau 'ai noa mākou;
kēia pō hema momoe ka 'ai 'ana.**
- *On all other nights we eat either sitting up or reclining;
on this night we recline.*

ABOUT THE LANGUAGE:

Hawaiian

Number of speakers: 1,000
Rank: 5,050

Hawaiian (also called 'Olelo Hawai'i Makuahine) is spoken in the Hawaiian Islands, mainly Ni'ihau Island and the Big Island of Hawai'i, with some speakers on all the other islands.

Hawaiian first appeared in the early 19th C in writing using a Latin alphabet version developed by missionaries, who started to visit the Hawaiian islands from 1820 onwards. After Hawaii was annexed by the USA in 1899, the Hawaiian language was banned from schools and went into rapid decline – by the 1980s, there were only 2,000 native Hawaiian speakers, most of whom were elderly. Since 1978, when Hawaiian was made an official language along with English, there has been a revival of interest.

ABOUT THE TRANSLATOR AND SPEAKER:

Lara Puamae'ole Mui Cowell

Age: 27   Recorded: 1997
Town: Honolulu, HI

Lara was born and raised in Honolulu. She took three years of college-level Hawaiian and had the rare opportunity to practice with native speakers of Hawaiian. She currently teaches English and Speech at the high-school level.

Aerial view of Kauai coast

Oahu's Ilani Palace, dressed up for King Kalakaua Day

Hausa

Waya daren nan ke da banbanci da sauran daren?

■ *Why is this night different from all other nights?*

Sauran daren mu na cin brodi maigishiri kwo kwuma mu ci masa; amma daren nan masa kawai.

■ *On all other nights we eat either leavened bread or matzah; on this night only matzah.*

Sauran daren mu na cin kwo wani irrin itatuwa; amma wannan daren masu daci kawai mu kaci.

■ *On all other nights we eat all kinds of herbs; on this night only bitter herbs.*

Sauran daren bamusamu loma ba kwo so daya; amma dadaren nan har so biyu.

■ *On all other nights we do not dip even once; on this night we dip twice.*

Sauran daren mu na ci azaune kwo kwa akwance; amma daren nan akwance.

■ *On all other nights we eat either sitting up or reclining; on this night we recline.*

Sauran daren mu na ci kamar bakwamai; amma dadaren nan mun ci cikin biki.

■ *On all other nights we eat in an ordinary manner; on this night we dine with special ceremony.*

ABOUT THE LANGUAGE:

Hausa

Number of speakers: 24,988,000
Rank: 42

Hausa is the most commonly spoken language of Nigeria, and the official language of its northern region. There is a pidgin Hausa spoken in Nigeria's markets. Hausa also has many speakers in Niger, Sudan and Cameroon.

Since the beginning of the 17th C, Hausa has been written with an Arabic script known as *ajami*. Most of the early writing in Hausa was Islamic poetry or on Islamic themes. Beginning in the 19th C, Hausa was spelled using the Latin letters shown here, using a spelling system called *boko*.

ABOUT THE TRANSLATOR AND SPEAKER:

Ibrahim Adoke Yakubu

Age: 36   Recorded: 2006
Towns: Zaria, Nigeria / Ottawa, Ontario / Athens, Greece

Ibrahim studied Political Science as an undergraduate at Nigeria's Ahmadu Bello University, also receiving a Masters Degree in International Affairs and Diplomacy. After getting a certificate in Conflict Resolution at the University of St. Paul, he is now a doctoral student at the University of Athens in Conflict Management in Africa. Ibrahim currently writes for a monthly African magazine in Athens. Hausa is his first language.

Drawing by Cydney Ilana Elkin, 5th grade, W Caldwell, NJ

Miriam's tambourine and the theme of freedom in the Seder

Haitian Creole

Pouki nouit cilàs diféran dé lòt nouit you?
- *Why is this night different from all other nights?*

Pandan tout lòt nouit yo, nou mangé pin ak lévin oubyin pin san lévin; min nouit cilàs cé pin san lévin.
- *On all other nights we eat either leavened bread or matzah; on this night only matzah.*

Pandan tout lòt nouit yo, nou mangé tout kalité fey; min a souèa nou mangé fey anmé.
- *On all other nights we eat all kinds of herbs; on this night only bitter herbs.*

Pandan tout lòt nouit you, nou pa tranpé fey di tou; min a souèa nou tranpé de foua.
- *On all other nights we do not dip even once; on this night we dip twice.*

Pandan tout lòt nouit yo, nou mangé chita douàt ou byin nou panché; min a souèa nou panché.
- *On all other nights we eat either sitting up or reclining; on this night we recline.*

Pandan tout lòt nouit you, nou mangé comm a lòdinè; min a souèa nou mangé ak on cérémoni espésial.
- *On all other nights we eat in an ordinary manner; on this night we dine with special ceremony.*

ABOUT THE LANGUAGE:

Haitian Creole

Number of speakers: 7,701,640
Rank: 99

Haitian Creole, also called Haitian Creole French and Fablas, is the national language of Haiti and is also spoken in the Dominican Republic and a half dozen other countries. In 1961, Haitian Creole was granted official legal and educational status.

ABOUT THE TRANSLATOR AND SPEAKER:

Ray Monel

Age: Unavailable   Recorded: 1995
Location: Haiti

Mr. Monel hails from Haiti.

Photo by Bernard Cloutier (berclo.net)

Solar cooking demonstration in an alternative energy exhibition (1979) in Haiti

Gwere

Lwachi echire chorwati chenjawulo okubire ebindi?

■ *Why is this night different from all other nights?*

Omubire ebindi byonabyona tulya emigati emibimbye oba egitali emibimbye; Muchire chorwati mibimbye gyonkani.

■ *On all other nights we eat either leavened bread or matzah; on this night only matzah.*

Omubire ebindi byonabyona tulya shodo yenayena; Muchire chorwati tulya shodo akakia yenka.

■ *On all other nights we eat all kinds of herbs; on this night only bitter herbs.*

Omubire ebindi byonabyona tetukozya wade mulundi gumo; Muchire chorwati tukozya emilundi mibiri.

■ *On all other nights we do not dip even once; on this night we dip twice.*

Omubire ebindi byonabyona tulya tutyaime obanga twesigikire; Muchire chorwati tulya twesigikire.

■ *On all other nights we eat either sitting up or reclining; on this night we recline.*

Omubire ebindi byonabyona tulya nga buligyo; Muchire chorwati tulya mbaga.

■ *On all other nights we eat in an ordinary manner; on this night we dine with special ceremony.*

Bonus in the recordings: The DVD contains the remarkable story of the Abayudaya Jews.

ABOUT THE LANGUAGE:

Gwere

Number of speakers: 409,000
Rank: 603

Gwere, also called Lugwere, is spoken in the Pallisa District of Uganda, dominating 2 of the district's 4 counties.

ABOUT THE TRANSLATOR AND SPEAKER:

Rachel Namudosi

Age: 16   Recorded: 1999
Towns: Mbale / Nabugoye, Uganda

Rachel is the leader of *Kohavim Tikvah* (Stars of Hope) Choir, Abayudaya Congregation in Nabugoye, near Mbale, Uganda. She is a native speaker of Gwere. She was born in Mbale to an Emugwere father and was raised in a Bugwere environment.

Photo by Boris Kester

Seen on safari in Uganda's Queen Elizabeth Park, a white Egret rests on a Buffalo's back

Gusii

Ingi obutuko obo boberete obonga'o kubua obotuko bonde bwensi?

■ *Why is this night different from all other nights?*

Ase obotuko bonde bwensi, nigo tokori omogate na Matzah; rakini ase obotuko obo tokori Matzah yoka.

■ *On all other nights we eat either leavened bread or matzah; on this night only matzah.*

Ase obotuko bonde bwensi, nigo tokori emete emenge; rakini ase obotuko obo tokori emete emeroro yoka.

■ *On all other nights we eat all kinds of herbs; on this night only bitter herbs.*

Ase obotuko bwonde bwensi, ntori gotongeria nonye rimo; rakini ase obotuko obo igo togotongeria kabere.

■ *On all other nights we do not dip even once; on this night we dip twice.*

Ase obotuko bonde bwensi, nigo tokoragera toikaransete kose toegegete gochi magega; rakini ase obotuko obo igo tokorare toegegete rioka.

■ *On all other nights we eat either sitting up or reclining; on this night we recline.*

Ase obotuko bonde bwensi, nigo tokoragera muna potambe; rakini ase obotuko obo igo tokoragera muna riri tore enyangi.

■ *On all other nights we eat in an ordinary manner; on this night we dine with special ceremony.*

ABOUT THE TRANSLATOR AND SPEAKER:

Kimeli Willson Naiyomah

Age: 25 Recorded: 2002
Towns: Enoosaen, Kenya / Stanford, CA

Kimeli is a junior Maasai warrior. He was raised in Enoosaen, a village 10 miles from the Kenyan Game Reserve. His father is Maasai and his mother speaks Kalenjin. He also speaks Kiswahili. Kimeli spent 2 years in an Gusii-speaking village among the *Abagusii* people – he claims to be very good with languages and would be considered to speak Gusii without an accent. He checked his translation with a native Gusii speaker.

Kimeli was in the national news because of a donation of sacred cows. This Maasai warrior was in New York City during the attacks of the September 11, 2001. When he told his community in West Kenya about the attacks, the community elders wanted to donate sacred cows to America – a traditional Maasai symbol of consolation. (The cows couldn't be sent to the USA, so Kenyan crafts were later sent.)

He is currently writing a dictionary of Maasai and pursuing a pre-med program.

ABOUT THE LANGUAGE:

Gusii

Number of speakers: 2,120,300
Rank: 221

Gusii (called Kisii and Ekegusii by its speakers) is a language of Kenya. It is spoken in southwestern Kenya, south of Kavirondo Gulf, Kisii District and Nyanza Province.

Photo © Susan Hantman

A herd of Zebra at a watering hole in Tsavo National Park, Kenya's largest park

Gurage, Sebat Bet

 የምሳ ዘሁ ጮዛሬ ትሁ8ዝ ጮሣሬ በት ግ7ኪ9?
WHY IS THIS NIGHT DIFFERENT FROM ALL OTHER NIGHTS?

እን2 የቦግ ዲፖ ጮሣሬ ንበሩነ እኒ7ን ያሬ ዳፈ(ኮ7) በናፖም።
ON ALL OTHER NIGHTS WE EAT EITHER LEAVENED BREAD OR MATZAH; ON THIS NIGHT ONLY MATZAH.

እን2 ጮሣሬ ጮ ሣሬ እትፖ ትጮ ንበሩነ እኒ ጮሣሬ ግነ እ0ዐ ም እ7ፖ ቅር በ7ፖም።
ON ALL OTHER NIGHTS WE EAT ALL KINDS OF HERBS; ON THIS NIGHT ONLY BITTER HERBS.

እን2 ጮሣሬ ጮሣሬ ትጮሰዲ ፎ ትዶ ጨዕም ንበሩ እኒ ጮሣሬ ግን ጺ00ረ ቅር እ72 ወረፖም በናፖም።
ON ALL OTHER NIGHTS WE DO NOT DIP EVEN ONCE; ON THIS NIGHT WE DIP TWICE.

እን7 የርባተ8 ንበሩ ተጨ7ቅነፖም ንበሩ እኒ ጮሣሬ ግን ተትጨ7ቅ7ፖም በናፖም።
ON ALL OTHER NIGHTS WE EAT EITHER SITTING UP OR RECLINING; ON THIS NIGHT WE RECLINE.

ረሩ በጮሣሬ ተጨ7ቅ ነፖ ንበሩነ በነ እኒ ጮሣሬ ግን ፎን2 ጮሣሬ ይዕዝ ግቦዝ በናፖም።
ON ALL OTHER NIGHTS WE EAT IN AN ORDINARY MANNER; ON THIS NIGHT WE DINE WITH SPECIAL CEREMONY.

ABOUT THE LANGUAGE:

Sebat Bet Gurage *

Number of speakers: 2,320,000
Rank: 213

The Gurage cluster of languages are spoken in Ethiopia. There are a number of dialects, all spoken in the West Gurage region: Ezha (the dialect of our speaker) is spoken in Agenna, Chaha is spoken around Emdibir, Gura is spoken around Ch'eza and in the mountains north of Chaha and Ezha, Gyeto is spoken south of Ark'it' in K'abul and K'want'e. The largest population of speakers is for Chaha (130,000), with 120,000 speakers of Ezha.

* For additional information, see
Focus on ... pages.pdf' **on the DVD.**

Photo by Bernard Cloutier (berclo.net)

ABOUT THE TRANSLATOR AND SPEAKER:

Alem Adera

Age: Unavailable   Recorded: 2001
Towns: Ababa, Ethiopia / NJ

Alem was born near Ethiopia's capital, Addis Ababa, Ethiopia. He learned Gurage from his parents. He was 19 or 20 when he moved to the USA.

Circus Ethiopia began in 1991 when the photographer's cousin, Marc La Chance, taught a circus program for a celebration held by the Ethiopian Jewish (*Beta Israel*) community. Most of the original troupe left when a change of government prompted the community's exodus to Israel. A second group, who had seen the first performance, asked to start again and Circus Ethiopia's success grew. Circus Ethiopia now encompasses over 10 circus troupes and reaches 500,000 people annually

Gulla

Wha fa disya ain same as oda res a ednin?

■ *Why is this night different from all other nights?*

Oda res a ednin we nyam pun disya bread o one wha flat; dis ebnin e got disya flat one by e dry sef.

■ *On all other nights we eat either leavened bread or matzah; on this night only matzah.*

Oda res a ednin we da nyam pun pleny herb; dis ebnin de herb bitta an e by e dry sef.

■ *On all other nights we eat all kinds of herbs; on this night only bitter herbs.*

Oda res a ednin we an gwine chook one time; disya ednin wi da chook een two time.

■ *On all other nights we do not dip even once; on this night we dip twice.*

Oda res a ednin wi nyam da sit up; disya ednin we da mos lay doung.

■ *On all other nights we eat either sitting up or reclining; on this night we recline.*

Oda res a ednin we jus nyam; dis ebnin nyam da mek special.

■ *On all other nights we eat in an ordinary manner; on this night we dine with special ceremony.*

ABOUT THE LANGUAGE:

Gulla / Sea Island Creole

Number of speakers: 250,000
Rank: 782

Gulla is spoken by the Gullah/Geechee Nation in coastal regions from North Carolina to Florida, and the Sea Islands off the coast of Georgia. Though based on English, it is a Creole with strong influence from West and Central African languages. The Gullah have preserved more of their African heritage than any other African-American community.

ABOUT THE TRANSLATOR:

Kwame Sha

Age: Unavailable   Translated: 2007
Town: St. Helena Island, SC

Kwame works as Technical Coordinator for the Gullah/Geechee Nation headquarters on St. Helena Island. This translation is noted as being included by Queen Quet, Chieftess of the Gullah/Geechee Nation. Further information about the Gullah/Geechee Nation is freely available from GullahGeecheeNation@officialgullahgeechee.info and www.officialgullahgeechee.info.

Chieftess of the Gullah/Geechee Nation, Queen Quet in front of the national flag of the Gullah Geechee Nation

Gujarati

 આ રાત્રી બદી રાત્રી થી કેમ જુદી છે?

■ Aa ratri badhi ratri thi kem judi chai?

■ *Why is this night different from all other nights?*

બીજી બદી રાત્રીએ, અમે ફુલકા અથવ સુકિ રોટલિ જમિએ છિએ;
આ રાત્રીએ ખાલી સુકી રોટલિ જમિએ છીએ.

■ Biji badhi ratri-a, ame fulka athva suki rotali jami-a chi-a;
aa ratri-a khali suki rotali jami-a chi-a.

■ *On all other nights we eat either leavened bread or matzah;*
on this night only matzah

બીજી બદી રાત્રીએ, અમે ઘણિ જાતના સાક- ભાજિ જમિએ છીએ;
આ રાત્રીએ ખાલી કડવા સાક-ભાજિ જમિએ છીએ.

■ Biji badhi ratri-a, ame ghani jatna sak-bhaji jami-a chi-a;
aa ratri-a khali kadva sak-bhaji jami-a chi-a.

■ *On all other nights we eat all kinds of herbs;*
on this night only bitter herbs.

બીજી બદી રાત્રીએ અમે સાક-ભાજિ ને ડુબોડતા નથી;
આ રાત્રીએ બે વખાત ડુબોડિએ છીએ.

■ Biji badhi ratri-a, ame sak-bhaji ne dubodta nathi;
aa ratri-a bae vakhat dubadi-a chi-a.

■ *On all other nights we do not dip even once;*
on this night we dip twice.

બીજી બદી રાત્રીએ અમે સિદ્ધા બેસિને અથવ ટેકે બેસિને જમિએ છીએ;
આ રાત્રીએ ટેકે બેસિને જમિએ છીએ.

■ Biji badhi ratri-a, ame sidha besine athwa taykay besine jami-a chi-a;
aa ratri-a taykay besine jami-a chi-a.

■ *On all other nights we eat either sitting up or reclining;*
on this night we recline.

બીજી બદી રાત્રીએ અમે સામાન્ય રિતે જમિએ છીએ;
આ રાત્રીએ અમે ખાસ વિદ્ધિ કરી ને જમિએ છીએ.

■ Biji badhi ratri-a, ame rojindi ritae jami-a chi-a;
aa ratri-a ame khase vidhhi kari ne jami-a chi-a.

■ *On all other nights we eat in an ordinary manner;*
on this night we dine with special ceremony.

ABOUT THE LANGUAGE:

Gujarati

Number of speakers: 46,493,990
Rank: 25

Gujarati is spoken in the Indian states of Gujarat, Maharashtra, Rajasthan, Karnataka and Madhya Pradesh. It is also spoken in 16 other countries, from Fiji to the United Kingdom. Most speakers are in Kenya, Pakistan, Singapore, Tanzania, Uganda and Zambia.

ABOUT THE TRANSLATOR AND SPEAKER:

Amit K Munta

Age: 30s   Recorded: 1997
Towns: Akhi / Palanpur / Bombay, India / NJ

Amit spent his early childhood in a small remote town of Arkhi, in the state of Gujarat. During his high school years, he lived in the bigger town of Palanpur, also in Gujarat. As an adult, he lived in Bombay before coming to the USA.

Photo by Jignesh Patel

Akshar Deri Temple in Gondal, Gujarat, commemorating the cremation spot of Aksharbrahman Gunatitanand Swami, most honored disciple of spiritual leader Bhagwan Swaminarayan

Gua

De ɛmgbɛ ne sunɔ ayi mɔ ken?
- *Why is this night different from all other nights?*

**Gbeya anyi akoala ɛnegyi brodo ndoo maasa;
ɛlɛ gban anyi mɔ le ɛ, ɛne egyi maasa ken.**
- *On all other nights we eat either leavened bread or matzah;
on this night only matzah.*

**Gbeya anyi akoala ɛne gyi agbom file;
ɛlɛ gban anyi mɔ le ɛ, agbom ɛlɛ ne aketa ne ɛne egyie ɛ.**
- *On all other nights we eat all kinds of herbs;
on this night only bitter herbs.*

**Gbeya anyi akoala ɛne gyi ɔlɔkoala;
anyi mmɔ le ɛ, ɛne egyie ɔboroso.**
- *On all other nights we do not dip even once;
on this night we dip twice.*

**Gbeya anyi akoala ɛne kyinae ndoo ɛne kpesɛ ogyi;
anyi mmɔ le ɛ, ɛne kpesɛ.**
- *On all other nights we eat either sitting up or reclining;
on this night we recline.*

**Gbeya anyi akoala ɛne gyi mo de ɛlɛ ne daa ɛne gyi mo a;
anyi mmɔ le ɛ, ɛne egyi mo akɔse.**
- *On all other nights we eat in an ordinary manner;
on this night we dine with special ceremony.*

ABOUT THE LANGUAGE:

Gua

Number of speakers: 60,200
Rank: 1,509

Gua, also called Anum-Boso and Gua-Anum, is spoken in Ghana in an area within the Ewe-speaking population.

ABOUT THE SPEAKER:

Samson Okoh

Age: 25   Recorded: 2005
Towns: Akosombo, Ghana / Grand Rapids, MI

Samson's mother tongue is Gua and he also speaks Twi/Akan and English. He was raised in Akosombo, in the eastern region of Ghana. His parents were from the towns of Anum and Boso – Gua's alternate name is Anum-Boso. Samson was 20 when he came to the USA. He currently works as a systems engineer and is pursuing a Masters in Engineering Management.

Photo by Samson Okoh

A palm plantation in Ghana

ABOUT THE TRANSLATOR:

Margaret Abena Okoh

Age: Unavailable   Translated: 2005
Town: Anum, Ghana

Mrs. Okoh, raised in Anum, Ghana, is a native speaker of Gua. She is the speaker's mother.

Gronings

Translated from Dutch

Waorom ist vanaomd aans as aans?

■ *Waarom is het vanavond anders dan andere avonden?*

Aans aten wie stoet of matses;
vanaomd allineg matzes.

■ *Op alle andere avonden eten we of gerezen brood of matzoh; vanavond alleen matzoh.*

Aans aten wie verschainde kruud'n;
vanaomd allineg bittere kruud'n.

■ *Op alle andere avonden aten we verschillende soorten specerijen; vanavond alleen bittere specerijen.*

Aans worden kruuden neit stipt;
vanaomd stippen wie.

■ *Op alle andere avonden dippen we de specerijen helemaal niet; vanavond dippen we ze twee keer.*

Aans zitten wie overend of underuut;
vanaomd hangen wie underuut.

■ *Op alle andere avonden zitten we rechtop of leunen we achterover; op deze avond leunen we achterover.*

Aans aten wie gewoon;
vanaomd eten wie met seremonie.

■ *Op alle andere avonden aten we zoals altijd; vanavond dineren we op ceremonile wijze.*

Groningen's *Martinitoren*, completed in 1482, is one of the largest church towers in the Netherlands and is known among the locals as *d'Olle Grieze*, The Old Grey One

Photo by John-Luc Bakker

ABOUT THE LANGUAGE:

Gronings

Number of speakers: 592,000
Rank: 502

Gronings is spoken in Groningen province in The Netherlands. Gronings (also called Groningen) is one of the official languages of The Netherlands and is the primary language for many rural people.

Groningers have a reputation for being terse. One bit of folk wisdom is *Iemand die echt Gronings spreekt gebruikt korte zinnen; acht woorden per zin is al veel* ("Groningers make short sentences; 8 words per sentence is almost too much").

ABOUT THE TRANSLATOR:

John-Luc Bakker

Age: 35   Recorded: 2005
Towns: Groningen / Delft, The Netherlands / Flemington, NJ

John-Luc holds a Masters in Computer Science and works as a Research Scientist in programmable services for telecommunications. He was raised in Groningen until age 20, when he moved to Delft for his higher education. John-Luc moved to the USA at age 29.

This was translated with assistance from **Aly Tooms** (of Stadskanaal) and **Lukas Bakker** (born and raised in city of Groningen).

ABOUT THE SPEAKER:

Gine Bakker-Nienhuis

Age: 67   Recorded: 2005
Towns: Siddeburen / Groningen, The Netherlands

Gine was born in Siddeburen and currently lives in the city of Groningen. She is the mother of translator John-Luc Bakker.

Greek

Γιατί αυτή η νύχτα είναι διαφορετική από όλες τις άλλες νύχτες;

■ Giati ayti i nyhta einai diaforetiki apo oles tis alles nyhtes;

■ *Why is this night different from all other nights?*

Όλες τις άλλες νύχτες τρώμε ζυμωμένο ψωμί ή ΄μάτσα΄·
'αυτή τη νύχτα μόνο μάτσα.

■ Oles tis alles nyhtes trome zymomeno psomi i "matsa";
aytin ti nyhta mono matsa.

■ *On all other nights we eat either leavened bread or matzah;*
On this night only matzah.

Όλες τις άλλες νύχτες τρώμε κάθε λογής μυρωδικά·
αυτή τη νύχτα μόνο πικρά μυρωδικά.

■ Oles tis alles nyhtes trome kathe logis myrodika;
ayti ti nyhta mono pikra myrodika.

■ *On all other nights we eat all kinds of herbs;*
on this night only bitter herbs.

Όλες τις άλλες νύχτες δεν βουτάμε·
αυτή τη νύχτα βουτάμε δύο φορές.

■ Oles tis alles nyhtes den boytame;
ayti ti nyhta boytame dyo fores.

■ *On all other nights we do not dip even once;*
on this night we dip twice.

Όλες τις άλλες νύχτες τρώμε ίσια ή γυρτά·
αυτή τη νύχτα μόνο γυρτά.

■ Oles tis alles nyhtes trome isia i gyrta;
ayti ti nyhta mono gyrta.

■ *On all other nights we eat either sitting up or reclining;*
on this night we recline.

> **Translation and transliteration notes:** The original
> had αυτή την ("ayti tin") in second half of the first and
> fourth questions. There is a 'soft sound' rule that deletes
> a letter when the next word starts with the same sound.
> The punctuation is correct: Greek uses a semicolon to
> represent a question mark and raised dot for commas.

ABOUT THE LANGUAGE:

Greek

Number of speakers: 13,084,490
Rank: 67

Greek, the national language of Greece, is spoken in 35 other countries, primarily Cyprus, Egypt, Albania, Italy and Turkey.

The Greek alphabet has been in continuous use since about 750 BCE. It was developed from the Canaanite/Phoenician alphabet. For example, *alpha* comes from the Canaanite *aleph* (ox) and *beta* from *beth* (house); hence the similarity to modern Hebrew.

Local and different versions of the alphabet were used in antiquity; one developed into the modern Greek alphabet, while another eventually became the Latin alphabet. Around the 4th C BCE, local alphabets were replaced by the eastern *Ionic* alphabet, which is represented in the capital letters of modern Greek. Modern Greek's lower case letters, based on Byzantine script and cursive writing, first appeared after 800 CE.

ABOUT THE TRANSLATOR AND SPEAKER:

Manolis Tsangaris

Age: 30s   Recorded: 1995
Towns: Rhodes / Karpathos / Athens, Greece / NJ

Manolis was born in Rhodes but lived in Karpathos, Greece until age 18. He lived in Athens until age 23 when he moved to the USA. His accent is clearly affected by Athenian speech. He received his PhD in Computer Science at the University of Wisconsin and worked in the research departments of several telecommunications companies in the area of wireless technology and services. The text was typed in with help from **George Lapiotis**.

A Greek village in southwestern Greece on the Ionian Sea

Z Y X W V U T S R Q P O N M L K J I H **G** F E D C B A Λ

Gogo

Nhaule chiro achi sivihwanile na viro avi?

■ *Why is this night different from all other nights?*

Viro vyose chiro chikudya mkate wono utajiwe vihanzizo amira au wono usina amira; kwa chiro achi chodya mkate wono usina amira.

■ *On all other nights we eat either leavened bread or matzah; on this night only matzah.*

Viro vyose chiro chukudya Madera ghono gehivanire; chiro chezuaali chikudya Madera makali du.

■ *On all other nights we eat all kinds of herbs; on this night only bitter herbs.*

Viro vyose sichikuloweka hamba kamonga du; chiro chezwadi chikuloweka kegete.

■ *On all other nights we do not dip even once; on this night we dip twice.*

Viro vyose chiro chikudya chikaye au chegamie; chro chezwadi chikudya chegamie du.

■ *On all other nights we eat either sitting up or reclining; on this night we recline.*

Viro vyose chiro chukudya kwa chogopo cha wera wera; chiro che zuadi chikudya kwa nyamo.

■ *On all other nights we eat in an ordinary manner; on this night we dine with special ceremony.*

ABOUT THE LANGUAGE:

Gogo

Number of speakers: 1,440,000
Rank: 290

Gogo, called Kigogo by its speakers, is spoken in the Dodoma Region and Manyoni District of the Singida Region.

ABOUT THE TRANSLATOR:

Yohana Sharif

Age: 38   Translated: 2009
Towns: Dodoma / Dar es Salaam, Tanzania

Yohana, who runs a photography business in Dar es Salaam, is a native speaker of Gogo. Yohana's interests are sports, traveling and music.

Photo by Ilana Locker

Baobab tree, sometimes called the upside-down, bottle or monkey bread tree, in Tanzania's Ruaha National Park. The *Lion King*'s Rafiki makes his home in an African Baobab tree

ABOUT THE SPEAKER:

Joanita Ngaiza

Age: 38   Recorded: 2010
Town: Dar es Salaam, Tanzania

Joanita is a native speaker of Kihaya, fluent in Kihehe, and can read and write Gogo and the other languages she recorded. Her full biography is on the Sukuma page.

Gĩkũyũ

Nĩkĩ ũtukũ wa ũmũthĩ wĩna ũtiganu na matukũ maria magnĩ mothe?

■ *Why is this night different from all other nights?*

Mantukũ maria mangĩ tũriaga mũgate wa ũimbia kana Matzah; ũtukũ ũyũ, no Matzah.

■ *On all other nights we eat either leavened bread or matzah; on this night only matzah.*

Mantukũ maria mangĩ tũriaga nyeni cia mĩthemba yothe; ũtukũ ũyũ, no nyeni ndũrũ tu.

■ *On all other nights we eat all kinds of herbs; on this night only bitter herbs.*

Mantukũ maria mangĩ mothe tũtitobokagia ona rĩmwe; ũtukũ ũyũ, tũratobokia merĩ.

■ *On all other nights we do not dip even once; on this night we dip twice.*

Mantukũ maria mangĩ mothe tũriaga tũtĩnĩkĩte thĩ kana twĩtiranĩtie na mwena; ũtukũ ũyũ, nĩ twĩtiranĩtie.

■ *On all other nights we eat either sitting up or reclining; on this night we recline.*

Mantukũ maria mangĩ tũriaga na mũtugo ũria twĩmenyeretie; ũtukũ ũyũ, tũraria tarĩ igongona.

■ *On all other nights we eat in an ordinary manner; on this night we dine with special ceremony.*

Gĩkũyũ has seven vowels:
a = a in accept
e = e in elephant
i = i in ink
ĩ = a in angel
o = o in oxygen
u = oo in zoo
ũ = o in open

We thank Dr. Minkyu Lee at Lucent Technologies who processed the recording by power spectrum subtraction. While leaving some tonal noise, the processing greatly reduced the noise of the original recording.

About the Translator and Speaker:

Nene Mburu

Age: Unavailable   Recorded: 1999
Towns: Hola / Kiambu, Kenya / TX / GA / London, England

Nene, a native speaker of Gĩkũyũ and Kiswahili, was born in Hola of northeastern Kenya, a detention camp for the Maumau people where his parents were incarcerated during Kenya's struggle for independence. He was raised in Kiambu in central Kenya. After his university education, Nene joined the Kenyan army and was trained in Kenya, the USA (San Antonio, TX and Ft. Benning, GA) and Britain (Army Command and Staff College, in Camberley). Nene was decorated and retired from the Kenyan Army in 1996 to privately pursue further education. He has received a Bachelors degree in Political Science (University of Nairobi, Kenya), Diploma in American Language (Defense Language Institute, San Antonio) and Masters and PhD in War Studies (University of London).

He has done extensive research on the oral narratives of his people, the Gĩkũyũ, which he intends to publish soon. Nene speaks other languages of Africa with varying degrees of competence.

About the Language:

Gĩkũyũ

Number of speakers: 7,180,000
Rank: 104

Gĩkũyũ (also called Kĩkuyu) is spoken in west-central Kenya, in Kiambu, Murang'a, Nyeri and Kirinyaga districts of Central Province.

Photo © Niko Lipsanen

A view of Nairobi's skyscrapers from Uhuru Park

German

Warum ist diese Nacht nicht dieselbe, wie alle anderen Nächte?

- *Why is this night different from all other nights?*

Alle anderen Nächte essen wir Brot oder Matzah;
In dieser Nacht, essen wir nur Matzah.

- *On all other nights we eat either leavened bread or matzah;
  on this night only matzah.*

Alle anderen Nächte essen wir allerlei Kräuter;
In dieser Nacht, essen wir nur bittere Kräuter.

- *On all other nights we eat all kinds of herbs;
  on this night only bitter herbs.*

Alle anderen Nächte tunken wir keine Kräuter ein;
In dieser Nacht, tunken wir sie zweimal ein.

- *On all other nights we do not dip even once;
  on this night we dip twice.*

Alle anderen Nächte essen wir gerade sitzend oder zur Seite gelehnt;
In dieser Nacht, essen wir gelehnt.

- *On all other nights we eat either sitting up or reclining;
  on this night we recline.*

Alle anderen Nächte essen wir normalerweise;
In dieser Nacht, speisen wir mit besonderer Feierlichkeit.

- *On all other nights we eat in an ordinary manner;
  on this night we dine with special ceremony.*

ABOUT THE TRANSLATOR AND SPEAKER:

Maria Beguin

Age: 59   Recorded: 1998
Towns: Obersuhl, Germany / Springfield, NJ

Maria was born and raised in Obersuhl, near the former border of East and West Germany and moved to the USA at age 23. She speaks a combination dialect of Hessisch and Thuringian when speaking to family and villagers. In developing the translation, Maria consulted her German Jewish friend and poet, **Gertrude Halstead**. The translation was also worked on by **Dr. Dan Kahn** (Gillette, NJ) and **Dr. Heinz Richter** (Leipzig, Germany).

ABOUT THE LANGUAGE:

German

Number of speakers: 90,294,110
Rank: 10

German (called Deutsch by its speakers) is the national language of Germany and six other countries. There are significant numbers of speakers in 40 countries; outside of Germany, the largest numbers are in Austria and Kazakhstan. There are at least 12 major dialect groups, some not inherently intelligible with each other.

The earliest known examples of written German date from the 8th C and consist of fragments of an epic poem, *The Song of Hildebrand*, magical charms and German glosses in Latin manuscripts. A short Latin-German dictionary, *The Abrogans*, was written during the 760s. Standard German is one High German variety ("High" refers to dialects from the upper Rhine region), which developed from the chancery of Saxony. Standard German, now known as *Hochdeutsch* (High German), gained acceptance as the written standard in the 16th and 17th C.

Rabbis seated around the Seder table. Erna Michael Haggadah, circa 1400, Germany

Georgian

რატომ არის ეს ღამე განსხვავებული სხვა ღამეებისგან?

- ram-mnishvne-LOba ahm GRameet KVEla DAnarcheet GRamehbs?
- *Why is this ni0ght different from all other nights?*

ყველა სხვა ღამეს ჩვენ მჭამთ საფუარ პურს ან მაცას;
ამ ღამეს კი მხოლოდ მაცას:

- KVEla sHva GRamehbeet chvehn vt'chamt Poors ahn matsuhs;
  ahm GRameet MARto matsuhs.
- *On all other nights we eat either leavened bread or matzah;
  on this night only matzah.*

ყველა სხვა ღამეს ჩვენ ვჭამთ ყველა ბალახეულს ფხალეულს;
ამ ღამეს კი მხოლოდ ცხარე ბალახეულს:

- KVEla sHva GRamehbeet chvehn vt'chamt KVEla (mits)vanyeels;
  ahm GRameet MARto m'zhav (mits)vanyeels.
- *On all other nights we eat all kinds of herbs;
  on this night only bitter herbs.*

ყველა სხვა ღამეს ჩვენ არ ვაწობთ ბალახეულს მარილიან
წყალში არც ერთხელ;
ამ ღამეს კი ორჯერ ვაწობთ:

- KVEla sHva GRamehbeet chvehn ahra vsrolt mitsvanyeels;
  ahm GRameet chvehn vsrolt oorneet.
- *On all other nights we do not dip even once;
  on this night we dip twice.*

ყველა სხვა ღამეს ჩვენ გზამთ ან დამჭდარი არ რამეს მიყრდნობილი;
ამ ღამეს კი მხოლოდ ღამეს მიყრდნობილი:

- KVEla sHva GRamehbeet chvehn v'zeevart dah vt'chamt ahnu vt'svehbt;
  ahm GRameet chvehn MARto vt'svehbt.
- *On all other nights we eat either sitting up or reclining;
  on this night we recline.*

ყველა სხვა ღამეს ჩვენ ვჭამთ რამე ჩვეულებრივი მანერით;
ამ ღამეს კი ჩვენ ვვახშმობთ სპეციალური ცერემონიით:

- *On all other nights we eat in an ordinary manner;
  on this night we dine with special ceremony.*

ABOUT THE LANGUAGE:

Georgian

Number of speakers: 4,255,270
Rank: 146

Georgian (also called Kartuli and Gruzinski) is the national language of Georgia. It is also spoken in a dozen other countries, with the largest concentrations in Iran and Turkey.

Written Georgian first appeared in about 430 in an inscription on a church in Palestine. The current script *Mkhedruli*, dates from the 13th C. Prior to that, Georgian was written in various scripts: before the 9th C, *Mrglovani* or *Asomtavruli*, which was based on Greek, and later, *Nuskha-khucuri*.

ABOUT THE TRANSLATOR AND SPEAKER:

Helen Borenstein

Age: Unavailable   Recorded: 1997
Towns: Tbilisi, Georgia / Lake Hiawatha, NJ

Helen grew up in Tbilisi. She worked as a software engineer after moving to the USA.

Photo by Boris Kester

The beautiful towers of the 16th C Ananuri castle and church located at Georgia's Aragvi gorge

Z Y X W V U T S R Q P O N M L K J I H **G** F E D C B A

Transliteration notes: H = ch as in Bach • GR = fricative g almost like Bach's ch • KV = 'k' very deep in throat • P = aspirated 'p' • All r's are rolled
Stressed syllables are capitalized • There is no transliteration of the last question. The handwritten translation accidentally contained one letter (h) not in the Georgian alphabet. Based on the transliteration and where an identical word was used, the 'h' was replaced with the letter რ shown in grey.

Garifuna

Kä san uéigie àmu lubei àriabu le luwei sün àmu àriabu?

- *Why is this night different from all other nights?*

Sün àmu àriabu fein weigubon o keke;
Àriabule, keke rügüba weiga.

- *On all other nights we eat either leavened bread or matzah;*
  on this night only matzah.

Sün àmu àriabu sün luúyeri híduru geigúati weigúbei;
Àriabule, híduru rügüba gifiti, le geigúati, weiga.

- *On all other nights we eat all kinds of herbs;*
  on this night only bitter herbs.

Sün àmu àriabu mederútiwa lidan íradinaü ni aban wéyasu;
Àriabule, wederúba biama wéyasu.

- *On all other nights we do not dip even once;*
  on this night we dip twice.

Sün àmu àriabu ñurutiwa le weigi o wabàlatüñ;
Àriabule, balàrügü badiwa.

- *On all other nights we eat either sitting up or reclining;*
  on this night we recline.

Sün àmu àriabu hou wagia gumu;
Àriabule, weiribei adinaruni le.

- *On all other nights we eat in any ordinary manner;*
  on this night we dine with special ceremony.

ABOUT THE LANGUAGE:

Garífuna

Number of speakers: 195,800
Rank: 905

Garífuna (also called Black Carib and Caribe) is spoken in Belize, Guatemala, Honduras and Nicaragua. In Guatemala, it is a mixture of Carib and African languages. Garífuna peoples decended from African slaves taken from St. Vincent Island in 1796-1797.

ABOUT THE TRANSLATOR AND SPEAKER:

Victor Joseph Nicholas

Age: Unavailable   Recorded: 1998
Town: Barranco Village, coastal town in Toledo District of southern Belize. It is reachable mainly by boat; there are no roads from Punta Gorda, the major town north of Barranco.

Victor is a teacher at the local school and his wife (Angie) is its principal. As a measure of Victor's kindness, he gave **Donald Kissil** (who helped obtained this translation) a book of his English and Garífuna poems, "An Anthology of Poems from Vinland Barranco", published 1/15/97.

Victor wrote a book of poems
about life in his village

Ganda

Lwakyi ekyiro kyino kyanjawulo kubiro ebilala byonna?
- *Why is this night different from all other nights?*

Mubiro ebilala byonna tulya emigati emizimbulukuse oba egitali mizimbulukuse;
mukyiro kyino tulya emigati egitali mizimbulukuse zokka.
- *On all other nights we eat either leavened bread or matzah;*
  on this night only matzah.

Mubiro ebilala byonna tulya enva zonna zonna;
mukyiro kyino tulya enva ezikawa zokka.
- *On all other nights we eat all kinds of herbs;*
  on this night only bitter herbs.

Mubiro ebilala byonna tetukoza omulundi nogumu;
mukyiro kyino tukoza emirundi ebiri.
- *On all other nights we do not dip even once;*
  on this night we dip twice.

Mubiro ebilala byonna tulya tutudde oba nga tweganzise;
mukyiro kyino tulya tweganzise.
- *On all other nights we eat either sitting up or reclining;*
  on this night we recline.

Mubiro ebilala byonna tulya nga bulijjo;
mukyiro kyino tulya mbaga.
- *On all other nights we eat in an ordinary manner;*
  on this night we dine with special ceremony.

Bonus in the recordings: The DVD contains the remarkable story of the Abayudaya Jews.

ABOUT THE LANGUAGE:

Ganda

Number of speakers: 4,130,000
Rank: 149

Ganda, also called Luganda, is the national language of Uganda. It is spoken in the southeast, from the northwest shore of Lake Victoria to Lake Kyoga and the Tanzania border; primarily in Buganda Province. Ganda is also spoken in Tanzania.

ABOUT THE TRANSLATOR AND SPEAKER:

Gershom Sizomu

Age: Unavailable   Recorded: 1999
Town: Nabugoye, Uganda

Gershom acts as Rabbi of Moses Synagogue for Abayudaya Congregation in Nabugoye, near Mbale, Uganda. He is fluent in Ganda – reading, writing and speaking it for over four years.

Gershom is the most well-known proponent of the Abayudaya community and tries to get support for his small community of 600.

Gershom is currently studying at the University of Judaism in Los Angeles, CA.

Rabbi Gershom Sizomu
visiting the USA

Galician

¿Por que esta noite é diferente das outras noites?
- *Why is this night different from all other nights?*

**En tódalas outras noites, comemos pan levedado ou pan ázimo;
Nesta noite só comemos pan ázimo.**
- *On all other nights we eat either leavened bread or matzah;
on this night only matzah.*

**En tódalas outras noites, comemos todo tipo de verduras;
Nesta noite só verduras amargas.**
- *On all other nights we eat all kinds of herbs;
on this night only bitter herbs.*

**En tódalas outras noites, non as mergullamos nen sequera unha vez;
nesta noite mergullámolas dúas veces.**
- *On all other nights we do not dip even once;
on this night we dip twice.*

**En tódalas outras noites, comemos de pé ou sentados;
esta noite sentámonos.**
- *On all other nights we eat either sitting up or reclining;
on this night we recline.*

**En tódalas outras noites, comemos de xeito ordinario;
Esta noite ceamos cunha cerimonia especial.**
- *On all other nights we eat in an ordinary manner;
on this night we dine with special ceremony.*

ABOUT THE TRANSLATORS AND SPEAKERS:

Ruth Losada and Leandro Rodriguez-Linares

Age: Unavailable   Recorded: 1995
Town: Pontevedra, Spain

Dr. Rodriguez-Linhares is a Professor of linguistics and speech researcher at Universitario de Vigo in Pontevedra. Ruth is a researcher at the Ramon Pineiro Research Centre, of the Universities of Coruna and Santiago. A version of the translation was worked on by **Jesus Lopez**.

ABOUT THE LANGUAGE:

Galician

Number of speakers: 3,185,000
Rank: 177

Galician (also called Gallego) is spoken in the autonomous region of Galicia of northwest Spain; it is also spoken in Portugal. Galician lies between Portuguese and Spanish, although closer to Portuguese. It is an official regional language. There is an Academy of the Galician Language. Galician has had many decades of development as a language of serious literature, including poetry, essays and novels, and for all levels of education.

Galician emerged as a standardized literary language near the end of the 19th C when there was a revival in the language and culture of Galicia. Rosalía de Castro's poem *Cantares Gallegos*, written entirely in Galician in 1863, was important to the revival of Galician. In 1936, Galicia was granted autonomy and the Galician language given official regional status.

**Window in the Alhambra
district of Granada, Spain**

Gaddang

Saay se toye a gafi neduma siin namitta era a gafi?

■ *Why is this night different from all other nights?*

No namitta era a gafi inakkan etam no tinapay o matsah; udde toye a gafi no matsah.

■ *On all other nights we eat either leavened bread or matzah; on this night only matzah.*

No namitta era a gafi inakkan etam no sari-sari a gamo; udde toye a gafi noye mapet a gamo.

■ *On all other nights we eat all kinds of herbs; on this night only bitter herbs.*

No namitta era a gafi mettam nebata maski namitta; udde toye a gafi namidwa etam a nebata.

■ *On all other nights we do not dip even once; on this night we dip twice.*

No namitta era a gafi nangngan etam a nakataddag o nakatuttud; toye a gafi nakatuttud etam.

■ *On all other nights we eat either sitting up or reclining; on this night we recline.*

No namitta era a gafi nangngan etam no ordinaryo a ugali; toye a gafi mangan etam si espesyal a ceremonia.

■ *On all other nights we eat in an ordinary manner; on this night we dine with special ceremony.*

The second half of the first question was not spoken for the recording.

ABOUT THE LANGUAGE:

Gaddang

Number of speakers: 30,000
Rank: 2,029

Gaddang is spoken in the Philippines (who call the language Cagayan), in the areas of central Isabela and Bagabag, Solano and Bayombong in Nueva Vizcaya, Luzon. Most speakers also use Ilocano.

ABOUT THE TRANSLATOR AND SPEAKER:

Miriam Schlauch

Age: Unavailable   Recorded: 1999
Towns: Santa Maria, Pangasinan / Bagabag, Nueva Viscaya, Luzon, Philippines / MN

Miriam, a native speaker of Gaddang, was born in Santa Maria; when she was very young, her family moved to Bagabag, Luzon (the same island as Manila), where Gaddang is spoken. (Manila is located on the Island of Luzon.) She now lives in Minnesota.

Photo by Rody Torres

Typical garden wedding in Manila

Ga

Maaba srɔ gbɛkɛ nɛɛ yɛ gbɛkɛ fɛɛ aheɛ?
- *Why is this night different from all other nights?*

Gbɛkɛ fɛɛ, wɔ yɛɔ bodobodo loo masa;
shi gbɛkɛ nɛɛ, wɔ yɛ masa pɛ.
- *On all other nights we eat either leavened bread or matzah;*
  on this night only matzah.

Gbɛkɛ fɛɛ, wɔ yeɔ tsamɔ bai srɔtoi;
shi gbɛkɛ nɛɛ, tsamɔ bai ni dzoɔ pɛ.
- *On all other nights we eat all kinds of herbs;*
  on this night only bitter herbs.

Gbɛkɛ fɛɛ, wɔ tsɔɔ shikome po;
shi gbɛkɛ nɛɛ, wɔ tsɔɔ shienyo.
- *On all other nights we do not dip even once;*
  on this night we dip twice.

Gbɛkɛ fɛɛ, wɔ yeɔ ni beni wɔtashi loo beni wɔdamɔ shi;
shi gbɛkɛ nɛɛ, wɔdamɔ shi.
- *On all other nights we eat either sitting up or reclining;*
  on this night we recline.

Gbɛkɛ fɛɛ, wɔ yeɔ ni yɛ gbɛ ni wɔkɛ yeɔ daa;
shi gbɛkɛ nɛɛ, wɔto okplɔ yɛ gbɛ kusu naa.
- *On all other nights we eat in an ordinary manner;*
  on this night we dine with special ceremony.

ABOUT THE LANGUAGE:

Ga

Number of speakers: 600,000
Rank: 492

Ga is spoken in Ghana, where it is also called Accra, Amina, Ga-Adangme-Krobo and Gain ("Ga-een").

ABOUT THE TRANSLATOR:

George Amankwah

Age: 52   Translated: 2003
Towns: Accra, Ghana / Caldwell, NJ

George was born and raised in the capital city Accra, Ghana. He learned Ga (Accra) at home and Ga-Adangme in school. He moved to the USA at age 39. He is the chief custodian of Congregation Agudath Israel in Caldwell.

ABOUT THE SPEAKER:

Mavis Acqua

Age: 50   Recorded: 2003
Towns: Accra, Ghana / Caldwell, NJ

Mavis was born and raised in Accra, Ghana; she moved to the USA at age 39. She is married to George Amankwah.

George Amankwah (holding baby) with his brothers and sisters in Accra, Ghana

Frisian

Wêrom is dizze nacht oars as alle oare nachten?

■ vehrom ihz dihzX naHt oXz awz awlX oXrX naHtN?

■ *Why is this night different from all other nights?*

Alle oare nachten ite wy òf bôle òf matse;
Fannacht allinnich matse.

■ awlX oXrX naHtN ihtX vay awf bawlX of matsX;
fXnaHt awlihnXH matsX.

■ *On all other nights we eat either leavened bread or matzah;*
on this night only matzah.

Alle oare nachten ite wy allerhande soarten krûden;
Fannacht allinnich bittere krûden.

■ awlX oXrX naHtN ihtX vay awlXrhawndX soXtN krudN;
fXnaHt awlihnXH bihtXrX krudN.

■ *On all other nights we eat all kinds of herbs;*
on this night only bitter herbs.

Alle oare nachten dippe wy sels net ienris;
Fannacht dippe wy twaris.

■ awlX oXrX naHtN dihpX vay sehlz neht iXnrXs;
fXnaHt dihpX vay tvarXs.

■ *On all other nights we do not dip even once;*
on this night we dip twice.

Alle oare nachten ite wy rjochtop sittend of efteroerlynjend;
Fannacht lynje wy efteroer.

■ awlX oXrX naHtN ihtX vay ryoXtop sihtNt awf eftXruXrlihnyXnt;
fXnaHt lihnyX vay eftXruXr.

■ *On all other nights we eat either sitting up or reclining;*
on this night we recline.

Alle oare nachten ite wy hiel gewoan;
Fannacht ite wy mei in spesjale seremoanje.

■ awlX oXrX naHtN ihtX vay hihXl gXvoXn;
fXnaHt itX vay my Xn speshalX sirXmoXnyX.

■ *On all other nights we eat in an ordinary manner;*
on this night we dine with special ceremony.

Transliteration notes: X is schwa (first syllable of "about" • N is syllabic n (final syllable of "button") • H is gutteral ch of Bach.

ABOUT THE LANGUAGE:

Frisian

Number of speakers: 467,000
Rank: 573

Western Frisian (also called Frysk and Fries), an official language of The Netherlands, is spoken in Friesland in northern Netherlands. (The other members of the Frisian language family tree, Northern and Eastern, are spoken in Germany.)

ABOUT THE TRANSLATOR AND SPEAKER:

Tjeerd de Graaf

Age: 57   Recorded: 1995
Towns: Leeuwarden / Paterswolde, near Groningen, Netherlands

Dr. de Graaf was Associate Professor of Linguistics at Groningen University, and more recently is Senior Research Associate at the Frisian Academy in Ljouwert, both in The Netherlands. He is a board member of the Foundation for Endangered Language. One of his projects has been Voices from the Shtetl: The Past and Present of the Yiddish Language in Russia.

Professor de Graaf is fluent in Dutch and Frisian, and also speaks English, French, German, Hungarian, Japanese, Polish and Russian.

Illuminated lettering from a Haggadah published in the Netherlands

French Sign Language

The accompanying DVD contains a video of Bill Moody signing the Four Questions in French Sign Language.

ABOUT THE LANGUAGE:

French Sign Language

Number of users: 50,000 – 100,000 primary users
Rank: 1,634

French Sign Language originated in 1752 and was the first sign language in the western world to gain recognition as a language, in 1830. Sign languages were known in France in the 16th C and probably earlier. Many sign languages have been influenced by French Sign Language, although they are not necessarily intelligible with it. It has been reported that French Sign Language is partially intelligible with sign languages from at least Austria, Czech Republic and Italy.

ABOUT THE TRANSLATOR AND SIGNER:

Bill Moody

Age: Unavailable   Recorded: 1997
Town: New York, NY

Bill is a professional sign interpreter working in New York City since 1984. Prior to that, Bill lived in France for 7 years, where he interpreted for the International Visual Theatre in Paris, trained deaf actors to become sign language teachers, and wrote the first comprehensive book on the history and grammar of French Sign Language (*La Langue des Signes: Entre les Mains des Sourds*).

Bill interprets and lectures internationally. He has interpreted for the World Federation of the Deaf and other international organizations in 16 different countries over the past 25 years. A specialist in International Sign, Bill received a BA in Theater (Trinity University) and Master of Fine Arts in Theater (Chicago's Goodman School of Theater).

French

Pourquoi cette soirée se distingue-t-elle des autres soirées?

■ *Why is this night different from all other nights?*

Tous les autres soirs nous pouvons manger du pain levé ou du pain azyme; ce soir seulement du pain azyme.

■ *On all other nights we eat either leavened bread or matzah; on this night only matzah.*

Tous les autres soirs nous pouvons manger toutes sortes d'herbes; ce soir seulement des herbes amères.

■ *On all other nights we eat all kinds of herbs; on this night only bitter herbs.*

Tous les autres soirs nous ne trempons pas la nourriture même pas une fois; ce soir nous trempons deux fois.

■ *On all other nights we do not dip even once; on this night we dip twice.*

Tous les autres soirs nous mangeons assis droit ou accoudés; ce soir accoudés seulement.

■ *On all other nights we eat either sitting up or reclining; on this night we recline.*

Tous les autres soirs nous mangeons de manière ordinaire; ce soir nous mangeons de manière spéciale.

■ *On all other nights we eat in an ordinary manner; on this night we dine with special ceremony.*

ABOUT THE LANGUAGE:

French

Number of speakers: 67,838,450
Rank: 16

French is the national language of France (where it is called Français) and is spoken in at least 53 other countries. French is the official or national language of 41 countries.

ABOUT THE SPEAKER:

Mehryar Mohri

Age: Unavailable   Recorded: 1998
Towns: Teheran, Iran / Paris, France

Mehryar was born in Teheran and moved to Paris at age 10; he left for the USA at age 30. He is bilingual in Farsi and French.

ABOUT THE TRANSLATOR:

Maxine Eskenazi

Age: 40s   Translated: 1998
Towns: Pittsburgh, PA / Paris, France

Dr. Eskenazi moved to Paris at age 21, where she was a speech researcher in France for 20 years. This translation was developed with reference to French Haggadahs from both the Spanish (Sephardic) and European (Ashkenzic) traditions.

Maxine is Associate Teaching Professor at Carnegie-Mellon University's Language Technologies Institute.

Completed in 1889, the 986-foot Eiffel Tower is the most recognized symbol of France

Frafra

Bene ti y u'unkuna wa bɔna kyuima yuunɔ woo puan?

■ Why is the night different from all other nights?

**Yu'untuseto woo, tu na di la ma asa bii koose;
yu'unkuna wa, ma'asa ma'a.**

■ On all other nights we eat either leavened bread or beans cakes;
on this night only [Matzah] cakes.

**Yu'untuseto woo, tu nan di la zevɔɔrɔ buuri woo;
yu'unkuna wa, zevɔtooro ma'a.**

■ On all other nights we eat kinds of vegetables;
on this night only bitter vegetables.

Yu'untuseto woo, tu ka tu'm la bayila mɛ;

■ On all other nights we do not dip even once;

**Yu'untuseto woo, tu nan zia mɛ bii tu dele mɛ dita;
yu'unkuna wa, tu dele mɛ.**

■ On all other nights we are either sitting up or reclining;
on this night we recline.

**Yu'untuseto woo, tu di doose le aŋa yoo;
yu'unkuna wa, tu di ti malema kanjaŋl bini.**

■ On all other nights we eat in an ordinary manner;
on this night we dine with Special Ceremony.

Translation notes: The Frafra translation is missing a line in the third question. **Ma'asa ma'a** may be a cognate for Matzah. The gloss for the 4th question had "we are either sitting up or reading", but that seems to be an error, as **tu dele mɛ** was used in both phrases.

About the Language:

Frafra

Number of speakers: 845,100
Rank: 407

Frafra (also called Gurune, Talensi and Farefare) is spoken in Ghana, in the Northeast, Upper East Region around Bolgatanga, Frafra District, and as far west as Navrongo. There are 5 major dialects and many minor ones (some dialects are named after towns or localities). Frafra is also spoken in Burkina Faso.

About the Translators:

Juliana Azure and Akazuo Lawrence

Age: Unavailable   Recorded: 2005
Towns: Bolgatanga and Winneba City, Ghana

Juliana lives in Bolgatanga, Ghana and Akazuo is associated with the Martyrs of Uganda Parish in Bogatanga. The (unnamed) speaker is from the University of Education in Winneba City. The text was also translated by **Grace Tarata**, of Tema, Ghana.

Photo by Ayeley Mills-Tettey

The Kwame Nkrumah Mausoleum, the final resting place of Ghana's first president (1900-1972). Nkrumah was a famous pan-Africanist, helping form the Organization of African Unity, and dreaming of a "United States of Africa", still a goal of many on the continent

Fon

Translated from French

Gbadanu elɔ aniuwɛ eka gbɔnvo nu ɖe lɛɛ?

■ *Pourquoi cette soirée se distingue-t-elle des autres soirées?*

Wɔxuxu ee dotɔn alo wɔxuxu ma dotɔn biwɛ mi sixu ɖu gbadanu ɖu lɛ bi; wɔxuxu ma dotɔn kɛɖɛ nu gbadanu elɔ.

■ *Tous les autres soirs nous pouvons manger du pain levé ou du pain azyme; ce soir seulement du pain azyme.*

Aman ɖebu wɛ mi sixu ɖu ɖo gbadanu ɖe lɛ; gbadanu elɔ aman vivɛ kɛɖɛ.

■ *Tous les autres soirs nous pouvons manger toutes sortes d'herbes; ce soir seulement des herbes amères.*

Gbadanu lɛ biɔ mi man tlɛ nɔn nylɔn nuɖuɖu ɔ azɔn ɖokpo gee vɔvɔ; azɔnwe wɛ mi nɔn nylɔn ɖo gbadanu elɔ.

■ *Tous les autres soirs nous ne trempons pas la nourriture même pas une fois; ce soir nous trempons deux fois.*

Mi nɔn ɖu nu ɖo aʏijijɔn ɖo titeungbe alo ɖadaji gbadanu ɖe lɛ bi; ajaji kɛɖɛ wɛ mi nɔn nɔn gbadanu elɔ.

■ *Tous les autres soirs nous mangeons assis droit ou accoudés; ce soir accoudés seulement.*

Gbadanu ɖe lɛ ɔ mi nɔn ɖu nu ɖo jlɛmɛ; gbadanu elɔ gbɔnvo, ɖo mi ɖo nu kpɛɖɛ wawɛ.

■ *Tous les autres soirs nous mangeons de manière ordinaire; ce soir nous mangeons de manière spéciale.*

ABOUT THE LANGUAGE:

Fon

Number of speakers: 1,435,500
Rank: 291

Fon (called Fongbe by its speakers) is spoken in Benin in the south-central region: Weme, Atlantique and Zou provinces. Also spoken in the country of Togo. In both countries, most speakers are bilingual in Fongbe and French.

ABOUT THE TRANSLATOR AND SPEAKER:

Bertin Yèhouénou

Age: Unavailable   Recorded: 1997
Towns: Ouida, Benin / Provence, France

Bertin was born in Ouidah (40 km from Cotonou). His primary education was there until age 13, when he moved to Porto-Novo (30 km from Cotonou). At age 20, he joined the University of Cotonou. Bertin later did language research at CNRS's Laboratoire Parole et Langage in Provence, France.

Photo by Boris Keszer

Benin's Ganvie Village, often called the "African Venice", with 3,000 houses on stilts

Flemish

Waarom is deze avond anders dan alle andere avonden?

■ *Why is this night different from all other nights?*

Op alle andere avonden eten we ofwel gegist brood ofwel matses;
op deze avond alleen matses.

■ *On all other nights we eat either leavened bread or matzah;*
on this night only matzah.

Op alle andere avonden eten we alle soorten kruiden;
op deze avond alleen bittere kruiden.

■ *On all other nights we eat all kinds of herbs;*
on this night only bitter herbs.

Op alle andere avonden dippen we zelfs niet n maal;
op deze avond dippen we tweemaal.

■ *On all other nights we do not dip even once;*
on this night we dip twice.

Op alle andere avonden eten we rechtop zittend of achterover leunend;
op deze avond leunen we achterover.

■ *On all other nights we eat either sitting up or reclining;*
on this night we recline.

Op alle andere avonden eten we op een gewone manier;
op deze avond eten we volgens een speciale ceremonie.

■ *On all other nights we eat in an ordinary manner;*
on this night we dine with special ceremony.

ABOUT THE LANGUAGE:

Flemish / Vlaams

Number of speakers: 6,141,560
Rank: 116

Flemish is the national language of Belgium. There are also speakers in Canada, France, The Netherlands and the USA. It is often considered a variation of Dutch.

Provided under Creative Commons Attribution 3.0 Unported License

In the recordings: The recording ends with *"Dit is Jan Leys in het Vlaams"*, which means "This is Jan Leys speaking Flemish".

Brussels, the capital of Belgium, is considered the *de facto* capital of the European Union

Finnish, Tornedalen

Miksi(s) tämä ilta o(o)n erilainen ko muut iilat?

■ *Why is this night different from all other nights?*

Kaikina muina iltiona met syömä jompaakumpaa hapatettua leipää eli matzaa (= jästitöntä leipää);
tänä iltana vain matzaa.

■ *On all other nights we eat either leavened bread or matzah;*
on this night only matzah.

Kaikina muina iltiona met syömä kaikenlaisia ruuhokasvia;
tänä iltana vain kirpeitä ruuhokasvia.

■ *On all other nights we eat all kinds of herbs;*
on this night only bitter herbs.

Kaikina muina iltiona met emmä kasta dippikastekheesseen kertaakhaan;
tänä iltana kastama net kaks(i) kertaa.

■ *On all other nights we do not dip even once;*
on this night we dip twice.

Kaikina muina iltiona met syömä joko istaalthansa eli lepoasenossa;
tänä iltana lepoasenossa.

■ *On all other nights we eat either sitting up or reclining;*
on this night we recline.

Kaikina muina iltiona met syömä millä tavalisella laila tahansa;
tänä iltana met syömä murkinan vasitulsen seremonian mukhaan.

■ *On all other nights we eat in an ordinary manner;*
on this night we dine with special ceremony.

Translation note: Letters within parentheses indicate alternative wording or pronunciations.

ABOUT THE LANGUAGE:

Tornedalen Finnish

Number of speakers: 109,600
Rank: 1,167

Tornedalen Finnish (also called Torne Valley Finnish and (Meänkielelä) is spoken in northeast Sweden, County of Norrbotten, municipalities of Gällivare, Kiruna, Pajala, Övertorneä and Haparanda. These are areas of Sweden where Finnish speakers settled in the 12th C. There are 30,000 speakers in Finland. Many of the Saami people use Tornedalen Finnish as their second language. 5,000 people belong to the Swedish Tornedalian Association.

ABOUT THE TRANSLATOR AND SPEAKER:

Tage Ranängen

Age: Unavailable   Recorded: 1997
Town: Luleå, Sweden

Tage Ranängen is an instructor at Luleå University of Technology, located just south of the Arctic Circle in Luleå, Sweden.

Photo © Niko Lipsanen

Ramparts on Susisaari Island, built in the 18th and 19th C to defend Helsinki

Finnish

Miksi tämä ilta on erilainen kuin mikään muu ilta?

■ *Why is this night different from all other nights?*

**Kaikkina muina iltoina syömme joko hapatettua leipää tai hapattamatonta leipää;
tänä iltana hapattamatonta leipää.**

■ *On all other nights we eat either leavened bread or matzah;
on this night only matzah.*

**Kaikkina muina iltoina syömme kaikenlaisia yrttejä;
tänä iltana vain katkeria yrttejä.**

■ *On all other nights we eat all kinds of herbs;
on this night only bitter herbs.*

**Kaikkina muina iltoina emme kasta yrttejä kertaakaan;
tänä iltana kastamme kahdesti.**

■ *On all other nights we do not dip even once;
on this night we dip twice.*

**Kaikkina muina iltoina syömme istuen suorassa tai nojaten sivulle;
tänä iltana nojaamme sivulle.**

■ *On all other nights we eat either sitting up or reclining;
on this night we recline.*

**Kaikkina muina iltoina syömme tavalliseen tapaan;
tänä iltana syömme erityisen seremonian kanssa.**

■ *On all other nights we eat in an ordinary manner;
on this night we dine with special ceremony.*

ABOUT THE TRANSLATOR AND SPEAKER:

Juha Salin

Age: Unavailable   Recorded: 1996
Town: Redmond, WA

Juha, a native speaker of Finnish, is a speech researcher with Microsoft. A translation was also provided by **Kaija Wilson** of the Foreign Service Institute, US Department of State. Corrections were provided by linguist **Cristoffer von Bonsdorff** of Finland.

ABOUT THE LANGUAGE:

Finnish

Number of speakers: 5,009,390
Rank: 130

Finnish, also called Suomi or Suomea, is the official language of Finland. There are also significant numbers of speakers in Sweden and Russia.

Finnish started to appear in writing during the 16th C. The first Finnish published text was a translation of the New Testament in 1548. Finland was a part of Sweden until 1809 and Swedish was the official language. Starting in 1883, civil servants were obliged to use Finnish and issue documents in it. Finnish became an official language in 1892. Today Finland is officially bilingual in Finnish and Swedish.

Photo © Niko Lipsanen

The large beach at Pihlajasaari Islands in Helsinki

Fijian

Kä san uéigie àmu lubei àriabu le luwei sün àmu àriabu?

■ *Why is this night different from all other nights?*

Sün àmu àriabu fein weigubon o keke;
Àriabule, keke rügüba weiga.

■ *On all other nights we eat either leavened bread or matzah;
on this night only matzah.*

Sün àmu àriabu sün luúyeri híduru geigúati weigúbei;
Àriabule, híduru rügüba gifiti, le geigúati, weiga.

■ *On all other nights we eat all kinds of herbs;
on this night only bitter herbs.*

Sün àmu àriabu mederútiwa lidan íradinaü ni aban wéyasu;
Àriabule, wederúba biama wéyasu.

■ *On all other nights we do not dip even once;
on this night we dip twice.*

Sün àmu àriabu ñurutiwa le weigi o wabàlatüñ;
Àriabule, balàrügü badiwa.

■ *On all other nights we eat either sitting up or reclining;
on this night we recline.*

Sün àmu àriabu hou wagia gumu;
Àriabule, weiribei adinaruni le.

■ *On all other nights we eat in any ordinary manner;
on this night we dine with special ceremony.*

ABOUT THE TRANSLATOR:

Dr. Michael Ogden

Age: Unavailable   Translated: 1997
Town: Honolulu, HI

Michael is an Associate Professor in Communications at the University of
Hawaii at Manoa; he spent 2 years in the Peace Corps in Fiji at the University
of the South Pacific and has a Graduate Certificate in Pacific Islands Studies.

ABOUT THE LANGUAGE:

Fijian

Number of speakers: 336,960
Rank: 667

Fijian is primarily spoken in the islands around Fiji, Nauru, New Zealand, Vanuatu.

Island hut and
Fiji dancer on
Taveuni Island

Photos by Stephanie Goldhuber

Farsi / Persian

ABOUT THE LANGUAGE:

Western Farsi

Number of speakers: 23,879,300
Rank: 43

Western Farsi (known also as Persian) is spoken throughout Iran, with most speakers concentrated in the central, south central and northeastern regions. It is spoken in over two dozen countries, especially in Iraq, United Arab Emirates, Qatar, Tajikistan and Oman. As expected with a language with a wide geographical dispersion, there are many dialects – at least 17. Persian dialects blend into Dari (Eastern Farsi) in Afghanistan and Tajiki in Tajikistan.

Judeo-Persian or Dzhidi, Persian written in Hebrew characters, is one of the oldest and yet least-studied of all Jewish languages. It was spoken by Jews for the past 1,000 years living in the current areas of Iran, Afghanistan, Uzbekistan and parts of India. After Iran's 1979 Islamic revolution, most moved to Israel; about 30,000 are now in California.

Modern Persian appeared in the 9th C. Written in a version of Arabic script, it is full of words of Arabic origin. An even earlier manuscript is a 37-line merchant's letter dating from 750, the oldest example of Judeo-Persian writing. Throughout history, Persian was written with many different scripts, including *Old Persian Cuneiform, Pahlavi, Aramaic* and *Avestan*.

ABOUT THE TRANSLATOR AND SPEAKER:

Iraj Saniee

Age: 40s   Recorded: 1998
Towns: Karachi, Pakistan / Teheran, Iran / UK / NJ

Dr. Saniee was raised in Karachi and Teheran and received his higher degrees in the UK (Exeter and Cambridge Universities). He researches mathematical aspects of network design at Lucent Laboratories. Translations helped by **Behzad Benyamini** and **Alireza Tarighian**.

Photo by Mohammad Hafezi

Beautiful Mount Damavand, an inactive volcano, is less than 50 miles from Teheran. At 18,600 feet, it is the highest peak in Middle East and West Asia

Translation note: The 4th question uses "eating comfortably" as an idiom for "eating while reclining".

چِرَا امشَب با سایر شَبِها فَرق دارَد ؟
- Chera emshab ba sayere shab-ha fargh darad?
- *Why is this night different from all other nights?*

دَر سایِر شَبِها ، ما یا نان میخوریم یا مصا ؛
ولی در اَین شَب فَقَط نان مصاً میخوریم.
- Dar sayere shabha, ma ya nan mikhorim ya matza;
  vali dar in shab faghat nan-e matza mikhorim.
- *On all other nights we eat either leavened bread or matzah;
  on this night only matzah.*

دَر سایِر شَبِها ، ما هَمه گؤنه سَبزیجات میخوریم ؛
اما در اَین شَب مخصؤصا سَبزیجات تَلخ میخوریم.
- Dar sayere shabha, ma hameh ghoneh sabzi-jat mikhorim;
  ama dar in shab faghat sabzijat-e talkh mikhorim.
- *On all other nights we eat all kinds of herbs;
  on this night only bitter herbs.*

دَر سایِر شَبِها ، ما سَبزیجات را دُر آب نمك نمیزنیم ؛
ولی در اَین شَب ما دوبار سبزیجات را دُر آب نمك میزنیم.
- Dar sayere shabha, ma sabizi-jat ra dar ab-namk;
  nemizanim vali dar in shab ma dobar sabizi-jat ra dar ab-namk mizanim.
- *On all other nights we do not dip even once;
  on this night we dip twice.*

دَر سایِر شبِها ، ما مشسجهیا صکیه داده غَذا میخوریم ؛
ولی امشب فَقَط تكیَه داده غذا میخوریم.
- Dar sayere shabha, ma neshaste ya takieh dadeh ghaza mikhorim;
  vali emshab faghat takieh midehim.
- *On all other nights we eat either sitting up or reclining;
  on this night we recline.*

دَر سایِر شبِها ، ما خیلی مضمولی غَذا میخوریم ؛
اما امشب با مَراسم مَخصؤص غذا میخوریم.
- Dar sayere shabha, ma kheily maamuli ghaza mikhorim;
  ama emshab ba marasem maghsus ghza mikhorim.
- *On all other nights we eat in an ordinary manner;
  on this night we dine with special ceremony.*

Farsi, Eastern

About the Language:

Eastern Farsi

Number of speakers: 7,600,000
Rank: 100

Eastern Farsi, or Dari as it was called by its speaker, is spoken in Afghanistan (as a national language), in several of Iran's provinces and in Pakistan.

The dialect differences between Iran and Afghanistan cause little difficulty in comprehension. Most Afghan dialects are closer to literary Persian than are Iranian dialects. *Zargari (Morghuli)* is a secret language used among goldsmiths and perhaps others, which is based on a dialect of Persian. Most speakers are Sunni and Shi'a Muslim, but as of a couple decades ago, 70 Jews spoke the same dialect as Muslims. The Madaglasht community in Pakistan came from Badakhshan, Afghanistan 200 years ago.

About the Translator and Speaker:

Fareed Shirzai Wardak

Age: 32 Recorded: 2002
Towns: Khoshal-Khan Mina, Afghanistan / Livermore, CA

Fareed was born in Wardak Province west of Kabul, but from infancy through late teens he was raised in the town Khoshal-Khan Mina in Kabul, Afghanistan. He attended one year of Medical school at the Kabul Medical Institute and was forced to move to Pakistan for a year and a half; at the age of 19, Fareed moved to the USA. Both Dari and Pashto are his native languages. The text was typed by **Faramak Vakil**.

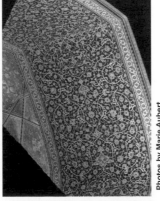

Completed in 1608, the Sheikh Lotfollah Mosque in Isfahan is decorated with the best mosaics of its era. Interior detail shown below

Photos by Marie Aubert

چرا لین شب با شب های دیگر فرق دارد ؟

■ Chera aeen shab ba shab-hai degar farq darad?

■ *Why is this night different from all other nights?*

در همح شب های دیگرو ما نان خمیر و یا فطیر میخوضیم
در لین شب صرف نان فطیر

■ Dar hama shab-hai degar, ma nan-e khameer wa ya fatir mikhorim;
Dar aeen shab serf nan-e fatir.

■ *On all other nights we eat either leavened bread or matzah;
on this night only matzah.*

در همح شب های دیگرو ما هر نوغ سبزیجات میخوضیم
در لین شب صرف سبزیجات تند

■ Dar hama shab-hai degar ma har nawaa sabzijat mikhorim;
Dar aeen shab serf sabzijat-e tond.

■ *On all other nights we eat all kinds of herbs;
on this night only bitter herbs.*

در همح شب های دیگرو ما حته یکمرتبح هم نان تر نکردیم
در لین شب ما و دو مرتبح نان تر کردیم

■ Dar hama shab-hai degar ma hata yak martaba ham nan tar nakardim;
Dar aeen shab ma dou martaba nan tar kardim.

■ *On all other nights we do not dip even once;
on this night we dip twice.*

در همح شب های دیگرو ما نشسته یا تکیه کرده نان میخوضیم
در لین شب ما تکیه کرده ایم

■ Dar hama shab-hai degar ma nashasta ya takya karda nan mikhorim;
Dar aeen shab ma takya karda aim.

■ *On all other nights we eat either sitting up or reclining;
on this night we recline.*

در همح شب های دیگرو ما بشکل معمولی نان میخوضیم
در لین شب ما با مراسم خاص نان میخوضیم

■ Dar hama shab-hai degar mo ba shakl-e maamolee nan mikhorim;
Dar aeen shab ma ba marasem-e khas nan mikhorim.

■ *On all other nights we eat in an ordinary manner;
on this night we dine with special ceremony.*

Faroese

Hví er henda náttin ólík øðrum?
■ *Why is this night different from all other nights?*

Allar aðrar nætur eta vit hvítt og ósúrgaðbreyð; í nátt fáa vit bert ósúrgað.
■ *On all other nights we eat either leavened bread or matzah; on this night only matzah.*

Allar aðrar nætur eta vit ymiskar urtir; í nátt fáa vit beiskar urtir.
■ *On all other nights we eat all kinds of herbs; on this night only bitter herbs.*

Allar aðrar nætur nýta vit ikki mat í saltlaka; men í nátt dyppa vit tvær reisir í lakan.
■ *On all other nights we do not dip even once; on this night we dip twice.*

Allar aðrar nætur sita vit upprætt ella hvíla afturá; í nátt hvíla vit afturá.
■ *On all other nights we eat either sitting up or reclining; on this night we recline.*

Allar aðrar nætur eta vit eins og vanligt; men í nátt er serligt hátíðarhald.
■ *On all other nights we eat in an ordinary manner; on this night we dine with special ceremony.*

ABOUT THE LANGUAGE:

Faroese

Number of speakers: 48,260
Rank: 1,702

Faroese, sometimes called Føroyskt, is spoken in the Faroe Islands, which are located between Denmark and Iceland. The language is closely related to Icelandic. The written form of Faroese, based on Icelandic, was developed in 1846.

The Faroe Islands were discovered and colonized in the 9th C by Norwegian Vikings and Norse colonies from the British Isles.

ABOUT THE TRANSLATOR AND SPEAKER:

Dr. Turið Holm

Age: 65   Recorded: 2007
Town: Hoyvik, Island of Streymoy, Faroe Islands

Turið, a native speaker of Faroese, was born and raised in the Faroe Islands. Her mother was Danish and her father was a Faroe Islander.

Turið performs with Yggdrasil, a long-established ensemble devoted to the folk songs and dances of the Faroe Islands.

This translation was developed with the assistance of **Rubekkur Rubeksen**, a native speaker who has studied Nordic and Faroese languages.

Photos by Hans Henrik Scheel

(Left) Tinganes – one of the world's oldest parliament meeting places, dating from 900 CE

(Right) Faroe Islands folkdance – The Common Dance

Ewondo

Alu ase ya'asi, bia'adi belet dza'avus ngeke matzah;
he dzam da alu dina, he nyen atzah nye bia'adi.

■ *On all other nights we eat either leavened bread or matzah;*
on this night only matzah.

Alu ase ya'asi, bia'adi kan bitutuga ese;
he dzam da alu dina, bia'adi he bitutuga bine ayol.

■ *On all other nights we eat all kinds of herbs;*
on this night only bitter herbs.

Alu ase ya'asi, bia'adzate kig to eyon dzia;
he dzam da alu dina, bia dzote biyon bida.

■ *On all other nights we do not dip even once;*
on this night we dip twice.

Alu ase ya'asi, abog ezin bia tobototoa abog ezin sikibi;
he dzam da alu dina, bia sikibi.

■ *On all other nights we eat either sitting up or reclining;*
on this night we recline.

Alu ase ya'asi, bia'adi zeze mama;
he dzam da alu dina, bia akak abok bidi.

■ *On all other nights we eat in an ordinary manner;*
on this night we dine with special ceremony.

ABOUT THE LANGUAGE:

Ewondo

Number of speakers: 578,000
Rank: 509

Ewondo (sometimes called Beti by its speakers) is spoken in Cameroon's Center and southern Provinces (except the eastern part of Mefou Division) and in the northern part of Ocean Division.

ABOUT THE TRANSLATOR AND SPEAKER:

Mengue Eka-Abila

Recorded: 2003
Locations: Cameroon / New York, NY

Mengue is a native Beti from Cameroon. Ms. Eka-Abila was born, grew up and lived in the Ewondo-speaking areas of Cameroon until moving to the USA in 1991.

Photo by Sister Mary Lynne, St. John the Baptist Convent

Baking bread in an oven for the Benedictine Sisters of Bethany, Bamenda, Cameroon

 Ewe

Nukatae egbea fe zã to vovo tso bubuwo katã gbɔ?

■ Why today's night is different from other ones all?

Le zã bubuwo katã me la míe ɖua aboloma ama a;
gake le zã sia me la akpɔnɔmemi koe.

■ In nights other all in we eat leavened bread;
but in night this in the biscuit-baked* only.

Le zã bubuwo katã me la míe ɖua ama vovovowɔ;
gake le zã sia me la amaveve koe míe ɖu.

■ In nights other all in the we eat herb different-different;
but in night this in the herb bitter only.

Le zã bubuwo katã me la míe medea ama tsi me zi ɖeka hão;
gake le zã sia me la míe dewo zi eve sɔŋ.

■ In nights other all in the we don't herb put water in even one not in;
but in night this in the we put them in twice all.

Le zã bubuwo me la míe nɔanyi ɖua nu dzidzemetɔe;
gake le zã sia me la míe ɖu nu dzidzemetɔe.

■ In nights other all in the we sit down eat thing relaxing way in;
but in night this in the we eat thing in relaxing.

Le zã bubuwo me la míe ɖua nu abe alesi ko mie ɖua nue ɣesiaɣi ene;
gake le zã sia me la míe ɖu nu ɖe azã e kɔnu me.

■ In nights other all we eat as we always do;
but in night this we eat thing festival way in.

---

* **Akpɔnɔmemi** refers to unleavened bread which is a negative cultural metaphor for someone or something lacking in energy, undeveloped, unrealized, or otherwise resembling the state of being "half-baked".

Ewe

Number of speakers: 3,112,000
Rank: 183

Ewe is spoken in the southeast corner of Ghana and southern Togo, where it is one of the national languages.

Kɔbla Ladzekpo

Age: 67   Recorded: 1998
Towns: Anyako, Volta region, Ghana / Accra, Ghana / Los Angeles, CA

Kɔbla has a Master's degree in Anthropology. For many generations, Kɔbla's family in Ghana has been highly regarded for musicians, poets, composers and dancers. Kɔbla, a native speaker of Ewe, developed his understanding and usage of the language from his Anyako upbringing. He lived briefly as a young adult in Accra and moved to the USA at age 33. Kɔbla worked on the translation with his wife, **Dzidzogbe Lawluvi**.

Photo by Ben Swets

Kɔbla holds a horsetail in this 1996 picture of Alan Eder and Friends (aka the "Pesach Posse") who sing and play on the Reggae Passover album. For yet another unique Passover experience, get Alan Eder's CD of Reggae and West African versions of Passover melodies from www.reggaepassover.com

Estonian

Miks on see õhtu erinev kõikidest teistest õhtutest?

■ *Why is this night different from all other nights?*

Kõikidel teistel õhtutel me sööme leiba või krõbinaid.
Sel õhtul ainult krõbinaid.

■ *On all other nights we eat either leavened bread or matzah;*
on this night only matzah.

Kõikidel teistel õhtutel me sööme igasuguseid rohttaimi.
Sel õhtul ainult mõrudaid rohttaimi.

■ *On all other nights we eat all kinds of herbs;*
on this night only bitter herbs.

Kõikidel teistel õhtutel me ei kasta rohttaimi.
Sel õhtul me kastame neid kaks korda.

■ *On all other nights we do not dip even once;*
on this night we dip twice.

Kõikidel teistel õhtutel me sööme istudes või kallutades.
Sel õhtul me kallutame.

■ *On all other nights we eat either sitting up or reclining;*
on this night we recline.

ABOUT THE LANGUAGE:

Estonian

Number of speakers: 1,048,660
Rank: 346

Estonian, the national language of Estonia, is also called Eesti and Viro. There is considerable mutual intelligibility between Estonian and Finnish. While Finnish has a lot of loan words from Swedish, Estonian contains many words of German origin, plus some words from Russian, Latin, Greek and English.

The oldest examples of written Estonian are names, words and phrases found in early 13th C chronicles. The earliest textbook appeared in 1637.

ABOUT THE TRANSLATOR AND SPEAKER:

Aita Salasoo

Age: 30s   Recorded: prior to 1995
Towns: Sydney, Australia / Bloomington, IN / Cedar Knolls, NJ

Aita's first language is Estonian. She grew up in the suburbs of Sydney, Australia, the daughter of Estonian-born immigrants to Australia. Aita first learned English when she went to primary school. She studied Estonian grammar in high school; at age 20 Aita moved to the USA and taught 2 years of Estonian at Indiana University as a Teaching Assistant.

Photos by Aita Salasoo

Tallinn, the capital of Estonia – a port on the Gulf of Finland – was settled by Finno-Ugric people about 3500 years ago

English

Translated from Hebrew

Why is this night different from all other nights?

◼ מַה נִּשְׁתַּנָּה הַלַּיְלָה הַזֶּה מִכָּל הַלֵּילוֹת?

On all other nights we eat either leavened bread or matzah; on this night only matzah.

◼ שֶׁבְּכָל הַלֵּילוֹת אָנוּ אוֹכְלִין חָמֵץ וּמַצָּה. הַלַּיְלָה הַזֶּה כֻּלּוֹ מַצָּה:

On all other nights we eat all kinds of herbs; on this night only bitter herbs.

◼ שֶׁבְּכָל הַלֵּילוֹת אָנוּ אוֹכְלִין שְׁאָר יְרָקוֹת הַלַּיְלָה הַזֶּה מָרוֹר:

On all other nights we do not dip even once; on this night we dip twice.

◼ שֶׁבְּכָל הַלֵּילוֹת אֵין אָנוּ מַטְבִּילִין אֲפִילוּ פַּעַם אֶחָת. הַלַּיְלָה הַזֶּה שְׁתֵּי פְעָמִים:

On all other nights we eat either sitting up or reclining; on this night we recline.

◼ שֶׁבְּכָל הַלֵּילוֹת אָנוּ אוֹכְלִין בֵּין יוֹשְׁבִין וּבֵין מְסֻבִּין. הַלַּיְלָה הַזֶּה כֻּלָּנוּ מְסֻבִּין:

On all other nights we eat in any ordinary manner; on this night we dine with special ceremony.

◼ שֶׁבְּכָל הַלֵּילוֹת אָנוּ אוֹכְלִין בְּצוּרָה רְגִילָה. הַלַּיְלָה הַזֶּה בְּרוֹב טְקָסִיּוֹת:

Photo © Eliot Cohen and Judith Jango-Cohen

The Statue of Liberty

Photo by Stephanie Goldhuber

Royal British Guard

ABOUT THE LANGUAGE:

English

Number of speakers: 328,008,138
Rank: 3

English is spoken in at least 105 countries and is the official or national language for at least 78 countries. There are nearly 3 dozen recognized dialects in Britain alone. English is closely related to Dutch, German and Frisian and has a significant amount of words from French, Latin, Greek and many other languages.

ABOUT THE TRANSLATOR:

Unknown

The earliest English translation was by A. Alexander, published in London in 1770. The earliest English Haggadah published in the New World was in 1837 from the first Jewish printer in New York, Solomon Henry Jackson, a native of England. Jackson's translation was based on a Haggadah first published in London in 1794 by David Levy.

Translations in various Haggadahs vary considerably. Some describe in more detail what is unleavened bread, what is dipped, the manner of reclining, etc. As described in the main text, some translate the initial sentence as a statement ("How is this night ...") rather than as a question.

This English translation is based on the original Hebrew, with the exception of the final question, for which some communities use a form similar to that shown here. The 5th Hebrew question is not original; it is back-translated from the English.

ABOUT THE SPEAKER:

John Simpson

Age: 45   Recorded: 1998
Town: Cheltenham, England
Dialect: Standard RP dialect, with a little hint of Gloucestershire
Title: Chief Editor of the Oxford English Dictionary (Co-Editor starting 1986, Chief Editor since 1990)

As Chief Editor of the Oxford English Dictionary, John presides over the world's largest-ever dictionary program. The OED is the accepted authority on the evolution of the English language over the last millennium. It is the premier guide to the meaning, history and pronunciation of over half a million words. It traces the usage of words through 2.5 million quotations from a wide range of international English language sources.

John is a world authority on proverb and slang. This recording is the first time the OED's Chief Editor had spoken the word matzah!

Ebira

Seve di 'rahu onon oya ananka anavo?

■ *Why is this night different from all other nights?*

**Irahu anavo ye ri bread di ri masa;
irahu onon dai ki masa kene yi rin.**

■ *On all other nights we eat either leavened bread or matzah;
on this night only matzah.*

**Irahu anavo voni ri abepochi;
irahu onon dai ka anayi 'rei kene yi rin.**

■ *On all other nights we eat all kinds of herbs;
on this night only bitter herbs.*

**Irahu anavo ye ma hiaku risa uponya;
irahu onon dai ka upeva ihiaku risan.**

■ *On all other nights we do not dip even once;
on this night we dip twice.*

**Irahu anavo ye yate risa di hutete risa;
irahu onon voni hutete risa.**

■ *On all other nights we eat either sitting up or reclining;
on this night we recline.*

**Irahu anavo voni tanwua risa ayi ordinari;
irahu onon voni rieche risa.**

■ *On all other nights we eat in an ordinary manner;
on this night we dine with special ceremony.*

ABOUT THE LANGUAGE:

Ebira

Number of speakers: 1,000,000
Rank: 358

Ebira is spoken by the Ebira people, who live in north-central Nigeria, and by speakers of many other languages who use Ebira to speak with them. The language is taught at Nigeria's College of Education.

ABOUT THE TRANSLATOR AND SPEAKER:

Ibrahim Adoke Yakubu

Age: 36   Recorded: 2006
Towns: Zaria, Nigeria / Ottawa, Ontario / Athens, Greece

Ibrahim studied Political Science as an undergraduate at Nigeria's Ahmadu Bello University, also receiving a Masters Degree in International Affairs and Diplomacy. After getting a certificate in Conflict Resolution at the University of St. Paul, he is now a doctoral student at the University of Athens in Conflict Management in Africa. Ibrahim currently writes for a monthly African magazine in Athens. He learned Ebira from his mother.

Drawing by Stephanie Black,
5th grade, W Caldwell, NJ

**The themes of the
Passover Seder**

Dutch

Waarom is het vanavond anders dan andere avonden?

■ *Why is this night different from all other nights?*

Op andere avonden eten we of brood of matses; vanavond alleen matses.

■ *On all other nights we eat either leavened bread or matzah; on this night only matzah.*

Op andere avonden eten we verschillende soorten specerijen; vanavond alleen bittere specerijen.

■ *On all other nights we eat all kinds of herbs; on this night only bitter herbs.*

Op andere avonden dippen we niet; vanavond dippen we twee keer.

■ *On all other nights we do not dip even once; on this night we dip twice.*

Op andere avonden zitten we rechtop of leunen we achterover; op deze avond leunen we achterover.

■ *On all other nights we eat either sitting up or reclining; on this night we recline.*

Op andere avonden eten we zoals altijd; vanavond dineren we op ceremoniële wijze.

■ *On all other nights we eat in any ordinary manner; on this night we dine with special ceremony.*

ABOUT THE LANGUAGE:

Dutch

Number of speakers: 21,730,290
Rank: 47

Dutch (called Nederlands by its speakers) is spoken in The Netherlands, as well as Aruba, Belgium, France, Netherlands Antilles and Suriname. Linguistically, Dutch is the closest language to English.

ABOUT THE TRANSLATOR AND SPEAKER:

John-Luc Bakker

Age: 35   Recorded: 2005
Towns: Groningen / Delft / Flemington, NJ

Dr. Bakker holds a Masters degree in Computer Science and works as a Research Scientist in programmable services for telecommunications. He was raised in Groningen until age 20, when he moved to Delft for his higher education. John-Luc moved to the USA at age 29.

Translations were also worked on by **Dr. Jan P. H. van Santen** (raised in Eindhoven and Amsterdam) and **Stefan Lubbersen** (South Africa).

Volendam, a small fishing village northeast of Amsterdam

Dogri

Aye raat dui raatain kola bakkharri kee aye?

■ *Why is this night different from all other nights?*

Dui raatain ee us khameeri rutti ya matza khanne aan;
iss raat sirf matza.

■ *On all other nights we eat either leavened bread or matzah;*
on this night only matzah.

Dui raatain ee us saari kism di jaadi-booti khanne aan;
ajj sirf kaudi booti khanne aan.

■ *On all other nights we eat all kinds of herbs;*
on this night only bitter herbs.

Dui raatain ee us ikk baar bi ni dobne;
iss raat do baar dobne aan.

■ *On all other nights we do not dip even once;*
on this night we dip twice.

Dui raatain ee us yaa te baitheeye ya tek laayie khanne aan;
iss raat us tek laayie khanne aan.

■ *On all other nights we eat either sitting up or reclining;*
on this night we recline.

Dui raatain ee us roze di tarah khanne aan;
iss raat us jashan manayie khanne aan.

■ *On all other nights we eat in an ordinary manner;*
on this night we dine with special ceremony.

We show only the transliteration of Dogri;
we were unable to get a written version
written in Dogri's native characters.

ABOUT THE SPEAKER:

Ajay Kapoor

Age: 32   Recorded: 2004
Towns: Srinagar, Jammu Kashmir, India / Edison, NJ

Ajay was born and raised in Srinagar, India. He learned Dogri from
friends at home and at school. Ajay came to the USA age 26. He works
as a software engineer.

ABOUT THE LANGUAGE:

Dogri

Number of speakers: 2,110,000
Rank: 223

Dogri (also known as Dogri-Kangri, Dhogaryali and other names) is one
of India's many official languages. It is spoken in the States of Jammu
and Kashmir, between the Ravi and Chenab rivers; Chandigarh; and West
Bengal. Dhogri is a Scheduled Caste in Himachal Pradesh and Punjab.

ABOUT THE TRANSLATOR:

Shailender Chohan

Age: Unavailable   Translated: 2004
Towns: Jammu City, India / Reston, VA

Shailender (Shally), a native speaker of Dogri, was born and raised in
Jammu City. He works as a software developer in Reston, VA.

Photo by Tony DeJoie

**Detail from ancient temple
in the Belur-Halebid area
near Bangalore**

Diriku

Morwanke matiku ghano ghana kushuvu na matiku na ghantje?

■ *Why is this night different from all other nights?*

Matiku naghantje, atwe kwalyanga mboroto ya ghushashu ndipo ya kupira ghushashu;
Matiku ghano, ya kupira ghushashu pentjanko.

■ *On all other nights we eat either leavened bread or matzah;*
on this night only matzah.

Matiku naghantje, kwa lyanga marudi naghantje ghandya;
Matiku ghano, ndya daghururu.

■ *On all other nights we eat all kinds of herbs;*
on this night only bitter herbs.

Matiku naghantje, narumweshi twa diviranga;
Matiku ghano, kudivira ruviri.

■ *On all other nights we do not dip even once;*
on this night we dip twice.

Matiku naghantje, kwa lyanga mujimandjindji ndipo kuyengama;
Matiku ghano, atwe kuyengama.

■ *On all other nights we eat either sitting up or reclining;*
on this night we recline.

Matiku naghantje, kwa lyanga pankedi ndjoyi yimwetupu;
Matiku ghano, kunali pankedi yayiwa.

■ *On all other nights we eat in an ordinary manner;*
on this night we dine with special ceremony.

ABOUT THE LANGUAGE:

Diriku

Number of speakers: 36,200
Rank: 1,891

Diriku, also called Rugciriku, Mbogedu and Shimbogedu by its speakers, is spoken in the Okavango region of Namibia. It is also spoken in Angola. The language is close to Kwangali.

ABOUT THE TRANSLATOR AND SPEAKER:

Robert Kuronga

Age: Unavailable   Recorded: 1998
Town: Kavango, Namibia

Robert grew up in Kavango, which is in the district of Nyangana. He is a native speaker of Diriku, which he calls Rugciriku.

Photo by Boris Kester

The giant Sossusvlei dunes are the highest in Namibia

Dene

Wēgonen wēndji bakanad awē tibikad onji kakina bakan tipikad?
- *Why is this night different from all other nights?*

Kakina bakan tipikad, nintamonan pakkwēsikanikan kēma pakkwēsikan; oma ka-tipikad, pakkwesikan ēta.
- *On all other nights we eat either leavened bread or matzah; on this night only matzah.*

Kakina bakan tipikad, kakina itō-ikana mashkosīwan; nintamonan wissakati-mashkosīyan oma ka-tipikad.
- *On all other nights we eat all kinds of herbs; on this night only bitter herbs.*

Kakina bakan tipikad, kawin goginassīmin pēsik; nintagoginanan nijing oma ka-tipikad.
- *On all other nights we do not dip even once; on this night we dip twice.*

Kakina bakan tipikad, niwissinan ēnamatapiyang kēma ēpimishimiang; oma ka-tipikad, ninpimishimonan.
- *On all other nights we eat either sitting up or reclining; on this night we recline.*

Kakina bakan tipikad, kawin pakan nintiwissiniminan; niwissinian gigi ka-itakamigak.
- *On all other nights we eat in an ordinary manner; on this night we dine with special ceremony.*

* For additional information, see *"Focus on ... pages.pdf"* on the DVD.

ABOUT THE LANGUAGE:

Dene *

Number of speakers: 9,030
Rank: 3,146

Dene is spoken in central and western Canada. The specific areas are northern Alberta, Saskatchewan, Manitoba and southeastern Northwest Territories. This specific dialect may be in Western Ojibwa, also called Sauteaux, one of the several languages/dialects of the Ojibwe people. It is sometimes known as Chipewyan, a term originally used by enemies.

ABOUT THE TRANSLATOR AND SPEAKER:

Charles Beauchamp

Age: Unavailable   Recorded: 1996
Town: Peguis Island Reserve, Hodgson, Manitoba

Charles is a native speaker of Dene. Peguis Island is on the southwest tip of Lake Winnipeg.

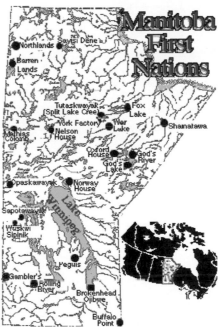

Map © 1996, Paula Giese.
Used by permission

Degema

Inu Ibirigena Ini   *The Four Questions*

Imo nụ ivuur nụ ạsu inina /ojza mạmu ạsu ạtire nụ ịdare yo?

■ Why is today's night not like the nights of the days that have passed?

Ạsu ạtire nụ ịdare yọ kịre, eni/ẹvon ubọ ẹyal ẹvo dị;
Ạsu inina dọ ubo ẹyal nụ eni ẹvo dịin.
Ạsu inina dọ mạtusa kpẹny nụ eni ẹdiin.

■ All the nights of the days that have passed, we ate lumps (loaves) of bread that were made with what causes them to swell (rise), or we ate 'matzah' (the ones that were made with what does not cause them to swell (rise); today's night, we ate only 'matzah'.

Ạsu ạtire nụ ịdare yọ kịre, eni ẹdin ạbitany nụ ekotun mụ ạbitany;
Ạsu inina dọ ạbitany nụ milom a kpẹny nụ eni ẹdiin.

■ All the nights of the days that have passed, we ate any named leaf (i.e. all kinds of leaves); today's night, we ate only bitter leaves.

Ạsu ạtire nụ ịdare yọ kịre, eni/ẹrov ekire ọvu kạa;
Ạsu inina dọ eni ẹrov n ekire eva.

■ All the nights of the days that have passed, we did not dip even once; today's night, however, we dipped twice.

Ạsu ạtire nụ ịdare yọ kịre, eni ejzan ụto gam omokaa ẹsirere vọ dịin;
Ạsu inina dọ ṣirere kpẹny nu eni ẹsirere vọ dịin.

■ All the nights of the days that have passed, we sat down or reclined while eating; today's night, we only reclined (while eating).

Ạsu ạtire nụ ịdare yọ kịre, eni/ẹvon ubọ ẹyal ẹvo dị;
Ạsu inina dọ ubọ ẹyal nụ eni ẹvo dịin.

■ All the nights of the days that have passed, we did not eat like during a feast; today's night, we ate like during a feast.

ABOUT THE LANGUAGE:

Degema

Number of speakers: 10,000
Rank: 3,000

Degema, also called Atala and Usokun, is spoken in Nigerian areas of the Rivers State, Degema, Usokun and Degema Town (Atala) communities. Many in the community now speak Kalabari (250,000 speakers). Some linguists claim Degema is an endangered language.

ABOUT THE TRANSLATOR AND SPEAKER:

Ethelbert Kari

Age: 34   Recorded: 2001
Towns: Usokun-Degema, Nigeria / Tokyo, Japan

Dr. Kari is a Degema linguist born in Usokun-Degema, Nigeria. His father was a Chieftain of the Degema people. Ethelbert received a Masters in Linguistics from the University of Port Harcourt (Nigeria) and a PhD from Tokyo University of Foreign Studies.

He dedicates his efforts to documenting Degema with the hopes of rescuing it from the linguistic pressures of Kalabari, English and Pidgin. Ethelbert describes that the uniqueness of the Degema culture includes its chieftaincy installation, coronation and annual festivals.

Photo © Damilare Onajole

The path to the Lagoon at the University of Lagos, a favorite relaxation spot for students

Danish

Hvorfor er denne nat forskellig fra alle andre natter?

■ *Why is this night different from all other nights?*

**På alle andre natter, spiser vi enten brød eller matza;
på denne nat kun matzah.**

■ *On all other nights we eat either leavened bread or matzah;
on this night only matzah.*

**På alle andre natter, spiser vi mulige urterge;
på denne nat spiser vi isør bitre urter.**

■ *On all other nights we eat all kinds of herbs;
on this night only bitter herbs.*

**På alle andre natter, spiser vi overhovedet ikke krydderier;
på denne nat dypper vi dem dobbelt.**

■ *On all other nights we do not dip even once;
on this night we dip twice.*

**På alle andre natter, sidder vi enten ret op eller tilbagelænet og spiser;
på denne aften sidder vi kun tilbagelænet.**

■ *On all other nights we eat either sitting up or reclining;
on this night we recline.*

**På alle andre natter, spiser vi med gode mannerer;
y aften er aftensmad med en special cermoni.**

■ *On all other nlghts we eat In an ordlnary manner;
on this night we dine with special ceremony.*

ABOUT THE LANGUAGE:

Danish

Number of speakers: 5,581,690
Rank: 124

Danish, called Dansk by its speakers, is the national language of Denmark. Significant numbers of speakers live in Germany and Greenland, and it is also spoken in Canada, Germany, Greenland, Norway, Sweden, United Arab Emirates and the USA.

Danish was the official language of Norway until about 1830 and Iceland until 1944. Danish is now the first foreign language learned in Iceland.

The first known written language of Scandinavia was Old Norse or *Dånsk tunga* (Danish tongue), which appeared in Runic inscriptions from about 700 CE onwards. Between 800 and 1050 CE a division began to appear between East Norse, which developed into Swedish and Danish, and West Norse, which developed into Norwegian, Faroese and Icelandic. The earliest work of Danish literature was *Gesta Danorum* (History of the Danes) written in Latin in about 1200 by Saxo Grammaticus.

ABOUT THE TRANSLATOR AND SPEAKER:

Jan Fischer

Age: Unavailable   Recorded: 1996
Towns: Copenhagen, Denmark / Sydney / NY

Jan grew up in Copenhagen. He lived in Sydney, Australia for a period of time before moving to the USA. He works at the United Nations.

Photos © Barry Hantman

Copenhagen's famous Little Mermaid
and a serene canal scene

Z Y X W V U T S R Q P O N M L K J I H G F E **D** C B A

Dagbani

Bɔ n-lee che ka yuŋ ŋɔ be di ko ka che yuŋ kam?

■ *Why is this night different from all other nights?*

Yuŋ kam ti ŋubirila bɔrobɔro shɛli din ka yiisi bee dim ka yiisi.

■ *On all other nights we eat either leavened bread or matzah;*
on this night only matzah.

Yuŋ kam ti dirila zevari balibu kam;
ameba yuŋ ŋɔ ŋun zevari din to pam.

■ *On all other nights we eat all kinds of herbs;*
on this night only bitter herbs.

Yuŋ kam ti' y'i susiri hali yiri gba;
amaa yuŋ ŋɔ ŋuna buyi ka ti susi.

■ *On all other nights we do not dip even once;*
on this night we dip twice.

Yuŋ kam ti yi diri bindirigu, ti ziinila chip bee tin zini dalini;
yuŋ ŋɔ ŋuna ti kuli zini dalim.

■ *On all other nights we eat either sitting up or reclining;*
on this night we recline.

Yuŋ kam ti dirila tin pun kuli diri shɛm;
yuŋ ŋɔ ŋuma ti dirimi ka chusu ka ti puhirila.

■ *On all other nights we eat in an ordinary manner;*
on this night we dine with special ceremony.

ABOUT THE LANGUAGE:

Dagbani

Number of speakers: 800,000
Rank: 422

Dagbani s one of the national languages of Ghana, spoken primarily in the northeast around Tamale and as far as Yendi.

ABOUT THE TRANSLATOR:

Mohamadu Alhassan

Age: Unavailable   Translated: 2005
Town: Tamale, Ghana

Mohamadu lives in Tamale, in the Northern Region of Ghana.

ABOUT THE SPEAKER:

Muntana Munatu

Age: Unavailable   Recorded: 2005
Town: Winneba City, Ghana

Muntana is a student at Winneba University in Winneba City. He called his dialect "Sanjina".

Photo by Ayikai Mills-Tettey

A mother and her children run to catch a bus in Kumasi, in the rain forest zone of Ghana

Dagaare, Southern

Bong la su ka zine teng-sɔg ba wãã a nga daari zaa teng suri?

■ *Why is this night different from all other nights?*

**Daari zaa teng sugɔ, ti ma dina boro bobo naba daabile bii maase;
kye zine ten sugɔ ti din a maasa.**

■ *On all other nights we eat either leavened bread or matzah;
on this night only matzah.*

**Daari zaa teng sugɔ, ti ma dina zevari iri iri;
kye zine deng zeva tuo.**

■ *On all other nights we eat all kinds of herbs;
on this night only bitter herbs.*

**Daari zaa teng sugɔ, ti mawa tung da yen gba;
kye zine tin sugɔ ti tung na bu yi.**

■ *On all other nights we do not dip even once;
on this night we dip twice.*

**Daari zaa teng sugɔ, ti ma zigna a dib ii a del;
kye zine ten sugɔ ti del la.**

■ *On all other nights we eat either sitting up or reclining;
on this night we recline.*

**Daari zaa teng sugɔ, ti ma bun na di;
kye zine ti di ni na ni laa fɛɛ longn.**

■ *On all other nights we eat in an ordinary manner;
on this night we dine with special ceremony.*

A/E

Z
Y
X
W
V
U
T
S
R
Q
P
O
N
M
L
K
J
I
H
G
F
E
D
C
B
A

About the Language:

Southern Dagaare

Number of speakers: 700,000
Rank: 451

Southern Dagaare is spoken in the northwest corner of Ghana and the western part of Upper West Region. It is closely related to another Ghanian language, Birifor, and is partially intelligible with it. The people who speak these languages are called the '*Dagaaba*'.

About the Translator and Speaker:

Joan Binza

Age: Unavailable   Recorded: 2002
Town: Tema, Ghana

Joan's translation appears to have some inconsistencies of spelling. Sometimes *tin* or *ten* is used, other times not. We cannot know if the differences are accidental or intentional.

Photo by Ayeley Mills-Tettey

Hawkers, pedestrians and vehicles vie for space at Makola market in central Accra, Ghana

Czech

Proč je tenhle večer jiný než všechny ostatní večery?

- Proch ye ten-hle ve-cher yi-nee nezh vsheh-ni o-stat-nyee ve-che-ri?

- *Why is this night different from all other nights?*

Ve všechny ostatní večery jíme bud' kynuty chléb nebo nekynuty chléb; tohoto večera pouze nekynuty chléb [maces].

- Ve vsheh-ni o-stat-nyee ve-che-ri yee-me budʸ ki-nu-tee hlép ne-bo ne-ki-nu-tee hlép; to-ho-to ve-che-ra pow-ze ne-ki-nu-tee hlép.

- *On all other nights we eat either leavened bread or matzah; on this night only matzah.*

Ve všechny ostatní večery jíme všechny druhy bylin; tohoto večera pouze hořké byliny.

- Ve vsheh-ni o-stat-nyee ve-che-ri yee-me vsheh-ni dru-hi bi-lin; to-ho-to ve-che-ra pow-ze horzh-ké bi-li-ni.

- *On all other nights we eat all kinds of herbs; on this night only bitter herbs.*

Ve všechny ostatní večery si nenámač íme ani jednou; tohoto večera si namácíme dvakrát.

- Ve vsheh-ni o-stat-nyee ve-che-ri si ne-naa-ma-chee-me a-nyi yed-now; to-ho-to ve-che-ra si na-maa-chee-me dva-kraat.

- *On all other nights we do not dip even once; on this night we dip twice.*

Ve všechny ostatní večery sedíme při jídle bud' rovně nebo se opíráme; tohoto večera se opíráme.

- Ve vsheh-ni o-stat-nyee ve-che-ri se-dyee-me prshi yeed-le budʸ rov-nye ne-bo se o-pee-raa-me; to-ho-to ve-che-ra se o-pee-raa-me.

- *On all other nights we eat either sitting up or reclining; on this night we recline.*

Ve všechny ostatní večery jíme obvyklým způsobem; tohoto večera jíme slavností večeři.

- Ve vsheh-ni o-stat-nyee ve-che-ri yee-me ob-vik-leem spoo-so-bem; to-ho-to ve-che-ra yee-me slav-nost-nyee ve-che-rzhi.

- *On all other nights we eat in an ordinary manner; on this night we dine with special ceremony.*

Transliteration notes: Word accent is always on first syllable. When there is a one-syllable preposition (as in *ve vshekh-ni*), the accent shifts to the preposition (*ve*). Accent marks in the transliteration indicate a longer vowel, not a different vowel. *h* indicates Czech's so-called hard h (sounding close to an English h); *kh* denotes Czech's soft h (close to ch in *Bach*).

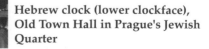

Hebrew clock (lower clockface),
Old Town Hall in Prague's Jewish
Quarter

Crow

Hinna áhpeesh sáapii áhpee ihée xaxúa kuk kootássuu?

■ As for this evening, why is it not like all other evenings?

Ahpee ihée xaxúa kuk ii baaxawuá púa ii díoo dak ii díassuua dak kuk buushíiluk.
Heehtaa hinna áhpee ii baaxawuá púa ii díassuua kuttáchik.

■ As for all other evenings, we eat bread made with, and not made with, yeast.
But this evening it is only bread not made with yeast.

Ahpee ihée xaxúa kuk hileen óosshee iiwaaiíkasshioo shíishiaahe kuk buushíiluk.
Heehtaa hinna áhpee baa ishía kuttáchik.

■ As for all other evenings, we eat various spices (lit. what-is-mixed-with-food).
But this evening it is only bitter ones.

Ahpee ihée xaxúa baa datchíissuua hawátteehtaa koótbaassuuk.
Heehtaa hinna áhpee dúuhpaa baa datchíishbuuk.

■ On all other evenings, we don't even once dip something.
But on this evening we dip something twice [as a rule].

Ahpee ihée xaxúa ámmaatuu xuh pátchetaa baaxapák baa buushíiluk.
Heehtaa hinna áhpee pátchetaa baaxapíiluk.

■ On all other evenings, we sit or lie on our sides and eat.
But on this evening we lie on our sides.

Ahpee ihée xaxúa shóosseehtaa baa buushíiluk.
Heehtaa hinna áhpee annámmaak baa buushíiluk.

■ On all other evenings, we eat in any old way.
But on this evening we eat befittingly.

Pronunciation notes:
ee pronounced as in bay, but at end of words is vowel of bed
ii pronounced as in key
oo pronounced as in code
uu pronounced as in sue
diphthongs *ia* (area) and *ua* (Nashua) sometimes spelled *iia, iaa* and *uua*
b often pronounced as w when beginning a word and following a vowel
(e.g. *baa buushíiluk*)
d sounds like l in similar circumstances (*ii díassuua dak*)
x is pronounced like ch in Bach
l pronounced like combination of English l and flapped d in "rider"
Doubled consonants have longer durations
Between vowels, *p* sounds like b, *t* like d, *ch* like j, *k* like g, *s* like z and
sh like zh (pleasure).
The first sentence ends with "?" which stands not for a punctuation mark,
but a glottal stop (middle of "uh-oh"). Accents indicate word intonation:
high pitch occurs when the accent is on the last vowel, falling pitch
occurs when the accent occurs on any other vowel.

ABOUT THE LANGUAGE:

Crow

Number of speakers: 4,280
Rank: 3,867

Crow, also called Apsaalooke, is spoken in southern Montana. Language use is quite vigorous: nearly all high school students and younger children can speak Crow. About one or two dozen of the elderly speak only Crow.

ABOUT THE TRANSLATOR:

Hu Matthews

Age: Unavailable   Translated: 1996
Location: Montana

Dr. Matthews is a linguist working for the Summer Institute of Linguistics among the Crow Indians in Montana. Hu has studied the Crow language many years.

ABOUT THE TRANSLATOR AND SPEAKER:

Sylvester Goes Ahead

Age: Unavailable   Recorded: 1996
Town: Pryor, MT

Sylvester, known as Cardy, is a native Crow speaker living in Pryor, MT, which is 40 miles south of Billings. He no longer can read Crow. The recording was created by Hu reading each line to Cardy, which he memorized and then read out loud. The recordings also contain a non-native (but clearer) reading by Dr. Matthews.

Photos by Meagan Thompson

Sarge Old Horn of the Crow Nation dances with his grandson in a powwow in Billings, MT

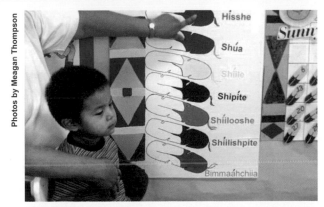

Elijah Not Afraid learns the Crow color names from instructor Kathy Dawes

Croatian

Zašto je ova noć različita od svih drugih noći?
■ *Why is this night different from all other nights?*

Sve druge noći jedemo kruh s kvascem ili beskvasni kruh; ove noći samo beskvasni.
■ *On all other nights we eat either leavened bread or matzah; on this night only matzah.*

Sve druge noći jedemo svakovrsno bilje; ove noći samo gorko.
■ *On all other nights we eat all kinds of herbs; on this night only bitter herbs.*

Sve druge noći ne umočimo niti jednom; ove noći umočimo dvaput.
■ *On all other nights we do not dip even once; on this night we dip twice.*

Sve druge noći jedemo uspravno sjedeći ili oslonjeni; ove noći se oslanjamo.
■ *On all other nights we eat either sitting up or reclining; on this night we recline.*

Sve druge noći jedemo bilo kojim redom; ove noći blagujemo po posebnoj ceremoniji.
■ *On all other nights we eat in an ordinary manner; on this night we dine with special ceremony.*

ABOUT THE LANGUAGE:

Croatian

Number of speakers: 5,546,590
Rank: 125

Croatian, also called Hrvatski, is the national language of Croatia. It is also spoken in Austria, Bosnia and Herzegovina, Germany, Hungary, Italy, Slovakia and Slovenia. It is closely related to Serbian and Bosnian. See entry for Serbian for fuller discussion.

ABOUT THE TRANSLATOR:

Josip Štilinović

Age: Unavailable   Translated: 1995
Town: Zagreb, Croatia

Josip was born and raised in the capital city, Zagreb, Croatia. He is a free-lance journalist based in Zagreb and a regular contributor to the Catholic World Report and other magazines.

ABOUT THE SPEAKER:

Željko Jergan

Age: 55   Recorded: 2010
Town: Varaždin / Zagreb, Croatia / Pittsburgh, PA

Željko is an internationally known choreographer and teacher. He was lead performer with Croatia's folk ensemble, *LADO* (at age 7, he vowed to dance with them after seeing them). He has created over 450 choreographies for groups and conveys his love of folk dance in workshops around the world.

Photo © Barry Hantman

View from Stari Most bridge, built in 1566 – Mostar, Croatia

Photo by Stephanie Goldhuber

Folkdance performance in Dubrovnik, showing hand-embroidered costumes

Crioulo

Pabia di qué cu manda nóti di ahós i ca djuntu cu tudu quil utrus nótis?

■ *Why is this night different from all other nights?*

Na tudu quil útrus nótis no cumé pón reforcadu ó bolacha;
Má ahós di nóti nó dadu só bolacha.

■ *On all other nights we eat either leavened bread or matzah;*
on this night only matzah.

Na tudu quil útrus nótis no ta cumé ba tudu coldadi di padja;
Má ahós di nóti é danu són pádjas malgós.

■ *On all other nights we eat all kinds of herbs;*
on this night only bitter herbs.

Na tudu quil útrus nótis nunca é ca púnu múdju;
Má ahós di nóti nó pudu madju dús biás.

■ *On all other nights we do not dip even once;*
on this night we dip twice.

Na tudu quil útrus nótis nó cumé ó sintadu ó ntón ngóstadu;
Má ahós di nóti anós túdu nó ngósta.

■ *On all other nights we eat either sitting up or reclining;*
on this night we recline.

Na tudu quil útrus nótis nó cumé súma cu no tarda ta cumé ba;
Má ahós di nóti nó cumé cu cirmónia.

■ *On all other nights we eat in an ordinary manner;*
on this night we dine with special ceremony.

About the Language:

Upper Guinea Crioulo

Number of speakers: 483,400
Rank: 561

Upper Guinea Crioulo (also called Portuguese Creole) is spoken throughout Guinea-Bissau, as well as the Bijagos Islands, Gambia, Senegal and the USA.

About the Translator and Speaker:

Joao Carlos Salvador Gomez

Age: Unavailable   Recorded: 1997
Locations: Guinea-Bissau / New York, NY

Joao, a native of Guinea-Bissau, is a journalist with the United Nations radio show "Scope".

Photo by Bernard Cloutier (berclo.net)

The Presidential Palace in downtown Bissau

A/E
Z Y X W V U T S R Q P O N M L K J I H G F E D C B A

Corsican

Parchi sta sirata e differenti di quid'altri serati?

■ *Why is this night different from all other nights?*

Tutti quid'altri seri pudemu manghjà u pani livitatu e u pani ághjimu; sta sera solamenti u pani ághjimu.

■ *On all other nights we eat either leavened bread or matzah; on this night only matzah.*

Tutti quid'altri seri pudemu manghjà tutti qualita d'arba; sta sera solamenti arba amara.

■ *On all other nights we eat all kinds of herbs; on this night only bitter herbs.*

Tutti quid'altri seri un femu mica funda a roba; manc'una volta; sta sera a femu funda dui volti.

■ *On all other nights we do not dip even once; on this night we dip twice.*

Tutti quid'altri seri manghjemu posendu, stichiti o appughjati; sta sera nienti che appughjati.

■ *On all other nights we eat either sitting up or reclining; on this night we recline.*

Tutti quid'altri seri manghjemu di manera simpliccia; sta sera femu una cirimunia spicciali.

■ *On all other nights we eat in an ordinary manner; on this night we dine with special ceremony.*

ABOUT THE LANGUAGE:

Corsican

Number of speakers: 402,000
Rank: 609

Corsican, also called Corsu, is spoken in France, in the regions of Corsica, Paris and Marseilles. Corsican has been recognized as a separate language by the French government. It is also spoken in Italy, with a few speakers in a half dozen other countries. Corsican is in the Tuscan group of Italian varieties. Southern Corsican (the dialect represented here) is closer to northern Sardinian or Gallurese than other Corsican dialects.

ABOUT THE TRANSLATOR:

Benoit Lagrue

Age: Unavailable   Translated: 1996
Town: Provence, France

Dr. Lagrue received a PhD in linguistics from the Universite de Provence.

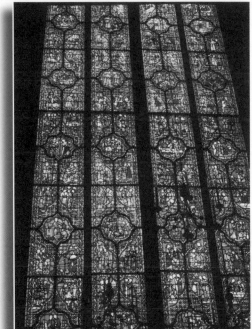

The famous 13th C windows of the Sainte Chappelle Church in Paris

ABOUT THE SPEAKER:

Gilles Giovannanjeti

Age: 40s   Recorded: 1996
Town: Corte, France

Gilles teaches the Corsican language at the University of Corsica at Corte.

Cornish

Prag yth yw an nosweyth ma dihaval orth pub nos arall?
- PRAHG ith ihw ahn NAWSS-wayth mah dee-HAH-vahl orth PB NAWSS AH-rahl?
- Why is the night this different to every night other?

Pub nos arall, y tybryn po bara gans burm po matzah;
an nosweyth ma, matzah hepken.
- PÜB NAWSS AH-rahl, ih TIH-brin paw BAH-rah gahnz BÜRM paw MAHT-sah; ahn NAWSS-wayth mah, MAHT-sah hep-KEN.
- Every night other (we) eat bread with yeast or matzah; the night this matzah only.

Pub nos arall, y tybryn losow a bub eghenn;
an nosweyth ma, losow hwerow hepken.
- PÜB NAWSS AH-rahl, ih TIH-brin LAW-soh ah BÜB EH-hen; ahn NAWSS-wayth mah, LAW-soh HWEH-roh hep-KEN.
- Every night other (we) eat herbs of every kind; the night this herbs bitter only.

Pub nos arall, ny droghyn kammenn vyth;
an nosweyth ma, y troghyn diwweyth.
- PÜB NAWSS AH-rahl, nih DRAW-hin KAHM-men VIHTH; ahn NAWSS-wayth mah, ih TRAW-hin DEEW-wayth.
- Every night other (we do not) dip step at_all; the night this (we) dip twice.

Pub nos arall, y tybryn po agan esedh po agan growedh;
an nosweyth ma, y hwrowcdhyn.
- PÜB NAWSS AH-rahl, ih TIH-brin paw AH-gahn EH-sedh paw AH-gahn GROH-wedh; ahn NAWSS-wayth mah, ih hwro-WEH-dhin.
- Every night other (we) eat or of our sitting or of our reclining; the night this (we) recline.

Pub nos arall, y tybryn yn maner gemmyn;
an nosweyth ma, y kinyewyn gans solempnyta arbennik.
- PÜB NAWSS AH-rahl, ih TIH-brin in MAH-nehr GEM-min; ahn NAWSS-wayth mah, ih keen-YEH-win gahnz SAW-lemp-NIH-tah ar-BEN-nik.
- Every night other (we) eat in manner ordinary; the night this (we) dine with ceremony special.

ABOUT THE LANGUAGE:

Cornish

Number of speakers: 5600
Rank: 5,396

Cornish is a Celtic language closely related to Breton and Welsh, spoken mainly in Cornwall (southwest England) and by a few people in Australia, Canada and the USA. It is used for some religious services. Several families raised children in Cornish-speaking homes, but many stop using it as they grow up.

Old Cornish was used from about 800-1250. By the late 19th C, Modern Cornish disappeared from everyday use – the last native speaker died in 1891. Several efforts tried to revive Cornish during the 20th C (Unified, Phonetic, Modern and Common Cornish). The language is taught in some schools and at the University of Exeter.

ABOUT THE TRANSLATOR AND SPEAKER:

Dr. Benjamin Bruch

Age: 33   Recorded: 2006
Towns: Kenosha, WI / Baltimore, MD

Dr. Bruch is a Post-doctoral Fellow in Celtic Languages and Literatures at Harvard University. Although not a native speaker, he is very fluent in Cornish. Ben has been studying and teaching the language for 11 years. He is probably in the top 10% of Cornish speakers in terms of proficiency, has very "by-the-book" pronunciations without noticeable accent, and is he is one of only a handful of fluent Cornish speakers in North America.

Ben corrected nuances in an earlier translation provided by **George Ansell**, the "official translator" for the Cornish Language Board in Wales. George, age 65, first studied Cornish at Cornwall College in the 1970s and has been involved with the Cornish language movement ever since. He was Grand Bard of the *Gorsedd* of Cornwall (1991-1994).

Dr. Benjamin Bruch

Cofán

Translated from Spanish

Jauiugae ja da fais´ë cusi a ca<u>e</u>n cusia ca<u>e</u>n micumba sët cambia?

■ *¿Por qué es diferente esta noche de todas las otras noches?*

**Pai cuseja, faise cusëja <u>a</u>fa p<u>a</u>maja shushuricquë s<u>e</u>i´chua;
ja´ñu cu´seja pama s<u>u</u>ichuja´a.**

■ *En todas las otras noches comemos pan hecho con levadura o pan ázimo;
en esta noche solamente matzah.*

**Pai cuseja, cu´anifae cu´seja <u>a</u>fa cuanitae shushubina´a;
ja´ñu cuani fai cusemaja shushuubima i<u> </u>´tsama <u>a</u>´fa.**

■ *En todas las otras noches comemos todas clases de hierbas;
en esta noche comemos hierbas amargas.*

**Cuanifai cuseja, inguija ni feinlli d<u>a</u>´tvi, shushubimaja;
ja´ñu cuse´eja shushubiaja feusiuda y cuanguise.**

■ *En todas las otras noches no sumergimos las hierbas de ninguna manera;
en esta noche las sumergimos dos veces.*

**Cuanifai cuseja, tansise yaipa <u>a</u>´fa;
ja´ñu cuseja pëbifapa <u>a</u>´fa.**

■ *En todas las otras noches comemos sentados rectos o inclinados;
en esta noche nos sentamos inclinados.*

**Maqui´faja egae yaifapa <u>a</u>´fa;
ja´ñu cuseja cara ´fapa ñucas<u>e</u>´e <u>a</u>´fa.**

■ *En todas las otras noches comemos de manera ordinaria;
en esta noche comemos con ceremonia especial.*

ABOUT THE LANGUAGE:

Cofán

Number of speakers: 1,700
Rank: 4,680

Cofán is primarily spoken in Ecuador, with more speakers in Colombia near the border with Ecuador. The locations are the Aguarico River and the Napo Province near Santa Rosa de Sucumbios.

ABOUT THE TRANSLATOR AND SPEAKER:

Gladys Lucifante

Age: 30s   Recorded: 2000
Village: San Pablo de Sionas Y Secoyas, in El Oriente, Ecuador

Gladys lives on the Aguarico River in Ecuador's jungle. She is the Cofán teacher for students in the village school, Colegio Tecnico Agropecuario Rio Aguarico, and is a native speaker of Cofán.

Happy visitors to Ecuador's jungle and rain forest

Choctaw

Chihowa im ubanublit ont la anumpa ilbasha asilha.

■ Chihowa im-abanablit ont ia anompa ilbasha asiła.

■ God -to them- Passover -goes and- talk humble beg.

■ *The Passover Prayer*

Katiohmi ho ninak elop at ninak inla ka itiminla ho?

■ Katiohmi-hõ ninak ilapp-at ninak ĩla kã itimĩla hõ?

■ How/is it night this night other -different from each other?

Ninak inla moma-kuno paska shatummi anoti paska ik shutmmo aienincht epa;
Ninak elopano paska ik shatummo ila epa.

■ Ninak gla moma-k-ano paska shatammi anõti paska ik-shatammo aiininchit ii'pa;
Ninak ilapp-ano paska ik-shatammo ila-ii'pah.

■ Night other all/of them/contrast bread leavened and bread neg/leavened -together with -we eat;
Night this/contrast bread neg/leavened -by itself we eat.

Ninak inla moma-kuno alba itim-inla moma epa;
Ninak elopano haiyukpulo homi ila epa.

■ Ninak ĩla moma-k-ano alba itimĩla moma ii'pah;
Ninak ilapp-ano haiõkpolo hommi ila ii'pah.

■ Night other all/of them/contrast herbs -other kinds- all -we eat;
Night this/contrast herbs bitter -by itself we eat.

Ninak inla moma-kuno himmona-kia nan-el-okachi keyo;
Ninak elopano hitokla oka elokachi.

■ Ninak ĩla moma-k-ano himmona-kia nana il-okachih kiiyo;
Nlnak Ilapp-ano hitokla oka Il-okachih.

■ Night other all/of them/contrast -not even once- something -we dip- not;
Night this/contrast twice water -we dip.

Ninak inla moma-kuno apissat e binohlih anoti nantaiyat binohli-hosh el-impah;
Ninak elopano nantiayat binohli-hosh el-impah.

■ Ninak ĩla moma-k-ano apissat ii-binohlih anõti nantaiyat binohli-hosh il-īpah;
Ninak ilapp-ano nantiayat binohli-hosh il-īpah.

■ Night other all/of them/contrast straight -we sit- and reclining sit/as -we dine;
Night this/contrast reclining sit/as -we dine.

Ninak inla moma-kuno pim-aialhpesa-kakosh el-impah;
Ninak elopano Nana kaniohmi fehna hosh okla el-impah.

■ Ninak ĩla moma-k-ano pim-aiałpiisa-k-akosh il-īpah;
Ninak ilapp-ano nana kaniohmi fiihna hosh okla il-īpah.

■ Night other all/of them/contrast -in our manner/being -we dine;
Night this/contrast something do certain/as -we dine.

Pronunciation notes:
a = short, central mid vowel
aa = long, low central vowel
ł = voiceless lateral fricative
i = short high central vowel
ii = long high central vowel
o = short mid round back vowel
oo = long mid round back vowel
Nasal vowels are marked with ~

ABOUT THE LANGUAGE:

Choctaw

Number of speakers: 11,400
Rank: 2,890

Choctaw is spoken in the USA, principally McCurtain County in southeastern Oklahoma, and east-central Mississippi; there are some speakers in Louisiana and Tennessee.

ABOUT THE TRANSLATOR AND SPEAKER:

Henry Willis

Age: 66   Recorded: 1996
Towns: West Purcell / Norman, OK

Henry was born near West Purcell to a monolingual Choctaw family. Although he was placed in the Goodland Indian Orphanage when he was 7, he retained his native language because he returned to his family on many occasions. Leaving Goodland at 21, he received a technical education in industrial electronics at the Oklahoma City and Oklahoma State Universities and the Elkins Radio School in Dallas. Mr. Willis worked as a television and radio station engineer and an industrial electrician. After retirement, Mr. Willis devoted himself to his two life-long avocations: native art and the Choctaw language. He has served as a Choctaw consultant for many linguists, including Choctaw linguist Marcia Haag and Aaron Broadwell at SUNY Albany. He also teaches advanced Choctaw courses at the University of Oklahoma.

In addition to his language research, Henry has traveled throughout rural Oklahoma and Mississippi recording, transcribing, and translating Choctaw folktales, and extensively researched his family's genealogy. He makes authentic miniatures of Native American artifacts, is active in Choctaw cultural and community affairs, and has served on many boards of directors and committees of local and regional associations. He helped establish the Norman First American United Methodist Church in 1995.

Transliteration of text was done by **Dr. Marcia Haag.**

Chinook

Kahta okoke polaklie huloima kopa konaway polaklie?

■ *Why is this night different from all other nights?*

Kopa konaway polaklie, nesika mukamuk piah sapolil pe matzah;
Kopa okoke polaklie, kopet matzah.

■ *On all other nights we eat either leavened bread or matzah;*
on this night only matzah.

Kopa konaway polaklie, nesika mukamuk konaway illahee tupso;
kopa okoke polaklie, kopet klilt illahee tupso.

■ *On all other nights we eat all kinds of herbs;*
on this night only bitter herbs.

Kopa konaway polaklie, nesika waket mahsh keekwullie kopa chuck ikt;
kopa okoke polaklie, nesika mahsh keekwullie mokst.

■ *On all other nights we do not dip even once;*
on this night we dip twice.

Kopa konaway polaklie, nesika mukamuk mitlite delate pe mitlite kahkwa
tikegh moosum;
kopa okoke polaklie, nesika mitlite kahkwa tikegh moosum.

■ *On all other nights we eat either sitting up or reclining;*
on this night we recline.

Kopa konaway polaklie, nesika mukamuk kahkwa waket huloima;
Kopa okoke polaklie, nesika mukamuk kopa kloshe tahmanawis.

■ *On all other nights we eat in an ordinary manner;*
on this night we dine with special ceremony.

ABOUT THE TRANSLATOR AND SPEAKER:

Scott Ford

Age: Unavailable   Recorded: 2000
Towns: Poulsbo, WA / Sitka, AK / Albion, WA

Scott is Apache by blood, but was adopted into the Raven moiety of the
Lingit by his Lingit stepmother. As his society is matrilineal in clan and
moiety membership, the adoption makes him Lingit. He learned Chinook
Jargon by himself and is said to know it well. Scott grew up in Poulsbo,
Washington and recently lived in Albion, after spending 6 years in Alaska.

ABOUT THE LANGUAGE:

Chinook

Number of speakers: 100
Rank: 6,130

Chinook Wawa (Chinook Jargon) is still spoken by a few speakers
scattered throughout Canada. It was formerly a trade or pidgin
language (although very much a language in its own right), used for
much of the 19th C along the Pacific coast from Oregon to Alaska,
between Indian and white people, and between speakers of different
languages.

Chinook has elements of Salishan, Wakashan, Chinookan, Kwakiutl,
English and French. It was still spoken by 100,000 people in 1875, but
went out of use in the early 20th C and is now understood by few.

Photo by Tom Judd

First Light at Victoria Glacier

Chinese

為什麼今晚與其他的夜晚不同？

■ *Why is this night different from all other nights?*

在其他的夜晚我們吃發酵的麵包或無酵餅；
今晚我們只吃無酵餅。

■ *On all other nights we eat either leavened bread or matzah;*
on this night only matzah.

在其他的夜晚我們吃各種各樣的香料；
今晚我們只吃苦味草。

■ *On all other nights we eat all kinds of herbs;*
on this night only bitter herbs.

在其他的夜晚我們什麼都不沾；
今晚我們沾兩次。

■ *On all other nights we do not dip even once;*
on this night we dip twice.

在其他的夜晚我們直坐著或斜靠著進餐；
今晚我們只斜靠著進餐。

■ *On all other nights we eat either sitting up or reclining;*
on this night we recline.

在其他的夜晚我們以普通的形式吃飯；
今晚我們以特殊的儀式進餐。

■ *On all other nights we eat in an ordinary manner;*
on this night we dine with special ceremony.

China's Great Wall, near Beijing

ABOUT CHINESE LANGUAGES:

Most researchers believe writing was invented in China during the latter half of the 2nd millennium BCE; there is no evidence suggesting writing was transmitted there from somewhere else. The earliest examples of written Chinese (on oracle bones) date from 1500-950 BCE (the *Shang* dynasty) and were inscribed on ox shoulder bones and turtle shells.

Compared to languages contained within other countries, the languages of China are unique. All major Chinese languages write words using the same characters – a book written in Mandarin or Hakka or Min-Bei would be identical. However, most Chinese languages differ from each other in the pronunciation of the characters; hence the languages are not mutually intelligible. Although the character for 'face' is always written as 臉, it is pronounced *li'-en* in Mandarin, *man* in Hakka, *meen* in Min-Bei, etc.

Chinese characters are known as *hànzi*. Each character represents a syllable of spoken Chinese as well as a meaning. The characters were originally pictures of people, animals or other concrete things but over the centuries they became increasingly stylized and now no longer resemble the things they represent. Many characters are actually compounds of two or more simpler symbols and many nouns are written with two or more characters. For instance, the characters representing the word university (大學) mean 'great learning', radio (收音機) is 'receive sound machine' and schizophrenia (精神分裂症) is 'split mind syndrome'.

Chinese writing is an open-ended system, meaning there is no upper limit to the number of characters. The largest Chinese dictionaries include about 56,000 characters, but most are archaic, obscure or rare variant forms. Knowledge of about 3,000 characters enables one to read about 99% of the characters in Chinese newspapers and magazines. To read Chinese literature, technical writings or Classical Chinese though, one needs to be familiar with about 6,000 characters. In Taiwan, Chinese is often written in vertical columns, while in China it is usually written horizontally (as shown here).

Four tones, or pitch contours, are used for Chinese syllables. Tone 1 has a level high pitch, tone 2 has a rising pitch, tone 3 dips downward then ends higher, while tone 4 has a falling pitch. Tones can change the meaning of identically pronounced syllables. For example, in Mandarin *ma1* (tone 1) means mother, *ma2* means hemp, *ma3* means horse and *ma4* means curse.

All of our Chinese translations are grouped together because they are written identically.

Photo by Stephanie Goldhuber

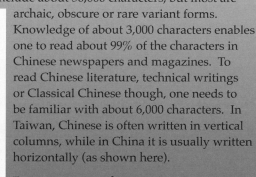

Yue/Cantonese

ABOUT THE LANGUAGE:

Yue Chinese

Number of speakers: 55,541,660
Rank: 22

Yue Chinese (Cantonese) is spoken throughout Guangdong, Macau, and in the southern part of Guangxi of China, with significant numbers of speakers in Vietnam, Malaysia, Singapore, Indonesia and a dozen other countries.

ABOUT THE TRANSLATOR AND SPEAKER:

Nim Cheung

Age: 55   Recorded: 2003
Locations: Hong Kong / NJ

Dr. Cheung was raised in Hong Kong and moved to the USA at age 23. Nim received his PhD from Cal Tech and held a variety of research and management positions at Bell Labs, Bellcore and Telcordia in optical and high-speed networking.

An earlier version was recorded by **Wah Chan Thom.** Ethnically Chinese, he was born and raised in Waiahole, Hawaii. Wah was in his mid-90s at the time of the recording.

Temple on coast of Guangzhou in Guandong province

Xiang/Hunan

ABOUT THE LANGUAGE:

Xiang Chinese

Number of speakers: 36,024,400
Rank: 31

Xiang Chinese (Hunan) is spoken in China's Hunan Province, over 20 counties in Sichuan and parts of Guangxi and Guangdong provinces.

ABOUT THE TRANSLATOR AND SPEAKER:

Jane Jiao

Age: 42   Recorded: 1997
Towns: ChangSha City / GuangZhou, China / Charleston, SC

Jane was born and raised in ChangSha City, Hunan; she moved to GuangZhou at age 21 and then to the USA at age 25.

China's Great Wall, near Beijing

Photos © Barry Hantman

Chinese
Wu/Shanghaiese
Nuosu/Sichuan

ABOUT THE LANGUAGE:

Wu Chinese

Number of speakers: 77,201,820
Rank: 12

Wu Chinese (also called Shanghaiese) is spoken in China's Jiangsu, south of the Changjiang River, east of Zhenjiang, on Chongming Island in the mouth of the Changjiang, and north of the Changjiang in the area around Nantong, Haimen, Qidong and Qingjiang, and in Zhejiang Province as far south as Quzhou, Jinhua and Wenzhou.

ABOUT THE SPEAKER:

Yibei Ling

Age: 40   Recorded: 2003
Towns: Shanghai, China / NJ

Dr. Ling was raised in Shanghai and moved to the USA at age 30. Yibei has the position of Senior Research Scientist, working in telecommunications. An earlier version was recorded by the wife of Californian **John Jiang**.

ABOUT THE LANGUAGE:

Nuosu Chinese/ Sichuan

Number of speakers: 2,000,000
Rank: 236

Yi Chinese (Sichuan or Nuosu) is mainly spoken in China's Greater and Lesser Liangshan Mountains, southern Sichuan and northwestern Yunnan. It is also spoken in 40 countries. In addition to using written Chinese, Sichuan Yi has an official script, the Yi syllabary, which is based on a traditional Sichuan Yi script and on the syllable inventory of a variety of Shengzha Yi spoken in Xide county. The Yi script is used in the Liangshan area, both in southern Sichuan and northwestern Yunnan.

ABOUT THE SPEAKER:

Wen-Lei Jiang

Age: 30   Recorded: 2003
Towns: Ba-Xian / ChongQing, China / Randolph Township, NJ

Wen-Lei Jiang was born in Ba-Xian and raised in ChongQing, both of which are in Sichuan province. She emigrated to the USA at age 23.

Photo © Barry Hantman

In the recordings: Yibei ends his recording with his name and the name of the language, spoken in Wu (Shanghaiese) and English.

Gold statue of Wei Tuo, the military protector of Buddhist scriptures. Located in Shanghai's Jade Buddha Temple

Illustration by Alysa Lerman

Sichuan Province is famous as the home of the Panda Bear

Chinese
Min-Nan/Taiwanese   Min-Bei/Foochow

ABOUT THE LANGUAGE:

Min-Nan Chinese

Number of speakers: 47,265,100
Rank: 24

Min-Nan Chinese, also known as Taiwanese and Fukienese, is spoken throughout China and has significant numbers of speakers in Taiwan, Singapore, Malaysia, the Philippines and Thailand. There are a large number of dialects.

ABOUT THE SPEAKER:

Fuchun Lin

Age: 48   Recorded: 2003
Towns: Kao-Hsiung, Taiwan / NJ

Dr. Lin was raised in Kao-Hsiung, in southern Taiwan. Fuchun (Joe) was 28 when he arrived in the USA. A computer scientist, Joe works in the research area of telecommunications, developing commercial opportunities for commercial and government organizations. An earlier version was spoken by **Ming Mei Lee** who grew up in Hong Kong within a family from Fukien province.

ABOUT THE LANGUAGE:

Min-Bei Chinese

Number of speakers: 10,304,000
Rank: 78

Min-Bei Chinese, also known as Foochow and Min Pei, is spoken in Taiwan and northern Fujian Province in 7 counties around Jian'ou. Min-Bei is also spoken in Singapore.

ABOUT THE SPEAKER:

Ping Jiang

Age: 34   Recorded: 2003
Towns: Fuzhou Province, China / NY

Ping was born and raised in China's Fuzhou province. He arrived in the USA at age 23. An earlier version of the text was recorded by **Samantha Chan**, who was born in a small village in Foochow province, moved to Hong Kong at age 4, and migrated to New York City at age 6. She retained language fluency through speaking with relatives.

Photo © Susan Hantman

Koxinga's Shrine, built in 1662, is the only Foochow-style temple in Taiwan. Koxinga (*Cheng Cheng-kung*) was a Ming Dynasty pirate-warrior who made great contributions to Taiwan's development

Chiang Kai-Shek Memorial Hall, a landmark of Taipei City, Taiwan. It was dedicated in 1980, 5 years after the leader's death

Photo © Susan Hantman

Chinese, Mandarin

wei shuh muh jeen wan ü chee ta duh yieh wan bu tong?

■ Why tonight is different from other nights?

tzai chee ta duh yieh wan, wao muhn chi fa shiao duh myen bao hwuh woo shiao beeng;

jeen wan wao muhn ji chi woo shiao beeng.

■ On other nights we eat leavened bread or unleavened flat bread;
tonight we only eat unleavened flat bread.

tzai chee ta duh yieh wan, wao muhn chi guh jong guh yuhng duh shiang liao;

jeen wan wao muhn ji chi koo wei tsao.

■ On other nights we eat all various kinds of spices;
tonight we only eat bitter herbs.

tzai chee ta duh yieh wan, wao muhn shuh muh do boo jan;

jeen wan wao muhn jan liang tsi.

■ On other nights we do not dip anything;
tonight we dip twice.

tzai chee ta duh yieh wan, wao muhn ji tzuo juh hwuh shieh kao juh jeen tsan;

jeen wan wao muhn ji shieh kao juh jeen tsan.

■ On other nights we sit up or lean while eating;
tonight we only lean while eating.

tzai chee ta duh yieh wan, wao muhn yee pu tong duh sheeng shi chi fan;

jeen wan wo muhn yee tuh shoo duh yee shi jeen tsan.

■ On other nights we have a meal in an ordinary manner;
tonight we have a meal in a special ceremony.

Transliteration does not follow standard Romanization of Chinese (e.g., *qi, xi*), as that is misleading for English speakers. "zh" often is closer to j sound • most vowels are quite short • "ee" indicates *very* short ee-sound (as in "see") • "i" (as in *ji, shi*, sometimes written *zhi*) indicates retroflex vowel (ee-vowel with tongue tip curled to back roof of mouth – [i] moving toward [ɚ] • "a" as in father, never as in bat • ü is ee vowel with oo-rounding, as in French *tu* or German *für Elyse* • "do" is word doe, not English word "do" • Different speakers will disagree what the best English representation is for consonants such as j, sh, ts, tz, etc. Tones are: • ("light", short), 1: — (straight tone, longer than light), 2: ✓ (like English question), 3: ∨ (more like English declarative), and 4: ＼ (shorter declarative).

ABOUT THE SPEAKER:

Dong Cui

Age: 47   Recorded: 2003
Towns: Hei Long Jiang Province, China / NJ

Dong grew up in Hei Long Jiang Province, a relatively dialect-neutral area of China. He came to the USA at age 42. An earlier version was recorded by **Chung Teh Fan**, an ethnic Chinese Mandarin speaker in Hawaii.

ABOUT THE LANGUAGE:

Mandarin Chinese

Number of speakers: 845,456,760
Rank: 1

Mandarin, the most commonly spoken language on the planet, is the official language of China. Although 265 languages are spoken in China, nearly all Chinese people around the world have a basic understanding of Mandarin, in addition to their "own" language. As would be expected in a single language spoken by over 1 billion people, Mandarin has many different dialects.

Most Mandarin speakers live in monolingual areas and are not conscious of other languages. Thus, relatively few speakers are bilingual.

Mandarin is known as *pǔtōnghuà* (common language) or *běijīnghuà* (Beijing language) in China, *guóyǔ* (national language) in Taiwan, and *huáyǔ* (Chinese language) in Singapore and Malaysia.

The word Mandarin comes, via Portuguese, from the Sanskrit word *mandari* (commander). The Portuguese used the term to refer both to the Chinese people and their language.

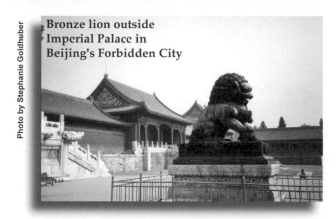

Bronze lion outside Imperial Palace in Beijing's Forbidden City

Photo by Stephanie Goldhuber

Mandarin Chinese Transliteration

嗎　你是他那　哈來了　哈澤　迷口勒　哈蕾漏特？
- ma nee-shuh-tah-nuh ha-lai-luh ha-tzuh mee-ko-luh ha-lay-lo-tuh?

靴北扣勒　哈蕾漏特　阿奴　歐赫林　哈梅測　嗚嗎測；
- sheh-bay-ko-luh hah-lay-lo-tuh ah-nu o-hhuh-leen hha-may-tsuh u-ma-tsuh;

哈來了　哈澤　枯樓　嗎測。
- hah-lai-luh hah-tzuh ku-lo mah-tsuh.

靴北扣勒　哈蕾漏特　阿奴　歐赫林　捨一爾　耶爾啊扣特；
- sheh-bay-ko-luh hah-lay-lo-tuh ah-nu o-hhuh-leen shuh-ee-err yieh-er-aa-ko-tuh;

哈來了　哈澤　嗎弱爾。
- hah-lai-luh hah-tzuh mah-ruo-err.

靴北扣勒　哈蕾漏特　阿奴　嗎特比林　啊飛盧　葩啊麼　誒哈特；
- sheh-bay-ko-luh hah-lay-lo-tuh ah-nu mah-tuh-bee-leen ah-fay-lu pa-a-muh ey-hha-tuh;

哈來了　哈澤　捨退　發啊敏。
- hah-lai-luh hah-tzuh shuh-tway fa-ah-meem.

靴北扣勒　哈蕾漏特　阿奴　歐赫林　編　油捨無瑩　無偉呢　麼淑餅；
- sheh-bay-ko-luh hah-lay-lo-tuh ah-nu o-hhuh-leen byehn yo-shuh-u-een u-way-nuh muh-shu-been.

哈來了　哈澤　枯拉奴　麼淑餅。
- hah-lai-luh hah-tzuh ku-lah-nu   muh-shu-been.

Transliteration notes: Most Chinese words do not end with consonants (except n, ng), so words that end with a consonant plus schwa-like vowel have been used; Mandarin has no 'v', so 'w' is used; the ma-ruo-err is actually very close to *maror*, as are many of the other constructions.

The word 誒 (Ey) [an exclamation of affirmation] is rarely seen, and might be mispronounced as ai or ee. Other less-used words may be 麼 (Muh) and 是 (Shuh). This transliteration uses traditional characters, which some in Mainland China are less experienced with, having been taught simplified characters.

As the Chinese transliteration only uses characters for words, the question naturally arises as to what do the words used for the transliteration mean?   The following gives an idea:
ma: **[question]*** *nee*: **you**   *shuh*: **are**   *tah*: **he**   *nuh*: **that**   *ha*: **"ha" [laughter]**   *lai*: **come**
luh: **[prior verb is past tense]***   *ha*: **laughter**   *tzuh*: **shiny gloss/pond**   *mee*: **confused/lost**
ko: **mouth**   *luh*: **force/compel****   *ha*: **laughter**   *lay*: **flower bud**   *lo*: **leakage**   *tuh*: **special**

* used only at end of sentence
** used mostly to transliterate foreign names

ABOUT THE LANGUAGE:

Chinese Transliteration

Unlike other living languages, traditional Chinese is unusual in not having a phonetic spelling mode – only full words can be used. Transliterations (like the one shown here or for foreign names) use the closest sounding character-words, which are spoken as a syllable. Thus, transliterations in traditional Chinese writing have a meaning (although usually non-sensical). For example, Lincoln is 林肯 [lin kuhn], two characters that mean 'forest' and 'willing-to'. *Bopomofo*, a method of phonetic spelling, is used in Taiwan, but not for transliterations.

The spellings used here are not the official Chinese Romanization, which is not a good approximation of the actual sounds spoken. Instead they are spellings of one of the authors, listening to pronunciations of native Mandarin speaker **Hong (Julia) Liao**, who was born in Jiang Xi Province.

ABOUT THE TRANSLATOR AND SPEAKER:

Yuu-Heng (Alice) Cheng

Age: 26   Recorded: 2003
Towns: Chung-Hwa / Kao-Hsiung, Taiwan / Piscataway, NJ

Alice was born in Chung-Hwa and was primarily raised in Kao-Hsiung, both in Taiwan. She first came to the USA at age 6 for 4 years and again lived in the USA starting at age 24. She has a Masters Degree in Computer Science and works as a Research Scientist in telecommunications. Adjustments were made by **Evan Chu** and **Binggong Ding**.

Photo by Stephanie Goldhuber

Another view of The Great Wall

Jews

THE JEWS OF K'AI-FENG FU:

For several centuries, there was a Jewish community in K'ai-Feng Fu, China. The Jews arrived in China from Persia, and their religious texts used a well-preserved form of Judeo-Persian. They also spoke Mandarin Chinese.

The earliest Judaic inscriptions in China date from 1489, and Jews may have lived in China even earlier. The last survivors of the Chinese community died in 1850.

ABOUT THE LANGUAGE:

Hakka Chinese

Number of speakers: 30,032,520
Rank: 38

Hakka Chinese is spoken in many parts of mainland China side by side with other dialects. The largest concentrations of speakers are in eastern and northeastern Guangdong, and in Fujian, Jiangxi, Guangxi, Hunan and Sichuan provinces. Hakka is also spoken in 15 other countries, most notably Taiwan, Malaysia, Indonesia, Singapore and Thailand.

ABOUT THE TRANSLATOR AND SPEAKER:

Xin-Mian Lu

Age: 66   Recorded: 2003
Towns: He San Shien, China / Parsippany, NJ

Xin-Mian was born in He San Shien, Guang-Dong province, China. Although a native Hakka speaker, at age 28 she stopped using Hakka regularly. Xin-Mian moved to the USA at age 48. She reports that her dialect is a "minor" version, not the standard Yue-Tai (*MeiXien*) version.

An earlier version was recorded by fluent but non-native speaker **Sandy Zhong**, who was born in Canton, China.

祖獨承天敬天因而念祖

הגדת יהודי סין

HAGGADAH
OF THE
CHINESE JEWS

Synagogue of K'ai-Feng Fu, China

From a Manuscript of the Seventeenth-Eighteenth Century C.E.

Modern reprint of Haggadah used by the Jews of K'ai-Feng Fu, China

Photo © Susan Hantman

Tianenmen Gate in Beijing

Chickasaw

Katihmihta himmaka' oklhilihookano oklhili ilaka ittimila?

■ Why is tonight different from the other nights?

Oklhili ilahookmano paska shatabli' paskikshatablo' tawáaho iipahminatookya himmaka' oklhilihookano paskikshatablo' illaho iipa'chi.

■ On other nights we eat both bread that rises and bread that doesn't rise;
but tonight we will eat only unleavened bread.

Oklhili ilahookmano nannokchamali iláyyo'ka mómaho iipahminatookya himmaka' oklhilihookano alba homi' illaho iipa'chi.

■ On other nights we eat all kinds of greens;
but tonight we will eat only bitter weeds.

Oklhili ilahookmano iitakaffihminatok ki'yohookya himmaka' oklhilihookano hitokla' iitakaffa'chi.

■ On other nights we do not dip them;
but tonight we will dip them twice.

Oklhili ilahookmano kanihmit iibiniilihookya ilimpahminatookya himmaka' oklhilihookano aaombiniili' atáyya'at iibiniilikmakoot ilimpa'chi.

■ On other nights we eat sitting any old way;
but tonight we will eat sitting leaning back against the chairs.

Oklhili ilahookmano kanihmit ilimpahminatookya himmaka' oklhilihookano aai'pa' holiito'pa' ilaaimpa'chi.

■ On other nights we eat any old way;
but tonight we will eat at a holy table.

ABOUT THE LANGUAGE:

Chickasaw

Number of speakers: 1,000 (possibly as low as 200 currently)
Rank: 5,033

Chickasaw is spoken principally in south-central Oklahoma, bounded by the towns Byng and Happyland (near Ada) in the north, by Davis and Ardmore in the west and Fillmore and Wapanucka in the east; speakers also live in Los Angeles, California.

The Chickasaws originally lived in Tennessee, Alabama and Mississippi, but were relocated to Oklahoma about 160 years ago by the Federal government in what became known as the "Trail of Tears". Because fluent speakers are elderly and younger members of the Nation are not learning the language, Chickasaw is regarded as a seriously endangered language.

ABOUT THE TRANSLATOR AND SPEAKER:

Catherine Willmond

Age: 74   Recorded: 1996
Towns: McMillan, OK / Los Angeles, CA

Mrs. Willmond was born in McMillan, OK; at age 37 she moved to Los Angeles. She is a direct descendant of Edmund Pickens and I. Hunter Pickens, two very important figures of the early Chickasaw Nation of Oklahoma. As a fundamentalist Christian, Mrs. Willmond fully enjoyed thinking about the translation.

The spelling is based on a system and dictionary developed by Mrs. Willmond with linguist **Dr. Pamela Munro** (through whom this translation was obtained), published by the University of Oklahoma Press. This translation is included in their textbook for learning Chickasaw.

In the recordings: Mrs Willmond ends her recording with the phrase "Passover Prayer" spoken in Chickasaw.

Pronunciation notes: *lh* is a voiced lateral fricative; *sh* is slightly retroflexed alveopalatal fricative; *ch* is voiceless alveopalatal affricate; apostrophe represents glottal stop; underlined vowels are nasalized.

Translation notes: Chickasaw is a polysynthetic language, in which a verb often expresses the whole idea contained in an English clause, and where verbs express concepts differently than in English. For instance, the noun for night *oklhili* is the same as 'to be night;' other nouns are derived from verbs as in *aaombinili'* (chair) means 'place one sits on' and *aaimpa'* (table) means 'place one eats'. Chickasaw's future tense expresses a potentially future habitual reference (and is particularly appropriate, for at the time of the questions, the activities mentioned have not yet occurred). *Takaffi* (dip) usually refers to a dipper or container cup; it is not possible to say 'we do not dip' in Chickasaw without an object ('them', for instance, the bitter herbs) in mind. With no word for recline, the Chickasaw translation gets very specific about the leaning (few translations mention leaning to the left, as this is a Rabbinic interpretation). Faced with no words for 'special ceremony', Mrs Willmond, like many others, appropriately chose to cast the ceremony with religious connotations.

Photo by Peter Lang

**Catherine Willmond
and Dr. Pamela Munro**

Cheyenne

Hénová'e tséhésenétàhéva'e hétsetseha taa'eva?

■ *Why is this night different from all other nights?*

Naa taa'évee'èstse néohkemésenone heováestse kóhkonòheóo tséhéso; naa oha hétsetseha taa'eva némésenone hé'tóhe kóhkonòheóo tsésáapóheotséháne.

■ *On all other nights we eat either leavened bread or matzah; on this night only matzah.*

Naa máto néohkemésenone netao'o hová'éhe tséhóné'o; naa oha hétsetseha tsévé'òhkeéno'ee'èstse éto'semésèstóvénèste.

■ *On all other nights we eat all kinds of herbs; on this night only bitter herbs.*

Naa máto néohkèsáasé'hasenéhema; naa oha hétsetseha taa'eva nésé'hasenémáne nexa.

■ *On all other nights we do not dip even once; on this night we dip twice.*

Naa máto néohketomòhtónoémáne náa máto héva néohkèheamáxenámáne mésèhétsee'èstse; naa oha hétsetseha taa'eva oha émàheheamáxenáhtove.

■ *On all other nights we eat either sitting up or reclining; on this night we recline.*

Naa máto ooxhesta néohkèhešeamemésèhémáne; oha hétsetseha taa'eva énétàhévo'eétàhéstove.

■ *On all other nights we eat in an ordinary manner; on this night we dine with special ceremony.*

ABOUT THE TRANSLATOR AND SPEAKER:

Louise Fisher

Age: 66   Recorded: 1999
Town: Busby, MT

Louise was born and raised in the area of Busby, Montana. She is very fluent in Cheyenne and all her siblings spoke the language fluently. The linguist who obtained the translation for us, **Dr. Wayne Leman,** said: "She should enjoy translating the Seder service since she (and a number of us in Busby) participate in a Seder service each Passover season. How interesting to have a Native American translating this. Cheyennes have deep respect for spiritual ceremonies."

* For additional information, see "*Focus on ... pages.pdf*" on the DVD.

ABOUT THE LANGUAGE:

Cheyenne *

Number of speakers: 1,720
Rank: 4,674

Cheyenne is spoken in Montana, in the Northern Cheyenne Reservation located in southeastern Montana; the southern Cheyenne live in western Oklahoma. Cheyenne is taught by 5 fluent speakers in a summer camp for children in Montana. In Oklahoma most speakers are at least middle-aged. The Cheyenne name for their language is *Tsêhést* and the Cheyenne people call themselves *Tsitsistas*.

Photo by Tom Judd

A common western scene

Cherokee

ᎾᎧ ᎭᏗᏃ ᏓᏍᎦ ᎵᏔᎴᎦ ᏬᎦᏫ ᏑᏃᏴ
- do nv hi ah no u su hi   dv da le ga wo wa dv su no ye
- Why   this   night   different   other   nights?

ᏬᎦᏫ ᏑᏃᏴ ᏣᏣᎴᏍᏗ ᏴᎲᏍᎪ ᎦᏚ Ꭺ ᎠᏑᏴ Ꭷ ᎾᏎᎦ
- wo wa dv su no ye o tsa le s ti yv hu s go ga du go ah su ye ah le ne ga sv nah
- All other nights   we eat   bread leavening mix   or   not;

ᎭᏗᏃ ᏓᏍᎦ Ꭺ ᎠᏑᏴ ᎾᏎᎦ
- hi ah no u su hi go ah su ye ne ga sv nah
- this   night   leavening mix   never.

ᏬᎦᏫ ᏑᏃᏴ ᏧᏓᎴᎾᏛ ᎡᎾᎦ ᏧᏕᏒᎯ ᏣᏣᎴᏍᏖ ᏴᎲᏍᎪ
- wo wa dv su no ye tsu da le na dv e nah ga tsu du sv hi o tsa le s te yv hi s go
- All other nights   all kinds   wild herb   grow   we eat;

ᎭᏗᏃ ᏓᏍᎦ ᎡᎾᎦ ᏧᏕᏒᎯ ᎤᏳᏍᏗ
- hi ah no u su hi e nah ga tsu du sv hi u yu s di
- this   night   wild herb   grow   bitter.

ᏬᎦᏫ ᏑᏃᏴ ᎦᏍᏗ ᏲᏤᎬᏍᎪ ᎠᏑᏴᎫ*
- wo wa dv su no ye ga s di yo tse gv s go ah su ye gu-o
- All other nights   we   dip   [negation];

ᎭᏗᏃ ᏓᏍᎦ ᏔᎴ ᏲᏤᎫᎩᏍᎪ
- hi ah no u su hi ta le o tse gu gi s go
- this   night   two   dip.

ᏬᎦᏫ ᏑᏃᏴ ᏲᏌᎾ Ꭷ ᏲᏌᎾᎪ ᏣᏣᎴᏍᏗ ᏴᎲᏍᎪ
- wo wa dv su no ye o tse nv ah le o tse nv go o tsa le s ti yv hi s go
- All other nights   sitting   or   lying   we eat;

ᎭᏗᏃ ᏓᏍᎦ ᏲᏌᎾᎪ
- hi ah no u su hi o tse nv go
- this   night   recline.

ᏬᎦᏫ ᏑᏃᏴ ᏲᏚᏗᎠᏤᎳ ᏣᏣᎴᏍᏗ ᏴᎲᏍᎪ
- wo wa dv su no ye o su ti ah ye ta o tsa le s ti yv hi s go
- All other nights   ordinary   we eat;

ᎭᏗᏃ ᏓᏍᎦ ᏌᎴᏍᎦᏓ ᎤᏳᎴᏛ ᏗᏂᏦᎯᏍᏗᏳ ᏣᏣᎴᏍᏗ ᏴᎲᏍᎪ
- hi ah no u su hi u le s ga da u ye le dv di ni tso hi s di yu o tsa le s ti yv hi s go
- this   night   special   manner   meeting   we eat.

* Written version had ᎠᎿᏴᏒ᷄ but transliteration and recording indicated the text shown.

Weaving demonstration at Oconaluftee Indian Village, Cherokee, NC

ABOUT THE LANGUAGE:

Cherokee
Number of speakers: 16,400
Rank: 2,584

Cherokee is spoken in eastern and northeastern Oklahoma, in the Cherokee Reservation located in the Great Smokey Mountains and western North Carolina. In Oklahoma, children are being raised speaking the language and there is vigorous use in some Oklahoma communities.

The Cherokee syllabary (a phonetic writing system consisting of symbols representing syllables) was introduced in 1819 by Sequoyah, Chief of the Cherokee nation. By 1820, thousands of Cherokees had learned the syllabary, and by 1830, 90% were literate in their own language. A constitution, books, religious texts, almanacs and newspapers were all published using the syllabary, which was widely used for over 100 years.

The syllabary is still used today, but only by relatively few people.

ABOUT THE TRANSLATOR AND SPEAKER:

Jeremiah Wolf
Age: Unavailable   Recorded: 2000
Town: Cherokee, NC

Jeremiah lives on the Cherokee Reservation and works as a greeter at the Museum of the Cherokee Indian, in the town of Cherokee.

Photo by Ian and Cheryl Bernstein

Chechen

Кхечу массо буьисанашкахь оха кхаллар;
я гIагIал доу, хIокху буса гIагIал.

- Other all nights [we (erg.)] bread or matza eat;
  this night matza.

Кхечу массо буьисанашкахь оха массо таипан бецаш ёу;
хIокху буса - кIаьхьа бецаш баи.

- Other all nights [we (erg.)] bread all types grasses eat;
  this night bitter grasses only.

Кхечу массо буьисанашкахь оха [даар туьханчу] ча Iуьтту;
хIокху буса - оха шозза Iутту.

- Other all nights [we (erg.)] [food into-salt] not dive;
  this night [we (erg.)] twice dive.

Кхечу массо буьисанашкахь оха охьахоишана я агIордоьвла ёу;
хIокху буса - тхо Iохку.

- Other all nights [we (erg.)] sitting or reclining eat;
  this night [we (Erg.)] lie.

Кхечу массо буьисанашкахь оха даím санна ёу;
хIокху буса къаьстíначу ламасте хьаьжжína ёу.

- Other all nights [we (erg.)] always like eat;
  this night [we (erg.)] special rule regarding eat.

> Erg = Ergative: Case or voice that indicates the subject of
> a transitive verb; e.g., no specific word for "we" is used.

ABOUT THE SPEAKER:

Osman Polatkan

Age: Unavailable   Recorded: 1997
Towns: Boskurt, Turkey / N Haledon, NJ

Osman (Todd) was raised in Turkey. His dialect is "old-style" Chechen, incorporating the speech styles when many Chechens emigrated to Turkey in the 1890s.

Translation note: The initial question was not translated.

Z Y X W V U T S R Q P O N M L K J I H G F E D **C** B A

ABOUT THE LANGUAGE:

Chechen

Number of speakers: 1,341,000
Rank: 301

Chechen, called Nokhchiin by its speakers, the Nokhchi, is spoken in Chechnya, in the north Caucasus area of Russia. It also spoken in Jordan (where 3,000 speakers live) and Georgia, Germany, Kazakhstan, Kyrgyzstan, Syria, Turkey and Uzbekistan.

ABOUT THE TRANSLATOR:

Mikhail Alekseev

Age: Unavailable   Translated: 1996
Town: Moscow, Russia

Dr. Alekseev, also known as Michael Alekseyev, is a Daghestanian language specialist at the Institute of Linguistics, Russian Academy of Sciences, in Moscow.

Mikhail's translation was sent before documents could be sent by email. The Cyrillic characters were coded by an arcane set of ASCII codes that many Russians used to communicate with others outside Russia.

Turkey is famous for the craftwork in its Turkish rugs

ABOUT THE LANGUAGE:

Chaouia

Number of speakers: 1,400,000
Rank: 296

Chaouia, also spelled Shawiya, also called Tachelwit, is spoken in Algeria, in the south and southeast of Grand Kabylie in the Aurès Mountains. Chaouia is one of the major Berber languages.

ABOUT THE TRANSLATOR AND SPEAKER:

Muhand Meziani

Age: Unavailable   Recorded: 1998
Towns: Chennawra, Algeria / Geneva / Reykjavik, Iceland

Dr. Meziani was born in Chennawra, a village in the community of T'kout, in the middle of Auresiennes (Aurès) mountains. The surroundings are a complete Chaouia-speaking area (Muhand's native language). Muhand lived in the area for 32 years. He received a PhD in Generative Linguistics at the University of Geneva. He is now extending his research of Berber languages to Icelandic.

We wish to thank an un-named informant living in Algeria and France (recruited by SIL worker **Frank Dieleman**) who also provided a Chaouia translation and recording.

The Chaouia's Arabic script was typed by **Abdelmounaam Rezgui**.

Photo by Bernard Cloutier (berclo.net)

The marina in Algiers

Translated from French

ماغف ايغ ضين يملـخظة نتن نيين

■ Mmaghef ida ur yelli ca am yidan inn i eiddan?

■ *Pourquoi cette soirée se distingue-t-elle des autres soirées?*

كل ايض ذقد انتش اكفيل نيغ المـغصوب
مبصح ايض ذين نتت المـغصوب

■ Idan inn qaei nella ntet ukfil d urexsas; ida kes urexsas berk.

■ *Tous les autres soirs nous pouvons manger du pain levé ou du pain azyme; ce soir seulement du pain azyme.*

كل ايض ذقد انتش سق كل اررار
مبصح ايض ذين نتت اررار ا قرراقن

■ Idan inn qaei nella ntet hizzuzut amek yex hella; ida kes n tizzuzut hmirzayt.

■ *Tous les autres soirs nous pouvons manger toutes sortes d'herbes; ce soir seulement des herbes amères.*

كل ايض اندقعش الماكلت لاك لمـرغث
مبصح ايض ذين ذقع سنت لمـراث

■ Idan inn qaei ur nneqqe ca ula d lemerret; ida nneqq sent n lemerrat.

■ *Tous les autres soirs nous ne trempons pas la nourriture même pas une fois; ce soir nous trempons deux fois.*

كل ايض نتت سوقيمى نيغ سوتاكى
مبصح ايض ذين نتت سوتاكى

■ Idan inn netett neqqim nbed nnegh nettekka; ida nettekka berk.

■ *Tous les autres soirs nous mangeons assis droit ou accoudés; ce soir accoudés seulement.*

كل ايض نتت امـكل وسان
مبصح من غير ايض ذين

■ Idan inn qaei ntett amw akkas; ida ntett am yid mensi.

■ *Tous les autres soirs nous mangeons de manière ordinaire; ce soir nous mangeons de manière spéciale.*

Cebuano

Nganong lahi man kining gabhiona sa ubang mga gabii?

■ *Why is this night different from all other nights?*

Sa ubang mga gabii, mokaon kitag pan nga may patubo o pan nga walay patubo; karong gabhiona, pan nga walay patubo lamang.

■ *On all other nights we eat either leavened bread or matzah;*
on this night only matzah.

Sa ubang mga gabii, mokaon kita sa tanang matang sa utanon; karong gabhiona, mga utanon nga pait lamang.

■ *On all other nights we eat all kinds of herbs;*
on this night only bitter herbs.

Sa ubang mga gabii, dili kita modudo bisag makausa; karong gabhiona, modudo kitag makaduha.

■ *On all other nights we do not dip even once;*
on this night we dip twice.

Sa ubang mga gabii, mokaon kita nga maglingkod ug tul-id o magsandig; karong gabhiona, mokaon kita nga magsandig.

■ *On all other nights we eat either sitting up or reclining;*
on this night we recline.

Sa ubang mga gabii, mokaon kita sa yanong paagi; karong gabhiona, kita mokaon uban sa pinasahing seremonyas.

■ *On all other nights we eat in an ordinary manner;*
on this night we dine with special ceremony.

ABOUT THE LANGUAGE:

Cebuano

Number of speakers: 15,807,260
Rank: 57

Cebuano, also called Cebu and several other names, is spoken in The Philippines (Negros, Cebu, Bohol, Visayas and parts of Mindanao) and in the USA.

Linguist Dr. Rubrico
in Quezon City

ABOUT THE TRANSLATOR AND SPEAKER:

Jessie Grace U Rubrico

Age: 45   Recorded: 1998
Towns: Mindanao / Diliman, Quezon City, Philippines

Dr. Rubrico has an MA in Linguistics and a PhD in Philippine Linguistics from the University of the Philippines. Jessie has done dozens of translation projects and serves as the English-Cebuano Translator for Radio Bible Ministries. Cebuano is *lingua franca* in her birthtown of Mindanao. Jessie helped obtain translations in 8 Philippine languages.

Catalan

Translated from Spanish

Per què aquesta nit és diferent de totes les altres?

■ *¿Por qué es diferente esta noche de todas las otras noches?*

Les altres nits podem menjar tota mena de pa, amb llevat o sense. Per què aquesta nit només pa sense llevat?

■ *En todas las otras noches comemos pan hecho con levadura o pan ázimo; en esta noche solamente matzah.*

Les altres nits podem menjar tota mena d'herbes. Per què aquesta nit només herbes amargues?

■ *En todas las otras noches comemos toda clase de hierbas; en esta noche comemos hierbas amargas.*

Les altres nits no mullem ni un sol cop els nostres aliments. Per què aquesta nit ho fem dues vegades?

■ *En todas las otras noches no sumergimos las hierbas de ninguna manera; en esta noche las sumergimos dos veces.*

Les altres nits podem menjar seient rectes o inclinats. Per què aquesta nit seiem inclinats?

■ *En todas las otras noches comemos sentados rectos o inclinados; en esta noche nos sentamos inclinados.*

Les altres nits mengem de manera ordinària. Per què aquesta nit mengem amb una cerimònia especial?

■ *En todas las otras noches comemos de manera ordinaria; en esta noche comemos con ceremonia especial.*

ABOUT THE LANGUAGE:

Catalan

Number of speakers: 11,530,160
Rank: 74

Catalan, also called Català, Bacavès and Catalonian is spoken in northeast Spain, in the region of Barcelona; Catalonia, Valencia Provinces, Balearic Islands, region of Carche and Murcia Province. (Other subdialects are located in different overlapping regions of Spain.) Catalan is also spoken in France, Andorra, and Italy, with a few speakers in 14 other countries.

ABOUT THE SPEAKERS:

Monica Estruch and Joan Torruella

Age: Unavailable   Recorded: 1996
Town: Barcelona, Spain

Monica Estruch and Joan Torruella live in Barcelona, Spain. They were both students at the Linguistics Department (*Departament de Filologia Espanyola*) at the Universitat Autonoma de Barcelona. Monica obtained an 'official' Catalonian translation from the Jewish Temple in Barcelona. The male voice in the recordings is Joan's (a male name in Catalan).

A translation was also worked on by **Jesus Lopez** in Spain.

Detail from 14th C El Transito Synagogue and Sephardic Museum in Toledo, Spain

Cajun French

Pourquoi cette nuit est différent que tout les autres nuits?

■ *Why is this night different from all other nights?*

Sur tout les autres nuits on mange le pain levain ou matzah; sur cette nuit on mange juste le matzah.

■ *On all other nights we eat either leavened bread or matzah; on this night only matzah.*

Sur tout les autres nuits on mange tout les herbes et les épices; sur cette nuit juste herbes amers.

■ *On all other nights we eat all kinds of herbs; on this night only bitter herbs.*

Sur tout les autres nuits on ne plonge pas, comme même juste une fois; sur cette nuit on plonge deux fois.

■ *On all other nights we do not dip even once; on this night we dip twice.*

Sur tout les autres nuits on mange assoiez avec le dos droist ou appuyé; sur cette nuit on appuyez.

■ *On all other nights we eat either sitting up or reclining; on this night we recline.*

Sur tout les autres nuits on mange n'importe de quoi; sur cette nuit on mange avec une certaine cerémonie.

■ *On all other nights we eat in an ordinary manner; on this night we dine with special ceremony.*

Translation notes: Obvious spelling errors were corrected by **Barry Ivker** of New Orleans who worked with Charles on the translation. Corrections were: omission of plural *s* on *nuits, amers* and *épices*; *just* for *juste*; *drois* for *droist*, *certain* for *certaine*; *un fois* for *une fois*. Based on its pronunciation, *n'importe de quoi* had been spelled as *ne parte de quoi*.

In the recordings: The recordings give a native pronunciation, showing major vowel shifts from Parisian French. The text affords few opportunities to demonstrate vocabulary shifts. Charles relied on a standard French dictionary for much of the spelling. Dialect and spelling variants are prevalent, such as the word for sitting. Charles recognized, but regularly mispronounced, the verb *appuyez*, indicating it is not part of his current vocabulary.

About the Language:

Cajun French

Number of speakers: 17,200
Rank: 2,554

Cajun French is spoken in southern Louisiana west of the Mississippi as far north as Avoyelles, Evangeline, Allen and Calcasieu Parishes. Cajun is recognizably different from the variety of *Broken French* used by 8,000 African Americans and of *Napoleonic Era French*, an archaic combination of French and English spoken near Houma and north of Theriot.

About the Translator and Speaker:

Charles Bourque

Age: 70s   Recorded: 2005
Town: St. Landry Parish, LA

Charles was raised and lives in St. Landry Parish in southwest Louisiana. All his relatives are Acadians. Charles is proud of his Cajun roots (he regularly goes to the *Congrés Mondiale* for the Cajun people). Although an observant Catholic, he is genetically one-fourth Jewish and is proud of his Jewish links.

Charles primarily spoke Cajun as a child. As the teaching of Cajun was discouraged during his upbringing, his writing is often ungrammatical. Some unfamiliar words are mispronounced because he doesn't use Cajun on a daily basis anymore.

Riding in New Orleans' French Quarter

Burmese

အဘယ်ကြောင့် ဤ ညဉ့် သည် အခြားသောညဉ့် များနှင့် ကွာခြားပါသနည်း။

■ ***Why is this night different from all other nights?***

အခြားညဉ့် များ၌ ငါတို့သည် တဆေးပါသော ပေါင်မုန့်အပျော့ကိုငှင်း တဆေးမပါသောပေါင်မုန့်အမာကိုငှင်း သုံးဆောင်ကြ၏။

ဤ ညဉ့် ၌ကား ငါတို့သည် တဆေးမပါသောပေါင်မုန့်အမာကိုသာ သုံးဆောင်ကြ၏။

■ ***On all other nights we eat either leavened bread or matzah;***
on this night only matzah.

အခြားညဉ့် များ၌ ငါတို့သည် ဆေးဘက်ဝင်သော သစရွက်သစ်မြစ်မျိုးစုံကို သုံးဆောင်ကြ၏။

ဤ ညဉ့် ၌ကား ငါတို့သည် ခါးသော ဆေးဘက်ဝင်သစ်ရွက်သစ်မြစ်တို့ ကိုသာ သုံးဆောင်ကြ၏။

■ ***On all other nights we eat all kinds of herbs;***
on this night only bitter herbs.

အခြားညဉ့် များ၌ ငါတို့သည် (ပေါင်မုန့်ကို) ဆားရေနှင့် တစ်ကြိမ်ပင် တို့၍ မစားကြချေ။

ဤ ညဉ့် ၌ကား ငါတို့သည် (ပေါင်မုန့်ကို) ဆားရေနှင့် နှစ်ကြိမ်ပင် တို့၍ စားကြ၏။

■ ***On all other nights we do not dip even once;***
on this night we dip twice.

အခြားညဉ့် များ၌ ငါတို့သည် ကိုယ်ကိုမတ်မတ်ထား၍ငှင်း စောင်းမှီ၍ငှင်း ထိုင်ကာ စားသောက်ကြ၏။

ဤ ညဉ့် ၌ကား ငါတို့သည် ကိုယ်ကို စောင်းမှီ၍သာ ထိုင်ကာ စားသောက်ကြ၏။

■ ***On all other nights we eat either sitting up or reclining;***
on this night we recline.

အခြားညဉ့် များ၌ ငါတို့သည် သမရိုးကျသာ စားသောက်ကြ၏။

ဤ ညဉ့် ၌ကား ငါတို့သည် ထူးခြားသော အခန်းအနားဖြင့် စားသောက်ကြ၏။

■ ***On all other nights we eat in an ordinary manner;***
on this night we dine with special ceremony.

Translation notes: U Thein-Tun provided two translations – one using the formal form of Burmese (shown here) and another using a more colloquial form of the language. The recordings contain both versions. To preserve the original Jewish cultural context, he provided a cross-language, not cross-cultural, translation: e.g., he used words for bread (although rice is typically used in Burmese meals) and dipping into salt-water (rather than curry gravy, sauce or paste).

Photo by Boris Kester

Destroyed in WW II, Mandalay's Royal Palace was built by King Mindon Min in 1857

About the Language:

Burmese

Number of speakers: 32,319,700
Rank: 36

Burmese, the national language of Myanmar (Burma), is spoken in its south, central and adjacent areas. Burmese is also spoken in Bangladesh, Malaysia, Thailand and the USA. Native speakers of Burmese seldom speak a second indigenous language. Burmese is also known by the names Bama, Bamachaka and Myen. There are 5 main regional dialects; some may be distinct enough to be defined as separate languages.

The Burmese script developed from the Mon script, which was adapted from a southern Indian script during the 8th C. The earliest known inscriptions of Myanmar script date from the 11th C.

About the Translator and Speaker:

U Thein-Tun

Age: Unavailable Recorded: 1994
Locations: Myanmar (Burma)/ Australia

U Thein-Tun, a native of Myanmar, was a linguistics student at La Trobe University, Bundoora, in Victoria, Australia when the translation was done.

Buriat

Translated from Russian

Ондоо hуни энэ hуни хоёр юугээрээ илгарнаб?
- Ondo huni ene huni khoyor yugeeree ilharnab?
- Чем отличается эта ночь от всех других ночей?

Ондоо hуни бидэн мацу угшьеhаа хара хилззмз здинзбди; харин знз hуни ганса мацу.
- Ondo huni biden matzu, ugyshehaa khara khilieeme edynebdi; Kharyn ene huni gansa matzu.
- Во все другие ночи мы едим либо квашеный хлеб либо мацу; а в эту ночь-только мацу.

Ондоо hуни злдзб янзын ногоо здинзбди; харин знз hуни гансал гашуун ногоо.
- Ondo huni eldeb yanzyn nogoo edynebdi; Kharyn ene huni gansal gashuun nogo.
- Во все другие ночи мы едим любую зелень; а в эту-только горькую.

Ондоо hуни бидэн ногоогоо уhан соо шзнгзздзг угыбди; харин знз hуни хоёр дахин шзнгзздзбди.
- Ondo huni biden nogogo uhan so shengeedeg ugybdi; Kharyn ene huni khoyor dakhyn shengeedebdi.
- Во все другие ночи мы вообще не обмакиваем зелени; а в эту ночь-обмакиваем ее дважды.

Ондоо hуни бидэн hуумгашаа угышьеhаа хзбтзн хоол баринабди; харин знз hуни hансал hуумгашаа.
- Ondo huni biden huumgashaa, ugyshehaa khebten knol barynabdi; Kharyn ene huni gansal humgasha.
- Во все другие ночи мы едим сидя или возлегая; а в эту ночь-возлегая.

Ондоо hуни здезмнзй юрзнхы хоол болодог; харин муноодзр здезмнзй ёho заншалта сайлган.
- Ondo huni edyemney yurenkhy khol bolodog; Kharyn munoder edyemney yogo zanshalta saylgn.
- Во все другие ночи мы едим как обыденно; а сегодня у нас ритуадьная трапеза.

Bonus in the recordings: Battuvshin, who performs internationally with Sayan, demonstrates Mongolian/Tuvin Throat Ginging (*Khoomei* and *Kargyraa* styles). He also demonstrates continuous breathing while playing the Mongolian flute (*Limbe*) non-stop for nearly 2 minutes. "Tuvsho" has been able to play continuously for over 3 hours, after which his neck muscles, which act like a pump, give out. Battuvshin was born in Bulgar province of Mongolia; was Grand Prize winner at All-Mongolian Flute Contest, Gold Medalist at the International Folk Music Festival in Korea; and has played in the well-known Buryat-Mongolian Folk Ensemble, *Baikal* Folk Ensemble, and *Badma Seseg* Folk Ensemble of Ulan Ude.

ABOUT THE LANGUAGE:

Buriat

Number of speakers: 64,900
Rank: 1,478

Buriat, also called Buriat-Mongolian and Northern Mongolian, is spoken in the state of Buryatia in Russia. It is also spoken east of Lake Baikal, Siberia and along the border with Mongolia.

Sayan playing *limbe*, the Mongolian flute

Photo by Natalia Honcharenko

ABOUT THE TRANSLATOR AND SPEAKER:

Sayan Zhambalov

Age: Unavailable   Recorded: 1998
Town: Aginskoye / Ulan Ude, Buryatia, Russia

Sayan is a native speaker of Buriat. He was born in Aginskoye in the Aginsk Autonomous Region and currently lives in the capital of the Republic of Buryatia, Ulan Ude. He is a nationally famous actor and musician in the Buriat National Theatre and accomplished throat singer. He won first prize at the International Contest of Singers in Ulan Bator, Mongolia. Sayan tours internationally, singing traditional Buriat and Mongolian music, and plays in the rock band *Urag Sha*. (When Sayan met one of the authors in the USA, a year after translating the text, his first question was "What number language was Buriat in the collection?"! [It was the 150th.] He remembered it immediately as the text with *Matzu* in it.)

Photo by Alexander Khantaev

Sayan and Battuvshin (front row) and the rock group *Urag Sha*

Bulgarian

С какво е по-различна тази нощ от всички останали нощи?

■ S kakvo e po-razlichna tazi nosht ot vsichki ostanali noshti?

■ *Why is this night different from all other nights?*

■ *Ма ништана алайла азе микол алайлот.*

Нали във всички нощи ние ядем квасно и неквасно;
а в тази нощ само неквасно.

■ Nali vuhv vsichki noshti nyeh yadem kvasno i nekvasno; a v tazi noshti samo nekvasno.

■ *On all other nights we eat either leavened bread or matzah; on this night only matzah.*

■ *Шебехол алейлот ану охлин хамец, умаца, алайла азе куло маца.*

Нали във всички нощи ние ядем различен зеленчук;
а в тази-само горчив.

■ Nali vuhv vsichki noshti nyeh yadem razlichen zelenchook; a v tazi, samo gorchiv.

■ *On all other nights we eat all kinds of herbs; on this night only bitter herbs.*

■ *Шебехол алейлот ану охлин шеар йеракот, алайла азе куло марор.*

Нали във всички нощи ние нито веднъж не мокрим (нашата храна);
а в тази нощ-два пъти.

■ Nali vuhv vsichki noshti nyeh nito vednuhzh neh mokrim; a v tazi noshti, dva puhti.

■ *On all other nights we do not dip even once; on this night we dip twice.*

■ *Шебекол алелот ейн ану матбилин афилу паам ехат, алайла азе штеи феамим.*

Нали във всички нощи ние вечеряме седнали или полегнали;
а в тази нощ-само полегнали.

■ Nali vuhv vsichki noshti nyeh vecheryameh cednali ili polegnali; a v tazi noshti, samo polegnali.

■ *On all other nights we eat either sitting up or reclining; on this night we recline.*

■ *Шебехол алейлот ану охлин бейн йошвин увейн месубин, алайла азе кулану месубин.*

ABOUT THE LANGUAGE:

Bulgarian

Number of speakers: 9,097,220
Rank: 87

Bulgarian is the national language of Bulgaria and is spoken in 10 other countries, primarily Greece, Moldova, Romania, Turkey and Yugoslavia.

The script below the English shows the Bulgarian transliteration of the original Hebrew text.

The Great Synagogue in Sofia, Bulgaria, constructed in 1910

Bulgarian street musicians in Sofia

ABOUT THE TRANSLATOR AND SPEAKER:

Vasia Benusi

Age: Unavailable   Recorded: 1995
Towns: Sofia, Bulgaria / Far Hills, NJ

Vasia grew up in the capital city of Sofia, Bulgaria. In the USA, she was an expert seamstress. Vasia's recording is of her own translation which differs from the text shown here, which is traditional.

Bukharic

Translated from Russian

Барои чи ин шаб аз дигар шабхо Фарқ дорад?

■ Чем отличается эта ночь от всех других ночей?

Ба ҳама шабҳои одди мо нони хамир бо хамиртуруш ёки масо бо намаку хамиртуруш мехурдем;
имшаб шаби (писхо) - пасха Фақат массо мехурем.

■ Во все другие ночи мы едим либо квашеный хлеб либо мацу;
а в эту ночь-только мацу.

Ба ҳама шабҳои одди мо кабути ҳархела мехурдем;
ба шаби песах Фақат кабутии талхи мехурем.

■ Во все другие ночи мы едим любую зелень;
а в эту-только горькую.

Ба ҳама шабҳои одди мо кабутиро ба намак об тар накарда мехурдем;
дар ин шаби песах ба намак об кабутиро тар карда мехурем.

■ Во все другие ночи мы вообще не обмакиваем зелени;
а в эту ночь-обмакиваем ее дважды.

Ба ҳама шабҳо хурок ва маёро шишта ва рос истода мехурдем;
дар шаби песах ҳамаи инро алал хусуе маёро такя карда мехурем.

■ Во все другие ночи мы едим сидя или возлегая;
а в эту ночь-возлегая.

Ба ҳама шабҳои одди ҳархела хурок мехурдем;
ба ин шаби песах ҳурокҳои махсус барои песах таёр карда шударо мехурем.
Чунки ин шаб шаби махсус аст.

■ Во все другие ночи мы едим как обыденно;
а сегодня у нас ритуадьная трапеза.

גְּי מַגְיִיר הַסְתְ. אָן שַׁבִי אָן אִין אַז הַמַהִי אָן שַׁב הָא. אָנגְ'י דַר
הַמַהִי אָן שַׁב הָא. נִיסְתַים אִימָא אַנְדַר וַנָאָן. אַגַרִי יַאֲנִי כַּבְתִי
יַפִי. וְאָן שַׁבִי אָן אִין. דִי כַּבַת הָא: אָנְגְ'י דַר הַמַהִי אָן שַׁב הָא.
אִימָא כֹּורָאָן תֻורוּש שׁוּדַח יָא פַּטִיר. וְאָן שַׁבִי אָן אִין גְ'יַמְלָהִי אוֹ
פַּטִיר: אָנְגְ'י דַר הַמַהִי אָן שַׁב הָא. אִימָא כֹּורָאָן כָּאקְנִיאַתִי סַבְזַה.
וְאָן שַׁבִי אָן אִין מַלְכַּה: אָנגְ'י דַר הַמַהִי אָן שַׁב הָא. אִימָא כֹּורָאָן
וְנוֹשָׁאָן. כָּאהֵי נִישְׁסְתַנְאָן. וְכָאהֵי מַקְיִיה פַּרְדַנְאָן. וְאָן שַׁבִי אָן אִין
גְ'יַמְלָהִי אִימָא מַקְיִיה פַּרְדַנְאָן:

From a 1929 Judeo-Tajik Haggadah: translation of the
traditional Four Questions using Hebrew letters

Bonus in the recordings: Izra Malakov
sings, in Hebrew, the *Ma Nishtana*,
Passover *Kiddush* and *Ha-Lachma* using
traditional Bukharan melodies.

ABOUT THE LANGUAGE:

Bukharic

Number of speakers: 110,000
Rank: 1,159

Bukharic, also called Bukharan and Judeo-Tajik, is a
language of Uzbekistan that is also spoken in Israel. It is
close to Judeo-Persian and Tajik Persian.

ABOUT THE TRANSLATOR:

Manahem and Izra Malakov

Ages: 67 and 61   Translated: 1999
Towns: Shakhrisabz City, Uzbekistan / New York, NY

Manahem and Izra are brothers born in Shakhrisabz City,
Uzbekistan. Both sing in the Bukharan Jewish Ensemble,
Shashmaqam, which has been performing music and dance
from their native Uzbekistan and Tadzhikistan since 1983.
Izra came to the USA in 1992; Manahem in 1993.

ABOUT THE SPEAKER AND SINGER:

Izra Malakov

Age: 61   Recorded: 1999

Information about Izra is above.

Photo by Martin Koenig

Shashmaqam, the Bukharan Jewish Ensemble

Breton

Perag eo an noz-mañ disheñvel diouzh an noziou all?

■ *Why is this night different from all other nights?*

An holl noziou all, e tebromp pe bara goell pe bara-kan;
An noz-mañ, mann med bara-kan.

■ *On all other nights we eat either leavened bread or matzah;*
on this night only matzah.

An holl-noziou all, e vez debret ganimp, louzou a bep seurt;
an noz-mañ, mann med louzou c'hwerw.

■ *On all other nights we eat all kinds of herbs;*
on this night only bitter herbs.

An holl noziou all, ne soubomp ket, memes ur wech;
an noz-mañ, e soubomp diw wech.

■ *On all other nights we do not dip even once;*
on this night we dip twice.

An holl noziou all, e tebromp pe sonn en hon c'hoazez pe harp hon c'hein;
an noz-mañ, harp hon c'hein.

■ *On all other nights we eat either sitting up or reclining;*
on this night we recline.

An holl noziou all, e tebromp en ur mod ordinal;
an noz-mañ, e koaniomp war an ton bras.

■ *On all other nights we eat in an ordinary manner;*
on this night we dine with special ceremony.

ABOUT THE LANGUAGE:

Breton

Number of speakers: 500,045
Rank: 535

Breton, also called Brezhoneg, is spoken within France in western Brittany; speakers are dispersed throughout eastern Brittany; there are Breton emigrant communities throughout the world, including the USA.

ABOUT THE TRANSLATOR AND SPEAKER:

Guy Mercier

Age: Unavailable   Recorded: 1998
Town: Lannion, France

Dr. Mercier is a linguist working for CNET, the French telephone company, in Lannion, France. Although French is his native language, because Guy's parents were native Breton speakers, his Breton is somewhat close to native speech. His parents spoke Breton exclusively with each other and not with their children, probably because it was forbidden at school.

(He notes that his recording is not as representative of native Breton speech as it could have been; to speak proper Breton, Guy said he needed to speak to other Bretons or to be in a Breton environment.)

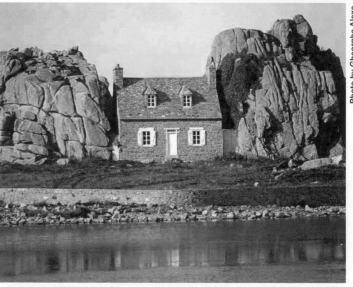

Photo by Gheorghe Alexe

One of the most well-known houses in Brittany, located in Plougrescant, is built between blocks of pink granite that permeate the coastal area

Bicolano, Central

Täno ta ining banguing ini kaiba sa ibang mga bangui?

■ *Why is this night different from all other nights?*

Sa ibang mga bangui, minakarakan kita nin tinapay na may libadura, o kaya matza; ngunyan na bangui, matza lang.

■ *On all other nights we eat either leavened bread or matzah; on this night only matzah.*

Sa ibang mga bangui, minakarakan kita ning gabos na klase ning yerba; ngunyan na bangui, mga mapait lang na yerba.

■ *On all other nights we eat all kinds of herbs; on this night only bitter herbs.*

Sa ibang mga bangui, nungka kita nagsawsaw; ngunyan na bangui, dowang beses kitang nagsawsaw.

■ *On all other nights we do not dip even once; on this night we dip twice.*

Sa ibang mga bangui, minakarakan kitang nakatukaw o nakahilay; ngunyan na bangui, nakahilay kita.

■ *On all other nights we eat either sitting up or reclining; on this night we recline.*

Sa ibang mga bangui, minakarakan kita sa ordinaryong paagi; ngunyan na bangui, may espesyal na seremonyas ang pag-aratubang ta.

■ *On all other nights we eat in an ordinary manner; on this night we dine with special ceremony.*

ABOUT THE LANGUAGE:

Central Bicolano

Number of speakers: 2,500,000
Rank: 206

Central Bicolano, also called Naga Bicolano and Bikol Naga is spoken in the Philippines, primarily Naga City and Legaspi City. It is also spoken in southern Catanduanes, northern Sorsogon, Albay, Camarines Norte and Sur, and Luzon.

ABOUT THE TRANSLATOR AND SPEAKER:

Clarita B Caraig

Age: 52   Recorded: 1998
Towns: Calabanga, Camarines Sur / Quezon City, Philippines

Clarita was born and raised in Calabanga. She currently works in Quezon City as an accountant.

Photo by Rody Toreres

At the Villa Escudero Resort in Batangas Province, visitors are offered BBQ pork, skewered fish and soups on buffet tables lined with banana leaves. Refreshing water runs underneath the tables where everyone eats

Bicolano, Albay

Nata ining bangging ini iba sa gabos na banggi?
- *Why is this night different from all other nights?*

Sa ibang mga banggi, nagkakaon kami ki tinapay o matza; ngunyang bangging ini, matza lang.
- *On all other nights we eat either leavened bread or matzah; on this night only matzah.*

Sa ibang mga banggi, nagkaon kita ki iba-ibang klase ki dahon; ngunyang banggi, mapait na dahon.
- *On all other nights we eat all kinds of herbs; on this night only bitter herbs.*

Sa ibang mga banggi, dai kita nagpalubog maski saro; ngunyang banggi, nagpalubog kita duwang beses.
- *On all other nights we do not dip even once; on this night we dip twice.*

Sa ibang mga banggi, nagkakaon kita na nakatukaw o nakaiigda; ngunyang banggi, nagkakaon kita na nakaigda.
- *On all other nights we eat either sitting up or reclining; on this night we recline.*

Sa gabos mga banggi, nagkakaon kitang ordinaryo; ngunyang banggi, nagkakaon kita na may espesyal na seremonyas.
- *On all other nights we eat in an ordinary manner; on this night we dine with special ceremony.*

The word *mga* was left out of some phrases in the recording. Those phrases represent the semantically similar "On other nights" rather than "On all other nights".

ABOUT THE LANGUAGE:

Albay Bicolano

Number of speakers: 1,900,000
Rank: 247

Albay Bicolano, also called Bikol Albay, is spoken in the Philippines, in Western Albay Province and Buhi, Camarines Sur and Luzon.

ABOUT THE TRANSLATOR AND SPEAKER:

Emmanuel A dela Rosa

Age: 20   Recorded: 1998
Towns: Legaspi, Albay / Quezon City, Philippines

Emmanuel was born and raised in Legaspi, Albay. He presently lives in Quezon City and was studying at the College of Music at the University of the Philippines.

In Manila's poorest area, Tondo District, children search garbage for valuables

Photo by Rody Torres

Bhojpuri

ई रात दूसर सब रात से अलग काहे बा?

■ Ee raat doosar sab raat se alag kahe ba?

■ *Why is this night different from all other nights?*

दूसर सब रात के हमनी के पावरोटी ना त रोटी खानी जा।
ई रात के हमनी खाली रोटी खानी जा।

■ Doosar sab raat ke humnee ke paawroti naa ta roti khani ja;
ee raat ke humnee khali roti khani ja.

■ *On all other nights we eat either leavened bread or matzah;*
on this night only matzah.

दूसर सब रात के हमनी के कुल तरह के जड़ी-बूटी खानी जा।
ई रात के हमनी खाली कड़ुवा जड़ी-बूटी खानी जा।

■ Doosar sab raat ke humnee ke kul taran ke jadee bootee khani ja;
ee raat ke humnee khalee kaduwa jadee bootee khani ja.

■ *On all other nights we eat all kinds of herbs;*
on this night only bitter herbs.

दूसर सब रात के हमनी के इकबार भी चटनी में बोर के ना खानी जा।
ई रात के हमनी दु बार चटनी में बोर के ना खानी जा।

■ Doosar sab raat ke humnee ke ekbaar bhee chutney mein bor ke naa khanee ja;
ee raat ke humnee doo baar chutney mein bor ke khanee ja.

■ *On all other nights we do not dip even once;*
on this night we dip twice.

दूसर सब रात के हमनी ऊपर बैठ के या कबो नीचे बैठ के खानी जा।
लेकनि ई रात के हमनी नीचे ही बैठ के खानी जा।

■ Doosar sab raat ke humnee oopar baith ke ya kabo neeche baith ke khani ja;
lekin ee raat ke humnee neeche hee baith ke khanee ja.

■ *On all other nights we eat either sitting up or reclining;*
on this night we recline.

दूसर कुल रात में हमनी के रोजें जइसन खानी जा।
ई रात हमनी के उत्सव मना के खानी जा।

■ Doosar kul raat mein humnee ke roz jaisan khanee ja;
ee raat humnee ke utsaw mana ke khanee ja.

■ *On all other nights we eat in an ordinary manner;*
on this night we dine with special ceremony.

ABOUT THE LANGUAGE:

Bhojpuri

Number of speakers: 38,546,000
Rank: 28

Bhojpuri is spoken in throughout India (Uttar Pradesh, Gorakhpur, Basti, Deoria and many other districts). It is also spoken by over 300,000 people in Mauritius and 1,700,000 people in Nepal.

ABOUT THE TRANSLATOR AND SPEAKER:

Binay Pandey

Age: 47   Recorded: 2007
Towns: Chapra (Bihar) / Jharkhand, India

Binay works as a senior manager for MECON, an architectural engineering firm in Jharkhand, India. An earlier translation was developed by **Sailesh Mishra**, Founder and President of Bhojpuri Association of North America.

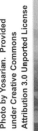

Photo by Yosarian. Provided under Creative Commons Attribution 3.0 Unported License

Kumbh Mela, a mass Hindu pilgrimage of 10 million people, is the largest gathering in the world. It takes place in Uttar Pradesh, located in the northern part of India

Bezhta

Вадло нішела водла' іле мӱх'чӓ иіякӓлас бӓбӓяги судалкӓс бӓбӓ;
Жеиса ніше мӱх'ча судалкас.

■ *On all other nights we eat either leavened bread or matzah;*
on this night only matzah.

Вадло нішела водла' іле ӥх'чӓ к'ацІо (батІі-батІіяб) бох;
Жеиса ніше ӥх'чӓ нік'аа бох.

■ *On all other nights we eat all kinds of herbs;*
on this night only bitter herbs.

Вадло нішела водлаа' іле цІя' гӓк'к'ана кен гіцІле'еш;
Жеиса ніше іле цІя' кІахна гіцІілло.

■ *On all other nights we do not dip even once;*
on this night we dip twice.

Вадло нішела водлаа' іле к'ей бечена ягі буватІія'к ӓӓ;
Жеиса ніше іле буватІца (буватІія'кӓа беясца).

■ *On all other nights we eat either sitting up or reclining;*
on this night we recline.

Вадло нішела водлаа' нітоназу беясцала'цой беясца;
Жеиса ніше іле бесца бесал нуцІоцала к'агІідалкӓ.

■ *On all other nights we eat in an ordinary manner;*
on this night we dine with special ceremony.

ABOUT THE LANGUAGE:

Bezhta

Number of speakers: 6,200
Rank: 3,488

Bezhta is spoken in southern Dagestan in Russia. It has no written language, so ' indicates a glottal stop after a vowel and doubled letters indicate lengthened durations.

ABOUT THE TRANSLATOR:

Mikhail Alekseev

Age: Unavailable   Translated: 1996
Town: Moscow, Russia

Dr. Alekseev, also known as Michael Alekseyev, is a Daghestanian language specialist at the Institute of Linguistics Russian Academy of Sciences, in Moscow.

Mikhail's translation was sent before documents could be sent by email. The Cyrillic characters were coded by an arcane set of ASCII codes that many Russians used to communicate with others outside Russia.

Photo © Susan Hantman

A view of the Kremlin in Moscow

Translation note: The initial question was not translated.

Bete-Bendi

Ekukolobo ele esene akukolo aso minde?

■ *Why is this night different from all other nights?*

Ekukolo okima aso biseledja mapa mo matzah; ekukolobo bisledja matzah nto.

■ *On all other nights we eat either leavened bread or matzah; on this night only matzah.*

Ekulolo okima eso biseledja ntchuosi; ekukolo bo biseledja ntchuosi ololo.

■ *On all other nights we eat all kinds of herbs; on this night only bitter herbs.*

Ekukolo okima aso bisekayo ntchuose ni; ekukolobo biseleyo ntchuosi mbale mwele.

■ *On all other nights we do not dip even once; on this night we dip twice.*

Ekuklol okima aso tous biseledja nto; ekukolobo biseledja njele njele mo nwara-nwara.

■ *On all other nights we eat either sitting up or reclining; on this night we recline.*

Ekukolo okima biselentchi; ekukolobo biselentchi njele njele nto.

■ *On all other nights we eat in an ordinary manner; on this night we dine with special ceremony.*

ABOUT THE LANGUAGE:

Bete-Bendi

Number of speakers: 36,800
Rank: 1,883

Bete-Bendi, called Mbete by its speakers, is spoken in Nigeria in Cross River State and the Obudu region.

ABOUT THE TRANSLATOR:

Larry Finkelstein

Age: Unavailable   Translated: 1996
Locations: NJ / Republic of Congo

Larry was raised in NJ. He worked in the Peace Corps, where he learned Mbete and Lingala while stationed in the Republic of Congo.

Photo © Damilare Onajole

At the sports complex of the University of Lagos, Nigerian children await their school's interhouse sports festival

Z Y X W V U T S R Q P O N M L K J I H G F E D C B A

Bengali

আজ রাত অন্নো কোন রাতের থেকে আলদা কেন ?

■ Aaj raat onno kono raater theke alada kono?

■ *Why is this night different from all the other nights?*

অন্নো কোন রাতে আমরা রুঠি বা মাট্যা খছি ,
কিন্তু আজ রাত আমরা শুধ মাট্যা খছি ।

■ Onno kono raate aamra ruti ba matzah khayi;
kintu aaj raate aamra shuddhu matzah khayi.

■ *On all other nights we eat either leavened bread or matzah;*
on this night only matzah.

অন্নো কোন রাতে আমরা নানান রকামর শাক শাবঝি খছি ,
কিন্তু আজ রাত আমরা একঠি বিশষ তেতো শাক খছি ।

■ Onno kono raate aamra naanan rokomer shaak shobji khayi;
kintu aaj raate aamra ekti bishesh teto shaak khayi.

■ *On all other nights we eat all kinds of herbs;*
on this night we eat bitter herbs.

অন্নো রাতে আমরা শাক শাক ডুবিায় খছি না ,
কিন্তু আজ রাত আমরা শাক ডুবার ডুবিায় খছি ।

■ Onno raate aamra shaak dubiye khayi na;
kintu aaj raate aamra shaak dubaar dubiye khayi.

■ On all other nights we do not dip herbs at all;
on this night we dip them twice.

অন্নো রাতে আমরা বাস হা শুয় খছি ,
কিন্তু আজ রাতে আমরা শুয় শুয় খছি ।

■ Onno raate aamra boshe ya shuye khayi;
kintu aaj raate aamra shuye shuye khayi.

■ On all other nights we eat either sitting up or leaning;
on this night we lean.

অন্নো রাতে আমরা সাধারন ভাবে খছি ,
কিন্তু আজ রাতে আমরা ফূর্তি ও উতসাবর সাঙা খছি ।

■ Onno raate aamra shadharan bhabe khayi;
kintu aaj raate aamra phurti o utshaber shonge khayi.

■ *On all other nights we eat in an ordinary manner;*
on this night we dine with special ceremony.

ABOUT THE LANGUAGE:

Bengali *

Number of speakers: 181,272,900
Rank: 6

Bengali is spoken in Bangladesh and in the West Bengal and Tripura regions of India, in Malawi, Nepal, Saudi Arabia, Singapore, United Arab Emirates, United Kingdom and the USA.

ABOUT THE TRANSLATOR AND SPEAKER:

Arindam Datta

Age: Unavailable   Recorded: 1997
Town: Hillsborough, NJ

Arindam was born and grew up in Calcutta, India and came to the USA at age 25. The text was typed by **Subir Das**.

* For additional information, see
"*Focus on ... pages.pdf*" on the DVD.

Photo c/o U.N. World Food Programme

Victims of the 1998 Bangladesh floods awaiting aid. These images remind us disasters can affect anyone in the world

Bemba

Ninshi uyu ubushiku tawulingenye na amasikuyonse?
- *Why is this night different from all other nights?*

Pa mashiku ena onse, tulalya umkate wa *bread* nangu *matzah*; pali uyu ubushiku, ni *matzah* fye.
- *On all other nights we eat either leavened bread or matzah; on this night only matzah.*

Pa mashiku ena onse, tulalya umnani uwa pusana pusana; pali uyu ubushiku, numunani walula fye.
- *On all other nights we eat all kinds of herbs; on this night only bitter herbs.*

Pa mashiku ena onse, tatutowela nangu kamo; pali uyu ubushiku, tulatowela imiku iwiri.
- *On all other nights we do not dip even once; on this night we dip twice.*

Pa mashiku ena onse, tulalya ninshi natuikele nangu natulala;
- *On all other nights we eat either sitting up or reclining;*

The Bemba translation received was incomplete.

ABOUT THE TRANSLATOR:

Zilore Mumba

Age: Unavailable   Translated: 2010
Town: Lusaka, Zambia

Zilore Mumba, born and raised in Zambia's capital city, Lusaka, works as the lead weather forecaster for an Africa-wide company. He speaks both Bemba and Nyanja.

ABOUT THE LANGUAGE:

Bemba

Number of speakers: 3,602,000
Rank: 165

Bemba is one of the two most common Zambian languages spoken around the capital city of Lusaka. Bemba is recognized for educational and administrative purposes, and is used widely.

Town Bemba (a variant includes English and neighboring Bantu languages) is widely used in urban areas, and has higher social status than other African languages. It is also spoken in Botswana, Democratic Republic of the Congo and Malawi.

Photo by Bernard Cloutier (berclo.net)

The international bridge between Zambia and Zimbabwe spans the Zambezi river a short distance downstream from Victoria Falls

Belarussian

Чаму гэта ноч адрознiваецца ад iншых начэй?
- Chamu geta noch adroznivaetsia ad drugih nachej?
- Why is this night different from other nights?

Ва ўсе iншыя вечары мы ядзiм хлеб прыгатаваны на заквасы або прэсны хлеб;
у гэты вечар толькi прэсны хлеб.
- Va wsie jinshyja viechary my jadzim hlieb prygatavany na zakvascy abo presny hlieb;
u gety viechar tolki presny hlieb.
- On all other nights we eat bread baked with yeast or unleavened bread;
this night we eat unleavened bread only.

Ва ўсе iншыя вечары мы ядзiм розную зелянiну;
у гэты вечар толькi горкую.
- Va wsie jinshyja viechary my jadzim roznuju zelianinu;
u gety viechar tolki gorkuju.
- On all other nights we eat all kinds of greens;
this night we eat only bitter greens.

Ва ўсе iншыя вечары мы не акунаем нават адзiн раз;
у гэты вечар мы акунаем двойчы.
- Va wsie jinshyja viechary my nie akunajemsia navat adzin raz;
u gety viechar my akunajemsia dvojchy.
- On all other nights we don't dip even once;
this night we dip twice.

Ва ўсе iншыя вечары мы ядзiм або сiдячы прама або адкiнуўшыся назад;
у гэты вечар мы адкiдваемся назад.
- Va wsie jinshyja viechary my jadzim abo siedziachy prama abo adkinuwshysia nazad;
u gety viechar my adkidvajemsia nazad.
- On all other nights we sit straight or lay back;
this night we lay back.

Ва ўсе iншыя вечары мы ядзiм у адвольнай манеры;
у гэты вечар мы абедаем з захаваннем асобага абраду.
- Va wsie jinshyja viechary my jadzim u advolinaj maniery;
u gety viechar my abiedajem z zahavanniem asobaga abradu.
- On all other nights we eat without following any formal structure;
this night we eat following a ritual.

Translation note: The recording uses акунаемся, which is the reflexive form of the verb to dip, e.g., *we don't dip ourselves.* Translation typing, gloss and translation note by **Valerij Glinskij** of Minsk, now living in South Brunswick, NJ, with additional corrections by **Valerie Rose Grier**, of Liga, Belarus, now in NJ.

ABOUT THE LANGUAGE:

Belarussian

Number of speakers: 8,618,630
Rank: 92

Belarussian is spoken in Belarus (literally "White Russia"), as well as in 15 other countries, such as Russia, Poland, Turkmenistan, Tajikistan, Urkaine, Canada and the USA. Jews and Yiddish played a prominent part of Belarus – until WW II, Yiddish was one of the four official state languages.

ABOUT THE TRANSLATOR:

Alexander Podluzhnyj

Age: Unavailable   Recorded: 1997
Town: Minsk, Belarus

Dr. Podluzhnyj is the Director of the Belarussian Linguistic Institute Academy of Sciences in Minsk.

ABOUT THE SPEAKER:

Boris M Lobanov

Age: Unavailable   Recorded: 1997
Town: Minsk, Belarus

Dr. Lobanov obtained the translation from Alexander Podluzhnyj.

Photo © Barry Hantman

Yanka Kupala's Park – monument to Belarus' most famous poet

Batak Toba

Boasa borngin on   asing   sian borngin na   asing?
- Why   night this different   from night   that's other?
- Boasa borngin on a'sik sian borngin na 'asing?

Di borngin na asing, ta-allang   do roti na   mar-ragi   manang roti tawar;
- On night   other,   we-eat bread that's with-yeast or   bread unleavened;

molo   borngin on, holan roti tawar do.
- as for night   this, only bread unleavened.
- Di borngin nasing, ta'allanggo roti na marragi manang roti tawar;
  molo borngin on, holar roti tawar do.

Di borngin na asing, ta-allang do sude na rata;
- On night   other,   we-eat   all   greens;

molo   borngin on, holan na   paet do.
- as for night   this, only ones   bitter.
- Di borngin nasing, ta'allanggo sude na ra'ta;
  molo borngin on, holanna paeq do.

Di borngin na asing, ndang boi   manombur   hita manang sahali;
- On night   other,   not allowed   dip   we   even   once;

molo   borngin on, manombur ma hita dua hali.
- as for night   this,   dip   we two   times.
- Di brongin nasing, dak boi manobbur hita manak sahali;
  molo borngin on, manobbur ma hita dua hali.

Di borngin na asing, boi hita mangan sambil hundul manang galle;
- On night   other, may we   eat   while   seated   or not straight (reclining);

molo   borngin on, hita ingkon galle.
- as for night   this, we   must   recline.
- Di borngin nasing, boi hita mangas sabbil huddul manang 'galle;
  molo borngin on, hita ikkon 'galle.

Di borngin na asing, hita mangan biasa;
- On night   other, we   eat ordinarily;

molo   borngin on, hita mangan mar-las   ni roha.
- as for night   this, we   eat with-happiness of heart.
- Di borngin nasing, hita mangab biasa;
  molo borngin on, hita mangam marlas ni roha.

The last lines illustrate pronunciations in fluent speech; e.g., *na asing* becomes *nasing* and *ta-allang do* becomes *ta'allanggo*.

ABOUT THE LANGUAGE:

Batak Toba

Number of speakers: 2,000,000
Rank: 232

Batak Toba is spoken on islands in Indonesia: Samosir Island and in north Sumatra, all areas of Toba Lake except the north.

Batak's syllabic alphabet, used only by the *Datu* (priests) for calendars and magical texts, is written from bottom to top in vertical columns running from left to right on strips of bamboo held together with string.

ABOUT THE TRANSLATOR AND SPEAKER:

Wilson Manik

Age: 46   Recorded: 1999
Towns: Sangkal, Simanindo, Lake Toba / Yogakarta, Java / Ithaca, NY

Wilson was born and raised in the village of Sangkal, Simanindo, located on the island of Samosir, Lake Toba. At age 17, he moved to Yogakarta in central Java to attend high school and college. Wilson came to the USA at age 27. Batak Toba is Wilson's first language.

Photo by Tom Judd

Washing dishes in the rural areas of Indonesia

Bassa

Mãnã gair amɔ mã akokaklo. Dɛkpa?

■ Tonight is different from other nights. Why?

Mã mã doh air bla ah di ble doo sɔ̃.
Gɛblɛ doo sɔ̃blɛ dia duado ɔ say jandair blay.
Kayma tiair moɛ̃ blɛ ɔ gnɔ̃ah deer ɔ blay jandair.

■ On other nights we eat two kinds of bread.
  One bread has yeast in it, and the other bread does not have yeast in it.
  Tonight the bread we eat does not have yeast in it.

Mã dwehbla saar day adiair vaor ɔ kiandi ɔ mɔ̃vaar kiandi;
mãnã gair vaar ah deer ɔ nɛ̃.

■ On other nights we eat different kinds of greens;
  Tonight the greens we eat, it bitter.

Bo mã gnonãgɛ apo adidior toniordo woka deer;
gayma kowear mã muɛ̃ didior adia apo nay didior tɔ̃moo kpa
sɔ̃wokay adiair.

■ On other nights we do not put our food in salt water before we eat it;
  Tonight we put our food in salt water two times before we eat it.

Mã niakɛ ah say yee koji kay ah kay day dee kay adidair;
mã niake muɛ̃ ah say yee kojo kay ah taydio kay adidair.

■ On other nights we can sit down and we can lie on our back when we eat something;*
  Tonight we must lie on our back when we eat something.

Mã gnonakair ah say bar kay adidair;
kairboma doo ma noo eh ah blay baba kpa dare way kar adidiar.

■ On other nights we do not have special ceremony when we eat something;
  Tonight we have special ceremony when we eat something.

---

* In *Bassa*, as in all Liberian languages, the verb 'eat' cannot stand alone, but must take an object; *adidiar* ('something') is used here. The reference to lying down is strongly reminiscent of the Roman custom of eating, which is the basis for our current terminology, 'reclining'.

Pronunciation guide:
ɔ as in "or" (short)
ɔ̃ as in nasalized "on" ("n" silent)
ɛ as in "air" (short)
ɛ̃ as in nasal "air" (short)

ABOUT THE LANGUAGE:

Bassa

Number of speakers: 408,730
Rank: 604

Bassa is spoken in central Liberia, in Grand Bassa, Rivercess and Montserrado counties. Bassa is also spoken in Sierra Leone.

Bassa was the first Liberian language in which the Bible was translated. It is the largest linguistic group that is indigenous to Liberia. (Liberia was founded by freed American slaves.)

Bassa was written in an indigenous *Vah* script, which fell out of use in the 19th C. In the 1900s, a Bassa named Dr. Flo Darvin Lewis discovered former slaves in Brazil and the West Indies were using *Vah*. Dr. Lewis revived the alphabet in Liberia; currently it is recognized only by the older men. A phonetic transcription is shown here.

ABOUT THE TRANSLATOR AND SPEAKER:

Madia Smith-Brown

Age: 57   Recorded: 2005
Towns: Buchanan, Liberia / Charlotte, NC

Madia was born in Grand Bassa County, in the city of Buchanan. She came to the USA at age 43.

The phonetic transcription was provided by Liberian **Jim Nyema-Davies**, currently of Greensboro, NC.

Photo by Jim Nyema-Davies

Eighth grade in the nationally prominent B.W. Harris school in Monrovia, Liberia. All Liberian schools require uniforms

Basque

Zergatik da gau hau beste guztiak ez bezalakoa?

■ all, every

■ *Why is this night different from all other nights?*

Gainerako gau guztietan ogi legamiatua edo matzah jaten dugu; gaur matzah bakarrik.

■ only

■ *On all other nights we eat either leavened bread or matzah; on this night only matzah.*

Gainerako gau guztietan moeta guzietako belarrak jaten ditugu; gaur belar mikatzak bakarrik.

■ *On all other nights we eat all kinds of herbs; on this night only bitter herbs.*

Gainerako gau guztietan ez dugu behin ere bustitzen;

■ even once

gaur bi aldiz.

■ *On all other nights we do not dip even once; on this night we dip twice.*

Gainerako gau guztietan zuzen eserita edo etzanda jaten dugu; gaur etzanda.

■ *On all other nights we eat either sitting up or reclining; on this night we recline.*

Gainerako gau guztietan era arruntean jaten dugu; gaur zeremonia bereziz.

■ *On all other nights we eat in an ordinary manner; on this night we dine with special ceremony.*

ABOUT THE LANGUAGE:

Basque / Eskara

Number of speakers: 658,960
Rank: 467

Basque, also called Euskara and Vascuense, is spoken along the border of France and Spain. There are three primarily Basque provinces: Alava (Araba), Biskaia (Biskay) and Gipuzkoa. In addition, Basque is spoken in the northern area of Navarra (Nafarroa) in north-central Spain. It also has speakers in Australia, Costa Rica, Mexico, Philippines and the USA.

Of the European languages, Basque is unique in not being linguistically related to any other language, a remarkable fact in light of how much is known about the movement of peoples into and within Europe.

ABOUT THE TRANSLATOR AND SPEAKER:

Miren Lourdes Oñederra

Age: Unavailable   Recorded: 1996
Town: Vitoria-Gasteiz, Spain

Dr. Oñederra is a linguist at the University of the Basque Country. He has published widely on the Basque language. He is a native speaker of Basque and Spanish and is proficient in English, French and German.

An earlier translation was provided by an unnamed friend of **Jesus Lopez** of Spain.

Photo © Niko Lipsanen

The village of Valcarlos in Spain's Basque country

Punapi wengine mangkin tios ring wengi-wengine sane lintang?

■ *Why is this night different from all other nights?*

Wengi-wengine sane lintang, iraga ngajeng roti utawi matsa; wengine mangkin, matsa kewanten.

■ *On all other nights we eat either leavened bread or matzah; on this night only matzah.*

Wengi-wengine sane lintang, iraga ngajeng saluir loloh; wengine mangkin, loloh pait kewanten.

■ *On all other nights we eat all kinds of herbs; on this night only bitter herbs.*

Wengi-wengi sane lintang, nenten apisan iraga nyelebang; wengine mangkin, iraga nyelebang ping kalih.

■ *On all other nights we do not dip even once; on this night we dip twice.*

Wengi-wengine sane lintang, iraga ngajeng sambilang melinggih utawi nyeleleg; wengine mangkin, iraga ngajeng sambilang nyeleleg.

■ *On all other nights we eat either sitting up or reclining; on this night we recline.*

Wengi-wengine sane lintang, iraga ngajeng abiasaan; wengine mangkin, iraga ngajeng maupacara.

■ *On all other nights we eat in an ordinary manner; on this night we dine with special ceremony.*

ABOUT THE LANGUAGE:

Bali

Number of speakers: 3,330,000
Rank: 171

Bali (or Balinese) is spoken in Indonesia (the islands of Bali and Java), as well as northern Nusapenida, western Lombok Islands and south Sulawesi.

Bali's original *Carakan* alphabet descended from ancient India's *Brahmi* script, by way of *Pallava* and *Old Kawi* scripts. The oldest known inscriptions date from the 11th C, but are thought to be reproductions of texts written even earlier on palm leaves. Few people can now read the original alphabet as the Latin alphabet has supplanted it.

An interesting aspect of Balinese, like Javanese, is its speech-level system. It has an elaborate vocabulary reflecting social aspects. For example, there are more than five forms for the first person pronoun, depending on whether the speaker is a low, middle or high caste and whether the listener / person talked about is low, middle or high caste. Clever speakers can relate subtle feelings and social dimensions.

ABOUT THE TRANSLATOR AND SPEAKER:

I Wayan Arka

Age: 30s   Recorded: 1995
Town: village near Denpasar, Bali / Sydney, Australia / Stanford, CA

Wayan grew up in a village 8 km north of the capital city of Denpasar. He was a linguistics student at the University of Sydney. Wayan, a native Balinese, acquired Bali first. As he was educated in Indonesian and has used it over a quarter of century, his Indonesian communicative competence is much better than Bali. The reason is Bali uses a speech level system that is hard to use. Wayan uses both Indonesian and Balinese with his family, and more recently, English with his daughter.

Photo courtesy of Tom Hoogervorst

A traditional procession at Kuta beach, on the island of Bali

Azerbaijani

Bu gece pütün ayrı gecelerden niye ferglidi?

- *Why is this night different from all other nights?*

**Pütün ayrı gecelerde biz ya mayali çöreyh yiverih ya da mayasız;
Bu gece de, tekçe mayasız.**

- *On all other nights we eat either leavened bread or matzah;
on this night only matzah.*

**Pütün ayrı gecelerde biz her cür sebziler yiyerih;
Bu gece de, tekçe acılı sebziler.**

- *On all other nights we eat all kinds of herbs;
on this night only bitter herbs.*

**Pütün ayrı gecelerde biz bir kere bile batırmanığ;
Bu gece de, iki kere batırariğ.**

- *On all other nights we do not dip even once;
on this night we dip twice.*

**Pütün ayrı gecelerde biz ya düz oturup yiyerih yada söykerereyh;
Bu gece de, söykenereyh.**

- *On all other nights we eat either sitting up or reclining;
on this night we recline.*

**Pütün ayrı gecelerde biz cürbecür halda horeyh yiyerih;
Bu gece de, bir merasimle yeyirih.**

- *On all other nights we eat in any ordinary manner;
on this night we dine with special ceremony.*

ABOUT THE LANGUAGE:

Azerbaijani

Number of speakers: 7,473,270
Rank: 103

Azerbaijani is spoken in Iran and Azerbaijan, as well as Afghanistan, Iraq, Jordan, Syria, Turkey and the USA.

ABOUT THE TRANSLATOR AND SPEAKER:

Ercüment Kılıç

Age: 38   Recorded: 1996
Towns: Ankara, Turkey / Centreville, VA

Ercüment Kılıç learned Azerbaijani from his parents. He was raised in Ankara, Turkey, came to the USA in 1977 to get a college education and graduated from the University of Texas at Austin. In 2004, he became President of the Assembly of Turkish American Associations, the umbrella organization for 57 Turkish-American associations across America.

Ercüment is known for his contributions to the promotion of Turkic culture worldwide. He received training in music and dance at an early age. Before arriving in the USA, he was also a member of the Turkish National Ensemble. Ercüment has presented seminars and lectures in all 50 states of the USA, and in Canada, England, Germany, Switzerland, Holland, Hong Kong, Taiwan and Japan. He has also produced a number of musical recordings with his orchestra, which have been made available to musicologists in many countries.

He has written various cultural articles that have been published in a number of languages.

Used by permission of Ercüment Kılıç

Ercüment performs dances of Azerbaijan in ethnic costume

Awutu

Idwo miɛna bɔ na ade enuntɔ mo maahata enuntɔ sɛnsie ne fuu a?

■ *Why is this night different from all other nights?*

Enuntɔ ko afa ane di paanoa nkaw ntoo maasa;
ade enuntɔ mo de maasa wire.

■ *On all other nights we eat either leavened bread or matzah;*
on this night only matzah.

Enuntɔ ko afa nkyɛane dɛmfetamfeta mforaforae bɔ ane edutɔ;
ade* enuntɔ ɔmo wire de ane di mfetamfeta abɔ wen.

■ *On all other nights we eat all kinds of herbs;*
on this night only bitter herbs.

Enuntɔ bratɛko bo a ane meedi atɔ kome mpo;
ade enuntɔ mo de ane di atɔ nwiɔ.

■ *On all other nights we do not dip even once;*
on this night we dip twice.

Enuntɔ ko afa ane sina ase di atɔ ntoo ane twer ase;
ade enuntɔ ɔmo wire de ane twer ase di atɔ.

■ *On all other nights we eat either sitting up or reclining;*
on this night we recline.

Enuntɔ ko afa ane di atɔ ko na ko afa;
ka enuntɔ ɔmo de ane dwuo ane ase bo nwora worae
edi amo bɔ ane atɔdi ne wo.

■ *On all other nights we eat in an ordinary manner;*
on this night we dine with special ceremony.

---

*ade was missing from two lines in
the original text, but was added by the
authors on the basis of consistency.

ABOUT THE LANGUAGE:

Awutu

Number of speakers: 180,000
Rank: 930

Awutu (also called Efutu and Senya) is spoken along
the coast of Ghana and west of Accra.

ABOUT THE TRANSLATOR AND SPEAKER:

Robert Mensah

Age: Unavailable   Recorded: 2002
Town: Winneba, Ghana

Robert works for the Effutu programme of Radio Peace.

Photo by Samson Okoh

**The Adomi Bridge, southern tip of
Lake Volta, in southeast Ghana**

Avar

Щай гьаб къасимех бугеб батӏияб дал късимехаялдаса?

■ ššay hab q'xsimex bugeb bat'ijab dal q'xsimexayaldasa?

■ *Why is this night different from all other nights?*

Дал къасимехаль нижь кунана чалалги мацаги;
гьаб къасимехлъ маца.

■ dal q'xasimexaɬ niž kunana čadalgi matsagi;
hab q'xasimexaɬ matsa.

■ *On all other nights we eat either leavened bread or matzah;*
on this night only matzah.

Дал къасимехаль нижь кунана баӏиял хурдул;
гьаб къасимехлъ тӏагӏан гьечил хурдал.

■ dal q'xasimexaɬ niž kunana bat'iyal xurdul;
hab q'xasimexaɬ t'ag'an xeč'il xurdal.

■ *On all other nights we eat all kinds of herbs;*
on this night only bitter herbs.

Дал къасимехаль нижь чуна цо нухалъ;
гьаб къасимехлъ нижь чуна кӏиго нухалъ.

■ dal q'xasimexaɬ niž čuna tso nuxaɬ;
hab q'xasimexaɬ niž čuna k'igo nuxaɬ.

■ *On all other nights we do not dip even once;*
on this night we dip twice.

Дал къасимехаль нижь кунана гӏодорчӏонги регунчи;
гьаб къасимехлъ нижь кунана речун.

■ dal q'xasimexaɬ niž kunana čodorč'ongi regunči;
hab q'xasimexaɬ niž kunana rečun.

■ *On all other nights we eat either sitting up or reclining;*
on this night we recline.

Дал къасимехаль нижь кунана гӏадаталда рекъон;
гьаб къасимехлъ нижь кунана батӏаго.

■ dal q'xasimexaɬ niž kunana čadatalda req'xon;
hab q'xasimexaɬ niž kunana bat'ago.

■ *On all other nights we eat in an ordinary manner;*
on this night we dine with special ceremony.

ABOUT THE LANGUAGE:

Avar

Number of speakers: 788,960
Rank: 427

Avar (also called Dagestani) is spoken in Dagestan in Russia, specifically southern Dagestan and the Terek and Sulak river areas. Avar is also spoken in Azerbaijan, Kazakhstan and Turkey.

Avar was written with the Old Georgian alphabet from the 15th C and with the Arabic alphabet from the 17th C until the early 20th C. Between 1928 and 1938, the Latin alphabet was used, then the Cyrillic alphabet became standard.

ABOUT THE TRANSLATOR AND SPEAKER:

Madina Vadachkoria

Age: Unavailable   Recorded: 1997
Towns: Gunib / Makhachkala, Daghestan / Seattle, WA

Madina was born in Gunib, Daghestan. When she was 5, Madina moved to the capital of Daghestan, Makhachkala, near the Caspian Sea. As an adult, she moved to the USA.

Young Russian dance students touring Bulgaria put on an impromptu performance

Asturian

Translated from Spanish

¿Por quénun siasemeya esta nueche a les otres?

■ *¿Por qué es diferente esta noche de todas las otras noches?*

Toles otres nueches xintamos pan fecho con formientu o pan ensin lleldar; esta nueche namái pan ensin formientu.

■ *En todas las otras noches comemos pan hecho con levadura o pan ázimo; en esta noche solamente matzah.*

Toles otres nueches tomamos toa triba de yerbes aromátiques; esta nueche namái yerbes marguxes.

■ *En todas las otras noches comemos todas clases de hierbas; en esta noche comemos hierbas amargas.*

Toles otres nueches nun les somorguiamos nin una vez; esta nueche somorguiámoles dos vegaes.

■ *En todas las otras noches no sumergimos las hierbas de ninguna manera; en esta noche las sumergimos dos veces.*

Toles otres nueches xintamos sentaos, derechos o inclinaos; esta nueche sentámonos inclinaos.

■ *En todas las otras noches comemos sentados rectos o inclinados; en esta noche nos sentamos inclinados.*

Toles otres nueches xintamos normal; esta nueche facémoslo d'un mou especial.

■ *En todas las otras noches comemos de manera ordinaria; en esta noche comemos con ceremonia especial.*

ABOUT THE LANGUAGE:

Asturian

Number of speakers: 125,000
Rank: 1,099

Asturian, also called Astur-Leonese, is spoken within Spain, in the Princedom of Asturias (outside the western areas where Galician is spoken), the western part of Cantabria and Leon and northern Castilla-Leon. Asturian is as different from Spanish as Galician and Catalan.

Asturian literature, in the form of poetry, ballads and oral novels, dates from the 17th C.

ABOUT THE TRANSLATOR AND SPEAKER:

Xosé Lluis García Arias

Age: 53   Recorded: 1998
Towns: Monticiellu (Teberga) / Oviedo, Spain

Xosé Lluis is a lecturer in Spanish Philology at the University of Oviedo, Spain. Dr. García Arias is the Director of the Academy of Asturian Language. (The Academy was formed in 1981 to revive a similar academy of the 18th C.)

Flamenco dancers in Seville, Spain

Assyrian

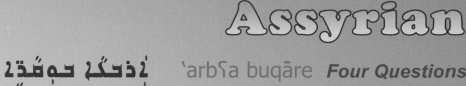

ܝ݇ܐܪܒ݂ܥܐ ܒܘܩܪ̈ܐ ‍ **'arbʕa buqāre** *Four Questions*

ABOUT THE LANGUAGE:

Assyrian *

Number of speakers: 219,330
Rank: 844

Assyrian (Neo-Aramaic) is spoken in Iraq and in 25 countries, including Armenia, Georgia, Iran and Syria. The Assyrian and Chaldean sects separated denominationally in the 16th C.

ABOUT THE TRANSLATOR AND SPEAKER:

Daniel Benjamin

Age: 73   Recorded: 2000
Towns: Mosul / Kirkuk, Iraq / Kuwait / Des Plaines, IL

Daniel is a native speaker of Assyrian. He was born in Mosul, in northern Iraq. He completed his studies of the Assyrian language at the Assyrian Seminary, run by the famous Assyrian Scholar, Reverend Joseph De Kelaita. He moved to Kirkuk, Iraq, and later lived in Kuwait. Daniel moved to the USA in 1988.

ܩܡ̇ܕܝ ܦܪܝܫܠܗ ܐܗܐ ܠܠܐ ܡܢ ܠܠܘܬܐ ܐ̣ܚܢܐ؟
- ■ qamṭdi prišele 'aha lele min lelawate xene?
- ■ *Why is this night different from all other nights?*

ܒܟܘܠܗ ܠܠܘܬܐ ܐ̣ܚܢܐ ܠܐ ܛܡ̇ܫܠܢ ܐܦܠܐ ܚܕܐ ܓܗܐ؛ ܐܝܢܐ ܒ ܐܗܐ ܠܠܐ ܛܡ̇ܫܠܢ ܬܪܬܐ ܓܗܐ.
- ■ bkeulle lelawate xene la ṭmišlan 'apla xda gaha; 'ina b 'aha lele ṭmišlan terte gahe.
- ■ *On all other nights we do not dip even once; on this night we dip twice.*

ܒܟܘܠܗ ܠܠܘܬܐ ܐ̣ܚܢܐ ܐ̇ܟ݂ܠܚܘܐ ܟܘܠܗ ܐܕ݂ܫܐ ܕ ܝܪܩܐ؛ ܐܝܢܐ ܒ ܐܗܐ ܠܠܐ ܝܪܩܐ ܡܪܝܪܐ ܒܠܟ݂ܬܕ.
- ■ bkeulle lelawate xene 'axlaxwa kulle 'adše d yarqe; 'ina b 'aha lele yarqe marīre balxṭd.
- ■ *On all other nights we eat all kinds of herbs; on this night only bitter herbs.*

ܒܟܘܠܗ ܠܠܘܬܐ ܐ̣ܚܢܐ ܐ̇ܟ݂ܠܚܘܐ ܠܚܡܐ ܚܡܝܥܐ ܐܘ ܦܛܝܪܐ؛ ܐܝܢܐ ܒ ܐܗܐ ܠܠܐ ܠܚܡܐ ܦܛܝܪܐ ܒܠܟ݂ܬܕ.
- ■ bkeulle lelawate xene 'axlaxwa laxma xmi'a aw patīra; 'ina b 'aha lele laxma patīra balxṭd.
- ■ *On all other nights we eat either leavened bread or matzah; on this night only matzah.*

ܒܟܘܠܗ ܠܠܘܬܐ ܐ̣ܚܢܐ ܐ̇ܟ݂ܠܝܚܘܐ ܝܕܥܝܕ؛ ܐܝܢܐ ܒ ܐܗܐ ܠܠܐ ܒܝܟ݂ܠܘܚ ܒܙܘܚܐ ܦܪܝܫܐ.
- ■ bkeulle lelawate xene 'axlixwa 'yada'id; 'ina b 'aha lele bixalewax bzawxa priša.
- ■ *On all other nights we eat in an ordinary manner; on this night we dine with special ceremony.*

ܒܟܘܠܗ ܠܠܘܬܐ ܐ̣ܚܢܐ ܐ̇ܟ݂ܠܝܚܘܐ ܘ ܐ̇ܚܢܢ ܬܝܘܐ ܐ̇ܘ ܓܝܢܝܐ؛ ܐܝܢܐ ܒ ܐܗܐ ܠܠܐ ܐ̇ܚܢܢ ܓܝܢܝܘܚ.
- ■ bkeulle lelawate xene 'axlixwa w 'axnan tiwe 'aw ginye; 'aina b 'aha lele 'axnan ginyewax.
- ■ *On all other nights we eat either sitting up or reclining; on this night we recline.*

In the recordings: Daniel ends his recording with his name and that of the language, spoken in Assyrian.

Pronunciation guide:
ã = vowels with macron indicates lengthening
š = "sh"
` = glottal stop
x = "ch" as in German word "nacht" or Arabic ح
ʕ = voiced pharyngeal fricative shown by Arabic ع
ṭ = an emphatic "t" found in Semitic languages shown by Arabic ط
q = hard guttural sound found in Semitic languages shown by Arabic ق

Photos © Jan Oberg

Playing cards, reading and talking in Baghdad's *Café Shah Bender*

Two men conversing in *Shah Bender*

* For additional information, see *"Focus on ... pages.pdf"* on the DVD.

Assamese

আজিব ৰাতিটো আন সকলো ৰাতিতকৈ কিয় বেলেগ?
- Aajir raatitu aan xokolu raatitokoi kiyo beleg?
- *Why is this night different from all other nights?*

আন ৰাতি আমি পাউৰুঠি বা মৎসা খাঙু।
আজি কেৱল মৎসা।
- Aan raati aami paauruti baa maat-suh khaaõ;
  Aaji kewal maat-suh.
- *On all other nights we eat either leavened bread or matzah;
  on this night only matzah.*

আন ৰাতি আমি সকলো শাক-পাচলি খাঙু।
আজি কেৱল তিতা শাক।
- Aan raati aami xokolu xaak-paasoli khaaõ;
  Aaji kewal titaa xaak.
- *On all other nights we eat all kinds of herbs;
  on this night only bitter herbs.*

আন ৰাতি আমি ধনীয়া শাক লোন পনীত নিতিয়াঙু।
আজি দুবাৰ তিয়াম।
- Aan raati aami dhoniyaa xaak lun-paanit nitiyaaõ;
  Aaji dubaar tiyaam.
- *On all other nights we do not dip even once;
  on this night we dip twice.*

আন ৰাতি আমি পোনহৈ বা আৰামকৈ বহি খাঙু।
আজি আৰামকৈ বহি।
- Aan raati aami punhoi baa aaraamkoi bohi khaaõ;
  Aaji araamkoi bohi.
- *On all other nights we eat either sitting up or reclining;
  on this night we recline.*

আন ৰাতি আমি সাধাৰনকৈ খাঙু।
আজি পৰম আড়ম্বৰেৰে।
- Aan raati aami xaadhaaronkoi khaaõ;
  Aaji param aaramborere.
- *On all other nights we eat in an ordinary manner;
  on this night we dine with special ceremony.*

About the Language:

Assamese *

Number of speakers: 16,818,750
Rank: 56

Assamese is one of the national languages of India. It is primarily spoken in the states of Assam, Meghalaya and Arunachal Pradesh. It is also spoken in Bangladesh and Bhutan.

About the Translator:

Jugal Kalita

Age: Unavailable   Translated: 1996
Towns: Assam province, India / Colorado Springs, CO

Dr. Kalita is an Assistant Professor at the University of Colorado in Colorado Springs.

* For additional information, see "*Focus on ... pages.pdf*" on the DVD.

Illustration by Alysa Lerman

Navagraha Temple, the temple of nine planets on Chitra Chal Hill, Guwahati, Assam. In ancient times, the temple was a great center for astronomy and astrology

ASL (American Sign Language)

The accompanying DVD contains a video of Marla Berkowitz signing the Four Questions in American Sign Language. She also explains the background behind Passover and the two new signs she created for its interpretation.

ABOUT THE LANGUAGE:

American Sign Language

Number of users: 100,000 – 500,000 primary users
Rank: 536

American Sign Language (ASL) is used in the USA and a few other countries. There are an estimated 2,000,000 profoundly deaf persons in the USA, with upwards of 15 million having some hearing handicap (hard of hearing). There is also a Black American Sign Language, a Tactile Sign Language (used by several hundred persons who knew ASL but lost their sight), and several systems of manually coded English, such as Signed English and Pidgin Signed English.

There are several schools devoted to the deaf, most notably Gallaudet University. Some elementary and high schools teach ASL; a few, such as St. Louis' Central Institute for the Deaf, are exclusively oral schools.

ABOUT THE TRANSLATOR AND SIGNER:

Marla Berkowitz

Age: 30s   Recorded: 1997
Town: New York, NY

Marla was born and raised in New York City. She studied at Gallaudet University and received a Masters in Deaf Education from New York University. Marla was the first deaf student at the Jewish Theological Seminary, where she received her second Masters in Jewish Education with a specialization in Jewish Deaf Education. Marla directs the deaf programming at B'nai Jeshurun Synagogue, is Chazzan of the Deaf for the larger community, and does crisis intervention support for Deaf, Deaf-Blind and Hard of Hearing programs for the New York Society for the Deaf (NYSD).

Arrernte, Eastern

Ingwe nhenhe ingwe arrpenhareyenge arrpenhe-ulkere iwenhengarle?

■ *Why is this night different from all other nights?*

**Ingwe arrpenhelareye anwerne merne uthene tampe uthene arlkweme.
Ingwe nhenhele tampante arlkweme.**

■ *On all other nights we eat either leavened bread or matzah;
on this night only matzah.*

**Ingwe arrpenhelareye anwerne atherrke-areye arlkweme.
Ingwe nhenhele atherrke irrkerteye ante arlkweme.**

■ *On all other nights we eat all kinds of herbs;
on this night only bitter herbs.*

**Ingwe arrpenhelareye anwerne thwekem-iletyakenhe.
Ingwe nhenhele atherrengare thwekeme-ileme.**

■ *On all other nights we do not dip even once;
on this night we dip twice.*

**Ingwe arrpenhelareye anwerne anemele arlkweme irlkanye intemele apeke.
Ingwe nhenhele, anwerne irlkanye intemele arlkweme.**

■ *On all other nights we eat either sitting up or reclining;
on this night we recline.*

**Ingwe arrpenhelareye anwerne akwetetharle arlkweparlkweme-arteke arlkweme.
Ingwe nhenhele anwerne ceremony impene-akertele arlkweme.**

■ *On all other nights we eat in an ordinary manner;
on this night we dine with special ceremony.*

ABOUT THE LANGUAGE:

Eastern Arrernte

Number of speakers: 3,820
Rank: 3,991

Eastern Arrernte, also called Aranda and Arunta, is spoken in Australia's Northern Territory, specifically the areas of Alice Springs, Santa Teresa and Hats Range.

ABOUT THE TRANSLATOR AND SPEAKER:

Veronica Dobson

Age: 56   Recorded: 2001
Town: Alice Springs, NT, Australia

Veronica's native tongue is Arrernte. She learned English as a child at the Catholic Mission. She works part-time at the Institute for Aboriginal Development.

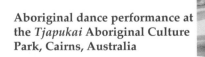

Aboriginal dance performance at the *Tjapukai* Aboriginal Culture Park, Cairns, Australia

Armenian

Ինչո՞վ է տարբերվում այս գիշերը բոլոր մյուսներից:

- Eenchov-eh tarbervoom aees geesheruh bolor meeyoosnereets?
- Why is this night different from all other nights?

Բոլոր Մյուս գիշերներն երը մենք կարող ենք ուրել թթխմորա կամ առանց թթխմորահացը,

իսկ այս գիշերը Միայն թթխմորահացը:

- Bolor meeyoos geesherneruh menk karogh-enk ootoom tuhtuhkhmora kam voch tuhtuhkhmorahatsuh; eesk aeesor meeaeen voch tuhtuhkhmorahatsuh.
- On all other nights we eat either leavened bread or matzah; on this night only matzah.

Բոլոր Մյուս գիշերները մենք ուտրում ենք ամեն տեսակի կանաչեղեն, իսկ այս գիշերը Միայն դառնահամ կանաչեղեն:

- Bolor meeyoos geesherneruh menk ootoom-enk ammen tesakee banjareghen; eesk aeesor meeaeen daruh kanacheghen.
- On all other nights we eat all kinds of greens; on this night only bitter greens.

Բոլոր Մյուս գիշերներ մենք ոչ մի անգան չենք թաթախում կանաչեղեն, իսկ այս գիշերը թաթախում ենք երկու անգամ:

- Bolor meeyoos geesherneruh menk voch mee angam chenk tatakhoom; eesk aeesor tatakhoom-enk krknagee angam.
- On all other nights we do not dip vegetables even once; on this night we dip twice.

Բոլոր Մյուս գիշերներ մենք ուտրում ենք նստաց կամ հենվաց, իսկ այս գիշերը Մենք բոլորս հենվում ենք:

- Bolor meeyoos geesherneruh menk ootoom-enk nuhstadz kam henvadz; eesk aeesor menk boloruhs henvoom-enk.
- On all other nights we eat either sitting up or reclining; on this night we recline.

Բոլոր Մյուս գիշերները մենք ուտրում ենք բնական Ձեւով, իսկ այս գիշերը Մենք Ճաշում ենք դարբեր նրշանակուրթյամբ:

- Bolor meeyoos geesherneruh menk ootoom-enk buhnakan dzevov; eesk aees geesheruh menk jashoom-enk masnavor araroghooteechamp.
- On all other nights we eat in an ordinary manner; on this night we dine with special manner.

Z Y X W V U T S R Q P O N M L K J I H G F E D C B A

ABOUT THE LANGUAGE:

Armenian, Eastern

Number of speakers: 6,376,520
Rank: 112

Armenian, called Hayeren by its speakers, is the national language of Armenia. There are two dialects: Eastern is spoken within Armenia, the Caucuses, Iran and China; Western Armenian is spoken elsewhere (Cyprus, Iraq, Israel, Jordon, Lebanon, etc.).

Around 404-406 CE, Mesrop Mashtots, a cleric at the Armenian royal court, invented the Armenian alphabet. He modeled the Armenian alphabet loosely on the Greek and possibly Assyrian alphabets.

ABOUT THE TRANSLATOR AND SPEAKER:

Tom Bozigian

Age: 60s   Recorded: 1998
Town: Los Angeles, CA

Tom was born in Los Angeles to Armenian parents from Gumri-Alexandropol and Kharpert (East Anatolya). He learned Armenian language, music and dance from his parents as well as Caucasian and Anatolian Armenians who immigrated to the San Joaquin Valley. Tom is fluent in English, Armenian and Russian.

An internationally recognized dance instructor, Tom graduated from the Armenian State Choreographic Academy and has degrees in Russian and Education. Invited by the Soviet Armenian government, he studied three years at the State Choreographic School, Sayat Nova. Tom has taught throughout America, Europe and the Orient.

Tom corrected a translation originally developed by **Mark Markish**. A Western Armenian translation was developed by **Lucy Piligian**, of Alexandria, Egypt.

Photo by Bernard Cloutier (berclo.net)

The state Opera and Ballet Theater in the capital of Armenia, Yerevan

Aramaic, Zakho (Kurdish)

ABOUT THE LANGUAGE:

Zakho Aramaic (Kurdish) *

Number of speakers: 7,500
Rank: 3,324

This variety of Kurdish, called Lishana Deni, Kurdit and Judeo-Aramaic, is spoken in Jerusalem and its vicinity, including Maoz Tsiyon. It originates from northwest Iraqi Kurdistan.

ABOUT THE SPEAKER:

Moshe Shimoni

Age: Unavailable   Recorded: 1996
Towns: Zakho, Kurdistan / Haifa, Israel

Native speaker Moshe Shimoni grew up in Zakho, Kurdistan within Iraq. He now lives in Haifa, Israel.

We also have a recording from **Dr. Hezy Mutzafi**, noted linguistics expert in Aramaic, who fluently speaks a half dozen Aramaic and Syriac dialects. Dr. Mutzafi is Linguistics Professor in the Department of Hebrew Culture Studies at Tel Aviv University. The translation is traditional, from a Haggadah in the Zakho dialect.

Photo by Dr. Zahed Sheikholeslami

A view of Sanandaj, the capital of Kurdistan, built on the site of old Sinneh, the ancient capital of Kurdistan in the Middle Ages

מַה מְגוֹיִרֵי לֵילֵי אוֹהָא מִן כֻּלּוּ לֵילֵיוָסָא?

- ma mgoyirre lele oha mɪn kulla lelewasa?
- *Why is this night different from all other nights?*

דִיד בְּד כֻּלּוּ לֵילֵיוָסָא לֵיס אַכְנַן גְטַמְשַׁך אֲפִילוּ נַקְלָא כָא,
וּלֵילֵי אוֹהָא - תְּרֵי נַקְלֵי.

- did bɪd kullu lelewawa les axnan kṭamšax afɪllu naqla xa;
  u-lele oha – tre naqle.
- *On all other nights we eat either leavened bread or matzah;
  on this night only matzah.*

דִיד בְּד כֻּלּוּ לֵילֵיוָסָא אַכְנַן כֶּכְלַך כְמִירָא יָאן פַטִירָא,
וּלֵילֵי אוֹהָא - כֻּלּוּ פַטִירָא.

- did bɪd kullu lelewawa axnan kɪxlax xmira yan paṭira;
  u-lele oha – kulle paṭira.
- *On all other nights we do not dip even once;
  on this night we dip twice.*

דִיד בְּד כֻּלּוּ לֵילֵיוָסָא אַכְנַן כֶּכְלַך שֶׁכְּלֵת גַלֵּי,
וּלֵילֵי אוֹהָא - מָרוּ.

- did bɪd kullu lelewawa axnan kɪxlax šɪklɪt gɪllale;
  u-lele oha – marur.
- *On all other nights we eat all kinds of herbs;
  on this night only bitter herbs.*

דִיד בְּד כֻּלּוּ לֵילֵיוָסָא אַכְנַן כֶּכְלַך וּכְשַׁתַך יָאן תִּיֵי וְיָאן תִּכְּיֵי,
וּלֵילֵי אוֹהָא - כֻּלּוּ תִּכְּיֵי.

- did bɪd kullu lelewawa axnan kɪxlax u-kšatax yan tiwe u-yan tɪkye;
  u-lele oha – kullenu tɪkye.
- *On all other nights we eat either sitting up or reclining;
  on this night we recline.*

Pronunciation notes:
ɪ   like English si̱ts
i   like English se̱ed
e   like English sa̱y
s   like English s̱he
x   like German Ba̱ch
ɣ   like Arabic غ
ṭ   like Arabic ط
q   like Arabic ق
Stress on penultimate (next-to-last) syllable

* For additional information, see "*Focus on ... pages.pdf*" on the DVD.

Aramaic, Lishanid Noshan (Kurdish)

ABOUT THE LANGUAGE:

Lishanid Noshan Aramaic (Kurdish)*

Number of speakers: 2,250
Rank: 4,438

Lishanid Noshan (also called Koyi Sanjaq, Kurdit and Judeo-Aramaic) is a variety of Aramaic Kurdish spoken in Israel's Jerusalem and vicinity, including Maoz Tsiyon. It was originally spoken in Iraqi Kurdistan, but all of its speakers moved to Israel many years ago.

ABOUT THE TRANSLATOR AND SPEAKER:

Ṣaliḥ Eliyahu

Age: Unavailable   Recorded: 2001
Towns: Koi Sanjaq / Suleimaniyah, Iraq / Jerusalem, Israel

Ṣaliḥ was born in Koi Sanjaq, Iraqi Kurdistan. He later moved to Suleimaniyah, where another Jewish Aramaic is spoken. Ṣaliḥ's dialect slightly influenced by Arbili Jewish Neo-Aramaic because his parents were born in Arbil, Iraq. He moved to Israel at age 28 and since then lived only in villages in Israel where his native tongue is the dominant language.

Photo by Dr. Zahed Sheikholeslami

A scenic view in southern Kurdistan

* For additional information, see "Focus on ... pages.pdf" on the DVD.

מַה פַּרְק לֵילֵי אִיָּא ־ מְכֻּלֵּי לֵילַוֵי?

■ ma farq leléʾiyya mə-kullé lelawé?

■ *Why is this night different from all other nights?*

אִי בְּכֻּלֵּי לֵילַוֵי לָא אַכְנַן מַטְבְּלֶך הַם גַּרְצִّי כָא גָّר,
וְלֵילֵי אִיָּא תְּרֵי גָّרֵי.

■ ʾay bə-kullé lelawé la ʾaxnán maṭbəléx ham garčí xá-jar;
ʾu lelé ʾiyyá tre jaré.

■ *On all other nights we do not dip even once;
on this night we dip twice.*

אִי בְּכֻּלֵּי לֵילַוֵי אַכְנַן כְּכְלֶך חָמֵץ יַן מַצָּה,
וְלֵילֵי אִיָּא כֻּלֵּיו מַצָּה.

■ ʾay bə-kullé lelawé ʾaxnán kəxlex ḥaméś yan maṣṣá;
ʾu lelé ʾiyyá kulléw maṣṣá.

■ *On all other nights we eat either leavened bread or matzah;
on this night only matzah.*

אִי בְּכֻּלֵּי לֵילַוֵי אַכְנַן כְּכְלֶך בָּקִّיד יֵרָקוֹת,
וְלֵילֵי אִיָּא כֻּלֵּיו מָרוֹר.

■ ʾay bə-kullé lelawé ʾaxnán kəxléx baqíyəd yeraqót;
ʾu lelé ʾiyyá kulléw marór.

■ *On all other nights we eat all kinds of herbs;
on this night only bitter herbs.*

אִי בְּכֻּלֵּי לֵילַוֵי אַכְנַן כְּכְלֶך וְשָתֶך צִ'י יְתִוֵי וצ'י תִּכְּיֵי,
וְלֵילֵי אִיָּא כֻּלֵּיו תִּכְּיֵי.

■ ʾay bə-kullé lelawé ʾaxnán kəxléx ʾu šatéx či ytiwé ʾu či təkyé;
ʾu lelé ʾiyyá kullán təkyé.

■ *On all other nights we eat either sitting up or reclining;
on this night we recline.*

Pronunciation notes:

i	like English s<u>ee</u>d
e	like English s<u>ay</u>
ə	like schwa in <u>a</u>bout
š	like English <u>sh</u>e
č	like English <u>ch</u>in
x	like German Ba<u>ch</u>
ṭ	like Arabic ط
q	like Arabic ق
ʾ	is a glottal stop
ṣ	like Arabic Sad ص (pharyngealized s)
ḥ	is pharyngeal unvoiced consonant, like Arabic Ha ح

Stress indicated by accent marks

About the Culture:

Yemenite

Yemenite is often not considered a language separate from Hebrew, but Yemenite's distinctive pronunciation and culture are a source of fascination. Their melodies, style of dance, elaborate wedding dress and prayer chants are unique in the world of Jewry. They are the only community that read the Torah in both Hebrew and Aramaic translation. Many scholars feel the Yemenite dialect is closest to ancient Biblical Hebrew.

Tradition holds that the earliest settlement in Yemen dates from the time of King Solomon. A Himyarite king, Abu-Kariba Asad-Toban, converted to Judaism in the 3rd C CE and many in the ruling family similarly converted. Jewish rule continued for more than a century until Ethiopian Christians ruled Yemen. Most Yemenite Jews now live in Israel; an estimated 200 still live in Yemen.

Passover Traditions:

The text of the Yemenite Haggadah for Passover is different than other communities. For instance, another passage is inserted between the Four Questions (*Ma Nishtana*) and We Were Once Slaves (*Avadim Hayinu*). The inserted paragraphs describe Pharaoh in unflattering terms and mentions the slaves' work of making bricks. Though written with Hebrew characters, this words are primarily Arabic. It is chanted by the youngest child – just like the Four Questions. During the chant, the child holds up the egg taken from the Seder plate.

There are several versions of this passage. One version, used by the general Yemenite community, is shown at the right; the smaller type is used by Jews of Iraqi descent. (Moshe Harir's chant, in the recordings, demonstrates yet another version of the text.)

In the recordings: Moshe Harir chants the uniquely Yemenite passage from the Haggadah, which recalls the slaves' work and describes their view of Pharaoh. Moshe begins by saying he'll now chant for us *Halaila Minjamia 'Aliali* (Arabic for "A Night Among All Nights"). The chant ends with *Avadim Hayinu* (We were once slaves), found in all traditional Haggadahs.

בֵּין יוֹשְׁבִין וּבֵין מְסֻבִּין.
וְהַלַּיְלָה הַזֶּה כֻּלָּנוּ מְסֻבִּין:

יש מוסיפין לומר זו

מָא כַּאן כְ'בַּר הַאדִי אַל
לַיְלָה מִן גָּמִיע אַל לַיַאלִי
כַּרְגוּ גְּדוּדְנָא וְאַבַּאנָא
מִן מִצְר מִן בֵּית אַל
עַבּוּדְיַּה מָא כַּאנוּ יִפְ'עַלוּ
יַכְדְּמוּ אַל פַרְעוֹן אַל
מַלְעוּן אִבֵּן אַל מַלְעוּן אַל
אָרוּר אִבֵּן אַל אָרוּר אַל
מְקוּלַל אִבֵּן אַל מְקוּלַל
בְּלְמִין וַאל לַבֵּן וַכַלְצָנָא
אַלְלָה מִנְהֹם בְּיַד שְׁדִידַה
וְאַדְרַע מַמְדוּדַ א
וְאַחְכַּאמַא עָצִימַה גֻּדָּא

מָא כַּאן כְּבַּר הַאדִי אַל
לַיְלָה מִן גָּמִיע אַל לַיַאלִי
לַיַאלִי כְּרְגוּ אַבַּרְנָא
וְאַנַבְּאדְנָא מִן בְּלָד מִצָר
מִן בֵּית אַל עַבּוּדְיֵה וּכַּאנוּ יַפְ'עָלוּ
כַּאנוּ יַכְ'לְטוּ אַל תִּבֵּן פַל
לִבֵּן וַאל לְבֵּן פַל תִּבֵּן.
לִמָן לְפַרְעָה אַל רַשַׁע
אַלְגַמוּר אַלְאָרוּר אִבֵּן אַל
אָרוּר אַל מְקוּלַל אִבֵּן אַל
מְקוּלַל וְאַרְסַל אַלְלָה עָלַא
אַל מִצְרִין אַלְדָּם. וָאל
צְּפַאדְע. וַאלְקַמֵל. וָאל
קוּמֵל. וַאלְוֻחֹש.
וַאלְפְנָא. וַאלְגָּרֵב.
וַאלְבְּרָד. וַאלְגָּרַאד.
וַאלצְּלַאם. וּמות

מַא כַּאן כְּבַּר הַאדִי אַל
לַיְלָה מִן נָמִיע אַל
לַיַאלִי כְּדְרוּ אַבַּרְנָא
וְאַנַבַּאדְנָא מִן כְּלָד מִצַר
מִן בֵּית אַל עַבּוּדַּיֵה וּכַּאנוּ
יַכְדְמוּ אַל פַרְעוֹן אַל
מַלְעוּן אִבֵּן אַל מַלְעוּן אַל
אָרוּר אִבֵּן אַל אָרוּר אַל
מְקוּלַל אִבֵּן אַל מְקוּלַל
בְּלְמִין וָאל לַבֵּן וַכַלְצָנָא
אַלְלָה מִנְהֹם בְּיַד שְׁדִידַה
וָאדְרַע מַמְדוּדַ א
וְאַחְכַּאמַא עָצִימַה גֻּדָּא
וָאֵיאת וּבְרַאַחִין עָלַא יַד
מוּסָא אִבֵּן עַמְרַאן אַל
נְבִיא אַל עָצִים כְּלִים רַב
רַחְמַאן עָלַיה אַל סְלַאם
וְהַדָא אַלְגֵּוַאב:

אַלָאבְּכַּאר. וְחַתַּא. וְעָגּוּז בְּגֵוַּג עָלַיְהַא אַלַף לַעְנָה תָּגוּז. כַּאן מְעַאהָא מַעְבּוּד מִן עִנְגָּה דְכַ'ל אַלְכַּלְבּ וְאַכְּלְהַא תָּם צַרְכֵ'ת פִי תְּלַד אַלְלַיְלָה צָרַאך' עָצִים לִקֹיֵם מַה שֶׁנֶּאֱמַר כִּי אֵין בֵּית אֲשֶׁר אֵין שָׁם מֵת. וְכַ'לַץ אַלְלָה בְּנֵי יִשְׂרָאֵל מִנְהֹם בְּיַד שְׁדִידָה וְאַדְרָאע מַמְדוּדַה וְאַחְכַּאמַא עָצִימַה וְאֵיאת וּבְרַאַחִין עָלַא יַד מוּסָא אִבֵּן עַמְרַאן אַלְנְבִּי אַלְעָצִים כְּלִים אַלְרַחְמַאן עָלַיה אַלסְלַאם:

וְהַדָא אַלְגֵּוַאב
תָּם יַנְוֻב אַל קַארִי וְיִחְכִּי מָא גְּרָא לְנָא בְּמִצְר וּמָא גְּרָא לְיַעְקוּב גְּדְנָא מְעַא לָבָן כַּאלַה וּכֵיף כַּאנַת צְפַאת אַל גָּאוּלָה עָלַא הַאדָא אַלנְצַ'ם:

עֲבָדִים הָיִינוּ לְפַרְעֹה בְּמִצְרַיִם. וַיּוֹצִיאֵנוּ יְהֹוָה אֱלֹהֵינוּ

A page from a Yemenite Haggadah showing the special passage after the Ma Nishtana

Z Y X W V U T S R Q P O N M L K J I H G F E D C B A

About the Language:

Arabic, Judeo-Yemeni

Number of speakers: 51,000
Rank: 1,616

Judeo-Yemeni Arabic, often called Yemenite, is spoken in Israel by Jews of Yemeni descent. There is a small community left in Yemen. Dialects of Yemenite are San'a, 'Aden, Bëda and Habban. The language varieties of Judeo-Yemeni are markedly different from the Muslim languages spoken in the same territories.

About the Chanter:

Moshe Harir

Age: Unknown   Recorded: 2005
Town: Kiryat Ata, Israel

A native-born Israeli, Moshe sings with the Yemenite group *Moshav Amka*. He learned Yemenite melodies from his father, who taught him the music and characteristic pronunciation of the Achduf region, which is close to Taiz, Yemen's second-largest city in southwest Yemen.

מַה נִּשְׁתַּנָּה הַלַּיְלָה הַזֶּה מִכָּל הַלֵּילוֹת?

שֶׁבְּכָל הַלֵּילוֹת אֵין אֲנַחְנוּ מְטַבְּלִין אֲפִילוּ פַּעַם אֶחָת.
וְהַלַּיְלָה הַזֶּה שְׁתֵּי פְעָמִים:

שֶׁבְּכָל הַלֵּילוֹת אֲנַחְנוּ אוֹכְלִין חָמֵץ אוֹ מַצָּה.
וְהַלַּיְלָה הַזֶּה כֻּלּוֹ מַצָּה:

שֶׁבְּכָל הַלֵּילוֹת אֲנַחְנוּ אוֹכְלִין שְׁאַר יְרָקוֹת.
וְהַלַּיְלָה הַזֶּה מְרוֹרִים:

שֶׁבְּכָל הַלֵּילוֹת אֲנַחְנוּ אוֹכְלִין בֵּין יוֹשְׁבִין וּבֵין מְסֻבִּין.
וְהַלַּיְלָה הַזֶּה כֻּלָּנוּ מְסֻבִּין:

Photo courtesy of Moshav Amka

Moshav Amka, the Yemenite Folklore Troupe, has been performing since the mid-1970s, preserving traditional Yemenite ethnic culture through its music and dance

The text shows the traditional order used in Sephardi communities, with some wording differences. Notable is the plural used for מְרוֹרִים instead of מְרוֹר (bitter herbs).

In the recordings: Moshe chants the Four Questions using the traditional chant of Yemenite Jews. He ends the chant with "*Chag Sameah l'Kol Am Yisrael. L'hitraot*" (Happy holiday to all people of Israel. See you again). Both are traditional salutations.

ABOUT THE TRANSLATOR, SPEAKER AND CALLIGRAPHER:

Nabil Khatib

Age: Unavailable   Recorded: 1997
Locations: Lebanon / Boston, MA

Nabil is a Lebanese-born Palestinian. He worked as a calligrapher and teacher of Arabic in Boston. A translation was also developed by **Kamil Taha,** who was raised in Deir-Debwan, Jordan.

The Arabic is shown in typescript form on the Tachelhit and Tarafit pages.

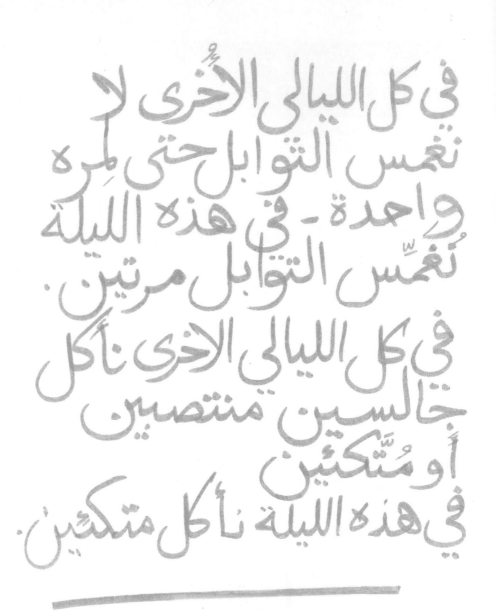

Tile inscription detail of Blue Mosque of Sultan Ahmet

■ *On all other nights we do not dip even once;
on this night we dip twice.*

■ *On all other nights we eat either sitting up or reclining;
on this night we recline.*

Arabic

لماذا تختلف هذه الليلة
عن كل الليالي الاخرى؟

في كل الليالي الاخرى نأكل
الخبز المخمّر أوالخبز الفطير
في هذه الليلة فقط
نأكل خبز الفطير.
في كل الليالي الاخرى نأكل
جميع أنواع التوابل الخضراء
في هذه الليلة نأكل فقط التوابل
المرّة.

ABOUT THE LANGUAGE:

Arabic

Number of speakers: 221,002,544
Rank: 4

Standard Arabic is spoken throughout the Middle East and north Africa. The largest Arabic-speaking populations are in Egypt (68M), Sudan (35M), Algeria (31M), Morocco (30M), Iraq (23M), Saudi Arabia (22M), Syria (16M) and Yemen (17M). Most countries have their own dialects or colloquial versions; linguists divide as to whether these are different languages.

The Arabic script evolved from the *Nabataean Aramaic* script. It has been used since the 4th C, but the earliest surviving document, an inscription in Arabic, Syriac and Greek, is from 512. There are two written forms: Classical, which is used for the *Qur'an* and classical literature, and Modern, which is the universal form understood by the Arabic-speaking world.

- Why is this night different from all other nights?
- On all other nights we eat either leavened bread or matzah; on this night only matzah.
- On all other nights we eat all kinds of herbs; on this night only bitter herbs.

Dome of the Rock, Jerusalem

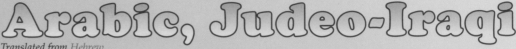

Arabic, Judeo-Iraqi

Translated from Hebrew

בְּמָא תְגַ׳יַירַת הָאדִי אֶל לֵילָא מִן כֹּל לְיַאלִי.

■ מַה נִּשְׁתַּנָּה הַלַּיְלָה הַזֶּה. מִכָּל הַלֵּילוֹת.

פִי כֹּל לְיַאלִי לֵיס נִחְנָא גַ׳אמְסִין לָאוּנוּ מַרָא וָאחְדָה.
וְהָאדִי אֶל לֵילָא מַרְתֵּין:

■ שֶׁבְּכָל הַלֵּילוֹת אֵין אָנַחְנוּ מַטְבִּלִין אֲפִילוּ פַּעַם אַחַת.

וְהַלַּיְלָה הַזֶּה שְׁתֵּי פְעָמִים:

פִי כֹּל לְיַאלִי נִחְנָא אַכְּלִין כְּמִיר יָא פְּטִיר.
וְהָאדִי אֶל לֵילָא כֻּלּוּ פְּטִיר:

■ שֶׁבְּכָל הַלֵּילוֹת אֲנַחְנוּ אוֹכְלִין חָמֵץ אוֹ מַצָּה.

וְהַלַּיְלָה הַזֶּה כֻּלּוֹ מַצָּה:

פִי כֹּל לְיַאלִי נִחְנָא אַכְּלִין כְצַ׳אר יָא מְרַאר.
וְהָאדִי אֶל לֵילָא כֻּלּוּ מְרַאר:

■ שֶׁבְּכָל הַלֵּילוֹת אֲנַחְנוּ אוֹכְלִין שְׁאַר יְרָקוֹת.

וְהַלַּיְלָה הַזֶּה מָרוֹר:

פִי כֹּל לְיַאלִי נִחְנָא אַכְּלִין וְשָׁארְבִּין בֵּין קָאעְדִן וּבֵין מִנְתִּכְּיִין.
וְהָאדִי אֶל לֵילָא כֻּלְתְּנָא מִנְתִּכְּיִין:

■ שֶׁבְּכָל הַלֵּילוֹת אֲנַחְנוּ אוֹכְלִין וְשׁוֹתִין בֵּין יוֹשְׁבִין וּבֵין מְסֻבִּין.

וְהַלַּיְלָה הַזֶּה כֻּלָּנוּ מְסֻבִּין:

ABOUT THE LANGUAGE:

Judeo-Iraqi Arabic

Number of speakers: 51,000
Rank: 1,616

Judeo-Iraqi Arabic was originally spoken in Iraq. Speakers now live in Israel, India, Iraq (less than a dozen speakers), United Kingdom and the USA. The language is close to Baghdadi Arabic and North Mesopotamian Arabic.

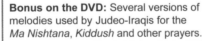

Bonus on the DVD: Several versions of melodies used by Judeo-Iraqis for the *Ma Nishtana*, *Kiddush* and other prayers.

Rahel Musleah

ABOUT THE TRANSLATOR AND SPEAKER:

Rahel Musleah

Age: Unavailable   Recorded: 2000
Locations: Calcutta, India / Great Neck, NY

Rahel was born in Calcutta and moved to the USA at age 6. Her father was Calcutta's first ordained rabbi. She is the 7th generation of her family to be born in Calcutta and can trace the family to 17th C Bagdad. Rahel is a graduate of Columbia University and the Jewish Theological Seminary of America, and promotes Judeo-Iraqi culture (its songs and recipes) through a wide variety of books.

Translation notes: Compared to the Ashkenazi version used in North America, the order of the questions and the Hebrew text is different:

אֲנַחְנוּ is used rather than אָנוּ,
וּמַצָּה instead of אוֹ מַצָּה,
וְהַלַּיְלָה ("and this night") instead of הַלַּיְלָה,
שְׁאַר יְרָקוֹת versus שְׁאָר יְרָקוֹת,
מְטַבְּלִין instead of מַטְבִּילִין,
פַּעַם אַחַת for פַּעַם אֶחָת
אוֹכְלִין בֵּין יוֹשְׁבִין ("and drink") is added within וְשׁוֹתִין

Apache, Western

Hant'é bighą dazhǫ́' dítł'é' ła' dáwa tł'é'híí bitisgo łahgo at'éé?

■ *Why is this night different from all other nights?*

**Ła' dáwa tł'é'gee bán sizíné dahyúgohíí matsah dahidąądą́';
áídą́' dítł'é'híí matsahzhą́ dahidąą.**

■ only matzah we eat.

■ *On all other nights we eat either leavened bread or matzah;
on this night only matzah.*

**Ła' dáwa tł'é'gee tł'ohdłádé dahidąą;
áídą́' dítł'é'híí tł'oh izee nch'i'i dahidąą.**

■ soft leafy vegetables we eat;
bitter (medicinal) herbs we eat.

■ *On all other nights we eat all kinds of herbs;
on this night only bitter herbs.*

**Ła' dáwa tł'é'gee doo dałaadn bidahit'áh da;
áídą́' dítł'é'híí nakidn bidahit'áh.**

■ (not) we dip it not;

■ *On all other nights we do not dip even once;
on this night we dip twice.*

**Ła' dáwa tł'é'gee nahaatąądą́' dahyúgohíí binahzhį' ádant'eego da'idąą;
áídą́' dítł'é'híí binahzhį' ádant'eego da'idąą.**

■ *On all other nights we eat either sitting up or reclining;
on this night we recline.*

**Ła' dáwa tł'é'gee daalínégo da'idąą;
áídą́' dítł'é'híí dázhǫ́' ízisgo da'idąą.**

■ *On all other nights we eat in an ordinary manner;
on this night we dine with special ceremony.*

Illustration by Alysa Lerman

ABOUT THE LANGUAGE:

Western Apache

Number of speakers: 12,700
Rank: 2,809

Western Apache, also known as Coyotero, is spoken in several reservations in east central Arizona.

ABOUT THE SPEAKER:

Willem J de Reuse

Age: Unavailable   Recorded: 1998
Locations: Belgium / San Carlos, AZ / Denton, TX

Dr. de Reuse is a linguist teaching Apache at the University of North Texas. His native language is Flemish. As the translator (Phillip Goode) was unable to be recorded, Willem read the text to him and in Phillip's estimation, Willem's version was pretty fluent. Phillip and Willem had worked together for many years. When Phillip died in 1999, Willem said of this translation, "it was the last piece of work he ever did for me."

ABOUT THE TRANSLATOR:

Phillip Goode

Age: late 40s   Translated: 1998
Town: San Carlos, AZ

Phillip was born and raised in San Carlos, within Arizona's Seven-Mile Wash area. He was part of the Pinal group of the San Carlos Apache. Philip, a fluent speaker of Apache, was also one of the most proficient and linguistically sophisticated writers on his reservation; his Apache was richer than most people his age. He had been an Apache language teacher at various schools in and near the reservation. Phillip's father, Britton Goode, was a knowledgeable historian and Bible translator, and descendant of one of the Apache scouts that General Crook used to chase after Geronimo.

Amharic

ይህ፡ለሊት፡ከለ ለቶች፡ሉ፡በምን፡ተለየ?።
- Yeah laelit kellaelitoch hullu bemin teleye?
- *Why is this night different from all other nights?*

በለ ለቶች፡ሉ፡ተቀመጠን፡ወይም፡ዘንበል፡ብለን፡ተዘናንተን፡እንበላለን፤
በዚህ፡ለት፡ግን፡ላችን፡ዘንበል፡ብለን።
- Belaelitoch hullu tekemeten woiem zenbel belen tezenanten enbelalenn;
  Bezeeh laelit gen hoolatchenm zenbel belen.
- *On all other nights we eat either sitting up or reclining;
  on this night we recline.*

በለ ለቶች፡ሉ፡ያልቦካ፡ወይም፡የቦካ፡ቂጣ፡እንበላለን፤
በዚህ፡ለት፡ግን፡ሉ፡ያልቦካ፡ቂጣ።
- Belaelitoch hullu yalboka woiem yeboka kita enbelallenn;
  Bezeeh laelit gen hullu yalboka kita.
- *On all other nights we eat either leavened bread or matzah;
  on this night only matzah.*

በለ ለቶች፡ሉ፡ለ ሎች፡ቀጠሎ ች ን ም፡እንበላለን፤
በዚህ፡ለት፡ግን፡ሉ፡መረር።
- Belaelitoch hullu laelotch ketelotchnem enbelallenn;
  Bezeeh laelit gen hullu merarra.
- *On all other nights we eat all kinds of herbs;
  on this night only bitter herbs.*

በለ ለቶች፡ሉ፡እንድ፡ገዘ ስ፡እንኳን፡እንነክርም፤
በዚህ፡ለት፡ግን፡ለት፡ገዘ ስ።
- Belaelitoch hullu annd gezae enquan annenkrem;
  Bezeeh laelit gen hulet gezae.
- *On all other nights we do not dip even once;
  on this night we dip twice.*

በለ ላ፡ምሸቶች፡ሉ፡እንደማንነኛ፡ውም፡ኔ ታ፤
በዚህ፡ሐ ሸት፡ግን፡የ ምንበላ ሙ ፡በሉ፡ሥ ር ን ት፡ነ ኡ።
- Belella mesheetoch hullu endemangnawoom hooneta enbelalenn;
  Bezeeh mesheet gen yemenbellaw seneseraat balew huneta naw.
- *On all other nights we eat in an ordinary manner;
  on this night we dine with special ceremony.*

Note that Amharic's questions are asked in a different order than Ashkenazi tradition.

ABOUT THE LANGUAGE:

Amharic

Number of speakers: 17,528,500
Rank: 54

Amharic, also called Abyssinian and Ethiopian, is spoken in north-central Ethiopia, Amhara region, and in the capital, Addis Ababa. It is also spoken in Egypt and Sweden, with a large population in Israel. The Ethiopian Jews call themselves *Beta Israel* (the term *Falasha* is pejorative).

The Ethiopic script developed from the script of Ge'ez, Ethiopia's classical language. The script has been in use since at least the 4th C CE.

ABOUT THE TRANSLATORS AND SPEAKERS:

Zerfe Kebede and Aberash Zwede

Ages: Unavailable   Recorded: 1999
Town: Addis Ababa, Ethiopia

Most of the text is traditional, from a Yaniv Enterprises Haggadah published in Israel. The reading and transliteration of the traditional Four Questions is by **Zerfe Kebede** who grew up in Addis Ababa and works in San Jose, CA. The final question was translated and read by **Aberash Zwede**, who was born and raised in Addis Ababa. She currently lives in Queens, NY and works at the United Nations. Also contributing: **Tiguist Fisseha**, from Addis Ababa, Ethiopia.

መኍ ሸ ታ ፈ ሃሳ ደ ሳ ሃዘ መኵ ል
ሃ ሴ ሎ ት ። ሸ በ ነ ል ሃ ሴ ሎ ት ኤ ን
ኣ ረ ሱ መ ጠ ቢ ሊ ን ኣ ረ ሱ
ፓ ዓ ም ኤ ሐ ት ሃሳ ደ ሳ ሃዘ ሸ ቴ
ፓ ዓ ሚ ም ።
ሸ በ ነ ል ሃ ሴ ሎ ት ኣ ኑ ኣ ህ ሉ ን
ሐ መ ጸ ው መ ጸ ሃሳ ደ ሳ ሃዘ ኵ ሎ
መ ጸ። ሸ በ ነ ል ሃ ሴ ሎ ት ኣ ኑ
ኣ ህ ሊ ም ን ሸ ኣ ር ይ ራ ቀ ት ሃሳ ደ ሳ
ሃዘ ኵ ሎ መ ፀ ር ር ሸ በ ነ ል ሃ ሴ ሎ ት
ኣ ኑ ኣ ህ ሉ ን ሽ ሸ ቲ ን ቤ ን ዶ ሸ ቢ ን
ው ቤ ን መ ሱ ቢ ን ሃሳ ደ ሳ ሃዘ ከ ሳ ኵ
መ ሱ ቢ ን

Amharic transliteration of the Hebrew

From Yaniv Enterprises Diaspora Haggadah

Aberash's notes: *Laelit/Laelitoch*(pl.) indicates night, not evening [akin to the Hebrew]. *Annenkrem* is awkward for "We do not dip"; *anateksem* is more appropriate. *Zenbel* indicates a tilted position, but not a comfortable eating position.

Alemannisch

Warum isch die Nacht andrsch als alle andra Nächt?
- *Why is this night different from all other nights?*

In allna andra Nächt essa mr entwedr suhrs Brot odr Matzah;
In dera Nacht nu Matzah.
- *On all other nights we eat either leavened bread or matzah;*
  on this night only matzah.

In allna andra Nächt essa mr alle Arta vo Krütr;
In dera Nacht nu bittre Krütr.
- *On all other nights we eat all kinds of herbs;*
  on this night only bitter herbs.

In allna andra Nächt tua mr net eh mol tunka;
In dera Nacht tunka mr zwäh mol.
- *On all other nights we do not dip even once;*
  on this night we dip twice.

In allna andra Nächt essa mr entwedr sitzat odr zruckglehnt;
In dera Nacht lehna mr üs zruck.
- *On all other nights we eat either sitting up or reclining;*
  on this night we recline.

In alla andra Nächt essa mr uf jede gwöhliche Art;
In dera Nacht schpeisa mr uf a bsundre Art.
- *On all other nights we eat in an ordinary manner;*
  on this night we dine with special ceremony.

ABOUT THE LANGUAGE:

Alemannisch

Number of speakers: 6,469,000
Rank: 111

Alemannisch, called Schwytzertütsch in Switzerland, Schwyzerdütsch in Germany and Alsatian in France (and Swiss German by many others), is spoken throughout the central regions of Switzerland and in various villages of Austria, France, Germany and Liechtenstein.

The varieties of Swiss are classified as High Alemannisch and Highest Alemannisch. The language is not very intelligible to speakers of Standard German. Separate varieties (between 20 to 70) are found in each canton, and occasionally in each village, many of which are unintelligible to each other. Only a few of them are listed as dialects or subdialects. The varieties have a strong social function, maintaining the borders of regions or cantons, or even to keep one village different from another.

ABOUT THE TRANSLATOR AND SPEAKER:

Stefan Riezler

Age: Unavailable   Recorded: 1997
Towns: Partenen, Austria / Tuebingen, Germany

Stefan speaks the Montafoneric variant of Alemannisch. He grew up in Partenen, a small village in Montafon valley, Vorarlberg, Austria. During primary school and in college he lived in various villages in Montafon valley, and used the Montafon dialect primarily with friends and Austrian-German with his family.

Photo © Barry Hantman

Lucerne's famous covered wooden bridge, the *Kapellbrucke* (Chapel Bridge) was built in 1300; its gable paintings were painted in the 17th C

Albanian

Pse kjo natë ndryshon nga të gjitha netët e tjera?

■ psā kyo natə endri'shon ngah tə jithah nehtet ā tyerah?

■ *Why is this night different from all other nights?*

**Në të gjitha netët e tjera ne hamë edhe bukë të mbrujtur edhe bukë ndorë;
te kjo natë, vetëm bukë ndorë.**

■ nə tə jeethah naytet ā tyerah neh hahmə bukə tə mbruitoor ehdeh ndawDmə;
nə kətə natə vehtem bookə ndawDmə.

■ *On all other nights we eat either leavened bread or matzah;
on this night only matzah.*

**Në të gjitha netët e tjera ne hamë gjithfarë barërash;
te kjo natë, hamë vetëm barëra të idhëta.**

■ nə tə jeethah naytet ā tyerah neh hahmə jith-farə baDəDash;
nə kətə natə hamə vehtem baDəDah tə eeDHətah.

■ *On all other nights we eat all kinds of herbs;
on this night only bitter herbs.*

**Në të gjitha netët e tjera nuk ngjyejmë në asgjë;
te kjo natë, ngjyejmë dy herë.**

■ nə tə jeethah naytet ā tyerah nook njyaymə nə as'jə;
nə kətə natə ne njyehmə dU hehrə.

■ *On all other nights we do not dip even once;
on this night we dip twice.*

**Në të gjitha netët e tjera, ne hamë kjoftë ulur kj ottë shtrirë;
te kjo natë, hamë shtrirë.**

■ nə tə jeethah naytet ā tyerah neh hahmə kyawftə ooloor kyawftə shtDiDə;
nə kətə natə neh hahmə shtDiDə.

■ *On all other nights we eat either sitting up or reclining;
on this night we recline.*

**Në te gjitha netët e tjera, ne hamë në mënyrë të zakonshme;
te kjo natë, hamë darkë me një ritual të veçant.**

■ nə tə jeethah naytet ā tyerah neh hahmə nə mənyDə tə za'kawnSmə;
nə kətə natə neh hahmə daDkə meh nyeh Ditu'al tə veh'chant.

■ *On all other nights we eat in an ordinary manner;
on this night we dine with special ceremony.*

ABOUT THE LANGUAGE:

Albanian

Number of speakers: 3,035,000
Rank: 187

Albanian, the national language of Albania, is also spoken in Turkey and a half-dozen other countries. The main dialect, Tosk, is the basis for the official Standard Albanian. In northern Albania, the primary dialect is Gheg Albanian, which is spoken mostly by the *Kossovars* in Yugoslavia.

ABOUT THE TRANSLATOR AND SPEAKER:

Giovanni M G Belluscio

Age: Unavailable   Recorded: 1995
Town: Rende, Italy

Dr. Belluscio is a linguist in the Department of Linguistica, at the Universita' della Calabria, in Rende, Italy.

Pronunciation key:
ā = long a, as in letter 'a'
ə = schwa, as in first syllable of 'about'; final schwas are very soft
DH = voiced th, as in 'that', not as in 'thin'
D = a flap; tapped 'r'
U = halfway between oo vowels in 'too' and 'book'
' is placed before stressed syllable; otherwise first syllable has stress

Photo by Bernard Cloutier (berclo.net)

Shkodra, Albania, one of the oldest cities in Europe, features the beautiful Sheik Zamil Abdullah al-Zamil Mosque, built in 1995

Akha

Translated from Burmese

Ahv* jayv meehf neh   nymmf chjeehxv ahv   yawv meehf yawv durhv nehv-ehf   mahv doohf layf tah?
■ Why   tonight   comparing to the other nights   different from?

Yawv meehf yawv durhv auhf ahv   doeuhv tsay kurhv urh hawv murh yaw byehxf auhf ghkawxv muuhv
■ In the other nights   either soft bread having yeast or
doeuhv tsayv mahv auhf urh hawv murh yaw rgauhf ghkawxv muuhv   ah duuh   dzahv urh mah;
■ either hard bread having no yeast   we   eat;
nymmf chjeehxv law nmmf ahv   doeuhv tsayv mahv auhf urh
■ tonight   having no yeast
hawv murh yaw rgauhf auhf dtehxv-ehf   ah duuh mahxv   dzahv urh mah.
■ only hard bread   we   eat.

Yawv yawv meehf durhv auhf ahv   jyahxf rgahv jyahxf loohf pyurhxv urh
■ In the other nights   being herbal medicine
ahf bpahxv doohv cheehf neeh   ah duuh mahxv   dzahv urh mah;
■ different types of leaves and roots   we   eat;
nymmf chjeehxv ah   hkahv urh   jyahxf rgahv jyahxf loohf pyurhxv urh
■ tonight   bitter   herbal medicine
ahf bpahxv doohv cheehf durhv auhf dtehxv-ehf   ah duuh mahxv   dzahv urh mah.
■ only leaves and roots   we   eat.

Yawv yawv meehf durhv auhf ahv   ah duuh mahxv hawv murh   auhf sahv durhxv dzahf uuhf nehv-ehf
■ In the other nights   we bread   with salty water
teehv bpohxf dtehxv   -ehf ghkawxv toeuhv lehxv hawf neh   mahv dzahv ah;
■ not even once   dip   not eat;
nymmf chjeehxv law nmmf ahv   ah duuh mahxv hawv murh auhf   sahv durhxv dzahf uuhf nehv-ehf
■ tonight   we bread   salty water
nyeehv bpohxf   gkurhxf neeh toeuhv lehxv dzahv urh mah.
■ even twice   dip and eat.

Yawv yawv meehf durhv auhf ahv   ah duuh mahxv   rgawf mawf auhf
■ In the other nights   we   to our bodies
dohf dehv neeh tahv hawf neh ghkawxv muuh   beeh heehf-ehf hkawv dahf neh ghkawxv muuhv   nuuhf neh dzahv urh mah;
■ either by keeping straightly   or by lying against   sit and eat;
nymmf chjeehxv law nmmf ahv   ah duuh mahxv   rgawf mawf auhf   beehf heehf dtehxv-ehf tahv hawf neh   nuuhf hawf   dzahv urh mah.
■ tonight   we   to our bodies   only lying against   sit   and eat.

Yawv yawv meehf durhv auhf ahv   ah duuh mahxv yawv jawf   nah hkahf dzahv urh lohxv-ehf   dzahv urh mah;
■ In the other nights   we   only rogular way   eat;
nymmf chjeehxv law nmmf ahv   ah duuh mahxv ahv chawv   auhf mahv doohf layf urh   ahf ghkahxf dawxf hawf   dzahv urh mah.
■ tonight   we   in strange way   with ceremony   eat.

─────────────────────────────────────

* The letters **f**, **xf**, **v** and **xv** at the end of words are tone markers and are not part of the word's spelling.

About the Translator and Speaker:

Mooh Jurh

Age: mid-40s   Recorded: 2001
Town: Burma, Myanmar

Mooh was born near Keng Tung and currently lives in the city of Burma. Both are in Myanmar's East Shan State. Akha was Mooh's first language. He used to be a Catholic Priest.

Working with **Matthew McDaniel** of the Akha Heritage Foundation, Mooh produced two Akha versions with formal and informal vocabularies. Although the ceremonial nature of the Four Questions nominally calls for formal language, the gloss of the informal version more closely matches the intentions of the text and is shown here. The translators worked from both English and Burmese translations of the text. The project was delayed two years by a war on the border between Thailand and Myanmar.

The Akha Heritage Foundation (www.akha.com) mentioned the Western Wall of Jerusalem. Matthew explained, "*The Akha are an orthodox people with traditions very similar to that of the Jewish Orthodox and they are attempting to preserve this tradition despite Western Protestant Missions who wish to destroy it, just as they wished to destroy Jews a few years back.*"

About the Language:

Akha

Number of speakers: 563,960
Rank: 514

Akha is spoken in Myanmar (Burma) and in China, Laos, Thailand and Vietnam.

Buddhist monks at a pagoda on Sagaing Hill, a frequent site for meditation

Photo by Bernard Cloutier (berclo.net)

Akan

Adɛn na anadwo yei akɔyɛ ne ho adadwo sonowonko korakora yi?

■ *Why is this night different from all other nights?*

Na anka anadwo biara yɛdi panoo a mmɔkaw wɔ mu anaa maasa;
Nso anadwo yei nko ara deɛ maasa nko ara na yɛredie.

■ *On all other nights we eat either leavened bread or matzah;*
on this night only matzah.

Na anka anadwo biara yɛdi nhahannuro ahodoɔ pii;
Nso anadwo yei nko ara deɛ nhahannuro a ɛyɛ nwono nko ara na yɛredie.

■ *On all other nights we eat all kinds of herbs;*
on this night only bitter herbs.

Na anka anadwo biara sɛ yɛredidi a, yɛdi no hunaa a yɛmfa mmɔ hwee mu;
Nso anadwo yei nko ara deɛ yɛde abɔ mu mprɛnu.

■ *On all other nights we do not dip even once;*
on this night we dip twice.

Na anka anadwo biara sɛ yɛredidi a, yɛtena ase sirenn anaa yɛpa da;
Nso anadwo yei nko ara deɛ yɛapa ada.

■ *On all other nights we eat either sitting up or reclining;*
on this night we recline.

Na anka anadwo biara yɛnnidi kwan sonowonko biara so;
Nso anadwo yei adidie yi yɛ sonowonko koraa.

■ *On all other nights we eat in an ordinary manner;*
on this night we dine with special ceremony.

The Volta River and surrounding mountains near
the town of Akosobo in southeast Ghana

ABOUT THE LANGUAGE:

Akan

Number of speakers: 8,300,000
Rank: 95

Akan is spoken in Ghana. The language is also called Fante when spoken by the Fante, and Twi when spoken by the Asante and Akuapem.

ABOUT THE TRANSLATOR AND SPEAKER:

Samuel Obeng

Age: 38   Recorded: 1997
Towns: Asuom, Ghana / Bloomington, IN

Dr. Obeng is a linguist at the University of Indiana. He was born in an Akan-speaking community in eastern Ghana. Both of his parents were Akan speakers, and he speaks and writes Akan very fluently. Samuel's 14 initial years of education were in an Akan-speaking community, and he studied Akan in high school and Akan linguistics in college. His BA and PhD theses were on Akan syntax and phonology respectively. He wrote a book in Akan about Akan poetry (published by the Bureau of Ghana languages), was chief examiner for West African Languages for West African Examinations Council in Accra for 6 years, and at the University of Ghana, he taught 6 years of Akan Linguistics and 2 years of Essays and Literature of Akan.

Afrikaans

Hoekom verskil dié aand van al die ander?

■ Hu-korm fer-skil dee arnt fuhn uhl dee under?

■ **Why does this night differ from all the others?**

**Op al die ander aande eet ons of gewone brood of matzah;
dié aand net matzah.**

■ Orp uhl dee under arnder eeyit orns off khe-voorner bru-it off matzah;
dee arnt neyt matzah.

■ **On all the other nights we eat either regular bread or matzah;
this night only matzah.**

**Op al die ander aande eet ons allerande kruie;
dié aand eet ons veral suur kruie.**

■ Orp uhl dee under arnder eeyit orns uhler-under krayer;
dee arnt eeyit orns fer-uhl su-yer krayer.

■ **On all the other nights we eat all sorts of herbs;
this night we eat bitter herbs.**

**Op al die ander aande doop ons glad nie die kruie nie;
dié aand doop ons hulle tweemaal.**

■ Orp uhl dee under arnder du-wip orns gluht nee dee krayer nee;
dee arnt du-wip orns huhler twee-yer-marl.

■ **On all the other nights we do not dip the herbs at all;
this night we dip them twice.**

**Op al die ander aande eet ons regop of leun ons;
dié aand leun ons.**

■ Orp uhl dee under arnder eeyit orns rekh-orp off lee-yin orns;
dee arnt lee-yin orns.

■ **On all the other nights we eat upright or we lean;
this night we lean.**

**Op al die ander aande eet ons in 'n gewone manier;
vanaand eet ons met spesiale plegtigheid.**

■ Orp uhl dee under arnder eeyit orns in a khe-voorner muhneer;
fuhn-arnt eeyit orns met speshi-arler plekh-tikh-heyt.

■ **On all the other nights we eat in an ordinary manner;
tonight we eat with special ceremony.**

About the Language:

Afrikaans

Number of speakers: 4,934,950
Rank: 133

Afrikaans is spoken in South Africa, primarily in Pretoria and Bloemfontein; more are in Cape Town, Johannesburg, Durban and Port Elizabeth. Afrikaans is also spoken in 9 other countries, primarily Namibia, Botswana, Zambia and Malawi.

Afrikaans is a variant of the Dutch spoken by the 17th C colonists, with some borrowings from Malay, Bantu languages, Khoisan languages, Portuguese and other European languages. The ancestors of the current Afrikaans population were brought from Java 300 years ago.

About the Translator and Speaker:

Tim Jackson

Age: Unavailable   Recorded: 1994
Town: Johannesburg, South Africa

Tim's native language is Afrikaans.

Haggadah from the collection of Rabbi Arnold Zoref

Haggadah published in the Netherlands, containing illustrations from medieval Haggadahs in The British Library's collection.

Adyghe

Щыга мы уещыр щыщхьэθэр?

■ *Why is this night different from all other nights?*

НэмыкӀ сыдрэ чэщхэм хьалыгъоу тшхырэм кӀытэ хэльми хэмыльми мэхъу;
а чэщым кӀытэ зыхэль хьалыгъу тшхырэп.

■ *On all other nights we eat either leavened bread or matzah; on this night only matzah.*

НэмыкӀ сыдрэ чэщхэм сыд θэдэ хэтэрыкӀи тэшхы;
э чэщым хэтэрыкӀ дыдж нэмыкӀ тшхырэп.

■ *On all other nights we eat all kinds of herbs; on this night only bitter herbs.*

НэмыкӀ сыдрэ чэщхэм эыкӀи хэдгъаорэп;
а чэщым тӀо хэтэгъао.

■ *On all other nights we do not dip even once; on this night we dip twice.*

НэмыкӀ сыдрэ чэщхэм тышхэ хъумэ тыщысми тегъэкӀыгъэми мэхъу;
а чэщым тегъэкӀыгъэу тэшхэ.

■ *On all other nights we eat either sitting up or reclining; on this night we recline.*

НэмыкӀ сыдрэ чэщхэм сыд ишӀыкӀэу тышхэми мэхъу;
а чэщым хабзэ гъэнэθагъэ хэльэу тышхэн ретэгъэкӀокӀы.

■ *On all other nights we eat in an ordinary manner; on this night we dine with special ceremony.*

ABOUT THE TRANSLATOR AND SPEAKER:

Majdalin Hilmi

Age: Unavailable   Recorded: 1997
Locations: Jordan / New York, NY

Majdalin (Majida) was raised in Jordan. She is a
Circassian princess and enjoys substantial standing in
the Caucasian community. Majida is a native speaker
of two forms of Circassian: Adyghe (Bzhedukh dialect,
West Circassian) and Kabardian (East Circassian).

ABOUT THE LANGUAGE:

Adyghe, Bzhedukh dialect

Number of speakers: 499,300
Rank: 551

Adyghe, also called Circassian, Lower- and West-
Circassian, is the language spoken in the Russian
Republic of Adygea. It also has a significant
number of speakers in Turkey, Jordan, Syria,
Iraq, Israel and a few villages in Macedonia.

The Circassians (who call themselves *Adyghe*)
are the oldest indigenous people of North
Caucasus. The language has an unusual system
– its overabundance of consonants and scarcity
of vowels has stimulated much interest among
linguists. It has been referred to as a language
with *bewildering complexity*.

In the recordings: Majida ends her
recording with the name of the language,
which sounds like "anjaDO".

**Turkish children
performing in Yassaçal**

Adhola

Irango wori me opokere g'wori megi?

■ *Why is this night different from all other nights?*

Wori mdongi jie, wa chamo mugati madithowi kosa mongoye thowi (ma buuthowi); wori me mugati mabuuthowi kende.

■ *On all other nights we eat either leavened bread or matzah; on this night only matzah.*

Wori megi jie wachamo fufa mopokere opokere; wori me fufa makechi kende.

■ *On all other nights we eat all kinds of herbs; on this night only bitter herbs.*

Wori megi jie wakiluthi kada dichiel; wori me wa lutho diriyo.

■ *On all other nights we do not dip even once; on this night we dip twice.*

Wori megi jie wachemo monyo wabedo ka wabwowere kosa mawayala; wori me wabedo mawayala.

■ *On all other nights we eat either sitting up or reclining; on this night we recline.*

Wori megi jie wachemo paka kisandelo (kisindiri); wori me wachamo kalima manya kare.

■ *On all other nights we eat in an ordinary manner; on this night we dine with special ceremony.*

ABOUT THE LANGUAGE:

Adhola

Number of speakers: 360,000
Rank: 646

Adhola, called Dhopadhola by its speakers, is spoken in east Uganda, primarily the Tororo District.

The speakers are called Jopadhola ("people of Adhola") and their lands are called Padhola.

ABOUT THE TRANSLATOR:

Oketch Sam Otenge

Age: 35   Translated: 2010
Locations: Uganda / Nigeria / UK / Tororo, Uganda

Oketch speaks Dhopadhola, some Swahili, Ateso and Luganda. Although Ateso is his mother tongue, he lost it living in the Padhola land.

Oketch works as a health trainer for the Peace Corps in Uganda. Prior to training for health promotion in the UK, Oketch worked with Voluntary Service Overseas in Nigeria. His love is supporting people to achieve their dreams. He was assisted in the translation by **Anne Apio**, of Tororo District.

A/E
Z Y X W V U T S R Q P O N M L K J I H G F E D C B **A**
A/C

Photo © PlanUSA

Photo © Tororo District

"The Eiffel Tower is to Paris as the magnificent Tororo Rock is to Tororo District". **Tororo Rock is visible everywhere in the district**

Abkhaz

Уахатэи ацх егьырт ацхкъэа зегьы излареиҟшымзеи?
- ■ waHatwi atsH ageet atsH kwazeegy yuhzlaraypSHoomzay?
- ■ *Why is this night different from all other nights?*

Егьырт ацхкъэа зегь раан ҳара ма ача мамзаргьы амгьал ҳҩоит; уахатэи ацх азы [уаха] амгьал мацара* ҳҩоит.
- ■ aygeert atsHkway zeegyraan hara ma atsha mamzar-gyamgyal hfoit;
  waHatwee atsH azuh amgyal matsara hfoit.
- ■ *On all other nights we eat either leavened bread or matzah;*
  on this night only matzah.

Егьырт ацхкъэа зегь раан ҳара еиуеиҟшым ацаара архаагакъэа ҳҩоит; уахатэи ацх азы ицаау [архаага] мацара ҳҩоит.
- ■ aygeert atsHkway zeegyraan haraee ooweepSHem atsaara arHaagakwa hfoit;
  waHatwee atsH azuh eetsaoo matsara hfoit.
- ■ *On all other nights we eat all kinds of herbs;*
  on this night only bitter herbs.

Егьырт ацхкъэа зегь раан ҳара зныкгьы иацаҳшьуам; уаха сынтэгьы иацаҳшьуеит.
- ■ aygeert atsHkway zeegyraan hara znuhk-gyuh yats-ahshwam;
  waHa iyuntw'gyuh yatsahshwayt.
- ■ *On all other nights we do not dip even once;*
  on this night we dip twice.

Егьырт ацхкъэа зегь раан ҳара ма ҳтэаны мамзаргьы ҳианы акраҳҩоит; уаха ҳианы акраҳҩоит.
- ■ aygeert atsHkway zeegyraan hara ma htooanuh mamzer-gy' Hyanuh akrahfoit;
  waHa hyanuh akrahfoit.
- ■ *On all other nights we eat either sitting up or reclining;*
  on this night we recline.

Егьырт ацхкъэа зегь раан ҳара баша акраҳҩоит [ҳакрыҩашьа башоуп]; уаха ҳара хыла ҳацклаҟшны акраҳҩоит.
- ■ aygeert atsHkway zeegyraan hara baSHa akrahfoit;
  waHa hara Huhla hatsklapSHnuh akrahfoit.
- ■ *On all other nights we eat in an ordinary manner;*
  on this night we eat with special ceremony.

---

* The recording does not use **мацара** ("only")
in the first question.

ABOUT THE LANGUAGE:

Abkhaz

Number of speakers: 117,350
Rank: 1,138

Abkhaz, also called Abxazo, is spoken in the Abkhazia region of Georgia, Turkey and Ukraine. Abkhaz first appeared in writing in 1862 using a spelling system devised by Russian soldier-linguist Baron Peter von Uslar. Other spelling systems using the Georgian, Latin, and Cyrillic alphabets appeared during the 20th C. The current Cyrillic system, in use since 1954, is cumbersome with its 14 extra consonant letters and inconsistencies.

The first novel in Abkhaz was by Dârmit' Gulia (1874-1960), regarded as the Father of Abkhaz Literature.

ABOUT THE TRANSLATOR AND SPEAKER:

Zaira Khiba

Age: Unavailable   Recorded: 1997
Towns: Ochamchira, Abkhazia / London, England

Dr. Zaira Hewitt Khiba was born and raised in Ochamchira, Abkhazia. She spoke Abkhaz at home and learned Russian when she attended school; thus today, her 2 first languages are Abkhaz and Russian. At the Sukhum Pedagogical Institute, Zaira studied Abkhaz and German. Her postgraduate research was on consonant-complexes in Abkhaz. At the time of recording, she had lived in England 21 years.

Zaira is married to Dr. George Hewitt, Professor of Caucasian Languages, at the University of London's School of Oriental and African Languages.

Transliteration key:
- H = 'ch' of Bach
- h = hard, including "ah"
- SH = more narrowly focussed "sh"
- w = often like oo
- r = before consonants nearly silent

The Centenarian Choir, formed by the oldest members of the Abkhazian Folk Art Club, dressed in traditional Georgian costume

CONSTRUCTED LANGUAGES AND PARODIES

Our final section shows translations in Constructed Languages – languages that arose as an invention of one or two people, rather than from a community of people – as well as humorous Parodies.

Some languages have been constructed for noble purposes. The best known, Esperanto, was started with the idea that if nations spoke with one common language, people would more readily get along with each other. Codes such as Morse Code, Braille and Signal Flags aren't languages, but they aid communication when normal language cannot be used. Some languages were constructed for literary reasons: J.R.R. Tolkien's Elvish, Sindarin, etc. The 'language' of Klingon was developed for a commercial venture: Universal Pictures wanted some alien-sounding phrases to use in the *Star Trek* movies, however linguist Marc Okrand created an entire language with vocabulary, grammar and usage. And other 'languages' are just for fun: Valley Girl, Lawyerese and of course, Pig Latin and Israel's Abanibi are some of the many languages that have been constructed purely for enjoyment.

Some may take offense at these parodies of what is, at its core, a sacred text. Our answer is to quote Peter Schikele, the creator of PDQ Bach, expressing sentiments on his radio program (Schickele Mix) to enjoy good-natured humor in religious contexts, while being respectful of those who feel religion's passion:

"We're talking about keeping Christmas. So what does that mean? For some people, that means keeping it religious, and for others it means keeping it serious, and then there are people for whom those two things are the same thing. There are many folks who feel that there is no place for humor in religion at all. When I 'discovered' the Consort of Christmas Carols by PDQ Bach, I very much wanted them to be completely secular. I didn't want to ruffle feathers, I wanted audiences to enjoy themselves during a season of good cheer.

The first carol is called "Throw the Yule Log On, Uncle John" and it's about throwing the Yule log on Uncle John. The second is called "Oh, Little Town of Hackensack," and it's about Santa Claus coming to New Jersey. The last is called "Good King Kong," and that's what it's about.

As I said, these are, to my sensibility, completely secular pieces. But after they appeared in print, a woman contacted my publisher and said that she was never again going to order any piece of music published by them, because the title, "Oh, Little Town of Hackensack," is so blasphemous. Obviously, the title doesn't offend me, but I can appreciate the woman's discomfort, perhaps even anguish.

Here is a member of the Shaker community commenting on Simple Gifts, the hymn that has become well known due to its use by Aaron Copland in the music for Appalachian Spring: 'Although the world has made the song famous, we feel troubled that, in its fame, it is taken so lightly. To believers, it holds a real message, reminding us that we do have to "come down to the place just right" in order to live out Mother's gospel.'

One should never belittle great depth of feeling, especially when it's in the service of love, and anyway, it's always wise to avoid being blasé. But you also have to make room for the diversity of a society like ours. When we look at small, self-contained societies, as we sometimes longingly do, the absolute integration of religion into everyday life seems healthy and powerful. But when things get more heterogeneous ... well, we all know what people can do to each other in the name of religion. And have done. And for that reason, separation of Church and State seems absolutely necessary in a large country, such as ours."

Like Peter Schickele, we believe there is room enough in this world for good-natured fun as well as serious spirituality. Both co-exist for us in the same holiday observance: We read 'Pour out thy wrath' the same night we play Hide and Sock games with our children!

Valley Girl

Like, why is this night like, <u>totally</u> different from, like, all other nights?

It's like the rest of the time we eat this really fattening, like, bread stuff or crackers. But, like, tonight we eat only gnarly thin stuff — which is good, 'cause like it's <u>faster</u>, and I have to like get my nails done.

Like, the rest of the time, it's like we eat any kind of salad we want. But, like, tonight, we eat only grody bitter stuff that like brings tears to your like eyes, and like <u>RUINS</u> your mascara.

It's like all year you like put your veggies in the avocado dip once. But, like, tonight it's sort of like <u>total</u> greed — and you do it like twice.

It's like all year it's really gross, 'cause you have to sit up like straight ... 'cause your parents like <u>said</u> so ... and it's like you're only there in the first place 'cause like they wouldn't let you go out with that guy 'cause he's like from Van Nuys and you're from the nice part of Encino. Anyway ... tonight is like <u>awesome</u>, 'cause you can like sit up or like lounge around or do like anything you want, <u>fer sure!</u> And isn't that, like, great?   <u>Totally!!</u>

ABOUT THE LANGUAGE:

Valley Girl

Number of speakers: Too Many
Status: Poorly Constructed, unfortunately Still Alive

Although Valley Girl is, like, a language that dates back to, like, the late-1970s in the San Fernando Valley of Los Angeles, like, California, it really sounds like it's from another, like, planet. Unless you're from that planet, in which case what's spoken elsewhere is, like, totally, nowhere. See? If not, find a copy of Frank Zappa's 1982 hit song that made Valley Girls, like, totally infamous. Fer sure!

ABOUT THE TRANSLATOR:

Mel Powell

Age: 31   Translated: 1995
Town: Sherman Oaks, CA

Mel Powell is a comedy writer and recovering ex-attorney. He is so creative that he made his own name into a website. Mel is Licensed to Intimidate with Words by the State Bar of California and is Licensed to Entertain with Words by the Scriptwriters Network. He has written parodies, screenplays and several pieces of Jewish humor.

ABOUT THE SPEAKER:

Nicki Berthelson

Age: 18   Recorded: 2006
Location: San Fernando Valley, CA

Nicki was born and raised in the San Fernando Valley. If brought to a random location and blindfolded, Nicki could find any specific store in any shopping mall in southern California in less than five minutes. She currently attends college at the University of Southern California.

Photo © Gary J Wayne

Present and past views of San Fernando Valley's Sherman Oaks Galleria, best known as the home of the Valley Girl. The Galleria was where "*Fast Times at Ridgemont High*" (1982) was filmed, and is mentioned in Frank Zappa's novelty song "*Valley Girl*" (1982), both of which spawned the nationwide recognition of the Valley Girl culture

Upper East Side

When Jews ask the Four Questions on the Upper East Side:

1) Does it come in black?

2) Do you take American Express?

3) When can you deliver it?

4) Is it returnable?

Translation by Fred Miller of New York City

Alternates:

Dan Kahn suggests a parody closer in style to the Ma Nishtana:

Why is the Upper East Side different from all other neighborhoods?
In all other neighborhoods, you have a Super;
in this neighborhood we have a Maintenance Coordinator.

Can you come up with other parodies?

ABOUT THE LANGUAGE:

Upper East Side (NYC)

Status: Constructed
Number of speakers: Unknown

The precise geographic regions of the Upper East Side dialect have been a matter of debate for decades among Judeo-Socio-Linguistic scholars. Most agree the primary region ranges from 59th Street to 96th Street and 5th Avenue to the East River. If this is substantiated, the Upper East Side would include all of Lenox Hill, Yorkville, Carnegie Hill, and areas along Park Avenue, Madison Avenue and 5th Avenue. Some authorities express consternation at such a wide geographical extent; none feel the area needs to be expanded further.

Once called the Silk Stocking district, the area has some of the most expensive real estate in the world and likely contains the greatest concentration of individual wealth. Cultural institutions: Cooper-Hewitt (National Design Museum), Frick Collection, *Goethe Institut*, Metropolitan Museum of Art, Museum of American Illustration, Museum of the City of New York, National Academy of Design, 92nd Street Y, Jewish Museum, Asia Society, Guggenheim Museum and Whitney Museum. Also contains Gracie Mansion, residence of New York City's mayors. A neighborhood within the Upper East Side, Yorkville, was inhabited throughout most of the 20th C by people of German and Hungarian descent. Yorkville was also home to the Marx Brothers.

Some scholars discovered variations of UES in other areas of New York City. There have been a few reports of mimicry as far away as the bordering regions of New Jersey, Connecticut and Long Island. To date, however, these reports have been discounted by mainstream scientists as unsubstantiated mumblings of dilettante dialecticians.

Uncle Eli

Why is it only on Passover night
we never know how to do anything right?
We don't eat our meals in the regular ways,
the ways that we do on all other days.

`Cause on all other nights we may eat
all kinds of wonderful good bready treats,
like big purple pizza that tastes like a pickle,
crumbly crackers and pink pumpernickel,
sassafras sandwich and tiger on rye,
fifty falafels in pita, fresh-fried,
with peanut-butter and tangerine sauce
spread onto each side up-and-down, then across,
and toasted whole-wheat bread with liver and ducks,
and crumpets and dumplings, and bagels and lox,
and doughnuts with one hole and doughnuts with four,
and cake with six layers and windows and doors.
Yes -- on all other nights we eat all kinds of bread,
but tonight of all nights we munch matzah instead.

And on all other nights we devour
vegetables, green things, and bushes and flowers,
lettuce that's leafy and candy-striped spinach,
fresh silly celery (Have more when you're finished!)
cabbage that's flown from the jungles of Glome
by a polka-dot bird who can't find his way home,
daisies and roses and inside-out grass
and artichoke hearts that are simply first class!
Sixty asparagus tips served in glasses
with anchovy sauce and some sticky molasses--
But on Passover night you would never consider
eating an herb that wasn't all bitter.

ABOUT THE LANGUAGE:

Uncle Eli's Dr. Seuss-style

Status: Constructed

This verse is excerpted from Uncle Eli's Special-for-Kids, Most Fun Ever, Under-the-Table Passover Haggadah, ISBN 1-886411-26-3, (c) 1999 by Eliezer Segal. Reprinted with the permission of No Starch Press. Be sure to get it!

ABOUT THE AUTHOR:

Eliezer Segal

Age: 30   Translated: 1980
Town: Calgary, Alberta

Talmudic scholar Professor Segal (aka *Uncle Eli*) headed the University of Calgary's Religious Studies Department. Starting as a joke with the *Ma Nishtana* text, Eli parodied what the Haggadah would be like if it were rendered in playful verse. Many years later, the project became a very popular children's book. Segal "fools the protagonist into learning about Passover by giving him a version of the story that is flat-out fun" (Los Angeles Times).

And on all other nights you would probably flip
if anyone asked you how often you dip.
On some days I only dip one Bup-Bup egg
in a teaspoon of vinegar mixed with nutmeg,
but sometimes we take more than ten thousand tails
of the Yakkity-birds that are hunted in Wales,
and dip them in vats full of Mumbegum juice.
Then we feed them to Harold, our six-legged moose.
Or we don't dip at all! We don't ask your advice.
So why on this night do we have to dip twice?

And on all other nights we can sit as we please,
on our heads, on our elbows, our backs or our knees,
or hang by our toes from the tail of a Glump,
or on top of a camel with one or two humps,
with our foot on the table, our nose on the floor,
with one ear in the window and one out the door,
doing somersaults over the greasy k'nishes
or dancing a jig without breaking the dishes.
Yes-- on all other nights you sit nicely when dining--
So why on this night must it all be reclining?

Illustrations © Bonnie Gordon-Lucas

Sullen Teenager

Stage Direction – spoken in a whiny voice:

Why does this night have to be different from other nights?

Do I HAVE to eat that Matzah?

I'm not eating that horseradish. Besides, if I don't eat vegetables during the year, why should I eat anything tonight?

Can you tell Michael to get his hands out of my salt water?
(Alternate version) Can I just eat the Charoset?

(The fourth question cannot apply, since all teenagers do EVERYTHING *reclining:* eating, drinking, talking on the phone, IM'ing ...)

ABOUT THE LANGUAGE:

Sullen Teenager Language

Number of speakers: Too Many
Status: Constructed

Sullen Teenager Language (STL), as many a parent knows, is spoken by teenagers who are being forced against their will to participate in rituals that are really, really irrelevant to life, love and the real world.

ABOUT THE TRANSLATOR:

Gill Diamond

Age: 40s   Translated: 2005
Town: Millburn, NJ

Dr. Diamond is a genetics biochemist working at the University of Medicine and Dentistry of NJ, where he is an Associate Professor. At home, he is father to a lovely daughter who only occasionally reverts to STL.

Drawing by Alyssa Barnea, 5th grade, Millburn, NJ

Miriam's tambourine, themes of Passover

Structured Query Language

```
SELECT Tonight.item,

    Othernights.Description AS [All_Other_Nights],

    Tonight.Description AS [This_Night]

FROM Othernights

JOIN Tonight ON (Tonight.Item = Othernights.Item)

WHERE Othernights.Description <> Tonight.Description

Rows returned: 4

Item        All_Other_Nights        This_Night
========    ====================    ==========

Eat         Chametz and Matzah      Matzah

Herbs       Any                     Maror

Dip         Null                    2

Recline     Maybe                   Always
```

ABOUT THE LANGUAGE:

Structured Query Language (SQL)

Status: Constructed
Time Period: 1974 -Present

Structured Query Language (SQL, often pronounced as "sequel") is a standard programming language for querying and managing databases. Queries allow the user to specify which data to extract from a database, for example, all company employees older than 55 whose income is greater than a specified amount. Or, show the names of all Levites who participated in the creation and worship of the Golden Calf (this should be none).

SQL was created by Donald Chamberlin and Raymond Boyce, two computer scientists working for IBM.

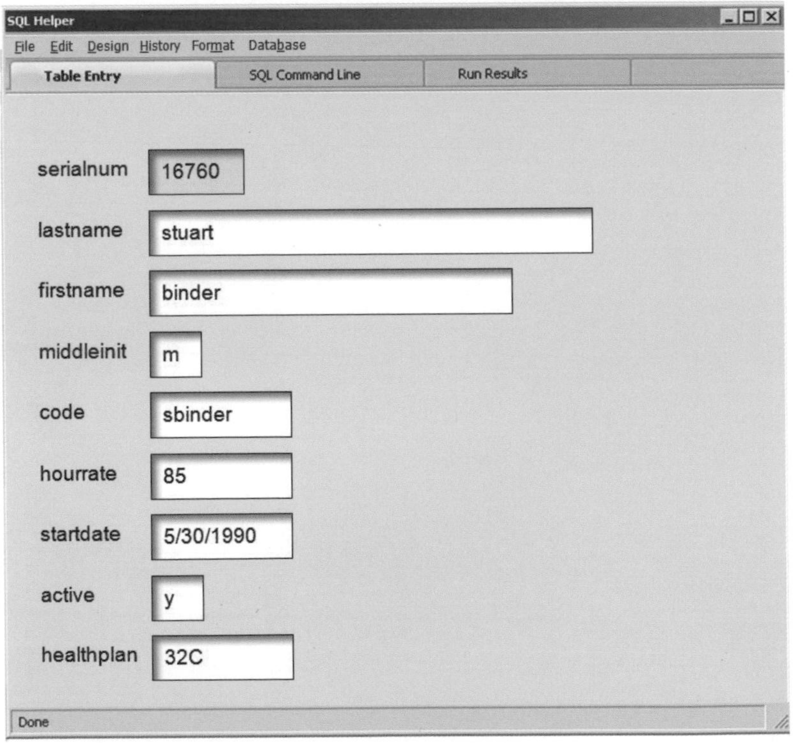

SQL Helper

File Edit Design History Format Database

Table Entry	SQL Command Line	Run Results

serialnum 16760

lastname stuart

firstname binder

middleinit m

code sbinder

hourrate 85

startdate 5/30/1990

active y

healthplan 32C

Done

Typical window for database entry

ABOUT THE TRANSLATOR:

Cantor Stuart Binder

Age: Unavailable   Translated: 2008
Towns: Bethlehem, PA / Chicago / Robbinsville, NJ

Cantor Binder is the cantor (and database administrator!) at Congregation Beth Chaim in Princeton Junction, NJ. Stuart obtained his BS from Iowa State University and his MS in sacred music from Hebrew Union College.

Stuart holds the unique distinction of creating a Four Questions version <u>while</u> listening to the authors' book talk at his synagogue.

Stenography

117

```
      P H A
T P H       EU R B
T           A        PB
T P H A
      H A
      HRA   EU
      HRA
      HR O            S
              U   PB
STKPWHR     E
      P H AO E
      K       O         L
      H A
      HRA   EU
      HR O               S
ST P H
I
S     H     E
      PW        EU
      K   H O           L
      H A
      HRA   EU
      HR O               S
              U   PB
T P H       U
      O E F P
      HR    EU  PB
K   H A         PL
      PHA   EU       TS
          AO
      P H A          TS
STKPWHRA
              R B G S
      HRA
      H A   EU
      HRA
      H A
STKPWHR     E
      K   AO
      HR    EU
      P H A          TS
STKPWHRA
```

```
P H
      H       E
      PW      EU
      K   H O         L
      H A
      HRA   EU
      HR O           S
              U   PB
P H           U
      O E F P
      HR    EU  PB
      H     EU
              U R
K W R       EU R
      R       U B G
K       O            S
              R B G S
      H A
      HRA   EU
      HRA
      H A
TKPWHR      E
      P H     U
      R   O   R
T P H
J
      H       E
      PW      EU
      K   H O         L
      H A
      HRA   EU
      HR O           S
      A   EU  PB
              U   PB
T P H         U
P H A             TS
      PW      EU
      HR    EU  PB
      A       F
T P
      HR    EU
      H R     U
TKPW    A         P L
      E F P
      H             S
```

118

```
      HRA
      HRA   EU
      HRA
      H A
STKPWHR     E
S     H     EU
      T       A  EU
      PW      EU
      A           P L
      P H     EU P L
ST P H
4
S     H     E
      PW      EU
      S   H O         L
      H A
      HRA   EU
      HR       U      S
              U   PB
T P H         U
      AO  EUF P
      HR    EU  PB
      PW  A EU  PB
K W R       UF P
      PW    EU  PB
      O E
      PW  A EU  PB
      P H     EU
S             U
      PW    EU  PB
              R B G S
      H A
      HRA   EU
      HRA
      H A
STKPWHR     E
      K   AO
      HR       U  PB
T P H         U
      P H     EU
S             U
      PW    EU  PB
ST P H
```

A modern stenography machine

Translation notes: The tape was created by the Stenograph model *Stentura 8000*. The letters are read from left to right. For example, the first phrase is represented as:

PHA – *Ma*	TPHEURB = *Nish*	HA = *Ha*	HA = *Ha*	PHAOE = *Mi*	HA = *Ha*
	TAPB = *Tan*	HRAEU = *Lai*	STKPWHRE = *Ze*	KOL = *Kol*	HRAEU = *Lai*
	TPHA = *Na*	HRA = *La*			HROS = *Los*

Sociology Professor

What functions are served by the departure from hegemonic practice on this occasion, in contradistinction to other, comparable occasions, most notably with regard to the preparations of grains without – and this is particularly deserving of our attention in this context – without, dare we say in the interests of humor, without "hot air", leavening with our humor, as it were, the questions regarding the unleavening of grains; and the further departure in the specific use of bitter – bitter being of course a relative concept, differently understood in different vocabularies of food consumption, but still, bitter in this context, bitter herbs; and then too, regarding the dyadic pairing of foods, notably the salt water immersions we repeatedly engage in; and finally the general aura of relaxation, perhaps not apparent to those who have engaged in frantic preparations for the past two weeks, but nonetheless, on this occasion, an aura of relaxation being normatively required?

What, then, are the functions of these practices?

ABOUT THE LANGUAGE:

Sociology Professor

Status: Constructed

Sociology Professor is spoken by, well, Sociology Professors, Assistant and Full, as well as students in Sociology and related sciences.

The language variety shown here is the Cultural Studies dialect.

ABOUT THE TRANSLATOR:

Barbara Katz Rothman

Age: 51   Translated: 1999
Towns: New York, NY / Groningen, Netherlands /
        Osnabrueck, Germany / Plymouth, United Kingdom

Dr. Katz Rothman is Professor of Sociology at the City University of New York. Her books, on birth, motherhood, genetics, race and adoption, have been translated into Japanese, German and Finnish. None of her writing is available in Sociology Professor. Her honors include Fulbright and Leverhulme Professorships.

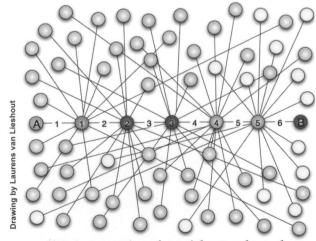

Drawing by Laurens van Lieshout

Artist's conception of a social network graph representing six degrees of separation

SMS / Twitter

YYYY THS NITE DIFRNT FRM AL OTHR NITES ?

Y DUWE ET ONLY MATSA ?

Y ONLI BTR ERBS ?

Y DIP X2 ?

Y ET LEENING ?

CUZ. :-)

ABOUT THE LANGUAGE:

SMS / Twitter

Number of users: Billions
Time Period: 1985-Present

SMS (Short Messaging Service) is the underlying mechanism for text messaging from mobile phones and similar devices. It was first proposed in 1985 as a standard for GSM handsets. The first SMS message, "Happy Christmas," was sent in 1992; its use has expanded to all cell, satellite and landline networks.

Tweets, 140-character messages posted on Twitter, are used for social networking and microblogging. They are posted on the user's profile page and sent to their followers. Because of the limit on the number of characters, messages for SMS and Tweets have evolved their own slang, abbreviations and language style.

ABOUT THE TRANSLATOR:

Ruthie Ben-Mayor

Age: 52   Translated: 2007
Towns: Albuquerque, NM / Kibbutz Ein-Shemer, Hefer, Israel

Ruthie submitted this parody in response to our contest. It is one of three she submitted within a week in "a flash of inspiration." She made *aliya* (emigrated to Israel) at 19 and majored in linguistics and English literature at Tel-Aviv University.

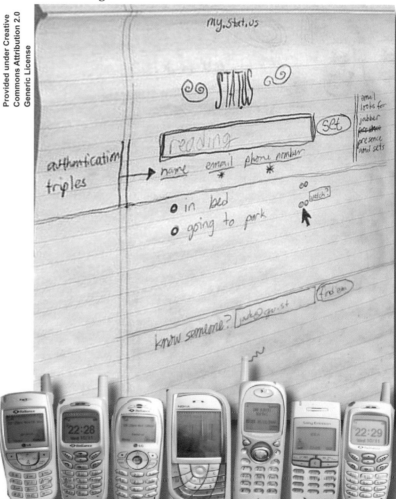

Sketch by the creator of Twitter, Jack Dorsey, envisioning in 2006 his SMS-based social network

Provided under Creative Commons Attribution 2.0 Generic License

Provided under GNU Free Documentation License

Mobile phone styles at the time of Twitter's creation

Shakespearean

We look from friend to friend and ask of them
Why dark of night is different to us
On this occasion, such that brings us here.

When time is of the norm we eat the bread
That rises, like Apollo in the morn,
Or else, we fill our plates without the chance
That yeast shall work its physic on our food.
But this night just the latter doth suffice.

When time is of the norm we eat the herbs
That fill our garden beds, with no regards
To sweet or sour. This night we apply
Only those whose bitterness doth remind
Us the somber tenor of the hour.

When time is of the norm we eat the herbs
That spice our evening feast as dry as bone.
But on this night we celebrate fortune
By wetting them, not once but twice, submerged
In briny tears for those remembered.

When time is of the norm no especial
Thought doth decide the manner of our feast.
So for this once we choose our seat with care,
And stand upon ceremony taught
By ancient wisdom from time long ago.

ABOUT THE LANGUAGE:

Shakespearean

Status: Constructed

Shakespearean aims to mimic the style and prose of William Shakespeare (1564-1616), who is often regarded as the greatest writer in the English language and in Western literature, as well as one of the world's most eminent dramatists. He wrote some 38 plays over the course of a quarter century. All are still performed, four centuries later.

Superlatives apply to this Shakespearean parody as well.

ABOUT THE TRANSLATOR AND SPEAKER:

Ralph Carhart

Age: 29   Translated: 2002
Town: New York, NY

Ralph is the Director of the Revolving Shakespeare Company, which has been called "New York's newest and hottest Classical Theatre company." They perform updated works of Shakespeare, Ionesco, etc. as well as cabaret pieces.

William Shakespeare

ABOUT THE LANGUAGE:

Sfat HaBet (B Language)

Number of speakers: Millions
Status: Constructed

This children's language is well-known in Israel. It became even more popular with Nurit Hirsh's song *Abanibi*, whose chorus is in 'B language'. *Abanibi* won the 1978 Eurovision song contest. The title is taken from the first line of the song, *Abanibi Obohebev Obotabach*, ("I love you"). Sfat HaBet has been traced to Kfar Saba in the 1950s; it may be quite older. The rules of Sfat HaBet add, after each syllable, a 'b' with the same vowel as the prior syllable. A similar Portuguese language, *lingua do P*, uses 'p' and was popular in Brazil.

As one might expect, there are a great variety of children's language games and in many languages. Most involve adding syllables, such as *ubb* (the language Ubbi Dubbi was popularized on the PBS show Zoom), *op* (called op-talk and Double Dutch), *ithig/ittig, boro* and other variants. Usually these are added before or after each word's syllable or at the end of each word.

Other games involve reversing the order of syllables (called *Verlan* in France, *Hablar al vesre* in Buenos Aires and *Fasa fahukha* in Israel), as well as more involved replacements for consonants. Play languages are documented for at least Burmese, Javanese, Kuna (Central America), Persian, Tagalog, Thai and Turkish.

ABOUT THE SPEAKER:

Miriam Tauil

Age: 40   Recorded: 2005
Towns: Mendoza, Argentina / Ganei Tikva, Israel / Berkeley Heights, NJ

A native Hebrew speaker, Miriam was born in Argentina, moved to Israel (outside Tel Aviv) when she was 8, and then to the USA when she was 28. This was the first time she spoke Sfat HaBet.

מַבַּה עִבְּשֶׁתְּבַּנֶּבַּה הַבְּלֵיבְּלֶבַּה הַבַּזֶּבֶּה מִבְּכֹּבֹל הַבְּלֵיבְּלוֹבֹת?

■ Maba nibishibitabanaba habalaybaylaba habazehbeh mibikobol habaleibeilobot?

■ *Whyby ihbis thibis nibight dibifferberehbent fruh-bum aball obuhtherber nibights?*

שֶׁבְּבְּבְּכֹּבֹל הַבְּלֵיבְּלוֹבֹת אֲבָנוּבוּ אוֹבוֹכְבֶּלִיבִּין חָבְמֵבֵץ וּמַבַּצְּבָּה. הַבְּלֵיבְּלָבָה הַבַּזֶּה בַּבֻּלּוֹבוּ מַבַּצָּבָה:

■ Shehbehbibikhobol habalaybaylobot abanubu obokhibileebeen khabamaybayts ubumabatsabah; habalaibailaba habazeheh kubulobo mabatsahbah.

■ *Obon aball obuhtherber nibights webe eabeat eibeitherber leabevebenebed brebed orbor mabatzahbah;*
obon thibis nibight obonlyby mabatzahbah.

שֶׁבְּבְּבְּכֹּבֹל הַבְּלֵיבְּלוֹבֹת אֲבָנוּבוּ אוֹבוֹכְבֶּלִיבִּין שֶׁבָּאבַּר יִבְּרַבְּקֹבוֹת הַבְּלֵיבְּלָבָה הַבַּזֶּה בַּבֻּלּוֹבוּ עָבָרוּבוֹר:

■ Shehbehbibikhobol habalaybaylobot abanubu obokhibileebeen shihbiahbahr yihbihrabakobot; habalaibailaba habazeheh kubulobo mabarobor.

■ *Obon aball obuhtherber nibights webe eabeat aball kibinds obof herberbs;*
obon thibis nibight obonlyby bibitterber herberbs.

שֶׁבְּבְּבְּכֹּבֹל הַבְּלֵיבְּלוֹבֹת אֵיבֵין אֲבָנוּבוּ מַבַּטְבֵּיבְּלִיבִּין אֲבַפֵּיבְּלוּבוּ פַּבַּעֲבַם אֶבֶחְבַּת הַבְּלֵיבְּלָבָה הַבַּזֶּה שְׁבְּתֵיבוּ פְּבֵעֲבְּמֵיבִּים:

■ Shehbehbibikhobol habalaybaylobot aybayn abanubu mabatbeebeeleebeen abafeebeelu pabaabam ehbekhabat; habalaibailaba habazeheh shihbitabay fihbihabameebeem.

■ *Obon aball obuhtherber nibights webe dooboo nobot dibip eebeeveben unbunce;*
obon thibis nibight, webe dibip twibice.

שֶׁבְּבְּבְּכֹּבֹל הַבְּלֵיבְּלוֹבֹת אֲבָנוּבוּ אוֹבוֹכְבֶּלִיבִּין בֵּיבֵּין יוֹבְּשֶׁבְּבִיבִּין וּבוּבֵיבֵין עֲבְסַבְּבִּיבִּין. הַבְּלֵיבְּלָבָה הַבַּזֶּה בַּבְּלָבְנוּבוּ עֲבְסַבְּבִּיבִּין:

■ Shehbehbibikhobol habalaybaylobot abanubu obokhibileebeen baybayn yoboshihbihveebeen ubuvaybayn mihbihsububeebeen; habalaibailaba habazeheh kubulabanubu mihbihsububeebeen.

■ *Obon aball obuhtherber nibights webe eabeat eibeitherber sibittibing ubup obor rebeclibinibing;*
onbon thibis nibight webe rebeclibine.

שֶׁבְּבְּבְּכֹּבֹל הַבְּלֵיבְּלוֹבֹת אֲבָנוּבוּ אוֹבוֹכְבֶּלִיבִּין בֵּיבֵין בְּבְצוּבוּרְבָה רָבְגֵיבִּלְבָה. הַבְּלֵיבְּלָבָה הַבַּזֶּה בְּבְּרוֹבוּב עֲבְקַבְּסִיבִּיוֹבוֹת:

■ Shehbehbibikhobol habalaybaylobot abanubu obokhibileebeen bihbitzuburaba rahageeheelaba; habalaibailaba habazeheh bihbihrobov teebeekihbiseebeeobot.

■ *Obon aball obuhtherber nibights webe eabeat ibin aban orbordibinabary mabannerber;*
obon thibis nibight webe dibine wibith spebecialbul ceberebemobonyby.

Semaphore, Hebrew

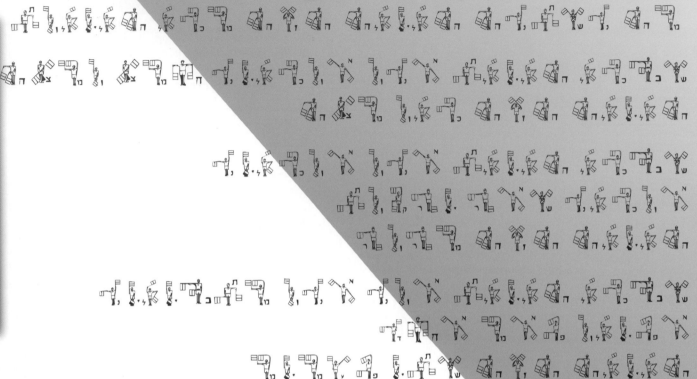

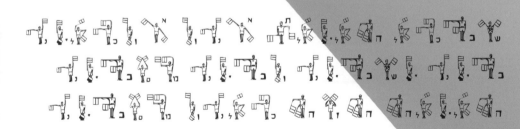

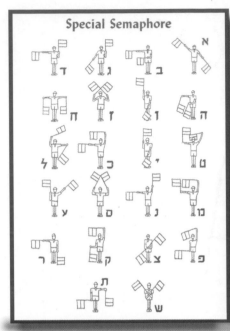

Special Semaphore

The original *World Over*
page published in 1954

ABOUT THE CODE:

Hebrew Semaphore

Status: Constructed

Semaphore is a signaling system which involves waving a pair of
hand-held flags in various positions to indicate letters of the alphabet
or numerals. The flags used in modern semaphore are usually square,
red and yellow and divided diagonally with the red part on the top
left. Semaphore in various forms has been used to send messages over
distances since at least Roman times.

The semaphores shown here were used by the Israeli Army, Navy and
Scouts at some point and were printed in *Israel Vista*, the magazine of the
Jewish National Fund's Education Department. These were found by
Rickey Stein when they were reprinted in 1954 by *World Over*, a magazine
published by the Jewish Education Committee Press (New York).

On the DVD there is a file you can print containing a
larger version of the Hebrew Semaphore. Have your
guests spell out the *Ma Nishtana* using Israeli flags!

Sandorian

hRlind Cid doCE Det flrek lorlok fedE Deten?

■ h'va-yind sid da-see shet fai-rik lar-lock fedee sheten?

■ *Why is this night different from all other nights?*

**nod GrBf fedE Deten yUd DrIn bEzuflOkom zUAlu rod motzu;
nod doCE Det inCitin motzu.**

■ nod grouf fedee sheten yood shrine bee-zu-flo-kum zoo-ay-la rod matza; nod da-see shet insi-tin matza.

■ *On all other nights we eat either leavened bread or matzah; on this night only matzah.*

**nod GrBf fedE Deten yUd DrIn GrBf Rritulen rod brAuren;
nod doCE Det inCit lRurd brAuren.**

■ nod grouf fedee sheten yood shrine grouf vritulen fod brayeren; nod dosee shet insit ayverd brayeren.

■ *On all other nights we eat all kinds of herbs; on this night only bitter herbs.*

**nod GrBf fedE Deten yUd flrek nalEtEd trofA gapCno;
nod doCE Det yUd nalEtEd cekCno.**

■ nod grouf fedee sheten yood fay-rek nal-ee-teed traw-fay jap-sna; nod da-see shet yood nal-ee-teed check-sna.

■ *On all other nights we do not dip even once; on this night we dip twice.*

**nod GrBf fedE Deten yUd iCit bEzuflOkom pud ruk;
nod doCE Det yUd iCit ruk.**

■ nod grouf fedee sheten yood isit bee-zu-flow-kum pud ruck; nod dosee shet yood isit ruck.

■ *On all other nights we eat either sitting up or reclining; on this night we recline.*

**nod GrBf fedE Deten yUd DrIn nid jo trAdalEak krakin rARam;
nod doCE Det yUd DrIn srok Ontuc CpiR.**

■ nod grouf fedee sheten yood shrine nid ja tray-da-lee-ack krackin ray-tham; nod dosee shet yood shrine throck own-touch spith.

■ *On all other nights we eat in an ordinary manner; on this night we dine with special ceremony.*

ABOUT THE LANGUAGE:

Sandorian

Number of speakers: 3
Status: Constructed
Time Period: 1986 - Present

There are many single-minded efforts at constructed/artificial languages. One finalist in the reknowned Westinghouse Science Talent Search (now sponsored by Intel) had created one and spoke it nearly exclusively, much to the annoyance of his co-finalists.

Brett Quist and Alex Sandor created Sandorian in 1986-1987, after a fascination with homespun codes and the Cyrillic alphabet. Sandor began scrawling oddly shaped characters and assigning sounds. Sandor and Quist soon created secret naughty words using the alphabet. With the Sandorian Renaissance (c. 1989-1994), a dictionary was developed, with writing rules, an elaborate grammar and eloquent Haikus. When Daniel Singer began studying Sandorian in 1992, it had truly become a vibrant, living language. Daniel, Brett and Alex communicated almost exclusively in Sandorian with each other at the University of Wisconsin-Superior. During the 1980s, their Nation of Ventnor (a tiny area near Nemadji River, Wisconsin) briefly claimed independence from the USA. The language fell into disuse when its three fluent speakers moved to three different states. This Four Questions translation is the first published communication in Sandorian.

Photo by Tiffany Follett

The Nemadji River, near the ancestral home of the Nation of Ventnor

ABOUT THE TRANSLATOR AND SPEAKER:

Cantor Daniel Singer

Age: 33   Recorded: 200
Towns: Superior, Wisconsin / New York, NY

Daniel Singer serves as the senior cantor at the Stephen Wise Free Synagogue in New York City. Cantor Singer obtained Masters degrees from the University of Michigan (vocal performance) and from the Hebrew Union College (sacred music). Before becoming a cantor, Daniel was Voice Department Chair and Opera Workshop Director at the Flint (MI) School for the Performing Arts. He also was a resident artist with the Toledo Opera, the Israel Vocal Arts Institute and the Brevard Music Center. Daniel's solo debut was in *On Second Avenue* with the Folksbiene Yiddish Theater.

Daniel began a tradition of chanting the book of Esther in Sandorian at the Stephen Wise Free Synagogue; it has not yet led to his sacking as a cantor there.

Reggae, Jamaican

Chorus sung after each verse:
Ah seh yeah! (Ah seh yeah!) Ah seh yeah! (Ah seh yeah!)
Ah seh hear me now! (Ah seh yeah!)
Listen what ah seh! (Ah seh yeah!)
What, mek-a dis night, so diff-a-rent, from all other night?
What, mak-a dis night, so diff-a-rent, from all other night?

On all other night, I and I eat Jah bread,
With de yeast and de leavening like all natty dread.
But tonight special night I and I confused Rasta,
Me lookin' for Jah bread all me find is de Matzah.

On all other night, me havin' all kind of herb,
Me plantin', me eatin', me smokin'-a de herb,
But tonight me have a bite, me gettin' red in de face,
Because Jah herb me have tonight, has got bitter taste.

On all other night, me takin' de food,
From de plate into de mouth, by directest route.
But tonight special food takes detour on de trip,
Karpas and Maror, gets de dip.
Dip it to me one time! (Uh!)
Dip it to me two times! (Uh Uh!)

On all other night, me eat like me please,
Me sittin', me leanin', whatever I please,
But tonight me have right to be treat like a king,
Reclinin' like royalty, me lay back and lean.

So all praise to God, who splitted de sea,
Who lead us to freedom from the land of slavery,
Who lead I and I from darkness to light,
So me brothers and me sisters, celebrate this night.

All praise to God, creator of Heaven and Earth.

> **In the recordings:** Heshy and the group
> Reality Shock sing *What mek-a dis night*.

ABOUT THE MUSIC:

Jamaican Reggae

Time Period: Late 1960s - Present

Reggae is a rhythmic style of Jamaican music characterized by accents on the off-beat. Its most revered performer, Bob Marley, is credited with spreading Jamaican music to a worldwide audience.

The infectious beat of Reggae influenced music around the world, including a Jamaican-African themed CD, *Reggae Passover*.

The song *What mek-a 'dis night* was featured in *When Do We Eat?*, the 2006 comedy film about a seriously dysfunctional family at a Seder.

ABOUT THE SINGER:

Heshy Rosenwasser

Age: 29
Recorded: 1996
Locations: Long Beach, NY / LA

Frederick "Toots" Hibbert

Age: 23
Recorded: 1968
Town: Kingston, Jamaica

The Reggae Four Questions was created by Heshy ("The Hesh"), who nurtured rock 'n' roll dreams in Jerusalem and emerged as the singer and keyboardist for a jazz-blues-rock band and hasn't stopped since. The first portion of the chorus is based on *54-46 That's My Number* by noted Reggae artist, Toots Hibbert.

Heshy masquerading as a
Jewish Soul Brother on Purim

Toots Hibbert in concert

RAP

A-chee a-chee a-chee a-chee a-chee pa-PAA

Well,
I look around the table and see there's something MISSIN'
Something you won't even find in the KITCHEN.
I ain't DISSin' you. No matter where I LOOK
I can't find no bread with leaven in it like in the BOOK
The Haggadah ...
So tell me home boys, Mah NishTANA
Ha layla hazeh mikol haleylot?
Now let's talk about them yerakot.

'Cause on all other nights, we can eat all kinds of VEGGIES:
Tomatoes corn and beets and peas and beans and brocCOLi!
But tonight when Elijah walk through our front DOOR
Our primary vegetable is DA MAROR
So I ask you again, homes, and tell me RIGHT
What makes this night so different from every other NIGHT?

A-chee a-chee a-chee a-chee a-chee pa-PAA

Kadesh.

Urchatz.

Karpas.

Kick it!

Now after we take the middle matzah and we RIP IT
We stick our food in charoset, yeah, that's right, we DIP IT!
Which ain't at all ILL which means it's kinda NICE
But I think it's overkill to be dippin' it TWICE!
So I'll repeat my kasha oh mah nishtaNAH
Mikol haleylot ZEHHHH lay-i-lah?

And another rule we added in our little CRIB
Has to do with when we sit to chow down our PRIME RIB
Yes another thing I noticed 'bout our fine cuiSINE
We can't eat it sittin' up, no man we gotta LEAN!

So give me an answer oh chacham son,
What make this night so different from every other one!
Answer now that The Mah Nishtanah Rap is DONE.

Mah Nishtanah Rap © Saul A Resnikoff

ABOUT THE LANGUAGE:

Rap

Number of speakers: At least several thousand
Status: Creative constructions

Rapping is the speaking or chanting of rhymed lyrics. Rap is distinct from poetry because it is performed in time to a beat. Although strongly associated with hip hop music, Rap predates the culture of hip hop by several centuries.

Wandering musicians / poets of West Africa (griots) delivered stories rhythmically. Some historians claim that Blues music was delivered in rap form as early as the 1920s. Jazz poetry and beat poetry are precursors, as is Jamaican toasting. One of the first rappers, DJ Clive Campbell (aka Kool Herc), delivered calls in the 1970s to dancers in a rapping style. Rap exists for most major languages and is an indication of a language's vitality. Rap being used in one endangered language was a sign to linguists that the language was valued.

ABOUT THE TRANSLATOR AND RAPPER:

Saul E Resnikoff

Age: 45   Translated: 1990   Recorded: 2010
Towns: Monsey, NY / Centennial, CO

Saul has played musical theater and enjoys getting caught in the rain. Growing up in Monsey, Saul loved the annual seders at his New Jersey cousins. One tradition everyone followed was reciting the Mah Nishtanah in as many languages as they knew (or could make up!). Two months after his father died, as the seder was about to move on to Avadim Hayinu, Saul broke the flow and introduced the Mah Nishtanah Rap. Saul hopes its distribution will be a merit for his father.

Bonus on the DVD: Learn from Saul how to do his rap, and learn additional raps for use at the Seder on the DVD.

Photo by Richa'd Alexander Caraballo. Provided under Wikipedia Commons freely licensed media

The Genesis rapper, Kool Herc

Quenya

Manen lóme sina ume ve neune lómi?

■ How (is it that) this night is not like other/following nights?

Ilye neune lómissen, matilve tiuyaina massa var matsa; lóme sinasse, er matsa.

■ On all second/other nights we eat either swollen bread or matza; on this night only matza.

Ilye neune lómissen, matilve ilye nossion laicar; lóme sinasse, er sáre laicar.

■ On all second/other nights we eat greens; on this night only bitter greens.

Ilye neune lómissen, lá mixalve mine lusse; lóme sinasse, mixalve atta lussen.

■ On all second/other nights we do not wet one time; on this night we wet two times.

Ilye neune lómissen, matilve hárala var caitala; lóme sinasse, caitalve.

■ On all second/other nights we eat sitting or lying; on this night we lie.

Ilye neune lómissen, matilve sanyave; lóme sinasse, matilve meryave.

■ On all second/other nights we eat normally; on this night we eat festively.

Illustration by Allison Ryan

King Thranduil of Mirkwood, also called the Elvenking

ABOUT THE LANGUAGE:

Quenya / High Elvish language of *Lord of the Rings*

Status: Constructed

Quenya was one of the languages created by J.R.R. Tolkien, writer of the well loved Lord of the Rings trilogy. Tolkien invented Quenya around 1915. It is considered to be "High Elvish".

ABOUT THE TRANSLATOR:

Helge Fauskanger

Age: Unavailable   Translated: 2004
Town: Island of Askøy, Norway

Helge has a Masters in Linguistics in Nordic languages. She lives on the Island of Askøy, which is outside the town of Bergen. Helge has ("with some persistence") studied what is available and written a number of articles about what can be inferred about Tolkien's languages. She is responsible for the website www.Ardalambion.com.

Although others frequently refer to her as an expert in Tolkien's languages (and only a few others, she adds), she says "so much of Tolkien's material still remains unpublished and unavailable that nobody can be an 'expert' on these languages – I don't even know all forms of the verb 'to be'!"

Helge states this translation should not be seen as a scholarly work. Tolkien would surely have translated it quite differently, if only because he felt freer to coin new words.

Helge wrote a treatise comparing different versions of Norwegian Bible translations.

Earlier versions of the translation were worked on by **Gildor Inglorion** in Greece and author Rickey Stein's daughter, **Robyn Stein**, in NJ.

For Tolkien fans, Helge's translation notes: The word "other" is a problem; we have a word for "other" in Tolkien's very early material, but it clashes with a later word for "dirty, soiled". Helge sometimes used *neuna* (pl. *neune*), glossed by Tolkien as "second" and derived from a root meaning "follow, come behind". Matzah may simply be Quenyarized as *matsa* (it is similar to one Quenya word for "bread", *masta*, and may even be Tolkien's inspiration for this word – in later material we have *massa*, though). "Leavened bread" is difficult. Gildor used *tiuca* "fat". A related verb is *tiuya-* "swell, grow fat". Helge suggested *tiuyaina massa* for "swollen bread". For "herbs" Helge used *laicar* "greens", the word *laica* "green" inflected as a noun -- though Tolkien may have intended it as an adjective only. There is a word for "herb" in early material, *nesse*, but its conceptual validity may be questioned since *nesse* means "youth" in later material. Helge adopted Gildor's idea of using the adjective *mixa* "wet" as a verb **mixa-* "to wet". There are some Tolkienian precedents for using adjectives in -a as verbal stems. Another possibility could be to derive a longer verb *mixata-* "make wet"; if so, it should also take the ending *-lve* "we". (Gildor used *-mme* here.) Tolkien himself is responsible for the chaotic pronoun tables, so it is hard to say what is strictly right or wrong. Gildor used a passive participle *caitaine* instead of the active participle *caitala*; both may work here. Gildor's use of *havaine* for "sitting" might have confused Quenya *ham-* "sit" with its Sindarin cognate **hav-* "sit". (Not given in Tolkien, but David Salo derived this likely cognate for a line occurring in the Jackson movies: At one point Aragorn tells Legolas, *havo dad* = "sit down".) Helge used another word for "sit", *hra-* or possibly *har-*, which occurs in a later source: active participle *hrala* "sitting". Helge adopted Gildor's idea of deriving adverbs (with ending -ve) from the adjectives *sanya* "normal" and *merya* "festive".

Poetry, E.B. Browning

Why — Do I ask thee? Let me count the queries.

I ask thee of the length and width and height [1]

Of a crumbly, flakey matzo slice;

I ask thee of the bitterness of herbs

Ingested, swallowed in a trice.

I ask thee of the fashion put to use [2]

By salty brine immersed in twice;

I ask thee of leaning and idle grace [3]

In reclining, feeling rather nice.

Smiles, tears, of all my life! - and, if I choose,

I shall but ask again being more precise.

Parody notes:
1. Original had: the depth and breadth and height.
   Of course, on Passover we must not refer to <u>breadth</u>!
2. Original had: passion put to use
3. Original had: Ideal Grace

ABOUT THE LANGUAGE:

E B Browning Poetry

Number of speakers: 1
Time Period: 1806 – 1861
Status: Poetic

Elizabeth Barrett Browning famously wrote her *How do I love thee* poem in the mid-1840s. She published throughout her life: her first poem was written when she was 6 or 8; her last, shortly before her death.

ABOUT THE TRANSLATOR:

Ruthie Ben-Mayor

Age: 52   Translated: 2007
Towns: Albuquerque, NM / Kibbutz Ein-Shemer, Hefer, Israel

Excited by the parody contest offered on this book's website, Ruthie fired off three remarkable parodies within a week. "I really want this book!" she exclaimed. The authors declared this and *Do Re Me* as the most artful parodies and awarded Ruthie the winning prize. Ruthie majored in linguistics and English literature at Tel Aviv University.

Pig Latin

אֵמָא אִשְׁתַּנְנָא אֲלַיְלָהָא אַזֶהָא אִכֹּלְמָא אֲלֵילוֹתְהָא?

■ **Amay ishtanahnay alaylahay azeh-hay ikolmay aleilot-hay?**

■ *Y-way isyay isthay ightnay ifferentday omfray allyay otheryay ightsnay?*

אֶבְכָלְשָׁא אֲלֵילוֹתְהָא אָנוּיָא אוֹכְלִיְנַיָא אָמַצְחָא וּמַצְיָא
אֲלַיְלָהָא אַזֶהָא אֲלֹכָא אַצַמָא:

■ **Ehbkholshay ahlaylot-hay ahnuyay okhleenyay ahmayts-khay umahtsahyay; alailah-hay ahzeh-hay ulokay ahtsahmay.**

■ *Onyay allyay otheryay ightsnay eway eatyay eitheryay eavenedlay eadbray oryay atzahmay; onay isthay ightnay onlyyay atzahmay.*

אֶבְכָלְשָׁא אֲלֵילוֹתְהָא אָנוּיָא אוֹכְלִיְנַיָא אַארְשָׁא יְדָקוֹתְיָא.
אֲלַיְלָהָא אַזֶהָא אַרוֹרְמָא:

■ **Ehbkholshay ahlaylot-hay ahnuyay okhleenyay ihahr-shay ihrahkot-yay; alailah-hay ahzeh-hay ahrormay.**

■ *Onyay allyay otheryay ightsnay eway eatyay allyay indskay ofyay erbs-hay; onyay isthay ightnay onlyyay itterbay erbs-hay.*

אֶבְכָלְשָׁא אֲלֵילוֹתְהָא אָנוּיָא אוֹכְלִיְנַיָא אַטְבְּלִיְנְמָא אָפִילוּיָא אַטְעֵפָא אֶחְתָיָא.
אֲלַיְלָהָא אַזֶהָא אָתְשָׁא אַטְעִיעֵפָא:

■ **Ehbkholshay ahlaylot-hay aynyay ahnuyay ahtbeeleenmay ahfeeluyay ahahmpay ehkhatyay; alailah ahzeh-hay ihtay-shay ihahmeemfay.**

■ *Onyay allyay otheryay ightsnay eway o-day otnay ipday evenyay once-way; onay isthay ightnay eway ipday ice-tway.*

אֶבְכָלְשָׁא אֲלֵילוֹתְהָא אָנוּיָא אוֹכְלִיְנַיָא בֵּייְנַיָא יוֹשְׁבִיְנַיָא וּבֵייְנַיָא אַסְבֵּייְנַמָא.
אֲלַיְלָהָא אַזֶהָא אֲלֵעוּכָא אַסְבֵּייְנַמָא:

■ **Ehbkholshay ahlaylot-hay ahnuyay okhleenyay aynbay oshveenyay uvaynyay subeenmay; alailah-hay ahzeh-hay ulahnukay ihsubeenmay.**

■ *Onyay allyay otheryay ightsnay eway eatyay eitheryay ittingsay upyay oryay eclining-ray; onay isthay ightnay eway ecline-ray.*

אֶבְכָלְשָׁא אֲלֵילוֹתְהָא אָנוּיָא אוֹכְלִיְנַיָא אַצוּרְבָּא אַגִילְרָא.
אֲלַיְלָהָא אַזֶהָא אָרוֹבְבָּא אַקְסִיוֹתְעָא:

■ **Ehbkholshay ahlaylot-hay ahnuyay okhleenyay ihtzurahbay ahgeelaray; alailah-hay ahzeh-hay ihrovbay eekseeot-tay.**

■ *Onyay allyay otheryay ightsnay eway eatyay inyay anyyay ordinaryyay annermay; onay isthay ightnay eway ine-day ithway ecial-spay eremony-cay.*

ABOUT THE LANGUAGE:

Igpay Atinlay

Number of speakers: Millions and millions
Status: Constructed

Igpay Atinlay (Pig Latin) is often the first constructed, private or secret language spoken by children, typically in the USA, Canada, Britain and English-speaking countries around the world. Similar language games are used in other languages. Some Pig Latin phrases have achieved official slang status, notably ixnay and amscray. There are several Pig Latin dialects, primarily differing in the syllable (ay, hay, way or yay) added for words beginning with vowels. The dialect used here adds yay.

The Pig-Latined Hebrew involved spelling changes to accommodate the phonetization rules of Hebrew, e.g., אֵמָא for מַה.

Ere-thay isyay onay ubstantiatedsay ate-day orfay e-thay originyay ofyay Igpay Atinlay, althoughyay one-yay eference-ray atesday ityay o-tay idmay 18th-yay entury-cay Englandyay.

ABOUT THE SPEAKER:

Joshua (Jack) London

Age: 12   Recorded: 2005
Town: Highland Park, NJ

Born and raised in Highland Park, Jack is a seventh grader at Yeshiva Shaare Tzion in Piscataway, NJ. He enjoys reading and plans to be an architect when he grows up.

Picture Communication Symbols, Hebrew

About the Code:

Hebrew Picture Communication Symbols (PCS)

Number of users: Unknown
Status: Constructed

Many children with motor disabilities use Augmentative and Alternative Communication (AAC) systems to communicate. They might use technology (a voice output device or computer) or low-tech methods: pointing in some manner to pictures, symbols or words on a communication board or in a communication book.

The system of Picture Communication Symbols (PCS) is easy to learn, even by children with cognitive difficulties, and is used world-wide. Originally developed by Mayer-Johnson, PCS has been translated into 40 different languages.

Approximately 1.1% of Israeli children and adults have physical disabilities; a smaller fraction (fewer than 25,000) have no speech capability and could benefit from augmentive systems.

About the Translator:

Lynn Kra-Oz

Age: Unavailable   Translated: 2009
Town: Ra'anana, Israel

Lynn is a speech pathologist, working with special-needs children, some of whom cannot speak due to Cerebral Palsy, Muscular Dystrophy or other causes.

She wrote the Four Questions in Hebrew using the Boardmaker program and Picture Communication Symbols. Shown here is a symbol in each square, the format that would be on a communication board.

מה	נשתנה	הלילה	הזה	מכל	הלילות?

שבכל	הלילות	אנו	אוכלין	חמץ	ומצה.

הלילה	הזה	כולו	מצה:

שבכל	הלילות	אנו	אוכלין	שאר	ירקות.

הלילה	הזה	מרור:

שבכל	הלילות	אין	אנו	מטבילין	אפילו פעם	אחת.
					 	1

הלילה	הזה	שתי **2**	פעמים:

שבכל	הלילות	אנו	אוכלין	בין	יושבין	ובין	מסובין.

הלילה	הזה	כולנו	מסובין.

Fìtxon na ton alahe nìwotx pelun ke lu teng?

■ This-night like nights other all why not is same?

Tonìri alahe awngal yom hametsìt yom matsat ke tsranten; fitxon yom matsat nì'aw.

■ As-for-nights other we eat hametz eat matzah not matter; this-night eat matzah only.

Tonìri alahe awngal yom fkxenti lerìk nìwotx; fitxon yom sat a lu syä'ä nì'aw.

■ As-for-nights other we eat vegetable-food leafy all; this-night eat those that are bitter only.

Tonìri alahe awnga ke yemfpay si keng 'awlo; fitxon yemfpay si melo.

■ As-for-nights other we not dipping do even once; this-night dipping do twice.

Tonìri alahe awngal yom wutsot tengkrr hereyn nìpxim tengkrr teruvon, ke tsranten; fitxon yom tengkrr teruvon.

■ As-for-nights other we eat meal while sitting erect while leaning not matter; this-night eat while leaning.

Tonìri alahe awngal yom wutsot nìfya'o letrrtrr; fitxon yom nì'eoio.

■ As-for-nights other we eat meal in-manner ordinary; this-night eat ceremoniously.

Notes on the translation:
Vocabulary added for a Na´vi seder:
hametsì: 'hametz'; *matsa*: 'matzah'; *yemfpay*: 'dipping, immersion'; *fkxen*: 'food of vegetable (as opposed to animal) origin'; *pxim*: 'erect, straight up and down'; *tuvon*: 'to lean'; and '*eoio*: 'ceremonious'.

ABOUT THE LANGUAGE:

Na'vi / Language in the movie *Avatar*

Status: Constructed
Language of: The moon Pandora
Time Period: 2005-Present
Biblical Quote: Eliyahu Ha-*Na'vi*

Na'vi was created by Dr. Paul Frommer for the lovely **blue aliens** in the 2009 blockbuster hit movie, *Avatar*. It is intended to sound both alien and pleasant. Na'vi fit the concepts of James Cameron (*Avatar's* director and writer) of what the alien language should sound like, to be learnable by the human characters in *Avatar*, and of course to be pronounceable by the actual actors – all this while not closely resembling any existing human language.

Although Dr. Frommer loosely based Na'vi's grammar on Polynesian languages, the Na'vi language has several elements that are uncommon for human languages, such as putting verb modifiers in the middle of words. Na'vi also has ejective consonants, spelled *px, tx* and *kx*, which sound a bit like "spat" consonants. (These are quite obvious in Dr. Frommer's recording.)

Avatar was a most successful movie, earning more money worldwide than any other at that point. While *Avatar* wasn't the first popular 3D movie, its smash success ushered in a new interest in 3D movies and 3D home televisions.

ABOUT THE CREATOR, TRANSLATOR AND SPEAKER:

Professor Paul R Frommer

Age: 65   Recorded: 2010
Towns: New York, NY / Malaysia / Iran / Los Angeles, CA

Professor Emeritus Paul Frommer retired from the Marshall School of Business at the University of Southern California in 2010. Throughout his life, Paul has had wide-ranging passions: based on an early interest in astronomy, he started college by majoring in astrophysics but ended up with a degree in math. While working for the Peace Corps in Malaysia, teaching math and English (in the Malay language!), Paul realized another passion, linguistics. He enrolled in USC's doctoral program for linguistics, taking time out to teach English in Iran. He learned Persian there, which led to his dissertation topic. It was then only a couple Frommerian-sized steps from Malay and Persian to USC's Business School.

Dr. Frommer also created the Martian language for the Disney film *John Carter of Mars* (Release date 2012).

Paul Frommer, creator of Avatar's Na'vi language

Morse Code, Hebrew

ABOUT THE CODE:

Morse Code

Status: Constructed

Morse code was invented in 1835 by Samuel Morse (1791-1872), a Professor of Art and Design at New York University. He used pulses of current to deflect an electromagnet, which moved a marker, producing written codes on a strip of paper – Morse code. The following year it was modified to emboss paper with the dots and dashes. The first news story sent by Morse code was the Whig Party's nomination of Henry Clay on May 1, 1844. It was sent 20 miles from Annapolis Junction to the Capital. The first demonstration to Congress, on May 24, was the phrase "What Hath God Wrought?" In 1858, the first transatlantic message was sent from Queen Victoria to President Buchanan. When Morse died in 1872, there were 680,000 miles of telegraph cable on land and undersea.

Trained Morse operators were able to transmit 40-50 words per minute. Automatic transmission, introduced in 1914, more than doubled that speed. In 1999, the international maritime community stopped using Morse code (the SOS) as acceptable communication for ships in distress. Morse code still thrives among amateur radio operators.

When spoken, the dash is represented as 'da' and the dot as 'dit'.

Hebrew Morse Code

There are Morse codes defined for many languages. Hebrew's Morse Code only represents consonants and ignores distinctions between ב and ב, כ and כ, פ and פ, ו and ו, ש and ש (which experienced readers do not need). The Hebrew codes are often mapped to their closest English equivalent, for instance: . (t) for ת.

The Israeli Navy reportedly maintains a station (call letters 4XZ) in Haifa that broadcasts in Hebrew Morse Code.

■ מה נשתנה הלילה הזה מכל הלילות
■ *Why is this night different from all other nights?*

■ שבכל הלילות אנו אוכלין חמץ ומצה הלילה הזה כלו מצה
■ *On all other nights we eat either leavened bread or matzah; on this night only matzah.*

■ שבכל הלילות אנו אוכלין שאר ירקות הלילה הזה מרור
■ *On all other nights we eat all kinds of herbs; on this night only bitter herbs.*

■ שבכל הלילות אין אנו מטבילין אפילו פעם אחת הלילה הזה שתי פעמים
■ *On all other nights we do not dip even once; on this night we dip twice.*

■ שבכל הלילות אנו אוכלין בין יושבין ובין מסבין הלילה הזה כלנו מסבין
■ *On all other nights we eat either sitting up or reclining; on this night we recline.*

■ שבכל הלילות אנו אוכלין בצורה רגילה הלילה הזה ברוב טקסיות
■ *On all other nights we eat in an ordinary manner; on this night we dine with special ceremony.*

The DVD contains a page showing the English Morse Code version of the Four Questions.

First Morse Code message from Washington to Baltimore: "What Hath God Wrought?" often cited incorrectly as the first-ever telegraph message

Maritime Signal Flags

■ *Why is this night different from all other nights?*

■ *On all other nights we eat either leavened bread or matzah; on this night only matzah.*

■ *On all other nights we eat all kinds of herbs; on this night only bitter herbs.*

■ *On all other nights we do not dip even once; on this night we dip twice.*

■ *On all other nights we eat either sitting up or reclining; on this night we recline.*

■ *On all other nights we eat in any ordinary manner; on this night we dine with special ceremony.*

About the Code:

Maritime Signal Flags

Status: Constructed

Maritime Signal Flags (also called the International Code of Signals) is a signaling system of flags that is used by ships around the world. The current system, published in 1857 by the British Board of Trade, was gradually adopted by most seafaring nations. A 1932 revision extended it to English, French, German, Italian, Japanese and Norwegian. Several earlier systems co-existed prior to 1857. For instance, the Elford Telegraph system, which was used along the Atlantic Seaboard, consisted of only 7 flags and was easy to read, since only blue and white colors were used.

Strung end to end and hung bow to stern from a ship's rigging, Signal Flags or Pennants dress the ship for ceremonial and festive occasions. The individual flags, used singly or in combination, more typically represent special messages, such as "Man overboard" (GW), "I am altering my course to starboard" (E) or "Keep clear of me, I am maneuvering with difficulty" (RU).

Logic, Symbolic

$$\forall x \forall y [\, Nx \cdot Tx \cdot Ny \cdot \neg Ty \;\to\; x \neq y\,]$$

■ **Nights other than this night are different from it.**

$$\forall x [\, Nx \cdot \neg Tx \;\to\; [\exists y (Cy \cdot Eyx) \land \exists y (My \cdot Eyx)]\,] \;\land$$
$$\forall x [\, Nx \cdot Tx \;\to\; [\exists y (My \cdot Eyx) \land \forall y (Eyx \to My)]\,]$$

■ **On nights other than this one we eat both chametz and matzah;
on this night we eat matzah and only matzah.**

$$\forall x [\, Nx \cdot \neg Tx \;\to\; \forall y (Hy \to Eyx)\,] \;\land$$
$$\forall x [\, Nx \cdot Tx \;\to\; \exists y (By \cdot Eyx)\,]$$

■ **On nights other than this one we eat all kinds of herbs;
on this night we eat bitter herbs.**

$$\forall x [\, Nx \cdot \neg Tx \;\to\; \neg \exists y Dyx\,] \;\land$$
$$\forall x [\, Nx \cdot Tx \;\to\; \exists y \exists z (Dyx \cdot Dzx \cdot (y \neq z) \cdot \forall w [Dwx \to (w=y \lor w=z)])\,]$$

■ **On nights other than this one we don't dip even once;
on this night we dip exactly twice.**

$$\forall x [\, Nx \cdot \neg Tx \;\to\; (Sx \lor Rx)\,] \;\land\; \forall x [\, Nx \cdot Tx \;\to\; Rx\,]$$

■ **On nights other than this one we eat either sitting up or reclining;
on this night we eat reclining.**

$$\forall x [\, Nx \cdot \neg Tx \;\to\; Ox\,] \;\land\; \forall x [\, Nx \cdot Tx \;\to\; \neg Ox\,]$$

■ **On nights other than this one we eat in an ordinary manner;
on this night we eat with special ceremony.**

Intended interpretations:

Nx: x is a night
Tx: x occurs today
Cy: y is chametz
My: y is matzah
Hy: y is an herb
By: y is bitter herbs
Eyx: we eat y during x
Dyx: y is a dipping during x
Sx: we eat sitting up on x
Rx: we eat reclining on x
Ox: we eat in an ordinary manner on x

Moses parting the Red Sea

Drawing by Ethan Meth, 4th grade, W Caldwell, NJ

ABOUT THE LANGUAGE:

Symbolic / Predicate Logic

Status: Mathematical
Time Period: 1887 – Present

Giuseppe Peano is the founder of symbolic logic (also called mathematical logic) and set theory. Although essentially the logic of Aristotle, symbolic logic seeks to represent knowledge, premises, deductions and conclusions in a mathematically rigorous form. **Gottlob Frege**, **George Boole** (the circuitry of digital computers embodies Boolean logic), **Augustus De Morgan**, **Bertrand Russell** and **Alfred North Whitehead** all made major contributions.

The translation shown is Predicate Logic, a subset of Symbolic Logic

ABOUT THE TRANSLATOR:

Dr. Larry Denenberg

Age: 53   Translated: 2008
Towns: Omaha, NE / Newton, MA

Dr. Deneberg received Bachelors and Doctorate degrees in Applied Mathematics from Harvard (thesis topic: Computational Logic). He has taught courses in computer science and math at Tufts and Harvard, and has written a college textbook in computer science. Larry has held the positions of Senior Scientist and CTO at several high-tech companies. An avid folkdancer, Larry has taught and performed at many venues.

An earlier translation was developed by **Johnathan P Reale.**

Leet Speak

About the Translator:

Cory Davia

Age: 15   Recorded: 2002
Town: Maplewood, NJ

Cory attends Columbia High School in Maplewood, NJ. In addition to Internet gaming, his interests include tennis, word games, philosophy, music and getting into college.

\/\/|-|y 15 7h15 /\/1g|-|7 |)1ff3|2r3/\/7 f|20/\/\ 4|| 07|-|3r /\/19|-|75?

0/\/ 4|| 0t|-|3r n19/\/75, \/\/3 347 317|-|3|2 |34\/3/\/3d 8r34|) 0|2 /\/\47z4|-|;
0/\/ 7|-|i5 /\/i9h7, 0n|y /\/\4tz4h.

0/\/ 4|| 0t|-|3r n19/\/75, \/\/3 34t 4|| k1n|)5 0f |-|3r85;
0/\/ 7|-|15 n16/\/7, 0/\/|y 81t73r |-|3|2b5.

0/\/ 4|| 07h3|2 /\/ig/\/75, \/\3 |)0 /\/o7 |)1p 3v3/\/ 0/\/c3;
0/\/ 7h15 /\/1g|-|t, \/\/3 d1p 7w1(3.

0/\/ 4|| 07h3|2 /\/ig/\/75, \/\3 347 317|-|3|2 5i77i/\/6 |_|p 0|2 r3c|1n1/\/9;
0/\/ 7|-|15 /\/i9h7, w3 |23c|i/\/3.

0/\/ 07|-|3r /\/1g|-|75, \/\/3 34t 1/\/ 4/\/ 0rd1/\/4|2y, m4/\/n3|2;
0/\/ 7|-|i5 /\/19|-|7, w3 d1/\/3 \/\/1t|-| 5p3c14| (3r3/\/\0/\/y.

At great personal risk, we reveal the secret Leet Alphabet:

A = 4 or @	N = /\/
B = 8	O = 0
C = (	P = |>
D = |)	Q = q
E = 3	R = |2
F = f	S = 5
G = 9	T = 7
H = |-|	U = |_|
I = 1	V = \/
J = j	W = \/\/
K = |<	X = x
L = |	Y = y
M = /\/\	Z = z

There is some disagreement in the online community regarding some letters. Some use @ instead of 4 for "A". Some use 1 for "L" rather than the vertical bar. There are at least three versions of "G". The list goes on. The alphabet above represents the most "proper" version of the code.

About the Code:

Leet Speak

Number of speakers: Unknown
Status: Constructed

Leet Speak (written as |337 5p34k in Leet Speak) codes English letters to make them more visually appealing and Internet savvy to the gaming community. Leet Speak is not the dialect used in Instant Messaging (IM), which shortens words to an extreme degree. Leet Speak evolved from the desire to hide forbidden hacker terms and profanity from automated searches.

Those who play real-time strategy games, where competing players play simultaneously in a shared environment, first meet in a chat room to organize terms for the game. Leet was created by experienced players to trade taunts in a way people newer to the Internet wouldn't be able to follow. Theoretically, the slang was more intimidating. Leet has evolved into the preferred language of Internet gamers and hackers. Those using Leet proficiently on gaming message boards are taken more seriously. The code is not used for long strategy explanations, but phrases are occasionally tossed in to look competitive.

The code's name was created by experienced gamers as a slang for "Elite". It was respelled because "Lite" looked like a diet cola product. The code uses combinations of keyboard symbols that mimic the letters. Those letters that cannot be mimicked are left in lowercase for visual effect. Many times letters are left untransformed, as in |33t 5pe4k rather than |337 5!>34k. Additional steps sometimes add slang terms associated with |337, but none were appropriate for the Four Questions. Spelling variants, as was used for "this night" (7|-|i5 /\/i9h7, 7h15 n16/\/7, etc) add to the code's "allure".

Lawyerese

1.0 Why is this night defined as that period of time commencing at sundown according to readily established almanac norms for sunrise and sundown and continuing until sunrise according to said established norms, different or unlike in substantive and material ways from all other nights as defined hereinabove?

1.1 On all other nights as defined hereinabove, save the particular night on which these questions are asked or stated, we eat and/or consume for quasi-nutritional purposes bread, including but not limited to rye, pumpernickel, whole wheat, multiple grain, sesame bun, bagel, bialy, English muffin or muffin from anywhere within the Commonwealth of Britain, or other form of bread product, or matzah; but on this night as defined hereinabove, only, solely, and limited to matzah.

1.2 The remaining questions shall be prepared in writing, served upon all interested parties, and submitted to later decision and/or appellate review.

ABOUT THE LANGUAGE:

Lawyerese / Legalese

Number of speakers: Too many Millions
Status: Constructed

Lawyerese is spoken by Attorneys, some of their staff clerks and secretaries, and commentators on Court TV. Legal secretaries are among the few who can translate Lawyerese to English and back again. A *pidgin* version is spoken by many non-lawyers who watch too much court-related television Judge shows and all 74 different versions of *Law & Order*. Although not their primary communication medium, it is understood by Judges and most politicians. It is the only known language where a listener is actually billed by the word.

Every major language group with a developed legal system has their own Lawyer dialects.

ABOUT THE TRANSLATOR AND SPEAKER:

Mel Powell

Age: 26   Translated: 1990
Town: Sherman Oaks, CA

Mel Powell is a comedy writer and recovering ex-attorney (but still licensed, don't mess with him) who spends most of his time helping people under the umbrella of the top legal services and identity theft protection company in North America, without having to be a lawyer himself. He is gradually re-learning how to speak English. He is so creative that he made his own name into a website.

Mel has written parodies, screenplays and several pieces of Jewish humor.

Courtesy of Rounder Records

Z Y X W V U T S R Q P O N M L K J I H G F E D C B A

Klingon

ꞌᕕᐢᕔᕙ ᔿᔭᐦᕕᐢᕔꞌ ᔿᕮᐦᕙᕮᐢ ᔿᕮᐦᕮᐢᕔ ᕵᕮᐢᕵᕮ ᔿᕤ

- qatlh pimlaw' ramvam rammey latlh je?
- *Why is this night different from all other nights?*

ꞌᕕᐢᕵᕮᐢᕵᕮᐢ ᔿᕮᐦᕮᐢᕔ ᕵᕤᕙ ᕵᕮᐦᕤᕵᕵ ᕕᕮᔿᕵᕮ ᔿᕤ ᔭᕵᕔᕤ
ꞌᕮᕙ ꞌᕕᐢᕵᕮᐢᕵᕮᐢ ᔿᕮᐦᕙᕮᐢᕔꞌ ᕕᕮᔿᕵᕮ ᕮᕵᕙ ᕵᕵᕔᕤ

- qaStaHvIS rammey Hoch "Hametz" "Matza" je DISop;
  'ach qaStaHvIS ramvam'e', "Matza" neH wISop.
- *On all other nights we eat either leavened bread or matzah;*
  on this night only matzah.

ꞌᕕᐢᕵᕮᐢᕵᕮᐢ ᔿᕮᐦᕮᐢᕔ ᕵᕤᕙ ᕙᕤ ᕵᕤᕙ ᕵᕵᕔᕤ
ꞌᕮᕙ ꞌᕕᐢᕵᕮᐢᕵᕮᐢ ᔿᕮᐦᕙᕮᐢᕔꞌ ᕙᕤ ᕵᕮᔭ ᕮᕵᕙ ᕵᕵᕔᕤ

- qaStaHvIS rammey Hoch, tI Hoch wISop;
  'ach qaStaHvIS ramvam'e', tI wIb neH wISop.
- *On all other nights we eat all kinds of herbs;*
  on this night only bitter herbs.

ꞌᕕᐢᕵᕮᐢᕵᕮᐢ ᔿᕮᐦᕮᐢᕔ ᕵᕤᕙ ᔭᕮᕵᕵᕤᕙ ᕵᕮᕵᔭᕮᐢ ᕵᕮᐢꞌ ᕵᕵᕮᕵᕵ
ꞌᕮᕙ ꞌᕕᐢᕵᕮᐢᕵᕮᐢ ᔿᕮᐦᕙᕮᐢᕔꞌ ᕙᕮᕵᕵᕤ ᕵᕮᐢꞌ ᕵᕵᕮᕵᕵ

- qaStaHvIS rammey Hoch paghlogh taSDaq vay' wIlan;
  'ach qaStaHvIS ramvam'e', cha'logh vay' wIlan.
- *On all other nights we do not dip even once;*
  on this night we dip twice.

ꞌᕮ ᕵᕮᕵᕮᐢᕵᕮᐢ ᔿᕮᐦᕮᐢᕔ ᕵᕤᔭᕮᕵ ᕵᕮᕵᕔᔭᕮᐢᕵ ᕵᕮᔭᕵᕤ ᕵᕵᕤ ᕵᕮᕵꞌ
ꞌᕮᕤᔭ ꞌᕕᐢᕵᕮᐢᕵᕮᐢ ᔿᕮᐦᕮᕮᕵꞌᕵ ᕵᕮᔭᕵᕤᕵꞌ ᕵᕵᔭᕵᕵᕵ

- qa StaHvIS rammey Hoch, maSopDI', maQot qoj maba';
  'ach qaStaHvIS ramvan'e', maQotba' Hochma'.
- *On all other nights we eat either sitting up or reclining;*
  on this night we recline.

ꞌᕮ ᕵᕮᕵᕮᐢᕵᕮᐢ ᔿᕮᐦᕮᐢᕔ ᕵᕤᔭᕮᕵ
ꞌᕮᕤᔭ ꞌᕕᐢᕵᕮᐢᕵᕮᐢ ᔿᕮᐦᕮᐢᕔꞌ

- qa StaHvIS rammey Hoch, mIw motlh wIpab;
  'ach qaStaHvIS ramvam'e', tay le' wIpab.
- *On all other nights we eat in an ordinary manner;*
  on this night we dine with special ceremony.

Illustration by Alysa Lerman

Klingon / Language of the *Star Trek* series

Status: Constructed
Language of: The Klingon planet, Kronos

Klingon, language of the Klingon home planet, was constructed by linguist Marc Okrand for Paramount Studios' *Star Trek* movies. While there are other artificial languages, and other languages crafted for fictional beings, Klingon was the first time a trained linguist was called upon to create a language for aliens. Marc did not simply invent a few words to make Klingons sound alien, but a complete language with its own vocabulary, grammar and usage. Many linguists consider Klingon a fully represented language. KLI.org has members in 45 countries.

Mark Shoulson

Age: 28   Recorded: 1996
Towns: W Caldwell / W Orange / Highland Park, NJ

Mark is a) one of this world's most accomplished Klingon speakers, and as Assistant Director of the Klingon Language Institute (KLI.org), has given several museum lectures on how to speak (or swear) properly in Klingon, b) pursuing a Doctorate in Computer Science at Rutgers University, and c) keenly interested in languages, particularly constructed languages (Esperanto, Lojban, Klingon).

He translated the Book of Jonah and other portions of the Bible into Klingon and is editor of *Hamlet, The Restored Klingon Version*.

Jibberish/Ubbi Dubbi

Mubah nubeeshtubahnubah hubahlubilubah hubahzubeh mubeekubol hubahlubaylubot?
■ Whuby ubis thubis nubight dubiffuberubent frubom uball ubothuber nubights?

Shubehbubekhubol hubahlubaylubot ubahnubu ubokhlubeen khubahmubayts ubumubahtsubah;
hubahlubilubah hubahzubeh kubulubo mubahtsubah.
■ Ubon uball ubothuber nubights wube ubeat ubeithuber lubeavubenubed brubead ubor mubatzubah;
ubon thubis nubight ubonluby mubatzubah.

Shubehbubekhubol hubahlubaylubot ubahnubu ubokhlubeen shubihubahr yubihrubahkubot;
hubahlubilubah hubahzubeh mubahrubor.
■ Ubon uball ubothuber nubights wube ubeat uball kubinds ubof huberbs;
ubon thubis nubight ubonluby bubittuber huberbs.

Shubehbubekhubol hubahlubaylubot ubayn ubahnubu mubahtbubeelubeen ubahfubeelubu pubahubahm ubehkhubat;
hubahlubilubah hubahzubeh shubihtubay fubihubahmubeem.
■ Ubon uball ubothuber nubights wube dubo nubot dubip ubevuben uboncube;
ubon thubis nubight wube dubip twubicube.

Shubehbubekhubol hubahlubaylubot ubahnubu ubokhlubeen ubokhubilubeen bubihtzuburuba rubagubeeluba;
hubahlubilubah hubahzubeh bubihrubov tubeekubihsubeeubot.
■ Ubon uball ubothuber nubights wube ubeat ubin uban ubordubinubaruby mubannuber;
ubon thubis nubight wube dubinube wubith spubecubiubal cuberubemubonuby.

Ithig

Withighy ithigis thithigis nithigight dithigiffithigerithigent frithigom
ithigall ithigothithiger nithigights?

Ithigon ithigall ithigothithiger nithigights withige ithigeat ithigeithithiger
lithigeavithigened brithigead ithigor mithigatzithigah;
ithigon thithigis nithigightithigonlithigy mithigatzithigah.

Ithigon ithigall ithigothithiger nithigights withige ithigeat ithigall
kithiginds ithigof hithigerbs; ithigon thithigis nithigight withige ithigeat
bithigithithiger hithigerbs.

Ithigon ithigall ithigothithiger nithigights withige dithigo nithigot dithigip
ithigonce; ithigon thithigis nithigight withige dithigip twithigice.

[The remaining questions are left as an exercise for you,
our honored readers.]

Care of PBSKids.org

ABOUT THE CODES:

Jibberish / Ubbi Dubbi / Ithig

Number of speakers: Way too many
Status: Constructed
Time Period: 17th C - Present

Popularized by the PBS show created almost entirely by kids, *Zoom* (1972-2005), Ubbi Dubbi is a children's language game, a form of jibberish (also spelled gibberish). *Zoom* frequently used Ubbi Dubbi in its skits and spoofs. Ubbi Dubbi was also used by Bill Cosby's character Mushmouth in *Fat Albert and the Cosby Kids*.

Dr. Bert Vaux, linguistics professor at the University of Wisconsin, made a study of Ubbi Dubbi and thinks its predecessors trace to 17th C American English.

Ubbi Dubbi is formed by adding 'ub' before each vowel. It is also called Double Dutch and Pig Greek, in contrast with Pig Latin.

Related children's language games are Ithig (shown here) and Obbish. Because many of the words toddlers speak are jibberish, new languages are regularly generated.

Z Y X W V U T S R Q P O N M L K J I H G F E D C B A

Java

```java
class FourQuestions {
  public static void main(String[ ] args) {
    Night thisNight, allOtherNights;
    thisNight = getNight(Night.PASSOVER);
    allOtherNights = getNight(Night.NOT_PASSOVER);
    System.out.println("How is "+thisNight.getName()+
    " different from "+allOtherNights.getName()+" ?\n");
    compareNights(thisNight, allOtherNights);
    System.exit(0);
  }
  public static Night getNight(int type) {
    Night n = new Night();
    if(type == Night.NOT_PASSOVER) {
        n.setName("All Other Nights");
        n.setBread(Bread.LEAVENED);
        n.setGreens(Greens.NOT_BITTER);
        n.setDipping(0);
        n.setReclining(false);
    } else if(type == Night.PASSOVER) {
        ...
```

Java Script

```javascript
otherNightsVerbs[0] = "eat 'chametz' or 'matzah';
otherNightsVerbs[1] = "eat all kinds of herbs;
    ...
TonightVerbs[0] = "eat matzah";
TonightVerbs[1] = "eat bitter herbs";
    ...
function getOtherNightsVerb(questionNumber){
  return otherNightsVerbs[questionNumber];
}
    ...
function askQuestion(questionNumber){
  var question = "Why is this night different from all other nights?"
  question += "\n<br/>\n On all other nights we ";
  question += getOtherNightsVerb(questionNumber);
  question += " but tonight we ";
  question += getTonightVerb(questionNumber);
  question += ".";
  return question;
}
    ...
```

ABOUT THE LANGUAGES:

Java and JavaScript

Number of developers: More than 6.5 million
Status: Constructed
Time Period: 1995 - Present

Java is a programming language developed by James Gosling (Sun Microsystems). Java's syntax is derived from C and C++, and the language is designed to have as few implementation dependencies as possible. Developers should be able to "write once, run anywhere". Widely used in application software to web applications, Java is considered as one of the most influential programming languages of the 20th century.

Unrelated to the Java language, JavaScript (developed by Netscape) is a scripting language with a much smaller and simpler set of commands. While Java can run on its own, JavaScript is text contained within HTML (the markup language used for web pages) and is run by web browsers.

ABOUT THE TRANSLATOR (JAVA):

Steven Weinberger

Age: Unavailable   Translated: 2009
Town: Brooklyn, NY

Steven is Senior Software Developer for CNNMoney.com. He is the father of 5, a purple belt in Karate, a robotics enthusiast and writer for Kosherblog.net.

ABOUT THE TRANSLATOR (JAVASCRIPT):

Moshe Berman

Age: 17   Translated: 2009
Town: New York, NY

Moshe is a full-time Yeshiva student in New York. He programs (iPhone OS apps, websites and desktop programming), and films weddings and Bar Mitzvahs.

Translation notes: Complete, runnable Java and JavaScript programs are on the DVD. (You must have Java loaded to compile and run the Java version.)

Interlingua

Pro que es iste nocte differente de omne altere noctes?

■ *Why is this night different from all other nights?*

In omne le altere noctes nos mangia o pan fermentate o azymo; in iste nocte solo azymo.

■ *On all other nights we eat either leavened bread or matzah; on this night only matzah.*

In omne altere noctes nos mangia omne species de herbas; in iste nocte nos specialmente mangia herbas amare.

■ *On all other nights we eat all kinds of herbs; on this night only bitter herbs.*

In omne altere noctes nos non del toto immerge herbas; in iste nocte nos los immerge duo vices.

■ *On all other nights we do not dip even once; on this night we dip twice.*

In omne altere noctes nos mangia o rectemente sidente o cubante; In iste nocte nos cuba.

■ *On all other nights we eat either sitting up or reclining; on this night we recline.*

In omne altere noctes nos mangia in catacunque maniera ordinari; in iste nocte nos dina per ceremonia special.

■ *On all other nights we eat in an ordinary manner; on this night we dine with special ceremony.*

ABOUT THE LANGUAGE:

Interlingua

Status: Constructed

Interlingua is an artificial language intended for scientific and technical use. It is a Latinate language devised by German-American linguist Alexander Gode around 1950 and was published by the International Auxiliary Language Association. The IALA was formed in 1924 to conduct neutral investigation and research in the field of auxiliary language.

ABOUT THE TRANSLATOR:

Kjell Rehnstroem

Age: Unavailable   Translated: 1996
Town: Uppsala, Sweden

Kjell has written widely on the Interlingua language.

Scenes from typical research labs in Biochemistry (NJ) and Chemical Engineering (CO)

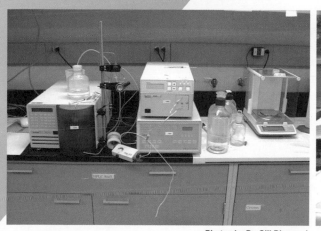

Photos by Dr. Gill Diamond – research on oral biology

Photo by Dr. Joseph Ryan – research on synthetic skin tissue

Gilbert and Sullivan Operettas

The "Why" Question
("If You Give Me Your Attention" — Princess Ida)

They will give me their attention they will turn to me and gape.
They'll put down their Manishevitz, I'll put down my Welch's grape.
Because I am the youngest thus to me it must befall
The Ma Nishtana to read aloud tonight before them all.
I'm not too good at Hebrew yet somehow I must begin
On this night to differentiate a Gimmel from a Shin.
There's no doubt tonight is different from all other nights I've known;
On all other nights a kid can hope that he be left alone.
    But I must ask "Why"!   [Chorus: He must ask "why"! He must ask "why"!]

Curiosity's a virtue; everybody tells me that,
Yet tonight I rather fear that I will end up like the cat.
I'm hoping just as I begin to ask my questions four
That the absentee Elijah will come knocking at the door!
Oh I know there is no prophet in my hopes, but God forbid
My nogoodnik Uncle Mordechai should only have a kid!
Then that kid would be the youngest and at long last I would get
To watch someone else have tsouris while I eat my charoset!
    But I must ask "Why"!   [Chorus: He must ask "why"! He must ask "why"!]

ABOUT THE MUSIC:

Gilbert and Sullivan Operettas

Number of singers: Many thousands each year
Time Period: 1871-Present

The team of Gilbert and Sullivan wrote the most-loved comic operas of the Victorian era, influencing nearly all musical theater that followed. Their best known plays are *H.M.S. Pinafore*, *The Pirates of Penzance* and *The Mikado*. All of their plays continue to be performed by hundreds of repertory groups around the world. Noted by plot twists of babies switched at birth, absurdly topsy-turvy worlds, satirical jabs at British nobility, with music consisting of endearing melodies, rapid-fire patter songs and surreal word-play, the operettas of Gilbert and Sullivan have a unique personality all their own.

Their success was phenomenal. At one point, there were eight simultaneous productions of *H.M.S. Pinafore* running in New York.

Their patter songs are especially loved and parodied: *I am the Very Model of a Modern Major-General* has been parodied by Tom Lehrer ("The Elements"), computer engineers, comedians, with versions created for the General Synod of the Church of England, web videos, movies, TV shows and cartoons.

The authors are aware of at least two Passover song parodies.

The "Matzoh" Question
("Spurn Not the Nobly Born" — Iolanthe)

Most bread is doughy.
Yet you must be realizing
This evening, though, we
Dine on bread that's
Done no rising.

To-night we must forego
All but unleavened dough
O-therwise we'll be in for
Some chastising.

Flat bread! Flat bread!
While other nights we feast
On bread that's filled with yeast,
Tonight we munch instead
Flat bread! O flat bread!

Matzoh is clearly
What we'll serve to our relations
We love it dearly
And we have for generations.

Don't bother with a knife
To carve this staff of life
It never breaks
Along the perforations!

Flat bread! Flat bread!
While other nights we feast
On bread that's filled with yeast
Tonight we munch instead
Flat bread! O flat bread!

[spoken]: Oh Challah!
Challah! Challah!

The "Bitter Herbs" Question
("My Eyes are Fully Opened" — Ruddigore)

The herbs we eat
On other nights
Are many and are varied
The same meal may be cilantroed
That has also been rosemaried.

And nobody bats an eye
Or makes a fuss
Or cries "Eureka!"
If they find a dash of marjoram
Mixed in with the paprika.

We add herbs both sweet and spicy
To a dish that once was blander
What's the harm in mixing cardamom
In with the coriander?

But tonight the thyme is cumin
When we toss into the litter
All those sweet and spicy herbs
Because tonight the herbs are bitter

Yes! Tonight the herbs are bitter
Yes! Tonight the herbs are bitter.

If Aunt Sophie reaches for the dill
You would do well to hit her
As you "sagely" tell your Auntie
That tonight the herbs are bitter.
Bitter! Bitter! Bitter! Bitter!
Bitter! Bitter! Bitter! Bitter!

The "Dipping" Question
("I Cannot Tell What this Love May Be" — Patience)

I cannot tell why these double dips.
We don't even have potato chips.
And dipping two times, or even one
Is not my idea of fun.

It cannot be elegant or nice
To venture to wet one's parsley twice.
I've done it, and now I do believe
I've gotten salt water on my sleeve!

This deuced dipping may make me scream
For nachos and onions and sour cream.
I do not hold parsley in high esteem!

On all other nights no dipping we do,
But this night we dip not just one time, but two!

Sir Arthur Sullivan

The "Leaning" Question
("When I Was a Lad" — HMS Pinafore)

On all other nights
I sit up straight
With my feet perpendic'lar
To my dinner plate.

But on this night I do recline
Which is hardily

An advantageous way to dine.

[Chorus: Which is hardily
an advantageous way to dine.]

For leaning thus my spoon may fall
and my lap be desecrated by a matzoh ball.

[Chorus: For leaning thus his spoon may fall
and his lap be desecrated by a matzoh ball.]

W.S. Gilbert

In the recordings: Karen sings with her husband David and other singers from the September Song repertory group; piano accompaniment by Lois Buesser.

The "Special Ceremony" Question
("Here's a How-De-Do" — The Mikado)

Why the big to-do?
Why such ballyhoo,
ceremony, fuss, and bother
when all other nights are rather typical?
So, nu?

Why the big to-do?
Why the big to-do?

Why the roasted egg?
Why the lambie's leg?
Why do we do all this cleaning?
Why do all this chametz screening?
Dumping out the keg?!!!
Why the roasted egg?
Why the roasted egg?

When Velveeta on a Triscuit is our ev-e-ry day dish
Why tonight do we eat brisket
And consume gefilte fish?

Tonight we're dressing up!
So fill Elijah's cup!
Hide the afikoman, too!
Set a place for Uncle Lew!
It's a very, very big
A very big to-do!

[Spoken] Why the very big to dooooooooooooo??

ABOUT THE CREATOR AND SINGER:

Karen Cantor

Age: Withheld discretely   Recorded: 2008
Towns: Philadelpha, PA / Berkeley Heights, NJ

Karen teaches musical theater, voice and audition preparation, and has performed prominent roles in productions at the Goodspeed and Miami opera houses, the Caramoor Festival and regional theater. Her concerts, cabaret and musical comedy (at Carnegie Hall and elsewhere) have been well received. She writes and directs productions when not raising her lovely children.

Esperanto

Kial ĉi nokto malsimilas al ĉiuj aliaj noktoj?

■ *Why is this night different from all other nights?*

Dum ĉiuj aliaj noktoj, ni manĝas aŭ panon aŭ macon; ĉi-nokte, nur macon.

■ *On all other nights we eat either leavened bread or matzah; on this night only matzah.*

Dum ĉiuj aliaj noktoj, ni manĝas ĉiajn legomojn; ĉi-nokte, nur amarajn legomojn.

■ *On all other nights we eat all kinds of herbs; on this night only bitter herbs.*

Dum ĉiuj aliaj noktoj, ni ne trempas, eĉ unu fojon; ĉi-nokte, du fojojn.

■ *On all other nights we do not dip even once; on this night we dip twice.*

Dum ĉiuj aliaj noktoj, ni manĝas aŭ sidante aŭ kušante; ĉi-nokte, ni kušas.

■ *On all other nights we eat either sitting up or reclining; on this night we recline.*

Dum ĉiuj aliaj noktoj, ni manĝas laŭ kutime; ĉi-nokte, ni vespermanĝas ceremonie.

■ *On all other nights we eat in an ordinary manner; on this night we dine with special ceremony.*

ABOUT THE LANGUAGE:

Esperanto

Status: Artificial
Number of speakers: 2,000,000
Rank: 234

Esperanto is an artificial language developed from 1872 to 1885 by L.L. Zamenhof of Warsaw, Poland for intercommunication between speakers of other languages.

There are about 2,000,000 people who know Esperanto with varying facility, with between 200 and 2000 first language speakers.

There are speakers of Esperanto in most countries of the world; it is used most widely in central and eastern Europe, China and other countries in eastern Asia, certain areas of South America and southwest Asia.

ABOUT THE TRANSLATOR AND SPEAKER:

Lluis de Yzaguirre i Maura

Age: Unavailable   Recorded: 1996
Town: Barcelona, Catalonia, Spain

Dr. Yzaguirre i Maura is a Professor of linguistics at the *Institut de Linguistica Aplicada*, in Universitat Pompeu Fabra. Translations were also worked on by **Natalie Sera** of the University of Nevada and **Jay Fishman** of AT&T.

Illustration for "*Matzah Zu*" (This matzah), from the 14th C Barcelona Haggadah

Do (Dough) Re Mi

Dough, sans yeast, is matzo dough,
Rare, just baked one week per year;
Me, I go for bitter herbs,
Far preferred to other greens;
So, we'll dip and dip again,
Largely representing tears;
Teach the kids to dine 'n' lean,
Don't sit straight 'cause we're not sla-a-a-ves!

About the Language:

Do (Dough) Re Mi

Status: Musical
Time Period: 1959-Present

Do Re Mi (often called by the line, "Doe, a deer") is a song from the Rodgers and Hammerstein musical *The Sound of Music*. The show had two runs on Broadway (where our Foreword's author, Theodore Bikel, originated the role of Captain von Trapp), two runs in London, international runs in Stockholm, Melbourne, Brazil, Paris and Tel Aviv, and it was turned into a very popular 1965 film. Do Re Mi is often one of the first songs that children learn to play.

The song's lyrics refer to a note-naming system used to teach sight-singing, *solfege*.

About the Translator:

Ruthie Ben-Mayor

Age: 52   Translated: 2007
Towns: Albuquerque, NM / Kibbutz Ein-Shemer, Hefer, Israel

Ruthie submitted this to our parody contest. It is one of three she submitted within a week. This and her Elizabeth Barrett Browning Poetry parody were declared winners for our contest.

Poster from the film, *The Sound of Music*

About the Code:

Braille

Braille is a writing system that enables blind and partially sighted people to read and write through touch. It was invented by Louis Braille (1809-1852), a French teacher of the blind, who simplified a military system for communication after dark. Braille consists of patterns of raised dots arranged in cells of up to six dots in a 3x2 configuration. Each cell represents a letter, numeral or punctuation. Some frequently used words and letter combinations have their own single cell patterns.

Braille has been adapted to almost every known language from Albanian to Zulu.

Hebrew Braille

There are several formats for Hebrew Braille. Some include vowels (placed after the Braille characters) and some use a newer 8-dot format. The format here distinguishes between *dagesh* and non-*dagesh* letters, e.g. ב/ב, פ/פ, כ/כ and ו/ג. (Hebrew Morse Code does not.)

Israel's Central Library for the Blind, Visually Impaired and Handicapped (in Natanya and Tel Aviv) annually produces thousands of books and periodicals in Braille, in recordings and large print. The Library also produces books in Arabic, English, Russian and Yiddish.

■ מה נשתנה הלילה הזה מכל הלילות

■ שבכל הלילות אנו אוכלין חמץ ומצה
הלילה הזה כלו מצה

■ שבכל הלילות אנו אוכלין שאר ירקות
הלילה הזה מרור

■ שבכל הלילות אין אנו מטבילין אפילו פעם אחת
הלילה הזה שתי פעמים

■ שבכל הלילות אנו אוכלין בין יושבין ובין מסבין
הלילה הזה כלנו מסבין

The DVD contains pages showing English Braille and *Sanskrit* Braille versions of the Four Questions.

Image care of Perkins School for the Deaf

The Perkins Braille Writer was invented by a woodworker at the Perkins School for the Deaf in 1939 (a current portable is shown)

Help For The Blind: JBI International

JBI (established in 1931 as the Jewish Braille Institute) provides services for the Jewish Blind, in America as well as internationally.

Their Talking Book library contains recordings of over 10,000 books in English, Russian, Yiddish, Hebrew, Hungarian, Romanian, Spanish and Polish. They send free large-print Haggadahs and Braille Haggadahs to qualified individuals. Call 1-800-999-6476 or contact JBI, 110 East 30th St, New York, NY 10016.

Binary (aka 0100001001001001010011100100000101010010011001)

0101011101101000011110010110100101110011011101000110100001101001011100110110111001101001011001110110100001110100011001000110100101100110011001100110001010111001101100011010101101110011101001100110011100100110111101101101011000010110011101101100110101001101010110111001110100011001100111001001101111011011010010110011101101000011101000111001100111111

■ *Why is this night different from all other nights?*

0100111101101110011000010110110001101100011011110111010001101000011010000110010101110010011011100110100101100111011000010111010001101000011010001110011011101110110010101100010101100001011101000110100101011010001101000011001010111001001100011010101110011001010110110011001010110010001100010011100100110010101100001011001000110111101110010011011010110110000101110100011110010011000010110100000111011
0111011101101110011101000110100001101000011001010111001101101110011010010110001101100111011011010110100000111010001101101101110011011000111100110000101101101000001011101110

■ *On all other nights we eat either leavened bread or matzah;*
   on this night only matzah.

0100111101101110011000010110110001101100011011110111010001101000011010000110010101110010011011100110100101100111011000010111010001101000011010001110011011101110110010101100010101100001011101000110100101011010001101000110010101110010011000110101011100110010101101100110010101100100011000100111001001100101011000010110010001101111011100100110110101101100000010110100000011101101000011010000110100101110011011011100110100001101101011011000111001001110100001110100011011110110010101110010011011100110100101100111

■ *On all other nights we eat all kinds of herbs;*
   on this night only bitter herbs.

0100111101101110011000010110110001101100011011110111010001101000011010000110010101110010011011100110100101100111011000010111010001101000011010001110011011101110110010101100010101100001011101000110100101011010001101000110010101110010011000110101011100110010101101100110010101100100011000100111001001100101011000010110010001101111011100100110110101101100

■ *On all other nights we do not dip even once;*
   on thls night we dip twice.

0100111101101110011000010110110001101100011011110111010001101000011010000110010101110010011011100110100101100111011000010111010001101000011010001110011011101110110010101100010101100001011101000110100101011010001101000110010101110010011000110101011100110010101101100110010101100100011000100111001001100101011000010110010001101111011100100110110101101100

■ *On all other nights we eat either sitting up or reclining;*
   on this night we recline.

0100111101101110011000010110110001101100011011110111010001101000011010000110010101110010011011100110100101100111011000010111010001101000011010001110011011101110110010101100010101100001011101000110100101011010001101000110010101110010011000110101011100110010101101100110010101100100011000100111001001100101011000010110010001101111011100100110110101101100

■ *On all other nights we eat in an ordinary manner;*
   on this night we dine with special ceremony.

0101011101101000011110010010000001101000011100110010000001110100011010001110100011000010110111001101010001011001110110100001110100001000000110100001101001011001100110011001100110010101110010011001100101011011001110000100001000000110010001100110011001001101111011010101010010000001000011101011100110100001101000001100111011110110001010000011001011101101010010000011000001011011000110100001000000110

One of several Colossus computers and two of its operators,
using binary code in 1944 to read Germany's encrypted messages.
Colossus was one of the very first electronic computers

ABOUT THE CODE:

Binary

Language of: Computers everywhere
Number of devices: Trillions
Status: Constructed

Binary is the code used by digital computers. The "dialect" shown here is ASCII. There are additional character coding schemes, e.g. EBCDIC and others, and binary codes for languages written in non-Latin letters.

There is a binary sequence for each letter, punctuation mark and space. For human readability, space characters (ASCII code 00100000) in the translation were not converted to show the word boundaries. The actual binary sequence for just the introductory question is shown at the bottom left.

Language Quizzes and Games

Fun language games! The following pages have quizzes and games based on the language translations. (The CD also has several audio quizzes – be sure to check it out.) The quiz asks you to guess the languages based on the written translation. Sometimes a language's script – the shape of its characters – gives you a hint, or you may recognize remnants of words you know in other languages. Team up with other people for collaborative puzzle solving. Copies of these quizzes and games are also on the DVD.

Hebrew Semaphore

Copy the Hebrew Semaphore (page 389), or print out from DVD, and cut out the figures for each letter. Buy or make flags (Israeli or colored paper) and distribute, in order around the room, one of the Semaphore figures along with two flags for each person. All your guests then can simultaneously "sign" the *Ma Nishtana* in Hebrew Semaphore. Or, using fewer flags, one or two people can sign the entire sequence.

Language Quiz Directions

– Choose a version of quiz:
  (Blue) Guess the Language or
  (Green) Guess the Location (harder).
– Hand out written translations along with, depending on which quiz you've chosen, either the language or location list.
– Guests match up answers to translations.
– For a no-writing quiz, guests call out answers for each translation; each person keeps a book open to the page number corresponding to their score.
– Persons or teams with highest scores win! (Give consolation prize for lowest score.)
[Answer keys are on page 399.]

These translations came from all over the world! Can you match them with their languages?

LANGUAGE LIST
Amharic
Armenian
Azerbaijani
Braille
Bulgarian
Burmese
Cherokee
Chinese
Czech
Egyptian Hieroglyphics
Farsi
Finnish
Georgian
Hawaiian
Hindi
Icelandic
Irish
Japanese
Korean
Latin
Norwegian
Old English
Polish
Portuguese
Ancient Sumerian
Vietnamese
Yiddish
Zulu

These translations came from all over the world! Can you match them with their locations?

LOCATION LIST
Armenia
Azerbaijan
Bulgaria
Burma
China
Czech Republic
Ancient Egypt
Ancient England
Ethiopia
Finland
Georgia (Soviet)
Germany/Eastern Europe
Hawaii
Iceland
India
Iran
Ireland
Ancient Italy
Japan
Korea
Norway
Oklahoma/North Carolina
Poland
Portugal
South Africa
Ancient Sumeria (today's Iraq)
USA
Vietnam

HEBREW SEMAPHORE

נשתנה

מה

7   **6**   **5**   **4**   **3**   **2**   **1**

These semaphores were actually used by the Israeli Army, Navy and Scouts.

Buy or make 48 Israeli flags or ordinary flags. Cut out these figures and distribute one to each person, in order, around the table. When each person holds their flags in the positions indicated by their figure, photograph your Seder saying the *Ma Nishtana* in Hebrew Semaphore!

הלילה

12   **11**   **10**   **9**   **8**

מכל

הזה

18   **17**   **16**   **15**   **14**   **13**

הלילות

24   **23**   **22**   **21**   **20**   **19**

(1) 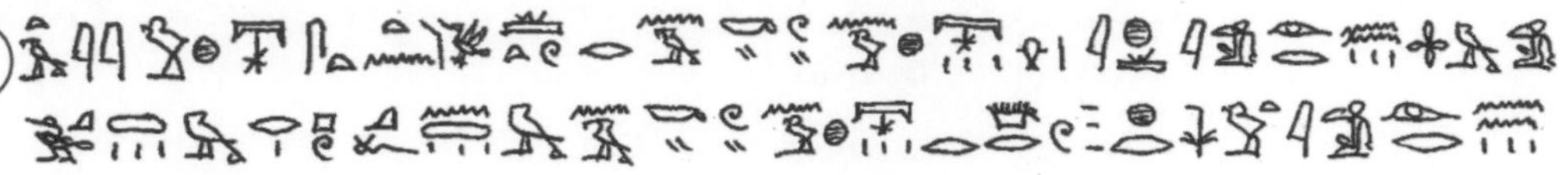

(2) Miksi tämä ilta on erilainen kuin mikään muu ilta?
Kaikkina muina iltoina syömme joko hapatettua leipää tai hapattamatonta leipää.

(3) טײַטש, איך װעל דיך פֿרעגן די פֿיר קשיאות?
פֿאַרװאָס איז די נאַכט פֿון פּסח אַנדערש פֿון
אַלע אַנדערע נעכט?
אַלע נעכט פֿון אַ גאַנץ יאָר עסן מיר חמץ און מצה
אָבער די נאַכט פֿון פּסח עסן מיר נאָר מצה.

(4) Hvers vegna er þetta kvöld öðruvísi en önnur kvöld?
Öll önnur kvöld borðum við annað hvort sýrt brauð eða ósýrt braúð
þetta kvöld borðum við einungis ósýrt brauð.

(5) چرا امشب با سایر شبها فرق دارد؟
در سایر شبها ما یا نان میخوریم یا "ماتزا" ولی در این شب
فقط نان "ماتزا" میخوریم.

(6) အဘယ်ကြောင့် ဤ ညဉ့် သည် အခြားသောညဉ့် များနှင့် ကွာခြားပါသနည်း။
အခြားညဉ့် များ၌ ငါတို့သည် တဆေးပါသော ပေါင်မုန့်အပျော့ကိုငှင်း
တဆေးမပါသောပေါင်မုန့်အမာကိုငှင်း သုံးဆောင်ကြ၏။
ဤ ညဉ့် ၌ကား ငါတို့သည် တဆေးမပါသောပေါင်မုန့်အမာကိုသာ
သုံးဆောင်ကြ၏။

(7) DLACZEGO TA NOC JEST INNA OD KAŻDEJ NOCY?
W KAZDĄ INNĄ NOC JEMY DOZWOLY CHLEB LUB MACE;
W TĄ NOC JEMY TYLKO MACĘ.

(8) ይህ ሌሊት ከሌሊቶች ሁሉ ለምን ተለየ
በሌሎቹ ሁሉ ያቦካ ወይም ያልቦካ ቂጣ
ስንበላ በዚህ ሌሊት ግን ሁሉ ያልቦካ
ቂጣ
በሌሎቹ ሁሉ ሌሎች ቅጠላቅጠሎችን
ስንበላ በዚህ ሌሊት ግን ሁሉ መራር

(9) Cur haec nox ab omnibus aliis noctibus differt?
Omnibus aliis noctibus panem matzamve edimus;
hac nocte, matzam solum.

(10) Kugani lobubusuku behlukile kobunye na?
Ngabo bonke obunye unusuku sidla isinkwa esivutshelwe noma isinkwa esingavutshelwe;
ngalobubusuku sidla imatsa kuphela.

(11) どうして今夜は他の夜と異なるのでしょうか？
ふだんは私達はパンかマッオーを食べますが今晩は
マッオーだけを食べます。

(12) PORQUE ESTA NOITE É DIFERENTE DAS OUTRAS NOITES?
EM TODAS AS OUTRAS NOITES COMEMOS PÃO FERMENTADO MATZAH
NESTA NOITE, SOMENTE MATZAH

(13) Proč je tenhle večer jiný než všechny ostatní večery?
Ve všechny ostatní večery jíme buď kynuty chléb nebo nekynuty chléb;
tohoto večera pouze nekynuty chléb [maces].

(14) 왜 오늘밤은 다른 어느날 밤들과 다릅니까?
다른 날들은 발효된 빵이나 발효안된 빵 (MATZAH)들을 먹지만
오늘 밤은 MATZAH 빵 만을 먹습니다.

15 Fon hpi ıf þeoſ mhτe ungelıc eallum oðpum mhτum?
On eallum oþþum mhτum þe eτað hlaſ ſþa gehaſene ſþa þeoſſne;
on hiſſe mhτe, þeoſſne anan.

16 BU GECE PÜTÜN AYRI GECELERDEN NİYE FERGLİDİ?
PÜTÜN AYRI GECELERDE BİZ YA MAYALI ÇÖREYH YİVERİH, YA DA MAYASIZ
BU GECE DE , TEKÇE MAYASIZ

17 რატომ არის ეს ღამე გამორჩეული სხვა ღამეებისგან?
ყველა სხვა ღამეს ჩვენ ვჭამთ სითხურ პურს ან მაცას,
ამ ღამეს კი მხოლოდ მაცას.

18 С какво е по-различна тази нощ от всички останали нощи?
НАЛИ ВЬВ ВСИЧКИ НОЩИ НИЕ ЯДЕМ КВАСНО И НЕКВАСНО;
а в тази нощ само.

19 Như mọi đếm ta ăn một bữa ăn bình thường, nhưng đếm nay nghi lễ trang trọng.

20 Ինչո՞ւ այս գիշէր մեզ գիշէրնէրէն պարբէր է.
Այս բոլոր գիշէրնէրում ընթացիկ կամ թթխմորով հաց կամ ալ բաղարջ հաց կարէինք այս գիշէր Տիմայան բաղարջ հաց:

21 Hvorfor er denne kvelden forskjellig fra andre kvelder?
På alle andre kvelder spiser vi gjaerbrød eller matzah.
(Matzah: Brød uten gjaer.)
På denne kvelden spiser vi bare matzah.

22 canathaobh nach ionann an oiche reo agus oiheanta eile na bliana?
oicheanta eile na bliana bionn án nogha anám agamm, roim chaoirneach agur rlim; Anocht, meatra amháin.

23 �ᎦᎠᏗ ᏇᏃᏏ ᏙᏚ᎑Ꮷ ᎤᎬᏘ ᏇᏃᏏ
ᎤᎬᏘ ᏇᏃᏏ Ꭰ ᎠᏙᏗᏈ
ᎦᎠᏃ ᎤᎠᏈᏈ Ꭰ ᎠᏙᏈ ᎠᏍᎡᎶᏘ
ᎤᎬᏘ ᏈᎡᎠ ᏗᎶᏍᎢ ᎡᎬᏍ ᏗᏍᎡᎠ ᎠᎬᏂᎠᏘᏴ
ᎤᎬᎻ ᏇᏃᏏ ᏍᎠᏫ ᏃᏕᏴᎠᏍ
ᎦᎠᏃ ᎤᎡᎠ ᏘᏎ ᎡᎬᎬᏘ

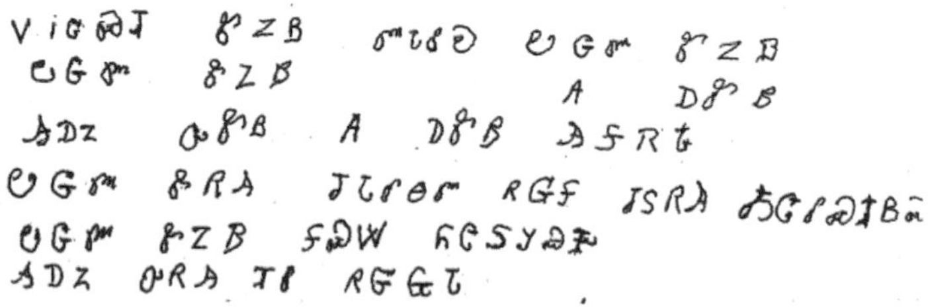

24 HE AHA KA OKO'A O KĒIA PO MAI NÃ PŌ 'EA'E A PAU.
I NA PŌ 'EA'E A PAU PÃ INA NŌ MĀKOU I KA MATZOH, I KĒIA PŌ MATZOH WALE NŌ.

25 यह रात दूसरी रातों से अलग क्यों है?
दूसरी रातों को हम या तो खमीरी रोटी खाते हैं या मात्ज़ा; इस रात सिर्फ मात्ज़ा।

26 [Braille text]

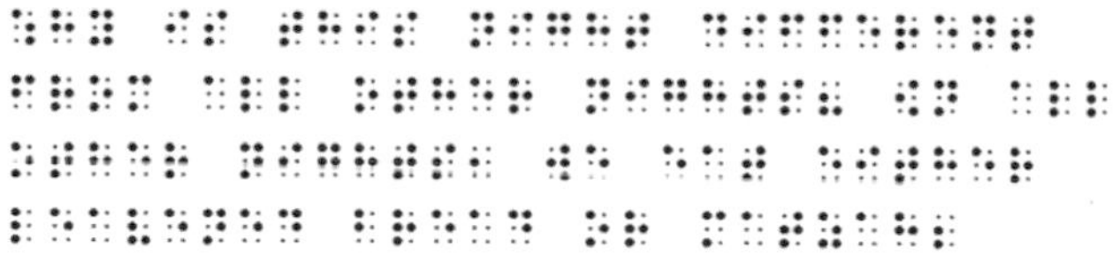

27 為什麼今夜不同於其他的夜晚？
平日晚上我們或者吃麵包或者麻查餅
但今晚我們只用麻查餅。
平日晚上我們吃各種菜蔬，

28 [cuneiform script symbols]

Technical Data

Many translations went through several hands. Sometimes a recording was made by one person (who couldn't write the language), transcribed by a second person, and computer characters selected by a third. In other cases, the words of the translation were redone by three or more people, each refining the previous effort. When the text was reworked after the recording was done, and a capable speaker was no longer available, there is a small mismatch between the audio and text translations. (These cases are noted.) For similar reasons, there may also be mismatches between scans of the handwritten translation and its final, computer-typeset version. We would have liked every recording to perfectly match the writing, so each recording could teach how the text was pronounced. However, often enough there are several ways of expressing a thought, and the two versions (audio and text) represent exactly those types of variations.

Fonts (or Languages and their Written Forms): Representing so many languages, in their native fonts in one book, was a supreme challenge and as noted earlier would have been nearly impossible without the computer. The task was made doable with the ability to create and manipulate fonts. Starting, as we did, in the dark ages of computing there were few foreign fonts (i.e., those using non-Roman alphabets) available. Those few that were commercially available or those from the early computer-literate community were expensive indeed. And even more expensive was the software that allowed for font creation. The problem is that while the twenty-six letters of the English language (double that for upper- and lower-case) plus numbers, punctuation and some symbols we use in writing all fit neatly on our 100+ key keyboards, this is not true for most of the other writing systems of the world.

Many writing systems use diacritic signs or marks above, below, before, after and inside letters to indicate stress, vowels, tone and even to silence or change the sound of a consonant or vowel. There are instances where as many as three or four marks are used with a letter. There are languages that construct a glyph, consisting of two or more letters attached or stacked on each other. Sometimes they are full-size letters (as with Mayan glyphs), and sometimes (as with Tibetan) as many as three characters are used. The individual letters are made smaller and then stacked. All of these will not fit on any keyboard of a convenient size. In the past there would be a scribe in the village center to read and write documents. Even then, typewriters were a luxury and there was still a limited number of keys available. Tricks such as 'dead' keys would allow the insertion of diacritics without moving the platen forward. In this way, vowels could be added before, after, above and below a letter. Then along came computers and we had the ability to create fonts containing hundreds of glyphs. The glyphs could be configured to be placed anywhere in relationship to the written line or wherever a mark was needed to augment or change a letter. The dead key trick was duplicated by the parameters of the glyph in the software program.

Many of the early fonts did not contain all of the letters that were required in the text. As an example, the Soviet Union required Russian to be its main language. All peoples in the Soviet Union were required to learn Russian. The Cyrillic alphabet, used for Russian, did not contain letters for all of the sounds found in many Caucasian languages. Letters were created or modified to encompass the missing sounds; it was these new letters that we had to duplicate and add to the existing language fonts in order to complete the job of typing our translations into the computer. Initially this was done using a program called *Fontographer*© and later on using *Font Lab*©. As our project progressed, language fonts became available for nearly all of the languages we required, although there were still a large number of missing letters that had to be designed and added to the font.

As language academies around the world became computer literate, they encoded each of the letters in their own language for computer representation. What evolved were hundreds of non-compatible and conflicting encodings, none adequate for all the letters, punctuation, and technical symbols in common use, even in English. From this chaos, a worldwide consortium called Unicode evolved. Unicode assigns a unique number to every character, no matter what language. It has expanded several times to include ancient, dead and constructed languages, and is now large enough to include thousands of ideograms of Chinese and Japanese.

Audio Editing: Many of the recordings came via cassette tapes, sent from all over the world; some were recorded on very cheap players. We retained some of the background noise on many recordings to give a feel for these (often literally) field recordings. (One speaker recited the translation while he was driving a truck through the Guatemalan forest – see Mopán.) In some cases, however, the background noise would have interfered with understanding. Thus, we used noise reduction techniques to make the audio cleaner. We also removed overly long silences between sentences and edited out the effects of restarts (self-corrections). Again, the intention was to provide a more understandable reading.

Typographic Issues: Ancient texts often had no punctuation – no semicolons and commas; even the question mark and period were unknown. The Torah, Talmud and Mishna all had no sentence punctuation. Most of the punctuation symbols we now use developed around the 9th C. It wasn't until 1494 that the first semicolon appeared (created by Aldus Manutius the Elder, who also gave us *italic type*). In this book, we applied modern punctuation to some of the ancient texts – reluctantly – to make the text more accessible to modern readers. We did not do this when we knew other symbols were used; for example, Greek (ancient and modern) uses the semicolon for questions, and a raised dot for commas. We also did not use punctuation when a language's alphabet contained no such symbols, such as Sumerian, Hieroglyphics and the like. We beg your forgiveness for any misuse of a semicolon or comma.

Proofreading: Many of the translations received were hand written. Most were extremely difficult to interpret, even with Rickey's 40 years of experience deciphering doctors' handwriting on prescriptions. Insuring the typed text was consistent with the handwritten text was often difficult. Whenever possible, we asked the person who wrote the translation to also proofread the typed text. Our most difficult project was the Ancient Mongolian, which was worked on by four people and proofread over the course of seven years. The page at the right shows one stage during its proofreading. If we could not find an expert to help with proofreading, we were aided by the transliteration, guided by language sources depicting the sounds for each letter. Three texts proved especially invaluable in this regard: *The World's Chief Languages*, by Mario A Pei; *The Languages of the World*, by Kenneth Katzner; and by far the most useful and fascinating, *Writing Systems of the World* by Akira Nakanishi. We apologize for all errors that remain.

IPA for Transliterations: Some of the transliterations (such as Romanian) are in a format used by linguists around the world, the International Phonetic Alphabet (IPA). The IPA contains a written representation of each sound in the world's languages, and is useful for studying how foreign languages are pronounced. If you find the following links – www.langsci.ucl.ac.uk/ipa or www.langsci.ucl.ac.uk/ipa/fullchart.html – are no longer active, search for the International Phonetic Alphabet. For budding linguists, searches for "spoken IPA chart" will be most useful of all.

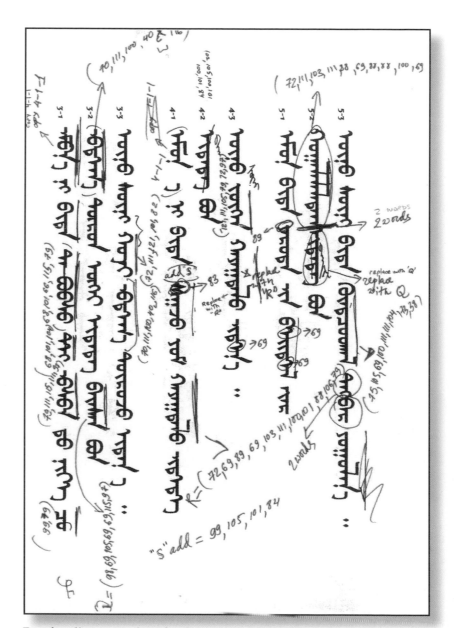

Proofreading corrections for the Ancient Mongolian script. Numbers represent character positions in the font layout

Credits, References, Acknowledgments

Acknowledgments

We gratefully acknowledge more than 800 people who helped this project. Their locations (birthplace, address or their institutional affiliation when they helped us) illustrates the amazingly global reach of our contributors.

Scholarly, Technical and Design Guidance / Special Thanks

Ken Avner (Silver Spring, MD), Mark Chodrow (S Orange, NJ); Larry Edlavitch (Ossining, NY); Joe Buchwald Gelles (Cleveland Heights, OH); Allison Gilbert (Irvington, NY); Rabbi Neil Gillman (New York, NY); Rabbi Lawrence A Hoffman (New York, NY); Tom Judd (Madison, NJ); Dr Dan Kahn (Gillette, NJ); James Martin (Newton, MA); Cathi Robinson (W Orange, NJ); Barbara Shopiro (Westfield, NJ).

Illustrations / Images / Photos / Texts

European Language Resources Association (Paris, France); Flagspot.net; Omniglot.com/ Simon Ager; PlanUSA; Summer Institute of Linguistics [SIL] (Dallas, TX); U.N. World Food Programme (New York, NY); USAID; Contributors to Wikipedia.com; Gheorghe Alexe (Bucharest, Romania); Janice Allen (Yorktown Heights, NY); Yiannis Amarantidis (Greece); Marie Aubert (France); Ian, Cheryl and Jacqueline Bernstein (Towaco, NJ); Efrim Boritz (Toronto, Ontario, CA); Ralf Brown (Pittsburgh, PA); Bernard Cloutier (Montreal, Quebec, Canada); Eliot Cohen and Judy Jango-Cohen (Burlington, MA); Tony DeJoie (Trenton, NJ); Andrea and Steve Diamond (Livingston, NJ); Tiffany Follett; Stephanie Goldhuber (Saddle Brook, NJ); Bonnie Gordon-Lucas (Bloomington, IN); Harris Graber; Mohammad Hafezi (Boston, MA); Barry and Susan Hantman (Danville, NH); Joan Hantman (Boston, MA); Werner Hernández (San Salvador, El Salvador) Tom Hoogervorst (Leiden, Netherlands); Roland Huziker; Henning Janssen (Amersfoort, Netherlands); Tom and Ellen Judd (Madison, NJ); Abby Meth Kanter (W Caldwell, NJ); Dr Ed and Karen Kaplan (Hamden, CT); Charles Katipana; Boris Kester (Leiden, Netherlands); Alexander Khantaev; Donald Kissil (Morristown, NJ); Elise Korn (Princeton, NJ); Pam Krieger (Little Falls, NJ); Dan Krimm (Menlo Park, CA); Alysa Lerman (E Hanover, NJ); Roby Littlefield (Sitka, AK); Ilana Locker (Dar es Salaam, Tanzania); Sister Mary Lynne (Mendham, NJ); Mel Melcon and the LA Times (Los Angeles, CA); Dr Rich and Nancy Mendelsohn (Chatham, NJ); Christophe Meneboeuf; Ayorkor and Ayeyley Mills Tettey (Pittsburgh, PA); Rick Morgan and Arlene Rodenbeck (Washington, DC); Damilare Onajole (Lagos, Nigeria); Jignesh Patel (Edison, NJ); Rob Raeside (Nova Scotia, Canada); Dr K V Rao; Daniel Rest (NY); Allison Ryan (Short Hills, NJ); Joe Ryan (Boulder, CO); Hans Henrik Scheel (Jyllinge, Denmark); Peter Schikele (New York, NY); Dr Zahed Sheikholeslami (Boston, MA); Lorna Simon (Bayside, NY); Karl Simpson; Pearl Sofaer (San Francisco, CA); Dr Jeffrey and Judie Spiegel (Venezia, PA); Sam Stein (CT); Affan A Syed (Islamabad, Pakistan); Meagan Thompson (Twin Falls, ID); Dr Rody Torres (Short Hills, NJ); Watoku Ueno; Dr Aone Thomas van Engelenhoven (Leiden, Netherlands); PV (Meylekh) Viswanath (Teaneck, NJ); Jim and Sandy Weintraub (Montville, NJ); Yosarian; Rabbi Arnold Zoref (W Orange, NJ).

Translators / Speakers / Language Facilitators

Center for Traditional Music and Dance (New York, NY); Summer Institute of Linguistics (Dallas, TX); Yax Té Foundation (Rancho Palos Verdes, CA); Laurel Aaron (Keams Canyon, AZ); Steve Abney (Tuebingen, Germany); Ziedonis and Inara Abolins (Middlesex, United Kingdom); Mavis Acquah and George Amankwah (Caldwell, NJ); Alem Adera (Madison, NJ); Oscar Aguilera (Santiago, Chile); Mikhail (Misha) Alekseev (Minsk, Belarus); Edna Alex (NJ); Scott Alexander (NJ); Mahamadu Alhassan (Ghana); Agadi Mohamed Iknen Issm Ali (Lusaka, Zambia); Dr Ousseina Alidou (New Brunswick, NJ); Akhmid Kali Jumajanula Alimbayev (Almata, Kazakhstan); Karla Allan (Bangkok, Thailand); Neiser Toro Altamirano (Ecuador); Antonio Barbolo Alves (Nice, France); Habjouqa Ammar (Vienna, Austria); Sigrun Andradottir (Atlanta, GA); Rolf Andvik (Syvde, Norway); Anna (United Kingdom); Pastor Annoshian (Tenafly, NJ); Rashid and Rasheeqa Ansari (Chicago, IL); George (Jori) Ansell (Wales); Cristian Carrillan Anton (Temuco, Chile); Anne Apio (Tororo, Uganda); Chuck Appel (Bloomfield, NJ); Antonio Arce (Provo, UT); Rtte Desiderio Arce (Salta, Argentina); Diana Archangeli (Tucson, AZ); David Argoff (Washington, DC); Xosé Lluis (Jose Luis) Garcií Arias (Oviedo, Spain); I Wayan Arka (Palo Alto, CA); Dr Mark Aronoff (Stony Brook, NY); Bishop Ben Arreak (Kuujjuaq, Canada); Moses Ashkenazi (Los Angeles, CA); Lydia Assen-Jackson (Ghana); Bishop Atagotaaluk (Yellowknife, Northwest Territories, Canada); Chris Atwood (Bloomington, IN); Kenza At Yaagun and Dr Yazid Djerbib (Yazid At Yaagun) (Quebec, Canada); Dr Yiwola Awoyale (Ilorin, Nigeria); Mesfin Ayaleen (Jerusalem, Israel); Juliana Azure (Bolgatanga, Ghana); Boris Bababekov (New York, NY); Souleymane Bah (Pita, Guinea); Moshê M Baitsewe (Bachbrecht, Namibia); Mark Baker (Quebec, Canada); John-Luc Bakker (Flemington, NJ); Eddie Baladjay (Lebak Cotabato, Philippines); Dr Catherine N Ball (Washington, DC); Eoghan Craig Ballard (Philadelphia, PA); Khun Bang-on (Bangkok, Thailand); Tonglaga Bao (Laie, HI); Felicia Emerenciana Baran (Newark, NJ); Abdirahman A Farah Barwaqo (Ottawa, Ontario, Canada); Inta Batsman (Middlesex, United Kingdom); Zanet Battinou (Athens, Greece); Hermenegildo Bautista Bautista (San Handrés Cohamiata, Jalisco, Mexico); Duane Hollow Horn Bear (Mission, SD); Charles Beauchamp (Hodgson, Manitoba, Canada); Dr Deborah Beck (Swarthmore, PA); Erie Beemsterboer (New Providence, NJ); Maria Beguin (Springfield, NJ); Dr Giovanni Belluscio (Honolulu, HI); Dr Byron Bender (Honolulu, HI); Daniel Benjamin (Des Plaines, IL); Ruthie Ben-Mayor (Hefer, Israel); Vasia Benusl (Basking Ridge, NJ); Behzad Benyamini (Cliffside Park, NJ); Marla Berkowitz (New York, NY); Dr Howard M Berlin (MD); Chanie and Moshe Berman (New York, NY); Melissa Bernstein (Rochester, NY); Simon Bernstein (Redmond, WA); Nicki Berthelson (San Fernando Valley, CA); Bhagyavati (Bangalore, India); Yeshoda Bhat and Rajaram Bhat (Middletown, NJ); Suraj P 'Raj' Bhatia (NJ); Anju Bhattrai (Muncie, IN); Pema Bhum (Bloomington, IN); Theodore Bikel (W Hollywood, CA); Lloyd N Binder (Inuvik, Northwest Territories, Canada); Cantor Stuart Binder (Princeton Juction, NJ); Joan Binza (Tema, Ghana); Josef Bitan (Livingston, NJ); Chester Bitissine (White Mesa, UT); Sue Black (Nanuet (NY); Duane Blanchard (China); Victoria Blay (Tema, Ghana); John and Susan Blood (Minneapolis, MN); Laura Bloomenthal (UT); Matthew Bloomfield (Athens, OH); Helen Blum (Glen Ridge, NJ); David Blumsohn (Glenhazel, South Africa); Gary Blumsohn (New York, NY); Maurice Blumsohn (South Africa); Frank Boateng (New Haven, CT); Charlotte Boje (New York, NY); Helen Borenstein (Lake Hiawatha, NJ); Tim Borzell (Hong Kong); Cuido Bosco (Castagnole Monferrato, Italy); Charles Bourque (St Landry Parish, LA); Shirley Bowman (Crownpoint, NM); Tom Bozlyian (La Mirada, CA); Yaara Brahm (New York, NY); Professor Michael Brame (New York, NY); Bill Brescia (Bloomington, IN); Tamara Brooks (Syracuse, NY); Louise Brown; Dr Benjamin Bruch (Cambridge, MA); David and Jullian Emma "Silkie" Burger (New York, NY); Souleymane and Rebecca Camara (Conakry, Guinea); Fodé Camera and Rebecca Rhodes (Takoma Park, MD); Wilfred L Camilleri (Ontario, Canada); Karen Cantor (Berkeley Heights, NJ); Alfred Capelle (Majuro, Marshall Islands); Ilan Caplan (Caldwell, NJ); Clarita B Caraig (Quezon City, Philippines); Ralph Carhart (New York, NY); Chetna Cariapa (Edison, NJ); Esther Lee M Caruncho (NJ); Evelyn Caruncho (W Orange, NJ); Hipolito Peralta Ccama (Cuzco, Peru); Kamal Chadha (Philadelphia, PA); Ritu Chadha (Hillsborough, NJ); James Chambala (Shinyanga, Tanzania); Alan Champion (Bensalem, PA); Professor Ailbhe Ni Chasaide (Dublin, Ireland); Yuu-Heng (Alice) Cheng (Piscataway, NJ); Nim Cheung (NJ); Beth Chia-Rubin (Saddle Brook, NJ); Miwako Kato Chiaet (Caldwell, NJ); Carlo Mario Chierotti (Asti, Italy); Venancio Chimbo (El Oriente, Ecuador); Charles Chipps (Wanblee, SD); Shailender (Shally) Chohan (NJ); Yaacov Choueka (Ramat-Gan, Israel); Evan Chu (Fremont, CA); Solongo Chuluunbaatar (Laie, HI); Gloria Churchill (Ketchikan, AK); Fiorello (Fred) Cicala (Washington, DC); Peter Claus (Hayward, CA); Stephen Coates (Alice Springs, Northern Territory, Australia); Angela Cockburn (Australia); Craig Cockburn (United Kingdom); Dr Harvey Cohen (Middletown, NJ); Dr Abigail Cohn (Ithaca, NY); Dr John Colarusso (Hamilton, Ontario, Canada); Dr Patrick Conner (Morgantown, WV); Serafin Coronel-Molina (Drexel Hill, PA); Charlie Courtney (Madison, NJ); Lara (Puamae'ole Mui) Cowell (Honolulu, HI); Beth Craig (NJ); Ronald Jay Cristal (Bangkok, Thailand); Dong Cui (HI); Jean Daigrepont (New Orleans, LA); Khun (Mrs) Namrin Dampan (Bangkok, Thailand); Philimon Darmo (Sydney, Australia); Rabbi Allen Darnov (Marlboro, NJ); Subir Das (NJ); Arindam Datta (Hillsborough, NJ); Cory Davia (Maplewood, NJ); Valerie Davia (Maplewood, NJ); Ian Wendell Davis; Richard Davis (NY); Keith Dawson (Northford, MA); Thomas F Dawson (Beaufort, NC); Joao Gabriel de Barros and Loubato Maria Pinto (Lisbon, Portugal); Inge De Bleecker (Boston, MA); Scott Deerwester (Hong Kong); Tjeerd de Graaf (Groningen, Netherlands); Tom De Herdt (Ghent, Belgium); Bert de Jong (Amsterdam, Netherlands); Joshibiah Gaa de Juan (Manila, Philippines); Victoriano de la Cruz Cruz (Zacatecas, Mexico); Emmanuel A dela Rosa (Quezon City, Philippines); Joe Delaney (Montclair, NJ); Brenda Dellinger (Cullowhee, NC); Dr Cristina Delogu (Rome, Italy); Dr Larry Denenberg (Newton, MA); Luis Caldas de Oliveira (Lisbon, Portugal); Christine Zachary Deom (Kahnawake Mohawk Reserve, Quebec, Canada); Willem J de Reuse (Denton, TX); Rishi Desai (Chicago, IL); Terry (Deerwoman) Dever (Martin, SD); Dr Lluis de Yzaguirre i Maura (Barcelona, Spain); Dr Gill Diamond (Short Hills, NJ); Helen Diaz (Quezon City, Philippines); Frank Dieleman (Marseille, France); Dr Steven C Dinero (Philadelphia, PA); Binggong Ding (Beijing, China); Michael Dobrovolsky (Calgary, Alberta, Canada); Veronica Dobson (Alice Springs, Northern Territory, Australia); Brian Doherty (Canada); Luan Lam Doniger (HI); Mamady Doumbouya (USA); Dr Edwin Duncan (Baltimore, MD); Alan Eder (Valencia, CA); Christopher Dost (Waterbury, CT); Martin and Elisa Eiger (Montville, NJ); Mengue Eka-Abila (New York, NY); Abderrahman El Aissati (Tilburg, Netherlands); Moncef Elaoud (NJ); Salih Eliyahu (Israel); Tereza Elizarova (Brooklyn, NY); Eric Elliott (CA); Ahmed Elmagarmid (W Lafayette, IN); Anwar Elwalid (New York, NY); Ashok and Shobha Erramilli (Old Bridge, NJ); Maxine Eskenazi (Pittsburgh, PA); Monica Estruch (Barcelona, Spain); Phuzile Eveline (Sasolburg, South Africa); Michel Everson (Ireland); Grazio Falzon (Sandusky, OH); Shehu Farinwata (Detroit, MI); Helge K Fauskanger (Askø, Norway); Larry Feinson (Ewing, NJ); Jan Fischer (New York, NY); Jay Fishman (USA); Tiguist Fisseha (Addis Ababa, Ethiopia); Curt Fissel and Ellen Friedland (NJ); Pat Folan (Connemara, Ireland); Shannon Foley (Nairobi, Kenya); Ted Folke (Westport, CT); Scott Ford (Albion, WA); Edward Foster (Matieland, Zambia); Brenda Francis (Orem, UT); Lawrence H Francis (Rooseveltown, NY); Kelley Moonwater Frederick (Parsippany, NJ); Dr Victor Friedman (Chicago, IL); Wilma Friedman (New York, NY); Dr Paul R Frommer (Los Angeles, CA); George Fulford (Winnipeg, Canada); Reinhart Gaeb (Windhoek, Namibia); Zenaida Garcia (NJ); Arnold I Garlick, III (San Clemente, CA); Bruce Gelder (W Jordan, UT); Professor Stephen Geller (New York, NY); Dr Alex Gelman (Princeton, NJ); Olivier Georg (Switzerland); Neil and Adele Gerace (Perth, Australia); Debbie Gerber (Highland Park, NJ); Gary Gibian (Potomac, MD); Dr Duncan

MacRae Gibson (Aberdeen, Scotland); Julia A Gimenez (Barcelona, Spain); Thamar Gindin; Gilles Giovannanjeti (Corte, France); Valerij Glinskiy (S Brunswick, NJ); Sylvester (Cardy) Goes Ahead (Pryor, MT); Etan G Goldman (Los Angeles, CA); Howie Goldman (Suffern, NY); Heshy Rosenwasser (Beverly Hills, CA); Joao Carlos Salvador Gomez (New York, NY); Professor Gaspar Pedro Gonzalez (Guatemala City, Guatemala); Phillip Goode (San Carlos, AZ); Yitzchak (Zuki) Gottlieb (NY); Geoffrey Graham (New Haven, CT); Christine Grant (Raleigh, NC); Barbara (Gray Deer) Gray (Tempe, AZ); Jenny Green (Alice Springs, Northern Territory, Australia); Edy Greenblatt (Los Angeles, CA); Stacey Greenstein (Hopatcong, NJ); Jack and Valerie Rose Grier (Randolph, NJ); Jeffery Gritz (Baltimore, MD); Malgorzata Groos (Zurich, Switzerland); Rabbi Daniel Grossman (Laurenceville, NJ); Colonel R Neil Grove (Wellington, New Zealand); Alexandra (Sandi) Gubin (Boston, MA); Dr Marion Gunn (Dublin, Ireland); Piadad Gutierrez (Caldwell, NJ); Matthew Gutman (Israel); Richard Gwananji (San Jose, CA); Professor Wilfrid Haacke (Windhoek, Namibia); Dr Marcia Haag (Norman, OK); Hiroka Hagishita (NJ); Moshe I (Moshiko) Halevy (Tel Aviv, Israel); Dr David Hallegua (Los Angeles, CA); Dr Ian Hancock (Manchaca, TX); Khurram Haneef (NJ); Moshe Harir (Kiryat Ata, Israel); Paavo Hasheela (Windhoek, Namibia); Murray Hasson (Randolph, NJ); Allison Hauptman (Princeton, NJ); Professor R J Hayward (London, United Kingdom); Ahmadshah Hazrati (Kandahar, Afghanistan); Dr Ning-Ji He (Charleston, SC); Desiewaar (Desie) D N Heita (Windhoek, Namibia); Prakash Hemrajani (Marlboro Twp, NJ); Alex Heppenheimer (Brooklyn, NY); Zoltan Herczegh (Stockholm, Sweden); Professor George Hewitt and Zaira Khiba (London, United Kingdom); Mia Kissil Hewitt (Bernardsville, NJ); Dr Sarah Higley (Rochester, NY); Markus Hiller (Tuebingen, Germany); Majdalin (Majida) Hilmi (New York, NY); Liudmilla Hirsch (New York, NY); Dr Dee Ann Holiksy (Fairfax, VA); Turið Holm (Hoyvik, Faroe Islands); Natalia Honcharenko (Franklin Park, NJ); Graham Hopwood (Windhoek, Namibia); Uri Horesh (Herzliya, Israel); Ahsan Hundal (Edison, NJ); Supharidh Hy (New York, NY); Marcia Haddad Ikonomopoulos (New York, NY); Dr Bruce Ingham (London, United Kingdom); Gildor Inglorion (Athens, Greece); Arian Ishaya (San Jose, CA); Tafiqual Islam (Queens, NY); Lazarus Issala (Windhoek, Namibia); Peter Ivanov (Sofia, Bulgaria); Barry and Fran Ivker (Birmingham, AL); Jan Jackson (Boston, MA); Tim Jackson (Johannesburg, South Africa); Mercy Jacob (Santa Clara, CA); Anna Janowska (New York, NY); Anthony and Nessy Jayakumar (Somerset, NJ); Roger Jefferson (Columbus, OH); Patricia Jeng (NJ); Željko Jergan (Pittsburgh, PA); John Jiang (CA); Ping Jiang (NJ); Wen-Lei Jiang (NJ); Jane Jiao (Charleston, SC); Dr Michael Job (Marlburg, Germany); Tsendsuren (Cindy) Tumnee Johnson (Provo, UT); Dr Rhys James Jones (Swansea, Wales); Matt Juan (Phoenix, AZ); Dr Alimhan Junisbekov (Almata, Kazakhstan); Mooh Jurh (Burma, Myanmar); Doreen Kahn (Silver Spring, MD); Benjawan Kanyaphan (Midvale, UT); Ajay Kapoor (Edison, NJ); Tuula Karabin (Schenectady, NY); Ethelbert Kari (Tokyo, Japan); Michael Karu (W Orange, NJ); Esther Kasenga (Kwimba Mwanza, Tanzania); Godlief Katipana; Nathan Katz (Miami, FL); Daniel Kaufman (New York, NY); Simon Kaufman (New York, NY); Zerfe Kebede (San Jose, CA); Joab Jonadab (JJ) Keki (Mbale, Uganda); Phil Kelly (Isle of Man); Norma Kennedy (Oneida, NY); Aldean and Wanda Ketchum (White Mesa, UT); Chodura N Khandy (Kizil, Republic of Tuva); Nabil Khatib (Boston, MA); Banzragchiin Khurelbat (Bloomington, IN); Justo Kib (Maya Center, Belize); Izzy Kieffer (Brooklyn NY); Ercüment Kılıç (Centreville, VA); Dr J Kim (Princeton, NJ); Mumo Kimanthi (Nairobi, Kenya); Alan R King Zarautz, The Basque Country, Spain; Dr Alexander King (Charlottesville, VA); Dr George Anton Kiraz (Murray Hill, NJ); Donald Kissil (Morristown, NJ); Baruch Klar (W Orange, NJ); Melvin Klassen (British Columbia, Canada); Rick Kleiner (Santa Monica, CA); Jessica Knapp (Pittsburgh, PA); Dagmar (Dasha) Katlandova Koenig (Seattle, WA); Gregory Koch (Poughkeepsie, NY); Professor Minas Kostis (Mytilene, Greece); Dr Rozi Kovesdi (NJ); M Krishnakumar; Jim Kruper (NJ); Lynn Kra-Oz (Ra'anana, Israel); Liliya Krasner (NJ); Moti Krauthamer (Seattle, WA); Robert Kuronga (Windhoek, Namibia); Kobla Ladzekpo

and Dzidzogbe Lawluvi (Valencia, CA); Benoit Lagrue (Provence, France); Ron Lahti (Boston, MA); Andrej Lajovic (Ljubljana, Slovenia); Dr Jaro Lajovic (Ljubljana, Slovenia); Marvin Lalo (Kykotsmovi, AZ); John Lampert (Carlstadt, NJ); George Lapiotis (Piscataway, NJ); Anastasia Lapsui (Helsinki, Finland); Paul Lareau; Amar Lathi (Bridgewater, NJ); Dr Bhagawandas P Lathi (Carmichael, CA); Mary Lau (NJ); Michael K Launer (Tallahassee, FL); Judy Lauter (TX); Akazuo A Lawrence (Bolgatanga, Ghana); Chiao-Wei Lee (NJ); Jessica Lee (N Brunswick, NJ); Ming Mei Lee (NJ); Dr Minkyu Lee (Murray Hill, NJ); Malgorzata Wojtaszek Legnica (Trenton, NJ); Wayne Leman (Busby, MT); Lesley Leposo (Pittsburgh, PA); Alan and Pricilla Levine (Potomac, MD); Rebecca Levine (White Meadow Lake, NJ); Philip Lew; Erin Lewis (Tororo district, Uganda); Jan Leys (W Orange, NJ); Peter (Shih-Wei) Li (NJ); Hong (Julia) Liao (NJ); Fuchun (Joe) Lin (NJ); Leandro Rodriguez Linares (Vigo, Spain); Dr Marc Lindy (Wellington, New Zealand); Yibei Ling (NJ); Dr Joyce Lionarons (Collegeville, PA); Rob Lisch (Jamaica Estates, NY); Chaim Litewski (New York, NY); Roby Koolyeik Littlefield (Sitka, AK); Dr Joaquim Llisterri (Barcelona, Spain); Ariadna Font Llitjós (Pittsburgh, PA); Boris M Lobanov (Minsk, Belarus); Ilana Locker (Dar es Salaam, Tanzania); Jeffrey Loewenstein (NY); Jesús López (Spain); Ruth Losada (Vigo, Spain); Dr Naima Louali-Raynal (Lyon, France); Julie Lovins (CA); Leonard Løvoll (Ålesund, Norway); David Lowe (Brookline, MA); Xin-Mian Lu (Parsippany, NJ); Stefan Lubbersen (South Africa); Gladys Lucifante (El Oriente, Ecuador); Dr Judy Lumb (Caye Caulker, Belize); Pastor Allan Luna (Quezon City, Philippines); Kimvuemina Luvuma (Philadelphia, PA); Maria J Machuca (Barcelona, Spain); Dr Duncan Macrae-Gibson (Aberdeen, Scotland); Sindiwe Magona (Riverdale, NY); Dr Tulsi Maharjan (Somerville, NJ); NJ); Dr Frith Maier (Seattle, WA); Jan Maier (Waltham, MA); Timon Onjero Maingi (Nairobi, Kenya); Izra and Manahem Malakov (Forest Hills, NY); Ezekiel Isaac Malekar (New Delhi, India); Fabien Malouin (Ottawa, Canada); Wilson Manik (Ithaca, NY); Ruth Manor (Kfar-Saba, Israel); Daye Mara (Kissidougou, Guinea-Bissau); Professor David Marcus (New York, NY); Danielle Marin (Lawrenceville, NJ); Mark Markish; Judith Markowitz (Evanston, IL); Laura Martin (Cleveland, OH); Reverend Barth Masa (Quezon City, Philippines); Phil and Rachel Mason (Framingham, MA); Issac Mathew (NY); Andrew Matjila (Caprivi, Namibia); Sol Matsil (N Woodmere, NY); Raymond Matson (North Island, New Zealand); Hu Matthews (Billings, MT); Professor Claude Mauron (Provence, France); John Mayer (Israel); Derek Mbatha (New York, NY); Loide Mbenzi (Windhoek, Namibia); Nene Mburu (London, United Kingdom); Matthew McDaniel (Salem, OR); Susie McKay (Friendswood, TX); Professor Damian McManus (Dublin, Ireland); Gopal Meempat (E Brunswick, NJ); Rajiv Mehta (Piscataway, NJ); Robert Mensah (Winneba, Ghana); Guy Mercier (Lannion, France); John Merrill (Redmond, WA); Dr Yemani Mesfun (NJ); Matthew Meyer (Wilmington, DE); Muhand (Muhamed) Meziani (Geneva, Switzerland); Rabbi Bennett Miller (New Brunswick, NJ); Fred Miller (USA); Jason Miller (Caldwell, NJ); Dr Miriam Youngerman Miller (New Orleans, LA); Naomi Miller (Wayne, NJ); Sailesh Mishra (India); Matua Moeke (North Island, New Zealand); Mehryar Mohri (NY); Raymond Monel (NJ); Bill Moody (New York, NY); Barbara Moss (NY); Veena Motwani (Freehold, NJ); Right Reverend (Bishop) David Moxam (Hamilton, New Zealand); Antery C Mswete (Iringa, Tanzania); Dick Mueller (E Lake, CO); Zilore Mumba (Lusaka, Zambia); Muntana Munatu (Bolgatanga, Ghana); Dr Pamela (Pam) Munro (Los Angeles, CA); Amit K Munta (Paramus, NJ); Wangari Muooria (London, United Kingdom); Monica Murphy (Bethel, AK); Rahel Musleah (Great Neck, NY); Dr Hezy Mutzafi (Tel Aviv, Israel); Professor Pieter Muysken (Amsterdam, Netherlands); Osward Mwitika (Mbeya, Tanzania); Dr Djafar Mynbaev (Fair Lawn, NJ); K Krishna Naik (Bengaluru, India); Kimeli Willson Naiyomah (Stanford, CA); Hermien Nakare (Windhoek, Namibia); Hangula Vistorina Namkuaya (Oshakati, Namibia); Rachel Namudosi (Mbale, Uganda); Sanjai Narain (Madison, NJ); Sudha Narain (New Delhi, India); Harold Nayda (Alice Springs, Northern Territory, Australia); Nurdin Nayopa (Dar es Salaam, Tanzania); Godfrey Ndagala (Stony Brook, NY); Dr Barbara Need (Chicago, IL);

Brenda Needle (Jerusalem, Israel); Charlotte Nichol (Whitemouth, Manitoba, Canada); Victor Joseph Nicholas (Barranco Village, Belize); Dr Johanna Nichols (Berkeley, CA); Joanita Ngaiza (Dar es Salaam, Tanzania); Vedasto Gasto Ngaiza (Bukoba, Tanzania); Phuzile Eveline Ntshumayelo (Sasolburg, South Africa); Liz Nunan (Decatur, GA); Jacque Nunez (CA); Professor Howard Nusbaum (Chicago, IL); Jim Nyema-Davies (Greensboro, NC); Sue Nyoni (Morristown, NJ); Dr John O'Meara (Thunder Bay, Ontario, Canada); Dr Virginia (Vaitekonis) Obando (Elizabeth, NJ); Samuel Gyasi Obeng (Bloomington, IN); Dr Michael R and Safaira Kua Ogden (Honolulu, HI); Richard Ogden (London, United Kingdom); Kabu Okai-Davis (Newark, NJ); Edward Okeke (New York, NY); Samson Okoh (Holland, MI); Jocobus Alwyn Kruger (Jako) Olivier (Sasolburg, South Africa); Mary Olson (Dover, NJ); Katherine Olstein (New Brunswick, NJ); Zakir Omarov (N Miami Beach, FL); Miren Lourdes Onederra (Virona-Gasteiz, Spain); Samuel Opare (Accra, Ghana); Irit Opher (Tel Aviv, Israel); Boris Orlovsky (NJ); Asako Oshiro (Santa Barbara, CA); David Osofsky (Boston, MA); Nicholas (Nick) Ostler (Bath, United Kingdom); Professor Shozo Ota (Tokyo, Japan); Oketch Sam Otenge (Tororo, Uganda); Hassan Ournahim (Tilburg, Netherlands); Panui (New Zealand); Kirthika Parmeswaran (NJ); Abdul Mateen Patel (Montville, NJ); Sarvar Patel (Montville, NJ); Smita Patel (Lawrenceville, NJ); Francene Patterson (USA); Anna Paun (Somerville, NJ); Guillermo Payahuaje (El Oriente, Ecuador); George Petty (Denville, NJ); Paul Pickard (Hodgson, Manitoba, Canada); Maureen Pierce (Wales); Lucy Piligian (Englewood Cliffs, NJ); Susan Pilshaw (Morristown, NJ); Sompol Piromyothee (Bangkok, Thailand); Kem Piseth (Shinkawa, Japan); Professor David Pisoni (Bloomington, IN); Elisavet Pliakas (Astoria, Queens, NY); Roberto Plomp (Netherlands); Aleksander Podluzhny (Minsk, Belarus); Osman (Todd) Polatkan (N Haledon, NJ); Dr Bob Port (Bloomington, IN); Mel Powell (Sherman Oaks, CA); Tony Pritchard (New Zealand); Priyono (Sydney, Australia); Queen Quet (Sea Island, SC); Ietje Rahakbauw-Rahanra (Overijssel, Netherlands); Muralidharan Ramaswamy (NJ); Tage Ranängen (Luleå, Sweden); Prakasa Rao (Bangalore, India); Jonah Ratsimbazafy (Stony Brook, NY); Dr Marina Rautenbach (Stellenbosch, Zambia); Vololontiana (Tiana) Razafindratsita (Stony Brook, NY); Johnathan P Reale (Mine Hill, NJ); Dominic Recchione (Largo, FL); Dr Michael Recchione (Nutley, NJ); Kjell Rehnstroem (Uppsala, Sweden); Sasha Reichstein (Helsinki, Finland); Professor Gary A Rendsburg (Highland Park, NJ); Saul A Resnikoff (Centennial, CO); Abdelmounaam Rezgui (W Lafayette, IN); Mort Rich (Blairstown, NJ); Dr Heinz (Hync) Richter (Leipzig, Germany); Stefan Riezler (Tuebingen, Germany); Steve and Zobeida B Roitstein (Miami, FL); Frank and Malgorzata Roos (Zurich, Switzerland); Dr Lauren Rose (Tivoli, NY); Heshy Rosenwasser (Brooklyn, NY); Dr Barbara Katz Rothman (Stony Brook, NY); Rubekkur Rubeksen (Tørshavn, Faroe Islands); Professor Aaron Rubin (University Park, PA); Jessie Grace U Rubrico (Quezon City, Philippines); Jack Rushing (Liberty Corner, NJ); Valeriu Rusu (Provence, France); Janet Rutledge (Washington, DC); Nathan Ryan (Sterling, VA); Dr Ashok Sabata (Sea Bright, NJ); Bikash Sabata; Peter Salamon; Aita Salasoo (Cedar Knolls, NJ); Daowd Ibrahim Salih (New York, NY); Juha Salin (Redmond, WA); Dr Tapani Salminen (Helsinki, Finland); Adrian Samareanu (Bucharest, Romania); Professor Liliana Sanchez (New Brunswick, NJ); Kathy Sandoval (CA); Iraj Saniee (Berkeley Heights, NJ); Sam Sankaran (Regina, Saskatchewan, Canada); Ernesto and Aurora Garcia Saqui (Maya Center, Belize); Francis Sarguis; Fantaye E Sarka and Dabela Olana (Calgary, Alberta, Canada); Vijeet Sarma; Lan-Ting (Alicia) Say (Taipei, Taiwan); Leonel Say (Hollywood, CA); Lisa Schachner (New York, NY); Vicky Schenandoah (Oneida, NY); Bert and Miriam Schlauch (Minneapolis, MN); Leila Schneps (France); Professor Ora R Schwarzwald (Ramat Gan, Israel); Dr Michael Scordilis (Patras, Greece); Isil Sebuktekin (Parsippany, NJ); Benyamim Sedaka (Holon, Israel); Professor Eliezer Segal & No Starch Press (Calgary, Alberta, Canada); Luisa Selis (Rome, Italy); Gunter Senft (Nijmegen, Netherlands); Natalie Sera (Reno, NV); Yael Shaffir (Quebec, Canada); Mughees Shaikh; Daya Shakya (Portland, OR); Barbara Shalit (Morristown, NJ); Rashbil Shamayev (Brooklyn, NY); Dr Sherrie (Shaunie) Shammass (Rishon Lezion, Israel); Yohana Sharif (Dodoma, Tanzania); Shanti Shashidhara (Princeton Junction, NJ); Denis Shelden (Alakanuk, AK); Joyce Shenloogian (Blauvelt, NY); Ang Chokpa Sherpa (Flemington, NJ); Ngawang (Dawa) Norbu Sherpa (Jackson Heights, NJ); Phurba Gyalzen Sherpa (Croton Falls, NY); Hyong Sop Shim (NJ); Moshe Shimoni (Haifa, Israel); Mark Shoulson (New York, NY); Adam Shwartz (Haifa, Israel); Asher Siebert (New Brunswick, NJ); Matthew A Siegler (Pittsburgh, PA); Carol Silverman (Eugene, OR); Dr Kim Silverman (Mountain View, CA); John Simpson (Oxford, United Kingdom); Cantor Daniel Singer (New York, NY); Tarun Singh (Santa Maria, CA); John Singler (New York, NY); Suvan Sitibong (Midvale, UT); Rabbi Gershom Sizomu (Mbale, Uganda); Dr Harold Charles Slengard (Zoetermeer, Netherlands); Eric Slone; Ahmed Munda Smart (New York, NY); Dr Graeme Smith (Stoneham, MA); Madia Smith-Brown (Charlotte, NC); Richard Smith; Dianne Snake (Moraviantown, Ontario, Canada); Thor Soreland (New York, NY); Professor Elliot Sperling (Bloomington, IN); Dr Jeffrey Spiegel (Pittsburgh, PA); Toby Lee Spiegel (Phoenix, AZ); Mike Stein (Washington, DC); Alyson and Robyn Stein (N Brunswick, NJ); Pam Stein (Philadelphia, PA); Sam Stein (CT); Inacio (Issar) Steinhardt (Israel); Steve Stevens (Midvale, UT); Josip Stilinovic (Zagreb, Croatia); Dr Justin Straus (Tenafly, NJ); Dr John Sullivan (Zacatecas, Mexico); Tetyana Sumaro'kova (Almata, Kazakhstan); Sumer (USA); C M Sunita (Bengaluru, India); Liv Svendsen (Point Pleasant, NJ); Cade Swinger (USA); Sylvia (NJ); Masimba Tafirenyika (Queens, NY); Kamil Taha (Hillsdale, NJ); Hany N Takla (Los Angeles, CA); Milton Tan (Singapore); Grace Tarata (Tema, Ghana); Alireza Tarighian (Millburn, NJ); Marie-Lucie Tarpent (Canada); Miriam Tauil (Berkeley Heights, NJ); Hui Mian Tay (Honolulu, HI); Everson Gunn Teoranta (Éire, Ireland); Bruno Tersago (Belgium); U Thein-Tun (Bundoora, Victoria, Australia); Wah Chan Thom (Honolulu, HI); Daniel Thompson (Rooseveltown, NY); Donna Thompson (AZ); Mikael A Thompson (Bloomington, IN); Anastasia Lapsui Timofeevna (Helsinki, Finland); Manasi Tirodkar (Brooklyn, NY); Magdalena Tjiroze (Windhoek, Namibia); Maria Tokarz (Chatham, NJ); George Tomov (Woodside, NY); Chief Peter Guanıkeyu Torres (Millville, NJ); Dr Ljiljana Trajkovic (British Columbia, Canada); Cong Luan Ngo Tran (United Kingdom); Sebastiano Triglla (Italy); Manolis Tsangaris (Greece); Roz Tunis (Oakland, CA); Reverend Fàafili Tusani (Apia, W Samoa); Mr Tweya (Windhoek, Namibia); Shlomi Tzion (Israel); Fera Ubro-Rahantoknam (Overijssel, Netherlands); Dr Christofer Jürgen Uhlich (Dublin, Ireland); Gordon McKay and Linda Uljon (El Lago, TX); Mai Britt Utsi (Guovdageaidnu, Norway); Madina Vadachkoria (Seattle, WA); Pierre Vaillancourt (Quebec, Canada); Andrew Vakhutinsky (NJ); Faramak Vakil (NJ); Dr Aone Thomas van Engelenhoven (Leiden, Netherlands); Dr Jan P H van Santen (Brooklyn, NY); H van Wyk (Windhoek, Namibia); Aaron Vaughn (Provo, UT); Paul Vedder and Hetty Kook (Leiden, Netherlands); Dace Veinberga (Canada); Dr Jean Véronis (Provence, France); PV (Meylekh) and Meena Viswanath (Teaneck, NJ); Eva Vogel (NJ); David Voluck (Sitka, AK); Christoffer von Bonsdorff (Finland); Dr Julie Vonwiller (Sydney, Australia); Julie Vreones (Phoenix, AZ); Sally Roesch Wagner (USA); Jenifer Wairumu (Nairobi, Kenya); David Wald; Karen Wallace (Nutley, NJ); Martin Wallraff (United Kingdom); Fareed Shirzai Wardak (Livermore, CA); Dr Samarada "Sam" Weerahandi (Millington, NJ); Jim Weintraub (Montville, NJ); Steven Weinberger (New York, NY); Dr Alan and Rabbi Judy Weiss (Millburn, NJ); Daniel Wemali (Nairobi, Kenya); Astrid Werner (Princeton, NJ); Rune Westerlund (Luleå, Sweden); Tom Willett (TX); Dr Briony Williams (Edinburgh, United Kingdom); Roseann Willink (Corrales, NM); Henry Willis (Norman, OK); Catherine (Pickens) Willmond (Los Angeles, CA); Kaija Wilson (Washington, DC); Jeremiah Wolf (Cherokee, NC); Min Fa Xu (Flushing, NY); Dr Tal Yadid (Tel Aviv, Israel); Firuza Yagodaeva (Brooklyn, NY); Maya Yajnik (NJ); Ibrahim Adoke Yakubu (Athens, Greece); Bonnie Yazzie (Crownpoint, NM); Bertin Yèhouènou (Provence, France); Celia Yitzhak (Arava, Israel); Teiko Yonaha-Tursi (Berlin, NJ); Yoko Yoshida (New York, NY); Amanda Young (Wellington, New Zealand); Ray and Eileen Young (Tauranga, New Zealand); Mark Yun (Queens, NY); Mor Nicholovos Zachariah (New York, NY); Dora Zaidenweber (Minneapolis, MN); Tariq Zawahir (Chicago, IL); Sayan Zhambalov (Ulan Ude, Republic of Buryatia); Sandy Zhong (Rockaway Borough, NJ); Paul Zolbrod (Albuquerque, NM); Abeberash (Abi) Zwede-Demissik (New York, NY).

Footnotes

Preface: The Jewish Theological Seminary in New York contains the largest collection of Haggadahs ... Searching the website of JTS' Library, one finds Haggadahs in at least these languages: Amharic, Arabic, Chinese, Czech, Dutch, English, Farsi, French, German, Greek, Hebrew, Hungarian, Italian, Judeo-Arabic, Kurdish/Aramaic, Ladino, Latin, Marathi, Persian, Polish, Portuguese, Provençal, Romanian, Russian, Slovenian, Spanish, Swedish and Yiddish.

Why Translate the Four Questions? "It's not that I go looking for people to invite based on what languages they speak ..." "Celebrating Diversity," by Barbara Katz Rothman, from *Weaving a Family: Untangling Race and Adoption* (Beacon, 2005). Used with permission.

How Translations Were Obtained: ... publisher of African textbooks, who provided nine languages spoken throughout Africa. One of the authors contacted the online site of Namibia's newspaper, seeking someone knowledgeable for an obscure language. The editor replied they had no one, but posted our notice in their national newspaper. Soon we started receiving letters from all over Namibia! Over the next 2 years, the leading publisher of African textbooks, Gamsberg Macmillan, provided translations in nine languages.

The Task of Translation: Flatbreads can be made from every grain ... From *Flatbreads and Flavors*, by Jeffrey Alford and Naomi Duguid (Willliam Morrow and Co., 1995). ISBN 0-688-11411-3.

The root סבב (*sovev*, 'to go around') is puzzling ... *A Comprehensive Etymological Dictionary of the Hebrew Language*, by Ernest Kline (Carta, Jerusalem, 1987) ISBN 965-220-093-X.

Mystique of the Number Four: The four core symbols on the Seder table: The Paschal lamb, matzah, bitter herbs and charoset. The four promises of redemption: I will take you out of the labor in Egypt, and free you from slavery; I will liberate you; and I will take you to Me [Exodus 6:6-8]. The four Hebrew names for Passover: *Chag Ha-Pesach* (The Festival of Passover); *Chag Ha-Matzot* (The Festival of Unleavened Bread); *Chag Ha-Aviv* (The Festival of Spring); *Ze'man Cherutenu* (The Festival of Freedom).

Fir Kashes vs. Qushiyot ... *kashes* are <u>more</u> than just a question. From *Born to Kvetch*, Michael Wex (Martin's Press, New York, 2005) ISBN 0-312-30741-1. Nechama Leibowitz expands this idea to say *qushiyot* are sharper questions, which require a deeper answer than does answering *sh'elot*. *Qushiyot* are the type of questions encountered in Torah study. From *Studies on the Haggadah: From the Teachings of Nechama Leibowitz,* edited by Reiner Yitshak and Shmuel Peetless (Urim publications, 2002) ISBN 978-9657108383.

Community Variations in the Text: *Chameits o matsah.* Examples of Haggadahs using אֹו מַצָּה (*o matsah*) from one author's 3 dozen Haggadahs: Cuban, Farsi, Greek, Italian, Judeo-Iraqi and 2 different Ladino Haggadahs.

Bread on Passover?: Permission to prepare food ... Exodus 12:16

... the food must be consumed on that day itself. Talmud *Betzah* 15b and 17a.

This caused the error. From editor's notes in the reprinted Haggadah of the Bene-Israel of Israel.

Language Extinction: ... half of the world's 5,000-7,000 languages will be gone in a hundred years. *Saving Dying Languages*, by W Wayt Gibbs, Scientific American (August, 2002) is an excellent overview of the endangered languages.

Samantha Stoma, age 8, Caldwell, NJ

Having a hand in the Seder

Answers to Puzzles
Quiz answers for the puzzles on pages 388-391

LANGUAGES ANSWER KEY

1. Egyptian Hieroglyphics
2. Finnish
3. Yiddish
4. Icelandic
5. Farsi
6. Burmese
7. Polish
8. Amharic
9. Latin
10. Zulu
11. Japanese
12. Portuguese
13. Czech
14. Korean
15. Old English
16. Azerbaijani
17. Georgian
18. Bulgarian
19. Vietnamese
20. Armenian
21. Norwegian
22. Irish
23. Cherokee
24. Hawaiian
25. Hindi
26. Braille
27. Chinese
28. Ancient Sumerian

LOCATIONS ANSWER KEY

1. Ancient Egypt
2. Finland
3. Eastern Europe (past) / USA & Israel (current)
4. Iceland
5. Iran
6. Burma
7. Poland
8. Ethiopia
9. Ancient Italy
10. South Africa
11. Japan
12. Portugal
13. Czech Republic
14. Korea
15. Ancient England
16. Azerbaijan
17. Georgia (Soviet)
18. Bulgaria
19. Vietnam
20. Armenia
21. Norway
22. Ireland
23. Oklahoma/North Carolina
24. Hawaii
25. India
26. USA
27. China
28. Ancient Sumeria (today's Iraq)

For additional copies of this book ...
To replace worn-out copies of the CD ...
For additional translations and corrections ...

Visit our website – _WhyIsThisNight.com_ – to get more copies of this unique book, to buy (inexpensive!) additional copies of the CD or DVD, or check back for even more translations in the future. Send us your novel uses for this collection – we'll post the best replies we get.

Have an idea for a great parody that we've missed? Send it in and we'll post the best on our website.

300 Ways to ask the Four Questions
Murray Spiegel and Rickey Stein
From Zulu to Abkhaz
Translations & Recordings
Includes CD and DVD with Language & Speaker Highlights
Suggestions to Enrich your Seder Puzzles and Games
Foreword by Theodore Bikel

Guide to Accompanying Media

CD Tracks

1 Welcome
2 Introduction to Audio Language Quiz
3 Audio Language Quiz: Identify languages, in Z→A order
4 Answers to Language Quiz
5 Introduction to Old English Quiz: Which language is 10th C Old English?
6 Old English Quiz
7 Answers to Old English Quiz
8 Introduction to Highlights Recordings
9 Click Languages: Zulu, Xhosa (!Hosa), Sotho, Khoekhoegowab (4 clicks!)
10 Chants around the World: Judeo-Iraqi, Yemenite, Aramaic, Libyan, Bukharan

Extinct Languages (Highlights)

11 Ancient Greek: Scholar of Ancient Greek living in Rhodes; 5th C BCE
12 Late Egyptian: Exodus time, language of Moses & Pharaoh; 1700-800 BCE
13 Manx: From Isle of Man; no first-language speakers since 1974

Living Languages (Highlights)

14 Adyghe: From Caucuses in Russia; speaker is Circassian Princess
15 Basque: Unique language related to no other European language
16 British English: Chief Editor, 20-volume OED (definitive authority on English)
17 Bukharic: From Uzbekistan; lead singer of Bukharan group, Shashmaqam
18 Crow: Speaker couldn't read Crow; text was memorized then spoken
19 Ewe: Speaker from highly regarded family of musicians from Ghana
20 Georgian: Speaker from Tbilisi, capital of Soviet Georgia
21 Hawaiian: Only 2,000 first-language speakers left
22 Inuktitut: Inuit Eskimo Priest in far northern Quebec
23 Kanjobal: Professor of Mayan literature, renowned Mayan novelist
24 Ladino: Vanishing language of Sephardi Jews; speaker's family from Rhodes
25 Lenape: Just 6 surviving speakers (at age 61 she is youngest native speaker)
26 Maasai: Junior Maasai warrior from Kenya (national attention after 9/11/01)
27 Malayalam and Marathi: Languages of Indian Jews (Bene Israel and Cochin)
28 Mandarin Chinese: Most common language (over 1 billion speakers)
29 Mongolian: Linguistics Professor at Jawaharlal Nehru University
30 Nenets: From Northern Siberia, freezing temperatures 260 days each year
31 Pitcairn: Language from mutineers of HMS Bounty and their Tahitian wives
32 Saami: From all around the 'top' of the world above Arctic circle
33 Tamil: Orthodox trilingual 7-year old (Yiddish, Tamil, English)
34 Tuvin: From Republic of Tuva; widely admired for throat-singing techniques
35 Welsh: Well-loved for its complex speech sounds
36 Xhosa: Most famous click language of South Africa
37 Yiddish: Actor Theodore Bikel chants the language of Eastern Europe

DVD

How to use on DVD Player DVD will show 4 Sign Language videos. (PC content will not play.)

How to use on MAC/PC Go to DVD's file menu. In directory *Bonus* within the *BLEND_TS* directory, double click __*CLICK HERE TO START*. If your default video player doesn't autoplay the DVD, double click the various *.IFO* files inside the *VIDEO_TS* directory (or open within your player).
On Windows XP: DVD's own display program will auto-install after a minute. Click on videos or "PC Content" button. Move cursor beneath video for video controls and player menu (the □). *For additional instructions and help for problems, see DVD Tutorial/FAQ on* <u>WhyIsThisNight.com</u>.

Videos 4 Sign Languages: ASL (American Sign Language), Israeli Sign Language, French Sign Language and Signed English. Captions show what is being signed. (Most videos are silent during the signing.)

Recordings 390 recordings of the Four Questions, Chants, Songs, Music from other lands, Parody Songs, and more!

Games Wave Hebrew Semaphore flags!

Quizzes Play the written-language quizzes!

CD Tracks (Continued)

Parodies and Constructed Languages (Highlights)

38 Donald Duck: Hebrew perhaps chanted by Disney's beloved Donald Duck
39 Transliterations of Hebrew: Chinese, Japanese and Panjabi
40 Klingon: Language created for the *Star Trek* series
41 Pig Latin: Kosher version by Yeshiva student
42 Uncle Eli: Fun poetry in Uncle Eli's Special-for-Kids, Most Fun ... Haggadah
43 Valley Girl: A true Valley Girl, from San Fernando Valley
44 Wrap up

Melodies on clarinet played by Cantor Joel Caplan

Please do not copy the CD or DVD. You hurt the independent publishers who offer them at very reasonable prices. Additional low-cost CDs and DVDs are available from our website: WhyIsThisNight.com